PARTNERS IN COMMAND

PARTNERS IN COMMAND

GEORGE MARSHALL and DWIGHT EISENHOWER
in War and Peace

MARK PERRY

THE PENGUIN PRESS
NEW YORK

THE PENGUIN PRESS
Published by the Penguin Group
Penguin Group (USA) Inc., 375 Hudson Street, New York, New York 10014, USA • Penguin Group
(Canada), 90 Eglinton Avenue East, Suite 700, Toronto, Ontario M4P 2Y3, Canada (a division of Pearson
Penguin Canada Inc.) • Penguin Books Ltd, 80 Strand, London WC2R 0RL, England • Penguin Ireland,
25 St Stephen's Green, Dublin 2, Ireland (a division of Penguin Books Ltd) • Penguin Group (Australia),
250 Camberwell Road, Camberwell, Victoria 3124, Australia (a division of Pearson Australia Group Pty
Ltd) • Penguin Books India Pvt Ltd, 11 Community Centre, Panchsheel Park, New Delhi–110 017, India
• Penguin Group (NZ), 67 Apollo Drive, Rosedale, North Shore 0745, Auckland, New Zealand
(a division of Pearson New Zealand Ltd) • Penguin Books (South Africa) (Pty) Ltd, 24 Sturdee Avenue,
Rosebank, Johannesburg 2196, South Africa

Penguin Books Ltd, Registered Offices:
80 Strand, London WC2R 0RL, England

First published in 2007 by The Penguin Press,
a member of Penguin Group (USA) Inc.

ISBN 978-1-59420-105-9

Printed in the United States of America

Designed by Stephanie Huntwork
Map illustrations by Jeffrey L. Ward

Book Club Edition

FOR BOBBY MULLER

Happy is the man who has learned the causes of things.

— VIRGIL

CONTENTS

A section of photographs follows page 236.

CHRONOLOGY

DECEMBER 31, 1880 George Marshall is born in Uniontown, Pennsylvania.

OCTOBER 14, 1890 Dwight Eisenhower is born in Denison, Texas.

SEPTEMBER 1897 George Marshall enters the Virginia Military Institute.

FEBRUARY 1902 George Marshall is commissioned an officer in the U.S. Army.

MAY 1902 Marshall serves as an officer in the Philippines.

AUGUST 1906 Marshall attends the Army Staff College at Fort Leavenworth.

JUNE 14, 1911 Eisenhower enters the U.S. Military Academy at West Point.

JUNE 12, 1915 Eisenhower graduates from the U.S. Military Academy.

JULY 1, 1916 Eisenhower marries Mamie Geneva Doud.

SEPTEMBER 13, 1915 Eisenhower serves as a second lieutenant with the 19th Infantry in Texas.

JUNE 1917 Marshall serves in the 1st Division in France.

JULY 1917 Marshall is promoted to captain.

JULY 1918 Marshall is appointed assistant chief of staff for operations of the American Expeditionary Force and meets Fox Conner.

NOVEMBER 1918 Dwight Eisenhower serves as a tank instructor at Fort Meade.

MAY 1919 Marshall is named aide-de-camp to General John J. Pershing.

AUGUST 1924 Marshall serves as executive officer of the 15th Infantry in Tientsin, China.

AUGUST 1927 Eisenhower attends the Army War College at Fort Leavenworth.

AUGUST 1927 Elizabeth Coles Marshall dies.

SEPTEMBER 1927 Marshall serves as an instructor at the Army War College.

NOVEMBER 1927 Marshall is assistant commander of the Infantry School at Fort Benning.

OCTOBER 1930 Marshall marries Katherine Tupper Brown.

JULY 1933 Marshall serves as commanding officer of District I of the Civilian Conservation Corps.

JULY 1938 Marshall is named assistant chief of staff of the U.S. Army and is head of the War Department's War Plans Division.

JULY 1939 Marshall is named acting chief of staff, U.S. Army.

SEPTEMBER 1, 1939 Marshall is sworn in as the chief of staff of the U.S. Army; that evening, Germany invades Poland. World War II begins.

FEBRUARY 1940 Eisenhower is chief of staff of the 3rd Division in San Antonio.

DECEMBER 18, 1941 Eisenhower is called by Bedell Smith and is assigned to the Office of the Chief of Staff, War Plans Division, Washington, D.C.

DECEMBER 1941 Arcadia Conference is held in Washington.

FEBRUARY 16, 1942 Dwight Eisenhower is promoted to head of the War Plans Division.

MARCH 16, 1942 Eisenhower memo on the strategy for the war is adopted by George Marshall.

MARCH 23, 1942 Eisenhower is named assistant chief of staff of the Operations Division by Marshall.

JUNE 24, 1942 Dwight Eisenhower is named commander of the European theater of operations.

JULY 7, 1942 Eisenhower is promoted to lieutenant general and shortly thereafter begins planning for Operation Torch.

NOVEMBER 8, 1942 Operation Torch: U.S. and British forces land in North Africa.

JANUARY 14–23, 1943 Marshall and Eisenhower attend the Casablanca Conference.

FEBRUARY 19, 1942 U.S. forces are defeated by Rommel at the Battle of Kasserine Pass.

MARCH 2, 1943 German forces begin their withdrawal from Tunisia.

MARCH 1943 Lloyd Fredendall is succeeded by George Patton.

MARCH 16, 1943 The Battle of El Guettar, Patton defeats Rommel.

MAY 1, 1943 The Battle of Hill 609 ends the North Africa campaign.

MAY 12–25, 1943 Trident Conference in Washington, D.C.

JULY 9–10, 1943 Operation Husky: The U.S. and its allies invade Sicily.

JULY 25, 1943 The fascist Italian government is overthrown.

AUGUST 10, 1943 George Patton slaps a soldier in Sicily.

AUGUST 17, 1943 Patton's troops enter Messina in Sicily.

AUGUST 1943 Quadrant Conference in Quebec.

SEPTEMBER 9, 1943 Operation Avalanche: Allies invade Italy at Salerno.

SEPTEMBER 11, 1943 Germans occupy Rome.

SEPTEMBER 17, 1943 Dwight Eisenhower confers with Mark Clark at Salerno.

NOVEMBER 1943 George Patton is reprimanded by Eisenhower.

NOVEMBER 17, 1943 Eisenhower-Churchill meeting at Malta.

NOVEMBER 19, 1943 Marshall, Churchill, Roosevelt, and Eisenhower meet in Tunis for a full briefing on the war.

NOVEMBER 23, 1943 Sextant I meeting in Cairo.

NOVEMBER 28, 1943 Eureka Conference in Tehran; Roosevelt, Churchill, meet with Stalin.

DECEMBER 7, 1943 Roosevelt informs Eisenhower of his command of Overlord.

JANUARY 2, 1944 Dwight Eisenhower confers with George Marshall in Washington.

JANAURY 13, 1944 Eisenhower returns to England.

JANUARY 21, 1944 Bernard Law Montgomery presents his plan for Overlord.

JANUARY 22, 1944 Operation Shingle: U.S. and British troops land at Anzio.

FEBRUARY 16, 1944 Germans counterattack at Anzio.

JUNE 5, 1944 Allied forces capture Rome.

JUNE 6, 1944 Allied armies invade France at Normandy.

JULY 19, 1944 British troops capture Caen.

JULY 25–30, 1944 Operation Cobra begins and the Allies break out of the Normandy beachhead.

AUGUST 15, 1944 Operation Dragoon: U.S. and British forces land in southern France.

AUGUST 20, 1944 The Battle of the Falaise Pocket begins.

AUGUST 25, 1944 Allied troops enter Paris.

SEPTEMBER 1–4, 1944 Allies liberate northern France and most of Belgium.

SEPTEMBER 13, 1944 Allied forces reach the Siegfried Line.

SEPTEMBER 17, 1944 Operation Market Garden begins.

DECEMBER 16, 1944 The Ardennes offensive. German Panzer divisions attempt to crush the Allied center in Belgium.

DECEMBER 26, 1944 Elements of Patton's Third Army relieve Bastogne.

JANUARY 28, 1945 Marshall and Eisenhower meet at Château Valmonte.

FEBRUARY 4–11, 1944 Stalin, Churchill, Roosevelt meet at Yalta.

MARCH 7, 1945 Allied units cross the Rhine River on the Ludendorff Bridge at Remagen.

APRIL 1, 1945 Allied troops surround the Ruhr Pocket.

APRIL 12, 1945 President Roosevelt dies; Harry Truman becomes president.

APRIL 18, 1945 German forces in the Ruhr surrender.

MAY 8, 1945 V-E Day.

JUNE 5, 1945 Allies assume governmental control of Germany.

JULY 16, 1945 The Potsdam Conference begins.

AUGUST 6, 1945 First atomic bomb dropped on Hiroshima.

AUGUST 9, 1945 Second atomic bomb dropped on Nagasaki.

AUGUST 14, 1945 Japan agrees to unconditional surrender, bringing World War II to an end.

NOVEMBER 19, 1945 Eisenhower replaces Marshall as Army chief of staff.

DECEMBER 20, 1945 George Marshall begins his mission in China.

JANUARY 21, 1947 George Marshall takes office as U.S. secretary of state.

JUNE 5, 1947 George Marshall gives a speech at Harvard University introducing the European Recovery Program.

NOVEMBER 17, 1947 Congressional hearings on the Marshall Plan.

FEBRUARY 7, 1948 Dwight Eisenhower replaced by Omar Bradley as Army chief of staff.

JUNE 7, 1948 Dwight Eisenhower becomes president of Columbia University.

JANUARY 1949 George Marshall resigns as secretary of state.

AUGUST 1950 Harry Truman appoints George Marshall as secretary of defense.

SEPTEMBER 1, 1951 Marshall resigns as secretary of defense.

MAY 31, 1952 Dwight Eisenhower resigns from the Army.

JUNE 4, 1952 Eisenhower announces his candidacy for the presidency.

OCTOBER 3, 1952 Eisenhower refuses to denounce Joseph McCarthy during a speech at a campaign stop in Milwaukee, Wisconsin.

NOVEMBER 4, 1952 Eisenhower elected president of the United States.

JANUARY 20, 1953 Eisenhower inaugurated.

MARCH 1953 George Marshall wins the Nobel Peace Prize.

NOVEMBER 6, 1956 Dwight Eisenhower is elected for a second term.

OCTOBER 16, 1959 George Marshall dies at Walter Reed Army Hospital.

JANUARY 17, 1961 Dwight Eisenhower gives his farewell address.

MARCH 28, 1969 Dwight Eisenhower dies at Walter Reed Army Hospital.

LIST OF MAPS

PROLOGUE:
"IKE" AND "THE GENERAL"

HERE IS, in the holdings of the Museum of the Confederacy in Richmond, a painting. *The Last Meeting of Lee and Jackson* shows the two mounted generals conferring behind the rebel lines at Chancellorsville in May 1863.[1] The grim-faced Lee, his white-gloved right hand open with fingers extended, is giving his lieutenant instructions. The caped Jackson leans forward, rising slightly in his saddle, his eyes on Lee. He is listening intently. By the spring of 1863, Robert E. Lee, the southern commander, is already a legend, as is Thomas Jonathan Jackson, who has earned the nickname "Stonewall" for his stand at Bull Run. In the painting, Lee's horse, Traveler, is restless, his head thrown sideways, while Jackson's mount, Little Sorrel, paws the stony ground, anxious for battle. In the background, three soldiers gaze in apparent awe at their commanders. There is blue sky beyond, but it is twilight. The day is ending.

Everett Julio's painting became an icon of the Lost Cause and is reproduced extensively today for Civil War aficionados. The painting adorns coffee cups and T-shirts, and its reproductions are sold at stores on battlefields. It has come to symbolize that last great moment in the history of the Confederacy, before the terrible defeat at Gettysburg, when victory was still possible. It is the most well-known representation of the relationship between a great commander and his brilliant subordinate. Historians of the era know the moment well: Jackson is about to ride off to lead his corps in a great march around the Union army. That evening Jackson will launch a flank attack on the Union line, and before dark he will have won the South's greatest military victory. In the darkness, Jackson will be mistakenly fired on by his own men and will die of his wounds less than a fortnight later. Lee will go on to Gettysburg, and Appomattox, without him.

As a student at the Virginia Military Institute, future chief of staff, and General of the Army, George Marshall was steeped in this history. Jackson had taught mathematics at VMI and only left the Institute to take up his duties for the South. When he died, his body was brought back to the school, where it lay in state and was buried. "His fabled marches, his tragic death, as well as his eccentricities, were already legend in Marshall's time," historian Forrest Pogue tells us. Adjoining the VMI parade ground was Washington and Lee University. Jackson's former commander served as its president following Appomattox, and the Lee Chapel at Washington and Lee held his remains. Lee's and Jackson's service was as much an example to VMI cadets as the sacrifice of a part of their corps at the Battle of New Market, at which ten VMI cadets were killed. Each May 3, the names of the VMI dead were read aloud. As their names were repeated a first classman would step forward and announce: "Died on the field of battle."[2]

George Marshall, an undistinguished boy from a modest family that hailed from a small town in Pennsylvania, arrived at VMI in 1897 and was immediately drawn to its southern traditions. In time he came to revere Lee and Jackson, and throughout his life he named them as the two men he admired most. "For Marshall, both Jackson and Lee were inspiring figures," Marshall's best-known biographer tells us, "both great and austere generals, the one an infantry commander of fanatic drive, the other, a soldier-statesman whose brilliance in war was capped by his demonstration in peace of how a general could live honorably and constructively in defeat."[3] The ghosts of the defeated Confederacy were brought to life at VMI, and it was said that late on some nights it was possible to see a lamp lit in Jackson's classroom. If you were stealthy enough, you might be able to spy his shadow standing before the blackboard, working out problems. Marshall remembered that there was "an old fellow with a scraggly beard" who sold nuts in the institute's "sally port." When cadets complained about his disreputable dress, they were told to leave him alone— he was a veteran of Lee's Army of Northern Virginia "with a very fine record, and he could sit in that arch till he died."[4]

The lives of Lee and Jackson were celebrated at VMI, their example ever present in the young minds of its cadets. It would not be surprising to suppose that some of these young men would imagine how their service might reflect the values of these two and how someday in battle they might replicate their great heroism. They might even imagine how in some future battle there might come a time when at twilight, they would meet with a commander to plot the defeat of an enemy, and so be forever remembered in the annals of the nation.

But more serious-minded cadets like George Marshall understood that the sweep of history is complex and cannot be relived and that Everett Julio's painting, while powerful, is more a representation of an idea than of an actual moment. It is not history. Here is what Shelby Foote says: Lee and Jackson met at sundown on horseback, but Lee did not give the younger man his orders, for he had none to give. Instead, the two withdrew into a nearby clump of trees. Lee did not wear gloves, was not clad in a full uniform, but wore a simple gray coat. Jackson had no cape but was dressed in a bright newly tailored uniform that sparked laughter from his soldiers. The two seated themselves on a log, then lay down to rest in a nearby grove. When they awoke, they conferred, studying a map. "General Jackson," Lee asked, "what do you propose to do?" Jackson stared at the map and traced his route. "Go around here," he said. Lee thought for a moment. "What do you propose to make this movement with?" Jackson barely paused: "With my whole corps."[5]

George Marshall was a not a student of war when he came to VMI, but he was intimately familiar with Lee and Jackson's campaigns by the time he left the institute and received his Army commission. He understood that while it had been only four decades since the meeting of Lee and Jackson at Chancellorsville, war had changed. Conflicts were now fought by soldiers armed with repeating rifles in armies organized by faceless bureaucracies and buried their dead in unmarked trenches. Within two decades of Marshall's graduation, iron behemoths were deployed in battle, poison gas filled the air, and machine guns killed more men in minutes than had been killed at Chancellorsville in a day. The dead of the battles numbered not in the thousands but in the tens of thousands. Nor would great commanders meet at twilight within rifle shot of their soldiers but instead would gather with their staffs in large rooms to plan movements over hundreds of miles of terrain. Commanders arrived at battlefield conferences in different uniforms, spoke different languages, and represented different countries. They would not confer, they would argue.

George Marshall prepared himself for such a war and was convinced that it was coming. He saw in World War I the outlines of a coming global conflict so bloody and horrible that its breadth would dwarf anything that had happened before. He knew that he would play a central role in this conflict, so he began to write the names of officers he respected in a little black book that he kept with him at all times. When he was finally placed in a position to build the army that would defend his nation, he referred to the names in his book and chose the generals he thought would be his nation's greatest commanders: Omar Bradley, Mark Clark, Joseph Collins, Jacob Devers, Leonard Gerow, Courtney Hodges, George Patton, Walter Bedell Smith, Maxwell Taylor, Lucien Truscott—and Dwight David Eisenhower.

Of these, "Ike" Eisenhower was to become George Marshall's Stonewall Jackson. Marshall trusted Eisenhower as much as Lee had trusted Jackson and placed in his hands the movement of men to fight and win battles. Yet, any comparison between Marshall and Eisenhower and Lee and Jackson must be as inexact as Everett Julio's symbolic study of the twilight conference on the eve of Chancellorsville. George Marshall was not Robert E. Lee, who carefully calculated his loyalties and fought for his state. Marshall would not have done so. And Eisenhower was not Stonewall Jackson. The eccentric Jackson was a quiet man who rode into battle in a dilapidated coat while sucking on a lemon. Eisenhower was voluble but proper; his greatest attribute was his ability to expertly manage the disparate personalities of commanders who made their plans while standing at a conference table.

Still, there is great truth in Julio's painting. The history of the Army of Northern Virginia in its greatest moment is defined by the partnership of Robert E. Lee and Thomas Jonathan Jackson. Their meeting at Chancellorsville, both real and symbolic, marked the apogee of that partnership, the moment when the two men saw clearly on the map before them the road to victory. Lee chose Jackson to lead the fight because he knew that in Stonewall he had found a perfect reflection of his own vision and a man who understood, as he did, what was at stake. So too, in Dwight Eisenhower, George Marshall found a commander with the insight to direct the army that he built. In time, the partnership grew even beyond that of Lee and Jackson so that Marshall and Eisenhower needed no map between them but understood instinctively what needed to be done and how to do it. Just as the greatest victory in the history of the South is defined in the partnership of Lee and Jackson, so too the greatest victory in the history of our nation is defined in the partnership of Marshall and Eisenhower.

This is their story.

THE WPD

"We must take great risks. . . ."
"I agree with you. Do your best to save them. . . ."[1]

O N THE MORNING OF December 12, 1941, less than one week after the
Japanese attack on Pearl Harbor, Dwight Eisenhower received a telephone call on the Third Army's direct telephone line linking San Antonio
to Washington.[2] On the other end was Eisenhower's friend, Colonel Walter
Bedell "Beetle" Smith, an assistant at the War Department. "Is that you Ike?"
Smith asked. Eisenhower was pleased to hear from his old friend and the two
exchanged pleasantries. Then Smith got to the point: "The Chief says for you
to hop a plane and get up here right away," he said brusquely. "Tell your boss
that formal orders will come through later."[3] Eisenhower could hardly hide his
disappointment. He had missed World War I and then, over the next two
decades, was unceremoniously shuttled from one staff position to another. Like
every other Army officer, Eisenhower wanted to train and command soldiers,
but the opportunity never seemed to come.

Eisenhower's most agonizing years were spent in the Far East, where he
served for five years as "assistant to the military advisor, Commonwealth of the
Philippine Islands." That was a fancy title for serving as the "horse holder" for
General Douglas MacArthur, one of the most disagreeable, self-centered,
blustering—and brilliant—commanders in the Army. Now, Eisenhower be-

lieved, he would be just another one of the innumerable staff assistants in Washington, no more than a "good second" to yet another senior commander or, worse still, "an assistant to an assistant," even though this time he would be serving the highest-ranking officer in the military—Army Chief of Staff George Catlett Marshall. "Heavy-hearted," he later recalled, "I telephoned my wife to pack a bag, and within an hour I was headed for the War Department."[4]

Eisenhower's commander in San Antonio, the sixty-one-year-old Prussian-born Lieutenant General Walter Krueger, was not surprised by Smith's call. Krueger, a veteran of both the Spanish-American War and World War I (he had enlisted as a private in 1901), had constantly urged Eisenhower on his colleagues among the senior American leadership, citing his strategic intuition, his willingness to take chances, and his intangible battle instincts.[5] Just months before, in August 1941, Krueger's Third Army (the "blue" force) had "destroyed" Lieutenant General Ben Lear's Second Army (the "red" force) in a series of war games called "the Louisiana Maneuvers," a field exercise involving tens of thousands of men in nineteen divisions that was monitored closely by Marshall.[6] The Third Army's plan was drawn up by Eisenhower, whose bold use of infantry blunted Lear's armored columns (commanded by Eisenhower's old friend, tank commander George Patton), pinned them against the Red River, then cut them off from their source of supplies.[7] The Louisiana Maneuvers were a victory for the irascible Krueger, but the plan was Eisenhower's.[8] In their wake, Marshall culled the senior military ranks of those who he deemed had done poorly in Louisiana and promoted those who had done well. Over the next months, literally dozens of senior officers were retired by Marshall, and younger men were moved up in the ranks, including Eisenhower, who became Brigadier General Eisenhower.[9]

While disappointed with Smith's call from Washington, Eisenhower was relieved that he was at least being given a senior position. Over the years he had seen many of his closest friends take on important assignments while he remained in the background, marginalized or shunted aside. Always, it seemed to him, his requests for a command were somehow ignored, while his closest colleagues were rewarded with the best assignments. While Omar Bradley, Mark Clark, J. Lawton Collins, George Patton, Joe McNarney, "Beetle" Smith, Carl Spaatz, Lucien K. Truscott, and Nathan Twining were charged with training and commanding actual infantry units or rising quickly in the increasingly important Army Air Corps, Eisenhower was busy writing reports or accompanying older and more senior luminaries.[10] Even those in the West Point classes behind him were being promoted faster. Among those now being considered as commanders of combat units were a large number of Eisenhower's personal friends, many of whom had actually been praising Eisenhower's abilities — including a lieutenant general named Leonard T. Gerow.

"Gee" Gerow was the head of the War Department's War Plans Division, the WPD. The WPD was Marshall's in-house think tank for designing America's war strategy. Along with Krueger, Gerow had been pressing Marshall to bring Eisenhower to Washington. He knew that Marshall had been impressed with Eisenhower when he first met him in Washington, back in 1930. The Marshall-Eisenhower meeting came about after General John Pershing, the then-head of the American Battle Monuments Commission, asked Eisenhower, who was serving as his assistant, to read and comment on a part of his memoirs, which were based on his personal World War I diaries. Eisenhower read what Pershing had written and suggested that the general abandon the diary style he had adopted in telling about two of the key battles involving American forces in France. Eisenhower advised Pershing to tell about the battle "as seen from his position as the commander of the American Expeditionary Forces."[11] Pershing was not overjoyed with Eisenhower's recommendation, but he agreed with his criticism. He asked Eisenhower to rewrite the chapters. Eisenhower agreed to do so, and Pershing passed them on to Marshall. Marshall read Eisenhower's work and huddled with Pershing when Marshall came to Washington. Eisenhower was not invited to the meeting.

"When his conference with the General was done, he [Marshall] came out through my office," Eisenhower recalled. "For the first time in my life, I met George Marshall. He did not sit down but remarked that he had read over my chapters. 'I think they're very interesting. Nevertheless, I advised General Pershing to stick with his original idea. I think to break up the format right at the climax of the war would be a mistake.' "[12] Eisenhower smiled, nodded, but politely disagreed with Marshall. He understood very clearly that continuity was important in the kind of book that Pershing was writing, he said to Marshall. But then he added: "I still think that each of the two battles ought to be treated as a single narrative with the proper annotations to give it authenticity." Marshall thought about this, but he would not let Eisenhower have the last word: Eisenhower's idea was good, he said, but General Pershing was happy with his original way of handling the material. Eisenhower nodded and there was a silence. Later in his life, reflecting on the meeting, Eisenhower noted that Marshall did not smile during their conversation and never again mentioned the meeting to him—though there were plenty of opportunities to do so.[13]

There is a sense of puzzlement in Eisenhower's later reflections on this first meeting with Marshall, an intangible yet uncomfortable feeling that somehow something had gone wrong. Indeed, while it is clear that Marshall regularly rewarded disagreement among subordinates, there can be little doubt that he did not welcome Eisenhower's views on the Pershing book. It may well have been that Marshall could brook no criticism, implied or direct, of a commander he so deeply admired.[14] Whatever the reason for their obvious discomfort, it was as if this first meeting between the two set the tone for their future relationship. For while Marshall and Eisenhower were to forge a close and successful partnership, an unbreakable professional kinship, neither man would ever have claimed they were close friends.

That was hardly unusual for Marshall. He maintained a strictly cordial relationship with all of his fellow officers, and not just with those whom he outranked. This had nothing to do with Eisenhower, as Marshall's approach to his colleagues was always strictly and purposely professional, sometimes to the point of being rude. "I have no feelings except those I reserve for Mrs. Marshall," Marshall once said. And while the first meeting between Marshall and Pershing's assistant may have been tepid or uncomfortable, it did not keep Marshall from inviting Eisenhower to join his staff at the Infantry School at Fort Benning, Georgia. Eisenhower turned down the invitation, but only because he already had his orders. Nor did the meeting keep Marshall from putting Eisenhower's name in his famous little black book, alongside the names of other promising officers, such as Mark Clark, George Patton, and Omar Bradley.[15] Even so, it was luck as much as purpose that eventually made the Army chief decide that he wanted Eisenhower on his staff: Marshall was planning to give Gerow a field command and promote a young colonel to replace him, but at the last minute the colonel unexpectedly died. Marshall told Smith to give Eisenhower a call.

EISENHOWER ARRIVED at Union Station in Washington on the morning of December 14 and was met by his brother Milton. Milton wanted to take Ike to his home in Virginia, but Eisenhower had no intention of keeping Marshall waiting and had Milton drive him the short distance to Marshall's office in the Old Munitions Building, an unsightly concrete-and-glass behemoth that bestrode the National Mall facing the White House. Eisenhower waited in Marshall's outer office for only a minute before being admitted. Marshall barely looked up. He spoke in clipped sentences: The U.S. military position in the Pacific was dire. American forces in the Philippines were in danger of being overrun and at least half of the U.S. Navy was at the bottom of Pearl Harbor. The U.S. lacked men and matériel. Training facilities were in short supply and America's supply lines were stretched to the breaking point. Everywhere, the powers of Germany and Japan were on the march. The situation was bad and bound to get worse. "We have got to do our best in the Pacific and we've got to win this whole war," Marshall said. He looked bluntly at Eisenhower, unsmiling, his face set. "Now, how are we going to do it?" Eisenhower hesitated for only a moment: "Give me a few hours."[16]

Eisenhower was greeted outside Marshall's office by Gerow, the deputy chief of staff for war plans, now Eisenhower's new boss. The two old friends had been students together in 1927 at the Army War College, then located in Washington. In that era, Ike and Mamie Eisenhower and Gee and Katie Gerow had been part of an informal and movable social club of Army officers and their wives that was dubbed "Club Eisenhower." The group included (depending on their assignments) George and Beatrice Patton, Mark and Maureen Clark, and a CBS executive, Harry "Butch" Butcher, and his wife, Ruth, among others.[17] Like Marshall, Gerow had seen combat in World War I and was known for his exacting staff work. And like Marshall, Gerow was a graduate of the Virginia Military Institute. But there the similarities ended: the soft-spoken Gerow seemed oddly out of place among Marshall's more vocal staff deputies; was exhausted by the sixteen to eighteen hours he had spent in his office each day since the Japanese attack; and he seemed distinctly uncomfortable, even intimidated, by the chief of staff.[18] Gerow was hoping that his old friend Eisenhower would lift some of his burden.

After telling Gerow about his meeting with Marshall, Eisenhower was shown to a desk and provided with a pen and several sheets of yellow copy paper. Eisenhower stared at the paper, and his thoughts turned to his old mentor, the imposing and unflappable Fox Conner, under whom he had served in the

Panama Canal Zone for two years in the early 1920s. Conner was responsible for Eisenhower's military education, liberally sharing his library of military treatises with the young major and unceremoniously shearing the military essays he assigned him to write of unnecessary ornamentation. All but forgotten now, Conner was one of America's greatest military thinkers and the man responsible for shaping Marshall's and Eisenhower's approach to warfare. "In the new war we will have to fight beside allies," Connor had told Eisenhower, "and George Marshall knows more about the techniques of arranging allied commands than any man I know."[19] Eisenhower admired Conner, who had also served as one of George Marshall's mentors and whom he described to Eisenhower as "a genius." Eisenhower stared at his blank sheet of paper and thought for only a moment more: What George Marshall wanted, he decided, was a paper that was "short, emphatic, and based on reasoning in which I honestly believed. No oratory, plausible argument, or glittering generality would impress anyone entitled to be labeled [a] genius by Fox Conner."[20]

Eisenhower headed the paper "Assistance to the Far East," and then under "Steps to be Taken" he began his narrative: "Build up Australia, a base of operations from which supplies and personnel (air and ground types) can be moved into the Philippines. Speed is essential." Next: "Influence Russia to enter the war." Then: "Initially, utilize the bombs and ammunition now in Australia and to be carried on carriers and fast merchant vessels with planes. Establish fast merchant ship supply service from U.S. to Australia for maintenance. Ferry from Australia to Philippines." All of this was quite predictable and could have been seen from simply looking at a map, but Eisenhower knew that his words reflected a larger strategic program that was shaped by the growing pressure of continual Japanese victories. There was no talk of an offensive, of ultimate triumph, of a strike that could suddenly resolve the crisis. The Philippines were lost, and with them thousands of American and Philippine soldiers. It would be many months, perhaps years, before those in Japanese captivity could be liberated. But the effort had to be made, and whatever would be done had to be done quickly. When Eisenhower was finished he had typed no more than three hundred words.[21]

Several hours later, Eisenhower presented his plan to Marshall. Seated before the Army chief of staff, he supplemented his paper with an oral briefing of the deteriorating situation: "General," he said, "it will be a long time before major reinforcements can go to the Philippines, longer than any garrison can hold out without any direct assistance, if the enemy commits major forces to their reduction, but we must do everything for them that is humanly possible. The people of China, of the Philippines, of the Dutch East Indies will be watching us. They may excuse failure but they will not excuse abandonment. Their trust and friendship are important to us." Marshall listened without comment.[22] Eisenhower continued. "Our base must be Australia, and we must start at once to expand it and to secure our communications to it. In this last we dare not fail. We must take great risks and spend any amount of money required." Marshall listened closely and finally, after a lengthy pause, spoke: "I agree with you. Do your best to save them." Eisenhower nodded and turned to leave, but Marshall stopped him: "Eisenhower," he said, "the Department is filled with able men who analyze their problems well but feel compelled always to bring them to me for final solution. I must have assistants who will solve their own problems and tell me later what they have done." Eisenhower got the message—he was there to make decisions. With his first full session with Marshall concluded, Eisenhower returned to his desk. He was to learn shortly that he was now, officially, the head of the Pacific and Far East Section of the WPD. He was convinced that the Army chief of staff had simply given him a test and that somehow he had passed: "His tone implied that I had been given the problem as a check to an answer he had already reached," he later reflected.[23]

AT THE moment Dwight Eisenhower was directed by George Marshall to write his memo on U.S. strategy in the war against Japan, things could not have looked worse: America's largest battleships were at the bottom of Pearl Harbor; Guam had fallen and Wake Island had been bombed; Burma and Indochina were occupied; the Philippines, Thailand, and the Netherlands East Indies had been invaded; most of China and north Malaya were lost (Malaya's defenders, the 10th and 11th Indian divisions, were decimated); the British battleship *Prince of Wales* and the cruiser *Repulse* had been sunk; and Japanese troops were moving south into the Admiralty, Bismarck, Gilbert, and Marshall Islands. Australia was threatened and might fall before the Japanese onslaught. The Americans had three aircraft carriers in the Pacific, the Japanese ten. On the morning that Eisenhower wrote his memo for Marshall, the Japanese began their second landing of troops on Luzon in the Philippines. It had been a week since the attack on Pearl Harbor, but the Japanese landings were unopposed.[24]

The situation was as bleak in Europe. Belgium, the Netherlands, Norway, Denmark, and France had been conquered. With France went all of North Africa. Poland had been invaded and conquered, and all of Eastern Europe had been lost. The Soviet Union was on the edge of defeat: German divisions surrounded Leningrad, were on the doorstep of Moscow, and had reached into the oil-rich Crimea. Hundreds of thousands of Soviet troops were already dead or captured, and the Red Army was fighting for its life amid the ruins of Stalingrad. Hungary and Romania had joined the Tripartite Pact. Tons of shipping was being lost in the North Atlantic. Britain was under siege. But for the first time since the fall of France, as a result of the German declaration of war against the United States on December 8, Britain was no longer alone.

Starting in 1939, the United States had begun the slow process of transforming its industries to a war footing and rebuilding a denuded peacetime military establishment. Still, on the eve of December 7, the U.S. military had only 267,000 officers and enlisted men in its army's ranks and 2,470 aircraft in the Army Air Corps while the Navy had five carriers, eighteen heavy cruisers, nineteen light cruisers, sixty-one submarines, and just hundreds of lighter specialized ships — patrol craft, gunboats, and submarine chasers.[25] To defeat the Axis, the United States required ten million men in uniform, and they had to be trained, equipped, fed, and shipped to the battlefield. The combat troops of the U.S. would be supported by thousands of bombers, fighters, and transport aircraft and thousands of ships: from the smallest landing craft to the largest troop transport to aircraft carriers capable of penetrating the Japanese defensive shield and destroying the Imperial Japanese Navy.[26] A bomber fleet would have to be created — virtually from scratch. But that would not be enough: the nation would be required to create a second army of engineers and scientists to design the war's weapons, and manufacturers, suppliers, and workers would have to be found to build them.

Perhaps most important, at least to George Marshall's mind, the men and women who were recruited or drafted for military service needed to be taken into battle by experienced, intelligent, selfless, and courageous leaders. Marshall viewed this requirement—identifying the right military commanders and putting them in a position where they could succeed—as his most important task. Fortunately, it was one he had prepared for his entire life. Two years before the attack on Pearl Harbor and just days after he became Army chief of staff, Marshall began the arduous task of building a command structure capable of fighting Germany and Japan, the two most well-armed and well-trained military establishments in human history. "I do not propose to send our young citizen-soldiers into action, if they must go into action, under commanders whose minds are no longer adaptable to the making of split-second decisions in the fast-moving war of today, nor whose bodies are no longer capable of standing up under the demands of field service," he explained to reporter George Fielding Eliot in an interview in his office in 1939. "They'll have their chance to prove what they can do. But I doubt that many of them will come through satisfactorily. Those that don't will be eliminated."[27]

Marshall could be ruthless. Harry Hines Woodring, who served as Franklin Roosevelt's secretary of war from 1936 until succeeded by Henry Stimson in 1940, once observed that Marshall "would sell out his grandmother for personal advantage," while one officer's wife bitterly remembered how Marshall had sidelined her husband on the eve of World War II: "He was once our dear friend, but he ruined my husband."[28] Marshall struck many as stiff-necked, remote, unreachable, and quick to judge, but he could also be surprisingly informal, even self-effacing. Marshall disdained officers who used their rank to bully or posture at the same time that he criticized others for a lack of toughness. He was a mass of contradictions and, for even his closest friends, an enigma.[29] He was tall for his time, at just under six feet, and rugged—"a magnificent looking man," as a British military colleague once noted—with intense blue eyes. A man of quirky habits and odd turns of phrase, Marshall constantly misplaced his reading glasses (his orderly at the War Department bought replacements by the handful) and butchered the names of his closest assistants. He called his secretary, Mona Nason, "Mason" and the secretary of his staff, Colonel Frank McCarthy, "McCartney." When Marshall repeatedly mangled McCarthy's name, his staff secretary corrected him, then related the story to a Colonel Young, a War Department officer, who responded "While you were about it, I wish you had told him that I am Young, not Maxwell Taylor."[30]

Born in 1880, Marshall was the second son of a Uniontown, Pennsylvania, small businessman whose Virginia and Kentucky family was descended from the legendary Supreme Court justice John Marshall. As a young boy, Marshall was regaled by his father with stories of the American Revolution and the Civil War. One summer, he and a close boyhood friend built a fleet of boats at a nearby creek, and boys came from the town to see their matchstick "Great White Fleet"—the pride of the U.S. Navy—fight naval battles. Athletic and precocious but not driven, Marshall worried his parents, who believed the indifference he showed toward his studies would keep him out of college. But when Marshall's older brother Stuart entered VMI, George determined to follow him, believing he would enjoy the life of a professional officer. Stuart was not so sure. "I overheard Stuart talking to my mother; he was trying to persuade her not to let me go because he thought I would disgrace the family name," Marshall later recalled. "Well, that made more impression on me than all the instructors, parental pressure, or anything else. I decided right then that I was going to wipe his face, or wipe his eye."

Marshall was named for his father, a gregarious man who built a company producing bricks for coke ovens. Marshall senior's partner was Arthur Bliss, an Alabama bookkeeper.[31] At first Bliss, Marshall and Company was a success and the business expanded; in 1876 the company was one of the largest coke oven manufacturers in western Pennsylvania. Pressed by competition, Marshall's father sold the company and invested the considerable profits he had made in establishing a land-speculation firm in Luray, Virginia. But that company went bankrupt, and Marshall's father was responsible for paying off hundreds of thousands of dollars in debt.[32] The family never recovered. It was a painful time for young George, but the greatest weight fell on his mother, Laura Bradford Marshall. Unlike Marshall's father, Laura Bradford Marshall was patient and soft-spoken. Marshall was intimidated by his father, but he had close emotional ties to his mother that he maintained throughout his life.[33]

The formation of Marshall's considerable military skills, his ability to communicate confidence and discipline, his talent for making others believe in his vision—in short, his ability to command—came from his experience as a cadet at VMI. The personal traits that were shaped by his years at VMI defined his place in history. Marshall did not stand on ceremony, did not expect flawless behavior or perfect results, but assumed that men would follow him. This self-confidence and self-possession emerged during his last year at the Institute and became the foundation of his stature as a military commander. The two men he admired most, Generals Robert E. Lee and Stonewall Jackson, had this same quality: they simply expected that when they gave an order it would be obeyed. Marshall was not a great student, but he drove himself relentlessly, discovering within himself an untapped reservoir of ambition. During his last year at VMI, Marshall was named the Institute's first captain, the highest cadet rank. He paid a price for his self-discipline and ambition: he found that his inner drive isolated him from others and made close friendships nearly impossible.

Marshall was commissioned an officer in the U.S. Army in January 1902 and one month later married Elizabeth Carter "Lily" Coles, a Lexington native whom he met while attending the Institute. In April he was shipped to the Philippines, then in the grip of a cholera epidemic, where he was "virtually the governor of the southern end of the Island of Mindoro."[34] After nearly two years in the Philippines, Marshall returned to the U.S., was assigned to Fort Reno, and then won an appointment to the prestigious Army Staff College at Fort Leavenworth, Kansas. "I just worked day and night," Marshall later recalled. "My great trouble was going to sleep at night. I remember I used to get up and shine my boots in order to wake up. So I had very shiny boots at the early period. I finally got into the habit of study, which I never really had had, but I revived what little I had carried with me out of college and I became pretty automatic at the business. It worked out all right because in the end I came out number one."[35] Marshall stayed on at the college as an instructor before being reassigned to the field: with the 24th Infantry in New York and San Antonio, then with the 4th Infantry in Arkansas, and then with the 13th Infantry back in the Philippines. In the fifteen years following his commissioning in 1902, Marshall held nearly every significant staff job in the U.S. Army—he had been a staff assistant, supply officer, paymaster, trainer, and instructor. In that time, he had built a reputation as a competent, even brilliant, officer. But the true test of command comes in war.

In June 1917, Marshall was assigned as the assistant chief of staff for the 1st Division of the American Expeditionary Force in France. In July he was promoted to captain and tasked with putting the first American doughboys into the trenches against the Germans. "I became very much involved with all these things at the start. And I was also involved in locating the first four divisions to arrive in France. I was just given the job of locating them and seeing what they needed. So I had to figure out what was required in the way of mess halls and bunkhouses and headquarters and hospital buildings and everything of that sort. Nobody advised me. They didn't have time. They just told me to do it,"[36] he later recalled. By May 1918, Marshall was America's premier combat planner, answering directly to General John J. "Black Jack" Pershing, the commander of the AEF. Marshall's experience in commanding troops was undoubtedly invaluable, but when asked years later about these experiences, he focused not on the battles with Germany but on America's struggle to cooperate as a part of a large coalition. The war, he mused, "shows how difficult it is for armies of different nations to work with full harmony."[37] It was a theme he would return to again and again during World War II.

O N T H E face of it, Dwight Eisenhower was a very different man from George Marshall. Marshall was proper, distant, and matter-of-fact; Eisenhower was talkative, social, and opinionated. While Marshall regularly entertained his colleagues and their wives, he seemed uncomfortable doing so; Eisenhower loved to socialize. Marshall was always viewed as the Army chief of staff—or "the General"—while Eisenhower was thought of as the commander of "Club Eisenhower" and affectionately known as "Ike."[38] Marshall loved to ride and hunt, to be alone for hours with his guns and dogs. He was a crack shot. Eisenhower hunted and fished, but his fondest entertainment was bridge— which he played expertly. Marshall made few close friends, perhaps no more than a handful in his entire life, while Eisenhower was at the center of an expanding network that included his family, his fellow officers, his boon buddies, and his childhood friends. Marshall could be wry and ironic, but he was never described as witty, while Eisenhower regaled his friends with long stories and ribald jokes. Eisenhower was outgoing, effusive, and backslappingly pleased with the success of others, while Marshall seemed incapable of praise. A job well done, he believed, was expected and its own reward. "The nearest that he ever came to saying [anything] complimentary directly to my face was, 'You are not doing so badly so far,'" Eisenhower once noted.[39]

Marshall's sense of propriety, dignity, and self-worth might have been offputting for those who worked most closely with him, but he was beloved nonetheless. While Marshall seemed impersonal, even peremptory, he rarely forgot to note a staff birthday or anniversary. He had a habit of picking up and chatting with War Department personnel stranded at cold or rainy bus stops, a worrisome eccentricity for his security-minded personal assistants. He became adept at maneuvering training and recruitment bills through the House and Senate, standing for hours engaged in what he viewed as the distasteful requirements of glad-handing and back-patting. He was different among military officers, of course, because he had to be. He was the highest-ranking man in the Army. But despite his stature and rank, Marshall gave a direct order only when deeply angered. These displays, while rare, were unforgettable. "I've never seen a man who apparently develops a higher pressure of anger when he encounters some piece of stupidity than does he," Eisenhower commented.[40] "Yet the outburst is so fleeting. . . . he doesn't get angry the way I do—I burn for an hour."[41]

Marshall's leadership style was designed to make subordinates feel that they had a stake in their chief's success. There is no record that he ever publicly upbraided anyone who worked with him, but in private his remarks could be chilling. When a fellow officer he had known for many years told him that he would have to delay his departure for Europe because his wife was gone and the furniture was not yet packed, Marshall was dumbfounded. The officer was suddenly apologetic. "I'm sorry," he said, to which Marshall responded: "I'm sorry too, but you will be retired tomorrow."[43] To be sure, Marshall was often cold and almost always seemed detached, but for every bitterly disappointed officer that Marshall ruthlessly culled from the ranks, there were dozens of others whom he nurtured and promoted. There is also weighty evidence that his trust, once gained, was conferred unfailingly thereafter, even in the face of sometimes blatant failure. The thousands of telegrams, papers, memoranda, and radio communications that Marshall wrote or dictated during America's four-year war with the Axis contained few blunt directives. His views were presented as "wishes" and "suggestions" or even more indirectly as expressions of concern. Marshall sprinkled his words with seemingly patronly advice, couching his own obvious disappointment in phrases like "Don't you think you should" or "perhaps you had better . . ." or "it was recently suggested that . . ."

Historians may search the volumes of American war correspondence, memoranda, battle reports, radiograms, and coded cables without finding a single communication from a senior commander to a subordinate that actually takes the tone of an apology. But there is one from Marshall, written in the midst of the European war in the spring of 1944. Marshall's message, transmitted from Washington to Europe by code, was sent to Lieutenant General Jacob Devers, a man with whom neither Marshall nor Eisenhower ever seemed comfortable. The Marshall message followed months of exchanges between the two men over a number of Devers's ill-advised combat and staff decisions, which exasperated the increasingly impatient chief of staff. But one day, and quite suddenly, Marshall drew back—as if realizing that his criticisms had only worsened the situation or that he might even have been unfair: "Have just read your letter of April 15th," Marshall wrote. "I like its tone and I have great confidence in what you are doing. I fear, in fact I feel certain that my radios regarding certain details have given you the idea of lack of confidence on my part and in effect thrown you on the defensive. Disregard such ideas because they are wholly incorrect. Be assured that I have great confidence in you."[43] Marshall's message had its desired effect; Devers led his army group "efficiently and well" thereafter, solidifying his reputation as a "solid, dependable, and capable general."[44]

Perhaps Marshall's greatest talent was his enormous capacity to give his full attention to a single subject for long periods. In the course of a single day, Marshall might dictate thirty separate memoranda, write ten personal letters, study dozens of battle reports, attend half a dozen meetings, and still spend hours bent over maps or poring over industrial-production figures. The pace that he set was physically and emotionally draining. While Marshall was nominally the Army chief of staff, he was clearly the senior officer of the American high command and, as such, became Franklin Roosevelt's most trusted military adviser.[45] His colleagues on the Joint Chiefs of Staff—Chief of Naval Operations Admiral Ernest King, Army Air Corps commander Henry "Hap" Arnold, and Roosevelt's military aide Admiral William D. Leahy—often deferred to Marshall's judgment. America's overall strategy for fighting the war was in his hands. As the military's unofficial coordinator, Marshall was bombarded with demands: for more planes, transports, ships, tanks, trainers, and soldiers. The demands of the war's first weeks, as the nation seemed to move from catastrophe to catastrophe, took their toll on him, and his close associates feared he would reach the end of his strength.

In fact, Marshall was well aware of his limits and, while working long and intense hours in the immediate aftermath of Pearl Harbor, he was also working to lessen his own decision-making burdens. He turned over all Army recruiting and training issues to Lieutenant General Lesley McNair, gave him the staff and resources to do the job, and then left him alone. McNair, an organizational genius, designed the course of study that, in thirteen weeks, would provide men capable of fighting the Germans and Japanese, then established the Army's specialty schools that trained tank commanders and airborne troopers. McNair, perhaps the most self-effacing officer in Army history (he once read a press release that mentioned his name—and crossed it out), regularly provided Marshall with a list of officers whom he deemed unfit for command, a kind of "little black book" in reverse. Marshall and McNair consulted on most command decisions, producing a skeleton leadership cadre for each new division, then spoke in detail about the qualities of the subordinate commanders they needed to appoint to support them. At the height of the war, the United States was producing four divisions of fourteen thousand men each month and shipping them to England and the Pacific. Marshall rarely questioned McNair's decisions, never intervened to redo his training regimen, and rarely disagreed with his command judgments.

The roots of this unusual willingness to show confidence in subordinates, to leave decisions in their hands, and to recruit them to his cause as a part of a team, came from the fact that others had done the same for him—even when Marshall's blunt questioning of authority might have ended with his retirement. The first such incident came in late 1917, when the U.S. military staff in France was conducting a combat exercise for AEF commander John Pershing. Pershing was in "a foul humor," and after the exercise was completed he asked for a critique from an officer who had arrived late for the demonstration. The critique was not to Pershing's liking, and he impatiently interrupted the officer and ordered a critique from a subordinate. When the subordinate's presentation also proved inadequate Pershing "rather contemptuously" dismissed those in attendance and stalked off. Marshall intervened:

> He didn't want to talk to me. He shrugged his shoulders and turned away from me. And I put my hand on his arm and practically forced him to talk. I said, "General Pershing, there's something to be said here, and

I think I should say it because I've been here longer." And he stopped
and said, "What have you got to say?" "Well," I said, "to start with, we
have never received anything from your Headquarters. When I was down
there two months ago, as a matter of fact, three months ago, I think, I
was told about this Platoon Chiefs' Manual that was coming up. It's
never come out yet." He turned to one of these officer and he said,
"What about that, So and So?" And So and So said, "Well, General,
we've had trouble with the French printers. You know they are very difficult to deal with." General Pershing turned to me and said, "You know
we have our troubles." I said, "Yes, I know you do, General, I know you
do. But ours are immediate and every day and have to be solved before
night. Now we never have gotten the Platoon Manual. We have made
the best we can of this thing."[46]

Marshall remembered the incident years later, citing it as a turning point
in his career. "Some of my bosom friends came up to me and said, of course,
I was finished and I'd be fired right off. I said, 'All I can see is that I may get
troop duty instead of staff duty, and certainly that would be a great success.' "[47]
In fact, Marshall was rewarded. "General Pershing never mentioned this thing
to me until years afterwards, and then he recalled it and his comment on me
was that I was pretty hot," Marshall later remembered. "Well, as a matter of fact,
it made quite an impression on me, because instead of ruining me, he sent for
me quite frequently. . . . So far as I could see, it helped me rather than
harmed me."[48]

A second incident has now become a part of U.S. military lore. On
November 14, 1938, George Marshall, then the deputy chief of staff, was invited to a White House conference on American war preparations. There
were twelve officials at the meeting, including Treasury Secretary Henry
Morgenthau, Roosevelt's adviser Harry Hopkins, Secretary of War Harry
Woodring, and Army chief of staff Malin Craig. Marshall sat on the sidelines
of the meeting, saying little. Roosevelt started the meeting and dominated it.
With Germany rearming and Europe moving closer to war, Roosevelt argued,
the U.S. must do everything that it could to protect its borders. Building a large
strike force of aircraft would do just that and so must be a top priority. Roosevelt
proposed that the U.S. commit itself to building seven aircraft plants, adding

that building a large ground army could wait until later. Pleased with these expert recommendations, Roosevelt smiled at those in attendance and asked for
their opinion. They all readily agreed—building an army could wait.

The meeting should have ended there, but quite unpredictably Roosevelt
turned to Marshall: "Don't you think so George?" he asked. Marshall bridled
at Roosevelt's "misrepresentation of our intimacy," and the room turned to hear
his answer. "I am sorry, Mr. President," Marshall said, "but I don't agree with
that at all." As the room went silent, Roosevelt nodded toward Marshall but did
not respond. Marshall's remark ended the conference. "The President gave me
a startled look," Marshall recalled, "and when I went out they all bade me
good-by and said that my tour in Washington was over."[49] Of course, it was not.
Like Pershing before him, Roosevelt was dismayed by Marshall's open disagreement, but he wasn't prepared to dismiss someone with the courage of his
convictions. Marshall remembered the incident, as he remembered his confrontation with Pershing, for the rest of his life, and while it is difficult to conclude that the Roosevelt-Marshall relationship was ever close, their ability to
work together dates from that disagreement. In fact, the disagreement may well
have been decisive in Roosevelt's decision to name him chief of staff in 1939.
"I want to say in compliment to the president that that didn't antagonize him
at all," Marshall later remembered. "Maybe he thought I would tell him the
truth so far as I personally was concerned, which I certainly tried to do in all
of our later conversations."[50]

The Marshall-Pershing standoff of 1917, and the Marshall-Roosevelt confrontation of 1938, reinforced in Marshall a belief that the best way to command
was to delegate authority and then, having delegated authority, to tolerate disagreements. This ability to reward skepticism was what marked Marshall as an
unusually successful commander. In fact, Marshall was so concerned that his
subordinates might hesitate to disagree with him that he purposely reminded
them to do so: "You may be completely frank with me in expressing your own
opinions," he wrote again and again to his commanders. Even so, Marshall's
command experience in World War II reflects that while he forgave failure and
tolerated dissent, he would rarely tolerate a refusal to act—a fear of failure.
When the war began, then, Marshall not only culled the Army officer corps
of those too old to command; he attempted to identify those commanders
who could act independently and make decisions in the sure knowledge that

their orders would cost lives. There was only one other requirement that Marshall deemed necessary for an Army officer to ascend to high command, and it came from Fox Conner. In the future, Conner had insisted, Army officers needed to be able to work with the senior commanders of other nations. What would be needed, Conner said, was a new kind of general, a diplomat as well as a fighter. But by late December 1941, Marshall had yet to identify such an officer.

MARSHALL'S WILLINGNESS to confront authority when he believed doing so served the truth was a quality he used sparingly. No successful officer could do otherwise. So while historians have focused on this side of his character, a closer examination of his career shows that the primary reason for his climb through Army ranks had more to do with his considerable capabilities and his willingness to take on tough assignments. Marshall first came to the attention of the U.S. high command in World War I, when he seemed to be everywhere at once: not simply making plans but then traveling to the front to implement them. A relative unknown in 1917, by the end of the war Marshall had become one of the most highly respected officers in the U.S. Army. On July 4, 1919, Marshall rode in triumph on the Champs-Elysées as the newest member of General Pershing's personal staff then returned with Pershing to the U.S. and served at his side. It was Marshall's relationship with Pershing that marked him for high command, and Pershing's impact on Marshall was decisive. A man of careful judgment and measured opinions, Pershing served as Marshall's mentor and supporter.

In July 1921, Pershing was named Army chief of staff and appointed Marshall as his assistant. Marshall's five years with Pershing were his first in Washington and gave him essential experience in dealing with the nation's civilian leaders. He briefed Presidents Harding and Coolidge and he rubbed shoulders with the secretary of war. There was no one in the upper echelons of the military he did not know. At the end of his tour, in 1924, Marshall was appointed a staff commander with the 15th Regiment in Tientsin, China—a city that was an island of calm in China's sea of political instability. Marshall immediately put the regiment on special guard duty, fearful that the war to the north would come south. The next three years were among the most rewarding that Marshall spent in the Army. His counsel that the U.S. should stay strictly neutral in the civil conflict was heeded in Washington—which left Marshall to look after his troops. He built a new recreation hall and planned regimental activities, attempting to keep the 15th Infantry (which had the highest rate of venereal disease of any American unit) as busy as possible. Marshall stayed long enough in China to meet Major Joseph Stilwell, who would later serve as the U.S. commander in China during Marshall's tenure as Army chief of staff. In 1927, Marshall accepted a teaching post at the Army War College and returned to America.

MARSHALL'S WIFE, Lily, was overjoyed by Marshall's reassignment to the States. She looked forward to decorating her new home at the Washington Barracks with the Chinese vases, rugs, screens, and wall hangings they had accumulated during their stay in Tientsin. But in August 1927, Lily became ill. A heart condition that had plagued her throughout her life worsened. The doctors at Walter Reed Army Medical Center told Marshall that his wife needed an operation. On August 22, Lily underwent heart surgery. In its aftermath, her doctors were optimistic and expected a full recovery. Lily agreed, telling her husband that she felt stronger and healthier than she had in many years. On September 15, the doctors at Walter Reed told her she would be released the next day. She sat down at her desk to write her mother the good news. She never finished the letter: a nurse found her, dead, slumped over her desk. Marshall was grief-stricken. John Pershing, who had also lost his wife, immediately sent his condolences: "No one knows better than I what such a bereavement means and my heart goes out to you very fully at this crisis in your life." Marshall responded honestly: "The truth is, the thought of all you had endured gave me heart and hope. But twenty-six years of most intimate companionship, something I have [not] known since I was a mere boy, leaves me lost in my best effort to adjust myself to future prospects in life."

Lily's death focused Marshall's attention as few other events. He filled his rooms with pictures of her, so that everywhere he turned he was reminded of her. Only his work seemed to keep his sense of loss in check, if only temporarily. "At the war college desk I thought I would explode," he later reflected. So he moved: first to the Infantry School at Fort Benning (an assignment he had wanted for many years), then to Fort Screvin, Georgia (where he served as the commanding officer of the 8th Infantry), then to Fort Moultrie, South Carolina (where he served as commander and head of District I of Franklin Roosevelt's Civilian Conservation Corps), and then to become senior instructor with the Illinois National Guard in Chicago. At each step along this arc of successive commands, Marshall implemented what he had learned from his experiences through thirty years of military service. And at each step that he took he was promoted, from major to lieutenant colonel and then to colonel (in 1933), and then to brigadier general (in 1936). The penultimate promotion came in July 1938, when he headed the War Plans Division of the War Department. Less than three months later, he was named deputy chief of staff of the U.S. Army.

Through the 1930s, with the nation in the midst of the Great Depression, the U.S. Army was nearly last on a list of federal appropriations. But Marshall was able to gain valuable experience in working with young men hired in public works programs for the Civilian Conservation Corps. In many instances, Marshall was supervising the men who would storm the beaches at Normandy, who would come ashore at Tarawa, who would fight the Germans in North Africa and the Japanese on Guadalcanal. The army was given a major role in launching the CCC and implementing its programs: in 1933, the U.S. Army processed nearly three hundred thousand CCC members and organized 1,330 camps. An old colleague from World War I, General Douglas MacArthur, was then Army chief of staff and the CCC's most vocal supporter. He was also impressed with Marshall's work with the CCC and thought it a miscarriage of justice that Marshall had not yet held some of the military's most senior posts. When the army needed a commander to head the 33rd Division, MacArthur reached into the upper officer corps and picked Marshall for the job. "He has no superior among infantry colonels," MacArthur said at the time.[51]

On his trip to Chicago to command the 33rd, Marshall was accompanied by Katherine, his new wife. They had met at a dinner in 1929, when Marshall was at Fort Benning. Katherine Boyce Tupper was the daughter of a Baptist minister and had become a Shakespearean actress touring England and Ireland. She pursued her career in the United States before marrying Clifton Brown, a prominent Baltimore lawyer. They had three children together—Molly, Clifton Jr., and Allen—before Clifton was shot and killed by an angry client. Katherine was devastated by her husband's death. Like Marshall, she could not reconcile herself to her loss and entered an extended period of grieving. That ended at Fort Benning, where Katherine met Marshall. They were nearly inseparable from the very beginning. The only bar to their marriage, it seemed, was Katherine's twelve-year-old son Allen, who preferred that his mother not re-marry. But when he met Marshall, who proposed to visit his mother at her home on Fire Island, he changed his mind: "I hope you will come to Fire Island," he wrote. "Don't be nervous, it is O.K. with me. A friend in need is a friend indeed." Marshall and Katherine were married in Baltimore on October 15, 1930—with Pershing serving as the best man. Lily's brother and Marshall's sister Marie were in attendance.

In the years that followed, Marshall and Allen would become as father and son, with Marshall showing an affection toward the young man that he could never show toward his fellow officers. Katherine, Molly, Clifton, and Allen be-came his touchstone and support, providing him with the quiet he needed out-side of the pressures of the War Department. Marshall was close to all three children but closest to Allen. As with his officers, Marshall allowed Allen the independence needed by a precocious adolescent. Unlike Lily, whose health was a constant concern, Katherine was a vibrant and engaging wife whose abil-ity to support Marshall's career allowed him to meet the social demands of being a senior Army officer. It helped that she was politically adept. When Franklin Roosevelt appointed Marshall Army chief of staff she, unbeknownst to her husband, wrote him in gratitude. "Ever since your appointment of my husband—as your next Chief-of-Staff—I have wanted to write you. It is diffi-cult for me to put into words what I really feel. For years I have feared that his brilliant mind, and unusual opinion, were hopelessly caught in more or less of a tread-mill. That you should recognize his ability and place in him your con-fidence gives me all I have dreamed of and hoped for. I realize the great re-sponsibility that is his. I know that his loyalty to you and this trust will be unfailing."[52] Marshall took the oath of office as Army chief of staff on the af-ternoon of September 1, 1939. Some hours earlier, Hitler had invaded Poland.

AFTER FIVE DAYS at his new post, Eisenhower found time to write to his old commander Walter Krueger: "My immediate assignment is as an assistant to Gerow to lighten the burden of this office," he said. "The rapid, minute-by-minute activities of the Army seem to be centered through this place, because no one else is familiar with everything else that has been planned in the past. As quickly as this work can be centralized properly the pressure should ease up some, but there is no prospect of it becoming 'normal.' "[53] Eisenhower lived with his brother Milton and Milton's wife and children across the Potomac River in suburban Virginia, though he most often arrived at Milton's home late at night, well after everyone had gone to bed. Years later, Milton remembered that Ike would let himself in and "would go at once to our children's bedroom, wake them, and have a relaxing chat."[54] Eisenhower hoped this would be a temporary arrangement, as he continued to press for a position as a commander of one of the new divisions being formed under the unforgiving gaze of Lesley McNair. Eisenhower might have been lonely—his wife, Mamie, remained in San Antonio, while his son John was at West Point—but he was enthralled by his work in spite of the killing sixteen- to eighteen-hours-a-day pace of the War Department. "Every day the same, 7:45 a.m to 11:45 p.m.," he wrote in his diary.[55]

Eisenhower saw Marshall every day, and often several times a day, as he put the finishing touches on the expansion of his original "Steps to Be Taken," memo. On December 17, Eisenhower developed his plan for an Allied buildup in Australia, detailing the numbers and types of aircraft, transport ships, and ammunition that should be used to build the "Australian Base."[56] He then wrote coded radiograms to Douglas MacArthur on Marshall's behalf listing the "pursuit planes, crews, ammunition and other supplies" headed from the West Coast to the Philippines. Many of the coded radiograms were sent out over Gerow's signature, even if it was now clear that Eisenhower, who had been in the War Department less than a week, was in charge of planning the American war in the Far East. Gerow was being eclipsed, primarily because he remained cautious and uncertain around Marshall. Eisenhower was not. Make the decisions and tell me later, Marshall had said; so Eisenhower shipped men and matériel to Australia, monitored the planned reinforcement of the Philippines, and recommended command assignments to the newly forming Army divisions.

Eisenhower's apparent ability to make snap decisions involving thousands of troops frightened Gerow, who often sent Eisenhower's decision memos up the line to Marshall—slugging them as "recommendations." Eisenhower was nonplussed: "Gee, you have got to stop bothering the Chief with this stuff,"

Eisenhower said one day. Gerow shook his head: "I can't help it, Ike," he responded. "These decisions are too important. He's got to make them himself."[57] The difference between Gerow and Eisenhower consisted simply in this: although both feared that a wrong decision might cost lives, Eisenhower was able to act in spite of this knowledge, while Gerow wasn't. It was perhaps this indefinable quality that made Eisenhower so valuable to Marshall, for whom the ability to make life-and-death decisions was a crucial requirement of high command.

One anecdote illustrates this quality in Eisenhower and illuminates how, in just a few months, Eisenhower was promoted by Marshall over 350 senior officers to take his place as the single most important commander in World War II. Within hours of arriving at the Old Munitions Building, Eisenhower was scrambling to find reinforcements for the South Pacific. While it was not difficult to find units that could quickly be shipped to build the Allied base in Australia, it was nearly impossible to find adequate shipping to transport them. After hours of searching, Eisenhower located the *Queen Mary*, requisitioned her, ordered the boarding of a fifteen-thousand-man division, and sent her on her way—across the Atlantic and around the Cape of Good Hope to Brisbane. Eisenhower was unconcerned with German submarines, because he believed that the *Queen Mary* could outrun them; then too, of course, the Germans had no idea that the *Queen Mary* was crossing the Atlantic. But one morning, Eisenhower arrived at his office to find a cable from an Italian official in Brazil to his government in Rome. The cable was decoded, translated, and delivered to Eisenhower's desk. "The *Queen Mary* just refueled here," the cable said, "and with about fifteen thousand soldiers aboard left this port today steaming southeast across the Atlantic." It was too late for Eisenhower to stop the ship, but he thought about the fate of the fifteen thousand defenseless Americans nearly every day. He dared not tell Marshall and only did so after the ship arrived safely in Australia. Marshall allowed himself one wry smile: "Eisenhower," he said, "I received that intercept at the same time you did. I was merely hoping you might not see it and so I said nothing to you until I knew the outcome."[58]

In less than two weeks, by Christmas 1941, Eisenhower had become one of Marshall's most important staff officers. It was an astonishing accomplishment. Eisenhower had not only proven that he was a talented strategist (he had established an Allied base in Australia, organized the relief effort for the

Philippines, and built a command structure for the Pacific); he had shown that he was "one of those assistants" who would, in Marshall's words, "solve their own problems" and tell Marshall "later what they have done." In none of this had he shown that other quality so admired by Marshall, the ability to dissent from Marshall's views, to stand up to authority, to be "completely frank" with him when it came to expressing his own opinions. And as Marshall knew, Eisenhower had to pass one more test as well: Eisenhower had to prove that could work well with Allied commanders—that he was as good a diplomat as he was a soldier.

ARCADIA

"Eisenhower you're not going to get any promotion. . . ."
"General, I don't give a damn. . . ."

B RITISH PRIME MINISTER Winston Churchill and a retinue of senior British officers arrived in Washington just after dark on December 22 for a conference with Franklin Roosevelt and the American high command. Code-named "Arcadia," the conference was requested by Churchill to coordinate British-American war planning. Roosevelt was initially skeptical about the wisdom of holding a conference on such short notice, but he finally agreed at Churchill's insistence, then warmed to the idea after reading a number of dispatches Churchill wrote to him enroute.[1] Churchill arrived in Washington fit, hale, and confident and had every reason to be: the Americans were now in the war.[2] Over drinks with Roosevelt at the White House, with a fire crackling on the other end of the room, Churchill talked of the war and his plans for winning it. Roosevelt sat silently across from him, the ice tinkling reassuringly in his drink, listening carefully. Churchill leaned forward in his chair, his eyes blazing. The U.S. should send three divisions to Ireland to relieve British troops stationed there, Churchill said. The British troops would then be shipped south, to invade North Africa from the west. The British Eighth Army was in Egypt and headed into Libya, and the two forces could eventually link up, providing a base for operations in the Mediterranean. Churchill was voluble, excited, expansive, nearly irrepressible. He wanted to take the fight to the Germans immediately, defeating them in North Africa. Though the U.S. president was noncommittal, he seemed to like the idea.[3]

Churchill went on to his second point, outlining his plan for gaining control of the South Pacific. There was no reason why Allied forces could not regain the offensive against Japan in early 1942, he said. He bubbled with enthusiasm, gesturing with his pudgy hand, fixing Roosevelt with his gaze. He seemed to dismiss Japanese military prowess. Again, Roosevelt was noncommittal. Undeterred, Churchill plunged on: the U.S. and Great Britain should begin planning for the invasion of Europe now, he said, so that the landings on the French coast could take place by mid-1943. Roosevelt nodded his understanding but not his agreement. Churchill was unconcerned with the president's silence, confident that Roosevelt had accepted his plans. The next morning, he reported on the meeting by coded cipher to his war cabinet in London: "The President said that he was anxious that American land forces should give their support as quickly as possible wherever they could be most helpful, and favoured the idea of a plan to move into North Africa."[4]

Churchill's proposal would have shocked George Marshall had he known of it. He was greatly worried that Churchill's excitable personality and his well-earned reputation as a master politician might overawe Roosevelt, leading the President to accept unwise military initiatives.[5] And Churchill was famous for grand plans, like his scheme during World War I to land troops to capture the Dardanelles and defeat Turkey. The resulting disaster at Gallipoli nearly ruined Churchill's career. The prime minister was undeterred by judgments on his martial prowess, believing it was the task of military commanders to put their troops where the enemy wasn't. But George Marshall viewed such simplistic theories as downright dangerous. Churchill, Marshall knew, was obsessed with the idea of exploiting what he called "the soft underbelly" of Europe. Marshall was not. The last thing he wanted was to squander Allied strength and American lives by chipping away at the European periphery. Churchill's strategy for defeating Germany contradicted that most fundamental of American military principles: to relentlessly pursue and destroy the enemy's military in the quickest way possible with overwhelming force and the least number of casualties. The doctrine had been a pillar of American military thinking since the days of Ulysses S. Grant, who, in his final drive against Marshall's hero, Robert E. Lee, had instructed his commanders to make Lee's army their objective: "Wherever Lee goes, there you will go also," he had said.[6] Hitler was in Germany, not North Africa.[7]

Marshall's worries about the British strategy deepened the next afternoon, when Roosevelt and Churchill convened a high-level strategy meeting at the Oval Office.[8] Roosevelt sat at his desk with Churchill beside him. Arrayed around the room in clusters were the U.S. Joint Chiefs of Staff (Marshall, Admiral Harold Stark, Air Chief Henry "Hap" Arnold) and their staff and the British Chiefs of Staff (Field Marshal Sir John Dill, Lieutenant General Sir Hastings Ismay, Admiral Sir Dudley Pound, and Air Chief Marshal Sir Charles Portal), and their staff. Secretary of War Henry Stimson and Secretary of the Navy Frank Knox stood by to help and advise Roosevelt, while Churchill was aided by Max Aitken (Lord Beaverbrook), a Fleet Street millionaire and powerful minister of supply. Other aides and assistants, including Eisenhower, sat in the background. The room was filled, its various clusters murmuring greetings and shuffling papers.[9]

The British began the meeting by focusing on what they called their "five points": an armaments buildup, the maintenance of communications between the U.S. and Britain, "closing and tightening a ring around Germany," wearing down German resistance by bombardment, and holding off further Japanese advances in the Pacific.[10] Identifying the importance of these five points seemed natural enough; their purpose, the British explained, was to build up military strength before going on the offensive. Marshall was surprised and skeptical. He was worried that his British counterparts had not begun with a discussion of general strategy and frowned at their use of the phrase "closing and tightening a ring around Germany." This seemed vintage Churchill, nipping and sawing at Europe without going for Germany's jugular. Confirming Marshall's fears, Churchill announced that U.S. troops bound for Ireland would free Allied divisions for an invasion of North Africa, a necessary precursor to an invasion of Europe itself.[11] Roosevelt responded, carefully weighing his words: he did not oppose Britain's five points and confirmed that the U.S. would send troops to Ireland. But he would not endorse Churchill's plan for an assault on North Africa until it had been studied more fully. Now it was Churchill's turn to be surprised. The prime minister had thought that he had already won Roosevelt's approval for an invasion during their discussion the night before. He expressed his disappointment. But Marshall was almost visibly relieved. After a short but sharp discussion, the decision was put in the hands of a subcommittee for further study. Marshall silently agreed with the decision: he had not won the first round, but he had not lost it either. Eisenhower, when he heard of this proposal, was also surprised: "I've been insisting that the Far East is critical—and no sideshows should be undertaken until air and ground there are in a satisfactory state." An invasion of North Africa was, for him, a "sideshow."[12]

The real work of Arcadia began the next day, December 24, when senior American and British officers met to hammer out the general understandings they had reached at the White House. It was no easy task: the Americans were uncomfortably aware that their British counterparts had been at war since 1939 while the Americans had stayed on the sidelines. The British, for their part, lacked confidence in U.S. military power.[13] The meetings got off to a rocky start when the room set aside for the delegations at the Federal Reserve Building proved to be too small. Marshall, Stark, Arnold, Dill, Pound, and Portal stood in a hallway until another room was located.[14] An unspoken rebuke hung in the air: if this was American planning, how could the Allies ever hope to invade Europe in 1943? When the group finally convened, the slight whiff of distrust that permeated the two delegations could not be dispelled. At times, on this day and in the future, discussions on resources, plans, supplies, and war goals became so rancorous that Marshall despaired that the two nations might ever agree on anything.

The disagreements came as a surprise to Marshall because the British and the Americans agreed on a common guiding principle for fighting the war—a "Europe First" strategy, dictating that the largest portion of men and matériel should be given over to the defeat of Germany.[15] The devil was in the details: whether the U.S. could agree with a British proposal, code-named "Gymnast," to fight the Germans in North Africa in 1942, whether to build up Allied resources in England ("Bolero") for a full cross-Channel invasion in 1943 (code-named "Roundup"), or in the case of the imminent collapse of the Red Army, to divert Allied resources to gain a small foothold in Europe ("Sledgehammer"). The disagreements over strategy often reflected American prejudices. There was, Marshall later noted, "too much anti-British feeling on our side; more than we should have had. Our people were always ready to find Albion perfidious."[16] These suspicions were mirrored by the British, who openly doubted

American combat prowess. Marshall worked with British general Sir Charles Portal to dampen British-American disagreements.[17] At key moments in the conversations, the British literally looked down their noses at their counterparts, issuing lectures to the Americans on the realities of fighting the Germans.[18] Senior Americans would often respond bitterly. Marshall listened calmly, then waited for Portal to intervene. "We can't blow up on something like this," Portal said at one point. "Something has to be done which one side or the other isn't going to agree on. Let's get on with it."[19]

IT WAS soon clear to Marshall and to the rest of America's senior officers that the differences between the British Chiefs of Staff and the American Joint Chiefs of Staff had little to do with petty points of national pride. What the British feared most of all was that the Americans would run the war. The fear was justified: the United States had vast resources and a large pool of soldiers. If American influence became so pervasive, not only would the Americans set Allied strategy but American officers would lead British soldiers in battle. What the British hoped, therefore, was that they could delay a final decision on overall command, allowing an informal system of "cooperation" and "liaison" to take hold. Marshall disagreed. Such a system would not work. It had not worked in World War I, and the crisis now was even greater. What Marshall wanted was not "cooperation" but "coordination" under a single commander. The British might command their own troops in their own peripheral theaters, but an invasion of Europe would take full unity of arms.

Marshall not only disagreed strongly and vocally with British opposition to a unified command, he took issue with their strategy to fight the Germans on Europe's periphery, as well as with their constant attempts to postpone an invasion of the continent.[20] There were murmurings among his own senior staff— including Eisenhower—that British proposals to fight in North Africa and the Middle East were a means of securing their colonial possessions.

Marshall and Eisenhower had studied a paper, written by Lieutenant Colonel Edwin E. Schwein three months before Pearl Harbor, that identified the French province of Calais as a likely landing point for Allied troops attempting to liberate the Continent.[21] Schwein had written that "the only possible method of approach to an ultimate victory of the democracies [was the] area in France between Dunkirk and Le Touquet."[22] To invade North Africa, or the Middle East, or even Scandinavia (a plan given the code name "Jupiter") would be to waste resources that could be stockpiled in Britain for an invasion of France in 1943. Only an invasion of France, and a fight against Germany on its borders, would lead to "the ultimate victory." Marshall was adamant; he would not agree to dispersion of effort and he would press relentlessly for unity of command. The meeting of the twenty-fourth, a conference in which both British and Americans gingerly explored each other's position, adjourned with only one agreement: that the Allies would adopt a Europe First strategy. But there was no agreement on a command structure that would make that possible.

After the end of the meeting, Eisenhower reported to Marshall, was briefed on the afternoon session, then wrote a short memo on what Marshall had told him.[23] Eisenhower then turned his attention to getting ships, aircraft, and men to Australia. On Marshall's instructions, Eisenhower continued his daily radio communications with Douglas MacArthur, his old commander in the Philippines.[24] Eisenhower's messages reassured the Far East commander that everything was being done to reinforce him while never mentioning that the troops, tanks, and aircraft MacArthur needed would never arrive either in time or in the numbers needed to stave off catastrophe.[25] "So far as possible," Eisenhower wrote to MacArthur, "critical items listed in your recent messages are being shipped to Australia for delivery as quickly as circumstances will permit."[26] With this done and with a cold winter's night settling on the nation's capital, Eisenhower sent a radiogram to senior commanders from Marshall: "The Chief of Staff particularly directs that units and troops located in all exposed positions avoid any relaxation in precautions and alertness because of the incidence of the holiday season," he wrote.[27]

Finally, though it was getting late, Eisenhower turned his attention to a paper that Marshall had told him to draft at the outset of Arcadia and that now, in the wake of the December 24 meeting, was vitally important. The purposely undated memo was Marshall's trump card in his negotiations over the question of a unified command.[28] The draft was headed "Memorandum for the Chief of Staff." The paper dictated a complex unified command structure for the Southwestern Pacific theater. Eisenhower began the memo by reviewing command decisions that Marshall had made in building up U.S. forces in the region, then listed Allied forces available for combat operations. Finally, Eisenhower innocuously reported on Allied theater cooperation: "The Commander of Task Force 5, of the Asiatic Fleet, has held a conference with Dutch naval authorities and has made an agreement for the coordination of Dutch and American naval effort in the whole region." This was Marshall's trump card: it was no longer a matter of whether the U.S. and its allies should adopt unity of command—it was already happening. Eisenhower, understanding the sensitivities of the British, built his case slowly. Paragraph 5 was the clincher:

> The strength of the allied defenses in the entire theater would be greatly increased through a single intelligence command. The many organizations enumerated in paragraph 1 cannot possibly operate at maximum effectiveness so long as cooperation alone dictates their employment, no matter how sincere a purpose may inspire the cooperative effort.
>
> Because of the number of independent national interests represented, to say nothing of the separate organizations represented in each nation's defense forces, real unity of command cannot be achieved suddenly and without well thought-out preliminary agreements among the heads of the military, naval and air arms of the several powers. Such unity of command could be readily achieved, however, with respect to a more localized theater, such as Singapore.[29]

This was a nasty bit of business—as Marshall and Eisenhower knew. Eisenhower made it sound as if his mention of Singapore were an afterthought, as just one among many examples of the threats being faced by the Allies. But Marshall and Eisenhower surely knew the British viewed Singapore as their most important possession in the Far East. The sun might never set on the British Empire, but it would certainly be dimmed without Singapore. The only way to save the colony, Marshall and Eisenhower seemed to suggest, was to ensure that it could be resupplied. And *that*, the memo claimed, could be effectively accomplished only if "allied defenses in the entire theater" could be unified under a single commander. Marshall and Eisenhower's underlying message was but a very thinly veiled threat: Singapore could be saved and the Americans would try to help the British save it, but the price for the salvation would be unity in command. Eisenhower put the finishing touches on the memo, then walked out into the night. It had been an unseasonably warm day in Washington, but now a chill had set in. It was Christmas Eve.

IT MUST have seemed ironic to Eisenhower that, after more than two decades serving his country, during which time he repeatedly felt himself cut out of the real action, he would now find himself at the very center of its decision-making process—and at the side of George Marshall. Eisenhower had always yearned for a command of his own. Like every Army officer, he knew that successive command assignments assured successive promotions. Command was the route to the top. But Eisenhower always seemed to miss his main chance, spending his most formative years as a staff assistant to older and more experienced leaders. In the end, though, while others were promoted on the basis of command, Eisenhower's success was attributable in no small part to what he learned from the three military giants under whom he served. At the same time, he gained invaluable insights and built a lasting friendship with a brilliant but mercurial colleague. The giants were Fox Conner, Douglas MacArthur, and George Marshall. The friend and colleague was George Patton. For Dwight Eisenhower, each of them was a model of achievement, a tower of strength, and an example of how it might be possible through sheer willpower to climb the greasy pole to ultimate success.

It is also fair to say that each of them stood in stark contrast to the single most important other male in Eisenhower's life, his father. While Dwight Eisenhower certainly loved his father, and remembered and celebrated his simple honesty, there seemed little else in him to hold up for emulation; his lack of affection and ambition, eruptions of physical violence, sullen personality, and odd eccentricities made him a distant and difficult figure.

David Jacob Eisenhower was a hardworking, upright, and religious man who at times seemed oddly listless.[30] The son of Mennonites, a pacifist and student of engineering, David left college to marry Ida Stover, a music teacher from Staunton, Virginia, who had followed her two brothers to Kansas. When David and Ida were married, David's father gave him enough money to start a store in Hope, Kansas, not far from Abilene, where they lived.[31] David found a partner, Milton D. Good, and for a time the two did well. But the bleak vicis-

situdes of Kansas farm life ruined their business, and David headed south to
Texas, alone and humiliated, where he was hired as an engine wiper
in Denison.[32] Ida followed soon after. When Dwight D. Eisenhower was born
in a shotgun shack up from the railroad tracks along the Red River, his mother
named him D. Dwight Eisenhower—the D. in the birth certificate left oddly
blank, unspecific. Eventually the young couple returned to Abilene, where
David worked in a creamery. But David was a changed man—his failure at the
general store made him suspicious and narrow-minded, a person who not only
would never take a chance, but who didn't think others should either.

David Eisenhower awoke each morning and walked to the Belle Springs
Creamery in Abilene, where he looked after the business's refrigeration units.
The creamery was only a few blocks from the small Eisenhower home, but
David never came home for lunch. Ike and his brothers might go for days without speaking to him. If David Eisenhower fished or hunted with his sons, if he
urged the arts or athletics on them, there is no evidence of it. His abiding interest was the study of a book he owned on the Great Pyramid. He drew a chart
of the Great Pyramid and hung it on the wall of the family home. "He tried to
prove prophecies for the future as well as prophecies in the *Bible* that had been
fulfilled," Ike's older brother Arthur once said. "By extending the lines of the
pyramids, the passageways, the mechanical measurements, and all that sort of
thing, he provided to his own satisfaction that the *Bible* was right in its prophecies." Dwight Eisenhower was not close to his father and never spoke of him.[33]
Aksel Nielsen, one of Eisenhower's lifelong friends, said that in all of the
decades they knew each other Dwight never mentioned his father. "It just
wasn't his favorite subject," he said. At a very early age, D. Dwight Eisenhower
made the decision that his mother hadn't; he called himself Dwight D.
Eisenhower, settling not only what he would be called, but what he wouldn't.
No matter what his name, it would not be his father's.

Eisenhower idolized his mother, who gave him his earliest and strongest
guidance. Like Laura Bradford Marshall, Ida Stover rarely reproved Ike or engaged in the violent outbursts that marked Ike's relationship with his father. She
was filled with homilies: "God deals the cards," she told her children, "and we
play them."[34] Eisenhower grew up in a family of boys. There were seven sons—
Arthur, Edgar, Dwight, Earle, Milton, Paul, and Roy—and the small house the
Eisenhowers rented in Abilene was crowded. Ike's childhood was filled with

school, baseball, football, chores—and fighting. Coming from "the other side of the tracks" in Abilene often meant facing down boys from other parts of the town. The Eisenhowers fought each other and then teamed up to fight others. Ida later admitted that Dwight was the most difficult to handle and had the worst temper.[35] He would have agreed, and he worked diligently for years to control his sudden outbursts. By his third year in high school, Ike had become an outstanding student. When he graduated, his classmates deemed that he would become "a professor of history at Yale," while his brother Edgar would be "President of the United States."[36] Eisenhower spent another year in Abilene brushing up on his math and English skills, and in October 1910 he took the West Point entrance exam. He won an appointment to the academy from Kansas Senator Joseph Bristow.

Eisenhower spent his first years at the academy flaunting its simplest disciplines, piling up demerits for minor infractions and showing a marked indifference to the spit and polish of cadet life. Later in life he admitted he "looked with distaste on classmates whose days and night were haunted by fear of demerits and low grades."[37] He played for the junior varsity football team, worked on an indoor track to improve his speed, and met and became friends with Omar Bradley, an outstanding student and a star of the West Point baseball team.[38] Eisenhower played football against Jim Thorpe, perhaps America's greatest athlete, and was described by the New York Times as "one of the most promising backs in Eastern football."[39] But his football career ended when he twisted his knee and was told by doctors that he would never play football again.[40] When he graduated in 1915 as a part of "the Class the Stars fell on" (his class had the highest proportion of generals of any in West Point history), Eisenhower signed up for the infantry and was told to report to Fort Sam Houston in San Antonio, Texas, a leisurely post where a young lieutenant might coach a few of the local football teams—and fall in love. Eisenhower did both, serving as head coach of both the Peacock Military Academy and the St. Louis College football teams and meeting and falling in love with Mary Geneva Doud—"Mamie"—a Denver native who visited San Antonio during her winter vacations. It was a whirlwind courtship: Mamie thought that Ike was "about the handsomest male I have ever seen."[41] The Douds were as attracted to Eisenhower as their daughter. Eisenhower proposed to Mamie on Valentine's Day 1916, and they were married in the Doud home in Denver on July 1.[42]

In mid-1917, with the nation at war, Eisenhower was promoted to captain, but instead of being assigned to a combat unit destined for the battlefields of France, he was ordered to Fort Oglethorpe, Georgia, to train officer candidates. It was there that he and Mamie celebrated the birth of a son, whom they named Doud Dwight Eisenhower. Mamie nicknamed him "Ikky." Eisenhower deluged the War Department with requests for a transfer to France, but he was far too valuable to the army as a trainer. In December, Eisenhower was transferred to Fort Leavenworth, Kansas, where he trained young second lieutenants, and then, in February 1918, he was ordered to Fort Meade, Maryland, to take over command of the 301st Tank Battalion. He was ecstatic. The tank was a new weapon and no one knew what it could do. Eisenhower immediately requested battle reports from Europe about the first tank battle of history, at Cambrai. He pored over the reports and realized that he had in his hands a weapon that could transform the European war from a stand-up slaughter to one of open maneuver with tanks slashing into the enemy's rear. But before he could begin putting his new theories into practice, Eisenhower was shipped off once again, this time to Gettysburg, Pennsylvania, where he was put in charge of the newly created Tank Corps at Camp Colt.

On October 14, 1918, his twenty-eighth birthday, Eisenhower was promoted to lieutenant colonel and given orders to report to New York for embarkation to France. He was finally getting what he wanted—he was going to war. But it was not to be. Three days before he was set to sail, the war in Europe ended and Eisenhower's orders were rescinded. Now, without the combat experience that he needed for promotion, he was certain he would be sidelined. "I suppose we'll be spending the rest of our lives explaining why we didn't get into this war," Eisenhower bitterly remarked to a colleague in New York. "By God, from now on I am cutting myself a swath and will make up for this."[43] Eisenhower was once again set adrift. The thousands of men he had commanded at Camp Colt melted away, leaving a skeleton command. He reverted to his prewar rank of captain, though he was promoted soon after to major. It was hardly a palliative. Eisenhower knew that he faced years of hard work to make his next grade, of lieutenant colonel, and that he would serve in a wilderness of posts, with little or no attention from his commanders or his government. It would be twenty years, from the end of World War I until 1938, before Eisenhower was again promoted. Historians have often looked on this period of his life as one in which he was marking time, when his services were undervalued, when

America's military slept while Europe seethed. This view is too one-sided. For one thing, after being transferred to Fort Meade, Eisenhower met a fellow officer named George Patton.

Like Eisenhower, Patton believed that tanks would transform warfare. He commanded the light tanks of the 304th Brigade at Fort Meade, while Eisenhower was deputy commander of the 305th. They became good friends. Patton was a West Point graduate (class of 1909), but unlike Eisenhower he was a decorated war hero. He had been seriously wounded in the first day of the Meuse-Argonne offensive, and had seen in battle what Eisenhower had learned at Camp Colt: that the tank would dominate future battlefields. Colonel George Patton was already viewed as one of the Army's most successful officers, destined for high command. No one would say that of Eisenhower. "Everybody thought from the beginning of Georgie's career that there were no limits to the heights he might achieve," one Eisenhower biographer has noted. "For most of his life very few people thought that Eisenhower would achieve anything much."[44] But the two shared a love of horses, athletics, history, and tanks, and Mamie and Beatrice Patton became lifelong friends.

PATTON AND Eisenhower began to experiment with the tanks at Fort Meade, laying out doctrines for their use that were viewed as revolutionary. Tanks were to be used in support of the infantry, Army doctrine then dictated, and were not viewed as a major offensive force. "George and I and a group of young officers thought this was wrong," Eisenhower reflected. "Tanks could have a more valuable and more spectacular role. We believed . . . that they should attack by surprise and mass. . . . We wanted speed, reliability and firepower."[45] Eisenhower and Patton were not alone in their musings. At the same time that they were reflecting on how America might use massed tank formations in a future war of maneuver on the open plains of Europe, a World War I veteran by the name of Heinz Guderian was doing the same thing in Germany. The debate in both nations followed the same lines. One of Guderian's students, a German officer with the same rank as Patton and the same age as Eisenhower, was facing the same opposition from his own senior officer corps as his future enemies were an ocean away: "There was a particular clique that still fought bitterly against any modernization of methods and clung fast to the axiom that the infantry must be regarded as the most important constituent of any army,"[46] he later remembered. Eisenhower and Patton would have heartily agreed with the young tank commander, a man named Erwin Rommel.

In the summer of 1920, Eisenhower and Patton commandeered one of their Liberty Mark VIIIs, stripped it piece by piece to determine how it worked, and reassembled it. They experimented with mounting new weapons on the tank, testing their firepower and range, and attempted to give more power to its engine. A tank should be able to race across a battlefield, spreading destruction and fear among the enemy, they thought, so it needed to be fast. "These were the beginnings of a comprehensive tank doctrine that in George Patton's case would make him a legend," Eisenhower later wrote. "Naturally, as enthusiasts, we tried to win converts. This was not easy but George and I had the enthusiasm of zealots."[47] Eisenhower underestimated the power of his and Patton's ideas. Their most important convert was Fox Conner, then a brigadier general. In the autumn of 1920, Patton invited Ike and Mamie to lunch at his quarters at Fort Meade. When Eisenhower arrived, Patton introduced him to Conner, whom Patton had met while serving in World War I.[48] After lunch, Patton, Eisenhower, and Conner toured Fort Meade, and the two friends explained their theories of tank warfare. Conner was mesmerized.[49] He urged Patton and Eisenhower to continue their experimentation with tanks and made a mental note to keep an eye on Eisenhower's career.

At the end of 1920, both men wrote articles for the *Infantry Journal*, the Army's leading theoretical periodical.[50] Their articles were immediately controversial, and were followed by others, including Eisenhower's "Tanks with Infantry"—an unpublished monograph that was circulated at the Army's higher levels. Eisenhower's arguments were widely viewed as heretical. His beliefs did not pay proper obeisance to current Army doctrine, a nearly liturgical faith in massed infantry attacks, and earned him a verbal reprimand from Major General Charles Farnsworth, the Army's chief of infantry. Inevitably, Eisenhower was summoned to Washington, where Farnsworth told him to keep his ideas to himself. They were not only "wrong, but dangerous." Remain silent, Farnsworth said, or face a court-martial. Both Eisenhower and Patton were stunned by the Army's intellectual paralysis, but both obeyed Farnsworth's order. Eisenhower maintained his silence for the next ten years, while Patton, fearful for his own career, worked for a transfer back to the cavalry. But both believed their time would come.[51]

With Patton now transferred and with Farnsworth's reprimand fresh in his mind, Eisenhower did what he could to maintain the morale of his command at Fort Meade. But in late 1920, that was becoming more difficult. Mamie and Dwight's son, Doud—a popular mascot among the troops of the Tank Corps and a child paraded proudly by his father during his official rounds—became feverish and ill. An Army doctor was called and Doud was examined. The doctor was uncertain in his diagnosis. Mamie, frantic with worry, demanded that a physician from Johns Hopkins Medical Center in Baltimore be called. The doctor was blunt: Ikky had scarlet fever. "We have no cure for this," he said. "Either they get well or you lose them."[52] Ikky was quarantined and for a time seemed to recover. But the scarlet fever developed into meningitis, and on January 2, 1921, Doud Eisenhower died at the Fort Meade hospital. He was only three years old. Ikky's body was transported to Denver, where it was interred in the family plot. When Mamie and Ike returned to Maryland, they realized their marriage had changed. "I was on the ragged edge of a breakdown," Eisenhower later reflected. Mamie retreated into a world of sullen isolation while Ike attempted to lose himself in his work, as Marshall had done when he lost his wife. But with his good friend Patton now gone, that was nearly impossible. Worse yet, as far as Eisenhower could tell, no one seemed to notice what he and Patton had done at Fort Meade and what it might mean for America's ability to fight future wars. But Eisenhower was wrong. Fox Conner, the man who called George Marshall a "genius," had noticed.

THE STRATEGIC ideas that motivated Dwight Eisenhower during his first weeks in working with George Marshall did not bloom unbidden into his thinking, but were the result of long years of study and discussion with an older generation of officers who had held senior command assignments in World War I. The most prominent and influential of these was Fox Conner, whose friendship with Marshall and mentoring of Eisenhower provided a foundation for their strategic approach to the war with Japan and Germany. After meeting Eisenhower at Fort Meade, the then–brigadier general requested that he serve as his staff assistant in the Panama Canal Zone. Eisenhower arrived in Panama with Mamie in January 1922. While Eisenhower liked Conner, he and Mamie were stunned by Panama's fetid environment and by their bug-infested living quarters, separated from Conner's residence by an overgrown hedge. But

Eisenhower was impressed by his new commander. The first thing he noticed, after he and Mamie climbed through the hedge to introduce themselves to their neighbors, was the enormous number of books that Conner had brought with him to Panama. Nearly wet with humidity, the books lay moldering on their shelves. While Virginia Conner took a moment to reassure Mamie that, with a little work, her small tin-roofed house next door would be more than comfortable, Eisenhower admired Conner's library.

Conner had requested Eisenhower as an assistant for a reason, but the reason had nothing to do with Eisenhower's duties. While maintaining and policing the Panama Canal Zone had been an American responsibility from the days of Teddy Roosevelt, only one regiment was stationed in the Canal, and it needed little supervision. While Eisenhower spent his days commanding his troops as Conner's executive, he spent his nights reading, writing, and talking with Conner about leadership, command, strategy, and war. This is exactly what Conner had had in mind and why he had called Eisenhower to Panama. The tutoring began immediately: as Eisenhower stood admiring Conner's library, the brigadier general reached into the shelves and pulled out a book, and then another, and another. Take this, and this, and this, he said. They were odd choices, all fiction, and all about command and battle. Read them, Conner said, and tell me what you think. Eisenhower set up a command classroom on the second floor of his own home, complete with bookshelves, pens, papers, and campaign maps.

Conner found in his young executive officer a willing mind of almost limitless mental endurance. Eisenhower would read a book and then review it with Conner. He was studying at the feet of one of the military's most creative strategic thinkers, a man who insisted that Eisenhower understand what was happening in the world. Conner told Eisenhower that he had to prepare himself for the future. There would be another war with Germany in Europe, Conner said, and it would be fought by a coalition of allies that would operate under a unified command. Eisenhower bought a map of Belgium and Holland, pinned it to his wall, and studied it. Conner rarely lectured Eisenhower, but when he did, the lessons he gave were blunt: the Treaty of Versailles made a future war with Germany inevitable, and it would come soon.[53] Conner spread his hands out over northern France. This is where the next war will be fought, he said, and where it will be won—or lost.

Conner made the same points to George Marshall. The two had discussed their ideas about warfare, the future of the Army, and the prospect for another conflict in the wake of the Allied victory in World War I when both had served on General Pershing's staff. The two men were intellectually compatible and shared a common experience of conflict. Both understood the vital importance, and difficulty, of building a unified command. Nor did either shy from the political implications of their beliefs. The United States was a democracy, and the simple and unalterable truth was that democracies could not stand alone against tyrannies. They needed to form an alliance, to act in concert. The American military's central principle—that it was and always would be under the command of and answerable to an elected civilian government—meant that in times of war, it would have to depend for its strength on a conscripted army of citizen-soldiers. Conner's and Marshall's beliefs might well be best expressed in a simple aphorism: Never fight unless you have to, never fight alone, and never fight for long.

Eisenhower soon realized that his time in Panama would provide invaluable training for combat command. Mamie was less excited by her surroundings, and less intellectually engaged. She hated the climate and found the social life of the Canal Zone stifling. She left to live with her family in Denver, and it was there, on August 3, 1922, that she gave birth to John Sheldon Doud Eisenhower. Ike was present when this second son was born and was overjoyed with John's birth—this second son eased his sorrow over the loss of Ikky and made him proud that he was once again the head of a growing family. After some hesitation, Mamie returned with Ike to Panama, where they continued their routine: Mamie would visit with Virginia Conner and her daughter; Ike and General Conner would make their rounds of the post, almost always on horseback, talking of world politics and strategy. Under Conner's direction, Eisenhower read and reread Clausewitz's masterpiece, *On War*, until he had mastered its principles. He studied the lives of Grant, Sherman, and Napoleon, and followed their campaigns.

At the end of the summer of 1924, Eisenhower requested assignment to the Infantry School at Fort Benning. But Conner had bigger things in mind for his protégé. "One of the most capable, efficient, and loyal officers I have ever met," Conner wrote of Eisenhower in his efficiency report. "Upon completion of his foreign service tour he should be sent to take the course at the Army Services

School at Fort Leavenworth."[54] But Eisenhower was not immediately sent to Leavenworth. Instead, he was ordered back to Fort Meade. Conner wired him, urging patience: "No matter what orders you receive from the War Department, make no protest. Accept them without question." Eisenhower trusted in Conner but was confused by his note, particularly when the War Department assigned him as a recruiting officer at Fort Logan, Colorado. Once again, in spite of Conner's telegram, Eisenhower believed he was being ignored, and once again he was wrong. Not only had Conner taught Eisenhower the principles of strategy; now he was giving his protégé a long-distance education in just how the Army worked. Conner patiently explained the reason for the Fort Logan transfer in a letter Eisenhower received just after his arrival in Colorado: as a recruiting officer, Conner wrote, Eisenhower would be assigned to the Office of the Adjutant General, where two slots had just opened up for attendance at Leavenworth. Several days after Conner's letter, another arrived from the War Department, ordering Eisenhower to the Command and General Staff School. Eisenhower was delighted and also pleased to learn that his time at Fort Leavenworth would be spent in the company of his good friend Leonard "Gee" Gerow. Gerow and Eisenhower made a pact: unlike many other students, they would study neither alone nor as a part of a "study committee." They would be a team. Both liked the arrangement, Gerow especially, for Eisenhower had brought with him the study sheets of a previous Leavenworth graduate — George Patton. Patton had graduated with honors. Eisenhower would do better. Like Marshall, he graduated at the top of his class.

IF GEORGE PATTON was a lifelong friend and Fox Conner an aging mentor, the place held by Douglas MacArthur in this unlikely trinity is that of constant crucible. "Flamboyant, imperious, and apocalyptic," biographer William Manchester wrote, "he carried the plumage of a flamingo, could not acknowledge errors, and tried to cover up his mistakes with sly, childish tricks. Yet he was also endowed with great personal charm, a will of iron, and a soaring intellect."[55] Eisenhower met MacArthur in Washington in 1931, when Eisenhower was assigned to serve in the Office of the Assistant Secretary of War. Eisenhower had just emerged from a half decade of indifferent service: with the 24th Infantry in Georgia, as a member of the American Battle Monuments

Commission, and as a graduate of the Army Industrial College. He was anxious for a command of his own. MacArthur had other ideas. The then–Army chief of staff was impressed with Eisenhower and insisted that he serve as one of his assistants.

Controversy had followed MacArthur through his career and followed him even when he was Army chief of staff in the years of the Great Depression. With the nation mired in an economic crisis, World War I veterans lobbied to be paid the bonus promised them when they had signed up to fight in France. A "Bonus Army" of veterans descended on Washington to pressure Congress to act, but in July 1931 the Bonus Bill failed. Encamped in the swampy Anacostia Flats, the Bonus Army (some five thousand strong, including women and children, all living in hovels) became increasingly militant, greeting police patrols with bricks and stones.[56] At the end of July 1931, Secretary of War Patrick J. Hurley ordered MacArthur to intervene: "Proceed immediately to the scene of disorder. . . . Surround the affected area and clear it without delay."[57] Summoned to the chief of staff's office, Eisenhower was ordered to accompany MacArthur at the head of the troops. Eisenhower was skeptical: "I told him that the matter could easily become a riot and I thought it highly inappropriate for the Chief of Staff of the Army to be involved in anything like a local or street-corner embroilment."[58] MacArthur waved off Eisenhower's warning: there was incipient revolution in the air, he said, and he was going to do something about it.[59]

With MacArthur in the lead, troops under the command of George Patton used tear gas to disperse the camp. The decision brought howls of protest from a nation that remembered the use of gas in the Great War. Told by President Hoover to use restraint and to stay out of Anacostia Flats, MacArthur later claimed that he never received such an order. That was a lie, and MacArthur and Eisenhower knew it. MacArthur had received the order; he just refused to obey it. Eisenhower was horrified by MacArthur's actions, but he defended them, writing an official report for MacArthur that was a model of discretion. But the difference between the two was obvious for all who saw them at Anacostia Flats: "There is MacArthur in full regalia, complete with several decks of ribbons, looking sternly upon the 'battlefield,' with the look of eagles in his eyes," a reporter later reflected. "Next to him is Ike, dressed in a regular unadorned uniform. If you take a close look at the expression on Eisenhower's face, you realize it is one of cold, caustic contempt. This is the closed Eisenhower, who later observed he had learned acting from MacArthur."

Eisenhower was enraged by MacArthur's actions, telling the historian Stephen Ambrose in an interview toward the end of his life, "I told that dumb son of a bitch not to go up there."[60]

"I wasn't really an aide," Eisenhower said when recalled his years with MacArthur. "The job really didn't have a name. I called myself his good man Friday. My office was right next to his, and he could just call me at any time. He gave me chores—for example, I'd prepare the annual report of the Chief of Staff. He gave me a few ideas and I'd work them up."[61] Eisenhower's writing was so facile, MacArthur found, that he could often express precisely what the chief of staff wanted. He was invaluable. But Eisenhower's views of MacArthur were not tempered by working with him; he complained about his mercurial moods, his petty tirades, his ego. He called him "General Impossible." MacArthur, on the other hand, realized that in Eisenhower he had a loyal and dedicated officer whose service was still underappreciated: "The numbers of personal requests for your services brought to me by heads of many of the Army's principal activities during the past few years furnish convincing proof of the reputation you have established as an outstanding soldier," MacArthur wrote in his evaluation of Eisenhower's service. "I can say no more than that this reputation coincides exactly with my own judgment."[62]

Evaluations aside, in 1935 Eisenhower, at the age of forty-five, was still a major. By contrast, his brothers were prospering. Milton was the most successful. He served as an aide to Secretary of Agriculture Henry Wallace and sat in on meetings in the Oval Office. Eisenhower, meanwhile, was strapped for money and considered leaving the military to take a job as a military correspondent. At Milton's urging he decided against it. But Major Eisenhower still had hopes for high command. With MacArthur leaving his position as chief of staff in 1935, he believed he would finally get the assignment he had always wanted. But just as he seemed destined for a field assignment, MacArthur lowered the boom, asking Eisenhower to accompany him to the Philippines, where he had been assigned as a military adviser to the Philippine president-elect, Manuel Quezon. Eisenhower agreed, though as he reflected, "I was not ecstatic about the prospect." But there was something in the former Army chief of staff that Eisenhower admired: MacArthur was the consummate public leader, a man who almost genetically understood the power of the press and the cinema, of posing for the public, of exuding a tough but dignified confidence. Then too, as Eisenhower had learned from Fox Conner, the next war would be a truly world war, and the War Department was chock-full of experts on Europe with few who could claim any experience in the Pacific. On July 1, 1936, Eisenhower was promoted to the rank of lieutenant colonel, and he was now earning a salary from the Philippine government. While Mamie and young John remained in Washington, Ike was able to send a considerable sum home. But serving with MacArthur in the Philippines proved considerably more difficult than serving with him in Washington. The carnival atmosphere that surrounded MacArthur greeted Eisenhower's arrival in Manila. There were constant dinners and speeches, receptions and parties, while the obsequious deference that everyone paid him fed MacArthur's already inflated ego.

By mid-1936, Eisenhower's relationship with MacArthur was deteriorating. Their arguments were occasionally epic. Their most bitter argument took place after MacArthur decided to accept a position as field marshal in the Philippine Army. Eisenhower thought the honor and title meaningless: "General, you have been a four-star general. This is a proud thing. There's only been a few who had it. Why in the hell do you want a banana country giving you a field-marshalship?" MacArthur was enraged by such talk. "Oh, Jesus, he just gave me hell," Eisenhower recalled.[63] The relationship continued to disintegrate; sometimes Eisenhower dared MacArthur to fire him: "I told him again and again, 'Why in the hell don't you fire me? . . . Goddamnit, you do things I don't agree with and you know damn well I don't.' "[64] But MacArthur would not fire Eisenhower; he was simply too valuable. Then too, while MacArthur might be a preening and self-important egomaniac, Eisenhower never doubted his dedication. He watched MacArthur in awe and knew that for all of his negative qualities, MacArthur was absolutely dedicated to his job. In the face of public and congressional attempts to cut Army appropriations, MacArthur peppered Congress with letters and cajoled close friends to lobby for more men, more money, more weapons. He was particularly keen to build up the Philippine military, though he dismissed any threat to the islands from Japan. During a trip to the United States with Quezon, his disdain for Japanese power was apparent: "Never in word or deed, so far as I know, has Japan given any indication of a desire to absorb the Philippine Islands," he said confidently. "Propaganda to that effect is generally traceable to those who have some ulterior motive to be served."[65] He gave this advice to anyone who listened, while Republican senators and congressmen stood by nodding their approval.

In 1940, MacArthur was told that he would be retired from active service. He wrote a gracious letter to Army chief of staff Malin Craig, but he was determined to remain as Quezon's adviser. His plan was to continue cultivating his friends in the Republican Party, then return at the end of Franklin Roosevelt's term to run for the presidency. He never doubted that he was destined to fill America's top office, that his popularity in the Philippines was matched only by his popularity in America. Eisenhower, on the other hand, believed MacArthur was nearly delusional about his political prospects, and dared to say so. His relationship with MacArthur was now more than strained, as the two engaged in daily arguments; he not only hoped that he would finally get the command he so desperately wanted, he looked forward to getting away from MacArthur forever. Once again, it was not to be. Eisenhower was urged by the Philippine president, Manuel Quezon, to remain in Manila. It was not a request: Quezon was desperate that Eisenhower continue as a buffer between the Philippine government and the imperious American. So for another painful two years, from mid-1937 until May 1939, Eisenhower stayed at Quezon's side, arguing sullenly and constantly with MacArthur. He was now nearly comfortable with the belief that he was destined to remain a lieutenant colonel and, with war looming, thought it likely that he would continue to be deskbound. Why would he get a field command, he reflected, as he had never had one? His only hope was to be assigned as an executive officer, a second in command, to a senior commander who needed a politically savvy assistant with a background as a troop trainer. In May 1939, Eisenhower got his wish: he was ordered to Fort Lewis, Washington, to begin service as a regimental executive to the 15th Infantry. Two years later, in June 1941, he made another step up the Army's ladder: he was assigned as the chief of staff to General Walter Krueger of the Third Army. Less than six months later, he was in Washington sending radiograms back to Douglas MacArthur, who was vainly organizing the defense of Manila against a nation he had once claimed had never given "any indication of a desire to absorb" the Philippines.

ON CHRISTMAS morning of 1941, Dwight Eisenhower was at George Marshall's side as the two set off for a meeting at the White House, accompanied by Army Air Corps chief Hap Arnold and Secretary of War Henry Stimson.

Marshall was intent on speaking to Roosevelt about his apparent decision to divert U.S. forces intended to reinforce the Philippines to Singapore to help the British. What Marshall had long feared, that Roosevelt was proving susceptible to Winston Churchill's charms, had finally happened: in a private discussion just hours before, Marshall had learned that Roosevelt had agreed to the diversion, something that neither Marshall nor Eisenhower could ever approve.[66] It was one thing to forge a global coalition, Marshall felt, and quite another to sacrifice American soldiers to it. Surely the worst had happened: Churchill had cast one of his spells on Roosevelt. It didn't help that Churchill was staying at the White House, and that he and Roosevelt would talk at odd hours. In fact, Marshall learned, the president and prime minister were talking constantly; at one point, Roosevelt even burst in on Churchill when the prime minister was emerging, stark naked, from the shower. Marshall was so upset that he was prepared to argue with Roosevelt, something that he believed no Army chief of staff should ever do. But as it turned out, Marshall's fears over the diversion of reinforcements intended for MacArthur were exaggerated. Seated facing his chief of staff in the Oval Office, Roosevelt insisted that he had made no such agreement, and Churchill, sitting nearby, backed him. The British prime minister was most adamant: he had only suggested that if American troops could not make it to MacArthur, then they would prove quite useful in the British defense of Singapore. Marshall was mollified, but he had made his point; such major strategic decisions should be made only after seeking the advice of senior Allied officers.[67]

Marshall and Eisenhower returned to their offices at the Old Munitions Building, but Marshall left soon after. He and Katherine had invited a group of senior British officers to their home, Quarters No. 1 across the river at Fort Myer, for a holiday lunch. Christmas or not, Marshall intended to press his point about unity of command with his British guests and was hoping that, having lured them to his home, he could get them to accept a proposal that had so far met with their outspoken disapproval. Marshall's Christmas dinner guests were Great Britain's most senior military and diplomatic leaders, including the British ambassador to the United States, Lord Beaverbrook; Lord and Lady Halifax; Admiral Sir Dudley Pound; Air Marshal Charles Portal; and Field Marshal Sir John Dill. A sprinkling of Americans, including Admiral Ernest King and his wife, filled out this large contingent.[68]

It was Dill—a man comfortable with Americans and as dedicated as Marshall to U.S.-British cooperation—who was Marshall's target. By softly convincing Dill of the importance of a single command arrangement, Marshall believed, he could open a wedge in the British Chiefs of Staff and win their approval for his idea of forming a unified command. It helped that Christmas Day was also "Jack" Dill's birthday, a fact that sparked Katherine Marshall into a last-minute search for a birthday cake, adorned with British and American flags (made in Japan, Marshall ruefully noted) and blazing candles. After his guests arrived, Marshall gave a short speech that focused on American-British cooperation. He smiled at Portal and the others, his eyes sweeping the room. But he kept his focus on Dill, then, almost slyly and in the midst of his toast of friendship, he suggested that just as the cooperation of the two nations would be melded together by the heat of battle, so too both nations could go forward under one command. The room remained silent. Marshall hesitated for only a moment and changed his tone. He spoke more formally, as if recognizing the difficulties those British officers present might have with such an arrangement. Marshall conceded these difficulties: the task ahead, he said, would be very difficult. But, he added, the lack of a unified command had caused enormous difficulties during World War I. It had cost lives. By deciding for a unified command now, at the outset of the war, Marshall said, the Allies could avoid enormous problems. This was an odd way to greet his guests, but Marshall forged ahead and finished by repeating his central point. "If we could decide on a unified command now, it would be a great advance over what was accomplished [in World War I]," Marshall said.[69]

While Marshall's British guests were shocked by this blunt assessment, Dill knew that Marshall's presentation had been planned. Dill would later remembered this meal with deep emotion, gratified that Marshall would take the time to celebrate his birthday. It was the first such celebration he had had since childhood. But while softened by this extraordinary show of friendship, Dill was still not convinced by Marshall's argument, largely because he sensed that America's senior commanders had not been prepared for Arcadia while the British had come with a view of the war that was detailed in several long papers.[70] The lack of preparation shocked the British. A unified command? What did the Americans know of command? Dill's own pessimistic judgment was given to Field Marshal Sir Alan Brooke, the new chief of the Imperial General

Staff: "Everything is done on a grand scale," he said. "I have never seen so many motor cars, but I have not seen a military vehicle. . . . And yet amid all this unpreparedness the ordinary American firmly believes that they can finish off the war quite quickly—and without too much disturbance. . . . This country has not—repeat not—the slightest conception of what the war means and their armed forces are more unready for war than it is possible to imagine."[71]

Marshall was to later reflect that his Christmas plea was a mistake and only served to solidify British suspicions and opposition to his ideas.[72] He vowed to make up for his misstep in the meetings that followed by deftly playing to British pride. After the Christmas lunch, Marshall and his senior commanders met to take up the issues they had left unresolved from the day before.[73] Facing his staff, Marshall reviewed his discussion with Roosevelt and Churchill. After a short description of the controversy over reinforcements in the Pacific, Marshall bored in on his point: questions like this, he said, "would come up again and again until unity of command" was decided on. Marshall then made an odd admission, noting that part of the problem the Americans faced in convincing the British of the importance of command unity was that senior U.S. commanders had not yet resolved an even more fundamental problem. Interservice rivalry was so intense, he said, that that it was clear that simply promoting "liaison and consultation" with America's allies would never be enough.[74] "With differences between groups and between services," he declared, "the situation is impossible unless we operate on a frank and direct basis."[75] Early the next morning, December 26, Marshall made the same argument to the British: unity of command was an essential component in ending interservice rivalries in both the U.S. and Great Britain. How could a battlefield be managed unless one commander had control over ground, sea, and air forces?

The British had no good answer, but still they hesitated. Air Marshal Charles Portal, heretofore a Marshall ally, took the lead, saying that he believed the current forum was inappropriate for a full discussion of the topic, implying that Marshall's initiative should be decided on by the president and prime minister. The meeting was once again adjourned without a decision. Early that afternoon, the two staffs met again, and again Marshall pushed his point. "I am convinced that there must be one man in command of the entire theater—air, ground and ships," he reiterated. "We cannot manage by cooperation. Human frailties are such that there would be emphatic unwillingness to place portions of troops under another service. If we can make a plan for unified command now, it will solve nine-tenths of our problem."[76] If Marshall's point could have been won through sheer force of personality, the Army chief of staff would have convinced the British. But they remained adamant. Again, it was Portal who took the lead: a unified command was not needed, he said, for when general directives were accepted by all the commanders, the machinery of the military would begin to run smoothly. He then asked that the discussion be postponed so that the British Chiefs of Staff could confer with their prime minister. Marshall agreed, reluctantly.[77]

By midafternoon of December 26, a clearly frustrated Marshall decided to change his tack. Turning to Dwight Eisenhower, he directed him to draft a model "letter of instruction" to a theater commander to accompany Eisenhower's earlier Christmas Eve memo on building a unified command for Asia. He suggested that Eisenhower draft the letter as if it came from a unified commander in the Far East, where Australian, British, Dutch, and American (ABDA) soldiers and sailors would be forced to fight together. But Marshall sensed that such a letter would still not be enough to convince the British. There had to be something more, something that would convince them that his proposal was not some kind of trick to put American officers in charge of British troops. So Marshall instructed Eisenhower to make sure that his draft letter could be signed by a commander who would have control over all Allied troops in the Far East Asia theater—and that that commander be General Sir Archibald Wavell, one of Great Britain's most highly respected senior combat officers. Eisenhower understood immediately what Marshall wanted, returned to his office for a short time, and then gave the letter to Marshall in time for the last afternoon session of the British and American chiefs.

Marshall made one last plea for a unified command with Eisenhower looking on. He waved the letter that Eisenhower had composed, telling the British that a unified command was the only way to stop the Japanese onslaught in East Asia. And who should be the commander in East Asia? Wavell's battle-tested experience and his service in the Far East made him a perfect candidate for the job, Marshall said. Still the British were skeptical, suspecting that Marshall was offering the job in the Far East to a British officer because the Far East was the least likely region to see an Allied victory. Wavell, the British thought, was being set up to be a scapegoat while the Americans would reap the easy victories.[78] Marshall retreated, but he would not yet concede defeat. In a private discussion in the Oval Office on the morning of December 27, Marshall persuaded Franklin Roosevelt to endorse his initiative. He then convened the American high command at his office in the Old Munitions Building and persuaded them to stand behind him when American and British senior commanders met that afternoon.[79] Surely, Marshall thought, the British would have to surrender under the onslaught of not only the U.S. Joint Chiefs of Staff but also Franklin Roosevelt.

The most stubborn opponents facing Marshall on the twenty-seventh were senior commanders of the British Navy, who feared that under his proposal they would have to answer to an infantry officer. What did the infantry know of battleships? Marshall gave ground, but he did not concede the point. Any unified commander would have to have full technical knowledge of all the services, he said.[80] He then added that in the Far East, ABDA forces faced a unified enemy, a single nation in which all the services worked together. That had been the secret of Japanese success, he said. To counter that success the Allies needed to build a similar structure. It was the turn of the British to concede the point, but to Marshall's surprise they added that the Eisenhower directive was too restrictive; if there was to be a unified commander, they said, then he should be given great powers over the troops under his command, no matter what their nationality.[81] Marshall was taken aback, but quickly agreed. Admiral Harold Stark, who had hesitated to endorse the Marshall proposal until a meeting with the Army chief of staff that morning, added his own caveat: the important thing was to approve of the concept, he argued, and then to revise it to fit specific conditions. Suddenly, shockingly, and in silence, the British and American chiefs of staff had agreed. The room went silent. Across the table, the chief of the imperial staff eyed Marshall and nodded that he too now agreed. Marshall had won.

Over the next days, no single decision would loom as large as that made by the chiefs of staff on December 27, but no agreement would have been reached on the twenty-seventh if Marshall and Eisenhower, working together, had not shaped a command structure that could work on paper. Eisenhower's Christmas Eve memo proved to be a key document, for it showed how Marshall's theory was already being applied in practice. Even Churchill, skeptical of an arrangement in which an American officer commanded British troops, finally assented. Seated on the edge of his bed in his room at the White House, Churchill argued, then wavered, then argued again and raised his voice and even wagged his finger at Marshall, as if lecturing him: "What the devil does a naval officer know about handling a tank?" he bellowed.[82] Marshall bellowed back: if we don't do something right away, he said, we are finished in the war. This silenced Churchill, who was not accustomed to hearing someone respond so quickly. Churchill told Marshall he would think about his proposal, and that afternoon he wired Marshall's idea to his war cabinet in London, adding: "I will send you my considered advice." By the next day, he had shifted his ground: "I have agreed with President, subject to Cabinet approval." The British cabinet waited for Churchill's bellow to reach across the Atlantic. It never came. The day following the cable announcing that he would give his "considered opinion," he made Marshall's idea sound like his own: "I have not attempted to argue the case for and against our accepting this broadminded and selfless American proposal," he wired his cabinet.[83]

As ARCADIA ground on, Eisenhower continued his breakneck pace, arriving at his office early each morning and working late into the night. His sleep was fitful and he would awaken at odd hours, get dressed, and return to his silent office before sunrise to review, add, edit, or pen commands. His secretary, Helen Dunbar, often arrived at work to find him seated at his desk, deep in reading. The work was fascinating, particularly on the sidelines of Arcadia, where Eisenhower served on a special committee of military officers designated by a special Combined Chiefs of Staff (composed of the British Chiefs of Staff and the U.S. Joint Chiefs of Staff) to undertake planning designed to stem the Japanese advance in the Far East. Eisenhower wrestled with the daunting problems of providing troops and supplies to Australia while attempting to reinforce MacArthur's hard-pressed army in the Philippines. But Arcadia had worn him down. Eisenhower was frustrated by the seemingly endless discussions that led nowhere. "What an effort," he scribbled on a note card to himself during one meeting. "Talk, talk, talk."[84] At the end of another meeting he confided that there were "a lot of amateur strategists on the job, and prima donnas everywhere."[85]

One of Eisenhower's closest friends in the Army, Lucien Truscott, came to visit Eisenhower in Arcadia's wake and was awed by the amount of work that was being done: "There was everywhere the sense of urgency, of hurry," he reflected, "as though time were pressed, and everywhere an air of mystery as though all could tell of deep dark secrets."[86] Truscott, destined for a key senior combat command in Europe, noted Eisenhower's increased importance and his place at Marshall's side. But Eisenhower had not changed from the time they had served together at Fort Lewis: "Every problem was carefully analyzed. There was the same extraordinary ability to place his finger at once on the crucial fact in any problem or the weak point in any proposition. There was the same ability to arrive at quick and confident decisions. And the same charming manner and unfailing good temper," he later wrote.

As the New Year approached, Eisenhower reflected on his time in Washington. It was clear that in spite of Marshall's impenetrable distance, the two were growing closer. Eisenhower had passed a series of tests. Marshall had demanded that Eisenhower make decisions on his own without asking for guidance, and Eisenhower had done so. Marshall had demanded that Eisenhower use his considerable skills to support the chief of staff in the Europe First strategy, and Eisenhower had done so. Marshall had demanded that Eisenhower prepare memos on Allied strategy that reflected his own thinking, and Eisenhower had done so. By early 1942, Eisenhower's ability to not only read Marshall's thoughts but add to them had slowly transformed Marshall's strategy for winning the war into *their* strategy for winning the war. Moreover, Eisenhower had passed perhaps the most important test that Marshall could set for him. Marshall had demanded that Eisenhower put aside his desire for combat command—in effect, to put aside his career—to serve the chief of staff.

Years later, Eisenhower remembered the test: "I was in his [Marshall's] office one day and he got on the [subject] of promotion. He said, 'I want you to know that in this war the commanders are going to be promoted and not the staff officers.' After going into this homily for about two or three minutes, he turned to me and said, 'You are a good case. General Joyce wanted you for a division command and the Army commander said you should have corps command.' . . . 'Eisenhower [Marshall said,] . . . you're not going to get any promotion. You are going to stay right here on this job and you'll probably never move.'" Eisenhower responded: "General, I don't give a damn about your promotion. I was brought in here to do my duty. I am doing that duty to the best of my ability and I am just trying to do my part in winning the war." With that Eisenhower got up, turned on his heel, and began to leave Marshall's office. But on his way out the door he turned to assess the effect of his words on the chief of staff: "It was just one of those things," he later remembered. "I happened to turn around and there was a little quirk of a smile [on his face] and I grinned and I left. I just had to grin.' "[87]

BOLERO

". . . our first major offensive should be Germany. . . ."
"All right. It is persuasive to me."

T HE FATE OF MACARTHUR'S forces on Luzon was sealed on January 5, 1942, when American and Philippine forces retreated to a defensive line at the base of the Bataan Peninsula.[1] It was now only a matter of time before the Japanese overran the American positions. From his office at the Old Munitions Building Eisenhower monitored the retreat, all the while struggling to build up Allied forces in Australia. Five days later, the Imperial Japanese Army made its first surrender demand, which was firmly rejected by America's Philippine commander.[2] Over the next three days, the Japanese slowly tightened their hold on the American-Philippine lines, landing an amphibious force halfway down the peninsula on the fourteenth, the same day that the Arcadia Conference ended in Washington.[3] On January 22, under the tide of this offensive, MacArthur ordered a new retreat to a position farther south in the vain hope that a constriction in his defensive line would stem the Japanese onslaught. It did not.

On February 6, Marshall appointed Eisenhower as Gee Gerow's replacement at the head of the War Plans Division. Suddenly, Eisenhower's horizons were expanded; while he continued to fret over America's untenable position on the Bataan Peninsula, he was now forced to balance his previous demands for more men and more matériel for the Far East with the larger strategic concerns of a global battlefield. The exhausted Gerow, who had proven incapable of making the kinds of independent decisions demanded by Marshall, was given command of the newly forming 29th Infantry Division.[4] Gerow shook his head at Eisenhower on his way out the door: "Well, I got Pearl Harbor on the book, lost the Philippine Islands, Singapore, [and] Sumatra. Let's see what you can do," he said.[5] The irony was not lost on Eisenhower: Gerow's reward for his inability to satisfy Marshall was command of the new division, a billet Eisenhower would have done nearly anything to get. Eisenhower had once again proven his value, but his work had not led to his appointment to the command he wanted. "I'd give anything to be back in the field," he confided to his diary.[6]

Eisenhower almost immediately missed his old sidekick. "Gee and I have really played tag with each other all along the line; but this is the first time I really envy him," Eisenhower wrote to one Army commander in the wake of Marshall's decision to make him America's premier war planner. "My heart is in the field and it is hard to sit at a desk on days such as these. The powers that be have put me in this backbreaking job—so all I can do is hope."[7] Eisenhower adopted a lighter touch with his old friend George Patton, who was now commanding I Corps, yet another job that Eisenhower wanted. "We will eventually beat hell out of those bastards," Patton wrote, perhaps sensing Eisenhower's frustration at being stuck in Washington. "You name them; I'll shoot them."[8] Eisenhower appreciated Patton's vintage bonhomie and responded in kind: "I don't have the slightest trouble naming the hellions I'd like to have you shoot; my problem is to figure out some way of getting you to a place to do it. . . . It was a personal disappointment to me to come to Washington [but this war] is too serious to worry about anyone's personal preferences, so I have wrapped up in cotton batting all my ideas about troop training and laid them away in mothballs. You'll have to do that end of the job."[9]

Unbeknownst to Eisenhower, however, George Marshall's "promotion" of Gerow was effected simply to get Ike's former boss out of the way—and make room for Eisenhower's eventual promotion to a more senior position. While Marshall had earlier threatened Eisenhower that he would keep him in a permanent staff position in Washington, the Army chief of staff conceded to one colleague that Eisenhower's performance since his arrival at the War

Department marked him for one of the military's highest ranks: "We're going to put a new man in charge of War Plans who may at some stage be destined for pretty high command," Marshall told Assistant Secretary of War John J. McCloy.[10] That Marshall had a plan for fighting the war did not come as a surprise to anyone, but that Eisenhower was a key part of that plan did. Only much later did Marshall expand on his reasons for promoting Eisenhower, albeit with his characteristic understatement.

> When I brought him in to head the Operations Division after Pearl Harbor, I put him in the place of a good officer [Gerow] who had been in that job two years. I felt he [Gerow] was growing stale from overwork and I don't like to keep any man on a job so long that his ideas and forethoughts go no further than mine. When I find an officer isn't fresh, he doesn't add much to my fund of knowledge, and, worst of all, doesn't contribute to the ideas and enterprising push that are so essential to winning the war. General Eisenhower had a refreshing approach to problems. He was most helpful.

This was backhanded praise. It was not simply that Gerow was "growing stale" or that Marshall needed the kind of "fresh" thinking that Eisenhower offered. The telltale phrase (that Marshall needed someone whose "forethoughts" would go "further" than his own) was the Army chief of staff's way of confirming that Eisenhower's view of war was visionary; for Marshall that was an essential quality for any officer aspiring to high command. The two now worked more closely together than Marshall had ever worked with anyone, barring the possible exception of Marshall's time with General John J. Pershing. And while the two might not have formed an abiding and deep friendship (as had, for example, the Union commanders Ulysses S. Grant and William T. Sherman during the Civil War), Marshall seemed more comfortable in Eisenhower's company than in the company of any other officer. Indeed, from the date of Eisenhower's appointment as Gerow's replacement to the last day of the conflict, the Eisenhower-Marshall relationship took on the characteristics that were to define it as perhaps the most successful partnership in the history of modern warfare. On the one side was the taciturn, seemingly detached, but easy-to-anger Marshall, "the organizer of victory." On the other was the outgoing and deeply driven Eisenhower, the diplomat-planner who was now Marshall's alter ego.

EISENHOWER'S NEW responsibilities brought new challenges; Marshall expected that he would now give his attention to an entirely different set of problems. While Eisenhower's gaze had once been cast over the vastness of the Pacific, he now understood that his strategic senses had actually been circumscribed. Even so, while his planning encompassed the entire globe as a battlefield, his primary and most immediate focus was once again on the Philippines. The march of the Japanese Imperial Army could not be stemmed, as evidenced by the drumbeat of field reports coming from the Bataan Peninsula. From February 10 to February 13, U.S. and Philippine forces mounted a small offensive and actually succeeded in reducing Japanese salients on the Bataan Peninsula. But the temporary victory was dwarfed by the enormity of the task that lay before the outgunned Allies. By February 14 the Japanese were again pressing in on MacArthur and his men. Eisenhower was despairing because he knew that the Philippines could not be relieved. A rescue force of 1,500 aircraft and 125 ships could turn the tide, but deploying them across the Pacific would mean stripping ships from the battle of the Atlantic, and that simply could not be done. "For many weeks—it seems like years—I've been searching everywhere to find a feasible way of giving real help to the P.I.," he noted. "I'll go on trying, but daily the situation grows more desperate."[11]

Perhaps even more disturbing, though it could not have come as a surprise to either Eisenhower or Marshall, was Douglas MacArthur's reaction to the impending debacle. MacArthur retreated to his headquarters, bored deeply inside a railroad tunnel on the island of Corregidor, and peeked out only for highly photogenic inspection trips of the positions of his soldiers on Bataan. Geoffrey Perret speaks for many historians when he reflects that MacArthur's physical courage was never in doubt; it was "moral courage that he lacked."[12] However, MacArthur's primary combat deputy, Jonathan Wainwright, was cut from a different cloth. Spare, focused, and soft-spoken, Wainwright remained a constant presence among his hard-pressed troops. It was his strategy that had saved the vast portion of the American garrison in the earliest days of the war, as he engineered a fighting withdrawal down the Bataan Peninsula, where he then designed and defended the interlocking defenses that cost the Japanese an easy victory. But even Wainwright could see the weakness of his position. Hunger, dysentery, and malaria swept through Wainwright's ranks, and ammunition began to run low. American and Philippine troops were exhausted.

In Washington, the Philippine crisis focused Franklin Roosevelt on MacArthur's fate. With the situation in the Philippines deteriorating, Roosevelt determined that he could not afford to allow the prestigious and politically powerful former Army chief of staff to become a prisoner of the Japanese. On February 22, Roosevelt decided that Marshall should order MacArthur to slip through the Japanese blockade and make his way south to Australia, and safety.[13] Informed by cable of Roosevelt's decision, MacArthur gallantly resisted, imagining himself, pistol in hand, defending Corregidor's Malinta Tunnel to the last barricade. Eisenhower put MacArthur's fantasy in context in a memorandum-for-the-record that he wrote for the War Department files: "ABDA [America, British, Dutch, Australia] area is disintegrating! We have concocted a message to MacArthur directing him to start south to take command of the Australian area, etc. . . . We've dilly-dallied along about Burma, India and China. Now, with Singapore practically gone and the Japs free to move as they please, we're getting scared. I think, too late! Circumstances are going to pull us too strongly to the Australian area. We've got to keep Russia in the war—and hold India!! Then we can get ready to crack Germany through England."

Later that same day, Marshall's cable directed MacArthur south: "The President directs that you make arrangements to leave Fort Mills and proceed to Mindanao. You are directed to make this change as quickly as possible. . . . From Mindanao you will proceed to Australia where you will assume command of all United States troops."[14] To assuage MacArthur's "outrage" at not being granted a combat death, Marshall recommended him for the Medal of Honor. MacArthur's transfer, his lengthy and somewhat feigned protests, his sense of personal insult, and finally Marshall's decision to recommend him for the military's highest honor enflamed Eisenhower. The day after Marshall's cable to MacArthur, Eisenhower boiled over, though he made certain that his views were kept private; he memorialized them in writing and hid them away in his personal papers—where they would remain unread for the balance of the war.

Message to MacA was approved by Pres. and dispatched. In a war such as this, where high command invariably involves a Pres., a Prime Minister, 6 Chiefs of Staff and a horde of lesser "planners" there has got to be a lot of patience—no one person can be a Napoleon or a Caesar! And certainly there's no room for a Pope or a Gates! It's a back breaking job to get a single battle order out—and then it can't be executed for from 3–4 months!!![15]

At sunset on March 11, Douglas MacArthur and eighteen others (including thirteen Army officers, two naval officers, a staff sergeant, and the MacArthurs' Cantonese nurse) boarded four sleek patrol boats for the 2,500-mile open-ocean escape from Corregidor. Jonathan Wainwright met with MacArthur for final instructions just hours before his commander's departure. "If I get through to Australia you know I'll come back as soon as I can with as much as I can," MacArthur told the leathery and rail-thin Wainwright, who nodded his understanding. "In the meantime, you've got to hold."[16] Wainwright, just off the battle line, looked blankly at MacArthur and said that holding Corregidor was "our aim in life." It was Wainwright who reassured his commander: "You'll get through," he said.[17] That evening, MacArthur set out toward Mindanao as Japanese naval vessels, alerted to his escape, scoured the seas hoping to find him. On March 17, MacArthur and his party flew from Mindanao to Australia.[18]

While Eisenhower was careful to keep his views of MacArthur concealed, he knew they were shared by Marshall. The Army chief of staff had recommended the Philippine commander for the Medal of Honor only out of concern for his political power. The astute Marshall was, in fact, acting on behalf of Roosevelt, who was always interested in protecting his vulnerable right flank from the constant skirmishing of anti–New Deal Republicans for whom MacArthur was a political icon. This was another lesson for Eisenhower, who was learning quickly that the term "global war" was not simply a geographic nicety; a worldwide conflict involved diplomats and statesmen as much as soldiers and commanders, and while the war might be global, many of its most important battles would be fought in the back rooms of Washington and London. Maneuvering through Washington's political minefields might have been old hat for Marshall, who was justly viewed as one of Washington's most adept political insiders, but it was new for Eisenhower, whose career as a staff officer had kept him away from the vicious intrigues of the capital.

Eisenhower was lucky to have an outgoing personality, but he was also fortunate that in Marshall he had the most adept political teacher available. It was one thing to flash a smile and proffer a hand (Eisenhower had mastered that art form), but he had not yet disciplined his temper to the same degree as the chief of staff—as was obvious from his often volcanic diary entries. "One thing that might help win this war is to get someone to shoot [chief of naval operations Admiral Ernest J.] King," he wrote soon after taking over as Marshall's chief planner. "He's the antithesis of cooperation, a deliberately rude person, which means he's a mental bully. . . . This fellow is going to cause a blow-up sooner or later, I'll bet a cookie."[19] The often prickly King, whom Marshall had spent an inordinate amount of time soothing, had returned an envelope addressed to "Rear Admiral Ernest J. King" unopened, with the word "Rear" circled. This was his way of saying that a full admiral had his prerogatives, and being offended by such inadvertencies was one of them. "And that's the size of man the Navy has at its head," Eisenhower confided to his diary.[20]

IRONICALLY, the author of the letter was Henry Harley "Hap" Arnold, a West Point graduate of 1907 who had been an indifferent student, a forgettable infantry officer, and a tactless and headstrong senior commander who paid as little attention to command prerogatives (as King had learned) as he did to West Point academics. Arnold found his niche with the military by accident. While visiting Paris in 1909 en route from the Philippines to his new billet on Governor's Island, New York, he looked up to spot "a queer contraption overhead"—and, as he later remembered, wondered what England would do "if you were to put a bomb on one."[21] When he arrived in New York, Arnold signed up for a course in aeronautics and then made his way to Dayton, Ohio, where he was given an eleven-hour lesson by the Wright brothers on flying. By 1938 he was the commanding officer of the Army Air Corps, an embarrassingly backwater assignment in a part of the military woefully unprepared for war. In 1938, when Arnold took command of the Air Corps, America's bomber and fighter fleet consisted of several hundred patched-together boxes with wings, and twenty thousand airmen.[22]

Irreverent and prankish though Arnold might be, by 1942 he was shaping a bomber and fighter force that would eventually number eighty thousand aircraft and hundreds of thousands of fliers, navigators, bombardiers, mechanics, and support personnel ("the cook, baker, military policeman, signal personnel, medics—all of it," as Arnold once said)[23] that would consume nearly one-quarter of all American military expenditures. Arnold was perfect for the job: like Marshall, he kept a list of fliers and planners who had impressed him, and like Marshall he was absolutely committed to unity of command. Arnold also had a friend in Franklin Roosevelt, who was so convinced that air power would be decisive in any future conflict that as early as 1938 he demanded that Congress approve funds for building ten thousand aircraft.[24] Fortunately for Arnold, Marshall's support gave him almost complete control of what was technically a part of the Army. Beginning in 1942, Marshall was including Arnold in every meeting between the Army and Navy—and treating his Army Air Corps as a separate service. By making Arnold a virtual equal on the American Chiefs of Staff, Marshall was placing the Air Corps in Arnold's hands, a nearly unprecedented command decision that all but guaranteed that in the wake of World War II the Army Air Corps would become the U.S. Air Force. "I tried to give Arnold all the power I could. I tried to make him as nearly as I could Chief of Staff of the Air without any restraint although he was very subordinate," Marshall later remembered. "And he was very appreciative of this. My main difficulties came from the fact that he had a very immature staff. . . . Arnold's role was a very difficult one because he had a budding air force. It had a terrific expansion rate to it."[25]

Arnold's devilish side appealed to Eisenhower, and the two became close friends in the period immediately following Eisenhower's appointment to head the War Plans Division. It was a fortuitous friendship for Eisenhower, who cribbed Arnold's prodigious sense of global strategy in intense Sunday-morning sessions. The two would meet at Arnold's quarters, where the head of the Army Air Corps spread maps out on the dining-room table where the two could study them. "For two or three hours they'd pore over maps, trying to memorize the geography of the entire world in excruciating detail," Arnold's biographer, Geoffrey Perret notes. "There were scores of remote peninsulas, obscure mountains and far-flung islands that were to become militarily important in the years ahead. They intended to know them almost as well as if they'd walked over them."[26] The lessons were invaluable for Eisenhower, who was being pressed by Marshall to lay out American military strategic priorities.[27] Marshall's pressure was unrelenting. Japan, Germany, and their allies had conquered nearly half the world and had not yet been stopped. Russia and Great Britain were under siege; in the Philippines tens of thousands of American and Filipino troops would soon surrender. Marshall pushed Eisenhower: he needed plans and options and detailed battle orders for air, sea, and ground operations in the South Pacific, Africa, Asia, and Europe—and he needed them now.

DWIGHT EISENHOWER'S father, David, died on March 10, at the age of seventy-eight. He had been ill for many years. The family had shown increasing concern over his state of health, and Eisenhower had known for some time that his father's life was slipping away. Eisenhower received the news from Mamie in the middle of a workday. Late that afternoon, while seated at his desk, he wrote a simple entry in his diary: "Father died this morning. Nothing I can do but send a wire." In spite of their rocky relationship, and his father's lifelong detachment from his sons, Eisenhower's emotions were deep. He had not known his father well and was much closer to his mother, and his duty was his paramount responsibility. He decided to stay in Washington: "I have felt terribly," he confided, emotionally, and bluntly, to his diary. "I should like so much to be with my mother these days. But we're at war. And war is not soft, it has no time to indulge even in the most sacred emotions. I loved my dad. I think my mother is the finest person I've ever known. She has been an inspiration for dad's life and a true helpmeet in every sense of the word. I'm quitting work now, 7:30 p.m. I haven't the heart to go on tonight."[28]

David was buried on March 12. In Washington, Eisenhower closed his office door to pray. He added a note to his previous diary entry, saying that he was "proud" of his father, while admitting that "it was always difficult to let him know the great depth of my affection for him." The same sentiment might well have been uttered by David. Ida Eisenhower and a number of Ike's brothers attended the funeral in Kansas, later writing to Ike about it. His mother was frail now and aging, nearing the end of her own life. Her pride was in her sons, nearly all of whom had become great successes in their lives and respected members of their communities with families of their own. A friend of Ida's moved in with her to keep her company, and her sons visited often. But many of them, like Milton and Ike, were too far away to visit, and she had to rely on their letters. Only Roy and Arthur remained in Kansas and, shortly after David's death, Roy died suddenly and unexpectedly at the age of fifty-one.[29] The death of one of her sons, so close by, seemed to make Ida fade quickly. She began to live more and more only with her memories, and her always youthful looks quickly faded. It was only when faced, later, by a bevy of reporters anxious to hear her judgment on her "famous" son that she showed a spark of her legendary feistiness. Which son are you talking about? she asked, and flashed a withering smile, adding: all of my sons are famous.[30]

While historians have focused on the pressures suffered by Dwight Eisenhower in the early months of 1942—the worsening situation in the Pacific, his struggle to gain control of his planning division, the death of his father, the worries over his mother—Eisenhower was also concerned with his brother Milton, whose own mental health was besieged. A man of great intellectual gifts, Milton Eisenhower had made his way through the federal bureaucracy to a position of stature and strength. He had served for thirteen years as the director of information for the Department of Agriculture, where his considerable talents had come to the attention of successive presidents. In March 1942, Franklin Roosevelt asked him to take on the controversial job of heading the War Relocation Authority, responsible for the internment of thousands of Japanese Americans.[31] Milton considered the task onerous and was blunt in his assessment of it with Roosevelt, who nodded his understanding and settled on his own judgment—the "relocation centers," he told Milton, were "concentration camps." But Milton did the job, relocating 120,000 Japanese Americans to ten camps, despite his hesitations. Even so, the task took its toll, and Milton became distant, nearly unapproachable.[32] Ike worried about him.

March 1942 was also a difficult month for George Marshall. His wife, Katherine, was slow to mend from an injury suffered in November of the previous year, when she had slipped on a rug on their porch and broken four of her ribs.[33] The ribs were only now beginning to heal, and her movements were slow and painful. Marshall worried about the constant whirlwind schedule that she kept, attending dinners and meetings and fund-raising events. It seemed to George Marshall that being the wife of the Army chief of staff was exhausting her. He wrote of this to his stepson Allen: "The trouble is, I cannot persuade her to lighten her own burdens, telephone, mail, and committees. She resents my ideas of procedure and suffers accordingly. Her mail has become voluminous, telephone calls more numerous than ever, and demands on her to attend meetings a daily matter. Added to this are her own affairs, those normal to the house."[34] Marshall went on to note Katherine's other worries, though they were also his, about his two stepsons, Clifton and Allen, and his stepdaughter, Molly, and about the wider family. In many respects, Marshall's nearly obsessive worry over his wife's health was reminiscent of his lingering wound over the death of Lily, who had been in poor health for many years prior to her death.[35] He didn't want to revisit that pain.

The four-month-old war was taking its toll on both men. Eisenhower and Marshall worked backbreaking hours, though Marshall always attempted to maintain a healthy regimen, no matter what the crisis. He watched his health, Katherine later noted, "as though he were a runner in training for a long race."[36] And while Marshall attempted to adopt an even-tempered approach to all of his friendships and in all social environments, he had purposely cut back on the round of dinners and receptions that are common to senior military officers. On more than one occasion he feigned having to answer an important telephone call simply in order to leave a dinner or reception early, and as biographer Forrest Pogue noted, he became expert at avoiding Washington's social requirements. The cost of the war on Marshall's nerves might not have been obvious to official Washington, but Katherine noticed. During their regular evening walks she often found herself alone as he began talking to himself, as if ticking off in his own thoughts the intrusive requirements of his position. "It was as though he lived outside himself and George Marshall was someone he was constantly appraising, advising, and training to meet a situation." Such detachment was perhaps to be expected in such circumstances, when thousands were dying and thousands of others were being trained to kill or die. Marshall himself recognized this. "I cannot afford the luxury of sentiment," he told Katherine one evening; "mine must be cold logic. Sentiment is for others."[37]

The degree to which Marshall was detached and silent was the degree to which Eisenhower was outgoing and voluble. Eisenhower might work long hours and endure incredible pressures, but outwardly, at least, he seemed unfazed by the demands of his work. At the same time, he and Mamie were getting along better than ever; the rocky relationship that had developed as a result of Ikky's death and Ike's constantly shifting deployments was now well behind them. When her husband came to Washington, Mamie expressed her irritation at yet another move, and she headed south, to San Antonio, to pack up yet again. "I feel like a football—kicked from place to place," she had written to her parents from Washington, but added, "Now that the break is made, I am glad to be here."[38] When Mamie arrived, Eisenhower moved out of Milton's home and joined her in a small apartment in Washington's Wardman Park Hotel. Mamie enjoyed her new surroundings and the obvious benefits of being the wife of one of Washington's most senior Army officers. But the nights of socializing with the Butchers, Gerows, and Pattons over cocktails and bridge were over. The world had changed forever. "You must have some inkling of the real pressure under which I am now working," Eisenhower wrote to a friend. "The days are all too short. I rarely leave this rabid room in the daylight. We can never accept a social invitation, unless someone will invite Mamie to dinner and has me drop past later to pick her up."[39]

Eisenhower was also concerned about his son, John, then in his plebe year at West Point. John was closer to Mamie than to his father, who seemed to be repeating the detached, affectionless attitude that David had visited on him. The two were noticeably stiff with each other, and Ike's letters to his son were filled with advice laden with the privilege taken by every father—of lecturing and, sometimes, finding fault. The same Eisenhower who had regularly flaunted West Point's rigid routine and even ridiculed the academy's more staid traditions was now concerned that his son not follow in his footsteps. At the same time, Eisenhower could use his son as a confidant. Once he confided to John his fear that he would be stranded for years at the War Department as a brigadier general. "I think Dad was sort of apologizing to me," John later reflected, "that he was going to be a brigadier for the rest of his life. Hell, that sounded pretty good to me."[40] But these moments were unusual. Normally, Eisenhower eschewed any shows of affection, both in person and in his letters; he was sensitive that his son would be living in his shadow and was anxious that John find his own way.[41] Yet in time, his relationship with his son would grow even more distant.

Marshall and Eisenhower accelerated their planning through March. Marshall was particularly intent on continuing his program of streamlining the War Department and his own staff. Now that the war was on, Congress and the

White House would agree to nearly every reorganization they recommended, and Marshall moved quickly to put in place a command structure that would meet the war's needs. Marshall's transformation at the War Department was preceded by the appointment of Lieutenant General Joseph McNarney "as the man to put the reorganization into effect."[42] Known for his candor (he had once responded to one of Marshall's suggestions by blurting out "Jesus, man, you can't do that"), McNarney was thick-skinned and uninterested in the inevitable power politics among Marshall's staff. Like Eisenhower and Patton, McNarney's name had been in Marshall's little black book. Marshall's mandate to McNarney was simply stated: "It was taking too long to get a paper through the War Department. Everybody had to concur. About twenty-eight people had to pass on matters." As if there were any doubt, he added: "I can't stand it."[43]

McNarney's changes were sweeping. In just two weeks he eliminated the War Department's staid bureaucracy, eviscerated the old General Staff system, downgraded the General Staff divisions, subordinated the supply chiefs, and liquidated the welter of training and doctrine staffs so that now there would be one "czar" charged with overseeing all the training of new recruits of all the service branches. Reorganizing any federal department was politically charged, the War Department perhaps more so than any other. At one point Marshall joked to McNarney that his powers were so great that the committee he had put together to effect the changes had as much power as the Soviet politburo. McNarney nodded: that's exactly what he wanted. Democracy was fine for the rest of the country, but it would be death for the military. The reorganization even affected Dwight Eisenhower. By the end of March, the number of senior officers reporting to the Army chief of staff had been whittled from sixty to six. Eisenhower, who was promoted to major general, was one of the six, one of Marshall's inner circle. Additionally, Eisenhower learned, he was no longer in charge of the War Plans Division. It was now called the Operations and Plans Division (OPD), and it had been given even more power under Eisenhower's leadership. Joining Eisenhower in this new arrangement were three other commanders: Army Ground Forces commander Lesley McNair, Army Air Forces commander Henry "Hap" Arnold, and Army Service Forces (commander) Lieutenant General Brehon B. Somervell, charged with supplies.

McNarney's transformation of the War Department ruffled feathers and enflamed officers who believed they had lost their prerogatives. It led to suspicions among naval officers that the Army chief of staff intended to run the war by himself. Marshall moved in mid-March to allay these fears, suggesting to Roosevelt that the Joint Chiefs of Staff needed a chairman. Prior to mid-March, King, Marshall, and Arnold had shared the duties of running their respective services (and ironing out the almost constant interservice difficulties of roles and missions), and the system had worked well. But Marshall believed that it had not worked well enough. Nor, he believed, had the system given the Navy as much power in making military decisions as that branch would have liked. The problem was that the Army actually had two votes inside the JCS, while the Navy had only one. While Army Air Corps chief Hap Arnold was charged with commanding the nation's semiseparate Air Corps, he still reported to Marshall — and was his subordinate. Marshall remedied the situation by recommending that Admiral William D. Leahy, the former chief of naval operations and Franklin Roosevelt's nominal military adviser, be appointed as JCS chairman, a show of magnanimity that some believed was unnecessary: "Marshall is a far better man than any man in sight," Secretary of War Henry Stimson later reflected. But Marshall wanted to head off any interservice bitterness before it began, and his suggestion was approved by Roosevelt.

It was done then: the Allies — the United Nations, as Roosevelt and Churchill had dubbed them — had created a combined command, and the War Department had been restructured. Everywhere in America, hundreds of thousands of young men were moving from the nation's recruiting offices to their training bases, where Lesley McNair and his staff were preparing them for war. Even as Dwight Eisenhower and George Marshall were working to save the ill-fated soldiers on the Bataan Peninsula, and as Douglas MacArthur was preparing for his run across the seas to Australia, thousands of men were already aboard ships bound for the South Pacific and across the Atlantic to England. America's war economy was beginning to produce the thousands of rifles, tanks, ships, and aircraft that would be needed to assure victory. And the British and Americans had reached a broad agreement: they would fight Germany first, then turn their attention to Japan. But just when and how this fight would take place and who would command it had yet to be decided. George Marshall gave the job of shaping this strategy to Dwight Eisenhower.

ON MARCH 25, 1942, Major General Eisenhower submitted a memorandum to the Army chief of staff outlining the strategic goals of the Allies in World War

II. Known as the Marshall Memorandum (or, alternatively, the Eisenhower Doctrine), Eisenhower's outline of Allied goals (formally entitled "Critical Points in the Development of Coordinate Viewpoint as to Major Tasks of the War") became the premier planning document for the United States and Great Britain in its war with Germany and Japan.[44] In three succinct pages, Eisenhower identified Allied vulnerabilities, how they could be overcome, and when and how the Allied forces could begin offensive operations in Europe. Three paragraphs state its central precepts:

We are principally concerned in preventing the rise of any situation that will automatically give the Axis an overwhelming tactical superiority; or one under which its productive potential becomes greater than our own.

The loss of either England or Russia would probably give the Axis an immediate ability to nullify any of our future efforts. The loss of the Near East or England would probably give the Axis a greater productive potential than our own.

Consequently the immediately important tasks, aside from protection of the American continent, are the security of England, the retention of Russia in the war as an active ally, and the defense of the Middle East.[45]

Eisenhower then fleshed out the details of this overall strategy, noting that "it is considered that the principal target for our first major offensive should be Germany, to be attacked through western Europe." None of this was a surprise, of course; the general outlines of the strategic plan had been put in place by Eisenhower for Marshall over the previous month in a series of planning documents on each theater of combat. Then too, the Arcadia meeting had determined that the defeat of Germany should be a priority of the Allies, a fact simply reiterated by Eisenhower in his memo. But the Marshall Memorandum was the first time that a senior American planner had actually put in writing a plan to win the war. In many ways, Eisenhower's paper was the culmination of U.S. military thinking that had its roots in Marshall's work to rebuild U.S. military capacity, which he and Hap Arnold had begun in 1938.

Nor was the Marshall Memorandum written in a vacuum. Throughout February and into the middle of March, Marshall and Eisenhower had met to talk through their conception of the war and the command arrangements that would guide its most important military operations—conversations which were followed by Eisenhower's planning documents laying out the military goals for each theater. The first of these documents, circulated on February 28, focused on "Strategic Conceptions and Their Application to Southwest Pacific."[46] Subsequent planning documents established the status of the "United States Army Air Forces in the United Kingdom,"[47] fixed the command "responsibility" of U.S. and UK forces stationed in Great Britain,[48] created a new "Southwest Pacific" command structure,[49] and provided guidance to Marshall in his delicate dealings with the Navy and the always sensitive Admiral Ernest King. Eisenhower was particularly concerned that Marshall tread softly when handling the Navy's deep-seated conviction that it should be responsible for all operations in the Pacific and that, since this was "the Navy's lake" (and because the Navy was—as King would have it—the most important military service), the war against Japan should take precedence over any offensive operations in Europe. While King had acceded to the Europe First strategy laid out as a result of the Arcadia meetings, that did not mean that he would agree to the continued diversion of resources from the Pacific to Great Britain. Beginning in February and then for the next several months, King mounted a veritable siege of Marshall, pummeling him with requests for increased aircraft, soldiers, and ships. King's siege was abetted by the "Pacific First" views of Douglas MacArthur. Europe would come first, King argued repeatedly, but not "to the extent that we find ourselves unable to fulfill our obligations to implement our basic strategic plan in the Pacific Theatre, which is to hold what we have against any attack that the Japanese are capable of launching against us."[50]

Marshall placated King when he could, ignored him when he had to, and granted his demands when King was right. But King's constant bombardment did not deter Marshall or Eisenhower from their continued focus on Europe. While King might be disturbed by the amount of time, effort, and resources that a European strategy would consume at the expense of his plans for the war against Japan in the Pacific, the Marshall Memorandum was unswerving in designating the war on Germany as a priority. Nowhere in the memorandum was Japan mentioned: if America was to lose the war it would not be because it had failed to defeat Japan but because it had failed to defeat Germany. The three areas where failure could doom Allied efforts had to do with Germany: ". . . the security of England, the retention of Russia in the war as an active ally, and the defense of the Middle East." Eisenhower's memorandum concluded: "Our first major offensive should be Germany." The document was approved by Marshall on the last day of March. "All right," Marshall told Eisenhower. "It is persuasive to me."

The Marshall Memorandum did not simply reflect the more specific tasks that the War Department believed lay before the Allies, it also reflected Marshall and Eisenhower's conception of how the United States should fight modern wars, even those that the nation would face once Germany and Japan were defeated. Both believed strongly in the need for the U.S. to build a strong political coalition to wage the war; both believed strongly in discarding the need for peripheral operations ("We've got to go to Europe and fight," Eisenhower had said, "and we've got to quit wasting resources all over the world");[51] both believed that defeating the enemy in the shortest possible time was essential; and both believed that the United States should bring all of its resources to bear on the enemy. In the particular case of defeating Germany in Europe, Marshall and Eisenhower were putting in place a conception of warfare that was to dominate American military thinking for the next half century: with a war now forced upon it, the United States was required to engage the enemy in the shortest amount of time with the largest force possible—with a concentration of men and matériel in Great Britain which, when landed on the northwest coast of France, would engage Germany's greatest military resource, its panzer divisions, on the plains of northern Europe. This was Marshall's dream and it was also Eisenhower's: that America's greatest tank commanders, men like George Patton, would defeat Germany's greatest tank commanders, in a battle that would decide the conflict.

Eisenhower's final draft of the Marshall Memorandum was given to Franklin Roosevelt on April 1.[52] Roosevelt, who had had at least one conversation with Marshall before he saw the actual memorandum, approved it. Roosevelt had initially been skeptical of the plan, largely because he found Churchill's argument that the Allies first face off against the Germans in North Africa compelling. But he approved the plan, thereby giving Marshall the go-ahead to begin its implementation. Marshall left the White House content that his conception's central principle, that the U.S. would build a force in Great Britain for an invasion of northwestern Europe sometime in 1943, was sound. The buildup of Allied forces in Great Britain provided the otherwise innocuous yet portentous military code phrase with which Eisenhower had headed his memo:

"OPD 381 Bolero, Case 6."[53] "Bolero" was the code name for the buildup of U.S. and Allied forces in Great Britain; "Sledgehammer" (which Marshall viewed only as an "emergency" operation)[54] would be the code name for an operation in Europe in 1942 to divert German resources should Russia collapse; and "Roundup" was the code name given the Allied plan for the invasion of France, now scheduled for 1943.[55]

WHILE BOLERO, Sledgehammer, and Roundup had been approved by Franklin Roosevelt, they had not yet been approved by Winston Churchill, so the president directed that George Marshall and presidential aide Harry Hopkins travel to London to meet with him. Marshall knew that convincing Churchill of the American plan would be difficult; Churchill's sights were set on confronting the German Army in North Africa or the Middle East prior to any European operation. Then too, Bolero called for the deployment of 5,800 combat planes and forty-eight divisions to Britain—numbers that were sure to startle the British, who had only twelve combat divisions available to lend to the planned invasion of France. Marshall and Hopkins arrived in England on April 7 and met immediately with Churchill at 10 Downing Street, then moved their discussions to Churchill's country home at Chequers. As expected, Marshall had difficulty persuading Churchill and the British Chiefs of Staff to adopt important aspects of the U.S. program—and, in particular, Marshall's support for Sledgehammer—which seemed ancillary to British concerns. Sir Alan Brooke, chief of the Imperial General Staff, was particularly outspoken in his opposition to Sledgehammer, saying that it would be simply impossible to mount any kind of offensive in Europe in 1942. Instead, he said, the Allies should plan to take on the Germans in the Middle East and North Africa until enough men and matériel could be gathered in England for an invasion of France. "All well . . . ," Hopkins cabled to Roosevelt, but that wasn't true. Through the long weekend Marshall pressed his point with Churchill and senior British commanders to little effect.[56]

Marshall and Hopkins left England with Churchill's approval for Bolero, but it was now clear that the British would not be swayed from their argument about North Africa. On April 14, the British Chiefs of Staff approved the broad outlines of Marshall's proposals for Bolero, Sledgehammer, and Roundup but insisted on adding that offensive operations against the Germans in 1942 would have to "await developments," a caveat that reflected British doubts that the Allies could muster the strength necessary to take on the Germans so early. That was good enough for Marshall: "It appears that our proposal will be accepted in principle," he wrote to McNarney upon his return from London, "but relative to avoidance of future dispersions particularly of planes, such acceptance will have to be considerably and continuously bolstered by firmness of our stand. . . . Virtually everyone agrees with us in principle but many if not most hold reservations regarding this or that."[57] The differences between the Americans and the British were, in fact, substantial. After the departure of the American delegation, Churchill cabled Roosevelt that any attack on Europe in 1942 might prove impossible: "I may say that I thought the proposals made for an interim operation in certain contingencies this year met the difficulties and uncertainties in an absolutely sound manner," he wrote. "If, as our experts believe, we can carry this whole plan through successfully it will be one of the grand events in all the history of war."[58] In this, then, was stored up much future disagreement: the British would smile and nod their approval, without fully believing that the American plan for a full early assault on "Fortress Europe" was feasible.

Indeed, after Marshall's departure, the British began planning a military operation that would focus Allied resources on defeating the Germans in North Africa, a strategy distinctly at odds with the American vision for the war. There is little doubt that the British were being underhanded with Marshall and Hopkins, that they never intended to support an American plan for an invasion in Europe in 1942, and that they were simply playing for time. They intended to bring as many Americans to Britain as possible and only then to disagree openly with American invasion plans for Europe.[59] "Our American friends went happily homewards under the mistaken impression that we have committed ourselves to both Roundup and Sledgehammer," British major general Hastings Ismay later admitted. "This misunderstanding was destined to have unfortunate results. For when we had to tell them, after the most thorough study of Sledgehammer, that we were absolutely opposed to it, they felt that we had broken faith with them."[60]

The British were also shocked by the sheer breadth of America's war plans. They had never commanded or even imagined the deployment of such an enormous force prior to 1942, their horizons limited by the lack of British manpower.

> We had come to be daunted by figures and had got into the habit of plan-
> ning everything on the improvised and shoestring basis which circum-
> stances had condemned us. Here were the Americans coming along to
> say that there was no shortage of manpower, and that there need be no
> shortage of anything else. The British planners gulped when they saw
> their modest twelve divisions neatly multiplied by four to make forty-
> eight, and their hundreds of landing craft translated into thousands; and
> it took them a little time to raise their sights.[61]

Churchill remained intent on sticking to his philosophy of pecking away at the Germans by conducting operations on the periphery of the Third Reich, and the Imperial General Staff supported him. This common British front set the stage for the American-British falling-out over immediate global objectives in the summer of 1942, but in April of that year neither Marshall nor Hopkins was even dimly aware that their foray to England was anything but a success. Indeed, the British turnabout, when it came, shocked Marshall and Roosevelt, who not only began to doubt British intentions in all future relations but thus learned that the canny Churchill, amid his nods and smiles, was capable of find-ing ways to impose his vision *regardless* of what the Americans thought. "I had to work by influence and diplomacy in order to secure agreed and harmonious action with our cherished Ally," he later admitted, "without whose aid nothing but ruin faced the world. I did not therefore open to any of these alternatives at our meeting on the 14th."[62] This was Churchill's way of saying that while he was "open to" any alternatives presented by the Americans, he was not open to acceding to their strategy. Sir Alan Brooke was Churchill's accomplice in this. Brooke felt threatened by the politically adept Marshall, and his diaries reveal the condescending gaze with which he viewed his opposite number:

> He is, I think, a good general at raising armies and at providing the nec-
> essary link between the military and political worlds, but his strategical
> ability does not impress me at all. In fact, in many respects he is a very
> dangerous man whilst being a very charming one. He has found that

King, the American Navy Chief of Staff, is proving more and more a drain on his military resources, continually calling for land-forces to capture and hold land-bases in the Pacific. . . . MacArthur in Australia constitutes another threat by asking for forces to develop an offensive from Australia. To counter these moves Marshall has started the European offensive plan and is going one hundred percent all out on it. It is a clever move that fits in with present political opinion and the desire to help Russia.[63]

And so, Marshall and Hopkins returned to Washington on April 19 well satisfied with their trip. Eisenhower was happy to see the chief of staff and pleased with the progress that he had made. "He looks fine," Eisenhower noted in his diary. "I hope that, at long last, and after months of struggle by this division, we are all definitely committed to one concept of fighting. If we can agree on major purposes and objectives, our efforts will begin to fall in line and we won't just be thrashing around in the dark."[64] Over the next week, Eisenhower was busy fulfilling the Marshall Memorandum's Bolero plan, dispatching an entire corps and two divisions to England, complete with a headquarters staff. The deployment would take upward of four months and include a full contingent of ten thousand men billeted aboard the *Queen Mary*.[65] The new deployments and the apparent success of Marshall's mission to London were brightened by news that on April 18, sixteen B-25s had successfully carried out the first American air raid of the war, bombing Tokyo, Kobe, Yokohama, and Nagoya. The bombings had a minimal impact on Japanese war-making capacity, but that had not been their goal. Instead, as everyone in the War Department knew, they were simply a signal to the Japanese leadership of what was to come. Marshall, Eisenhower, and the American high command were ecstatic.[66]

With the initial deployments for Bolero now under way, Eisenhower turned his attention once again to the Philippines, where the remnants of Wainwright's command, now clinging tenaciously to the rocky island of Corregidor in Manila Harbor, were coming under increased pressure from the Japanese. Wainwright was nearly at the end of his strength: his eleven thousand soldiers (those who had made it to safety from the divisions decimated on the Bataan Peninsula, which had surrendered on April 8) were under constant shelling, weakened by increasing disease, and running low on ammunition. Wainwright had promised

MacArthur that he would fight to the last, but it was now becoming apparent that continuing the battle would lead to his annihilation. His inability to continue was clear to both Marshall and Eisenhower in Washington. Marshall had Eisenhower cable Wainwright on May 2, asking for a "completely frank and confidential estimate" of the situation. Wainwright responded the next day: "I estimate that we have something less than an even chance to beat off an assault," he said. Marshall studied Wainwright's cable and wrote immediately to Roosevelt. "General Wainwright has performed a marvelous job and without even uttering a word of complaint," Marshall told the president. "I feel he has earned a commendation from you in the highest terms."[67]

On the night of May 5, Japanese forces under General Masaharu Homma landed four divisions on the island and began fighting overland to Wainwright's headquarters in the Malinta Tunnel. The assault was overwhelming and was accompanied by devastating artillery shelling that ripped through Wainwright's ranks. The island was "scorched, gaunt, leafless."[68] With nearly 10 percent of his command wounded and lying on hospital beds in the Malinta Tunnel, Wainwright knew that he had little choice but to capitulate to the Japanese. He surrendered on May 6. General Homma refused to concede to Wainwright's plea that he had little control over other American and Filipino forces in the archipelago, so, faced with the prospect that his soldiers might be harshly treated by Homma were he not to accede to Japanese demands, Wainwright surrendered all American and Filipino forces in the islands—some eighty thousand men in all.[69] In Australia, MacArthur was stunned by Wainwright's decision. Just days before, he had cabled the general that he expected him to fight to the last man and had provided a copy of the cable to Marshall: "Prepare and execute an attack upon the enemy,"[70] MacArthur had shrilly demanded of Wainwright. He then added his own judgment of Wainwright's command abilities in a personal note to Marshall. "It is of course possible that with my departure the vigor of application of conservation may have been relaxed." As a final gauge of his ego and shabbiness, when Marshall recommended Wainwright for the Medal of Honor, MacArthur refused to add his signature.[71]

4

SLEDGEHAMMER

". . . this is the paper you should read in detail. . . ."
"I certainly do want to read it. You may be the man who
executes it."

I T WAS A DARK May for the Allies. Not only had Corregidor fallen and the
Philippines surrendered, but the Japanese now controlled nearly all of East
Asia. Approximately eighty-four thousand Americans were prisoners of the
Japanese in the Philippines. Though Marshall and Eisenhower did not yet
know it, of that number ten thousand had already died as prisoners of war.[1] By
the beginning of May 1942, the British position in the Near East, which had
been uncontested for more than a century, was extinguished. The defeat was
not simply a matter of Japanese power: a British Imperial General Staff study
found that the defeat was the result of a lack of aggressive leadership, inadequate
armaments, the splitting of divisional strengths, and "the piecemeal tossing of
reinforcements into battle."[2] By the second week of May, all of central Burma
had been overrun and Mandalay had fallen. On May 8, the USS *Lexington* was
sunk in the Battle of the Coral Sea.[3] That same day the Germans began their
offensive in the Crimea.[4] The Red Army was reeling.

Surveying the continuing retreat of the Allied forces from his office in
Washington, Dwight Eisenhower struggled to gather the men and matériel for
Bolero. It had been easy enough to find divisions and ships for the buildup, but

it had been much more difficult to find the necessary support for a planned in-vasion of Europe in 1943. Eisenhower's notes for this period, accentuated by his diary entries, show that his struggles on Bolero far outweighed the worries that attended his three-month-long efforts to reinforce the Philippines.[5] On the morning of May 6, Eisenhower attended a meeting of a Bolero subcommittee convened to discuss the particularly knotty problem of finding enough landing craft to put at least several divisions of Allied troops ashore on the beaches of France. Following the meeting, Eisenhower wrote out his most important ques-tions on the issue in staccato form: "Who is responsible for building landing craft? What types are they building? Are they suitable for cross-Channel work? Will the number of each type be sufficient?"[6] No one seemed to know—even though Eisenhower understood that the answers to the landing-craft issue should have been available as early as February, when talk of a cross-Channel invasion dominated the British and American Chiefs of Staff. Just writing out the questions seemed to make him angry. "How in hell can we win this war un-less we can crack some heads?" he wrote in his diary.[7]

The same questions were plaguing George Marshall, who spent a number of days in mid-May giving attention to the landing-craft issue. Eisenhower's questions—who will build them, will they work, how many are needed—was the focus of a Marshall-Roosevelt meeting at the White House on May 15, and the subject of a message from Marshall to Eisenhower the next day. Interservice competition, Marshall conceded, was once again an issue. The Army was hav-ing difficulty convincing the Navy to set aside enough workers to produce land-ing craft for the European theater, the Army chief of staff told Eisenhower.[8] Marshall was once again in a delicate balancing act with the Navy's chief of naval operations, Admiral Ernie King, as "landing craft would have to be con-structed in many of the Naval ship yards which were occupied to the full with Naval projects."[9] Roughly translated: the answers to Eisenhower's questions would have to wait. The frustrations of providing landing craft for Europe were exacerbated, at least in Marshall's mind, by his continuing worries over the command structure of American forces in England. Marshall was particularly concerned that the U.S. commander in England, Major General James E. Chaney, was incapable of overseeing the U.S. buildup for the cross-Channel attack, and also lacked the necessary diplomatic skills to carry through the Marshall program with the British.[10] Marshall did not want to replace Chaney, at least not yet. But he had not been impressed with his work during his own trip to London and had concluded that a more structured staff was needed. Marshall called Eisenhower into his office on May 20 and directed him to fly to England to give his own assessment of the situation. You will be leaving in two days, Marshall told him.

"I'M TAKING off on the twenty-third with General Arnold and others for a trip to England," Eisenhower wrote in his diary. "We want to see how things are going there on our offensive plan. . . . My own particular reason for going is an uneasy feeling that either we do not understand our own commanding general and staff in England or they don't understand us. Our planning for Bolero is not progressing. We'll be gone about a week."[11] Accompanying Eisenhower was Ike's new friend Hap Arnold, who was to provide an independent assessment of Allied air needs leading up to a 1943 European invasion, Lieutenant General Brehon Burke Somervell (the commanding general charged with overseeing U.S. Army logistical needs), General William C. Lee (a trainer of airborne troops); Major General J. C. H. Lee (the head of the U.S. Army's supply division); Admiral John H. Towers (a Navy air specialist); and Major General Mark "Wayne" Clark, an old friend and cousin of George Marshall.[12] Marshall had told Clark to accompany Eisenhower because of Clark's close ties with Lesley McNair. Clark was a good trainer and under McNair's tutelage had become the best combat troop trainer in the American Army excepting McNair himself. Marshall was calculating that Clark's sophisticated eye for troop preparation would come in handy in England—where he could see firsthand whether the British were as well trained as they claimed and also whether the U.S. staff in London had made the proper provisions for billeting and upgrading the combat readiness of those troops that Eisenhower had sent to Europe over the previous weeks.[13]

Eisenhower welcomed Clark's addition to his delegation. The two had met at West Point three decades before and had become good friends.[14] Through the years, Clark became notorious in the Army as arrogant, egotistical, and a shameless self-promoter, but Eisenhower admired and envied him: while Eisenhower sat out World War I as a trainer, Clark was a battalion commander in France, where his reputation as a sound combat officer was enhanced by the fact that he was wounded. Sometime thereafter, Clark's name ended up in Marshall's little black book. Clark and his wife had been occasional members of Club Eisenhower, and in 1940 Ike had even recruited his friend to help him get an assignment as a senior officer to a combat division. Clark, for his part, was one of Eisenhower's loyal admirers and did everything he could to support him. In July 1941, Clark was promoted to brigadier general, ahead of Eisenhower, who was now required to salute his old friend and call him "sir." Clark's seemingly easy ascendance to high command clearly rankled Ike: "Why haven't I been promoted?" Eisenhower once wrote him. "It's in the works," Clark wrote back.[15]

Eisenhower, Arnold, Clark, and their delegation departed for London on May 23, flying first to Montreal and then to Goose Bay, Labrador. They arrived in Prestwick, Scotland, on the twenty-fifth. Taking a train south to London, Eisenhower reviewed his discussion with Marshall of the week before. His job was complex: he was not simply to pass judgment on the U.S. command in England, but also to assess the British senior command's commitment to Sledgehammer. Despite British agreement with Marshall that there should be an early invasion of France, the Army Chief of Staff sensed an underlying disquiet with the plan in the British high command. Eisenhower's job was to continue what Marshall had started: to press Alan Brooke and Winston Churchill to approve Roundup while keeping Sledgehammer alive. Eisenhower and his colleagues arrived at Victoria Station on May 26, where they were met by their escort—a young woman named Kay Summersby, who doubled as their driver—who took them to their rooms at Claridge's Hotel. This was the first meeting between Eisenhower and Summersby, whose relationship would grow throughout the war, leading to rumors that the two had had a romantic relationship. But for now, Summersby was simply Eisenhower's driver and nothing more. The three arrived at Claridge's late in the day, and Eisenhower instructed Summersby to come for them early the next morning. He was abrupt, almost impolite, and Summersby later remembered being miffed.[16] But Eisenhower was tired, had much on his mind, and was under pressure from Marshall; his meetings with the British Chiefs of Staff would begin the next morning.[17]

It did not take long for Eisenhower to determine that the British not only had doubts about Roundup, but believed Sledgehammer was a fantasy. The problem, Eisenhower determined, was not so much British hesitations as it was the ill-preparedness of the American staff, which was in chaos. Staff planners had little knowledge of either operation, and little planning for them had been done. At the center of these problems was Major General James E. Chaney, who seemed at a complete loss as to what he should be doing. Worse yet, he arrived for his meeting with Eisenhower in civilian clothes. Eisenhower was disgusted, and made a quick judgment: Chaney should be returned to the U.S. "on a slow boat, without escort."[18] Eisenhower took notes on his meetings with the American staff and began to shape his thinking on what would be needed. His plan was to make a series of recommendations to Marshall on restructuring the European staff when he returned to Washington. Eisenhower focused on the U.S. command structure in London, but he also worked diligently to make friends with his British counterparts. While Marshall had had his troubles with the British Chiefs of Staff during Arcadia, Eisenhower felt comfortable in their presence, and he made no secret of his admiration for their fighting skills. He attended a major British training exercise organized by General Bernard Law Montgomery, met and chatted with the legendary Lord Louis Mountbatten, and even seemed to get on with the normally aloof Sir Alan Brooke. But there were problems.

Eisenhower found Montgomery odd, distant, and at times even discourteous: when Montgomery was introduced to Eisenhower, the British general shook his hand stiffly and properly, but then said that he believed that overseeing a training exercise was beneath him. "I'm sorry I'm late," he said, "but I really shouldn't have come at all." When Eisenhower lit a cigarette, Montgomery was livid: "Who's smoking?" he asked. "I am, sir," Eisenhower said. Montgomery sniffed: "Stop it. I don't permit it here." Rude and officious, the wispy, hawk-nosed, peacock-sure Montgomery was widely admired in the British military and viewed as somewhat of a military genius. While these opinions seemed overblown, no one could argue with Montgomery's courage. Badly wounded in World War I, Montgomery served in some of the war's bloodiest battles, then returned to England to author the British Army's infantry-training manual. He later served courageously as a commander in Palestine, which provided him with the requisite colonial experience then common to all British commanders.[19] His fighting retreat to Dunkirk saved the lives of thousands of British soldiers who would provide the fighting core of the British Army.[20] Without

Montgomery there would not have been a British Army. He rose effortlessly through the ranks—his brusque style evidence, his colleagues thought, of his inherent genius. If anyone doubted his brilliance, Americans who met him believed, then Montgomery would clear it up in a few short sentences. There was little doubt that Montgomery knew how to fight, cared for his soldiers, and attacked only when the odds were with him. Great Britain's political leadership appreciated such care: after Dunkirk every British life mattered. Eisenhower was less impressed.[21]

While Brooke and Montgomery might have had their doubts about both Marshall and Eisenhower, Vice Admiral Lord Louis Mountbatten—already celebrated in the Royal Navy as a result of his exploits as a part of an Anglo-French expedition during the fight for Norway—became an Eisenhower partisan. The meeting between the two was accidental and even somewhat embarrassing for Eisenhower. During a briefing of senior British commanders on May 28, Eisenhower detailed the need for an early invasion of Europe and said, "The first thing to do is to name a commander for the operation."[22] After a short pause, one of the British commanders asked him who he thought could lead such an operation. Eisenhower thought only for a moment: "In America I have heard much of a man who has been intensively studying amphibious operations for many months," he said. "I understand that his position is Chief of Combined Operations, and I think his name is Admiral Mountbatten. I have heard that Admiral Mountbatten is vigorous, intelligent, and courageous, and if the operation is to be staged initially with British forces predominating I presume he could do the job." An uncomfortable but smiling silence followed Eisenhower's statement, until it was interrupted by General Brooke: "General, perhaps you have not met Admiral Mountbatten," Brooke said, with just the right amount of droll understatement. "This is he sitting directly across the table from you." Eisenhower joined the laughter then reiterated his point: "I still say that the key to success is to appoint a commander and give him the necessary authority and responsibility to carry out the planning and preparatory work that otherwise will never be done," he concluded.[23] Brooke was silent, but indifferently nodded his agreement.

Mountbatten was a central figure in Eisenhower and Marshall's plans. Found among Eisenhower's papers after his death was a note on Mountbatten written prior to the May 28 meeting that included discussion points he would raise with the admiral. It is now clear that Marshall had suggested these points during a meeting with Eisenhower prior to his departure for London—recommending Mountbatten as a likely supporter of American plans for Sledgehammer and Roundup. Eisenhower played on this knowledge, certainly at Marshall's insistence: the objective was to find a senior British officer who not only agreed with America's viewpoint on the war, but also was adept at the kinds of coalition operations that Eisenhower and Marshall envisioned. Mountbatten lived up to his billing: during the May 28 meeting Eisenhower learned not only that Mountbatten was as concerned with the landing-craft problem as the Americans, but that he had successfully created a joint staff that had resolved the nagging issue of interservice rivalries. Eisenhower was so impressed that he asked Mountbatten if he could assign a team of American officers as observers to study his system.[24] Eisenhower left the May 28 meeting believing that he had found a like-minded soldier, a "warm and firm friend." Eisenhower was also convinced that Mountbatten would be a strong voice among British senior commanders for the American program for fighting Germany.[25] But while Mountbatten could now be counted as an ally, the rest of the British staff refused to support any of Eisenhower's proposals, particularly his suggestion that Allied forces work under a single commander—an issue that, Eisenhower believed, had already been resolved during the Arcadia talks. Once again, as in their earlier meetings in Washington, the British suspected that in supplying most of the men and matériel for the war, the Americans would insist on a command structure dominated by men like Marshall, Eisenhower, Clark, and Arnold. Brooke, Montgomery, even Mountbatten, would be forced into the background. Still, the British were anxious to get on with the war and agreed with Eisenhower that it was "time to stop thrashing around in the dark."

Eisenhower met Lord Alan Brooke on the twenty-ninth and was subjected to a lecture on British capabilities and war planning. Eisenhower was affable, but underneath he was impatient and insulted. He believed Brooke's demeanor was intended to intimidate the American delegation and to position the British staff as superior fighters and commanders. Even so, Eisenhower kept his views to himself, remained pleasant, and only interrupted the chief of the Imperial General Staff to ask questions. His later judgment was harsh: "Brooke was mercurial, and though he seemed familiar with some of the best military books on strategy and the conduct of war, he was, I thought, governed more by preconceptions and rigid concepts rather than a profound study of modern war."[26] On the thirtieth, Eisenhower and Clark took a tour of British emplacements and training bases "so that," as Clark remembered, "we could see where their troops were and their defenses against a possible German invasion."[27] Kay Summersby acted as their chauffeur, pointing out in their cross-London travels where German bombing had done the most damage. Later that night, Eisenhower and his colleagues sequestered themselves around drinks at Claridge's and talked about Chaney's replacement. Arnold thought that a commander in Europe had to have the "experience and knowledge of our way of doing things," had to be "acquainted with our War Department," and had to have the confidence of George Marshall. Eisenhower agreed, but otherwise remained silent. Years later, Clark remembered Eisenhower's reaction: "He never said so, but it was clear to me that he very much wanted the job, very much."[28]

WHILE GEORGE MARSHALL left his office to be at home with his wife, Katherine, at a decent hour every night, the sheer number of decisions began to weigh on him. Marshall's worry was reflected in an unusually personal admission to Admiral Harold "Betty" Stark—an old and close friend who was born in Pennsylvania the same year as Marshall—in a letter he wrote to him in mid-June.[29] Stark ("Genial in manner and unobtrusive in personality" as one biographer described him)[30] had been replaced as chief of naval operations by Ernest King and publicly criticized for his failure to forward key intelligence to his subordinates in the days before Pearl Harbor. The criticism had no effect on Marshall, who believed the reports of Stark's oversight were exaggerated and politically motivated. He wrote Stark throughout the war, enjoyed his time with him when they met in England or the United States, and considered him a friend. "Each day grows more crowded than the last, and these battles in the Pacific, and the continued complications [against the Japanese in the Pacific] have not lessened the burdens," he wrote. "I am pulled and tugged in so many directions, China, India, Middle East, Bolero, East Coast, West Coast . . . that it is difficult to even dream of a peaceful day in the future." Perhaps fearful that he might be becoming too personal, or even complaining, Marshall quickly changed tack, reassuring his friend that he actually felt better "than I have for many years—I think because I am so very careful of my health and find op-

portunities at night to relax."[31] This was not exactly true, of course, as Stark—
as commander of U.S. naval forces in Great Britain certainly understood—but
he allowed his friend his little white lie.

The Marshall missive is important because it shows a side of George
Marshall that was rarely seen by the public and because it reflects Marshall's
reliance on Stark as his unofficial eyes and ears in England in the early months
of the war. Marshall's correspondence with Stark is not voluminous, but it
shows the Army chief of staff taking care to inform his decisions with first-hand
observations from those he trusted. The Eisenhower trip to London was an example of this. In the immediate aftermath of his decision to send the OPD head
to meet with the British, Marshall wrote to Stark about Eisenhower's impending arrival and solicited his opinion of him and the other visiting officers. Stark
gave the delegation his special attention, relaying word back to Marshall about
their capabilities. He gave them high marks: "I just wanted to let you know how
fine they have been in keeping me informed of their doings," he wrote in the
midst of their visit, "and having members of my staff with them so that we
would all be together. Of course it is the only way in the world to work and that
should be obvious; yet, we both know it has not always been the rule."[32]
Marshall was undoubtedly pleased with this, as he knew that if any of the officers had disappointed Stark, the former CNO would immediately have told
him. In truth, the delegation that Marshall had sent to London, as Stark undoubtedly understood, represented the core high command for the coming
war in Europe. These were officers Stark would have to work with for the du-
ration of the war. Stark's opinion of them was important: if he couldn't work
with Eisenhower and his colleagues, Marshall would have to find other officers
whom Stark could trust.

The burden on Marshall was eased by Stark's vote of confidence and also
by word of the American naval victory at Midway, fought over a period of three
days from June 4 to June 7, just as Eisenhower's group was returning the
Washington. Midway marked a turning point in the war against Japan and was
the first defeat of any Axis power following the debacle at Pearl Harbor. The
Japanese suffered a crushing blow, losing four aircraft carriers.[33] Marshall was
ecstatic, but no more so than Ernie King: "The first decisive defeat suffered by
the Japanese Navy in 350 years," King crowed in his official report, "it put an
end to the long period of Japanese offensive action, and restored the balance
of naval power in the Pacific." Marshall was somewhat more modest, remem-

bering years later that the victory was "the closest squeak," made possible by the courage of America's naval aviators, as well as by American intelligence intercepts of coded Japanese naval messages. Aware that the breaking of the Japanese naval code might become public, Marshall advised King to hold a press conference and face the question directly. "The purpose of the [press] conference would be to give you an opportunity, in a seemingly casual impromptu fashion, to offset the possibility of the Japanese suspicioning that we had broken their code. It would be a simple matter to plant the question, following your general statement. . . . 'You weren't caught by surprise this time, were you?' . . . Your answer, I think, might well be somewhat as follows: 'No, and for very good reason. We were morally certain that after the surprise raid on Japan proper we would be subjected to some sort of reprisal operations.'"[34]

Steeled by the victory at Midway, Marshall was also buoyed by the visit to the United States of Louis Mountbatten, who arrived in Washington for consultations with Marshall and Franklin Roosevelt even before Eisenhower and his delegation had returned from London.[35] Marshall's admiration for Mountbatten had been reflected in Eisenhower's views of the admiral during Ike's visit to Great Britain, so the Army chief of staff was pleased with Mountbatten's positive judgment of Eisenhower's abilities. Mountbatten told Marshall that Eisenhower had made a very favorable impression with senior British commanders during his visit. Mountbatten's praise for Eisenhower was reinforced by Hap Arnold and Mark Clark, who visited with Marshall one day after Mountbatten spoke with him at the War Department. Standing before Arnold and Clark in his office, Marshall froze them with his gaze, then told them that he had asked General Lesley McNair for his opinion on who should command U.S. troops in Europe. McNair had come up with three names: Major General George Patton, Lieutenant General Joseph Stilwell, and Major General Lloyd Fredendall. Do you agree with these recommendations? Marshall asked. Both men nodded: McNair had offered three good names, they said, and any one of them could do the job. Marshall turned to Clark: perhaps it would be best to consider a younger man, he said. Clark said he agreed. Well then, Marshall asked, who would it be? Clark's answer was immediate: "Eisenhower."[36]

DWIGHT EISENHOWER was undoubtedly aware of the recommendation of Arnold and Clark, but he was careful not to lobby openly for the top slot in

Europe. On the morning of June 3, just one day after his return, Eisenhower briefed Marshall on his visit to London and then prepared a paper for the chief of staff that detailed his recommendations on a new U.S. command structure in England.

> It is immediately necessary to dispatch to England the man who will be the Commander of the 1st Corps to take part in the assault. I have thought this matter over at great length, and, as a result, I recommend that General Clark be sent for this job. . . . During my visit to England, I also gave a great deal of study to the identity of the individual who should now be commanding our Forces in England. I was very hopeful that my conclusions would favor the present incumbent. For a variety of reasons, some of which I intimated to you this morning, I believe that a change should be made. I recommend General McNarney as the best-fitted individual to fulfill the various requirements enumerated in a previous memorandum to you on this subject, and who is, at the same time, thoroughly familiar with the exceedingly complex command and administrative arrangements by which the British Armed forces are controlled.[37]

Of course, as Marshall knew quite well, the same qualifications that Eisenhower found in McNarney, Marshall found in Eisenhower. Then too, as far as Marshall was concerned, it was far less important for a designated commander to be familiar with the "exceedingly complex command and administrative arrangements" of the British military than that he be familiar with the thinking of the American military—and most particularly with the thinking of George Marshall. It is quite likely that Marshall pocketed Eisenhower's recommendation and listened more closely to Mountbatten. If Eisenhower could get along with the British and understood the importance of combined operations to the degree that he was willing to dispatch an American team to learn about them from Mountbatten's staff, then he was actually more qualified than either McNarney or Clark. Three days later, Eisenhower added additional thoughts to his June 3 recommendation. He emphasized the importance of combined operations and noted that the U.S. commander in Europe would have to be "a Theatre Commander in every sense of the word" and then reiterated his belief that such a commander would have to be not only familiar with the British system, but also capable of showing patience in dealing with British officers, an indirect swipe, perhaps, at both Montgomery and Brooke. "Patience is highly necessary because of the complications of British procedure," Eisenhower wrote in his June 6 memo.[38]

McNarney was a good choice. Marshall knew McNarney well and trusted him. He had successfully reorganized the War Department and had then been named Army deputy chief of staff. He was competent, articulate, a good planner, and a careful thinker. But Marshall was not about to send him to England; he needed him right where he was. Eisenhower surely knew that McNarney was valuable to Marshall and that it was unlikely he would be assigned the theater command in Europe, but Ike insisted that Marshall pay attention to his views, for they reflected much of what he and Marshall believed about the war. For Eisenhower, the June 3 and June 6 memos, while important, simply reiterated what he had written and sent to Marshall just prior to his trip to London—on May 12—which laid out the requirements for Bolero and established the "Western European Theatre of Operations." Eisenhower called it "the Bible." The memo was, in fact, breathtaking in its designation of the powers that would be exercised by a commander stationed in Great Britain.

> The Theater Commander to be designated should be an officer qualified to organize and administer the theater and to organize, train, and command the combined forces of all arms and services set up in the Bolero Plan, and also qualified to act as the Chief of Staff of a future commander, should it become advisable at a later date, due to the expansion of the United States forces, to supersede him.

Marshall was silent on "the Bible" through all of May and into June, and also remained silent on Eisenhower's June 3 and June 6 memos. Nevertheless, now that Bolero was approved, Marshall was under pressure to appoint a U.S. commander for the European theater. We do not know how he made up his mind or when, but his opinion of Eisenhower and his work was inarguable. If he needed to be reassured, he could always refer to Harold Stark's letter, to the views of Admiral Mountbatten, to the opinions of Hap Arnold and Mark Clark. And he certainly knew that Eisenhower wanted the job, as Eisenhower himself had nearly come close to stating in his May 19 briefing paper. After all, it was likely that Marshall himself would eventually become the commander of all U.S. and European troops and would need someone who was "qualified to act as the Chief of Staff." As head of the Operations and Plans Division, Eisenhower was Marshall's most important staff officer and could serve in that position in London.

Marshall finally broached the topic of command in Europe in a meeting he had with Eisenhower on June 7, asking Eisenhower what kind of commander he thought the U.S. needed. Eisenhower responded by emphasizing the qualities that both he and Marshall admired and by reiterating what he had said in his three previous memos on the subject. Then he added one other qualification, saying that such a commander "must enjoy the fullest confidence of the Chief of Staff in order that he may efficiently, and in accordance with the basic ideas of the Chief of Staff, conduct all the preparatory work essential to the successful initiation of Bolero." Marshall nodded his agreement but said nothing, and the two then went on to other business. The next day, Marshall called Eisenhower into his office for yet one more conference on the Europe-command issue. By then, as his remarks would show, Marshall had made up his mind. In the middle of this conversation, as Eisenhower later remembered it, Eisenhower emphasized the importance of his May 19 briefing paper. "I remarked to General Marshall that this was one paper he should read in detail before it went out because it was likely to be an important document in the further waging of the war." Marshall nodded briskly then looked squarely at Eisenhower. "I certainly do want to read it," he said. "You may be the man who executes it. If that's the case, when can you leave?"[39] Eisenhower responded that he would leave as soon as the proper arrangements could be made, and Marshall nodded and dropped the subject. As far as Ike was concerned, Marshall had only held out the *possibility* that he would command in Europe. The appointment was far from certain. "The C/S told me this a.m. that it's possible I may go to England in command," Eisenhower wrote in an internal memo. "It's a big job—if U.S.-U.K. stay squarely behind Bolero and go after it tooth and nail, it will be the biggest job of the war. Of course command now does not necessarily mean command in the operation—but the job before the battle begins will still be the biggest outside of that of C/S/ himself."[40]

On June 11, Marshall's appointment was made public: Dwight Eisenhower was named commander of U.S. forces, European theater of operations. In a meeting with Marshall, Eisenhower was asked whom he would recommend as the theater's combat commanding general. "Clark," Eisenhower said.[41] This brought a rare smile to Marshall, who remembered that eight days earlier Clark had promoted Eisenhower as the theater commander. "It looks to me as if you boys got together," he said.[42] Eisenhower was exultant—he would be headed to England to command all U.S. ground forces by the end of the month. Over dinner with Mamie that night, Eisenhower could barely contain his jubilation, reviewing the command arrangements that Marshall was approving for Europe.

"What post are you going to have?" she asked.

"I'm going to command the whole shebang," he responded.[43]

Later, in his diary, he was laconic: "The C/S says I'm the guy," he wrote.[44]

MOMENTOUS AS Eisenhower's appointment as commanding general in Europe might have seemed at the time (Eisenhower was all but anonymous to the public and even in official Washington was commonly known as "Milton's brother"), George Marshall was struggling with a far more important issue, and one fatal to U.S. plans for an early invasion of Europe.[45] When Marshall greeted Louis Mountbatten on June 2, he had no idea that the admiral was carrying a message from Winston Churchill to Franklin Roosevelt. The message was delivered on the morning after Mountbatten's meeting with Marshall when the admiral saw Franklin Roosevelt in the Oval Office: the prime minister, Mountbatten said, opposed an invasion of Europe in 1942, preferring instead an invasion of northwest Africa. Mountbatten was as pugnacious as his prime minister in pointing out why an invasion of Europe in the coming months—Sledgehammer—was simply out of the question. The Germans had twenty-five divisions in France, Mountbatten said, while the Allies were still forming their divisions in England. Besides, Mountbatten said, there simply weren't enough landing craft available to mount a cross-Channel operation. Roosevelt was uncomfortable with Mountbatten's views. He worried that the failure to open a second front against Germany in 1942, no matter how difficult, might lead to the collapse of the Soviet Union. He "did not wish to send a million soldiers to England and find, possibly, that a complete collapse of Russia had made a frontal attack on France impossible," Mountbatten remembered. Mountbatten nodded his understanding and, when pressured by Roosevelt, allowed that it might be possible to mount Sledgehammer sometime in the late autumn, when the British would be ready to "follow up a crack in German morale by landing in France."[46]

Marshall spent the two days following Mountbatten's meeting in the Oval Office fuming at Roosevelt. Not only had he been excluded from the meeting but Roosevelt had failed to tell him about its results. Marshall had been informed only in a roundabout way—when John Dill said that he had received a summary of it from the British Chiefs of Staff, who had been informed of it by Churchill, who had been informed of it by Mountbatten himself. Victimized by Roosevelt's penchant for offhanded informality (Marshall also suspected that the president did not want to be the bearer of bad tidings), Marshall was stunned by what he viewed as the British senior military's abrogation of the pledge they had made at Arcadia. Marshall suspected, correctly, that the British had never intended to act on Sledgehammer but had simply agreed to it at the time to keep America tied to its Europe First strategy. The British had good reason for the subterfuge, Marshall reasoned, since Eisenhower had noted that if the Allies failed to agree on a landing in Europe in 1942, the United States would turn its attention to defeating Japan. Worse yet, angry as he was, Marshall could not let on that he knew about the British subterfuge, for to do so would endanger the position of his British spy, Sir John Dill. "I had to be very careful that nobody knew this—no one in the War Department and certainly not the [British] chiefs of staff," Marshall said. He then added: "If the secret [of Dill's back-channel communication] came to light, Dill would be destroyed in a minute."[47] So Marshall kept the knowledge of the Mountbatten-Roosevelt meeting to himself, but instructed Eisenhower to prepare a paper arguing against Gymnast—Great Britain's plan for an invasion of French North Africa.

As these machinations were reaching a crescendo in Washington, Winston Churchill was working behind the scenes in London. On June 10, Winston Churchill told visiting the Soviet foreign minister V. M. Molotov that the British opposed a cross-Channel attack in 1942. On the next day Churchill received his cabinet's opinion on Sledgehammer; it voted that an invasion of Europe would not be the recommended course of action until 1943 or later. There was only one caveat: Sledgehammer would go forward only if the Germans were so demoralized that such an operation would bring about their collapse.[48] Feeling certain that he now had enough political support to carry through his argument with Roosevelt, Churchill, accompanied by Sir Alan Brooke and Hastings Ismay—his personal chief of staff—scheduled a quick trip to Washington for a meeting with the president and the Joint Chiefs of Staff. Not yet realizing that John Dill had told Marshall about his prime minister's views, Churchill hoped to reach Washington before George Marshall could intervene to pressure Roosevelt. In fact, on June 17, just as Churchill was departing London for Washington, Marshall and Secretary of War Harold Stimson met with Roosevelt at the White House. Both men appeared steely-eyed before the commander in chief, fully prepared to do battle in defense of Sledgehammer. But Roosevelt was also prepared, and with fading British support for an early invasion of Europe, he was feeling political pressure. Roosevelt felt increasingly caught in the middle, between the need to satisfy a close ally and the need to satisfy his top military advisers. He began the discussion by coming to the point, preempting Marshall's own arguments. It might be best, he said, to "reopen" the subject of an invasion of northwest Africa. Stimson was aghast.

> The President sprung on us a proposition which worried me very much. It looked as if he was going to jump the traces over all that we have been doing in regard to Bolero and to imperil really our strategy of the whole situation. He wants to take up the case of Gymnast again, thinking that he can bring additional pressure on Russia. The only hope I have about it at all is that I think he may be doing it in his foxy way to forestall trouble that is now on the ocean bouncing towards us in the shape of a new British visitor. But he met with a rather robust opposition for the Gymnast proposition. Marshall had a paper already prepared against it for he had a premonition of what was coming. I spoke very vigorously against it.[49]

Marshall's defense of Sledgehammer and his attack on Gymnast had been prepared by Eisenhower, who was intent to arrive in London as the new Commanding General for the European theater with a plan in hand that focused on Europe, not North Africa. With Churchill's arrival now imminent, Marshall pressured Roosevelt to accept a simple military principle: The surest way to *defeat* Germany was to *attack* Germany. The Soviet Union was on the edge of collapse, Marshall argued, "which could only be avoided by opening a second front."[50] That meant that "tightening the ring" or "slowly strangling the Reich" (as Winston Churchill would describe it) was out of the question. So long as Germany was left unconquered, the war would continue.[51] But Roosevelt would not be shaken; Winston Churchill had grave doubts about Sledgehammer and would be arriving within a day for a second conference. Roosevelt said that he would hear him out.

Marshall would not be deterred. The morning after he and Stimson met Roosevelt in the Oval Office, Marshall convened his senior officers to gain their approval for a letter that Stimson would send to Roosevelt that argued against Gymnast. Eisenhower, Arnold, and McNarney studied the Stimson letter and gave it their approval. The entire senior leadership was now officially committed to Sledgehammer and opposed to Gymnast.[52] Stimson sent the letter on to Roosevelt, who was at his home in Hyde Park, New York. Churchill arrived in Washington on the eighteenth and departed for the president's summer retreat on the next morning, leaving behind his senior commanders to confer with the Americans. That same day, Marshall, Eisenhower, and their staffs huddled with Brooke, Ismay, and Dill at the Old Munitions Building. The British were distinctly uncomfortable; the day was "stinking hot" (in the words of Sir Alan Brooke), and the British knew that the Americans were prepared for a confrontation over war strategy. Marshall opened the presentation for the American side, but then called on Eisenhower to defend the Sledgehammer proposal. Eisenhower did his best, but Brooke was not moved: he was as concerned as Marshall and Eisenhower that Roosevelt and Churchill were "brewing up" a military operation for "North Africa and North Norway" for 1942 (both of which he opposed), but he did not think that Sledgehammer was the answer (he called it the "sacrifice operation" in the Channel). Instead, Brooke argued, 1942 should be set aside for building up U.S. and British military assets in England, so that an invasion of Europe in 1943 would be certain.

At least Marshall and Eisenhower could find in Brooke's arguments a certain palliative: the chief of the Imperial General Staff might oppose Sledgehammer, but at least he understood American fears that resources and men would be wasted by chipping away at the Axis periphery. If Brooke had his way Sledgehammer might not go forward, but neither would Churchill's

Gymnast. That was something, Marshall and Eisenhower thought, though not nearly enough. So Marshall and Eisenhower determined that they would continue to fight a two-front war: arguing to the British Chiefs of Staff that Russia's defeat could be staved off by an early invasion of Europe, while arguing to Roosevelt that Churchill's plan for an invasion of northwest Africa ran counter to every military principle they knew—as well as being an abrogation of the Arcadia understandings. "We were largely trying to get the President to stand pat on what he had previous agreed to," Marshall later recalled. "The President shifted, particularly when Churchill got hold of him. . . . The President was always ready to do any sideshow and Churchill was always prodding him. My job was to hold the President down to what we were doing. It was difficult because the navy was pulling everything toward the Pacific, and that's where the Marines were, and they got a lot of publicity. The President's tendency to shift and handle things loosely and be influenced, particularly by the British, was one of our great problems."[53]

At Hyde Park, Churchill continued to press Roosevelt, asking him a series of difficult military questions about the proposed European landing: How many troops would Sledgehammer take? he asked. Where would they land? How would they be transported? Who would command the operation? What was required of the British? *What was the plan?*[54] These were the same questions that Marshall had asked Eisenhower at the War Department on May 15. As yet, neither Marshall nor Eisenhower had any answers. Roosevelt too was stymied, and Churchill pressed his point. There were simply not enough naval transports for the operation, he told Roosevelt, and it would be foolhardy to go forward with Sledgehammer without them. Churchill leaned across to Roosevelt, his pugnacious demeanor now on full display, his eyes flashing, his voice tremulous and deep. He was speaking from the heart. Sledgehammer must be canceled, he said, as it would surely lead to a defeat. In any event, "in case no plan can be made in which any responsible authority has good confidence, and consequently no engagement on a substantial scale in France is possible in September 1942, what else can we do? Can we afford to stand idle in the Atlantic theater during the whole of 1942? Ought we not to be preparing within the general structure of 'Bolero' some other operation by which we may gain positions of advantage, and also directly and indirectly to take some of the weight off Russia? It is within this setting and on this background that the

French Northwest Africa operation should be studied."[55] Churchill stopped talking then, knowing that his argument had been compelling.

Roosevelt sat for a moment, then called Marshall and Ernie King and told them to be prepared to discuss what the U.S. planned to do if the Russians were near collapse by the end of the summer. Roosevelt hinted that any plan they proposed had to answer the tough questions about resources and men, but clearly implied that Sledgehammer was not an option. The U.S. and England could not stand idle in 1942, and a cross-Channel operation could not be launched so soon. That done, Roosevelt and Churchill returned to Washington by rail to be briefed by their military staffs. The next morning, June 21, the American and British chiefs met with Roosevelt and Churchill in the Oval Office. Marshall eyed the president and prime minister and prepared his briefing. But he had the disquieting sense that Sledgehammer was dead, that an attack on Europe would have to wait until 1943. Moreover, he sensed that Roosevelt and Churchill knew that something had to be done to take the pressure off of Russia, which meant there had to be an attack on the Germans somewhere in 1942. That meant that Gymnast—an attack on North Africa—was still very much under active consideration.

As if on cue, in the midst of this Oval Office meeting a Roosevelt aide entered the room and handed a slip of paper to the president.[56] Roosevelt read the message and silently handed it to Churchill. The news was devastating: Tobruk, the British garrison in Libya, had surrendered to Erwin Rommel's Afrika Korps.[57] Churchill directed Ismay to check the report then turned to Roosevelt. The president was effusive: the United States, he said, would help. Over the next eighteen hours, George Marshall and Dwight Eisenhower scrambled to put together reinforcements for the hard-pressed British troops in North Africa. Meanwhile, the full extent of the British debacle in North Africa became apparent: the Germans took thirty thousand British prisoners at Tobruk, and Rommel crowed about the victory: "I am going to Suez," he said.[58] By the morning of the twenty-second, Marshall was able to reassure Churchill that the U.S. would send an entire armored division to North Africa to buttress the shaky British position. Churchill knew that Marshall's initiative meant taking weapons out of the hands of American troops, stripping training divisions of their newest tanks, even paring down plans for reinforcements in the Pacific. Marshall did not deny this or seek to assuage Churchill but took the opportunity to cement an alliance that had begun to fray with Churchill's arrival in Washington: "It is a terrible thing to take the weapons out of a soldier's hands," he told the prime minister then added, "If the British need is so great they must have them."[59]

In the wake of the Oval Office meeting and news of Tobruk's fall, Harry Hopkins urged Churchill to meet "a couple of American officers" who would form the senior American command in England. Eisenhower and Clark duly presented themselves at the White House later that afternoon and were ushered in to meet Churchill. "I was immediately impressed by these remarkable but hitherto unknown men," he later recalled. "They had both come from the President, whom they had seen for the first time. We talked almost entirely about the major cross-Channel invasion in 1942, 'Round-up,' as it was then called, on which their thoughts had evidently been concentrated. We had a most agreeable discussion, lasting for over an hour."[60] The meeting merited little comment from Eisenhower, whose friendship with the prime minister lay in the future. Eisenhower later characterized the meeting as an "informal chat" that had "no military significance."[61] Even so, Eisenhower took time to assess his morale, which had been dealt a heavy blow by Tobruk's fall. But Ike could not discern any pessimism in the prime minister's approach and reflected later that Churchill was thinking of "attack and victory, not of defense and defeat."[62]

The fall of Tobruk, the divisions over Sledgehammer, and Marshall and Stimson's simmering anger with Roosevelt dampened what was thereafter referred to as the Second Washington Conference, but did not deter the Army chief of staff from putting the best face on Churchill's visit. Marshall not only rushed three hundred tanks (destined for Bolero) to hard-pressed British troops in North Africa, but provided his best show for Churchill and the British chiefs during a planned tour of U.S. training bases that followed the Oval Office meeting. Marshall, Churchill, Ismay, Dill, Brooke, and Stimson dutifully trooped off to Fort Jackson, South Carolina, where U.S. tank and infantry brigades staged a series of intricate field maneuvers designed to impress their visitors with American combat prowess. Churchill, cane at hand and cigar firmly in mouth—a little stooped perhaps, but as focused and irreverent as ever—nodded in appreciation while, nearby, an unimpressed Brooke attempted to keep his skepticism in check. The training maneuvers were a success,

Marshall believed, largely because he had put the hard-charging Major General Robert L. Eichelberger (as tough a combat commander as any in American history—as the future would show), who included in his maneuvers a parachute drop of six thousand airborne soldiers. Churchill was impressed, but Ismay remarked (under his breath, no doubt) that it would be murder to put such untrained men in harm's way. Never mind: Marshall had shown the prime minister that the United States was ready to meet its commitments, whether in Europe or (as Churchill insisted) against Erwin Rommel in North Africa.[63]

Churchill returned to England the day following his and Marshall's return from South Carolina. In spite of Tobruk, he had much to celebrate. The Americans were getting ready to face the Germans, and the American president, now a close friend, had agreed with him that they must be attacked in 1942. Marshall's views provide a stark contrast to Churchill's. He was sorely disappointed with the outcome of the Washington meetings but was satisfied that Bolero was going forward and that the United States now had a semblance of a command structure in place in London. Marshall was particularly pleased that Churchill agreed with his appointment of Eisenhower as the U.S. theater commander in London and that the prime minister had much praise for Clark. Marshall later said that Churchill's opinion was the final one he solicited, and that neither Eisenhower nor Clark would have gone to England without Churchill's approval: "He was extravagant in his estimate of them, so then I went ahead with my decision on Eisenhower," he told his biographer Forrest Pogue.[64] Marshall and Eisenhower spent the last days before Ike's departure for London in a series of meetings discussing the outcome of Churchill's visit to Washington and Eisenhower's new role as the commanding general in England. If Eisenhower ever thanked Marshall for his consideration there is no record of it. But then Eisenhower surely knew that Marshall's response would have been the same he gave to other officers when he received their gratitude: "Thank yourself," he would have said; "if you hadn't earned it you would not have received it."

MARSHALL'S DECISION to appoint Eisenhower as commander of U.S. troops in England marked a pivotal moment in Eisenhower's military career. It was one that could not have been predicted just twelve months before. The one-time staff colonel who had worked for thirty years for a combat assignment had now, at the age of fifty-two, become the command equal of Douglas MacArthur. He had done so in just over three years—he was promoted to colonel on March 11, 1939, and assigned as commanding general, European theater of operations/U.S. Army, on June 11, 1942. By any measure, his rise had been meteoric. The assignment of Eisenhower as America's commanding general in England was also a pivotal moment in the Marshall-Eisenhower relationship. For a little over six months, Eisenhower had served as George Marshall's unofficial aide-de-camp, planning under his guidance the response to the Axis challenge. Over that period the two had met dozens of times and exchanged dozens of papers. In all of those meetings and exchanges Marshall had not once found Eisenhower's conception of the war different from his. While Marshall might amend or edit an Eisenhower paper, he never rejected one; Eisenhower, for his part, never found Marshall's leadership wanting or his directives obtuse. Marshall's final judgment on Eisenhower is perhaps the most important: "If he hadn't delivered he wouldn't have moved up." [65] This is true: Eisenhower had "delivered." But Marshall had provided Eisenhower with that opportunity, as he had so many others. In Eisenhower, Marshall knew, he had the almost perfect model of a modern commander: part soldier, part diplomat, part administrator. Marshall knew the importance of this combination: Patton could fight, Dill was the perfect diplomat, McNarney was a brilliant administrator. Eisenhower was all three. Of course, Marshall might have reflected that it took a special kind of leader to recognize this in a commander and, at the same time, organize an entire nation for a global war. Only George Marshall could fill that role. Eisenhower might not have thanked Marshall for his promotion, but he understood the unequaled qualities that Marshall brought to his job and wrote of them to an old friend, Brigadier Spencer Ball Akin, who had escaped from Corregidor with Douglas MacArthur.

In a day or so I'll be leaving Washington. This has been a tough, intensive grind—but now I'm getting a swell command and, of course, am highly delighted that I got away with this job sufficiently well to have the Chief accord such recognition to me. Incidentally, the Chief is a great soldier. He is quick, tough, tireless, decisive and a real leader. He accepts responsibility automatically and never goes back on a subordinate. We're particularly fortunate in having him for a Chief of Staff. It has been a pleasure to work directly under him.[66]

For those myriad historians who have written on the American high command in World War II, the profound personal dissimilarities between Marshall and Eisenhower have provided a nearly insurmountable obstacle to explaining their relationship. In truth, however, Marshall and Eisenhower had much in common: both men spent most of their careers in staff assignments and understood the value of astute planning; both men were schooled by the same generation of commanders—Fox Conner and John J. Pershing; both men believed in the doctrine of combined-service warfare operating within a coalition in which there was joint command; both men admired the same predecessors (Robert E. Lee and Benjamin Franklin would later be mentioned by both as the greatest Americans); and both men had an innate feel for what could reasonably be asked of America's soldiers and of the American people—Marshall by his experience as an organizer of the Civilian Conservation Corps, Eisenhower by his successive assignments as a recruiter and troop trainer. "In retrospect, Marshall's appointment of Eisenhower seems remarkably casual," Marshall biographer Forrest Pogue has noted. Perhaps, but Marshall's decision to make Eisenhower the commanding general in Europe was a reflection of the depth of their common experiences and military beliefs. In the end, it was this— more than any other single factor—that brought the two together and gave their partnership its meaning.

ETOUSA

"You are generally familiar with my views. . . ."
"We stand on the brink . . . and must take the jump. . . ."

D WIGHT EISENHOWER ARRIVED IN England on June 24, took up residence at Claridge's[1] and began to plan the Allied invasion of Europe.
Less than twenty-four hours later, he wrote the first in a series of 108 letters to
George Marshall.[2] The letters, written over a period of three years, were personal and reflective and give an extraordinary insight into Eisenhower's views
on the war and its challenges. While Marshall rarely responded, and while the
two communicated over the war years primarily by means of hundreds of coded
cables, the Eisenhower letters provide a unique account of the Eisenhower-
Marshall relationship. It is perhaps precisely because of the collegial tone of
Eisenhower's letters that Marshall felt comfortable in reading them without
comment, as Eisenhower's blunt writing and detailed analyses allowed him to
turn his attention, often for relatively extended periods, to the war's other theaters, where his relationship with America's senior commanders was less intimate.

That Eisenhower would actually write to Marshall was unusual and well outside of military tradition. The decision to write the letters (to give Marshall "informal reports," as Eisenhower put it) was apparently Eisenhower's alone, and
undertaken to reassure the Army chief of staff that the work Eisenhower was

doing in England accorded with Marshall's vision. It may well be that Eisenhower, convinced that Marshall would one day come to England to take command of Allied forces himself, with Eisenhower as his chief of staff, thought it necessary to show Marshall that he was preparing the ground for his eventual arrival. That Eisenhower thought of himself as a placeholder until Marshall took command was implied throughout the first letters, as he told Marshall that one of his first acts on arriving in England was to inform his senior staff that they must satisfy two commanders, not just one: "I am quite certain that this staff and all commanders now realize that we have a unique problem to solve," he wrote, "that we have full opportunity and freedom of action in solving them, and that no alibis or excuses will be acceptable to you."[3]

That Eisenhower's letters reassured Marshall is apparent from the chief of staff's work in Washington over the next week. Rather than respond immediately to his new European commander, Marshall turned his attention to resolving a number of sticky problems in the Pacific. From Eisenhower's departure until early July, Marshall was consumed by a growing rift with Admiral King over command arrangements for the Pacific, a disagreement that contrasts sharply with his controversy-free relations with and trust in Eisenhower. The ever-sensitive King had once, in early 1942, stormed out of Marshall's office while waiting for him to finish a meeting. Realizing that he had insulted the naval chief, Marshall immediately went to King's office to apologize: "I think this is very important," he said. "Because if you or I begin fighting at the very start of the war, what in the world will the public have to say about us. They won't accept it for a minute. We can't afford to fight. So we ought to find a way to get along together."[4] King, chagrined, agreed.

After that moment, Marshall's disagreements with King were rare and never personal. But there was still a tension in the relationship, the outgrowth of a tenacious interservice rivalry that continued to hamper Pacific operations. "An unwritten agreement became apparent: King supported most of Marshall's proposals for the European and the China-Burma-India Theaters and in return asked for the main voice in Pacific matters," Marshall's biographer Forrest Pogue notes. "Although far more conciliatory than his bleakness of manner and rudeness in debate often indicated, he [King] was less disposed than the Army chief to seek agreement and was extremely jealous of the interests of the Navy."[5] The problem was not so much Marshall, as it turned out, but Douglas MacArthur.

The contentious general was a headache because he provided the Army's counterpoint to King's "extremely jealous" interest in the Navy. But MacArthur's problem with King was not simply that he had a jealous interest in promoting the Army; it was also that he had a jealous interest in promoting himself.

Just after Eisenhower's departure, MacArthur and King began a full-blown brawl over who would take command of an offensive against the Japanese in the southwestern Pacific. While Marshall had given MacArthur control of that theater, MacArthur also demanded control of U.S. Marine and Navy units for a planned summer offensive in the Santa Cruz and Solomon islands, specifically "one division trained and completely equipped for amphibious operations and a task force including two carriers."[6] Two carriers? Under Army control? King, his hackles raised, responded by flatly refusing to turn over the Navy's carriers to MacArthur's command. In a separate message he reminded Marshall that the Navy "had accepted Army primacy in Europe" in exchange for a free hand in the Pacific.[7] Was Marshall going to renege on that agreement? MacArthur's response to King through Marshall expressed his suspicion that what the Navy *really* wanted was not control of their carriers but "general command control of all operations in the Pacific theater."[8] Marshall watched this long-distance debate throughout June before intervening. The best solution was a bad compromise: the Navy's lead admiral in the southwestern Pacific, Chester Nimitz, would be in charge of the first part of the planned summer offensive before turning over command of the operation to MacArthur.[9] Additionally (though Marshall was careful never to say this so plainly), the Navy commander for the southwestern Pacific, Admiral William F. "Bull" Halsey, was to act under MacArthur's command in coordinating all land operations, even if naval assets were in use. The feisty Nimitz, meanwhile, was to lead the Navy in a charge across the central Pacific with all Navy and Marine Corps resources under his command.[10]

The politics of interservice rivalry was only one of Marshall's problems in attempting to form a unified command for the Pacific. Real politics, the politics of the 1944 presidential election, also intruded. MacArthur's name was being bandied about by Republicans, first as a "Generalissimo" of the armed forces of the United States then as a contender for the 1944 Republican nomination.[11] Whatever else Marshall might have believed about MacArthur (in truth, he believed he was a gifted organizer and commander), he certainly preferred Franklin Roosevelt as his commander in chief, which meant that MacArthur had to stay in Australia and that he had to be mollified.[12] Marshall admitted this bluntly after the end of the war: "He was of a very independent nature and he made himself a political factor from the start," Marshall reflected. ". . . And the President was very careful in handling him because of that. . . . Over there [in Australia], he made beautiful use of what he got, but he spent so much time scrapping with the Navy. Halsey tried his best to please MacArthur. He tried to cooperate all the way through. MacArthur was a very fine commander. He was . . . supersensitive about everything. He thought everybody had ulterior motives about everything . . ."[13]

One of the interesting and largely untold interior stories of World War II is of Marshall's constant battle to build interservice cooperation in the Pacific. At times it must have seemed to him that the defeat of Japan depended solely on his ability to balance a quartet of dynamic but competing egos: the insufferably megalomaniacal MacArthur, the dedicated and hard-charging Halsey, the Teutonic and wry Nimitz,[14] and the permanently dissatisfied and taut-as-a-wire King. After refereeing the intramural Pacific fistfight of June 1942, Marshall must have turned with some relief to the European theater, where, by comparison, everything seemed calm. But of course it wasn't. Just as one intramural controversy was being resolved in the Pacific, another, far more dangerous contest was starting in England. While the Pacific fight mediated by Marshall centered on interservice and interpersonal rivalries, the fight in England was much more serious—pitting the seemingly recalcitrant British Imperial General Staff and the tenacious British prime minister Winston Churchill against Marshall and his chosen European deputy, Dwight Eisenhower. Mediating the European dispute took a great deal of Marshall and Eisenhower's energies, but the stakes were high: if the U.S. and Great Britain could not agree on a strategy to defeat Germany and learn to work together, the war in Europe might well be lost. Finding a way to bring the British and Americans together on a common strategy would test Marshall's skill as both an organizer and a diplomat—a key reason he appointed Eisenhower as America's European commander.

THE BRITISH-AMERICAN disagreement about the overall strategy for winning the war in Europe dominates nearly all accounts of America's first months in World War II. Churchill argued ceaselessly for an Allied invasion of North Africa over the more direct straight-as-a-rifle-shot invasion of Europe favored by George Marshall and Dwight Eisenhower. The Afrika Korps must be engaged, Tobruk recaptured, Rommel defeated, and the Allies blooded and vindicated, Churchill said. It was his obsession. Marshall and Eisenhower drew their own conclusions from Churchill's personal experiences: it was not Allied arms that needed vindication—it was Churchill, eternally haunted by his failure at Gallipoli almost thirty years before.[15]

Marshall and Eisenhower resisted Churchill's obsession because it violated their most fundamental military belief: Find the enemy, fight him, and defeat him. A North African invasion would simply postpone this final reckoning, which would take place on the armor-friendly terrain of northwestern France. Marshall and Eisenhower envisioned a great battle, with Patton's tanks sweeping forward through France and with Germany's great tank commanders flanked and on the run. This was the American way of war, a tradition dating from Ulysses S. Grant and then polished and refined by Fox Conner: victory over the enemy consisted not in occupying his territory, but in defeating his army. Destroy Lee's army and you defeat the Confederacy, Grant had said, and his words and campaigns were taught at Leavenworth and tested in the great tank simulations of Louisiana, and had rung down through the annals of American military history: Find the enemy and destroy him was nearly genetically encoded in America's senior military leaders. They breathed it.

Yet, in truth, the debate over whether the Allies should divert their attention to North Africa turned far less on Churchill's obsession with "Corporal Hitler's" soft underbelly, and even less on British concerns that Erwin Rommel's Afrika Korps might find itself parading victoriously through the streets of Cairo. Though no one would state it so bluntly (with the possible exception of the ever-condescending Field Marshal Sir Alan Brooke), the British high command simply did not believe that American soldiers were ready to fight.[16] This lack of faith in America's soldiers found its way into a number of oft-repeated anecdotes that now infuse our understanding of British-American relations during the war. The most common of these anecdotes features a smiling, slightly sardonic, and lordly British "Tommy" facing off against a naïve, gum-chewing American "Mac." The British soldier asks his counterpart whether the Americans are ready for war. The offended American answers: We have been fighting the Japanese in the Pacific for many months. The British soldier laughs and shakes his head: Come now, mate, he says, fighting the Japanese is not fighting a war. You have not fought a war until you have fought the Germans.

The snide exchange finds truth in history, and in the reminiscences of both Marshall and Eisenhower. Marshall was keenly aware that Brooke had "led a corps in battle, while my experience, dating back to the First World War, was [as chief of operations] on an Army staff."[17] Eisenhower, too, was aware of his lack of battlefield experience. That he had worked diligently for two decades to gain such experience hardly mattered, for he had failed to do so. There was another side to this view, of course, though Marshall was polite enough not to mention it: Brooke had been a part of his country's most serious military disasters. In Flanders, in World War I, Brooke had witnessed the flower of British youth going up and over their entrenchments and not returning. And at the outset of World War II, Brooke had presided over the triumphant evacuation of the British Army from Dunkirk (a mere jaunt from the Somme through the cross-speckled rolling hills of northern France), a tactical retreat that saved thousands of British soldiers from annihilation. Nonetheless, the "miracle at Dunkirk" was merely the end point of an embarrassing strategic disaster resulting from a decisive German victory. The Somme and Dunkirk were fine British traditions, senior American commanders believed, but they were disasters. They made Tommy timorous.[18] The British, it was said, now lacked the stomach for the bloodletting that an invasion of Europe would require. They were cowed by the crosses of Flanders Field.

It was only with the passage of time that both Marshall and Eisenhower were able to admit that the British had the better of this debate: the Allies were woefully unprepared for Sledgehammer. Alan Brooke, for all his nose-in-the-air dramatics, was essentially right: this was a cross-Channel suicide operation. While Sledgehammer was viewed as a stopgap, a mere raid to force the Germans to shift troops to France from Russia (thereby keeping Stalin in the war), the most fundamental preparations for its implementation had yet to be put in place. At the end of June, by Marshall's own count (in a memo he had directed Eisenhower to write for Roosevelt) the United States had only "50,000 soldiers in the U.K." with forty thousand more due by August. That was hardly enough to provide a "permanent occupation" of a landing zone in France, particularly if (as Marshall also conceded) the "total carrying capacity" of the naval transports involved would put only twenty thousand Allied soldiers on the beaches of France.[19] Given these figures, it is no wonder that the British continued to oppose Sledgehammer while agreeing with its conclusion: "There is no reason why we should 'stand idle in the Atlantic Theater during the whole of 1942.'" There was no need to stand idle in 1942, Brooke, Ismay, and Churchill argued. There was plenty of war to fight, and there were plenty of Germans to kill if North Africa was invaded and Rommel was defeated before he could conquer Egypt.

The debate over Sledgehammer lay dormant even as Eisenhower began to build the staff and resources in his first weeks in London, but by June 30, when he composed his second personal letter to Marshall, Eisenhower was growing concerned that his inability to engage the British in any sort of planning for the operation was a clear signal that Churchill and the British Chiefs of Staff were dedicated to killing Sledgehammer forever and replacing it with Gymnast. Eisenhower's unease at his inability to get the British focused on Sledgehammer was apparent in his second letter:

I can discover little if any progress in the formulation of broad decisions affecting the operation as a whole. To force decisive action along this line is becoming my principal job; so far I have visited everyone except General Brooke who has been practically incommunicado since his return from Washington. . . .

There seems to be some confusion of thought as to the extent of the British commitment toward a 1942 operation. I have repeated to them emphatically your statement that we are ready to cooperate with everything available to us, and will do so by attaching our forces to appropriate commands of the British forces in order to get the job done. In this particular matter a decision must be quickly reached because of the length of time necessary to collect coastwise shipping and available landing craft.[20]

If there was any doubt in Marshall's mind that the British were simply "stiffing" Eisenhower, the next sentence of Eisenhower's letter erased it: "General Ismay told me that, because of the Prime Minister's preoccupation this week in political matters, he would appreciate it if I would put off my formal call until Monday or Tuesday." The same day that Eisenhower penned his letter to

Marshall, pressure was mounting on the chief of staff to provide some relief for the British in North Africa. Marshall told Roosevelt that the situation there was dire and that it was possible that Rommel's Afrika Korps would occupy Cairo within one week. It was very unlikely, Marshall conceded, that he could be stopped.[21] In London, the British Chiefs of Staff made the same calculation and, in so doing, decided to openly oppose Sledgehammer, even if doing so caused a break in their relations with the Americans. The decision, made July 8, was communicated through Dill, who gave it to Marshall. A follow-up coded message came from Eisenhower in London. "The British Staff and Prime Minister have decided that Sledgehammer can not repeat not be successfully executed this year," Eisenhower wrote. Later in the same memo he noted: "The British military authorities are most fearful that in making this decision they may be giving you a feeling that they have partially let you down."[22] Studying Dill's and Eisenhower's messages, Marshall decided to go once again on the offensive and immediately wrote to Roosevelt in an attempt to reverse the British decision. He could hardly cover his anger, and wrote and rewrote the Roosevelt memo to cast as dark a pall as possible on the potential for Allied offensive operations over the next two years: the decision to cancel Sledgehammer, he wrote, also meant an end to Bolero—the buildup of U.S. troops in England for an early invasion of France. The only choice now, he argued, was to shift American war priorities. Marshall dug out an old Eisenhower memo, using a Pacific First strategy to force British compliance with Sledgehammer: "My object is again to force the British into acceptance of a concentrated effort against Germany, and if this proves impossible, to turn immediately to the Pacific with strong forces and drive for a decision against Japan," he wrote in a July 10 memo to Roosevelt.[23]

But Marshall was bluffing, and Roosevelt knew it. From his home at Hyde Park, the president immediately called Marshall. "In view of your Pacific Ocean alternative," he said, "please send me this afternoon by plane, a detailed comprehensive outline of the plans, including estimated time and overall totals of ships, planes, and ground forces. Also, any proposed withdrawal of existing or proposed use of ships, planes, and ground forces in the Atlantic. Also, advise as to the effect of such an operation on Russian and Middle East fronts during the balance of the year."[24] Marshall, chagrined, was forced to respond to Roosevelt that a detailed plan for the Pacific had not yet been completed and that a change would "require a great deal of detailed planning which will take considerable time."[25] This was the closest that Roosevelt and Marshall would come to a falling-out over America's strategy for winning the global war. Roosevelt later characterized the Joint Chiefs of Staff's response that they would abandon a Europe First strategy as "taking up your dishes and going away." On July 14, Roosevelt directed Marshall, King, and Hopkins to travel to London to confer with Eisenhower and his staff on a possible invasion of North Africa. After that, Roosevelt said, America's senior commanders could confer with their British counterparts and report back to him. Marshall would still not give up, and he decided to press his point with Roosevelt. At a meeting at the White House on July 15, he raised his voice to the president, telling him that a diversion from an invasion of Europe was typical of Churchill, who was addicted to "half-baked" schemes.[26] Roosevelt sat grim-faced, unswayed.

Through all of this, Eisenhower and Marshall had been exchanging messages, with Marshall briefing Eisenhower on his dustup with Roosevelt and seeking data on ships and troops available for immediate movement to the Pacific. Marshall might have been bluffing when he told Roosevelt that the U.S. should substitute a Pacific First strategy if the British did not agree to Sledgehammer, but even asking Eisenhower to provide information on what troops could be sent immediately to MacArthur in Australia was likely to give Churchill and the British chiefs pause.[27] The day following the Roosevelt-Marshall argument, Marshall cabled Eisenhower about his pending visit and reiterated his opposition to a North African invasion. "If the United States is to engage in any other operation than forceful unswerving adherence to full Bolero plans," he wrote, "we believe that we should turn to the Pacific and strike decisively against Japan with full strength and ample reserves, assuming a defensive attitude against Germany except for air operations."[28] Warned that Marshall was on his way, Eisenhower gathered his staff and began producing planning papers that would show that the obstacles to a North African invasion were insurmountable. He had little time for preparation: Marshall and his delegation, which included Harry Hopkins and Ernie King, left Washington on July 16 and arrived in London the next evening. Marshall immediately closeted himself with Eisenhower, and despite their near certainty that Sledgehammer was dead, the two prepared to do battle with Winston Churchill.

WHEN MARSHALL arrived in London, he found that Eisenhower had made good use of the three weeks he had spent there: organizing his staff, improving relations with the British, and gaining control of the American buildup in England. Mark Clark had also begun the difficult work of preparing II Corps (the first full unit deployed in the European theater) for combat, while J. C. H. Lee, the supply and logistics czar, took hold of the nearly impossible job of fitting out the new American Army. Clark was a known quantity, and Eisenhower trusted him, but Eisenhower had little experience with Lee, whose imperious style and religious obsessions soon earned him the sobriquet "Jesus Christ Himself" Lee.[29] Eisenhower badgered Marshall to send Walter Bedell "Beetle" Smith to London as his chief of staff, but Marshall hesitated. Smith was the man Marshall used to cut through the War Department bureaucracy, and the chief of staff did not want to lose him. Eisenhower pleaded that he needed him for the same reason, to manage and energize a staff that was sure to grow to huge proportions. Marshall finally agreed to the transfer but said Smith's arrival would be delayed until he wrapped up his work in Washington. Smith would not arrive until September; he would prove perfect for the job—he was in a state of constant rage (which endeared him to Winston Churchill)—and soon became known as "Eisenhower's son-of-a-bitch"[30] and "a specialist in psychological bullying."[31]

Before leaving Washington, Eisenhower had requested that his old friend Harry Butcher—a CBS executive, Navy Reserve captain, and charter member of Club Eisenhower—be assigned as his personal assistant.[32] Marshall and CNO Ernie King fulfilled the request, and the gossipy "go-anywhere-do-anything-for-Ike" Butcher became a member of Eisenhower's official family. Upon his arrival in early July, Eisenhower gave Butcher three jobs: he was to be Ike's official friend (to tell him things no one else dared, as Eisenhower put it), to guard his door from interlopers and favor-seekers, and to keep a written daily diary of the Eisenhower headquarters. Butcher dutifully served Eisenhower in all three capacities and, following the war, published the diary as *My Three Years with Eisenhower*. While Ike fell out with "Butch" over the gossipy character of some of his diary entries (including an account of Eisenhower's imitation of Churchill, his chin nearly touching the table, "gurgling" soup), Butcher took his job seriously.[33] Joining Clark, Lee, and Butcher in Eisenhower's inner circle were Carl "Tooey" Spaatz, a West Point graduate and commander of the U.S. Army Air Corps in Europe,[34] and Marshall's old friend Harold "Betty" Stark, who had "several long talks"[35] with Eisenhower just after the ground commander's arrival.[36] Also joining the circle around Eisenhower was Kay Summersby, his driver from his first trip to London.[37]

Shortly after his arrival, Eisenhower moved from Claridge's to the Dorchester Hotel because he considered the former gaudy and because, as he was told, "Claridge's is a pile of sugar. A bomb and it'll dissolve."[38] The morning after his arrival in England, Eisenhower presided over his first staff meeting at the offices of the U.S. command and was angered by what he believed to be a lack of aggressiveness in both American and British commanders. He immediately issued his first in a series of hundreds of directives: "Pessimism and defeatism will not be tolerated. Any officer or soldier who cannot rise above the obstacles and bitter prospects that lie in store for us has no recourse but to ask for instant release from this theater. And if he shows such attitude and doesn't ask for release, he'll go home anyway."[39] The circular had the desired effect. The pace of work accelerated quickly at 20 Grosvenor Square, with most staffers mimicking Eisenhower's schedule by working seven-day weeks. Even so, all but Ike's closest colleagues were deeply skeptical that he could get the job done. In his first weeks in London the new commander seemed too predictably American; he was wide-eyed, overly aggressive, "Rotarian."

While Eisenhower's staff might wince at phrases they thought absurdly jingoist (we will "kill the Hun" he told one audience),[40] British citizens applauded his combativeness and flocked to his public appearances. Eisenhower celebrated Independence Day by speaking to a mixed group of Londoners and American Red Cross workers. His short speech, written by the rece tly arrived Butcher, played on Eisenhower's belief that hatred of the enemy was a requirement for victory. He was a hit: "Ike told me an old Englishwoman had come to him and said she had lost her husband and a son in the war," Butcher related. "She had been despondent and dejected, but said Ike's speech had cheered her up and given her the first real confidence in the war. She had been waiting for toughness."[41] Eisenhower enjoyed the compliment, but he shied away from such public appearances ("This is a hell of a way to fight a war," he said once, after standing in a receiving line for nearly two hours),[42] and so welcomed Marshall's appearance in London on July 18,[43] even though he had spent the three nights prior to the Army chief of staff's arrival overseeing a nearly around-the-clock schedule of briefings and planning sessions.[44]

While Marshall and Eisenhower were prepared to argue strenuously for Sledgehammer despite its markedly fading prospects, the British chiefs of Staff had spent as much time preparing to knock it down. Sir Alan Brooke calculated that, given the disagreements among the American staff, the British chiefs would win the argument: "Harry Hopkins is for operating in Africa, Marshall wants to operate in Europe, and King is determined to stick to the Pacific," he wrote in his diary.[45] Brooke's calculation was correct, but he underestimated Marshall and Eisenhower's influence on Hopkins and King, who were determined to remain united behind Sledgehammer in the face of British intransigence. When Marshall came to Grosvenor Square on the morning of the eighteenth, Eisenhower handed him a planning paper that presented a carefully constructed argument against any offensive in 1942 that was not aimed at gaining a lodgment in Europe. "The belief of this headquarters and of the principal subordinate commanders," Eisenhower wrote, "is that the Russian situation is at least sufficiently critical to justify any action on our part that would clearly be of definite assistance."[46] Marshall studied the paper and agreed with his subordinate; he immediately adopted it as a model for one that he wanted presented to the British chiefs, whom he, Eisenhower, King, Spaatz, and Stark would be meeting the next day. The American delegation spent all of the nineteenth preparing the Marshall paper[47] at the same time that the British Chiefs of Staff were closeted with Churchill at his home at Chequers.[48] On July 20, a full conference between the American delegation—accompanied by Eisenhower, Clark, Spaatz, and Stark—and the British was held in the office of the British cabinet room.

Marshall began the meeting by arguing strenuously that an Allied failure to strike in France in 1942 might be disastrous for the Russians, lacing his language with words from Eisenhower's memorandum: "We should not forget the prize we seek is to keep 8,000,000 Russians in the war."[49] Anything less would be "one of the grossest military blunders in all history." But the British could not be budged: "After lunch at 3 p.m. we met Marshall and King and had long arguments with them," Alan Brooke noted. "Found both of them still hankering after an attack across the Channel this year to take the pressure off the Russians. They failed to realize that such action could only lead to the loss of six divisions without achieving any results."[50] The British would not be convinced, and the Americans, mindful that Roosevelt was inclined to agree with them, retreated to review their options. Marshall and Eisenhower once again went through the American plans to see if they could be refined. "The last few days have been tense and wearing," Eisenhower admitted.[51] On the afternoon of the twenty-second, Marshall met with Churchill and reported that in light of the deadlock over Sledgehammer, he had asked Roosevelt for direction. Within several hours, Marshall had his answer. Roosevelt instructed Marshall and the American delegation to drop Sledgehammer and reach a decision with the British "on some operation which would involve American land forces being brought into action against the enemy in 1942."[52] Marshall was crestfallen, though hardly shocked. He had hoped that in the end Roosevelt would at least push for some better compromise. When told by Marshall that the president would side with the British, Eisenhower could hardly believe it. Later, he called July 22 "the blackest day in history."

Now there was no alternative. Even with a cross-Channel invasion years away, Marshall and Eisenhower knew that the Allies must do something, anything, to take the pressure off the Russians. North Africa was the only acceptable alternative. With Sledgehammer postponed, Marshall was forced to support the North African invasion, though it galled him to do so. He later remembered the series of events that led him to this conclusion.

> The British staff and cabinet were unalterable in their refusal to touch Sledgehammer. It looked like the Russians were going to be destroyed. . . . The successful defense of Moscow had not yet occurred. . . . So we were at a complete stalemate. Churchill was rabid for Africa. Roosevelt was for Africa. Both men were aware of political necessities. . . .
>
> One morning I sat down in my room and began to write. I recognized we couldn't do Sledgehammer and that there was no immediate prospect of Roundup. What was the least harmful diversion? I always had to bear in mind that we didn't have much and that much of what we had was in the amateurish stage—particularly Air. I started writing a proposal. It called for an expedition into North Africa with operations, limits, nature, and the like.[53]

With this strategy finally decided, Marshall, Eisenhower, King, Hopkins, and their staffs spent the next three days discussing the invasion of North Africa — "Torch" — with their British counterparts. The key meeting took place on the afternoon of July 25, when Marshall, King, and Hopkins met with the British Chiefs of Staff to decide on command arrangements for the new operation. It must have been an uncomfortable time for Marshall. The shelving of Sledgehammer was a bitter defeat for the Army chief of staff, who was now forced to turn his attention to what the British wanted. Eisenhower, had he been present, would have been even more uncomfortable. He had come to London to serve as ground commander of U.S. troops in Europe (as the commander of the European theater of operations, U.S. Army — the "ETOUSA," as he was officially designated), but now he would be commanding troops for an operation that no longer existed. If the British sensed any of Marshall's or Eisenhower's discomfort, however, they had the courtesy not to show it. In fact, now that Sledgehammer was no longer an option, they were willing to name an American as the commander of all Allied forces slotted for the North African campaign, including British forces. The British and Americans sat down to discuss Torch with one overriding question hanging, unspoken, in the air: Who would be in command? It was Ernie King who broached and then finally answered the question: "Well you've got him right here [in London]," he said, looking at Marshall. "Why not put it under Eisenhower?"[54]

Late that afternoon, Marshall directed Eisenhower to meet with him in his room. He wanted to talk over the Torch operation with him, he said. When Eisenhower arrived in Marshall's suite, the Army chief of staff was in the bathroom. The two talked through the door.[55] For the time being, Marshall said, Eisenhower would be designated as deputy Allied commander of Torch, with Marshall serving as the overall commander. Eisenhower was to stay in London and plan the operation. Of course, Marshall added, it might turn out that Eisenhower would become the operation's supreme commander. The final command arrangements, he said, would be determined later.[56] When Marshall emerged from the bathroom, he and Eisenhower had a drink, and he told Ike that he could keep his current staff in place. But now they were to plan a different operation. That night, Marshall left for Washington, while the newly named deputy Allied commander in Europe — and the newly promoted Lieutenant General Dwight Eisenhower — began planning for an Allied invasion of North Africa.

SENSING THAT his meeting at his hotel had left his deputy uncertain about his role, Marshall wrote a personal letter to Eisenhower the day following his return to Washington. "Dear Eisenhower," Marshall said, ". . . the matter of command control remains undecided as the President has not yet indicated his intentions. Under these circumstances I consider it necessary that you take the bull by the horns and endeavor to push through the organizational set-up on the basis that you will be Deputy for whoever is designated for supreme command. We cannot afford to drag along at this late date."[57] Marshall spent the next paragraphs giving detailed advice on how Eisenhower should set up his command, relating how he had begun rerouting landing craft from the Pacific for Torch, and expressing President Roosevelt's view that the Torch landings, officially scheduled for September 15, should take place "as soon as possible." Marshall finished his letter by returning to the topic of overall command, with a hint that he might eventually come to London to command the operation. If this were to happen, Marshall wanted to make sure that Eisenhower was not surprised. "You are generally familiar with my views and the circumstances under which the recent agreement [to sideline Sledgehammer in favor of Torch] was arrived at," Marshall wrote. "I think with this as a basis you are in a position to use your own judgment without fear of committing me in some manner contrary to my desire."[58]

Eisenhower needed little prodding. Immediately following Marshall's departure, he convened a senior planning committee for Torch at London's Norfolk House, which would now serve as the command headquarters for the North African operation.[59] While Eisenhower was still viewed as a provisional commander of the operation, he appointed the reluctant Mark Clark as his deputy, taking him away from the combat command he prized to serve in an administrative capacity.[60] Alfred Gruenther, a brilliant young colonel, arrived from Marshall's office as Eisenhower's chief planner, and on July 31, under his direction, the first strategic planning mission for Torch was convened. The operation's first plans called for "the seizure of two large and two small ports within the Mediterranean and a subsequent seizure of Casablanca" by four divisions reinforced by the later arrival of six to eight more divisions.[61] The purpose of the landings was to open a second front against Rommel's Afrika Korps then operating near El Alamein in Egypt. After the landings, the Allied force would move into central North Africa and recapture Tobruk, then (in cooperation with the British Eighth Army moving from Egypt to the west) destroy all German forces in North Africa. The Germans and their Italian allies would be difficult to defeat, the planners felt, unless American and British forces could be constantly reinforced and resupplied by opening ports controlled by the pro-German Vichy French government. The French, as both Marshall and Eisenhower knew, could be a major problem, as their soldiers might well be ordered to fight the Allies.

Despite reassurances from Marshall, Roosevelt, Churchill, and the British Chiefs of Staff that the North African invasion was essential, Eisenhower remained distinctly uncomfortable with the operation. Now that it was being planned his unease only increased. He remained convinced that postponing the European invasion would divert Allied efforts. Moreover, Eisenhower was not convinced that the Allies could plan and carry out the invasion so quickly. The operation was too complex, and the resources needed to ensure its success were still en route to England. Eisenhower was unusually public about his doubts, expressing them bluntly to his British colleagues. British air chief marshal Sir John Slessor remembered after the war that Eisenhower told him that Torch was "really crazy," though Eisenhower added that "no doubt we should get away with it."[62] Eisenhower was also concerned that with all the attention given to Torch the invasion of Europe (Roundup) had been put on hold. It was as if no one even remembered that the purpose of having U.S. troops in England was to prepare them for the showdown with Germany, which would assuredly not come in Morocco, Algeria, or Tunisia.[63] Eisenhower also expressed his hesitations to his old mentor, Fox Conner, who had warned him against supporting any diversion from fighting the Germans in Europe.

> I quite agree with you as to the immediate task to be performed by the Allies. I have preached that doctrine earnestly for the last six months— to everyone who would listen to me. . . . I believe in direct methods, possibly because I am too simpleminded to be an intriguer or to attempt to be clever. However, I am no longer in the places where these great questions have to be settled. My only job is to carry out my directives as well as I can. I sincerely trust that I will be able to do my duty in accordance with your own high standards.[64]

Eisenhower had his assignment, and soon he put the controversy of Sledgehammer in the past and bent his every effort to making Torch a success. In his third personal letter to Marshall, Eisenhower laid out a list of prospective commanders for Torch's armored and infantry divisions. Eisenhower was apparently comfortable enough with Marshall that he could now openly ask for command of the American forces, with the understanding that Marshall himself would be the overall supreme Allied commander: "I wonder who you will select to command the American part of Torch?" he asked. "It is an appointment in which I'll take keen interest but, needless to say, anyone you can name to important commands in that force will be completely acceptable to me."[65] Eisenhower ticked off the names of those he believed would command major units in the North African invasion, most of them from Marshall's little black book: George Patton, Omar Bradley, Robert Eichelberger, Alexander Patch, and Lloyd Fredendall were the most prominent. Then, as if explaining why he would promote himself as Torch's commander, Eisenhower deftly implied that Marshall himself would be the overall Allied commander, regardless of who commanded U.S. forces: "Whoever is selected as C.G. should come over here as soon as firm decisions and Supreme Commander [presumably Marshall] are announced," he wrote.[66]

A final decision on the command structure for Torch was made on August 6, when Roosevelt informed Churchill that Eisenhower—not Marshall—would be the "Commander in Chief, Allied Expeditionary Force" for the operation.[67] From that date, "the organization of the staff, selection of major commanders, elaboration of operational plans and orders, arrangements for specialized training, and provision of materiel and transportation" would be left in Eisenhower's hands.[68] Or so says the official history. Yet, over the next weeks, the Americans and British wrangled endlessly over the details of the operation, with Eisenhower, at Marshall's direction, arguing strenuously that Allied units be fused "into one integrated force" that included "the ground, sea and air elements of the two national military establishments."[69] The debate was exasperating for both Marshall and Eisenhower, who continually reminded the British that Arcadia had decided the question of a combined command. The British did not disagree with this, but in practice British senior commanders showed slight inclination to place their soldiers under an American officer, particularly one, like Eisenhower, who the chief of the Imperial General Staff regularly criticized as "having only the vaguest conception of war."[70] The usually taciturn Ismay would not go that far, but his own judgment was damning: Eisenhower was not yet an Allied commander, he said, but an American commander.[71] Sensing the truth of Ismay's harsh observation, Eisenhower struggled to sandwich American and British officers evenly among his staff's higher echelons and even sent a senior American commander home after overhearing him calling another officer a "British son-of-a-bitch." Eisenhower reflected that he did not mind so much that the officer used the term "son-of-a-bitch," it was that he insisted on appending "British" to it.[72] Eisenhower later conceded the difficulties the British and Americans faced in forging a cooperative relationship: "In the early days officers of the two nationalities were apt to conduct their business in the attitude of a bulldog meeting a terrier," he said.[73]

As the Americans were guests of the English in their own country, Eisenhower believed it was up to him and his commanders to be accommodating. This view was supported by Marshall. But such conciliation had its limits. As Eisenhower attempted to build a unified command throughout the weeks leading up to the North African invasion, the British struck a diffident attitude, underscored by their fear that full British participation in the initial landings would bring French troops firmly behind Rommel. The British were also weighed down by a nagging disagreement over just who should replace Field Marshal Sir Claude Auchinleck, who had been hectored nearly into retirement by Churchill for losing Tobruk and then for failing (as Churchill claimed) to launch an early offensive against Rommel.[74] Churchill appointed Field Marshal Harold Alexander to command British troops for Torch, but two days after his appointment Churchill changed his mind and sent Bernard Law Montgomery to Cairo. That made the new British commander under Eisenhower General A. N. Anderson, who was largely unknown to the Americans. The constant shifts gave Eisenhower an uneasy feeling. "Are the British really serious about Torch?" Eisenhower wondered.[75] The on-again, off-again views of the British proved a grim irritant to Marshall and Eisenhower, who had canceled Sledgehammer and adopted Torch at their request only to find that the British had lately realized that doing so meant that the invasion of France—Roundup—would be impossible to mount in 1943. Eisenhower, his anger barely in check, wrote to Marshall in late September, using Churchill's nom de guerre, "the Former Naval Person": "It appears that for the first time the Former Naval Person and certain of his close advisors have become acutely conscious of the inescapable time costs of Torch," Eisenhower told Marshall, his "we told them so" attitude seeping through. "The arguments and considerations that you advanced time and again between last January and July 24th apparently made little impression upon the Former Naval Person at that time, since he expresses himself now as very much astonished to find out that Torch practically eliminates any opportunity for a 1943 Roundup."[76]

The differences between the Americans and their British allies were worsened by the inability of the British Chiefs of Staff to make up their minds about the invasion's landing zones.[37] The British initially favored two landing zones — one for each nationality — but then had second thoughts and proposed that the two landing zones be composed solely of American troops.[78] They then shifted their position again, agreeing to three landing zones, two for the Americans and one for the British. Even then the British high command evinced doubts, shifting their opinions nearly daily at the same time they dragged their feet on implementing Eisenhower's command arrangements and debating with him about the relative strengths of each landing task force. These debates became the subject of nearly daily messages between Marshall and Eisenhower and were described vividly by Harry Butcher as a "Transatlantic Essay Contest."[79] For Marshall, the Eisenhower-British debates must have seemed eerily reminiscent of the exchanges Marshall had refereed between MacArthur and King in the Pacific, though these exchanges were much more complex: while the Pacific debate was waged between two military branches and their headstrong commanders, the Atlantic debate was fought between two national military structures and, within each nation, between and among three different military services — the Army, Navy, and Air Corps — and included the British prime minister and the U.S. president.

To make matters worse, Eisenhower was spending hours each day overseeing the housing of the tens of thousands of American soldiers then pouring into England and reviewing military police reports of soldierly behavior. As if to mirror the Eisenhower-British disagreements over Torch, a series of tit-for-tat ditties began to circulate in London's crowded bars, where British veterans of Dunkirk faced off against Americans on leave from their training bases. The Americans, the British famously said, were "overfed, overpaid, oversexed, and over here." The Americans returned the favor: the British were "underpaid, undersexed, and under Eisenhower."

A consensus on Torch operations was finally agreed to in early September.

There were to be three separate task force commands riding ashore against Axis targets at Casablanca, Oran, and Algiers. George Patton was placed in command of the Western Task Force, which would come ashore at Casablanca;[80] Lloyd Fredendall was placed in command of the Center Task Force, which would capture Oran;[81] and the British general A. N. Anderson was placed in command of the Eastern Task Force, which would capture Algiers.[82] If all went as planned, seventy-three thousand American and British troops would be ashore in North Africa sometime during the first week of November. Eisenhower was pleased with the planning, though he still believed the operation "of a quite desperate nature" depended on luck as much as on training, and on superb combat leadership.[83] In this, at least, Ike was overjoyed by the appearance of George Patton, who made his way to London and immediately telephoned Eisenhower: "Ike, Goddammit," he announced, "I've just arrived in this blasted town. I'm holed up in Claridge's and don't know what to do with myself."[84] Eisenhower invited him to Norfolk House, where Patton attended the daily planning briefings and rubbed shoulders with his old West Point buddies. He was not impressed. "We both feel the operation is bad and mostly political," he wrote. "However, we are told to do it and intend to succeed or die in the attempt. . . . With a little luck, it can be done at a high price."[85]

IN HIS office in Washington, George Marshall read and reread Eisenhower's cables and letters and determined that his theater commander was starting to feel the pressure. He took time to visit Mamie, then wrote to Ike about giving her a copy of a military periodical that featured her husband's picture on the cover. Eisenhower was relieved, writing Marshall of his appreciation.[86] Marshall also reassured Eisenhower of his support, writing again and again that he approved of all that he was doing and disagreeing only once, when Eisenhower recommended the promotion of an Army Air Corps senior officer. Even then, Marshall's criticism was tempered with an expression of confidence. "You have my full confidence and I heartily approve of everything you have done," he wrote on September 26.[87] He repeated the reassurance two days later: "When you disagree with my point of view, say so, without an apologetic approach; when you want something that you aren't getting, tell me and I will try to get

it for you. I have complete confidence in your management."[88] The last thing
that a beleaguered Eisenhower needed now, Marshall clearly believed, was a
tyrannous commander in Washington criticizing his every move.

By early October, Eisenhower was consuming three packs of cigarettes a day,
and at times he seemed bent and weary. His shoulder ached. "He was not the
cheerful man I remembered," Colonel Gruenther observed, "and he had aged
ten years."[89] Butcher was anxious to take Eisenhower out of the limelight and
away from the bustle and media attention of central London, so he rented
"Telegraph Cottage"—a personal retreat for Eisenhower and his staff—in
Kingston, forty miles outside of the city. Surrounded by woods, with five bedrooms and a central bath, Telegraph Cottage became a second command headquarters for Eisenhower and a place where he could relax. "Our cottage is a
godsend," Ike wrote to Mamie. "Butch says I'm human again."[90] Eisenhower
insisted that his retinue remain small and trusted. In addition to Harry Butcher,
Eisenhower grew close to his driver, Kay Summersby; his valet, John Alton
Moaney; and John "Johnny" Hunt, his cook. A direct telephone line connected
Eisenhower to the American headquarters at 20 Grosvenor Square.

As the pace of planning for Torch accelerated through late September and
into October, Eisenhower's routine quickened; each Tuesday he and Mark
Clark lunched with the prime minister at 10 Downing Street, and most week-
ends found him alone with Churchill at Chequers. During one lunch, with the
date for Torch still undecided, Churchill asked Eisenhower when he thought
it would take place. "November 8," Eisenhower predicted flatly. "These meetings seemed to be a success," Churchill later wrote of his discussions with
Eisenhower and Clark. "I was nearly always alone with them, and we talked all
our affairs over, back and forth, as if we were all of one country. I set great value
on these personal contacts. . . . We also had a number of informal conferences
in our downstairs dining-room, beginning at about ten o'clock at night and
sometimes running late. Several times the American generals came for a night
or a weekend to Chequers. Nothing but shop was ever talked on any of these oc-
casions."[91] With Eisenhower and Churchill drawing ever more close, the division of labor between Marshall and Eisenhower was becoming clearer:
Roosevelt was Marshall's responsibility, while the "Former Naval Person" was
Eisenhower's. Marshall's bet had paid off: Eisenhower's natural bonhomie won
over the British PM to such a degree that criticism of him by Brooke and his

staff made little difference. Churchill's trust also had a decided impact on Eisenhower's ability to gain British agreement for Allied training regimens and for the final shaping of Torch's minute details. The transformation in British attitudes toward Eisenhower was so noticeable that he mentioned it in a late-October letter to the chief of staff.

> I must say that the British have been constantly ready to meet me more than half-way and have been most considerate in their treatment of my opinions, suggestions and recommendations. . . . From the day I came over here, I have dinned into the British the fact that you considered unity of command to exist only when the Commander of the Allied Force had the same authority—so far as it was legal to confer it upon him—with respect to all troops involved, as he had to those of his own nationality. I am now benefiting from this crusade because, in many instances, the British are ready to go much further than some American officers in accepting and abiding by the principle.[92]

Marshall's relief at hearing this must have been palpable, even if, in the same letter, he took note of his subordinate's worries over the American training regimen. Eisenhower told Marshall that he had just returned from Scotland, where he had witnessed an amphibious exercise involving one of the American assault divisions. "The exercises that I witnessed had, as usual, both encouraging and discouraging aspects," Eisenhower wrote. "The men looked fine and, without exception, were earnestly trying to do the right thing. I spoke to scores of them, in the pitch dark, and found that their greatest weakness was uncertainty! Most of them did not know exactly what was expected of them. . . . We are short in experience and trained leadership below battalion commander, and it is beyond the capacity of any Division Commander or any Colonel to cure these difficulties hurriedly. Time is essential."[93]

Marshall never responded directly to this letter, undoubtedly concluding that with the North African invasion just two weeks away, there was little either he or Eisenhower could do to remedy the shortcomings apparent among American troops. The "experience" and "trained leadership" would come in time and under fire. Like all armies, the American Army would learn by doing, by being blooded by the Germans. Marshall knew that all the training in the world would never fully prepare a soldier for what he would face on the battlefield and that, in war, the unpredictable and the unlikely were the most predictable and most likely things to happen. Marshall knew this so well that he never had to state it, while Eisenhower took the unusual step of putting his fears in writing, confiding them in uniquely reflective language to his mentor and teacher in Washington.

I do not need to tell you that the past weeks have been a period of strain and anxiety. I think we've taken this in our stride and, so far as I can see, all of my principal subordinates are up on the bit and ready to go! The real strain comes from trying to decide things for which there is no decision—such as, for example, what is to be done if the weather throughout that whole region simply becomes impossible along about the time we need calm seas. If a man permitted himself to do so, he could get absolutely frantic about questions of weather, politics, personalities in France and Morocco, and so on. To a certain extent a man must merely believe in his good luck and figure that a certain amount of good fortune will bless us when the critical day arrives.

At the end of October 1942, the three task forces set sail for North Africa. In all, some 300 warships and 370 transports ferried 107,000 American soldiers to North Africa's battlefields. Patton's forces came the farthest distance, sailing from Norfolk and Hampton Roads, Virginia, before being deposited in Morocco. Few of the great speeches of the commanders of this vast invasion force have been saved for posterity except those of George Patton, who had an aide nearby at every moment, scribbling his every word. In a warehouse in Norfolk, Patton faced his officers and senior Navy commanders, giving them a blistering warhawk speech that ranks as one of his best. "I'm under no illusion that the goddamn Navy will get us within a hundred miles of the beach or within a week of the date set for landing," he said. "It doesn't matter. Put us in Africa. We'll walk."

There were no grand martial speeches for the Army chief of staff. Marshall was not an anxious man, nor would he have revealed it if he was. For him, the key to success in North Africa was secrecy, so he breathed not a word of the invasion to anyone. Even in the two weeks leading up to the landings, Marshall barely mentioned the landings to Eisenhower, perhaps in the belief that anything that could be done was being done. Even so, the chief of staff was not only keen for the Americans to get into the fight but busy setting the groundwork for the cross-Channel invasion that would now most likely come in 1944. He warned Roosevelt in an unusually blunt memo to keep the Army at peak performance, pointing out that the figures the president had submitted to the Bureau of the Budget would mean the disbanding of fourteen divisions, divisions that Eisenhower might need if the divisions coming ashore at Casablanca, Oran, and Algiers were slaughtered.[94] But Marshall never thought once of defeat and continued his routine of rising early and driving himself to the Old Munitions Building, and from time to time he stopped to savor some good news. By the end of October it was clear to Marshall, and the world, that the Red Army was turning Stalingrad into a German killing ground, bringing to an end the successive waves of triumphs that had brought Hitler's legions to the edge of victory. And on November 4, Bernard Law Montgomery's Eighth Army had begun an all-out assault against Rommel's Afrika Korps along the El Alamein line. On November 6, Marshall penned a short cable to Eisenhower for delivery to Churchill: "Please send the following personal message from me to a certain naval party: 'Having been privileged to witness your courage and resolution on the day of the fall of Tobruk I am unable to express to the full my delight over the news from the Middle East and my admiration for the British Army."[95]

Still, in war—as Marshall knew—things that could go wrong could be counted upon to do so. The wild card in Africa was the French, who could not be trusted to join the Allied effort after the landings. In an attempt to salve French feelings embittered by civilian deaths resulting from British bombing raids, the Americans insisted that only U.S. troops participate in the initial landings. This was a convenient fib, as British troops formed the bulk of the assault force at Algiers. Even that might not be enough. The French garrison in North Africa was well armed, and its commander, Admiral Jean-Louis Darlan, was a volatile egoist susceptible to German flattery. "I serve Vichy," he told all comers, unblinkingly believing that such words marked his honor.[96] Nor were the French the only problem. Eisenhower's plan called for American forces to seize Tunisia before the Germans could be reinforced from Italy. That sounded only slightly plausible: if German aircraft were shifted suddenly to Sicily in anticipation of an American invasion or even crossed through Italy to occupy Gibraltar, Allied units could be caught on the beaches and cut to pieces. Nor was this the least of it. German U-boats were creating havoc in the North Atlantic, sending thousands of tons of munitions to the bottom. If they shifted south they would find Patton and his fine green troops fresh out of Virginia somewhere in the mid-Atlantic.

On November 2, George Marshall cabled Eisenhower that he and his men sailed to North Africa "with the hopes and prayers of America. For months you have planned, trained, and conditioned yourselves for the great task ahead. God speed to your success." In a more personal note at the end of the cable, Marshall once again expressed his "complete confidence" in Eisenhower's leadership.[97] Eisenhower circulated Marshall's memo to his staff, then, on November 5, at the invitation of Winston Churchill, he and his senior commanders flew to Gibraltar to establish the Allied headquarters. The landings on North Africa were scheduled for 1 a.m. on November 8, just three days later. Eisenhower arrived in Gibraltar convinced that the hundreds of cargo ships, warships, and troop transports now just a few dozen nautical miles from his own position would be discovered and attacked, but all was quiet. Eisenhower's command post was deep inside Gibraltar's rock, an eight-by-eight cell at the end of a chiseled tunnel blasted out by two companies of Canadian engineers.[98] On the night of November 7, Eisenhower sat down to write to Marshall about the coming invasion. His thoughts quickly turned to the subject of British-American cooperation. With Patton, Fredendall, and Anderson poised to leap at Tunisia, halfway across the continent from Montgomery, it must have seemed as if all of the work of the previous weeks was finally coming into focus.

We are standing, of course, on the brink and must take the jump— whether the bottom contains a nice feather bed or a pile of brickbats! Nevertheless, we have worked our best to assure a successful landing, no matter what we encounter. As I look back over the high pressure weeks since July 24th, I cannot think of any major item on which I would now, if I had the power, change the decision we made at the time. . . . If, of course, some unexpected development should make this operation appear as a failure, much of the work that has been done will be discredited by unthinking people, and the methods that have been followed will be cited as erroneous. I do not believe that a final success or failure, which is going to be determined by a number of factors beyond anyone's control, should blind us to the fact that before this war is won the type of thing that we have been doing for the past many weeks will have to become common practice between the British and American services.[99]

Eisenhower finished his letter—adding "I am weary" as a postscript—and went to bed. Less than twelve hours later, the first American troops went ashore in Africa.

| 6 |

TORCH

"I have no intention of ever giving you an alibi for failure. . . ."
"I have grasped your idea. . . ."

O N THE NIGHT OF November 8, 1942, Katherine Marshall watched the Washington Redskins play football at Griffith Stadium. She was sitting alone and unnoticed in the stands. And she was irritated. Her husband had excused himself from her company yet again, as he had often during the previous month, and she was worried about him. Just the week before, they had had a rare tiff on the hours he kept, when he announced during dinner that he would have to return to the War Department. That was now becoming a habit. She had resisted: "You are tired," she said, "and must get some relaxation." But he remained adamant: "This matter is very important," he said. She had lost her temper: "Oh! Every little thing is important to you," she snapped and with that she left the room, slamming the door behind her.[1] Now, as the Redskins offense drove down the field, the public address announcer interrupted the game. "The President of the United States of America announces the successful landing on the African coast of an American Expeditionary Force. This is our Second Front." The crowd roared, and the Redskins played on.[2] Smiling to herself, Katherine Marshall watched the rest of the game, then returned to Fort Myer and her husband. "Was this the important thing you were talking about?" she asked him. He nodded.[3]

That same night, Mamie Eisenhower was in her apartment at the Wardman Park Hotel. As far as she knew her husband was in London planning for the invasion of Europe. She had had a busy week, with many callers. Mamie did not like the public limelight and went to great lengths to stay away from reporters. She was helped in this by Ruth Butcher, Harry Butcher's wife, who lived across the hall. The two were good friends and spent many hours together.[4] Mamie was not in good health: she spent many sleepless nights, worrying, and was plagued by an undiagnosed malady that affected her balance. The resulting rumors of her alcoholism embittered her toward the press, and she felt increasingly lonely. "I find myself worrying about you a lot," she wrote her husband at one point. "Hope I'm not getting old maidish, but every once in a while I can begin to imagine a lot of things happening to you and then I get the cold chills."[5] Ike sensed Mamie's isolation and attempted to relieve her worries. As American soldiers were going ashore in North Africa, Eisenhower took time to write her from his rock-encased room at Gibraltar, reassuring her that the war would someday come to an end and they would be together: "We have got to steel ourselves to these things in war and just get down to earth and work as hard as we can so as to get the damn thing over quickly."[6]

If seemingly unsympathetic to his own wife's concerns, George Marshall was clearly aware of Mamie's worries. He called Mamie occasionally to check up on her, wrote to Eisenhower and reassured him of her good health, and visited her every time he returned from seeing Ike overseas. Both Mamie and Ike appreciated these visits. Marshall's concerns over Mamie also reflected a growing paternalism toward Eisenhower—Butcher commented that their partnership was much like that between a father and son.[7] As the North African campaign continued over the coming months, Marshall became more solicitous of Eisenhower's needs, requesting that his closest aides keep him informed of Eisenhower's sleep habits and general health. "You must look after him," Marshall told Butcher. "He is too valuable an officer to overwork himself."[8] At times, Marshall seemed almost obsessive about Eisenhower's ability to deal with crisis. "You must keep him refreshed," he told Butcher, "but knowing him as we do it will take ingenuity. It is your job in the war to make him take care of his health and keep that alert brain from overworking, particularly on things his staff can do for him."[9]

As KATHERINE MARSHALL watched a football game in faraway Washington, Eisenhower sat silently in his command headquarters in Gibralter. For him, November 8 was cloaked in silence, mystery, and isolation. With American and British transports unloading landing barges filled with soldiers into the surf and onto the beaches of North Africa, all that the Allied commander could do was wait and read the innumerable cables that updated him on the pace of operations. "Landing successful, A, B, and C Beaches, Eastern Task Force," the earliest read.[10] "Ike and Clark got in their cots to get some sleep," Harry Butcher noted in his diary. "I had an hour around 3:30, under the table."[11] Eisenhower, fitful, couldn't sleep and so appeared again at Butcher's side, eyeing the cables. Where's Patton's report? he asked. At 5:45 in the morning, Fredendall radioed from his position off Oran: "Landing continues unopposed." Eisenhower took time then to write a report to the Combined Chiefs of Staff, bringing them the latest information on his efforts to neutralize North Africa's French garrison, and steeling them to expect a spike in Allied casualties: "Latest news that we have been able to get from North Africa indicated that we may expect considerable resistance," he wrote.[12] Eisenhower then sat down to write a more detailed report to Marshall, passing the message to "Beetle" Smith in London for transmission to Washington. Eisenhower knew that the Army chief of staff was anxious for some news, no matter how uncertain.

To this hour, 9:30 a.m. Sunday, everything appears to be going ahead about as anticipated. Naval units and navy manned batteries are resisting and from secondary information it appears that Patton [landing in Morocco] may be having some trouble on air fields. Information directly from task forces is meager but I do not care to worry commanders at this stage by demanding reports. But I'd give a month's pay for an accurate report this minute from each sector. We do know that we are fairly solidly ashore at eastern and central points and that western attack began as scheduled.[13]

In Washington, Marshall read Eisenhower's cable and included it in his report on the landings to Franklin Roosevelt. As always, Marshall did not respond

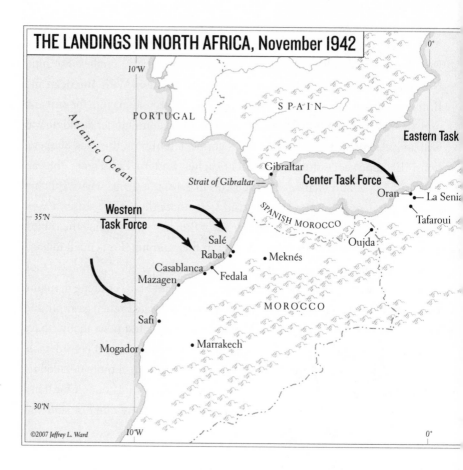

directly to Ike's cable, believing that the commander on the ground had a better feel for the situation and would know how to handle any problems. But
Marshall understood Torch's importance and decided that he would make a
public speech on Allied cooperation, a foray into explaining to the American
people the crucial importance of coalition warfare. It was vitally important that
the British and Americans were killing Germans in North Africa, he determined, but the successful landings could also be used to teach Americans
about the importance of fighting as a part of a coalition, about not going it
alone. Looking at his calendar, Marshall decided that he would accept an in-

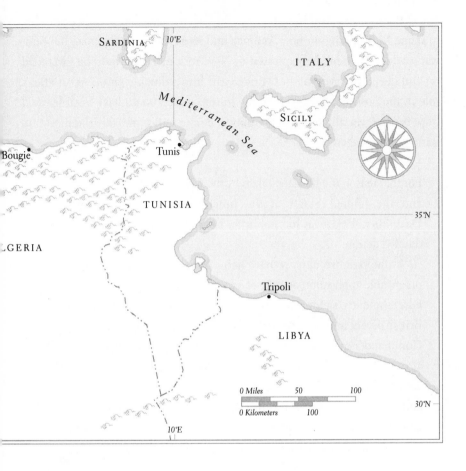

vitation to speak at the Academy of Political Science, an association of political science thinkers, teachers, and theorists that was holding a convention in
New York on November 10. The meeting would provide a public forum for
Marshall to air his ideas, and considering the headlines from North Africa, he
believed the American public would be vitally interested in what he had
to say.

Marshall spoke to the Academy of Political Science at the Astor Hotel on
the evening of November 10.[14] His remarks were memorable not simply because he focused on the importance of building a broad coalition to fight the

Axis powers, but because now the Army chief of staff was thinking ahead to the end of the war. It is clear from his remarks that Marshall was already beginning to shape his thinking on how America and its allies would organize the post-war world. The views he expressed in New York in 1942 would be expanded on and deepened over the next three years into a durable vision of America's role in the postwar world: "Of all the lessons which could have been learned from the last war, the question of unity of command is probably the most out-standing," he began.

> For that reason the first step taken by the Chiefs of Staff of Great Britain and the United States at the initial meeting in Washington in December, 1941, was to establish a basis of procedure to secure coor-dinated action. . . .
>
> In the past two days we have had a most impressive example of the practicable application of unity of command, an American Expeditionary Force, soldiers, sailors, and aviators, supported by the British Fleet, by British flyers and by a British Army, all controlled by an American Commander-in-Chief, General Eisenhower, with a Deputy Commander also an American Army officer, General Clark. They are served by a combined staff of British and American officers, of soldiers and sailors and aviators. Officers of the British Army and Navy senior to General Eisenhower, men of great distinction and long experience, have, with complete loyalty, subordinated themselves to his leadership.

Warming to his topic, Marshall projected his summary of Allied cooperation into the future, telling his audience that the "unity of command" that he and Eisenhower had insisted on in wartime would be used to create a structure that would assure peace in the postwar era.

> We are in a terrible war and our every interest should be devoted to win-ning the war in the shortest possible time. However, in view of your in-terest in the science of government and the intimate relationship that it bears to military requirements, I would ask your very careful considera-tion of these related military factors in whatever studies you make re-garding the readjustments which must follow this war. . . . How can we

so establish ourselves that we will not be doomed to a repetition of the succession of tragedies of the past thirty years? We must take the nations of the world as they are, the human passions and prejudices of peoples as they exist, and find some way to secure for us a free America and a peaceful world.

Marshall's brief November 1942 remarks seemed almost insignificant next to the events then taking place in North Africa. But Marshall's address is key to understanding the evolution of his political and military thinking. For as Eisenhower, Clark, Patton, Fredendall, and Anderson were commanding the "soldiers, sailors, and aviators" of Torch, Marshall was planning the peace he believed they would win—and outlining a postwar world in which their coalition would become institutionalized in the North Atlantic Treaty Organization—the foundation of the permanent Atlantic Alliance. In faraway North Africa that alliance was already being tested.

DESPITE HIS earlier reassurance to Eisenhower, Fredendall's task force had run into trouble at Oran, a key rallying point for the French.[15] A small mixed Allied force under British command was to storm the port, neutralize the French Vichy Navy, and seize the city. The operation was planned by the British. The Americans thought it suicidal, but in the name of Allied cooperation, Eisenhower had accepted British reassurances that it would work.[16] It was a debacle. In less than four hours, even before the sun rose, the American and British commando unit had been decimated and twenty-seven French vessels had been sent to the bottom of Oran harbor to keep them out of Allied hands. In the words of one after-action report, the French resistance at Oran had been "ruthless" and had "completely frustrated the daring adventure."[17] Of the seventeen officers and 376 enlisted men involved in the raid, only three officers and 44 enlisted men emerged unscathed.[18] In Gibraltar, Eisenhower focused on Oran, hoping that through sheer willpower he could move Fredendall's task force ashore. To Marshall, he was blunt: "My biggest operational difficulty at the moment is the slowness in straightening out the Oran region," Eisenhower wrote the Army chief of staff. "I must get it [done] soon."[19]

After the initial commando debacle, the weight of Allied numbers began to take hold, and Fredendall's task force moved ashore. Oran was finally seized on November 10, and Algiers was occupied soon after. Despite the good news, Marshall read Eisenhower's reports and worried: the Oran operation had been unnecessarily costly, and there were difficulties farther west, where the rough surf typical of the Morocco beaches might swamp Patton's landing craft, sending thousands of soldiers to their death. The British had opposed the landings, but Eisenhower ordered them forward. Marshall breathed a sigh of relief when he learned that Patton's troops had come ashore in some of the calmest seas that Moroccan natives could remember. Patton just smiled, writing to Marshall one week after the landings: "In spite of my unfortunate proficiency in profanity," Patton wrote, "I have at bottom a strongly religious nature. It is my considered opinion that the success of the operation was largely dependent on what people generally call 'luck,' but what I believe to be Divine help."[20] But none of the American and British commanders of Torch felt particularly lucky or blessed; the French stood and fought at Oran and Algiers, and in small skirmishing actions around Casablanca. And while the Allies had overcome the initial resistance of these Vichy forces, their landings were chaotic, delayed, and often mishandled. Marshall and Eisenhower were not surprised: this was the first test of Allied cooperation, and there were bound to be missteps. As Patton noted, if his troops had been fighting the Germans instead of the Vichy garrison, they would never have made it to shore.

Despite the difficulties of the landings, the most daunting problem facing Marshall and Eisenhower immediately after of the landings was political, not military. The key was to gain the agreement of the French to fight on the side of the Allies or, barring that, to lay down their arms. Shortly after Allied troops came ashore, Consul General Robert Murphy, the career diplomat charged with negotiating with the French, met with French general Alphonse Juin, the commander of French forces in North Africa, in the Hotel St. George in Algiers.[21] Murphy was confident that Juin would agree to a cease-fire, especially with nearly thirty thousand Allied troops closing in on Algiers. The negotiations would be short and simple, Murphy believed. But Juin hesitated, telling Murphy that there could no cease-fire until he had received word from his superior, Marshal Henri-Philippe Pétain in France. Frustrated by Juin, Murphy appealed to Admiral Jean-Louis Darlan, the commander of the French

fleet. Darlan was a typically proud French colonial officer and military bu-
reaucrat who held civilian officials in disdain because he mistrusted "the rab-
ble." On the afternoon of November 9, once again at the St. George, Mark
Clark and Murphy began negotiations with Darlan.[22] The negotiations dragged
on for days. At one point, Darlan—an open collaborator with Germany who believed the Third Reich was destined to win the war—even suggested that he
take command of all Allied troops, since he was the senior officer in North
Africa. Clark was dumbfounded. "What you are doing now means the killing
of more French and Americans," he screamed. "This is the time when we must
lean on our inclinations and not on our orders. Here is an opportunity for all
Frenchmen to rally and win the war. Here is your last chance."[23] Darlan, arms
crossed, nose in the air, merely shrugged. Rank was more than a reward for
competence, he felt; it was a sign of inherent worth. Raw Americans, un-
schooled in the traditions of the Old World, needed to learn that. Later, during a break in the negotiations, Darlan approached Murphy. "Would you mind
suggesting to Major General Clark that I am a five star admiral?" he said. "He
should stop talking to me like a lieutenant junior grade." With Clark's anger
rising by the minute, Eisenhower set out for Algiers, reassuring Marshall that
he would take a personal hand in the negotiations: "I am leaving at once for
Algiers in the effort to crystallize the confused political situation," he wrote from
Gibraltar. "The quarrels among the principal French personalities are exasperating and Clark needs help."[24]

Finally, on November 12, Murphy, Clark, and Darlan agreed that the
French would lay down their arms. In exchange, Darlan would serve as high
commissioner in North Africa.[25] The agreement also put aside any Allied intention to prosecute Darlan or any of his senior officers for collaborating with
the Nazis and left the French administration of the region intact. The agreement was bound to be controversial, but it took French forces in North Africa
out of the war and allowed Eisenhower's Allied armies to move east against the
Germans. "If we had come in here merely to whip this French Army,"
Eisenhower had written to Marshall, "I would be registering nothing but complete satisfaction at this moment. I am irritated though to think that every bullet we have to expend against the French is that much less in the pot with
which to operate against the Axis. Worse than that, every minute that we lose
will mean a week of reorganization and straightening out later, and I am so im-

patient to get eastward and seize the ground in the Tunisian area."[26] Eisenhower then penned a longer explanation to the Combined Chiefs of Staff, arguing strenuously that the agreement was needed for military reasons. Dealing with Darlan was hard for the Allies to swallow, but Eisenhower was convinced it had to be done. As the military commander, he was forced to deal with the cold realities of a difficult situation: "I am certain that anyone who is not repeat not on the ground can have no clear appreciation of the complex currents of feeling and of prejudice that influence the situation," he wrote.[27]

Unfortunately for Eisenhower, his willingness to do almost anything to sideline the French caused a firestorm of outrage in Washington. As soon as the Eisenhower-Darlan agreement was made public, American newspapers criticized Eisenhower's actions, and gave sustenance to Roosevelt's Republican critics.[28] Even the otherwise stalwart Henry Morgenthau, Roosevelt's treasury secretary, said that he was so disappointed he had nearly given up on the war.[29] In London, Churchill announced that he was "disgusted" by the deal and said that "Darlan ought to be shot." That was a strange statement for the prime minister, particularly as he and Roosevelt had told Eisenhower to negotiate an agreement, any agreement, with the French that would end their resistance. Indeed, as Churchill would later admit, what he said in public and what he said in private were two different things when it came to Darlan. "If I could meet Darlan, much as I hate him," Churchill admitted, "I would cheerfully crawl on my hands and knees for a mile if by doing so I could get him to bring that fleet of his into the circle of Allied forces."[30] Eisenhower was surprised by the outcry but was forced to admit that—having been promoted, at least in part, for his ability to handle people like Darlan—he had failed: "I do not understand anything about diplomacy," he said. As the storm of outrage built in the U.S. ("prostitutes are used, they are seldom loved," the *Nation* intoned), Marshall gathered his forces to defend his chief subordinate, then fired off a message of reassurance: "I am doing my utmost to support you by meetings with the press, with members of Congress, with [the] State Department and with the President. . . . Do not worry about this. Leave the worries to us, and go ahead with your campaign."[31]

A large number of senior commanders believed Eisenhower had misstepped and that his job was in jeopardy, but they were wrong; Marshall was convinced that Ike had done the right thing. The military's job was to fight and win. The critics who were now attacking Eisenhower had looked the other way when Joseph Stalin entered the war. Darlan was a nasty nuisance, not a monster. To counter the criticism of his deputy, Marshall ordered his staff to build friendlier relations with Charles de Gaulle, the leader of the Free French forces, and set out on a campaign in Congress to undermine Eisenhower's chief critics. Marshall then reassured President Roosevelt that Eisenhower's actions made military sense. The object was to win the war against the Germans, Marshall said, and Eisenhower's actions had saved American lives. Marshall bombarded Eisenhower with instructions on how to handle the criticism, garnered from years of handling the press and Congress as Army chief of staff. If people doubted that Eisenhower's actions were sound, Marshall suggested, then they needed to be reminded bluntly of the true cost of war. "I feel it would be tremendously helpful to the press and political pressures regarding Darlan, DeGaulle, Free French, et cetera if you would agree to my releasing the casualties," he wrote at the end of November. "I believe the critics of your action regarding Darlan et cetera have no conception of the serious nature of the fighting and therefore feel free to embarrass the War Department and you by superficial assaults on what we are doing."[32] Marshall and Roosevelt recruited Milton Eisenhower as an ally in his brother's cause and dispatched him to Algiers in the midst of the crisis to provide the Torch commander with some advice on how to handle the press. Milton's appearance fortified Ike, who turned over the most difficult public relations challenges to him so that he could get back to the war. Milton rallied his brother, lashed out at editors who implied that Eisenhower was giving comfort to fascists, and then showed up at the Hotel St. George to lecture Murphy, who had beaten a hasty retreat during the public controversy: "Heads must roll, Murphy!" he said. "Heads must roll."[33]

After meeting with Marshall on the controversy, Roosevelt publicly defended Eisenhower by describing the Darlan agreement as "the present temporary arrangement" and an "expedient, justified solely by the stress of battle."[34] Roosevelt's defense helped dampen the anti-Eisenhower public clamor, and in early December Marshall cabled his commander that from now on all relations with Darlan were to be handled on a military basis. Churchill followed Roosevelt's lead. After his initial eruption, Churchill was persuaded by his foreign secretary, Anthony Eden, that Eisenhower needed the sure hand of a seasoned diplomat to help him navigate the dangerous shoals of French politics.

Churchill agreed and assigned his government's most adept young diplomat, Harold Macmillan, to Algiers as minister of state. Still, the Darlan affair continued to roil American and British reporters well into early December, even as Patton's, Fredendall's, and Anderson's troops fought their way east to Tunisia. Eisenhower's dream was to capture Tunisia by the spring, with a quick seizure of Tunis and Bizerte.[35]

In mid-December, Eisenhower moved his headquarters to Algiers, taking up residence at the Villa Dar el Ouard, a kind of Telegraph Cottage on the outskirts of Algiers, where his brother had been successfully fending off reporters who thought they had taken the measure of Ike and were about to witness his dismissal.[36] Milton knew otherwise. In the first week of December, just as Marshall and Roosevelt were shaping a political strategy to answer Eisenhower's critics, Milton told Ike that the negative publicity he was receiving could be traced to an anti-Vichy radio station in Morocco—the only radio outlet of any consequence in North Africa—whose broadcasts were picked up by European reporters and often repeated verbatim. Milton organized a group of journalists to tell his brother's side of the story, purged the radio announcers in Morocco, lectured American reporters on their patriotism, then left Algiers for home. Before Milton departed, however, Darlan approached him remorsefully, keenly aware that his pro-Nazi past had forever tainted his place in history. "I know what you Americans think of me," he told Milton bitterly. "Your President thinks I'm a lemon to be held until all the juice has been squeezed out. Then the rind will be discarded. That is all right with me. I am cooperating with you not for the benefit of the United States or Great Britain, but for the good of France."[37] Milton listened without any show of emotion. Darlan, he believed, had simply failed to show any moral courage. Apparently, at least one of Darlan's countrymen agreed. On Christmas Eve 1942, Darlan was assassinated by a member of an Algiers French family, Bonnier de la Chapelle, who entered his office and shot him twice.[38]

THE CLUMSY handling of the Darlan affair and the problems with the Torch landings ("a hit and miss affair that would have spelled disaster against a well-armed enemy intent on resistance," as the 3rd Division's voluble commander Lucien Truscott described it)[39] couldn't eclipse the larger good news: the Allies were on the ground in North Africa and moving east. Ignoring Rommel's pleas that the Germans leave Tunisia and Libya to the Americans and their British allies and save their troops to fight another day, Hitler began reinforcing the Afrika Korps within days of the landings, shipping troops into Bizerte from Sicily and Italy and ordering reinforced air wings of German dive-bombers to North African airfields. In Italy, German commander Albert Kesselring (whose thin visage, flashing eyes, and constant grimace earned him the sobriquet "Smiling Al") organized Tunisia's defense, ordering the forty-seven thousand German and Italian soldiers to contest the coastal lowlands surrounding Bizerte and Tunis and the mountain ridges to the east. The rugged topography splitting the North African lowlands suited Kesselring, a keen defensive strategist, as did the Allied lines of approach along roads and railroads that hugged the coast.[40] Kesselring, a map fanatic, loved to identify the defiles and canyons that could be used by his soldiers for a good defensive fight. Every life squandered brought his beloved Reich closer to defeat, he said. Eight days after coming ashore, the first Allied formations bumped into the Germans, then recoiled, at Djebel Abiod, a small Tunisian town west of Bizerte.[41] The indecisive three-hour skirmish was convincing evidence that taking Tunisia would be neither easy nor swift. Within twenty-four hours of the skirmish, a new German commander, General der Panzertruppen Walther Nehring, arrived in North Africa to organize Tunisia's defense.[42] Nehring's appointment was temporary. The avatar of Hitler's decision to defeat Eisenhower, rescue Rommel from Montgomery, and salvage North Africa, Colonel-General Hans-Jürgen von Arnim took command on December 17, bringing with him the hard-bitten veterans of the Fifth Panzer Army.[43] Outspoken and tough, Arnim had little use for Erwin Rommel, whose nearly legendary status was, he believed, more the result of sophisticated press work than of exceptional tactical abilities. While he, Arnim, had been fighting through Russia's frozen bogs, Rommel had faced off against the hapless British; while he had been crushing the Red Army, the Württemberg schoolboy had been fighting a hapless delaying action against a second-class army.

The Germans probed the Allied lines and then fell back, awaiting attack. In the north, British lieutenant general Charles Allfrey's V Corps pitched into the Germans, but then took up defensive positions west of Bizerte. Allfrey had felt the fire, sensed the German strength, and took counsel of his fears: he recommended planning for a more general offensive before going forward. The delay in the march on Bizerte allowed Arnim to secure his defensive positions in Tunisia and bring more of his panzers across the Mediterranean from Italy. A large number of Arnim's soldiers were also veterans just arrived from fighting the Russians on the eastern front. Having been through the Red Army's meat grinder, they reversed the British maxim on combat to reflect their own experience: until you had fought Russians, they believed, you had not been in a war. The spindly Dunkirk-seared British would eventually be defeated, they believed, while the Americans were pushovers.

The Germans had reason to be confident. The most formidable force facing them in the west lay in the Allied center, held by British lieutenant general Kenneth Anderson's First Army. Anderson's front line was not developed in depth and was manned by the poorly equipped and demoralized French troops of General Alphonse Juin. In the south, Lloyd Fredendall's II Corps faced off against Erwin Rommel's famed Afrika Korps, who should have little trouble with the green Americans. Arnim took the measure of Anderson and believed he could be defeated, particularly as a large number of Rommel's panzers had recently arrived from Libya, after having built a line of defenses against the British Eighth Army.[44] The Allied line wove from north to south for 250 miles, through trackless deserts and among the defiles and canyons of Tunisia. To the east, in Arnim's rear, the Allies were opposed by a German and Italian line forming a bridgehead on the Mediterranean. Montgomery was there, preparing to pounce—but he was moving slowly, and if Arnim and Rommel could attack Eisenhower successfully and quickly, they could turn on him in strength. As Arnim studied his position his confidence grew.

Eisenhower thought differently. He was confident that despite the flood of German reinforcements, an aggressive Allied campaign could quickly overrun Tunisia. The key lay in the decision of British, American, and, now, French combat commanders. "As I told you before, I'm well satisfied with all my people," Eisenhower confidently told Marshall at the outset of the campaign. "I don't believe that any commander was ever sent to the field with his principal staff and command subordinates representing a higher average of professional ability and a higher sense of loyalty and devotion to duty than it has been my good fortune to have here. Long hours and incessant work roll off their backs like water off a duck."[45] The fulsome praise was temporary. By early December,

Allied units were bogged down by Tunisia's winter rains as much as by the surprising tenacity of the German defenses. Eisenhower urged his commanders
forward, telling them to ignore the mud and strain of combat and grapple with
the enemy. British general Kenneth Anderson's decision to support Allfrey in
establishing a defensive line in western Tunisia before pressing on to Tunis was
Eisenhower's chief irritant. By mid-December, despite his constant directives,
the Allied forces were stalled, with the Germans now firmly entrenched along
an unbroken defensive line that ran the length of Tunisia's jutting geographic
thumb. The failure was public, the source of constant comment in American
and British newspapers. Consequently, Eisenhower's short temper, just weeks
after his confident missive to Marshall, was on full display: "I think the best way
to describe our operations to date," he wrote at the end of December, "is that
they have violated every recognized principle of war, are in conflict with all operational and logistic methods laid down in textbooks, and will be condemned
in their entirety by all Leavenworth and War College classes for the next twenty-
five years."[46]

Watching all of this from afar, Marshall decided that Eisenhower had too
many worries: "I think you should delegate your international diplomatic problems to your subordinates and give your complete attention to the battle in
Tunisia and the protection of the Straits of Gibraltar," Marshall wrote on
December 22. ". . . You are doing a magnificent job and I want you to feel free
to give your exclusive attention to the battle particularly as German intentions
against your right flank seem evident."[47] They were evident as well to
Eisenhower, who traveled to the front to find out why Anderson and his commanders had stopped short of their goal. The problem, he quickly saw, had
nothing to do with the Germans: the Allies were bogged down by mud and rain
and the incessant breakdowns caused by the winter weather. His good friend
George Patton agreed, describing Tunisia as "the coldest damn place I have
ever seen."[48] Meeting with Anderson during the last week of the year,
Eisenhower agreed to call off a Christmas offensive aimed at capturing Tunis
because of the "absolute impossibility" of moving vehicles through the mud,
concluding that if the rains continued "the attack would have to be methodical shelling of enemy positions with artillery."[49]

The winter weather that had slowed the Allies brought with it a raft of
illnesses—including a flu bug that struck Eisenhower on New Year's Eve.

Ironically, Eisenhower took to his bed after deciding that he could not conduct the war from the rear and that, from now on, he would oversee the Allied offensive closer to the front.[50] Eisenhower flew to Algiers and took a suite of offices at the Hotel St. George, a gaudy and sprawling colonial monstrosity, one of the largest buildings in the city. It became the Allied Forces Headquarters— the AFHQ—and was soon buzzing with Torch's air, ground and naval staff and their secretaries.[51] Eisenhower hoped his arrival in Algiers would spark the Allied race to trap Arnim, but when he arrived he found the British and American staffs in full-blown competition over command and staff prerogatives, sniping at one another over minor matters that, Ike believed, could only impede the Allied effort. He spent his first days imposing order and discipline, shifting assignments, and dampening the anti-British ardor of senior American commanders. He was blunt, irritable, and impatient. His staff steered clear of these tantrums even as they strained to carry out his orders. "I sensed every individual was suspicious of everyone else—every man was sure all others were crooks and liars," Eisenhower wrote in a letter to Ismay. "I immediately started a personal campaign to establish for myself a reputation for the most straightforward, brutal talk that could be imagined."[52]

Eisenhower decided to move his command to Algiers not only because of his concern over Allied lack of movement, but because he had learned that Roosevelt, Churchill, and senior American and British officials and commanders, including Marshall, would be coming to Casablanca for a mid-January conference on the war.[53] The conference, cooked up by Roosevelt and Churchill, would be the first of its kind since Arcadia and would give Roosevelt a chance to tour the North African landing sites and visit American troops.[54] Marshall, Roosevelt, and the others in the American delegation would then be coming to Algiers to visit Eisenhower, who wanted to be prepared with a full report—including the reasons for Anderson's stalemate with German forces protecting Tunis. This would be the first time that Eisenhower had seen Marshall since their time together in London, and Eisenhower was anxious to confer with the chief of staff on any changes in America's military strategy. The death of Sledgehammer did not provide good memories for either man, but their mutual failure against the British had solidified their partnership, and now, with both Sledgehammer and Roundup apparently dead, Eisenhower must have wondered what political maneuver Marshall had up his sleeve.

He did not have to wonder for long. At the beginning of the second week of January, Eisenhower dispatched Al Gruenther and Mark Clark to join the American delegation at the Hotel Anfa in Casablanca, and they reported back to the commanding general regularly. The British arrived just after the Marshall delegation. Brooke, Portal, Pound, and Ismay formed a tight and dedicated circle of combat-experienced senior commanders who were convinced that their political battle against the Americans was as crucial in its way as Anderson's against Arnim. Meeting informally around a long table in the hotel's conference room, the American and British chiefs of staff exchanged papers and ideas on global strategy, the first meeting taking place on the morning of January 14.[55] The British immediately went on the offensive, casting aside American arguments for an early invasion of France by pointing to Arnim and Rommel's stout defense of Tunisia. Gruenther reported back to Ike that Marshall and his colleagues were having a rough time of it. Over a period of five days, Marshall and General Alan Brooke reopened nearly every topic having to do with the war that had been broached—and reputedly resolved—at Arcadia.[56] The disagreements were as deep and bitter now as they had been in 1941, and while the British claimed the differences arose out of their experiences in fighting in Europe, the Americans suspected the British were sensitive about the increasing American domination in arms, men, and munitions. The United States had nearly limitless resources. At the end of 1942, the U.S. fielded seventy-three divisions and 167 air combat groups, was fighting Japan in the central and southwestern Pacific by deploying half a dozen new aircraft carriers, and was reinforcing the Nationalist Chinese Army by means of a tenuous air link with South Asia. But such massive resources did not come close to exhausting America's potential: nearly one-quarter of all military matériel destined for the war against the Axis was being shipped from American factories directly to the Soviet Union.[57] The British were a weak partner by comparison: while the United States was still dipping generously into its barrel of manpower, the British had already reached the bottom.

The result of the resource chasm found its way into Marshall and Brooke's arguments over strategy: the U.S. saw no reason why the Allies should continue to postpone a direct assault on France, while the British disagreed—preparations for a full invasion took time and planning and could not be rushed. Meanwhile, the British argued, the Allies should capture North Africa and then turn their

attention to Sicily, Sardinia, or Corsica. Marshall was exasperated but hardly surprised. Having seen Sledgehammer destroyed, he knew that the British had now
set their sights on Bolero, hoping to divert its resources to Africa and the
Mediterranean. But the Army chief was in no mood to concede the point and
decided to change the topic. Intent on playing his "Pacific card," Marshall
asked Ernie King to present his views on the Allied war against Japan. Marshall's
message was hardly subtle: if the British did not want to use the Americans
against the Germans in France, they could be shipped to the Pacific, where they
would be only too happy to take on the Japanese. King understood Marshall's
ploy and laconically reviewed American naval operations in the Pacific. At the
end of his presentation, the chief of naval operations almost casually argued that
the Allies should increase their focus on building up their forces in Southeast
Asia, where there was a good prospect for success in an American-led offensive
in Burma. The British chiefs were aghast, wondering aloud if the American
chiefs were as committed to a Europe First strategy as they claimed. Marshall
smiled: If it's a Europe First strategy you want, he said, then why are you ob-
jecting to an early invasion of France? The meeting at once turned stormy—
the British could not admit that tolerating an American-led offensive against
Burma would undercut their postwar claims to the maintenance of their colonial empire, but they were loath to be part of a frontal assault that would pitch
their last infantry reserves into an all-out battle against the Reich. But Brooke
mastered his temper, finally, and calmly bowed to Marshall's viewpoint. An invasion would come, he agreed, certainly it would come, but only after Hitler's
legions were eroded to such a degree that any invasion would have a greater
chance for success.[58]

After six tense days, the British and Americans finally reached a compromise.
The final strategy document of the Casablanca Conference said that the
Americans and British would destroy the Germans and Italians in North Africa
before invading Sicily. The Europe First strategy would not be abandoned, and
an increasingly large number of Allied resources would be shipped to England,
where the buildup for an invasion of France would keep pace with Allied efforts in the Mediterranean. The Allies would continue the offensive in the
Pacific, but not to the point where any future operations against Germany
might be jeopardized. The compromise did not fully satisfy Marshall, who now
knew that a European invasion could not be launched until early 1944, but his

disappointment was modest. The United States was now in charge of the war effort, with the Army chief of staff the acknowledged "organizer of victory" and the Allies' most important war strategist. Marshall's standing was enhanced by the Casablanca Conference, for while he did not get everything that he wanted, he could leave Casablanca knowing that nothing would go forward without his approval.[59] Brooke had not been defeated, but he was in retreat, having conceded that America's military resources would now dictate the future course of the war.

Eisenhower was not surprised by Casablanca's outcome, nor by the Marshall-Brooke confrontation. He had been in the midst of such battles before, at Arcadia, and was confident that his mentor could more than hold his own. Also, he had seen some of the arguments up close, as he had conferred with his chief for a single day in the midst of the conference and received a report on its projected outcome from Marshall himself. Landing in Casablanca after a perilous flight from Algiers (an engine failed on Eisenhower's B-17 and the Torch commander strapped on a parachute and stood by the door just in case), Eisenhower had been met in Casablanca by his old friend George Patton, whose crusty summary of Marshall's mood set the tone for the ninety-minute meeting and lunch the two had that day. After his private meeting with Marshall (during which he reviewed Allied deployments against Arnim and Rommel), Eisenhower briefed British and American senior commanders on the North African fighting, bluntly laying out the difficulties of roads and weather and admitting to the surprising tenacity of German defenses. He then outlined his proposal for driving the Germans from Tunisia, an operation he had code-named "Satin," which depended on attacking the Germans on their left and driving them into a killing sack near the sea. The grand pivot would cut the Germans in half, he said.[60] The briefing was done without notes, with Eisenhower's characteristic matter-of-fact tones and clipped sentences oddly mesmerizing and reassuring to the British staff. Slouching in his chair, the droll Brooke watched Eisenhower, barely concealing his concern that this farm boy from Kansas could rise so quickly in the American ranks. Marshall, seated across the table, said not a word—Eisenhower would know how to deal with the supercilious Brooke. With Marshall looking on, Brooke sat up in his seat, eyed Eisenhower skeptically, then launched his attack. And just how would you coordinate this operation, this Satin? Brooke asked. Would not your plan be vulnerable to precisely the move from the Germans that you have proposed from the Allies? Brooke's "look-here-young-man" attitude irked Eisenhower, but the Torch commander was relaxed and self-confident as he answered his questions. Rommel would be watched, he said, by the 1st Armored Division—and he pointed to the placement on the map. The room fell silent, finally, a sign that Eisenhower was dismissed. He saluted and left. A "ridiculous plan," Brooke later said, one which only confirmed Eisenhower as incapable of brilliance. He carefully documented his views in his diary: "Eisenhower as a general is hopeless."[61]

Marshall remained unruffled, silently confident in his lieutenant. That night, as Eisenhower met alone with Roosevelt, Marshall met with senior American commanders at an informal dinner. Marshall loved these kinds of meetings—where Americans could discuss the war, their strategy, and their British counterparts. Marshall was reinvigorated by the bonhomie of Eisenhower's commanders. The same could not be said of Roosevelt, who believed Eisenhower "jittery," and who later during his Casablanca visit denied Marshall's request that Eisenhower be promoted to full general. Still, while Eisenhower might be "jittery," the president could not help but be impressed by Eisenhower's command of the facts. When will the Germans be defeated? the president asked him bluntly during their meeting. "May 15," Eisenhower said. Roosevelt was taken aback: why not the fourteenth or thirteenth. Eisenhower repeated his assurance, and considering his uncanny predictive abilities (he had been right when he told Churchill months before its planning was even completed that the North African invasion would take place on November 8), Roosevelt felt reassured.[62] But should he be promoted? Eisenhower had yet to prove himself, Roosevelt told Marshall, and would be promoted only when there was "damn good reason."[63] Marshall let the comment go, understanding that the president was both irritated that the Allies had not yet captured Tunisia and frustrated by the political problems of dealing with the French and the endless public headaches this had caused. The Darlan affair still rankled and soured relations between the new Western European triumvirate of Churchill, Roosevelt, and Charles de Gaulle, the leader of the Free French. Roosevelt's skepticism about Eisenhower was a surprise to Marshall, but it was not to be the last one to come out of the Casablanca Conference—in the midst of a meeting with the press at the end of the conference, Roosevelt had blurted out that the Allies would accept no terms from the Germans, Japanese, or Italians except "unconditional surrender." Marshall and his commanders agreed to

Roosevelt's formulation, though it meant fighting to the bitter end. The announcement steeled the Allies for the sacrifices ahead.[64]

EISENHOWER RETURNED from Casablanca to the bustling Allied Forces Headquarters in Algiers worried about the Allied lines in Tunisia and concerned particularly with his weakened right flank—the one that, as he had told Brooke, would be in the van of an effort to push the Germans into a killing sack around Tunis. He toured the battlefront and realized that with Rommel retreating toward Tunisia from the east, Fredendall's position on the Allied right flank might be endangered by Rommel's unforeseen arrival. Eisenhower huddled with Fredendall, Lucien Truscott, Kenneth Anderson, Carl Spaatz, and French commander Alphonse Juin at Tulergma Airfield in southern Tunisia on January 18 to determine the best course of action.[65] While his subordinates talked, Eisenhower assessed their command abilities. Short, stocky, booming-voiced, and outspoken, Fredendall was trusted by Marshall and Eisenhower. But in spite of his prominent inclusion in Marshall's little black book, his battlefield capabilities were yet to be assessed. That was not true of Lucien Truscott, whose command of American forces tasked with capturing Port Lyautey in advance of Patton's Casablanca landing on November 8 had been brilliant.[66] The tough-minded Truscott was rewarded with a promotion to major general and was named Eisenhower's deputy chief of staff. Anderson, on the other hand, was not nearly so outgoing as Truscott. Tall, handsome, and articulate, the British commander had the reputation of being a fighter, but Eisenhower suspected he had a case of "the slows"—a description Abraham Lincoln had applied to Union general George McClellan. Like McClellan, Anderson was always demanding more—more troops, trucks, tanks, bullets, rifles, food—all of which he surely needed, but he made his colleagues wonder if he would ever think he had enough. That left Eisenhower's air commander, Carl Spaatz (whose own abilities were not much in doubt), and Juin, who was a good enough commander, Eisenhower felt, but whose abilities were hampered by the poor condition of his troops. If Arnim were to attack, he would focus his panzers on Juin. Eisenhower could easily imagine the result—the center of his line along Tunisia's mountainous dorsal disintegrating like charred paper. Just give the French a little push, Eisenhower believed, and they would evaporate.

As the commanders exchanged information, Eisenhower determined that the Allies would maintain an "active defense," as any move forward now might lead to a slaughter, with Rommel falling on their right flank. Reluctantly, and with Brooke's suspicions in Casablanca ringing in his ears, Eisenhower called off Satin.[67] It was now official: Axis and Allied forces arrayed in Tunisia were stalemated and would remain that way for the time being, with both armies mired in the winter mud. In the wake of the Tulergma Conference, the frustrated Eisenhower was in full feather, his hackles up, his questions to his ground commanders curt and official. The stalemate was a problem, but there were others, not the least of them being the relationship between Lloyd Fredendall, Anderson, and Juin. Juin held Anderson in contempt, while Fredendall had little regard for any British officer. The disagreements outstripped anything Eisenhower had experienced in London (or the interservice dustups that exasperated Marshall in the Pacific) and were nearly paralyzing. It didn't help that Eisenhower's old friend Mark Clark was among the most blatant of America's Anglophobes, bruiting it about at AFHQ that he agreed with Napoleon's dictum "It was better to fight Allies than be one of them."[68] Clark's little laugh at such cleverness was grating. Eisenhower was also worried that American soldiers were not prepared for what lay ahead and viewed their contest with the Germans as "a sort of football game." Eisenhower knew that only sustained combat could harden the Americans, and that the real battle for North Africa was yet to come. Eisenhower toured the battlefield, from north to south—with Allfrey's V Corps in the north (facing Arnim), Fredendall in the south (facing Rommel), and a large French corps in the center—where a headlong plunge might, Eisenhower still believed, split the Germans. Farther south, Montgomery's vaunted Eighth Army would eventually lend weight to the assault when it came. In the meantime, Eisenhower did what he could to prepare his forces, to "get the battle properly organized, improve our airfields, and to bring up reinforcements, both in men and supplies."[69]

Eisenhower reviewed these deployments with Marshall and King at his villa on the outskirts of Algiers when the two arrived after the conclusion of the Casablanca Conference. Relaxed, finally, after the race to Tunis and the end of the conference, Eisenhower comfortably listed the problems the Allies faced now that they were stalemated in Tunisia. Marshall and King listened carefully, again impressed by Eisenhower's noteless briefing. But both men could tell that Eisenhower was disappointed in nearly every aspect of the Allied performance so far, disappointed with himself, and embarrassed about his public and out-spoken defense of the now defunct Satin. Brooke had been right and he had been wrong. Marshall and King sensed Eisenhower's disappointment, his feel-ing that he had been ignored at Casablanca, and both men worked to raise his spirits. Eisenhower said he appreciated their support, but he remained glum, musing that mud could not be used as an excuse for inaction. Eisenhower shrugged as if shaking off his malaise, then gave a blunt assessment of his com-manders, gleaned from his perceptions of their abilities at their Tulergma Conference. King reached out to the Torch commander in an unusual show of warmth. "We've seen what happens when commanders sit down and wait for the enemy to attack," he said. "Keep slugging!"[70] Marshall was also solicitous, particularly after touring the Allied rear areas, which he found chaotic, filthy, and lacking in the military snap that he so prized. The problem was not Eisenhower (Marshall commented that "he was almost in tears" over the situ-ation)[71] but the simple fact that he had too much to do. He counseled his most important lieutenant to "relax" and "get some rest" and to start delegating more authority to his subordinates. Marshall was more than offering a suggestion— his sentences amounted to an order. Eisenhower nodded his understanding. After their meeting, Marshall approached Butcher and ordered him to find Eisenhower a masseur. Marshall wasn't joking: "That will give him exercise and, most of all, relaxation." Marshall eyed Eisenhower closely: his subordi-nate's eyes were red-rimmed, his voice was raspy, and he choked back a nag-ging cough with nearly each sentence—he was smoking three packs of cigarettes a day.[72]

The father-son relationship that Butcher had identified as central to the Marshall-Eisenhower partnership seemed on full display in North Africa. George Marshall was proud of his own command prowess, of his uncanny abil-ity to identify the right person for the right job, and he was not about to have Eisenhower fail now. Anything and everything that could be done for him would be done, Marshall had vowed, and if that meant getting the Torch com-mander a masseur that too would be done.

The two men occasionally found things to laugh about together. Eisenhower had had Telek, his black Scottie, brought to Algeria from England, and Marshall thought it great sport that the undisciplined dog regularly urinated on Eisenhower's bed. The two roared with laughter, Eisenhower feigning anger.

Eisenhower's staff secretary, Sergeant Mickey McKeough, was supposed to keep track of the dog but never succeeded in housebreaking him. "Mickey," Eisenhower said, "when he does things like that, he's your dog."[73] But Marshall wasn't shy about dictating Eisenhower's schedule: get up at ten, conduct business of importance only, leave at noon, exercise at lunch, work, get a rubdown, return to the office, work, get dinner, and then relax. "After all," he said, "four or four and a half hours with the staff ought to be enough."[74] It was a lecture a much older man might give to his grown son; it feigned irritation, filling the void that the lack of open emotion left. Butcher noted that while Eisenhower always obeyed Marshall's orders, his directives on relaxing and taking care of his health were bound to be ignored—no matter what Marshall said.

While Marshall was privately solicitous and supportive of Eisenhower, in public he was careful to maintain the proper propriety toward his commander. He might be in Washington, but he was still the Army chief of staff. "General Marshall is about the only one who doesn't call him Ike," Butcher noted. "Calls him 'Eisenhower.' Admiral King calls him 'General.' The President and the PM and almost everyone I've ever heard of call him Ike."[75]

The one piece of good news that buoyed Eisenhower's spirit was Marshall's announcement of Field Marshal Sir Harold Alexander's appointment as Eisenhower's deputy, tasked with taking over as the combat ground commander in Tunisia. Alexander was the quintessential British imperial officer: tidy but rakish, smiling but tough-minded, given to understatement as a form of humor that conveyed bitterness. Like Patton, he was a fastidious dresser, with khaki trousers tucked into polished boots and a tipped-just-so combat cap with a red band.[76] The bone-thin Alexander also stood a full head higher than either Marshall or Eisenhower, towering over the two of them in official photographs—an exclamation point weighed down by medals. His appointment had been made to ease some of the pressure on Eisenhower and was welcomed as such. Marshall thought he would be a good addition to Eisenhower's team. Alan Brooke also agreed but, not surprisingly, had ulterior motives in appointing Alexander. The British commander's appointment as Eisenhower's deputy, Brooke calculated, would kick the Kansas farm boy into a coordinating role, with only nominal overall command of North Africa's forces. Alexander would be the man in charge, a reminder to the world that His Majesty's army still controlled the globe's battlefields. Marshall and Eisenhower talked of Alexander in Algiers, with Marshall emphasizing Alexander's battle experience (including four

wounds and three citations for bravery in World War I) and his ability to gain
the trust of subordinate combat commanders. He was a conciliator.[77] Alexander
would command the recently designated Eighteenth Army Group, which encompassed all the forces in the Mediterranean, while Eisenhower was designated as supreme Allied commander. "This development was extraordinarily
pleasing to me," Eisenhower later wrote, "because it meant, first and foremost,
complete unity of action in the central Mediterranean and it provided needed
machinery for effective tactical and strategical co-ordination."[78] The British
also urged that Eisenhower accept two other British subcommanders to run the
air and naval war in the Mediterranean: Air Chief Marshal Sir Arthur Tedder
and Admiral Andrew B. Cunningham. Brooke was cagey about the recommended appointments: they would allow Eisenhower to focus his efforts on the
overall war effort, he announced. In private, he chortled that now the British
would be running the war.[79]

   During their most recent consultation in Algiers, Marshall and Eisenhower
had turned their attention to the supply problems plaguing Allied forces. There
was only one major road resupplying Fredendall, and the ridges and stony
hillocks that provided a lifeline to Juin were treacherous. In this at least,
Eisenhower believed, Anderson was correct: he needed tanks, and lots of them,
and the Allied forces everywhere were short on supplies.[80] Everything—guns,
bullets, bread, water—had to be brought from damaged ports across hundreds
of miles of uncertain roads. The rest of the Allied forces also needed more of
everything. As Eisenhower ticked off his requirements, Marshall wrote them
down, his pinched handwriting reflecting his increasing concern that his commander was facing too many problems: Allied forces were demoralized; too few
of them were on the battlefront; some senior commanders were idling in the
rear (a bunch of "drugstore cowboys," Marshall called them),[81] America's soldiers had not yet been tested by the realities of combat ("the iron was not in their
souls," Marshall said),[82] and now the British, Marshall suspected, were going
to undercut Eisenhower by running the war in a series of committees, shelving
him while parading Alexander as the man of the hour.[83] Marshall counseled
Eisenhower to maintain his grip on the war, to impose his vision on Alexander,
and to make absolutely certain he maintained a high public profile. Marshall's
hunch that the British plan was to supplant Eisenhower and take credit for any
Allied victory could not have been more prescient.

   When the decision to appoint Alexander as Eisenhower's ground commander was made in Casablanca, Brooke crowed about his coup: "We were pushing Eisenhower up into the stratosphere and rarefied atmosphere of Supreme Commander," he wrote gleefully in his diary.[84] Eisenhower listened carefully to Marshall's warning and promised that he would fight the committee system and the British habit of promoting their views at the expense of the Americans: "I will be on my guard to prevent any important military venture depending for its control and direction upon the 'committee' system of command," he reassured his chief.[85]

EISENHOWER'S SIMPLE reassurance to Marshall was undergirded by Eisenhower's slowly simmering irritation with Brooke's attack on him in Algiers. Marshall was pleased by this anger, knowing that Eisenhower's patriotism would serve him well. It was one thing for Brooke to attack Satin, and quite another to show such bald disregard for America's prerogatives. Furthermore, Marshall believed, Eisenhower's frustrations with Brooke and the British were being fueled by Fleet Street suggestions that with Alexander's appointment, the stalemate in Tunisia would finally be broken. Marshall refused to dampen Eisenhower's anger, knowing that it made his subordinate more focused. Eisenhower could handle the job, he felt, staving off the British, the Germans, and the shortcoming of his own staff. Despite the enormous problems—the chaos in the rear areas, the lack of supplies, the constant sniping at Allied Forces Headquarters, the uncertainty about the fighting quality of American troops, the hesitations of Churchill and Roosevelt, the doubts of Brooke, the barrage of criticism from the British and American press, and, above all, the Allied loss of the race to Tunisia—Marshall believed that Eisenhower was the only American senior commander capable of managing the fractious Allied war effort. In any other war and at any other time Eisenhower might well have been dismissed for his failures in Tunisia, but at the end of their time together in Algiers, Marshall's confidence in Eisenhower remained unshaken. He might well have agreed with Churchill's diplomatic czar in North Africa, Harold Macmillan. Eisenhower, Macmillan said, had "an inherent goodness and firmness of his character. If sometimes impetuous, he was always fair."[86] Marshall felt that Eisenhower did not have the smallness of mind that characterized Clark's endless tiffs with the British or the unpredictable volatility of Patton or the hesitant uncertainties of Fredendall. His ability to balance contending and parochial national viewpoints while deftly subduing interservice rivalries made him invaluable. He was for the Mediterranean and Europe what Marshall was for the Pacific: an astute politician and diplomat around whom all nations and services could rally. Eisenhower did not need to be dismissed or sidelined or given a new assignment. He needed help.

In one of their last conversations, Marshall reiterated his confidence in his old OPD strategist but made it clear that his new job as supreme Allied commander meant that he had to get tougher—with the British and with his own staff. That would be difficult: a large number of senior American commanders were their friends. Marshall had faced that challenge when he became Army chief of staff, vaulting over dozens of other candidates who thought they should have the job. But the needs of the nation outstripped any of their personal feelings. When Eisenhower timorously noted that he was concerned that one of his commanders, an old friend, was not meeting his standards, Marshall turned on him. Eisenhower later remembered this sudden eruption. "He turned to me to say slowly and emphatically, 'Eisenhower, there is one thing that you must understand clearly. Retention under your command of any American officer means to me that you are satisfied with his performance. Any man you deem unsatisfactory you must reassign . . . or send him home!"[87] Marshall bore in on his supreme commander: "This principle will apply to the letter, because I have no intention of ever giving you an alibi for failure on the excuse that I forced an unsatisfactory subordinate [on you]. I hold you responsible."[88] Eisenhower did not respond at the time, but he later wrote to Marshall: "I have grasped your idea."[89]

7

KASSERINE

"I am disturbed you feel under the necessity to give personal time to us. . . ."
"Please do not look upon any communication . . . as a defensive explanation. . . ."

IN THE EARLY MORNING hours of February 14, 1943, armored units of the 10th Panzer Division under the command of German general Heinz Ziegler attacked from the mouth of Faid Pass, overrunning Allied units in their path.[1] The German attack cracked the center of the Allied II Corps position in Tunisia, on the right flank of Eisenhower's line. Later in the morning the attack was supported from the south by units of the 21st Panzer Division. German aircraft strafing American troops reinforced the sense of chaos on the battlefront. The German Stukas made a terrifying and unnerving sound when they screamed out of the sky, scattering Allied formations and sending American troops diving for cover in the hard desert underbrush. By nightfall, the Germans had reached the village crossroads of Sidi bou Zid, the German objective, and were within striking distance of Gafsa, a key crossroads city south of it.[2] With German armored units now poised to spill into the Tunisian plain west of Faid, British general Anderson ordered the abandonment of Gafsa in favor of the defense of Sbeitla and Kasserine, farther west. At least initially, Erwin Rommel believed, the so-far modest German offensive had succeeded, driving a thin but potentially fatal wedge between the Americans on the south and the mixed French-British contingent on the north.[3]

Eisenhower was surprised by the German attack and at first underestimated its impact. But by the morning of February 15, his full attention was on Fredendall and the worsening situation west at the Faid Pass. Just the day before, in touring Fredendall's front, Eisenhower had determined that the German push was no more than an attempt to punch at the Americans and was not an all-out attack.[4] Now, it seemed, the German thrust might turn into a sustained offensive. The fault in not fully protecting the pass, Eisenhower believed, lay with Anderson's decision to move Allied reserves north, leaving Fredendall vulnerable to a quick dash from Rommel's German and Italian tank units.[5] Anderson, however, could hardly be blamed for making the move, having been informed by English code-breakers bent over their desks in Bletchley, England, and in Algiers that German generals Jürgen von Arnim and Erwin Rommel would focus their forces on a push from the north.[6] Arnim and Rommel, the veteran slugger from the Russian front and the wily fox of the desert, surprised everyone, aiming their blow at the inexperienced Americans and their jittery commander, Lloyd Fredendall. It would be clear later, from after-battle combat reports, that Rommel's argument that the green Americans might scatter at the first sign of sustained killing was right: British soldiers scooped up by Rommel's soldiers along his panzer wedge's northern flank disparagingly called the Yanks "our Italians." Rommel's other hunch, that Fredendall was not up to the task of organizing any sustained defense, also turned out to be correct—as could be seen from the indifferent dispositions the American commander had made on the approaches to Tunisia's rocky hills, where American units were placed willy-nilly without any thought to the simplest military manual's directive of establishing interlocking fields of fire.[7] The American units that Fredendall placed fought isolated and ultimately failed battles—when they fought at all.[8]

So the real problem on Fredendall's front, Eisenhower soon determined, was not Anderson's dispositions but Fredendall's skittishness. Fredendall had gained a place in Marshall's little black book by dint of his vivacious cocksure demeanor and training skills, and Eisenhower was effusive about his abilities. Few would argue with Fredendall's understanding of war, and many admired his offhand analyses of complex tactical situations. But that is where Fredendall's expertise ended: in the field his arrogance wore thin and he became shrill and confused at the first sign of combat pressure.[9] Fredendall had arrived at his designated headquarters in Tebessa, in central Tunisia, many

weeks before. From that moment he seemed more intent on establishing a redoubt than in waging war and ordered an engineering regiment to tunnel his
command headquarters into a hill south of the city, which he dubbed
"Speedy Valley."[10] By the morning of February 15, Fredendall had all but taken
leave of his senses: first Arnim in the north and now Rommel in the south had
attacked—and the arrows on his map, flowing west from Faid, seemed aimed
directly at him. In Algiers, Eisenhower watched the growing German offensive
with increasing concern, though without panic, and remembered his inspection of Fredendall's position two days before. The old doubts about Fredendall
had resurfaced during Ike's inspection tour, though he could barely bring himself to think about relieving him. He turned his mind away from that possibility even now, with Arnim's tank blowing holes in Fredendall's preposterous
deployments. The loss of Gafsa was hardly worrisome, as it simply corrected a
nasty kink in the Allied line, but correcting kinks, Eisenhower knew, was not
what battles were about, and he began to grow short-tempered and irritable.
Harry Butcher summarized the attitude in Algiers. "We took a lacing on the central front last night," he wrote in his diary. "One of the combat teams is calling
for replacements of 50 Sherman tanks. Ike was worried at breakfast this morning, but in a phone call from him this afternoon, he was much more cheerful,
for the news from the fighting had turned better."[11]

Such confidence was short-lived, as events were taking a turn for the worse
at Speedy Valley, where the cave-bound Fredendall was attempting to counter
Arnim and Rommel's lunge by ordering Major General Orlando "Pinky" Ward,
commander of the 1st Armored Division (and a reputed artillery genius), to
counterattack the German forces and restore the line at Faid.[12] The order was
ludicrous, Ward believed, because his forces were dispersed and already engaged in heavy fighting. Ward, a self-effacing man with a dry humor who was
also a master of biting commentary, had little regard for the British (when the
British give an order, he said, the Americans "lie down on the ground and wig-
gle")[13] and even less for Fredendall. He received Fredendall's command and
thought momentarily of disobeying. "I don't like it much," he confided to his
diary.[14] Ward believed that sending understrength units toward Faid was suicidal. He was right; the armored battalion he sent to Faid to reconnoiter the
German attack was decimated, disappearing from the face of Tunisia as if suddenly swallowed by a desert storm. What little was left of the unit straggled limp-

ing and bleary-eyed to Sbeitla as Ward looked on, his seething anger apparent to his staff. Ward gazed grimly at the hollow-eyed soldiers spread thinly through the city and concluded, "If the enemy attacks again I will have to withdraw."[15]

By the seventeenth, the situation was dire. Nearly ninety German tanks were pressing on Sbeitla from the east and the town was in danger of falling. Ward, never a man to be stampeded, proceeded to mount a stout defense, bringing even French units south from Eisenhower's center.[16] Fredendall, a different kind of commander from Ward, was taking no chances: eighty miles to the west, he ordered his command post abandoned and a new one constructed at Le Kef, seventeen miles to the rear. Anderson, now beginning to size up the potential disaster the Allies faced, warned Eisenhower: "We are dangerously dispersed," he said. "It is wise to consider in good time whether we should voluntarily withdraw to the main ridge of the Grand Dorsal."[17]

At sunset on February 17, cigar firmly planted between his gritted teeth, Orlando Ward ordered the last American troops out of Sbeitla. The order came just as panzer units surging from the south came nipping at their heels, debouching into the western valley that fronted the pass at Kasserine.[18] Ward was philosophical: no commander liked a retreat, but none had fought better with less than Ward, who had graduated from West Point one year behind Eisenhower. While not in Marshall's book, he was as tough a commander as could be found in the American Army and hated to order his soldiers to the rear. If there was blame to be assessed, Ward was more than willing to take it, though he believed that Fredendall, then scuttering pell mell with his senior staff out of Speedy Valley, should take most of it. Farther east, field binoculars firmly placed to his disbelieving eyes, Erwin Rommel watched Ward's retreat while listening to a staff officer's report on the developing offensive. Initially skeptical that Arnim's attacks could yield a strategic victory, Rommel now saw before him a way to shift the entire war in North Africa—and force Eisenhower back to Algeria.[19] With that out of the way, Rommel could pivot and race back to face the British Eighth Army advancing slowly through Libya to the south and east. He cabled his superior, Field Marshal Albert Kesselring, the German commander in chief in the Mediterranean, recommending the envelopment of Tebessa. Kesselring disagreed, believing that Arnim's force should mount an attack in the north, while the newly renamed Group Rommel would support him from the south.[20]

What Kesselring believed, however, did not matter much to Rommel, who had his own ideas about how to win a war. He deployed his panzers along the valley floor leading to Kasserine and, on the morning of February 19, ordered them forward.[21] Responsibility for defending the pass was given by Fredendall to Colonel Alexander Stark, commander of the 26th Infantry Regiment. Stark arrived at the narrow defiles of Kasserine on the morning of February 19 to find his undermanned battalions facing thirty-five to forty truckloads of Germans, who had spilled out of their vehicles and were now engaging his understrength units. Stark's troops fought gallantly throughout the day but barely held the pass. An after-dark German-like order from British general Anderson—"The army commander directs that there will be no withdrawal from the positions now held by the First Army. No man will leave his post unless it is to counterattack"— didn't help: Stark's men could not have retreated if they had wanted to. They were pinned down and, in some cases, fighting hand to hand.[22]

The next morning, believing that time was working against him and that re-inforcements were on the way to the Americans, Rommel ordered six battal-ions into the pass in a last attempt to dislodge the Americans. The fighting was fierce. By midmorning the American position was disintegrating. By the morn-ing of February 21, Kasserine was in German hands. In the rear, experts from engineer regiments began rigging the supply depot at Tebessa with explosives. Around them, soldiers from Kasserine walked disconsolately to the rear. Historian Rick Atkinson writes of Lloyd Fredendall at this moment, seated in his command post at Le Kef whistling softly to himself, somberly cataloging the mistakes of the previous week. Sidi Bou Zid and Sbeitla were gone, the entire Allied line in central Tunisia was severed, Arnim was momentarily expected to press in from the north, and the vaunted Desert Fox had cut through Stark's units at Kasserine. Even fortified by a nip of bourbon, Atkinson writes, Fredendall looked and acted defeated—as he certainly was. While he vowed to hold on to Tebessa, Fredendall had taken to calling his nemesis "Professor Rommel," while gamely if intermittently telling his staff that all would yet be well. Still, he seemed oddly detached: "If I were back home, I'd go out and paint the garage doors," Atkinson quotes him as telling an aide. "There's a lot of pleas-ure in painting a garage door."

Into this morass stepped the tall but understated Harold Alexander, who ar-rived in Algiers at the outset of the offensive to take control of all ground combat forces as Eisenhower's commander in Tunisia. Alexander was stunned by the chaos that greeted him, though dismissive of the pessimism at Eisenhower's headquarters. Phlegmatic, articulate, and focused, Alexander is one of history's enigmas: a more talented and professional soldier than Bernard Law Montgomery—whom historians alternately denigrate and laud—and much less flamboyant (or profane) than George Patton, Alexander remains the most underappreciated British military leader of the war. Perhaps it was Alexander's dry wit or perhaps it was his startling ability to remain oddly silent when asked his views that led many to believe him "stupid." This judgment was lost on Winston Churchill, who believed that in Alexander, Britain had its greatest and most courageous captain. Alexander drove to the front, took one look around, and came to his own conclusion, which he dutifully inscribed in his battle diary. The Americans, he wrote, "lack the will to fight."

Just days after Rommel's piercing panzer breakthrough in Tunisia, Alexander took control of the front and began to plot an Allied counterattack. He started by reinforcing the shoulders of the Allied defense, pouring men and equipment into the wadis and hills northwest of Kasserine, where British armored units fought Rommel's panzers to a standstill.[23] Then Alexander reinforced American units into defensive positions east of Thala, where he believed Rommel would strike. The Americans held the high ground in strength, along a series of foothills called the Djebel el Hamra. The commander of the 1st Infantry Division, Major General Terry de la Mesa Allen, was in charge, with the 16th Regiment holding the line looking east. A West Point washout, Allen ("Terrible Terry," as he was called) was a fighter who gloried in his combat past, which included a test against a German machine gunner at Saint-Mihiel in World War I. A graduate of the Army War College (he graduated last in the same class as Dwight Eisenhower—who graduated first), the profane and quick-fisted Allen faced disciplinary charges, and imminent dismissal from the service, when Marshall plucked him from oblivion in 1941 and put him in charge of the American 1st Division—"the Big Red One."[24] Marshall admired Allen but worried about his personal habits, warning him more than once about his drinking. All of that, however, was in the past—Allen was now in his element, peering out over the top of the Djebel el Hamra at Rommel's advancing host. It was as if he had heard Alexander's assessment of America's soldiers and had set out on a personal mission to prove him wrong.

On the morning of February 21, Rommel attacked toward Thala with the 7th Panzer Regiment.[25] The panzers quickly ran up against a mixed unit under the command of Brigadier General Paul Robinette, which fought Rommel's tanks to a standstill. The desert to the east of Thala was soon speckled with the hulks of burned-out tanks and fallen soldiers. The U.S. 13th Armored Regiment, farther north, was also attacked with the same result. The German offensive had suddenly, and unexpectedly, ground to a halt. Rommel responded by deploying fighters to knock out the American artillery positions but by midafternoon had failed to move his tanks any farther westward.[26] On the night of the twenty-first, Rommel ordered an enveloping move to the south, hoping to skirt the hills east of Thala, surprise the dug-in Americans, and capture the town. At his headquarters in Thala, Allen countered the German move. But even he was surprised when, the next morning, German formations—which had lost their way in the desert—scraped up against the Americans at the Bou Chebka Pass. The fighting was intense, but the defense of Thala was ultimately successful when the British 26th Armored Brigade, which fought a daylong action against Rommel's 10th Panzer Division east of the city, countered Rommel's move by mounting a tenacious holding action. The stand of the 26th Armored was costly—the British lost fifteen tanks.[27] The battle had been touch and go, with the British infantry using their tanks as shields before withdrawing from ridgeline to ridgeline, exacting heavy German casualties as they withdrew. At the last ridgeline, with Thala at their backs, the British stood and fought throughout the afternoon of February 21. The official U.S. Army report describes their courage.

Soon the northern slope of the ridge was a scene of wild confusion. Burning vehicles, flares, pointblank fire from tanks, both German and British, and from the British artillery, provided a tumultuous melee. The enemy adroitly knocked out signal vehicles at the start, thus preventing prompt reports to Thala. Machine gunners following the tanks took positions along the heights and soon completed the job of wrecking the whole line of defense on which so much effort had been expended. At severe disadvantage, the British drew on every resource to hold the enemy, to destroy his tanks, and to throw him back. After three hours, the enemy offensive was stopped.[28]

On February 22, with reinforcements pouring into Thala and with the advantage in air support now shifting to the Allies, Rommel met with Kesselring at his headquarters northwest of Kasserine. His troops had ammunition for six days of fighting and rations for four.[29] His offensive had pierced the Allied line and pushed back American forces in western and central Tunisia. But his tank formations had been stopped. In the north, Arnim's own tanks had failed to give him any support, and when they did attack they had failed to make any headway against the British. The weather was worsening, with morning fog and afternoon rain turning the Tunisian desert into a quagmire. It would be impossible to mount further panzer assaults, Rommel said. With Kesselring's endorsement, Rommel ordered his troops back into Kasserine Pass. He and Kesselring now agreed: with the Americans bloodied and disorganized it was time for Rommel to turn east, to punish the British Eighth Army now arrayed before the Mareth Line.[30] In all, Rommel, with tardy help from Arnim, had succeed beyond his expectations, inflicting heavy losses in men and personnel on the Allied forces. The U.S. 1st Armored Division had been particularly roughly handled, suffering some 1,400 casualties—dead, wounded, and missing. Perhaps worst of all, haphazard Allied command arrangements had proven nearly fatal. The Battle of Kasserine Pass had gone into the history books as a U.S. defeat. The Germans had grasped at victory and nearly succeeded. But in the end and at key turning points in the battle, and just as German tanks seemed poised to roll westward unopposed, the British and Americans had stood and fought.

NEWSPAPER HEADLINES blared out the news of Kasserine: U.S. troops had been "routed," were in "full flight" and "demoralized" by the onrushing hellions of Rommel's Panzer Army Afrika. Marshall seemed oddly unconcerned. He thumbed through reports of the fighting before turning to Eisenhower's lengthy and personal summation.[31] If Marshall was at all concerned, it was with Eisenhower's tone. It seemed to him that his commander felt pressured to make a report, to explain exactly what was happening and why. Marshall diligently swept aside the bad news, cautioning Eisenhower against taking too much time to keep him informed: "I appreciate your lengthy detailed messages regarding present heavy fighting on your fighting front, but I am disturbed that you feel under the necessity in such a trying situation to give so much personal time to us," Marshall wrote; ". . . you can concentrate on this battle with the feeling that it is our business to support you and not to harass you and that I'll use all my influence to see that you are supported."[32] But Marshall's outward calm and his kind words to his chief subordinate veiled the blood-draining certainty that American boys, farm boys from Iowa and Wisconsin and Illinois, had died in North Africa in great numbers when a little more preparation and better leadership might have saved their lives. Marshall had nearly predicted this when, after the conference at Casablanca, he told General Lesley McNair—America's premier combat troop trainer—that Eisenhower was concerned that American soldiers were lax, sloppy, and complacent and disregarded even the simplest military duties. Marshall could see that in the results from Kasserine: "Some way or other," he said, "we must immediately enforce a more exacting discipline and bring all of these men to understand what it means and why it must be done. I don't know that we can accomplish this through a mimeographed order, but it must be done."[33]

Eisenhower put it differently, telling his staff that America's soldiers had not yet learned to hate their enemy, a situation he was confident would change after the mauling II Corps had taken from Rommel's panzers. But Eisenhower did not intend to leave it at that. The lost Battle of Kasserine Pass required that he shake up the American high command, a move he had pondered since the beginning of Rommel's offensive. Eisenhower recalled Marshall's blunt directive: "Retention under your command of any American officer means to me that you are satisfied with his performance. Any man you deem unsatisfactory you must reassign . . . or send him home!"[34] He now moved to send some top commanders home. After visiting Fredendall's headquarters on February 23, even as the burned-out hulks of American tanks lay smoldering along the desert trails leading west, Eisenhower was stunned by what he saw. Chaos reigned, the troops were poorly clad and clearly demoralized, and Fredendall was paralyzed, fearful, defensive. Eisenhower, his mouth set and eyes ablaze, could barely control his temper. He nodded curtly at Fredendall, listened in silence to his battle report, and then turned on his heels and walked away.[35] When he returned to his own headquarters at the Hotel St. George in Algiers on the night of the twenty-fourth, he was morose. Eisenhower aide Mickey McKeough painted a vivid portrait of the supreme commander.

He sat down at the piano in the house in Algiers the night we got back from that inspection trip. He had a habit, when there was a piano, of sitting down at it now and then and playing "Chopsticks" with two fingers. He looked worried and tired and the smile wasn't there—not in his eyes anyway. I thought it was strange that he should sit down to play "Chopsticks" which he usually did when he was feeling satisfied with the way things were going. He started to pick out notes, very slowly. It wasn't "Chopsticks." He picked out taps very slowly on the piano and then he got up, without saying anything, and went off to bed. I don't think I ever saw him lower than he was that night.[36]

In the aftermath of Kasserine, Eisenhower sacked his chief intelligence officer, British brigadier Eric Mockler-Ferryman, and replaced a number of the Army's senior combat officers, even some of those who had fought well. Mockler-Ferryman's sin had been to misread German intercepts and allow Anderson to place Allied reserves far to the north, just where Rommel had wanted them. Mockler-Ferryman's relief of duties was apparently unjustified—he had simply reported what the intercepts said. But Mockler-Ferryman had failed to check the intercepts against other independent reports, a dereliction that Eisenhower believed he could not forgive. Finally, but inevitably, Eisenhower replaced Lloyd Fredendall. The decision was Eisenhower's, but was supported by all of Eisenhower's best subordinates. Major General Ernest Harmon, a hard-fighting tanker whom Eisenhower had dispatched to check on Fredendall at the height of the German offensive, was the most damning. The permanently ill-tempered Harmon was known for his candid judgments and angry outbursts, which he rained on high and low alike. When Eisenhower said that he was sending Harmon to visit Fredendall, he told him he would have full control of the battlefront and could take command of either the "II Corps or the 1st Armored," whichever he thought necessary. Harmon couldn't help himself: "Well, make up your mind Ike, I can't do both."[37] Now, back in Algiers, Harmon was only too willing to issue his assessment of Fredendall. "He's no damn good," he said. "You ought to get rid of him." Never known as an officer at a loss for words, Harmon then told Eisenhower that Fredendall was a "common, low son-of-a-bitch" and a "physical and moral coward."[38] Even Eisenhower blanched.

Historians blithely repeat Harmon's words, though his most personal castigation—of "cowardice"—is difficult to support. True, Fredendall burrowed into the mountain at Speedy Valley and, at the height of battle, decamped to the rear. When Harmon arrived, Fredendall turned over command to him and took to his bed.[39] But later, sensing that he had lost control of events, he gamely spread his battle map on the hood of his jeep and attempted to retrieve the situation. He continued to issue orders, to visit the troops, to demand attacks and counterattacks.[40] Even so, Fredendall (who ranked high in Marshall's little black book) could not survive the judgment of Omar Bradley, who was assigned to North Africa by Marshall to be Eisenhower's "eyes and ears." Bradley, a soft-spoken but driven Missourian from Eisenhower's West Point class of 1915, could be direct and ruthless, as he was when Eisenhower asked him about Fredendall: "I've talked to all the division commanders," Bradley said after returning from the front. "To a man they've lost confidence in Fredendall as the corps commander."[41] Eisenhower shook his head in agreement. Less than one week later Fredendall was sent home to train troops in Tennessee.

While Fredendall had failed in combat, his failure unburdened Eisenhower of one of his command's most notorious Anglophobes. Fredendall had seeded his staff with anti-British officers, many of whom repeated their commander's all-too-public commentary on Eisenhower—that "Ike is the best commander the British have."[42] Eisenhower meant to clean out anyone and everyone who held such sentiments. British-American cooperation was a nearly sacred principle. Learned at the knee of Fox Conner, the message was reinforced by George Marshall. Not only did the United States need friends and Allies, Marshall believed, but the future of civilization itself depended on the ability of democracies to work together to guard the world's security. The showy words were proved by war's harsh reality, for it was not just boys from Iowa who lay on the valley floor below Kasserine. There were British soldiers there, and in large numbers. British-American cooperation was not simply a bilateral courtesy, it was the key to victory. Without unity of command, without American commanders trusting and depending on their British counterparts, there would be more Kasserines, more American deaths, and, in the end, defeat.

With Fredendall sent home, Harold Alexander sped reinforcements and supplies to the front line. Within a week of Kasserine, the Allied position had been retrieved. With Omar Bradley now in place as his eyes and ears, Eisenhower reflected on the lessons of Kasserine and concluded that the Allied defeat was the result of Anglo-French-American inability to quickly capture

Tunis. Allied intelligence services had not only failed to correctly read Axis intentions, they had performed poorly at the height of the battle. Moreover, Eisenhower concluded, Allied commanders had failed to "comprehend clearly the capabilities of the enemy." Worse yet, Allied armies suffered a result of American "greenness, particularly among commanders."[43] While Eisenhower penned this judgment in the immediate aftermath of Kasserine, when the pain of defeat was sharpest, his judgment was not softened by the passage of time. And when he spoke of misreading "the capabilities of the enemy" and "green commanders" he was speaking about no one more than Dwight Eisenhower. The failure at Kasserine was his; he had underestimated Rommel, overestimated Fredendall, and rivaled Mockler-Ferryman in the misreading of critical intelligence. Eisenhower admitted as much in print many years later, in commenting on his decision to send Fredendall home. "I had no intention of recommending Fredendall for reduction or of placing the blame for the initial defeats in the Kasserine battle on his shoulders," Eisenhower wrote. "Several others, including myself, shared responsibility for our week of reverses."[44]

Nor did Eisenhower make excuses to Marshall or betray any sense of disappointment in others. Rather, he responded to Marshall's view that he was taking too much time in writing to him about battlefield developments. "Please do not look upon any communication I send you as a defensive explanation," he wrote. "Not only do I refuse to indulge in alibis but, frankly, I feel that you have given such evidence of confidence in me, that I never experience the feeling of having to defend my actions. My communications, therefore, whether in letter or in telegraphic form, spring simply from my belief that in higher echelons the common understanding of problems is the most certain way to insure smooth functioning."[45] This must have made Marshall smile—the Eisenhower letters would continue, as would his subordinate's willingness to take the blame for Allied failures. For this reason alone Eisenhower retained Marshall's confidence despite the Kasserine setback, a fact reflected in the chief of staff's continued lobbying for Eisenhower's promotion to full general.[46] The promotion had come through on the eve of Kasserine and would not be reversed, no matter how loudly the American and British press criticized Eisenhower's North Africa Army. As was his habit, Marshall did not respond to Eisenhower's letter or mention it in any of his coded cables. But he approved of Eisenhower's decision to remove Fredendall and replace him with Patton.

Eisenhower flew to Algiers from Fredendall's headquarters on March 6, while Patton journeyed from Rabat, Morocco, to meet him. They met on the tarmac at Maison Blanche Airport in Algiers and stood talking for many minutes.[47] The two close friends—"Georgie" and "Ike"—were now, after many years, about to realize their ideal: Patton's tanks roaring to meet the enemy while Eisenhower stood nearby ready to help. It had been twenty-one years since the two had disassembled a tank at Fort Meade and put it back together, twenty-one years since they had played bridge together with their wives. Then, Patton had outranked Eisenhower; now he was his subordinate. Eisenhower's orders were detailed and blunt: There would be no criticism of the British. Patton would take his orders from Alexander. Patton would take over for Fredendall and get his army in shape. He would then link up with the British Eighth Army and move on Rommel. Eisenhower told Patton he would have full responsibility for II Corps—he was to "rehabilitate, re-equip, and train his troops to take advantage of lessons so far learned." Omar Bradley was now Ike's deputy, Eisenhower explained, and Patton could count on him. Finishing his presentation, Eisenhower cautioned Patton against any show of personal recklessness. "I don't need you dead on the battlefield," he said. Patton nodded his understanding and Eisenhower continued: be cold-blooded about removing officers who do not perform, he said, and "just send them back to me. I will take care of them."

Standing nearby, Harry Butcher, took in Patton's response.

> Ike and Patton, together with Brigadier General Hugh J. Gaffey, who was to be Patton's Chief of Staff, and Beetle, conferred standing up for half an hour at the airfield. Patton, who normally hates the Hun—as Ike says, like the devil hates holy water—and who now is all the more embittered because his son-in-law, Johnnie Waters [an armored officer] is reported missing in action—damned the Germans so violently and emotionally that tears came to his eyes three times during the short conference.[48]

Patton agreed with Eisenhower on every particular. He understood his assignment and left just hours later to take command at the front. He was ebullient. Finally, he would get his wish, he told Butcher. He was finally going to face off against Rommel, a man whom, he commented, he would now have a chance to personally shoot.[49]

Replacing Lloyd Fredendall was painful for both Marshall and Eisenhower, and they danced around the subject. When Fredendall's name did not appear on an Eisenhower promotion memo in early March, Marshall asked him whether Fredendall's actions at Kasserine had influenced his decision.[50] Eisenhower responded on March 4 that Fredendall was "a good fighter, energetic and self-confident" but had demonstrated "some weaknesses."[51] Eisenhower was being more than charitable, hoping perhaps that Marshall could read between the lines and that his action to relieve Fredendall the next day would not come as a surprise. Even so, particularly given Marshall's blunt directive that Eisenhower "reassign" or "send home" anyone whom the supreme commander found unfit, Eisenhower's handling of Fredendall's relief was surprisingly delicate: Eisenhower not only did not pass on Ernie Harmon's extreme judgment of Fredendall ("a moral and physical coward") to Marshall, he remained virtually silent on some of his command's more dramatic Kasserine failings. It may well be that Eisenhower calculated that Marshall could read the battle reports as well as anyone and knew of Fredendall's failures. Yet there is a sense that in letting Fredendall down easy, Eisenhower was attempting to do the same for Marshall. That might have been unnecessary, as Marshall never claimed infallibility, but Eisenhower knew the chief of staff was proud of the list he kept in his little black book, and was well aware that his own name was scribbled in its pages. Marshall agreed with Fredendall's recall without comment, saying he would be reassigned as a trainer of U.S. troops stateside. Eisenhower praised Marshall's decision, unnecessarily, in a personal letter of March 11. There was reason for Eisenhower to feel awkward, for he had once cabled Marshall that he was mightily pleased with Fredendall—"I bless the day you urged Fredendall upon me"—a particularly galling memory that neither he nor Marshall wanted to revisit.[52] Eisenhower added one more paragraph to the Fredendall saga, then let it drop.

Fredendall has left in response to your telegram of instructions, which were shown to him. I am quite certain that you are making the best use of him; he has the physical and nervous energy to keep on producing for a very considerable time and has very clear and specific ideas as to additional requirements in our training program. Under conditions of strain, he is not particularly successful in developing a happy family and complete teamwork, and I have personally cautioned him about one or two personal faults that have had a bad effect in the past. I believe he will be the most successful of any of your Army Commanders in obtaining the results you want.[53]

While Fredendall enjoyed the softest of landings—he was appointed commanding general of the U.S. Second Army and soon even promoted to lieutenant general—the delicate handling of the Fredendall case was not peculiar to Marshall or Eisenhower or unusual for the Army, where failed officers were often shuttled silently to the rear. The policy was a necessity for both Marshall and Eisenhower, who were overseeing officers who, like them, had suffered through long years of isolation in forlorn outposts with little pay. Combat failure was, neither man felt, necessarily a disqualification for high command (the common execution of failed commanders in the Red Army instilled fear but not loyalty), and Fredendall performed well in his next assignment. Then too both men were aware of the personal wreckages wrought by war. Myriad examples filled military textbooks: the unfair cashierings of otherwise intelligent men, the vicious sniping of armchair generals, the needless smearing of sound reputations.[54] Perhaps above all, Marshall and Eisenhower both knew that sometimes otherwise competent commanders simply do not perform well in battle. "He was a good colonel before the war," Beetle Smith said of Fredendall.[55]

It was with history in mind that both Eisenhower and Marshall were sensitive to claims of unfairness, particularly when it came to cleaning up the command mess and mending the bitter feelings sparked by the Kasserine defeat. In the midst of the battle, Fredendall sought the dismissal of Orlando Ward, the commander of the 1st Armored Division, whose sniping with Fredendall during the contest was outstripped only by his open disregard for the British. Ward survived Fredendall, but Eisenhower kept an eye on him, believing that his ability to insult nearly everyone he worked with would cost him his job. There was no question Ward was brave: during Kasserine, Ward had stood, binoculars firmly planted, as his tanks went into battle. He stood all day, in the middle of battle, trying to win back what had been lost. "The general, one of the finest men, stood on the skyline smoking a cigar, very calm, which was good on the nerves of a number of very jittery people, including me," a young sergeant remembered.[56] But for Marshall and Eisenhower bravery was expected, while insubordination was inexcusable. Now Ward was Patton's problem, and the two were destined to clash in spite of Ward's reputation as being "one of Marshall's men." In fact, Marshall thought so highly of Ward that he had promoted him two full grades shortly before the beginning of the war. For Ike, Ward was a little-black-book problem all over again and one that would, when the time came, demand the kind of remorseless treatment given to Fredendall. "Modern war is a very complicated business," Eisenhower wrote to his son John at West Point, "and governments are forced to treat individuals as pawns."[57]

That assessment included everyone, Eisenhower knew. Even his closest friends. The Kasserine defeat had taken a much greater toll than its numbers reflected. The German campaign to unhinge Fredendall accounted for six thousand American dead, wounded, and captured. The Germans later reported that two-thirds of the American casualties were prisoners.[58] The death toll sobered Americans, who had watched the advance of Eisenhower's army across the breadth of Algeria with nary a setback and so were shocked that German tanks could be allowed to plunge so effortlessly into his lines. Other casualty lists on other fronts, however, made Kasserine seem an almost minor skirmish—the Russians suffered the same number of casualties on the eastern front nearly every day, sometimes nearly every hour. But while the battle may not have reached the disastrous proportions now given it in American military lore, it provided valuable lessons for Marshall and Eisenhower, who moved quickly to put new commanders in charge of the Army's most important combat units while shifting other commanders to new duties. These shifts were neither revolutionary nor disruptive, adhering to the command calculus long upheld by Marshall and Eisenhower. For example, though he did not know it at the time, Mark Clark had fallen under Marshall and Eisenhower's cool gaze, the Army chief's pen poised metaphorically above the page of the black book that contained his name. It would not have taken much, in the spring of 1943, for Marshall to unceremoniously cross Clark from his list.

During his visit to North Africa, Marshall talked with Eisenhower about Clark, whom both liked and trusted. But Clark's judgment, Marshall believed, had recently proven suspect. Marshall was particularly disturbed by Clark's cultivated sense of self-importance, reflected in the long tail of reporters who, notebooks in hand, followed him through North Africa.[59] He had done nothing to deserve such attention, Marshall implied, except to call it to himself. Keep an eye on him, Marshall said. Eisenhower agreed that Clark "was becoming a bit consumed with a desire to push himself." Ike was concerned not only about Clark's ego, but about his constantly niggling and insulting criticism of the British.[60] During his time in Algiers, Clark had offended nearly every British officer he had come in contact with, loudly declaiming that Kenneth Anderson's battle plans for the Tunisia campaign were so flawed that he was prepared to recommend that Eisenhower withdraw all American troops from his command. Clark liked to quote Napoleon's dictum "It is better to fight an ally than be one" in front of British officers. Eisenhower was fed up with such talk, even from an old friend. So when Clark asked to be placed in command of the Fifth Army, then training in Morocco for the invasion of Sicily—now called Operation Husky—Eisenhower gladly accommodated him, telling Harry Butcher that Clark now had command of "his own manure pile."[61]

Eisenhower breathed a sigh of relief that Clark would no longer be a source of concern, but his transfer caused disruptions in the American high command. When Fredendall left, Eisenhower was forced to remove Patton from his indispensable position as a key commander of Husky to take over II Corps, though Ike certainly knew that Patton's views of the British were, if anything, more extreme than Clark's or Fredendall's. There would be no criticism of the British, Eisenhower had told Patton in Algiers, and Patton had agreed: "Yes sir." But Eisenhower knew that was very unlikely. Patton was a great trainer, disciplinarian, and fighter. But he was simply incapable of keeping his mouth shut, and Eisenhower surely knew that when Patton saluted and turned on his heel he was already muttering under his breath. So Eisenhower told him that he would be in command of II Corps only until mid-April, when Omar Bradley would take over.[62] Bradley's job was to keep Patton in line.

KASSERINE PROVIDED a reality check for Marshall and Eisenhower's command judgments and their leadership choices. Marshall's little black book was not infallible, Eisenhower's pledge to be ruthless was limited, and their common commitment to appointing officers who were utterly selfless was constrained by larger imperatives. Fredendall, Ward, Clark—and half a dozen other officers of lesser rank—had come up short. Some would be replaced and others would not. Still others, though transparently unsuited for the type of coalition warfare extolled by Fox Conner, John Pershing, George Marshall, and Dwight Eisenhower, would be rewarded. There was nothing that could be done about that just now, for the Americans were hungry for a battlefield triumph against the Germans. But eventually, Marshall and Eisenhower both knew, such men would have to be replaced, if for no other reason than to keep British commanders from open revolt.

Kasserine took its toll on the American high command and on Marshall and Eisenhower. While neither man would ever admit it, the British had been right at Arcadia and Casablanca. America's troops were well armed and well trained, but they were green. America's commanders were highly schooled, but only the pressures of combat could prove their worth. The weight of matériel had made a difference, to be sure, but battlefield success was predicated on lessons learned by the Greeks at Marathon—courage and tenacity made a difference. These unspoken calculations, clear to Marshall and Eisenhower, were hidden from the public. But other and much more important truths were hidden as well, not the least of which was that the embarrassment of Kasserine imposed its own judgment on Marshall and Eisenhower's strategic vision. Kasserine showed that the British judgment of Sledgehammer had been correct. The searing truth was that if the Americans and their British allies had fought in France as they had fought in North Africa, they would have been soundly defeated. The British had also been proven correct in their judgment that while fighting the Germans in France would have been preferred, fighting them somewhere— even in such an apparently peripheral theater as North Africa—would help the Russians, perhaps decisively. The truth of this was now clear on the eastern front, where the Russians were locked in a war of utter annihilation with the German Army. It would become clear only much later that British calculations had made it possible for the Red Army to score its most important triumph.

Twenty-four hours after German tanks seized Sidi Bou Zid,, German general Friedrich Paulus's Sixth Army surrendered at Stalingrad.[63] The battles at Kasserine and Stalingrad, separated by some 2,416 miles of nearly impassable mountains, desert, and sea, were vastly different in tactics and ground. The German Army stormed Stalingrad, pushing Soviet forces into a warren of factories and urban defiles, then fought through a nightmare of cold in an attempt to liquidate the remaining resistance.[64] German observation officers could see the Volga River just *there*, tantalizingly close, through their binoculars. But when German troops actually reached the Volga they were as far from victory as they had been when consigned to fighting among the city's factories. Its back to the river, the Red Army fought house to house while withdrawing among the ruins it had created, losing tens of thousands of soldiers. During one two-day period of the battle, in October 1942, the Red Army had more men killed in one action (in a fight for the Red October Factory) than the Allies lost during the entire North Africa campaign.[65] On November 19, 1942, the Red Army attacked from its positions outside the city in two huge pincer moves, from the north and the south, overwhelming units protecting the flanks of the German Sixth Army. This double envelopment, a strategist's dream, encircled twenty German and two Romanian divisions, some 280,000 soldiers in all, closing off Stalingrad from the west. In December, the Germans mounted a failed relief effort, attacking the Red Army with three tank divisions. In January, the German high command ordered a retreat, leaving the Sixth Army encircled in the city. Three months later, exhausted, emaciated, dispirited, surrounded, starving, the German Army was overrun and Paulus, told by Hitler to fight to the last bullet, surrendered. The German defeat was devastating: more than 150,000 German soldiers died; another 107,000 were taken prisoner. Of that number, only 6,000 survived the war. Stalingrad was a slaughterhouse.

Even before the battle on the Volga had ended, Colonel-General Jürgen von Arnim vowed that North Africa would not become another Stalingrad.[66] But Arnim's very presence in Tunisia, along with some 150,000 German and 60,000 Italian reinforcements, shipped quickly from the eastern front and then across the Straits of Messina from Sicily in the weeks after the Torch landings, fatally crippled German efforts in the east: German bombers deployed to stop Allied shipments of matériel into the Soviet Union at Murmansk were diverted to Tunisia, as was as a squadron of ninety bombers supporting the German offensive in the Caucasus.[67] The diversion of German bombers from their Murmansk assignment might well have been fatal: German troops fighting in Stalingrad reported capturing American-made tanks, some of them with their instruction booklets, written in English, still inside.[68] They had come across the

Atlantic, then been shipped south and pulled across the Volga. Arnim himself, the former commander of the 17th Panzer Division fighting its way east toward Moscow, was pessimistic about his North African command. He calculated that hundreds of thousands of tons of matériel would be needed to supply Germany's North African tank forces—but they were not available. It was not a surprise to Rommel, therefore, that his February offensive against Sidi Bou Zid and Tebessa was in the end fatally undermined by the lack of supplies. But he also blamed Arnim, who at a key moment in the battle had jaunted off to the north, deaf to Rommel's pleas for support east of Tebessa.[69] Arnim, it seems, had as little regard for Württemberg schoolboys like Rommel as Clark had for Sandhurst Tommies like Anderson.

Kasserine was a battle of what-ifs. What if there had been the supplies and fuel to exploit Rommel's opening? What if Arnim and Rommel had more closely cooperated? What if the Allies had not stiffened, but instead had panicked, lost their confidence, and fatally foundered? On the other hand, what if the 150,000 German troops in Tunisia had not been there at all. What if they had been in Stalingrad? Scrutinizing the North African battle maps from his office in the War Department, George Marshall might well have calculated these same what-ifs, and come to the conclusion that it was Torch that had saved Stalingrad. While he might have dismissed such a fantasy as mere speculation (for Stalingrad might have been lost to Germany despite the addition of 150,000 troops), Joseph Stalin, ensconced in his poorly lit office in the Kremlin, believed firmly that the German tide, which had once lapped at the outskirts of Moscow, was now ebbing. He also carefully, albeit quietly, noted that hundreds of transport aircraft resupplying German troops in Stalingrad had one morning mysteriously disappeared. Stalin later discovered that the German troop transports had been transferred to North Africa. German Luftwaffe commander Hermann Göring was despondent, believing the transfer fatally crippled German efforts in the East: "There died the core of the German bomber fleet," he moaned.[70]

Stalingrad was Kasserine's "victory" because it stripped badly needed German resources from the eastern front. But the Battle of Kasserine Pass was also a needed defeat, for it infused the American high command with a sense of purpose. The Americans needed seasoning, the British had said; they were green. They were ready to fight, to be sure, but they needed to be blooded. Now, after

Kasserine, the Allies, most especially the Americans, had taken the measure of their foe and knew what it would take to defeat him. "Our people from the very highest to the very lowest have learned that this is not a child's game," Eisenhower told Marshall, "and are eager to get down to the fundamental business of profiting by the lessons they have learned. I am going to make it a fixed rule that no unit from the time it reaches this theater until the war is won will ever stop training."[71] Eisenhower was right of course. But no armed force can substitute training for actual experience in combat, and in this Churchill had been right: if the Americans were to be blooded it would be far better for it to happen in the desert sands of North Africa than in the verdant hills of northern France.

PATTON KNEW what Eisenhower wanted and from the moment he arrived in Tebessa he worked ceaselessly to prepare his troops for battle. He stormed his way through II Corps, seeming to be everywhere at once. He cajoled and punished, he was profane and sympathetic, he listened and screamed—but mostly he imposed discipline.[72] "Each time a soldier knotted his necktie, threaded his leggings, and buckled on his heavy steel helmet," Omar Bradley, whom Patton insisted serve as his deputy, remarked, "he was forcibly reminded that Patton had come to command the II Corps, that the pre-Kasserine days had ended, and that a tough new era had begun."[73] When told that officers had removed their command bars from their helmets (to make them less conspicuous targets in battle), Patton was enraged. Better targets? "That's part of your job of being an officer," he insisted. Patton had once defended Fredendall, but after barely a week in command he changed his mind: "Discipline consists in obeying orders," he said. "If men do not obey orders in small things, they are incapable of being in battle. I will have discipline—to do otherwise is to commit murder. I cannot see what Fredendall did to justify his existence."[74] Bradley agreed; he supported Patton's disciplinary measures, believed in his military genius, was awed by his grasp of the American Army's tactical situation, supported him to subcommanders, defended him to Eisenhower—and despised him. "At times I felt Patton, however successful he was as a corps commander, had not yet learned to command himself," Bradley said.[75]

Eisenhower's ground commander in North Africa, British field marshal Sir

Harold Alexander, opened the Allied offensive to capture Tunisia on March 16 by giving Patton a secondary role: he was to capture the hill towns of Gafsa, Sened, and Maknassy, making up for the ground lost by Fredendall at Kasserine. The offensive would be coordinated with Montgomery, whose Eighth Army would attack Rommel in southern Tunisia. Montgomery would then join his forces with those of Alexander for the final drive north and east, toward Tunis.[76] Patton played his role, capturing Gafsa on March 17. With Rommel transferred to Germany, Arnim was now in command of all Axis troops in North Africa, and he drove them relentlessly from one defensive position to the next, taking the offensive only when Alexander showed weakness.[77] Six days after Alexander's attack and five days after Patton captured Gafsa, Arnim counterattacked the II Corps with the 10th Panzer Division. In an all-day battle on March 22, Patton's 9th Infantry Division, overlooking the highway east of El Guettar, cut the 10th Panzer Division to ribbons. Patton—"Old Blood and Guts" as the American press now dubbed him—was repelled by the slaughter, calling Arnim's tactics at El Guettar "a waste of good infantry."[78] In early April, Montgomery broke through the German defensive line and raced north while Alexander attacked eastward, penning Arnim into the Tunis bridgehead. Once again, Patton seemed everywhere. On April 4, Patton relieved General Orlando Ward (whom he had just awarded a Silver Star), commander of the 1st Armored Division, in a move that many in the division considered unjustified and purposely demeaning.[79] Eisenhower had seen it coming and remained silent. "The division has lost its nerve and is jumpy," Patton said in his own defense. "I fear that our troops want to fight without getting killed."[80]

Eisenhower was pleased and extolled Patton's successes, though he knew that sooner or later, his best tank commander's profane personality would lead to problems. They were not long in coming. Just days before firing Ward, Patton openly criticized British air support of his troops by noting in a situation report that "forward troops have been continuously bombed all morning. Total lack of air cover for our units has allowed German air force to operate almost at will."[81] Air Vice Marshal Arthur Coningham, a New Zealander with the improbable nickname of Mary, charged with overseeing all Allied tactical air assets in Tunisia, was enraged by Patton's criticism and responded by cabling his subordinates that they were to ignore him. The problem was not with air cover, he said, but with II Corps. It was "unbattleworthy."[82] Coningham also sent his cable to Eisenhower's headquarters and added that he hoped that Patton was not using the air force "as an alibi for lack of success on the ground." When Eisenhower's air chief for the Mediterranean, Sir Arthur Tedder, read this exchange, he moved quickly to end it, ordering Coningham to retract his words and apologize to Patton in person. That was not enough: Eisenhower's famous anger now spilled over in a towering rage—against Patton, against Coningham, and against himself—for his apparent inability to control his subordinates. For one of the few times during the war, Eisenhower was near to resigning, believing that he had failed in persuading his subordinate commanders to cooperate.[83] He was so disgusted, so despondent, so despairing that he wrote a letter of resignation to Marshall, but was persuaded by Beetle Smith to retract it. While Coningham personally apologized to Patton—afterward, in fact, the two men seemed to get on well—Eisenhower blamed himself for the controversy. Should Eisenhower have seen the disagreement coming? Both Marshall and Eisenhower knew about Patton's explosive temper; what they had not counted on was for the otherwise careful Coningham to spout off so carelessly.

Despite their differences, Bradley and Patton held a common disregard for the British, whose commanders were always willing to expend American blood, they felt, while taking the credit for American victories. American soldiers, Bradley and Patton believed, were not getting the credit they deserved, were being overlooked in Field Marshal Alexander's battle plan to capture Tunis, and were being regularly and snidely criticized for their fighting abilities. Both men chafed at Eisenhower's directive that criticism of the British end and that American commanders find ways to cooperate. Bradley's and Patton's views were not unjustified: criticism of the American Army started at the very top of the British leadership in North Africa, seeping down to subordinate commands. Alexander, for one, made no secret of his disdain for the fighting abilities of American soldiers, taking his lead from the officious Sir Alan Brooke, his good friend. The Americans were "soft, green and quite untrained" and "lacked the will to fight," he said.[84] Alexander's battlefield cables to Brooke in London fed his chief's anti-American sentiment and reinforced his indifferent attitude toward Eisenhower. "There is no doubt that they have little hatred for the Germans and Italians," Alexander wrote, "and show no eagerness to get in and kill them. Unless we can do something about it, the American Army in the European theatre of operations will be quite useless and play no useful part whatsoever."[85]

Neither Bradley nor Patton was privy to these views, but they sensed them, and they saw them reflected in Alexander's plan for the defeat of Arnim, in which the Americans would play only a supporting role. They seethed at the insult, revived Fredendall's loose anti-British talk, and blamed Eisenhower for coddling America's allies: "God damn all British and so-called Americans who have their legs pulled by them," Patton confided in his diary. "I will bet that Ike does nothing about it. I would rather be commanded by an Arab. I think less than nothing of Arabs."[86] But the enraged Patton kept appropriately silent in public (and especially with Eisenhower), even as he wrote in his diary, "Ike is more British than the British and is putty in their hands. Oh, God, for John J. Pershing."[87] Even Fredendall would not have gone this far. Bradley shared Patton's disdain for Ike, but he was more circumspect, knowing that Eisenhower "walked a chalk line to avoid being branded pro-American by the British command."[88] But while understanding Eisenhower's need to "avoid being branded pro-American" in public, Bradley ("the G.I.'s General," as journalist Ernie Pyle dubbed him; "a phony Abraham Lincoln," Terry Allen snorted)[89] had few kind words for his West Point classmate. After the war, he made these private feelings starkly public. "I shared Patton's misgivings about Ike, though I was less harsh in my private judgments and never criticized him before others," he wrote. "Ike was too weak, much too prone to knuckle under to the British, often . . . at our expense."[90]

Reassured by Coningham's apology and Patton's continued silence, Eisenhower swallowed his temper, withdrew his resignation letter, and began to take a more philosophic view of the dustup: "I realize that the seeds for discord between ourselves and our British Allies were sown, on our side, as far back as when we read our little red school history books," Eisenhower wrote to Marshall on April 5. "My method is to drag all these matters squarely into the open, discuss them frankly, and insist upon positive rather than negative actions in furthering the purpose of Allied unity."[91] Marshall might have been relieved by Eisenhower's message, but he had his own doubts now about the dangers of being overly cooperative. The Army chief could read the newspapers as well as anyone, and so far as he could discern, the only ones fighting in North Africa were the British. The United States needed a victory, he believed, and so in the wake of a conference in Washington to settle similar matters in the Pacific, Marshall began to shape an approach to the British in North Africa that would satisfy the put-upon personalities of his commanders while answering British criticisms that American soldiers could not fight. If it was glory that Patton and Bradley wanted, then that is what they would have. The strategy concocted by Marshall was hardly subtle—he was determined to do what he rarely did: order Eisenhower to insist that Americans be part of the final drive on Tunis, which meant that Eisenhower would have to give an order to Alexander. By insisting that American troops be put in the front lines, he would also strengthen Eisenhower's role as the Allied commander. So, in an unusually blunt directive to Eisenhower in the midst of the drive on Tunis, Marshall cited press reports that American troops were not taking the lead in the North African fight. He directed Eisenhower to "watch this very closely."[92] Reinforcing this message, he told Eisenhower that he was particularly disturbed that American soldiers had been consigned to "mopping up" operations, which "marked [a] fall in prestige of American troops in [the] minds of pressmen and in reaction of public."[93] Patton and Bradley also weighed in, with Bradley visiting Algiers and telling Eisenhower that Alexander's plans for taking on Arnim were unacceptable. "This war's going to last a long time, Ike, there'll be a lot more Americans in before we're through," Bradley said. "Until you give us the chance to show what we can do in a sector of our own, with an objective of our own, under our own command, you'll never know how good or bad we really are."[94]

Eisenhower got the message; he cabled Alexander to use II Corps "right up to the bitter end of the campaign," then met with Patton, Bradley, and Alexander at Alexander's headquarters to drive home Marshall's message. American prestige was now on the line, Eisenhower said, and if U.S. troops were sidelined it would have a negative impact on the European war effort. Under pressure from the U.S. public, Eisenhower added, American troops might be shifted to the Pacific. Eisenhower was stern in the face of Alexander's doubts. The U.S. would supply the bulk of the fighting forces in the war, Eisenhower reminded Alexander, and they needed confidence in their abilities. There was only one way for them to get it—and that was to have them fight, to send them into battle. Alexander expressed his doubts. Shifting II Corps meant pulling them out of their position and marching them across Anderson's line of supply, he said. Doing so would disrupt his battle plans. Even so, he added, he understood Eisenhower's point, and then quietly noted that because the Americans had failed at Kasserine he supposed they deserved another shot at fighting the Germans. Eisenhower held his temper, but just barely.[95] After a long silence, he simply ordered Alexander to turn over a key part of the front lines to the Americans. Chastened, Alexander agreed. With that accomplished, Eisenhower turned to Bradley. American troops must not fail, he said. "We have reached the point where troops *must* secure objectives assigned," he added, "and we must direct leaders to get out and lead and to secure the necessary results."[96]

AT THE end of April 1943, with II Corps now shifted north and under the command of Omar Bradley (Patton had been reassigned to finish the planning of the invasion of Sicily), Alexander launched his forces at Arnim's lines. The American troops were aimed at Bizerte, the British at Tunis. First contact was made on April 22 as II Corps pitched into the Germans. Arnim's troops held their positions tenaciously for ten days until, on May 1, Bradley's 34th Division fought its way up Hill 609.[97] The battle left dozens of Americans dead on the slopes of the hill, but the Germans broke and fled back toward Tunis. In the south, Anderson's First Army lunged northward, reinforced liberally by units from Montgomery's Eighth Army. The offensive in the south caught Arnim by surprise. Anderson drove relentlessly toward Tunis in an operation code-named "Strike." While the road to Tunis seemed suddenly opened, the Germans launched counteroffensives in the north, along the Tine River, hoping to retrieve their lost positions. Terry Allen's troops, caught near Hill 232, were badly bloodied. When reorganized and sent forward to reclaim their lost rifle pits they were bloodied yet again. The Americans were pushed off the hill. Bradley castigated Allen for the loss of 232, characterizing him as "an incorrigible rebel" who was "antagonistic to any echelon above that of division."[98] Which meant, of course, that Allen was antagonistic to the one person who outranked him: *Bradley*.

Allen's setback was temporary. On May 7, British troops entered Tunis, and just hours later the Americans captured Bizerte. On May 12, the First Italian Army surrendered en masse. That same day, with Allied troops closing in on his command headquarters, Arnim burned Rommel's mobile command headquarters, bequeathed to him one month earlier by the Desert Fox, then slowly walked toward the Allied lines to surrender.[99] Eisenhower was astonished at the numbers of surrendering Germans and Italians—some 275,000 in all, more than the Russians had captured at Stalingrad. The Allies had suffered over

70,000 casualties, including 11,000 dead. The precisely tabulated returns of 12,618 American dead, wounded, and missing did not tell the full story. Despite the victory in North Africa, whatever chance there was now of an Allied invasion of Europe in 1943 was finished. The German soldier was a tenacious fighter, and the German commanders were brilliant tacticians. As a result, a campaign that Allied planners had once believed might last only six weeks had lasted six months. It would be another year before Allied troops set foot in France. Still, North Africa was a victory. Most important, Marshall and Eisenhower's view that American soldiers would fight, and well, had been vindicated. "At the moment there seems to be nothing for me to say except to express deep satisfaction in the progress of affairs under your direction," Marshall told Eisenhower in a cable after the German surrender. "My interest is to give you what you need, support you in every way possible . . . and to leave you free to go about the business of crushing the Germans and gaining us great victories."[100]

8

HUSKY

". . . if he is not cured now there is no hope for him. . . ."
"Thank you for your generous attitude. . . ."

JUST AS GEORGE PATTON was taking command of II Corps in Tunisia, George Marshall did something unusual. He went on vacation.[1] While he would not admit it, mediating the arguments between the British and American high commands, dampening the continued interservice spats in the Pacific, and fighting to provide more of everything for everyone—not to mention the endless briefings and meetings, and, inevitably, the daily review of the long list of casualties from North Africa and the Pacific—left him exhausted. Marshall was also weakened by a winter cold that forced him to his bed. So he and Katherine decided to go to Miami, where they rented a large cottage on the ocean. Marshall was hoping for complete quiet, so he traveled incognito, sporting sunglasses and civilian clothes. He told Katherine that no one would recognize him out of uniform, and at first the disguise worked well. While Marshall was seated on the beach near his cottage after the sun had set one evening, a passing Coast Guard officer told him that regulations required that he fold up his chair and go inside.[2] Marshall ignored the command. Undeterred, the Coast Guard officer returned a few minutes later with a squad of men. The officer once again insisted that he move. "Don't you know there's a war on?" he asked.[3]

The next afternoon, Marshall and Katherine went into Miami to shop. The chief of staff was immediately recognized by two soldiers, who stopped their jeep to gawk at him. "Aren't you General Marshall?" one of them asked. "Yes, I am," Marshall said, "but you haven't seen me." The soldiers nodded, saluted, and left. A few moments later, as Marshall and Katherine shopped for beach shoes, a small crowd gathered to gawk at him. The owner of the store loudly pointed out that his customer was General George Marshall. Marshall smiled and attempted to leave the store without talking to anyone, but a crowd gathered around him, asking him questions and wishing him well. Smiling, shaking hands, and exchanging greetings, Marshall and Katherine retreated to a taxi with a crowd following. Later, Katherine laughed about the incident. You must be very happy with your disguise, she said.[4] Marshall focused on his work only during his last night in Miami, when he gave a radio address commemorating the founding of West Point. "Our success in this war now depends on leadership," he said. "We have the best equipment. We have the finest personnel in the world. Given adequate leadership, the victory is certain, and we will be spared unnecessary loss of life . . ."[5]

Marshall's otherwise innocuous address marked a new phase in his thinking about the war. The Army chief of staff had worked for sixteen months to organize, train, and ship America's soldiers, sailors, and airmen to the battlefields of Europe and the Pacific and provide them with the equipment necessary to engage the enemy. That effort was now successfully concluded. Given the numbers of men and amount of matériel deployed in combat theaters around the globe, Marshall knew, the Allies *should* win the war. Yet the issue remained in doubt. For Marshall, America's success at building, maintaining, and leading an international coalition ("to fight beside allies," in Fox Conner's simple dictum)[6] would determine whether the United States, Great Britain, and the other states of Roosevelt and Churchill's "United Nations" were ultimately victorious. "Our success in this war now depends on leadership," he had said, and the leadership he referred to was not confined to the American military; it included the senior commanders of America's primary allies. Marshall's simple calculus was Conner's and, now, Eisenhower's: If the United States could build and maintain a strong alliance it would be victorious; if it could not it would be defeated.[7] The victory of the United Nations depended on a leadership whose primary goal now was not only to fight the war, but to keep together the coalition that Roosevelt, Churchill, and Marshall had formed. From the end of the North

African campaign to the end of the war, the requirement of maintaining an international coalition was a permanent feature of Marshall's thinking; it was the reason he had appointed Eisenhower supreme Allied commander for the North African invasion and the reason he reconfirmed his leadership by keeping him as commander of Husky, the invasion of Sicily. Eisenhower was an instrument of Marshall's commitment to building a global military coalition to face the Axis; he was the one senior officer who best understood its importance.

The Marshall-Eisenhower relationship is key to understanding how America fought its war against the Axis; successfully decoding the Marshall-Eisenhower relationship is fundamental to decoding the larger American strategy. Yet a search for deeper meanings in Marshall and Eisenhower's partnership is more elusive. For Harry Butcher, Marshall and Eisenhower were like father and son, with occasional shows of affection and an abiding if unspoken personal commitment. Others saw between Marshall and Eisenhower simply an unusually close friendship that was deepened by working together during the war. Both views assume that Marshall and Eisenhower felt some intangible kinship. There is no evidence of this in any of Eisenhower's writings, and Marshall himself dismissed the claim, rejecting it with a simple statement of military professionalism: "If he [Eisenhower] hadn't delivered he wouldn't have moved up," Marshall said.[8] This is not the statement of a father about a son, or of a good friend's judgment on another. But if Marshall and Eisenhower were not like a father and son and if they were not close and deep friends, what are we to make of their relationship? Does it tell us anything new about America's role in World War II and in the era that followed? In the wake of the North African victory, evidence regarding the Marshall-Eisenhower relationship becomes richer, and it is easier to assess its depth and meaning.

Marshall and Eisenhower's communications, through correspondence and coded radiograms, provide the most important clues as to how the two worked together and viewed each other. It is worth repeating that while Eisenhower maintained his link to the Army chief of staff through a series of personal letters, Marshall always communicated to Eisenhower through official channels. Put another way, while Eisenhower was personal and familiar with Marshall, Marshall was rarely personal and familiar with Eisenhower. Then, too, while Marshall and Eisenhower maintained a studied propriety in their relationship, their behavior toward each other was proper in a particularly significant sense —

and was signaled by the otherwise mundane forms of address they used for each other. For Marshall, Eisenhower was never "Ike" and only occasionally "General Eisenhower." Rather, he was almost always simply "Eisenhower." The same was true in Marshall's relations with Eisenhower's colleagues. Clark, Patton, and Bradley were never "Wayne," "George," or "Brad," and normally Marshall even dispensed with their ranks. They were simply "Clark," "Patton," and "Bradley." These references were not unique to Marshall of course, nor do they necessarily reflect the Army chief of staff's notorious detachment or noted lack of personal feeling. They followed the traditions of the service academies and of military colleges like the Virginia Military Institute and the Citadel. For Marshall, Eisenhower was not a "son" or a close friend. He was an underclassman. For Eisenhower, Marshall was an upperclassman, whose last name must always be preceded by his rank. It is possible for an underclassman to write a personal letter to an upperclassman, but far less common for an upperclassman to do the same. An underclassman may be personal, even occasionally familiar. But an upperclassman? Never. The upperclassman-underclassman relationship is one way to understand Marshall's relationship with Eisenhower and Eisenhower's colleagues, nearly all of whom were one-half generation younger than Marshall and all of whom (with the exception of Douglas MacArthur and Walter Krueger) had graduated from America's military academies *after* Marshall.[9] The ritualistic pecking order of the service academies and like institutions is purposeful and important, as it allows a career military officer to use an accepted if unwritten tool of command—to be informal but not friendly, to offer guidance but not paternal advice. An upperclassman may be a mentor, a teacher, and a commander—but he may never be a friend.

North Africa was a test for both men, and in the midst of the fighting, the reason for Marshall's choice of Eisenhower as supreme commander (and the profound importance of their partnership to winning the war) became clear. "Ike is more British than the British and is putty in their hands. Oh, God, for John J. Pershing," Patton had said.[10] Omar Bradley now seconded this opinion, noting that Eisenhower was particularly susceptible to British flattery and that "Ike falls for it" and was "weak" and "too prone to knuckle under to the British."[11] Mark Clark was even more outspoken, roiling Eisenhower's headquarters with his quotes from Napoleon Bonaparte in spite of Eisenhower's explicit wish that he not do so. While the common postwar notion that

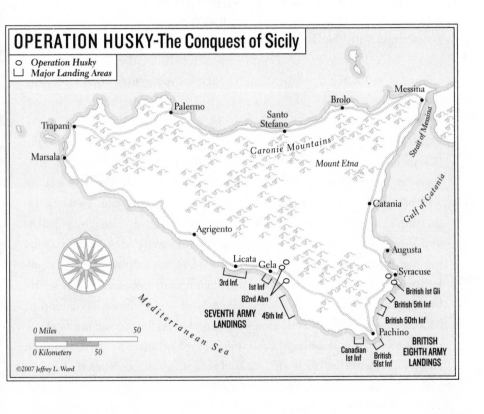

OPERATION HUSKY-The Conquest of Sicily

○   Operation Husky
▢   Major Landing Areas

Messina

Palermo   Brolo

Santo
Stefano

Trapani

Caronie Mountains

Marsala

Strait of Messina

Mount Etna

Catania

Gulf of Catania

Agrigento

Augusta

Licata   Gela

3rd Inf.   Ist Inf

82nd Abn

Syracuse

British Ist Gli

British 5th Inf

SEVENTH ARMY   45th Inf
LANDINGS

British 50th Inf

Pachino

0 Miles   50

Mediterranean Sea

0 Kilometers   50

Canadian
Ist Inf

British
5Ist Inf

BRITISH
EIGHTH ARMY
LANDINGS

©2007 Jeffrey L. Ward

the Americans and British fought each other as much as they fought the Nazis is exaggerated, unlike Patton, Bradley, or Clark, Marshall and Eisenhower shared a unique and special sensitivity to the importance of maintaining the American-British alliance, even if that meant doing so at the expense of promoting American prerogatives. Such cooperation had its limits, of course, but Eisenhower did give the British the benefit of the doubt, even when they least deserved it. Marshall was a corrective to this tendency, but prior to Husky he intervened only once to set Eisenhower on a new path, knowing that his subordinate was even more convinced than he of the necessity of American cooperation with the British. Then too, it is doubtful that John J. Pershing would have long tolerated Patton's open rebellion, Bradley's sotto voce criticisms, or Clark's sly barbs. That Eisenhower did so made his partnership with Marshall special—and it is in no small part why he became supreme commander.

By the end of the North African campaign, moreover, it was clear that the Marshall-Eisenhower partnership was diligently being maintained by both men not simply because of their belief that it was the only way to defeat the Axis powers, but in order to establish a postwar structure that would be aggression's strongest deterrent. The efficacy of such a deterrence, Marshall and Eisenhower understood, would not depend simply on America's ability to serve as the arsenal of democracy, but on America's ability to lead a coalition in which the separate national commands of democratic nations would have equal value and equal say. The germ of this idea was contained in Marshall's otherwise innocuous and understated address to the political science association in Washington and underscored yet again in his Miami radio address: it is what the Army chief of staff meant by "adequate leadership." In mid-1943, Marshall and Eisenhower were looking not only for leaders who would understand how to fight and win wars; they were also looking for military officers capable of working effectively with Allied commanders in responding to a common foe.

As the war progressed, Marshall and Eisenhower would spend an ever increasing amount of their time finding officers who could both fight *and* understand their larger vision. The exigencies of the crisis, of the need for victory, determined these choices as long as Germany and Japan remained undefeated. But once the war was won, those officers who proved incapable of transforming their parochial viewpoints would pass from view. They would be replaced by a new kind of military commander—one who could, like Marshall and Eisenhower, subordinate national interests to the needs of an entirely new American military doctrine: "collective security."

Marshall chose Eisenhower as the linchpin of his delicate effort to forge an international military coalition because—unlike Patton, Clark, Bradley, MacArthur, Stilwell, Devers, or any other single officer then serving in uniform—Eisenhower understood and was willing to nurture the Atlantic Alliance. Like Marshall, Eisenhower rarely (if ever) publicly castigated America's coalition partners, never once derided their abilities or questioned their commitment, never believed that America alone could defeat its enemies, and even viewed the submersion of national pride to international goals as necessary to victory. For Marshall, Eisenhower remained a singular presence in a generation of warriors. Eisenhower was a commander who believed that building and maintaining an international coalition of democracies was not a political nicety or a courteous bow to the blood shed by others in the years prior to 1941, but a matter of national survival. Not once, ever, in any single writing, did any other officer of Eisenhower's generation evince a comparable understanding of the importance of forging and maintaining such a coalition. Eisenhower's understanding of Conner's and Pershing's lessons of war and diplomacy placed him in unique company—not simply as Marshall's partner in command, but as a part of a special set of leaders that included Roosevelt and Churchill. It is this that gave Eisenhower's relationship with Marshall its special cast.

George Marshall did more than relax during his vacation in Florida; he spent time reflecting on the meaning of the war, the lessons it was teaching, and the structures that should emerge from it. While his ideas were yet to be fully formed, the traditions of international cooperation that he and Eisenhower were shaping would outlast the conflict with Germany and Japan and be institutionalized in the postwar world as the Marshall Plan and the North Atlantic Treaty Organization. And the Marshall and Eisenhower partnership would continue to affect Western policy for three generations, from the end of the war to 9/11. Of all the partnerships of World War II (Roosevelt and Hopkins, Roosevelt and Churchill, Churchill and Brooke, Marshall and Roosevelt, and many others), the Marshall-Eisenhower partnership would prove so resilient and significant that it would outlast its authors. It would leave a strong mark on the shape of the postwar world.

IN THE wake of the North African victory, Eisenhower sat down to write of his experiences to his wife and his son. "Today I write you with a lighter heart than I have carried in many a moon," he said in his letter to Mamie. "As the papers tell you . . . we have just about completed the current job, and though my confidence has been so complete that I predicted this victory, long ago, to take place in the middle of May . . . the fact that it is all done lifts a big load from my mind. I only wish that it were the final battle of this war and that I could be catching the next plane home and [to] you!! But I'm afraid that happy day is a long way off."[12] He alluded to John's West Point experience in his next letter: "This phase of the job is all done except for the shouting and cleaning up," he wrote. "We have been through the plebe course and now have to catch our breath while we think of starting the yearling grind."[13] Eisenhower's words were lighthearted and reassuring. He broadly and purposely hinted that with North Africa won, he might be able to take a respite from the war. But in a letter written at the same time to George Marshall, Eisenhower was already planning for the next campaign.

Unfortunately, I always anticipate and discount, in my own mind, accomplishment of the several steps and am, therefore, mentally racing ahead into the next one. The consequence is that all the shouting about the Tunisian Campaign leaves me cold. I am so impatient and irritated because of the slowness with which the next phase can unfold, that I make myself quite unhappy. I am convinced that if I could undertake Husky today with only two divisions, I could gain a bridgehead and an advantage that would make the further conquest a very simple affair. Just as I suffered, almost physically, all during January, February and March while the enemy was fortifying his positions in Tunisia, so now I resent every day we have got to give him to perfect and strengthen Husky defenses. I have gotten so that my chief ambition in this war is finally to get to a place where the next operation does not have to be amphibious, with all the inflexibility and delay that are characteristic of such operations.[14]

George Marshall took little solace from Eisenhower's missive, for he too was already on to the next campaign and wrestling mightily with the same issues that preyed on his lieutenant's mind in Tunisia. On May 12, 1943, the same day that Arnim surrendered in Tunisia, the Trident Conference opened in Washington, attended by all of the British senior military and political figures who had been at Arcadia, back at the beginning of the war, and then at Casablanca.[15] From Marshall's perspective, the victory in North Africa, while welcome, had not resolved the British-American disagreement over the invasion of France.[16] He knew that the fight to answer the question "what next?" would be bitter and divisive, and that his primary nemeses in this coming battle would be the British prime minister and the always imperious Field Marshal Alan Brooke. For his part, Winston Churchill arrived fit and stubborn in Washington after a cross-ocean voyage on the *Queen Mary.* He made it clear that he was ready for battle by launching into a well-rehearsed monologue on the war in his first private meeting with Roosevelt. This was Churchill at his best—arguing and cajoling and joking, hoping that the simple force of his personality could win the day. He was now just as he had been at Arcadia.[17] Husky must go forward, Churchill said, and be followed immediately by the invasion of Italy. Italy's defeat would "cause a chill of loneliness [to settle] over the German people, and might be the beginning of their doom."[18] And an invasion of France, across the English Channel? Churchill shrugged: that might well come, he allowed, but only if it offered "a reasonable prospect of success."[19]

When Marshall heard of this he sputtered to his aides that he had no idea what Churchill was talking about, repeating the pledge the British had made that the North African campaign would be followed by the invasion of France.[20] Over the next week, the British and Americans replayed the endless wrangling that had characterized both of their prior wartime summits, but this time the Americans more capably pressed their case. Marshall and Roosevelt now worked as a team, and Marshall's staff was more prepared than it had been during previous meetings. Marshall was also now inclined to confront more bluntly the British Chiefs of Staff, to draw them out on whether, in making their arguments, they were more concerned with holding on to their colonies after the war than they were with actually *winning* the war. And for the first time during the conflict, Marshall refused to ignore Alan Brooke's pithy anti-Americanisms, his well-aimed barbs. "I find it hard even now not to look on your North Africa strategy with a jaundiced eye," Marshall told Brooke during one particularly bitter session. Brooke was unaffected: "What strategy would you have preferred?" he asked. Marshall leaned toward Brooke across the table separating them: "Cross channel operations for the liberation of France and an advance on Germany," he answered. "We would finish the war quicker." Brooke was nearly rude: "Yes," he said, "but not the way we hope to finish it."[21] He gave a slight laugh, but no one else did. Marshall held his temper but continued to make his point, this time with the backing of Roosevelt: the United States would press for an invasion of France at the earliest possible moment. We want to end this war, Marshall said, and the only way to do it is to invade France and defeat the Germans in Western Europe. Italy is a sideshow. Brooke snapped back officiously—no invasion of France is possible, he said, until 1945 at the earliest.

By May 14, the Trident talks had nearly broken down.[22] The British continued to insist on degrading German military capacity prior to any cross-Channel effort. Their argument was based on their view that an early invasion of France was no longer necessary to keep Russia in the war. Russia was winning—it had little need for a front in northwestern France. Conversely, they said, the cost of such an invasion could prove prohibitive.[23] The number of divisions training for the invasion in Britain had shrunk to thirty-seven, while German divisions in France remained constant, at fifty-two. Invading Italy, on the other hand, would accomplish what had been accomplished in North Africa; it would draw German troops out of Eastern Europe and would subvert German morale. With Italy out of the war, the Germans would be left alone, huddled in their burned-out cities, waiting for the end.[24] The British believed an invasion of Italy would keep Hitler off balance, while further divisions were readied in Britain for the "eventual" invasion of France.[25] And if the Americans disagreed, Brooke thought, he could always point out that the reason there were only thirty-seven divisions in Great Britain was because Marshall, in a fit of pique against Churchill for having won the North Africa debate, had actually diverted the troops he needed for an invasion of Europe to the Pacific.[26] The Pacific bluff, he implied, would no longer work. Marshall could divert all the forces he wanted from Europe. The British would still cut and slash at Hitler's soft underbelly. Marshall listened to Brooke, his jaws clenched: "It is taking all Marshall's tact and adroitness to steer the conference through to a result which will not be a surrender but which will not be an open clash," Secretary of War Stimson commented.[27]

Despite the acrimony of the most intensive Trident sessions, by the morning of May 19 a compromise strategy was beginning to take shape. The key to
an agreement lay in the numbers of men, tanks, ships, and aircraft now available to the Allies that had not been available during the previous Arcadia and
Casablanca conferences. What had seemed nearly impossible just eighteen
months before now seemed not only possible, but likely. At the beginning of
the war, Roosevelt had said that the United States would need to produce ten
thousand aircraft to defeat Germany and Japan. His prediction was dismissed
as a fantasy. But that goal had not only been met by mid-1943, it had been surpassed. Rifles, uniforms, aircraft, tanks, fighters, bombers, destroyers, submarines, aircraft carriers, air transports, and nearly every kind of munition were
now being produced in almost astounding numbers. Additionally, Allied troops
were being fed better and more often than their enemy; were shod, transported,
and deployed faster and more capably; and were cared for in hospitals closer
to the front than in any previous conflict. The Axis powers, on the other hand,
had lost almost 1.5 million soldiers in two campaigns thousands of miles apart.
And in the Pacific, America was engaged in a relentless two-pronged offensive
that would soon bring Japanese cities under the sights of America's newest
four-engine bombers. It was no longer a question of which would come first,
Europe or the Pacific. It was now possible to do both. Even the never ending
and nagging problem of landing craft, Roosevelt told Marshall, could be resolved.[28] All that needed to be done was to order a crash production program.
America's workers would respond. The numbers were compelling, and a great
help in narrowing the strategic differences between the British and the
Americans. Both sides retreated. The British agreed to move up the date for the
invasion of France to May 1, 1944, while the Americans conceded "the possibility of continued operations in the Mediterranean" after the fall of Sicily.[29]
Bolero—the buildup of Allied strength in Great Britain—would go forward,
as would Husky and the invasion of Italy. The invasion of France, now called
"Overlord," would take place in 1944, with nine divisions, two of them airborne. Germany and Italy would meanwhile be pummeled around the clock
from the air.

Churchill was not pleased with the final Trident agreement, however, and
considered reopening the most important issues for discussion. The prime minister felt the conference had not emphasized the British commitment to a
Mediterranean strategy, and he noted that the invasion of Italy was almost an

afterthought and never even mentioned in the final agreement.[30] He scoffed at his own chiefs of staff, including the beloved Brooke, who he believed had been outfoxed by Marshall. It was only through the intervention of Harry Hopkins that Churchill decided to shelve his disagreement.[31] But while remaining silent, Churchill refused to concede defeat. On his final night with Roosevelt, he proposed that he travel to Algiers to meet with Eisenhower to discuss the next steps in the Mediterranean. Marshall should accompany him, he said. If Eisenhower was required to "plan such operations" that were "best calculated to eliminate Italy from the war," Churchill told Roosevelt, then he needed to see Great Britain's prime minister and to hear the results of the Washington conference from one of its principals. Unsubtle as this might have been, Roosevelt agreed, though he knew that Churchill believed that if he could see Eisenhower and Marshall alone, he could make them see the wisdom of his views—and still win a postponement of the invasion of France. Marshall reluctantly agreed to go along with this charade, thinking that at the very least, his chaperoning Churchill would keep him from exercising his wiles on Eisenhower. Marshall had wanted to travel to the Pacific to talk about war strategy with MacArthur and Nimitz, but Churchill was adamant: "I cannot let the matter rest where it is," he said. Secretary of War Henry Stimson was irritated by Churchill's request. The matter was decided, the conference paper was agreed to, and Marshall was needed to straighten out yet another Pacific dustup: "To think of picking out the strongest man there is in America, and Marshall is sure that today, the one on whom the fate of the war depends, and then to deprive him in a gamble of a much needed opportunity to recoup his strength and send him off on a difficult and rather dangerous trip across the Atlantic Ocean where he is not needed except for Churchill's purposes is I think going pretty far," he said.[32]

Dwight Eisenhower learned of the Marshall-Churchill visit only after being told of Marshall's imminent arrival by the ever watchful Beetle Smith, who had represented Eisenhower in Washington during Trident.[33] Marshall had remained silent on Trident's outcome, communicating with his chief lieutenant on only minor matters during the conference itself. Eisenhower's plan was to collar Marshall when the chief of staff landed with Churchill in Algiers to get an early report on Trident, but when the Marshall-Churchill party arrived on May 28, it was Churchill who did the collaring. Grabbing Eisenhower, he ushered him alone into a nearby limousine, plying him with compliments on his handling of the Tunisia campaign and pressing him to use his forces to jump the Straits of Messina into Italy once he had conquered Sicily.[34] Eisenhower was in the dark. Churchill's plan seemed like a good idea, particularly for a commander who had had to attend interminable staff meetings on Husky for nearly two months, two months that allowed the Germans to build up their forces in Sicily. Impatient, irritable, and angered by the long delays occasioned by the slow shipment of landing craft to North Africa, Eisenhower was prepared to give Churchill the benefit of the doubt. Churchill's limousine conference with Eisenhower was only the beginning, however. After arriving at the villa set aside for him outside of Algiers, Churchill, Eisenhower, Marshall, Ismay, and Brooke were led by Churchill to Eisenhower's porch, where the prime minister held forth to his bleary-eyed listeners on his post-Sicily strategy, his plan to discomfit "Herr Hitler."[35]

The next morning, Marshall was determined to keep his eye on Churchill, carefully monitoring the truculent prime minister's flirtations with his lieutenant.[36] Marshall had good reason to worry. Eisenhower's knowledge of the acerbic exchanges in Washington was incomplete, and Marshall knew that when Churchill turned on the charm he was nearly irresistible. The day passed uneventfully, however, as Eisenhower began to sense that Marshall's silence on the Italy venture signaled more than simple uncertainty. So Eisenhower remained coy, listening carefully to Churchill and nodding his understanding, though not his agreement. By now Churchill's strategy was no longer a secret, as he announced to Eisenhower that he had traveled to Algiers precisely because he had been unable to convince Roosevelt and Marshall that a full invasion of Italy should immediately follow Sicily's conquest. Churchill even admitted that the just concluded Washington meetings had determined that an invasion of Italy was only a "possibility." Still, Churchill insisted to Eisenhower, the Allies should "pursue the campaign in the Mediterranean, until the Italians are out of the war."[37] If sheer tenacity could win an argument, then Churchill would have won. "He makes no bones of his point of view," Harry Butcher confided, "and apparently regards the decision already taken [at Trident] as quite open to review and change. . . . The PM recited his story three different times in three different ways. . . . He talks persistently until he has worn down the last shred of opposition."[38]

Inevitably, Eisenhower fell into Churchill's trap. Or so it seemed. On the third day of the Churchill visit, during an informal midmorning conference at his villa, Eisenhower briefed his visitors on his plan for Husky, treating them to trays of food and coffee.[39] Churchill's cigar smoke filled the room as he, Marshall, Ismay, Brooke, and Eisenhower's senior staff and commanders for North Africa listened intently to Eisenhower's plan. The British would take the lead, Eisenhower said, with Bernard Law Montgomery commanding the invasion force. Churchill nodded his understanding but then plunged ahead, reopening his bid to convince Eisenhower that a full invasion of Italy should follow Sicily's fall. After showing little interest in his previous meetings with Churchill, Eisenhower was suddenly enthusiastic: if the invasion of Sicily went off without too much trouble, he said, then it would be quite possible to "go directly into Italy."[40] He went even further, saying that it was possible that by taking Italy out of the war, a cross-Channel invasion would be "a drop in the bucket." Churchill, pleased by Eisenhower's enthusiasm, was suddenly reassuring. He was not opposed to a cross-Channel invasion, he said. In fact, "the British people and the British army" were anxious to take on the Germans.[41] Marshall betrayed little surprise at Eisenhower's sudden enthusiasm, because he calculated that the Sicily invasion would not be as easy as Churchill supposed and that, in the end, his insistence that seven divisions be transferred to England six months after Husky was a part of the Trident agreement. Unlike an invasion of Italy, Overlord was confirmed in writing.

That Marshall and Eisenhower might have conspired to reassure the prime minister of their interest in Italy while agreeing that the cross-channel invasion must be a priority is likely. The two were as close now as they had been during Marshall's previous visit, with Eisenhower putting Marshall in his own larger bedroom in the villa and making certain the chief of staff was given a full tour of American units and briefed by all of Eisenhower's major commanders. Marshall was pleased by what he saw. American troops were disciplined, focused, and well trained; the chaos he had perceived in the rear areas during his previous visit was nowhere to be found. Patton and Bradley had done a magnificent job, and now, with Clark in Morocco, the Algiers headquarters was humming with activity. Morale was high.[42] Marshall talked with Butcher about

Eisenhower's health and inquired after Telek. "General Marshall has taken Ike's room again," Butcher wrote, "this time with only a mild protest. He has inquired as to the welfare and manners of Telek. I have informed him that Telek is about to become a father but is bearing up well. The General seems pleased that Ike has at least partly followed his instructions on care and refreshment of the human mind."[43]

British general Bernard Law Montgomery and British foreign minister Anthony Eden arrived in Algiers and on the afternoon of June 2, Montgomery briefed Marshall, Eisenhower, Churchill, and British and American senior commanders in Algiers on his plans for Husky.[44] Montgomery's staccato-voiced briefing was long and detailed, punctuated by the slap of his pointer on an easel-mounted map. Montgomery focused on Churchill, who interrupted him several times to ask questions. Marshall listened carefully, eyed from across the room by the wily Brooke. It was clear that Marshall did not like Montgomery and was put off by his attitude, dress, and easy confidence. Montgomery was oblivious, believing the briefing another in a string of triumphs.[45] Eisenhower did not like Montgomery any more than Marshall did, but he appreciated his strategic sense and admired his combat experience. The son of an Anglican priest dominated by an overbearing wife, Montgomery fled his home, graduated from Sandhurst, and was promptly wounded in the Great War. Shot through the lung and pronounced dead, he was thereafter convinced of his special place in British history.[46] Messianic, blessed by the star of combat in the Great War, Montgomery viewed himself the savior not just of the feckless Americans, but of King and Country—and Churchill. He treated everyone in Algiers, including the prime minister, the same: poorly.

While Montgomery's climb through the ranks was by no means meteoric, he found a patron in Brooke, who admired his ability to make believers of simple soldiers. His transformation of the Eighth Army in Egypt was legendary, as was his obsessive focus on writing detailed plans. Still, Montgomery seemed capable of swaggering while standing still, and his abrasive personality made enemies of his colleagues. Churchill had great confidence in him but found him overbearing. Montgomery seemed blithely unaware of this except, of course, when he ran into a commander who held his future in his hands. "I know well that I am regarded by many people as being a tiresome person. I think this is probably true," he had written to Eisenhower during the final days of the drive on Tunis. "I try hard not to be tiresome; but I have seen so many mistakes made in this war, and so many disasters happen, that I am desperately anxious to try to see that we have no more; and this often means being tiresome."[47] Montgomery was tiresome now, and boorish, explaining to Marshall and Eisenhower why the plan for Husky would succeed, as it ignored the ideas put forward by American senior commanders—a plan which, he said, reflected their "woolly thinking" about how infantry should be handled.[48] Not surprisingly, the plan that Montgomery presented on June 2 gave his own army a prominent role. Marshall remained purposely silent while, across the table, Brooke concluded that his student had unnecessarily made an enemy. His was a damning judgment. "He requires a lot of educating to make him see the whole situation and the war as a whole outside the Eighth Army orbit," Brooke wrote of Montgomery in the wake of the June 2 conference. "A difficult mixture to handle, brilliant commander in action and trainer of men, but liable to commit untold errors, due to lack of tact, lack of appreciation of other people's outlook. It is most distressing that the Americans do not like him, and it will always be difficult matter to have him fighting in close proximity to them."[49] Brooke was right—though he somehow failed to see Montgomery's weaknesses as resembling to no small degree his own.

In spite of his misgivings and his chief's clear distaste for the British commander, Eisenhower hesitantly approved Montgomery's plan for Husky. Churchill was thrilled. The end of the Montgomery briefing, and Marshall and Eisenhower's easy nodding agreement with everything that he had said, convinced the prime minister that the conquest of Sicily would be immediately followed by Eisenhower's commitment to knocking Italy out of the war. Overlord would be postponed, Germany would be pummeled from the air, and British soldiers would be saved from the awful consequences of a French invasion. The Somme and Marne would stay where they belonged, firmly if painfully in the past. Most important, Winston Churchill's strategy of pecking away at the Third Reich would be vindicated. Of course, Marshall and Eisenhower knew better; they had made no such commitment, but had only nodded their understanding of Churchill's viewpoint. "He [Marshall] is not opposed to the invasion of Italy now," Churchill crowed to his doctor, Lord Moran, at the end of the Algiers meeting. The ever skeptical Moran knew otherwise. Like Montgomery, he reflected, "Winston is so taken up with his own ideas that he is not interested in what other people think."[50] Marshall was loath to break Churchill's fantasy, and ended his visit with the prime minister by praising Allied cooperation. The real victory in Tunisia, he said, came from the sure knowledge that the Germans now understood that "the United States and Great Britain worked so well as a team."[51]

Marshall ended his visit with Eisenhower by meeting with the press—a briefing in which he intended to exude confidence and give proper praise to his commander and his colleagues. But the chief of staff must certainly have calculated that with Eisenhower's team looking on, he could draw stark differences between the manner in which an American commander gave a briefing and the way a man like General Bernard Law Montgomery did. It was a vintage Marshall performance; like Eisenhower he entered the room without notes and turned to the assembled group, giving focused attention to each questioner. His ability to command respect was on full display. "To save time," he said, "I'm going to ask each of you what questions you have in mind." And so, one by one, each of the thirty-plus reporters asked a question and waited until all had had their say. Marshall listened on in silence, nodding slightly from time to time, and then after only a moment's hesitation began to speak. He then talked in detail about the war, pointedly looking at a different reporter during each segment of his talk, until he finished—forty minutes later. It was a tour de force, what one reporter described as "a smooth, connected, brilliantly clear narrative that encompassed" all of the questions he was asked. The reporters were stunned not simply by Marshall's memory, for he seemed to have covered all of the questions he had been asked, but by his grasp of the war's details. Marshall's command of the subject was, in fact, uncanny: he could cite, in the same conversation, the numbers of marines deployed on Guadalcanal, the numbers of bombers lost over New Guinea, the problems associated with producing landing craft, the tactics employed by Russian commanders at Stalingrad, and the command experience of Hans Jürgen von Arnim.[52] Just two days later, Marshall was on his way home, aboard a C-54. His final round of meetings with Eisenhower and Churchill had gone as he had expected, and Marshall was pleased. His plan to transfer seven divisions from the Mediterranean to Britain to begin training for the invasion of France was now fully accepted. An invasion of Italy might tie up German troops, might take Italy out of the war, might so damage German morale that Hitler would be replaced, but in the meantime, the main focus would remain on France and, more immediately, on Sicily.

IN LATE April 1943, the body of a British officer, "Major Martin" of the Royal Marines, washed up on the east coast of Spain. Spanish intelligence officers quickly checked Martin's papers and pried open the briefcase that had been chained to his wrist. They concluded that Martin was an intelligence courier, that he had been in an aerial accident off Spain's coast, that he had drowned, and that the paper they found in his briefcase contained top secret instructions. The neatly folded paper, they determined, was actually a letter from the Foreign Office to General Harold Alexander outlining Allied strategic plans in the Mediterranean. The Spanish authorities passed the briefcase on to German intelligence officers in Madrid; the Germans read the letter with interest, then refolded it carefully, placed it back in the briefcase, and returned the briefcase to the Spanish. Spanish authorities then returned Martin's body, along with the briefcase, to the British. British intelligence officers minutely studied Martin's body, the briefcase, and the refolded note, and determined that their ruse (which included dispatching a submarine to deposit Martin's body in the ocean on Spain's eastern coast) had worked; the Germans now believed that Martin, who was really a British soldier who had died from pneumonia, was carrying papers laying out the Allied strategic plan to bypass both Sicily and Italy and invade Sardinia and Greece. On May 12, the British intercepted German coded messages directing their Greek and Sardinian commanders to take extra measures to bolster their defenses.[53]

On July 10, 180,000 American, British, and Canadian troops came ashore on the southern coast of Sicily.[54] The landings had been preceded by an airborne invasion intended to knock out coastal defenses and seize important transport areas near Syracuse.[55] The airborne assault was a disaster, with gliders and transports blown badly off course, scattering thousands of American and British soldiers over a wide area of southern Sicily. The American and British landings were much better, even though the 1st Infantry Division, landing at Gela, was forced to fight for two days against the relentless attacks of the well-trained and well-armed Hermann Göring Division, an elite veteran unit named for the German Luftwaffe commander. In spite of this, Allied intelligence officers concluded that their Major Martin operation had succeeded. The Germans were unprepared for the Allied invasion and had only 60,000 troops deployed on the island. The Sicilian invasion was spearheaded by Montgomery's Eighth Army, with Patton's Seventh Army shielding its left, in a subordinate role, protecting Montgomery's drive to the north. The planning for the invasion had left its scars on the Allied command. Patton believed he was being slighted by Eisenhower, who was once again bending over backward to satisfy the British and the loathed Montgomery. "The U.S. is getting gypped," Patton confided to his diary when he learned that Montgomery was to lead the primary assault. ". . . Churchill is running this war. . . . The U.S. must win—not as any ally, but as a conqueror."[56] His bitterness extended even to his old friend. "This is what you get when your Commander-in-Chief ceases to be an American and becomes an ally," he wrote in his diary.[57]

Inevitably, perhaps, Eisenhower and Patton clashed. On the night of July 11, transports carrying elements of the 504th Parachute Regiment of the 101st Airborne Division were shot to pieces by Allied naval antiaircraft gunners, who mistook the aircraft for airborne troopships ferrying German reinforcements. The 504th lost sixty pilots and crewmen and eighty-one paratroopers to friendly fire. Allied commanders immediately engaged in a round of finger-pointing, blaming the Navy, the paratroopers, Army planners, and Patton for the tragedy. Eisenhower, who knew that such mistakes endangered plans for the increased use of airborne troops in future operations, was enraged. He sent Patton a shrill cable demanding that he discipline those responsible.[58] While the fault for the mistake did not lie with the Americans, but with the sloppy coordination of Field Marshal Sir Harold Alexander's staff, Patton began an investigation. The next morning, July 12, Eisenhower saw Patton aboard his command ship, the *Monrovia*, and subjected him to a vicious and relentless tongue-lashing, telling him he was not satisfied with his reports on the incident. "Ike . . . stepped on him hard," Harry Butcher noted. "There was an air of tenseness. I had a feeling that Ike was disappointed. He said previously that he would be happy if after about five days from D-Day, General Bradley were to take over because of his calm and matter-of-fact direction."[59] Patton placidy accepted Eisenhower's rebuke, promised to get to the bottom of the incident, and then reported on his own command's progress. But underneath, he bitterly resented Eisenhower's rebuke.

Patton's resentment of Eisenhower mirrored a much deeper problem. Despite their mutual success in North Africa, the planning for Sicily seemed to reflect deepening divisions between British and American commanders. The casualties of the 504th symbolically mirrored these problems. Known for his eye for detail, Field Marshal Sir Harold Alexander, in overall command of the invasion, became unusually quiescent, reinforcing his staff's belief that at odd and usually inappropriate times, their commander simply lost his grip—went dead silent and seemed strangely indifferent to the course of the battle. Faced with battle reports and climbing casualties, Alexander seemed only to feign interest while emitting a slow and barely audible "hmm." This lack of interest had extended to Husky's planning. Despite the pleadings of his staff, Alexander had allowed Patton and Montgomery to plan two separate campaigns. Worse yet, Alexander refused to fill his traditional role as Montgomery's strategic conscience, guiding his dispositions and often not so gently arguing against his more outlandish proposals.[60] Alexander also simply refused to credit the Americans with any military prowess, once again letting slide, and often reinforcing, critical comments from senior British commanders on America's soldierly abilities. The effects of Alexander's strange detachment could be seen on the ground, where American and British forces slugged it out with German and Italian divisions without any apparent coordination, and with predictable results.

On the night of July 13, Montgomery's airborne troops assaulted a key bridge on the Plain of Catania, hoping that a quick strike would free British tanks for a triumphant and speedy move north toward Messina, along Sicily's eastern coast. But British intelligence had badly underestimated the bridge's defense and Montgomery's troops were bogged down for five days of brutal fighting. Frustrated by his lack of movement, Montgomery split his forces, a classic military mistake, hoping thereby to encircle German defenders entrenched below Mount Etna.[61] As Montgomery's Eighth Army maneuvered to carry out these orders, the German corps commander, General der Panzertruppen Hans Valentin Hube, reinforced his position and launched well-aimed delaying tactics that kept Montgomery's forces pinned to the series of ridgelines that led to Messina. Fearful that Montgomery's Eighth Army was in danger, Alexander agreed to his request that Patton's forces cede control of a key road that formed the boundary between the two armies—even though that meant that Patton would have to withdraw the American 45th Division to new positions farther south: a planned retreat over ground that American soldiers had bled to take. Bradley was stunned by Alexander's order. "My God," he yelled at Patton, "you can't let him do that."[62]

But Patton could let him do that—and did. The resulting retreat was nearly catastrophic, for it allowed the German XIV Panzer Corps to move south along roads recently vacated by the Americans and take up new and stronger positions. More careful than Patton, who showed his anger more publicly, Bradley considered appealing Alexander's decision. But that meant going over the head of Patton. For a professional soldier like Bradley, schooled in West Point's catechism of never subverting the chain of command, appealing over the head of Patton was unthinkable. So Bradley, his chin set, his eyes barely masking his anger, ordered the 45th Division into a new position. "We were ready to strike for Messina, the only real strategic prize on Sicily," he later wrote. "Now Monty would deny us that role, relegating us (as in southern Tunisia) to the demeaning and inconsequential task of protecting Eighth Army's flank and rear. Would George Patton sit still for such an outrageous decision?"[63] The question was rhetorical. In the wake of the airborne fiasco that had left the 504th Regiment badly crippled, Patton feared that if he pressed too hard, Eisenhower would relieve him. He was in no position to disagree with Alexander and he knew it.

But Patton's silent acceptance of Alexander's orders did not mean that he would sit still while Montgomery gained all the plaudits for conquering Sicily. On July 17, with Montgomery's forces pinned down in the east, Patton ordered II Corps to strike for Sicily's northern coast while the rest of the Seventh Army struck west, to clean up pockets of German resistance that might interfere with II Corps' march.[64] The purpose of the move was to take pressure off Montgomery from the north, allowing him to pierce the German lines around Mount Etna. In fact, Patton had no intention of ordering II Corps north; rather, he faced it northeast, on the road to Messina, believing that if he captured the city German resistance would end. He pushed his troops pitilessly, at times appearing in the front lines to help artillery commanders sight their guns. On July 21, Patton's armored spearheads liberated Palermo, then struck off on the road to Messina. Four days later, with his troops pressing eastward, Patton met with Alexander and Montgomery, and the three agreed to confirm what was already an established fact: Patton's II Corps would press on to Messina while Montgomery's Eighth Army continued to slug it out on the coast.[65] By early

August, Patton's armored spearheads were making steady progress along the north coast and closing in on Messina.[66]

The German defense of northern Sicily was sophisticated and well organized. The Axis commanders were nearly unmovable; they defended every ridgeline and gully, and exacted as many Allied casualties as possible. Allied tactics, on the other hand, were almost criminally unimaginative. Again and again, Patton and Montgomery sent their soldiers straight ahead in futile attempts to dislodge the Germans and Italians. To compound this disaster, the Allied commanders failed to seal off Sicily's northern reaches, giving German commanders the opportunity to organize a withdrawal of their forces to Italy.[67] Perhaps appropriately, particularly considering the poor planning and nearly nonexistent cooperation between the British and the Americans, the Allies missed an opportunity to bag tens of thousands of German prisoners. On the night of August 15, and for the two nights that followed, fifty-five thousand German soldiers escaped nearly unscathed to Italy, along with their ammunition and transports. The German's retreat epitomized their newfound abilities to fight while backing up.[68] While the days of panzer blitzkriegs were over, in the months ahead German forces were to prove tenacious defenders of Italian soil, using the fifty-five thousand soldiers who had escaped from Messina to exact a bloody penalty on British, Canadian, and American troops.[69]

The good news of the Sicily campaign arrived, finally, on the morning of July 26. The night before, Eisenhower learned, the Fascist Grand Council had placed Benito Mussolini under arrest.[70] Eisenhower quickly issued a "Message from the Allied Headquarters to the Italian People" praising the Italian people and urging them to expel their German allies. "We are coming to you as liberators," Eisenhower said. "Your part is to cease immediately any assistance to the German military forces in your country."[71] In Washington, Marshall scrambled to scrap Allied plans for the bombing of the Rome rail yards as a prelude to a general air offensive against the Italian and German troops. The bombing was intended to cut Rome off from the south, interdicting German reinforcements headed to the battlefields of Sicily.[72] It now seemed to both Marshall and Eisenhower that a quick end to the war in the Mediterranean was possible, giving Churchill the victory in Italy that he had long desired. But neither Marshall nor Eisenhower was yet ready to make a full commitment to an invasion of Italy. With the fall of Mussolini, Marshall went forward with his plan for the transfer of seven American and British divisions to England,[73] even though the German military moved quickly to take control of Rome and Italian military installations—and even as thousands of German soldiers, having faced Montgomery and Patton in Sicily, took control of southern Italy.

Studying the situation in the Mediterranean from his new headquarters on Malta, Eisenhower seethed over the minor and major catastrophes of Husky. It seemed nothing had gone right; from the first day of the invasion to Patton's entrance into Messina, the high command that he had spent so much time solidifying seemed at times on the edge of collapse. He raged at Patton and Bradley, sent exasperated messages to Montgomery, wondered at Alexander's odd detachment. But Ike remained oddly calm in his written reports, both to the Combined Chiefs of Staff in London and to Marshall. "Patton is doing well and, so far as I can determine, all the troops are handling themselves satisfactorily," he wrote the Army chief of staff on July 17. While he confirmed the steep loss in the 504th Parachute Regiment and conceded that "even in the daytime we have great trouble in preventing our own naval and land forces from firing on friend planes,"[74] Eisenhower continued to soft-pedal the difficulties of the campaign, even as German resistance stiffened. "The German defenses below Catania remain intact today, but I hope that we will have them knocked out shortly," he wrote on July 20. Marshall was certainly aware of Eisenhower's difficulties, as he constantly reviewed battle reports as they became available, but it was his habit to ignore the day-to-day obstacles faced by his ground commanders, believing (and this seemed especially true of Eisenhower) that they were "generally familiar" with his views. Later events would show that Marshall intervened only when he felt he had no choice. In Sicily, despite the problems, he felt sure that Eisenhower would take matters in hand.

On the morning of August 17, elements of Patton's 3rd Division marched into Messina. The city center was empty of German troops. The Allies could now celebrate another victory. Yet the triumphant parade that followed ("a goddamned waste of time," Patton fumed) was hollow.[75] The cost of conquering Sicily had been high, its lessons grim. The Allies had won, but only by carpeting their enemies with iron; Montgomery's tactics were uninspired and bloody. So were Patton's. The Allies had landed over five hundred thousand troops in Sicily, where they faced sixty thousand Germans. Eisenhower understood the failures of Sicily, for they were evident from the battlefield reports. Montgomery was too cautious, Patton too impetuous, Alexander too quiescent, Bradley too critical. Eisenhower had left the planning and conduct of the campaign to Alexander. He now understood that that had been a mistake. He had permitted his subordinates to plan the invasion, to decide on deployments, to pull and push the levers of command, to make fateful decisions on the ground, to compete for glory—to allow the battle to run itself. In any campaign where German forces were evenly matched against the Allies, such blunders would have proven costly, even decisive. In Washington, George Marshall surveyed the wreckage of Husky and concluded that the only way that he could help Eisenhower was to refocus Allied efforts by doing battle with the Germans in France. And the only way to do that was to do battle with the British. He wanted a showdown. "The allocation of additional forces to the Mediterranean is uneconomical and assists Germany to create a strategic stalemate in Europe," he wrote in preparation for yet another Allied summit.[76] It was time for a decisive effort against the Third Reich. Eisenhower would have agreed, but wondered whether, in light of the problems encountered in Sicily, his senior commanders would choose to settle their own battles in order to more effectively fight the Germans. Then too, Eisenhower was grimly aware that the Sicily campaign had been botched at the top: he had been in command, but he had not been in control. But there was worse to come.

ON THE morning of August 17, Dwight Eisenhower had his blood pressure checked by Brigadier General Frederic A. Blesse, the chief surgeon at Allied headquarters in Algiers. This was a part of Eisenhower's regular medical routine, and he was pleased by the results. While he was tired and overworked, Blesse told him, his blood pressure had fallen from his previous visit. That was good news and somewhat surprising, as Eisenhower was under continual stress and still consuming three packs of cigarettes a day. Blesse and Eisenhower were cordial and had come to know each other well. With this friendship in mind, during the checkup Blesse told Eisenhower that he had received disturbing information on the behavior of George Patton.[77] As Eisenhower listened silently, Blesse recounted that he had heard that Patton was vulnerable to disciplinary action, including a general court-martial, after striking two soldiers during a visit Patton had made to a number of hospitals in Sicily. Eisenhower was surprised and disturbed by this report and asked Blesse what he knew of the incidents. Blesse told Eisenhower that the first incident occurred when Patton made a scheduled visit to the 15th Evacuation Hospital on August 4, in the midst of the fight for Sicily. Visiting the wounded was a routine that Patton found emotional and trying, but that he considered his duty. During his visit, Blesse said, Patton spoke with infantryman Charles H. Kuhl, a soldier of the 1st Division. Patton stopped at Kuhl's bed and, apparently puzzled by his apparent physical well-being, inquired about his injuries. Kuhl was overwrought. He sank his head in his hands and responded: "I just can't take it, sir." Blesse told Eisenhower that when Patton heard this he flew into a rage, called Kuhl a coward, grabbed him by the scruff of his neck, and shouted to a nearby doctor. "Don't admit this sonofabitch." He stared down at Kuhl, his lips quivering, his face red: "You hear me, you gutless bastard? You're going back to the front at once."[78] Patton literally kicked him in the pants and dragged him out of the tent.

In fact, as Eisenhower later determined, Patton had been involved in three such incidents. On August 10, Patton visited the 93rd Evacuation Hospital and noted the visit in his diary. "At another evacuation hospital . . . saw another alleged nervous patient—really a coward," he wrote. "I told the doctor to return him to his company and he began to cry, so I cursed him well and he shut up. I may have saved his soul, if he had one."[79] Later, when Patton went down a line of cots he came upon a soldier from an artillery regiment that had seen some of the hardest fighting. The soldier was shivering. Patton asked him why he was in the hospital. "It's my nerves," the soldier responded. Once again, in a rage, Patton screamed at the soldier. "Your nerves, hell; you're just a goddamned coward you yellow son of a bitch." Patton's words tumbled out in a torrent: "You're a disgrace to the Army and you're going back to the front to fight," he screamed, "although that's too good for you. You ought to be lined up against a wall and shot. In fact, I ought to shoot you myself right now, goddamn you." Patton reached for his pistol, waved it in the soldier's face, then slapped him. Patton shouted at a nearby officer: "I want you to get this man out of here right away. I won't have these other brave boys seeing such a bastard babied."[80]

While Eisenhower hoped the incidents would go away, he did not underestimate their impact. After hearing Blesse's report he ordered the doctor to Sicily to investigate the charges against Patton, fortifying him with a letter to the general that censured his actions: "I clearly understand that firm and drastic measures were at times necessary to secure the desired objectives," he wrote. "But this does not excuse brutality, abuse of the sick, nor exhibition of uncontrollable temper in front of subordinates." He saved his harshest criticism for the letter's end, telling Patton that his job was now in danger. "I must so seriously question your good judgment and your self-discipline, as to raise serious doubts in my mind as to your future usefulness."[81] This sounded like Bradley. If Patton could not command himself, how could he ever hope to command others? Eisenhower ordered Patton to apologize to the soldiers he had slapped and to the hospital staff and headquarters staff who had been present, and to cooperate in an investigation of the incident.

Even before he received Eisenhower's letter, Patton acted quickly to head off any controversy. After Blesse's visit he doubled his efforts. He was worried that he had caused Eisenhower problems and wrote in his diary that he intended to make amends. Patton even went so far as to apologize to one of the soldiers on his own. He called the nurses and doctors of one of the evacuation hospitals into his office and told them that he had had a friend in World War I who thought he was a coward and committed suicide. Then, after receiving Eisenhower's warning, Patton made a number of speeches before various units and attempted to explain his actions to the First Army, a unit of eighteen thousand soldiers.[82] But Patton was required to go even further. Leaving nothing to chance, Eisenhower dispatched Major General John Porter Lucas, an old Patton friend, to Sicily to talk with the general. Lucas met Patton at the Palermo airfield and had a quiet but stern exchange with him. Eisenhower was disappointed by Patton, Lucas said, and insisted that he apologize personally to every division in the Seventh Army. Patton agreed, though suddenly realizing that even this might not be enough. If the incidents appeared in the press, Eisenhower might be forced to relieve him. Patton, now thoroughly frightened by the ramifications of what he had done, wrote Eisenhower an apology: "I am at a loss to find words with which to express my chagrin and grief at having given you, a man to whom I owe everything and for whom I would gladly lay down my life, cause to be displeased with me."[83]

In Algiers, Eisenhower was "sweating it out," as Butcher described it—attempting to get through the crisis without having to relieve his best tank fighter.[84] At the same time, he pleaded with a group of reporters who knew of the incidents to keep their reports on Patton out of the press. The last thing the U.S. needed, he told them, was to lose a fighter like Patton. The reporters reluctantly agreed and buried their stories. "Ike is deeply concerned and has scarcely slept for several nights, trying to figure out the wisest method of handling this dilemma," Butcher wrote at the time. "The United Nations have not developed another battle leader as successful as Patton, Ike thinks, yet he had to consider the very real possibility that he might be obliged to court-martial his old friend."[85] Eisenhower struggled to find the best way to inform Marshall about Patton, while not so disturbing him that it became his, and not Eisenhower's, problem. Eisenhower likely feared that Marshall would simply direct him to relieve Patton, if for no other reason than to head off any political problems the slapping incidents might cause. On August 24, Eisenhower penned a short letter to Marshall assessing U.S. combat leadership. The letter must have struck Marshall as strange, as most of it was taken up with praise for Patton. Eisenhower's telltale sign-off was also a hint that there was more to the letter than a commander's assessment. Of all the letters written by Eisenhower to Marshall during the war, Eisenhower's missive of August 24 seems the most puzzling, the most out of character. Certainly Marshall already knew about the leadership qualities of the commanders that Eisenhower mentioned. So why write about them now? Referring to Patton, Eisenhower wrote that he "has conducted a campaign where the brilliant successes scored must be attributed directly to his energy, determination and aggressiveness."[86]

Eisenhower's praise for Patton was effusive, but laced with caution. In one passage, Eisenhower indirectly alluded to the slapping incidents in Sicily, but without giving Marshall any details. "Now in spite of all this—George Patton continues to exhibit some of those unfortunately personal traits of which you and I have always known and which during this campaign caused me some most uncomfortable days," Eisenhower wrote. "His habit of impulsive bawling out of subordinates, extending even to personal abuse of individuals, was noted in at least two specific cases. I have had to take the most drastic steps; and if he is not cured now there is no hope for him. Personally, I believe that he is cured . . ."[87] This was a strange construction, Eisenhower's way of telling Marshall about Patton, but without really telling him. Eisenhower completed his letter with two other effusive assessments, of Omar Bradley and Mark Clark. But these assessments were sidelights, even afterthoughts, to his extended Patton narrative. Eisenhower finished the letter with an almost apologetic note: "I hope this letter does not strike you as being just a waste of time, I felt that you might like to have some of my thoughts concerned these things." Marshall did not respond to the letter immediately but used it to determine the command structure for Overlord, vaulting Bradley forward to major general. Marshall responded to Eisenhower by ignoring his Patton assessment and remaining silent on both Patton and Clark: "Thanks for your generous attitude regarding Bradley," he wrote, and then turned his attention to more pressing matters. But Marshall remembered Eisenhower's letter on Patton later, when Drew Pearson learned of the slapping incidents and reported them in his syndicated column. Marshall asked Eisenhower for all the details on the incident. Eisenhower responded and included an account of the steps he had taken to discipline Patton.

If Marshall was disappointed in Eisenhower's inability to be blunt, for trying to gloss over the incidents while cloaking them in an unnecessary command assessment, he did not show it. Marshall directed Eisenhower to provide him with as many details on the incidents as possible in order to head off a congressional investigation that could end Patton's career. Eisenhower's detailed account of the steps he had taken as Patton's commander was therefore quite welcome: it was the one way that Marshall could show that the Army had taken the steps necessary to discipline one of its own. Marshall also recruited Secretary of War Henry Stimson to reinforce this message. Stimson reviewed the incidents and the Eisenhower correspondence and wrote to Senator Robert R. Reynolds, the chair of the Military Affairs Committee, telling him that the incident was serious, that the Army was not underestimating its impact, that Patton had made amends, but that retaining Patton was essential to the war effort. This would become obvious, he said, in time. Stimson concluded that he hoped that Reynolds would postpone any action out of "national security necessity."[88] The secretary of war's plea was apparently convincing; Reynolds dropped the matter. Patton followed these events closely, deeply worried that he had irreparably harmed his reputation. He was unaware of Eisenhower's defense of his record and efforts to retain him in command. In the end, Eisenhower could excuse the fact that he had not informed Marshall by pleading that as the supreme Allied commander in the Mediterranean it was his decision to make. Still, Eisenhower may well have feared that Marshall's wrath about the incident would have removed Patton from his command. Patton was a fighter, and his old friend Ike needed him. So too did Marshall.

9

AVALANCHE

". . . You give the enemy too much time to prepare. . . ."
"I feel certain that some . . . look upon me as a gambler. . . ."

I
N AUGUST 1943, Franklin Roosevelt, Winston Churchill, and the
Combined Chiefs of Staff met in Quebec to chart the next steps in the war
in Europe and the Pacific. The Quadrant Conference, as it was called, was held
in Quebec's La Citadelle, an old British fortress that had once guarded the approaches to the city.[1] The meeting place seemed to symbolize Churchill and
Roosevelt's commitment to engage the world against Fascism. Tens of thousands
of Canadians and hundreds of thousands of Australians, New Zealanders,
Indians, Poles, and Filipinos (as well as thousands of other soldiers, sailors, and
airmen of the "United Nations") had joined with the Americans, British, and
Free French in fighting in Europe and the Pacific. The sheer weight of the
forces now arrayed against Hitler and Hirohito seemed to spell the eventual end
of the Axis. It had not been two years since the Japanese attack on Pearl Harbor,
but already the tide in the war had turned. The Red Army was moving inexorably toward Poland and the Balkans, and the United States was in the midst
of its island-hopping campaign in the central Pacific. Mussolini had been overthrown, and Italy's official capitulation seemed imminent.

Quadrant was vitally important for George Marshall, as it seemed likely
that he would finally have his way, reinforcing his preeminence as the war's

most important senior officer. Then too, Franklin Roosevelt was now firmly on his side in arguing for the invasion of France. Overlord, the president had decided, should take precedence over any other campaign.[2] As Marshall knew, Great Britain's opposition to Overlord now rested on shaky foundations—that Germany could somehow be defeated from the air, that its forces could be fatally degraded by attacks in the Mediterranean or the Balkans, that pinpricks at its periphery would spell an end to Hitler's Reich. Still, Marshall was inclined to give the British something; the Allies could continue operations against Italy so long as they did not detract from the Allied commitment to an invasion in France in 1944 and so long as the transfer of divisions from the Mediterranean to England went forward as planned and agreed to at Casablanca.[3] The month before the Combined Chiefs met in Quebec, therefore, Marshall conceded that an invasion of Italy would not hinder Allied operations in France and directed Eisenhower to begin planning for a landing of Allied troops at Salerno, near Naples.[4] Eisenhower's planning staff went to work on the operation on August 10, and soon thereafter Eisenhower reported to Marshall that he had some forty-eight divisions of American, British, Canadian, Indian, New Zealander, and Australian troops available for the central Italian front.[5]

Marshall arrived in Quebec triply armed: with his staff's recommendation that it was now time to carry out an invasion in France, with Eisenhower's reassurance that he had enough resources to move against the Germans in Italy, and with Franklin Roosevelt's commitment to confronting the British prime minister (if such a confrontation was necessary) with an American insistence that the time had come, finally, to fight the Germans in northwestern Europe. Marshall knew, of course, that the U.S. had made the arguments at Arcadia and Casablanca and again with Churchill in Algiers. And each time, he also knew, the British had deftly sidestepped the issue, postponing the invasion to some uncertain future date. Now, with Roosevelt firmly on his side, Marshall believed the British would have to face the inevitable. Roosevelt's willingness to finally confront Churchill was essential if Marshall was to win his battle against Brooke. Roosevelt's sudden shift in favor of Marshall would not have happened, however, if Secretary of War Henry Stimson had not pressured Roosevelt to weigh in against the British on Marshall's behalf. Before Quadrant, in a late-July meeting at the White House, Stimson argued strenuously that Roosevelt's strength with Churchill could turn the tide against the British prime minister.

It was time, Stimson said, for the president to "assume the responsibility of leadership" and decisively oppose Churchill's strategy of "pinprick warfare" against the Axis.[6] Stimson was more outspoken with Roosevelt than he had been before. It was not only time to take the final steps in ending the war, he argued; Roosevelt should also select George Marshall, "our most commanding soldier," as Overlord's leader. Stimson memorialized his argument in his diary just after his meeting with the president.

General Marshall already has a towering eminence of reputation as a tried soldier and as a broad-minded and skilled administrator. This was shown by the suggestion of him on the part of the British for this very post a year and a half ago. I believe he is the man who most surely can now by his character and skill furnish the military leadership which is necessary to bring our two nations together in confident joint action in this great operation. No one knows better than I the loss in the problems of organization and worldwide strategy centered in Washington which such a solution would cause, but I see no other alternative to which we can turn in the great effort which confronts us.

The president certainly was aware that Marshall's experience and reputation made him a natural choice for Overlord. His appointment as Eisenhower's successor was, in fact, long overdue; it would be a just reward for his years of service at Roosevelt's side. But while agreeing with Stimson's praise for Marshall, the president was unwilling to name an Overlord commander in mid-1943. That decision, he said, could come later. This was only half a victory for Stimson, but it was clear progress, and when the secretary of war left his meeting with Roosevelt that hot late-July day, he was pleased that at least Roosevelt was committed to standing up to Churchill in Quebec. So it was that just three weeks later the British found a united and strengthened U.S. high command that was less willing to compromise on European operations. The stage was set for yet another confrontation between George Marshall and Sir Alan Brooke, a face-off that was now a traditional part of every Anglo-American meeting. Indeed, the battle lines of Quebec were drawn early in the conference when the two commanders engaged in a heated and painfully blunt discussion on the invasion of Europe. As always, Brooke's soaring opinion of his own strategic sense served to deepen Marshall's suspicions, while the American chief's continued intransigence on Overlord seemed (at least to Brooke) yet another sign of American strategic simplicity. When Marshall insisted that the Combined Chiefs specify a date for France's invasion, Brooke fired a salvo at the American commander. This was the same old argument, he said, that was being put forward solely because of Marshall's amateurish understanding of warfare. The chief of staff simply did not "begin to understand a strategic problem."[7] Marshall responded heatedly. The problem was not America's, but Brooke's and his inability to understand that diverting resources from a cross-Channel attack to conquer Italy would not defeat Germany, but only postpone the ending of the war. Around the conference room at La Citadelle, Marshall's and Brooke's colleagues shifted uneasily in their chairs. "Our talk was pretty frank," Brooke later reflected.

And so it went, from August 12 to August 24, through twelve grueling days, with Marshall and Brooke, circling, parrying, then warily eyeing each other until yet another bout. Marshall would not give and slowly he began to wear down his opposition, as Brooke all but conceded in his diary: "A long and tiring day," he said on the thirteenth. "The end of a gloomy and unpleasant day," he wrote on the fifteenth, "Another poisonous day," he admitted on the nineteenth, "Another difficult day," he wrote on the twenty-first.[8] The American Chiefs of Staff had fought a tenacious battle until, on the twenty-fourth, they emerged triumphant. A compromise, Brooke said, had been reached, but he did not add that this time the compromise favored American and not British interests. Overlord was confirmed, and the date for the invasion was set for May 1, 1944.[9] While Eisenhower would lead his forces into Italy, the Allied command would begin to shift its attention to northwestern Europe. Troops and matériel destined for the Mediterranean would be diverted to England for the invasion of France, and their transfer would go forward no matter how tough the fighting became in Italy. The British, faced now with a united front of Marshall and Roosevelt, had no choice. They were committed, finally, to planning and carrying forward a cross-Channel operation. Brooke never conceded defeat, though his diary entries clearly signaled his disappointment. When the British carried the day the Americans were understanding and cooperative. When the British did not, the Americans were "stubborn," "petty," "stupid," and "pig-headed."[10] Still, in spite of Marshall's and Brooke's now open break, the British commitment marked a significant shift in Allied relations. For the first time since the entrance of the United States into the war, Churchill, Brooke, and the British Chiefs of Staff had lost the battle with the Americans. Italy would be invaded, but it would remain a sideshow even if, as now seemed likely, the Germans reinforced their armies on the peninsula. Brooke's defeat was total: he had not only lost the battle over the Mediterranean; on the last day of Quebec he was told by Winston Churchill that he would not be Overlord's commander. The commander of the cross-Channel invasion, Churchill told him, would be an American. Presumably that commander would be Brooke's longtime nemesis, George Marshall.[11]

IN THE midst of the Quebec meetings, Eisenhower cabled Marshall that the Germans had moved six extra divisions into Italy and seized Italian airfields. There followed several tense weeks as the Allies dickered with the new Italian government over the terms of its surrender. Eisenhower monitored the negotiations while overseeing the planning of the Allies' landings at Salerno—code-named Operation Avalanche. By early September, the new Italian government had collapsed and the German Army had seized the country. Churchill watched these events with growing alarm. Italy, he believed, was not out of the war after all, but was being revived as a German protectorate. So, for one last time, the British prime minister attempted to convince Roosevelt to postpone Overlord.[12] But it was too late, and Churchill retreated for the first time since the beginning of the war. He was heartbroken: "Italy was now to pass through the most tragic time in her history and to become the battle-ground of some of the fiercest fighting of the war," he later wrote.[13] On September 3, Allied forces under Montgomery crossed the Straits of Messina. Their purpose was to draw German divisions into the south prior to the landing of major Allied forces near Naples. Montgomery's landings in the south were nearly un-opposed, but Eisenhower was worried. The landings near Naples, he believed, had been hastily planned, and the Allies might be walking into a trap: "I am frank to state that there is more than a faint possibility that we may have some hard going," he confided to Marshall.[14] Despite these doubts, Eisenhower ordered Avalanche to go forward.

At 3:00 A.M. on September 9, 1943, American and British troops came ashore on the western coast of Italy, at Salerno. The landings were a disaster. The Fifth Army, comprising four divisions (two British and two American), landed on four different beaches ten miles apart. The landing zones were separated by the Sele River and overlooked by imposing bluffs.[15] At first the landings went well; the Germans had been taken by surprise. But within twenty-four hours, Allied troops came under withering fire from the 16th Panzer Division, dug in along Salerno's high bluffs. The Anglo-American force attempted to fight its way off Salerno's beaches, but the Allied landing zones were strewn with mines, slowing the American and British advance. German infantry dug into the hillsides and ravines, pinning down clusters of soldiers with sweeping machine-gun fire.[16] In Rome, Field Marshal Albert "Smiling Al" Kesselring, while taken by surprise by Eisenhower's move, quickly ordered the 26th Panzer and 29th Panzergrenadier divisions to Salerno to buttress the German defenses. The Allies, he believed, had finally made a fatal mistake. He would make them pay for it by pinning their forces on Salerno's beaches before deploying his panzers to exploit a breakthrough. The Americans and British would be more than bloodied—they would be cut to pieces and forced back into the bay.

Eisenhower's doubts about Salerno were reinforced by fears that Avalanche commander Mark Clark did not have enough landing craft or troops to overcome Salerno's German defenses (two divisions had been diverted to England for Overlord on the eve of Clark's landings, along with five hundred landing craft). To help Clark, Eisenhower scrambled to find more landing craft (diverting a number designated for Joseph Stilwell in Burma) and pressed air commanders to target German troops in marshaling areas near Naples.[17] Clark, in his first overall command, shared Eisenhower's worries, believing the Germans might quickly strengthen their defenses before he could bring additional units ashore. Watching the landings from his command post aboard a U.S. destroyer, Clark was relieved when all of his forces reached the shore, but later on that day noted the lack of movement on Salerno's beaches. Still, he believed, there was no reason to be overly worried. "Men squirmed through barbed wire, ground mines, and behind enemy machine guns and the tanks that soon made their appearance, working their way inland and knocking out German strongpoints wherever possible," Clark later wrote triumphantly.[18] This was nonsense. Allied troops were not making their way inland, but fighting their way across Salerno's beaches, which were crisscrossed by presighted German machine-gun fire and sighted by German antiaircraft artillery, whose muzzles were lowered to destroy incoming landing craft. The Germans were tenacious fighters. They did not want to give up their beaches so counterattacked across the shingle of Salerno on the two days following the Anglo-American deployment. All through the ninth and into the tenth the Anglo-American force struggled to conquer Salerno's bluffs, until finally—on the morning of September 11—the situation on the British beach became so desperate that Clark dispatched an American regiment to close the yawning Sele gap between the American and British sectors. Clark feared that the German panzer units would break through the gap and reach the bay. Their tanks would then roam the beaches at will, fulfilling Kesselring's Salerno fantasy.[19]

Part of the problem was that the Allies did not control the sky over Salerno. A hospital ship, large numbers of landing craft, a Liberty ship, and at least four transports were sunk on September 11.[20] For nearly a week after the landings, German aircraft, some 625 in all, swept the Anglo-American landing zones unopposed before winging their way west to attack American and British troopships and cruisers. Under the guns of the Germans, and constantly strafed from the air, Allied troops continued to fight for control of the bluffs that ringed the beaches and then, only tentatively, moved inland. The situation was so critical that on the evening of the eleventh, Clark considered withdrawing forces from the American beachhead before shipping them north to reinforce the British. As Clark ruminated, the Germans attacked. Panzer sorties for the first two days of the operation had been poorly coordinated and costly, but on the morning of September 12, the Hermann Göring Division, refitted after its heavy work against Patton in Sicily, launched a massed tank offensive aimed at exploiting the Sele gap.[21] The all-out assault struck the British X Corps with the force of a typhoon, nearly destroying the unit's cohesion and sending British Tommies scrambling for the rear. The Germans took a thousand British prisoners. Faced now with the distinct possibility that German tanks would head south, sweeping the Americans off their beaches, Clark came ashore to oversee the battle in person. The Germans greeted his arrival with yet another attack, targeting the entire front of Clark's dug-in VI Corps. Holed up in a villa east of the beaches, Clark cannibalized his units, sending cooks and clerks into the fight with rifles stripped from the Allied dead.[22] Artillerymen fired shells into advancing Germans at point-blank range while Clark, in the midst of the toughest fighting, directed units to plug holes in his defenses. At one point, Clark spotted members of a band standing idle. He ordered them to put aside their tubas, armed them, and had them man trenches on a key hill along the Salerno perimeter. The American lines held, but barely.

With the Germans pressing in from all sides, Clark was convinced that he would have to take extraordinary measures to save his troops. He desperately needed reinforcements. Clark ordered naval ships to steam in as close to shore as possible, shelling German troops still streaming westward into his lines. Then, pleading for increased air cover, Clark set his staff to planning for an evacuation and the shift of two entire American divisions to the north. Reinforced from their new position, the Allies could cut into Kesselring's panzers, who would be taken by surprise by the new onslaught.[23] Clark called his senior commanders—Generals Ernest J. Dawley, Fred L. Walker, and Troy Middleton—to meet with him at his command post to tell them about his plan. Dawley, exhausted from days of combat and under pressure from reports that Clark was disappointed with his combat decisions, protested his commander's plan.[24] The withdrawal should not be made, he said. Troy Middleton, the commander of the U.S. 45th Division and another of George Marshall's "little black book" generals, was appalled by the thought and by Clark's sudden lack of faith. Middleton was one of Eisenhower's most dogged fighters. Soft-spoken, selfless, efficient, and cool in combat, Middleton confronted Clark at this most crucial point in the battle for Naples, bluntly telling him that he would *not* move his division and would *not* evacuate his troops: "Put food and ammunition behind the 45th," he shouted at Clark as shells screamed overhead. "We're staying."[25]

Middleton's words and his insistence that the Americans could fight their way off the beaches gave Eisenhower's old friend confidence, providing a counterpoint to the pessimism that seemed to infect the American high command from the outset of the operation. In particular, Clark was enraged by Major General Ernest "Mike" Dawley's handling of VI Corps. Dawley had questioned the landings from the beginning, even to the point of quoting Fox Conner and John Pershing's dictum prior to a failed attack in the First World War: "Don't bite off more than you can chew." Dawley had cited this phrase to Clark during the planning for Avalanche, then nodded at a table map of the Bay of Naples and said that he doubted whether VI Corps could carry out its mission.

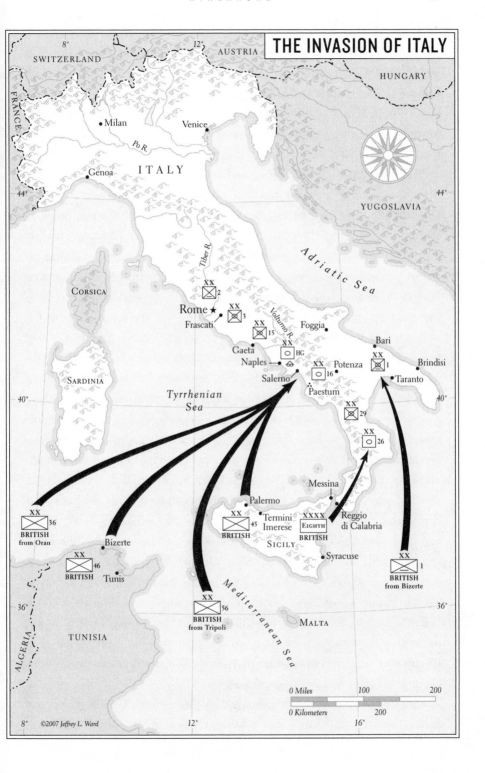

THE INVASION OF ITALY

SWITZERLAND
AUSTRIA
HUNGARY
FRANCE
Milan
Venice
Po R.
ITALY
Genoa
YUGOSLAVIA
CORSICA
Tiber R.
Adriatic Sea
Rome ★
Frascati
Volturno R.
Foggia
Bari
Gaeta
Naples
Potenza
Brindisi
SARDINIA
Salerno
Taranto
Tyrrhenian
Sea
Paestum
Messina
Palermo
Termini
Imerese
Reggio
di Calabria
BRITISH
from Oran
Bizerte
Syracuse
SICILY
BRITISH
BRITISH
BRITISH
Tunis
Mediterranean Sea
BRITISH
from Tripoli
MALTA
BRITISH
from Bizerte
TUNISIA
ALGERIA

0 Miles 100 200
0 Kilometers 200

©2007 Jeffrey L. Ward

Your plan is badly flawed, he told Clark. From that moment on, Clark viewed Dawley as a problem. Clark was ready to blame Dawley for nearly every catastrophe, so when the major general radioed Clark his report at the height of the Salerno fight, pleading that his troops were near collapse, Clark sputtered in anger: "Well, Mike," he asked, "what are you doing about it?" Dawley hesitated for only an instant: "I'm praying," he said. This was not the answer Clark wanted: "That's OK," he said, "but you had better do something else besides."[26]

Watching this from his bustling and now worried command headquarters, Eisenhower quickly realized that the Salerno landings might turn into a full-scale disaster—a Kasserine writ large. The supreme commander's quick assessment was that the Allies had only three ways of helping Clark save his four divisions: the British Eighth Army could more aggressively attack German positions in southern Italy (hoping thereby to force Kesselring to shift troops off the Salerno bluffs and pitch them south to face Montgomery), the Allies could increase their air and naval support at Salerno by shifting resources into the Bay of Naples, or the Salerno landing areas could be reinforced by one of four nearby divisions—the 82nd Airborne, the 3rd Infantry, the 1st Armored, or the 34th Infantry. Of these three options, a sudden lurch forward by Montgomery provided the best hope for immediate relief. If Montgomery could attack aggressively, he might be able to link up with Clark's Fifth Army, providing an unbroken line across the Italian peninsula.[27] With Clark being battered at Salerno, and Montgomery's troops crawling from bridge to bridge in the south, even the normally slumbering Harold Alexander was spurred to unusual action. He radioed Montgomery urging a quickened advance, then sent his chief of staff to deliver the same message in person. Montgomery pledged to do all that he could to move quickly but added, imperiously, that he was "administratively very stretched."[28] In Algiers, meanwhile, Eisenhower dispatched two cruisers to support the landings, then added two battleships anchored at Malta to provide close-in support for Clark's troops. There was another option. Prior to the Salerno landings, the 82nd Airborne Division had been designated to capture Rome in a surprise coup de main, but the operation had been canceled by Eisenhower when its commander determined that the attempt would be suicidal. The 82nd idled awaiting orders.

On the morning of September 13, with the already desperate fighting at Salerno having taken a turn for the worse, Clark scribbled a note to airborne commander Matthew Ridgway, ordering him to parachute a regiment of fighters onto the American beach after dark. "I want you to accept this letter as an order," he wrote. "I realize the time normally needed to prepare for a drop, but . . . I want you to make a drop within our lines on the beachhead and I want you to make it tonight. This is a must."[29] Several hours later Ridgway responded: "Can do." As Ridgway, who was known for his ability to improvise solutions to difficult battle scenarios, prepared his troops, he remembered the friendly-fire incident in Sicily that had sparked a week of recriminations between Eisenhower and Patton. In his return message to Clark, Ridgway emphasized the need for Allied control of its ground units. He did not want his troopers descending into the maw of sustained American and British volleys: "Vitally important," he wrote, "that all ground and naval forces . . . be directed to hold fire tonight. Rigid control of antiaircraft fire is absolutely essential for success." Ridgway then directed staff officers to visit commanders in the Salerno perimeter to make certain his instructions had been received and would be followed.[30]

At sunset, American soldiers filled five-gallon cans with sand and gasoline and laid them out in a T-shaped perimeter to guide the paratroopers to their designated landing zones. This was a desperate measure—most airborne assaults scattered at least a portion of their troopers well off target. Here, at Salerno, the landing grid encompassed a rectangle half a mile long and half a mile wide. If the troopships overshot the landing zone the paratroopers would be German prisoners, if they survived, but if they undershot their landing zones they would drown. Ridgway determined that his troopships should come in low and fast, complicating the drop, but it was the only way of ensuring success. The official U.S. Army history of the operation details the difficulties of bringing Ridgway's regiments into the battle.

A pathfinder group set up radar equipment to lead the flights toward the jump field, where ground troops furnished flare for further identification of the drop zone. At 2326, 13 September, four minutes ahead of schedule, men of the 2d Battalion, 504 Parachute Infantry, led the regiment in by jumping from thirty-five planes at a height of 800 feet. Most troops landed within 200 yards of the jump zone and all within a mile of it. Forty-one aircraft starting from Sicily several hours late because of mechanical difficulties dropped troops about 0130, 14 September. The pilots of some of these planes were unable to find the drop zone, and one company of paratroopers came to earth eight to ten miles away. Fourteen planes disgorging their troops still later completed the drop. In all, ninety planes brought about 1300 troops to the beachhead within fifteen hours of General Clark's request.[31]

At the same moment that Ridgway's troopers were floating down to the American beaches, U.S. troops were fighting for their lives in hand-to-hand combat to preserve the Salerno perimeter against sustained German attacks. The defenders were soldiers of the 158th and 189th Field Artillery. They were attempting to defend the most critical section of the Salerno perimeter until Ridgway's reinforcements could arrive. "Against the company of German tanks and the battalion of German infantry that had come roaring down the Sele-Calore corridor, the Americans fired a total of 3,650 artillery rounds in about four hours," the official U.S. Army history recounts. "Arriving during the height of the action, a battery of the 27th Armored Field Artillery Battalion added 300 rounds of fire. This, together with the shells of the tanks and tank destroyers and the resistance of the improvised infantry firing line built up at the base of the corridor, stopped the German attack."[32] The Germans withdrew. The next day, September 14, the Allies, fighting now alongside Ridgeway's paratroopers, shortened their lines, and resistance to German attacks began to stiffen. On the beaches, all of the unloading of transports ended and soldiers were told to grab a rifle and get into the firing line. The next day, the British 7th Armored Division came ashore, along with the last regiment of the 45th Division. On the night of the fourteenth, another two thousand paratroopers landed at Salerno. That day, realizing that the Allies would not be pushed into the sea, Kesselring ordered his commanders to withdraw to the north, where they would take up positions in defense of Rome.[33]

READING CLARK'S increasingly shrill battle reports in Algiers, Eisenhower remained publicly optimistic, but in private he was blunt about the possibility of defeat. He confided his worries to Marshall, writing the chief of staff twice in three days that the situation in Salerno was "touch and go."[34] He sent a blunt and detailed assessment to Marshall on the thirteenth:

We have been unable to advance and the enemy is preparing a major counter-attack. The 45th [Division] is largely in the area now and I am using everything we have bigger than a row boat to get the 3d Division in to Clark quickly. Ships that are unsuitable for going to Clark will carry reinforcements into Taranto. Unfortunately the 18 LST's finally given to us temporarily were already loaded for departure to India and it will be tomorrow night before the first eight are ready to move. It will take additional time to get the others unloaded. Many of them were carrying steel rails. In the present situation our great hope is the Air Force. They are working flat out and assuming, which I do, that our hold on southern Italy will finally be solidified, we are going to prove once again that the greatest value of any of the three services is ordinarily realized only when it is utilized in close coordination with the other two.[35]

Eisenhower's closing was pessimistic and uncharacteristically cavalier: "Considering for a moment the worst that could possibly develop, I would, in that event, merely announce that one of our landings has been repulsed—due to my error in misjudging the strength of the enemy at that place," he told Marshall. "But I have great faith that even in spite of currently grim reports, we'll pull out all right. Our Air Force, the fighting value of our troops, and strenuous efforts by us all, should do the trick."[36]

This almost shrugging acceptance of blame—that he would "merely" announce the failure of a U.S. operation (as if a defeat-by-press-release could dampen American and British horror at such a colossally botched operation)— was one of the few serious misjudgments Eisenhower made in any of his reports to Marshall. The chief of staff was not prepared to accept such an outcome. You do not "merely announce" a failure, nor explain away the deaths of thousands of Allied troops. But Marshall was not simply worried about the situation in Salerno; he was also concerned with the lack of tactical creativity shown by his chief European commanders and by the impact that operations in Italy would have on his plans for an invasion of France. It rankled Marshall that the Salerno landings had not turned out to be the "swift punch" that would take Italy out of the war (as Churchill had so confidently predicted in Algiers back in July), but now threatened to suck troops, ships, and landing craft into an Italian whirlpool. The British, Americans, Free French, and Canadians had been fighting together now for nearly two years and not once had Marshall's (or Eisenhower's) vision of an armored breakout, with tanks racing across an open countryside, been vindicated. And now the Germans were nosing the turrets of their Tiger tanks along the Sele River, pounding American and British troops sullenly clinging to the shingle of Salerno.

Marshall might have been mollified had he known that Eisenhower was as frustrated as he was by the Allies' lack of progress and by the increasing consumption of resources being siphoned off from Overlord. In Algiers, Eisenhower was giving his every waking moment to the Salerno crisis, was railing against Clark's lack of progress, was criticizing Clark's inability to relieve commanders who were not performing, was relentlessly questioning Clark's deployments, and was even raising questions about Clark's battlefield leadership. Eisenhower told his aides that if the Allies were defeated at Salerno, then Clark would have to "go down with the ship."[37] He realized, of course, that if that were to happen he would probably join his friend Wayne for the trip to the bottom, shipped with him "on a slow boat" back to Washington and on into oblivion. In the midst of the battle, Eisenhower spoke directly and desperately with his air commanders, praised them for their close-in support of U.S. and British troops mired in the sand at Salerno, and asked them for more. He ordered Lieutenant General Carl "Tooey" Spaatz, the deputy commanding general of the Mediterranean Allied Air Forces, to use heavy bombers in a tactical role, flying low against German panzer spearheads.[38] If Clark could not move, then at least Eisenhower would do everything he could to make certain he was not overwhelmed.

What Eisenhower could not then, or even later, admit was that his friend Mark Clark was simply the wrong man for the job. It was Clark who had bucked him up in Washington, it was Clark who praised him to Marshall, it was Clark who had given him confidence in the dark interwar years of endless soul-killing backwater staff assignments. And Clark was listed prominently in Marshall's book. To relieve him now, in the midst of battle, would be to admit that he had somehow misjudged Clark—and that Marshall had, too. Eisenhower swallowed his doubts, stuck with Clark, defended him to Marshall, and shipped him more men and matériel. Finally, on September 17, Eisenhower appeared at Clark's headquarters above the Salerno beach for a briefing. With the crisis subsiding, the two huddled under a tree, studying a map of the tactical situation. Eisenhower, his mouth set, listened carefully to Clark's plans, studied his deployments, and then gave his own recommendations. When German artillery shells landed dangerously close by, Clark's staff scrambled for their trenches, but Clark and Eisenhower barely raised their heads.[39] While it is not known precisely what Eisenhower told Clark at Salerno, Clark's actions thereafter became more certain, more focused, and more creative. With the beachhead saved and American and British reinforcements pouring ashore, Clark pushed his command forward, combined the American and British beachheads, and linked up with Montgomery's Eighth Army in the south. The situation was saved and Salerno went into America's history books as a victory. But Eisenhower knew that Salerno was—as Patton might have said—"a waste of good infantry" and a bloody and unnecessary attack.

"Clark continues to be what I have always told you—the best organizer, planner and trainer of troops that I have met," Eisenhower had told Marshall just weeks before. That begged the question. The Allies did not need an organizer, planner, or trainer at Salerno; they needed a tenacious and creative combat commander. Clark's lack of command experience weighed against him, for Salerno demanded that he improvise under enormous pressure at the same time that he managed a wide range of command personalities.[40] Temperamental and notoriously vain, Clark seemed more concerned with his place in history than with the placement of his troops. He strutted his expertise, his stars, his command position, for all the press to see, then downplayed the cost of his mistakes in his after-action accounts. Marshall knew this about him, as did Eisenhower—it is why they had transferred him to his own "manure pile" in Morocco in the midst of the North African campaign. Clark made certain that he was followed constantly by a photographer who was instructed to snap his shutter at the most opportune times: here's Clark talking with his commanders, here's Clark talking with his soldiers, here's Clark (eyes to binoculars) planning the victory. He instructed the photographer to make certain he was photographed from the left—"my good side."[41] A perhaps apocryphal story is told of Clark's staff urging reporters to serenade their commander with a special song, "Stand Up for General Clark," sung to the tune of "Stand Up, Stand Up for Jesus." The constant need for attention grated on his staff and on the British. Clark rewrote Clausewitz's famous dictum "War is an extension of policy by other means," one British commander quipped. What Clark believed was that war was "an extension of publicity by other means."[42] Another strategist compared Clark with Harold Alexander, noting, "Where Alexander would discuss endlessly and never give orders, Clark gave orders and refused to discuss them." Clark returned these damning judgments. Alexander was a "feather duster," the commander of the 1st British Division was "a good telephone operator," U.S. lieutenant General Jacob Devers was "a dope."[43] Why then did Eisenhower and Marshall, and even Alexander, defend him?

In the aftermath of the Salerno crisis, Eisenhower's assessment of the near failure corresponded almost exactly with Marshall's. While the Arsenal of Democracy had shown that it could supply everyone everywhere—that the United Nations could fight the Axis in Europe, the Pacific, Burma and even the Mediterranean—local conditions, geography, leadership, the intangibles of battle, and, of course, the brilliance of enemy commanders like "Smiling Al" Kesselring could all conspire to undermine the best-laid plans, to place in doubt the Allied enterprise, to threaten the lives of thousands, even tens of thousands, of American and British soldiers. In the end, battles were won as much by tenacity as they were by good planning or proper resources. Courage mattered, even for army commanders. And for all of his failings, courage is what Mark Clark had, and in abundance. While Bradley's reputation as the "the G.I. General" was exaggerated, Mark Clark was genuinely beloved by his troops. He contemptuously blamed Montgomery, Alexander, Churchill, and his subordinates for his setbacks. He even blamed Mike Dawley. But he never blamed his soldiers. Like Confederate general Jubal Early, whom Robert E. Lee called "my bad old man," Clark was a mediocre commander, widely disliked, and often questioned. But sometimes in war, the tipping point between victory and defeat rests not only on improvisation or command creativity, but on a commander's coldhearted calculation to expend blood in one last effort, one last attack. Clark could make these calculations. Then too, Eisenhower and Marshall knew that war leaves little time for experimentation and rarely rewards those who shift commanders endlessly looking for precisely the right one—the perfect commander. There is no such thing. Clark was a known quantity. If Lloyd Fredendall was "a good colonel" (to use Beetle Smith's description), then Mark Clark was a good sergeant. In Fredendall's case the judgment was damning; in Clark's it was the highest compliment. America's sergeants fought World War II, and Clark could often be seen, in the midst of battle, standing fearlessly beside them.

MARSHALL'S FRUSTRATIONS finally boiled over on September 23, when he cabled Eisenhower his views on Salerno, on the Italian campaign, and on what he viewed as Eisenhower's lack of creativity. It was a damning judgment, the most strident that Marshall had made of Eisenhower in all of their months together as partners in command. Marshall's message was harsh and blunt, its tone disapproving. Never before had the Army chief of staff showed his anger with anything his chief lieutenant had done. But this was different. The Salerno landings had been badly bungled. No one, it seemed to Marshall, had bothered with any of its details. Marshall told Eisenhower that he had been consulting with British field marshal Sir John Dill, and that they had agreed that the Salerno operation should have taken place prior to Montgomery's invasion across the Straits of Messina. This would have caught the Germans unprepared, Marshall said. Now, even if Eisenhower could solidify Allied lines south of Naples, the fight for Rome would be long and difficult, a bloody slugging match. Perhaps, Marshall said, Eisenhower should consider an amphibious assault farther north in Italy, to bypass German defenses. Marshall also expressed disappointment that Eisenhower had canceled a planned airborne assault on Rome—despite the clear dangers involved—on the eve of the Salerno landings. It was Eisenhower's mistake. "At long range," Marshall wrote, "it would seem you give the enemy too much time to prepare and eventually find yourself up against a very stiff resistance."[44] Eisenhower read the message and conceded that Marshall's criticism caused him "a great deal of mental anguish."[45] He was particularly upset that Marshall had not given him enough credit "for cracking the whip." He spent the whole day after receiving Marshall's message pacing, talking to himself, and dictating a response to Marshall's criticisms.[46] The Army chief's words struck deep and Eisenhower was wounded, fearing that now he had lost Marshall's confidence: "Ike has eaten no breakfast and passed up lunch," Butcher noted in his diary.[47]

Eisenhower's response to Marshall was direct and unapologetic. He took pains to defend his decisions, though it was plain that he did not want to offend the chief of staff. He did not say, as he would have liked, that the Salerno operation would have been much more successful had not Marshall been stingy with Allied resources, diverting divisions and aircraft to England in preparation for Overlord. Nor did he note that in the midst of the battle he had even been forced to request that the Combined Chiefs of Staff return three bomber groups destined for transfer to England at Marshall's direction. Eisenhower's view was obvious: given the resources he'd had, he told Marshall, his troops and commanders had done an exceptional job. "I want to say that we are looking every minute for a chance to utilize our air and naval power to turn the enemy positions. . . . I do not see how any individual could possibly be devoting more thought and energy to speeding up operations or to attacking boldly and with admitted risk than I do."[48] That afternoon, Eisenhower received a message from Winston Churchill complimenting him on his actions at Salerno. "I congratulate you on the victorious landing and deployment northward of our armies. As the Duke of Wellington said of the Battle of Waterloo, 'It was a damned close-run thing,' but your policy of running risks has been vindicated."[49] Eisenhower sent Churchill's note on to Marshall. "As a matter of interest to you I received from the Prime Minister a telegraph congratulating me on the success of my policy on running risks," Eisenhower wrote, poking gingerly but firmly at Marshall. "I feel certain that some of his correspondents in this area look upon me as a gambler."[50]

If George Marshall responded to or was angered by Eisenhower's missive it is not recorded, and it now seems likely that both men were too engaged in other matters to continue their sparring. The Salerno operation had been a near disaster, but Eisenhower, Alexander, Clark, and Montgomery had worked through the problems. By the end of September, the Allies had constructed a seamless front through central Italy, and on October 1, elements of Lucien Truscott's 3rd Infantry Division entered Naples unopposed.[51] In the east, Montgomery's Eighth Army occupied Foggia, gaining control of airfields from which Allied bombers could now be deployed against southern Germany. The following week, Allied forces probed northward, toward the mountainous terrain of central Italy, while Kesselring mounted a series of small probing offensives to cover his withdrawal. Clark and Alexander now had eighteen divisions facing Kesselring, whose thirteen German divisions girdled Italy's bony midriff south of Rome. Alexander's plan to breach this "Gustav Line" was to have Clark's forces drive on Rome by way of Monte Cassino, straight up "Route 6" through the Liri Valley. The straight-ahead assault against dug-in German troops would be aided by the landing of four British and one American division

at the beachhead of Anzio (an operation code-named "Shingle"), southwest of
Rome. These five divisions would link up with Clark's and Alexander's troops
and then both would sprint north, unhinge Kesselring, and take Rome by surprise. If all went well, Kesselring's forces would disintegrate in the resulting
northward retreat. The battle for Italy would be won.

Of course, Kesselring had other plans. The balding, grimacing winner of the
Iron Cross looked at a map of central Italy in his headquarters in Rome and determined that Clark and Montgomery would come at him by deploying their
tanks along Route 6. Kesselring, who seemed nearly prescient in anticipating
Alexander's, Clark's, and Montgomery's every move, prepared his forces accordingly. They were now dug in along the steep escarpment of Monte Cassino,
an abbey of the Benedictine order. The German position negated Allied
airpower. The Germans could kill the British, Americans, and Canadians as
easily as if they were shooting fish in a barrel. Kesselring was confident. The
Germans were now in a position to fight a long bloody campaign of attrition,
a trench-to-trench fight that rivaled anything the British, French, and Americans
had faced on the Western Front in World War I. Ironically, it was just the kind
of warfare that Churchill, in promoting his Mediterranean policy, had worked
so diligently to avoid.

As THE war bogged down in Italy, Eisenhower entertained a string of diplomats
who arrived, often uninvited, in Algiers to visit him. Averell Harriman, the U.S.
ambassador to Moscow, arrived in early October, along with his daughter. He
was followed by Secretary of the Treasury Henry Morgenthau Jr. and Secretary
of State Cordell Hull.[52] Eisenhower was now much in demand. The supreme
Allied commander had surmounted the Salerno crisis, and his armies were
now thought to be marching on Rome. To his disgust, Eisenhower was now
seen to be a diplomat as much as a soldier—having negotiated the recognition
of the successor government to Mussolini's, headed by Italian field marshal
Pietro Badoglio.[53] Like Jean-Louis Darlan, Badoglio was a committed Fascist;
he had supported Mussolini's war in Ethiopia and fought alongside Francisco
Franco's forces in Spain. As Eisenhower braced for yet another round of newspaper criticisms he would have been shocked at the power that even those closest to Roosevelt now believed he wielded. "I hope you will not encourage

Eisenhower to recognize Italy as a co-belligerent," Harry Hopkins wrote in a memorandum to Roosevelt.[54] Hopkins had made a simple slip—being "recognized" by Eisenhower was not the same as being recognized by the United States—but the gaffe symbolized how far Eisenhower had come. As a sign of his newfound fame, one of Eisenhower's friends forwarded a clipping from the New York Post: "Eisenhower Urged for President."[55] The Allied commander was enraged: "Baloney! Why can't a simple soldier be left alone to carry out his orders? And I furiously object to the word 'candidate'—I ain't and I won't."[56] In Washington, George Marshall (who had experience in such matters) might have smiled wryly, but to make certain that Eisenhower kept his mind on the war, he barraged him with messages—on building infantry morale,[57] on the quality of troop replacements,[58] on dispatching Patton to study the feasibility of troops landings in southern France,[59] and on a new unified command structure for the Balkans.[60]

There was more than enough to keep Eisenhower busy, as Allied soldiers fighting their way up Route 6 in Italy continued to grind their way through the winter mud. Clark and Montgomery, now fighting side by side, found it nearly impossible to unlock Kesselring's mountain positions. "The whole mountainous countryside had been organized into a series of defensive positions—the exact names and locations of which are still not well defined," one after-action report noted. "Demolitions and mine fields blocked every avenue of approach; machine gun and mortar positions were well dug in—many blasted out of solid rock—and camouflaged to disappear into the rugged scenery; German artillery had registered on all roads, trails, and possible sites for bivouac and assembly areas."[61] As Allied casualties mounted, Eisenhower applied the pressure Marshall had applied on him to Mark Clark, though to no avail. With Clark and Montgomery stuck in Italy, Eisenhower turned his attention to political matters, noting that the Allied leaders were beginning their almost seasonal maneuvers in anticipation of yet another summit on the war. This one was scheduled for Cairo in late November, and Eisenhower was given the task of finding accommodations for summit participants and ensuring their safety.[62] This was to be the most important summit since Arcadia, as it would decide on the final plan for the invasion of France, begin the long process of thinking about a postwar settlement, and determine the commander of Overlord.

On November 15, Eisenhower flew to Malta for a meeting with Winston

Churchill, who had arrived on the island aboard a British destroyer. The prime minister was fond of Eisenhower, and the two had gotten along ever since their first meeting, at the White House, two years before. The friendship had deepened in Algiers, and the two could now talk easily and bluntly to each other. Churchill supposed that his Malta stopover was an incidental rest stop on his voyage to Cairo, but he also wanted to take the measure of Eisenhower prior to his meetings with Roosevelt.[63] Churchill was suffering from a cold and had only a short meeting with the American commander, who was accompanied by Harold Alexander. Churchill gave them both a British campaign ribbon, approved by the king, for their service in Tunisia. Eisenhower was taken aback by the honor and effusive in his thanks. Churchill waved him off and got to the point. As Eisenhower later remembered:

He told me that originally it was intended that General Brooke should command in England and the Mediterranean command should remain undisturbed, he recalled. However, when the Americans, at Quebec, insisted upon American command in England, it became politically necessary (and the truth of this statement is obvious) that the British should have command in the Mediterranean. He said that later proposals of the president's were, however, to the effect that General Marshall should take over strategic direction of the whole European campaign, while General Brooke should actually command in England, and I should remain in command here. This, the prime minister said, he could not accept. There were many sidelights that the prime minister gave to me on the whole proposition. However, these were not particularly important, and at the time of my meeting him, he felt that the original proposal would go through as first approved; namely, that General Marshall would take command of Overlord in England and I would possibly go to Washington.[64]

Eisenhower responded to Churchill with his own long-held belief: that the decision on who would command Overlord rested with Franklin Roosevelt, that he assumed that George Marshall would be the commander, and that he would accept any position the president believed he should fill. Churchill's monologue on the command in Europe must have struck Eisenhower as odd, as it seemed to suggest that the decision had not yet been made. Eisenhower assumed that Marshall was fated to take his place as supreme Allied commander. Eisenhower might have been less surprised by Churchill's discussion if he had known that command of the invasion force had become a political issue in Washington, where Republican senators, anxious that Marshall not be promoted to a position that would add to his political luster, had recruited John Pershing to urge Roosevelt to keep Marshall as Army chief of staff.[65] "I am so deeply disturbed by the repeated newspaper reports that General Marshall is to be transferred to a tactical command in England," Pershing had written to Roosevelt, "that I am writing to express my fervent hope that these reports are unfounded." Pershing went on to note that transferring Marshall to a "tactical command in a limited area, no matter how seemingly important, is to deprive ourselves of the benefit of his outstanding strategical ability and experience."[66] Understanding the political nature of Pershing's letter, Roosevelt responded politely but firmly: "I think it is only a fair thing to give George a chance in the field—and because of the nature of the job we shall have the benefit of his strategical ability," he wrote.[67] Later, after the decision was made, Eisenhower would reflect on these unseemly political ploys and conclude that both he and the chief of staff were "a couple of pawns in a chess game, each compelled to await the pleasure of the players."[68]

Having done his duty to Churchill in Malta, Eisenhower hurried back to Oran, Algeria, where he met Roosevelt, Marshall, and Ernest King, who had come across the Atlantic aboard the newly minted battleship USS *Iowa*. From Oran, Eisenhower accompanied Roosevelt and his party to Tunis so that the president could visit his son, Elliott—then serving in a U.S. photo reconnaissance unit—and indulge his interest in history by visiting some nearby Carthaginian battlefields.[69] Leaving Marshall and King behind in a villa in Carthage, Eisenhower and Roosevelt toured the Tunisian plains, though neither of them could locate precisely where the legions of Scipio Africanus had devastated the armies of Hannibal. When they stopped for lunch by the side of the road, Roosevelt was in an unusually buoyant mood: "Ike, if one year ago, you had offered to bet that on this day the President of the United States would be having his lunch on a Tunisian roadside, what odds could you have demanded?"[70] The president then engaged in a long discussion of the events of the previous year and his admiration for Churchill. Command of Overlord remained unmentioned by Roosevelt.

But that evening, during a dinner with Marshall and King, Eisenhower was astonished to hear the chief of naval operations say that he opposed giving the Overlord command to Marshall, arguing that he "dreaded the consequences of Marshall's withdrawal from the Combined Chiefs of Staff." This was apparently the first inkling that Eisenhower had that Marshall might not get the command, and he and the Army chief of staff remained silent. Marshall, Eisenhower said, "seemed embarrassed."[71] As if to put a coda on King's statement, Roosevelt finally broached the subject of the Overlord command assignment to Eisenhower the next afternoon, just hours before he was due to depart for Cairo. It was now becoming apparent that Roosevelt was toying with the idea of keeping Marshall in Washington, no matter how painful that decision might be. He dreaded losing Marshall's help in Washington, he told Eisenhower, but then added: "You and I know the name of the Chief of Staff in the Civil War, but few Americans outside the professional service do."[72] Then, after a moment's hesitation, he added a wistful truism. "But it is dangerous to monkey with a winning team."[73]

George Marshall arrived in Cairo on November 21. Once again, the Army chief of staff was at the center of the negotiations, and once again, the topic under discussion was the invasion of France. But at this conference, Roosevelt and Churchill were hosting Chinese generalissimo Chiang Kai-shek, whose vitriolic relationship with American general Joseph Stilwell, the deputy supreme Allied commander to Vice Admiral Lord Louis Mountbatten in the South East Asia Command, was endangering the Allied position in China.[74] As during the American-British battle over the invasion of Europe, Marshall had been battling to put his own vision of the war in China in place. The problem in China was to get Chiang to focus his attention on fighting the Japanese instead of undermining Stilwell's efforts to arm and train Chinese units. Fearing that doing so would only fuel insurrection against his leadership, Chiang had worked against Stilwell at every turn. Marshall's task was delicate and demanded his every diplomatic effort. Marshall sympathized with Chiang and admitted that he was "constantly sold down the river by his advisors," but prosecuting the war against Japan in China was an Allied priority.[75] To help Chiang and Stilwell, Marshall pleaded for more resources for China. The British opposed Marshall's idea, arguing that resources destined for China could be put to better use in the Mediterranean. Marshall began yet another delicate dance with Churchill and Brooke. Watching this from his own position on the Joint Chiefs, Hap

Arnold shook his head in wonder. Marshall, he concluded, was nearly inde-structible. "He had more mature judgment [than his British counterparts], could see further into the future. I am sure that the President and Prime Minister both felt the same, because each one called on him for advice and counsel at all hours of the day or night."[76] When Roosevelt later approached Arnold for his views on who should command Overlord, the air chief noted Marshall's deft handling of Chiang and Churchill. He did not want Marshall to leave the Joint Chiefs of Staff, he said, but he thought he was the best man for the European command. His handling of the China negotiations in Cairo proved it.

Before the British and the Americans could come to any agreement on China, however, they suspended their discussions and traveled to Tehran, where Roosevelt and Churchill were to meet Soviet leader Joseph Stalin. This was the first meeting of the Big Three and the first time either Roosevelt or Churchill had met their Soviet ally. In Tehran, Roosevelt huddled with Marshall and his other advisers to determine what the Americans would say if Stalin insisted that more pressure be brought on the Germans prior to Overlord. Marshall said that Eisenhower could deploy forces farther north in Italy if need be, but he still op-posed promising an offensive in the Balkans. Every resource available must be given to Overlord. If necessary, Roosevelt should stand up to Stalin just as he had stood up to Churchill. Thus prepared, Roosevelt, Churchill, and their staffs met Stalin at the compound of the Soviet legation in Iran, where a mod-est conference room had been put aside for their meetings.[77] Stalin was impa-tient during the welcoming addresses and when they were finished waved his hand: "Now we can get down to business."[78] Stalin lived up to his billing. Brusque, temperamental, opinionated, quick to anger, with a sardonic sense of humor, the Soviet leader commanded the room. He was also filled with sur-prises. In his first meeting with Roosevelt and Churchill, Stalin peremptorily dismissed Churchill's talk of hitting Hitler's "soft underbelly." Overlord, he an-nounced, was his priority.[79] The next day Stalin's views were reinforced by Soviet marshal Kliment Voroshilov, who met privately with the American and British chiefs. An imposing man and veteran of the Soviet-German war on the eastern front, Voroshilov questioned Marshall and Brooke on the invasion of France. Brooke, as was his wont, was irritated by the questioning, thought that Voroshilov was being simplistic, and immediately dismissed him as a superfi-

Colonel Dwight Eisenhower
with Douglas MacArthur
after the Bonus March.
(Bettmann/CORBIS)

Presidential adviser Harry Hopkins, General Mark Clark,
U.S. President Franklin Delano Roosevelt, and General George S. Patton
eat lunch from mess kits after inspecting troops in North Africa.
(Bettmann/CORBIS)

1943, Casablanca, Morocco: President Franklin Delano Roosevelt and Prime Minister Winston Churchill (*seated*) pose with their staffs during allied conference at Casablanca. Standing (*left to right*) are: Lieutenant General H. H. Arnold, Admiral Ernest J. King, General George C. Marshall, Sir Dudley Pound, Sir Charles Portal, Sir Alan Francis Brooke, Sir John Dill, Lord Louis Mountbatten, and Brehon H. Somervell. Others are unidentified.
(*Bettmann/CORBIS*)

Field Marshal Erwin Rommel (*center*) in North Africa.
(*dpa/Corbis*)

Winston Churchill, Bernard Law Montgomery, and Alan Brooke near Tripoli.
(Bettmann/CORBIS)

Field Marshal Albert "Smiling Al" Kesselring *(right)* with his troops in Italy.
(CORBIS)

Dwight Eisenhower is shown with his staff: *Left to right, seated*: Air Chief Marshal Sir Arthur Tedder, General Eisenhower and General Sir Bernard Montgomery. *Left to right, standing*: Lieutenant General Omar Bradley, Admiral Sir Bertram Ramsey, Air Chief Marshal Sir Trafford Leigh Mallory and Lieutenant General W. Bedell Smith.
(Bettmann/CORBIS)

Dwight Eisenhower and Bernard Montgomery (*right*) in England planning for the invasion.
(Bettmann/CORBIS)

General Eisenhower speaking to paratroopers of the 101st Airborne Division in England, just prior to their participation in the first assault in the invasion of Europe.
(Bettmann/CORBIS)

Dwight Eisenhower in England prior to D-Day.
(Hulton-Deutsch Collection/CORBIS)

American troops land at Omaha Beach.
(Bettmann/CORBIS)

General Omar Bradley,
General Dwight Eisenhower
and General George Patton
survey war damage
in Bastogne.
(Bettmann/CORBIS)

George Patton and George Marshall in Europe in 1944.
(CORBIS)

Dwight Eisenhower and George Marshall at National Airport during Eisenhower's victory tour.
(Bettmann/CORBIS)

"Ja"—Colonel General Jodl signs the unconditional surrender of Germany at Rheims.
(Hulton-Deutsch Collection/CORBIS)

George Marshall and Dwight Eisenhower conferring on
Capitol Hill prior to testifying on the Marshall Plan.
(Bettmann/CORBIS)

cial thinker.[80] Voroshilov was not intimidated. Did Brooke support the cross-Channel invasion as much as Marshall or not? Brooke was silent, jaw set, clearly irritated by anyone who dared question his views—let alone a Russian. But he could no longer hedge. Yes, he said, he supported Overlord, but added, as if the question were of little moment, that the British had "always" considered Overlord essential.

On the afternoon of November 29, Marshall and Brooke briefed Stalin on the cross-Channel invasion plans, highlighting the potential pitfalls of the operation but emphasizing American and British agreement on its planning. Stalin sat silent, listening intently, eyeing the briefers. When they had concluded he asked only one question: "Who will command Overlord?" When Churchill, seated nearby, quickly interjected that he had already agreed that an American should be in command, Stalin nodded. That was fine, he said. He too had no intention of dictating who the commander would be; he just wanted to be given a name. Yet it was clear to everyone that the Soviet leader preferred Marshall. "He pressed for me all the time," Marshall later remembered. "And [he] made it quite a point, and I could take it or leave it as to whether it was just because he thought I was the man or whether he was trying to precipitate a second front."[81] Marshall knew about Stalin and was blunt in speaking about his reputation (he was "a tough SOB who made his way by murder" and "not a foreign service officer"), but Marshall was tickled by Stalin's continued needling of Churchill about Hitler's soft underbelly. "He was turning the hose on Churchill all the time," Marshall remembered, "and Mr. Roosevelt, in a sense, was helping him."[82] Inevitably, as the conference drew to a close, Stalin reiterated the importance of the cross-Channel operation. Overlord should be carried forward and not postponed, not for any reason, he emphasized. It should also be reinforced by landings in southern France, he said, and a supreme commander to head the operation should be named at once.[83]

MARSHALL AND the Combined Chiefs of Staff returned to Cairo to continue their discussions with Roosevelt and Churchill. The British again attempted to argue for another shift in emphasis—this time away from reinforcing Chiang Kai-shek in order to provide more resources for Overlord and for "Anvil," the proposed invasion of southern France. It now seemed to Marshall that anything the Americans wanted the British would contest. At issue was a proposed invasion of the Andaman Islands in the Bay of Bengal. The islands would be captured as a prelude to an invasion of Burma, siphoning off Japanese forces from China. The British favored canceling the operation, arguing that the Andaman invasion would divert landing craft meant for the cross-Channel invasion. The British proposal had enormous implications for the American war in the Pacific, as it would allow Japanese forces to withdraw from Southeast Asia to reinforce their commands fighting the Americans in the Pacific. The British decision would cost American lives, but it would add resources for the forces gathering in England. Marshall was for it, all in all, but Roosevelt was less certain. In confirming the Andaman operation, the Allies would be showing their commitment to China and tying down hundreds of thousands of Japanese troops. Still, after arguing strenuously with Churchill and Brooke, Roosevelt conceded the necessity of reinforcing Overlord. He agreed. The Andaman operation should be canceled. Europe must still come first.

Finally, Roosevelt turned his attention to naming the commander of Overlord. He had postponed the decision for weeks, but now it could not be postponed any longer. The decision was his and his only, since Churchill had agreed that an American should be in command, and Marshall had insisted that the Overlord commander should be a "supreme commander." Over a period of two years, from December 1941 to December 1943, George Marshall had argued incessantly for the important of a single unified command operating under a single commander. The British Chiefs of Staff were never fully comfortable with the Marshall concept and had at key moments attempted to undermine it—by pressuring Roosevelt through Churchill, by fighting for resources in regions important to the continuation of British colonialism, by attempting to "kick" Eisenhower into the "stratosphere." So too, at key moments and particularly during high-level meetings, the Americans had aggravated matters by commenting sotto voce and even openly about "limeys" and "Tommies" and by showing particular insensitivity to British hesitations about committing more soldiers to the German meat grinder. Through all of this incessant and sometimes painful wrangling, Marshall had remained unwavering. A single commander was a necessity, he said, and he undergirded his views by even suggesting that should the British oppose the concept of a supreme commander for Overlord from mistrust, they could take the command themselves—

so long as they named Sir John Dill to the post.[84] Finally, the British conceded. There would be one Supreme Allied Command for both Overlord and Europe—one "SACEUR."

But there was a problem, and it was not in naming a single commander or even agreeing to a unified command. The problem was Marshall. For, as the British quietly pointed out, if Marshall was named supreme Allied commander in Europe he would actually be holding two *different* supreme positions, as part of the Combined Chiefs of Staff and as the highest-ranking European commander. He would wield enormous power—too much power. And, the British pointedly asked, who would take Marshall's place as Army chief of staff? And would that new Army chief of staff outrank him—as, according to U.S. tradition and law—he must? Who would dare give George Marshall orders? The questions were politely and quietly put, but they were good questions, with no easy answers. And so, slowly but certainly, even before Roosevelt and Churchill met Stalin in Tehran, the sands began to shift under George Marshall, tilting the president and prime minister and the Combined Chiefs of Staff away from his candidacy. Inevitably Roosevelt's imprecation began to take hold. No one wanted to "monkey with a winning team." On December 4, Roosevelt sent Harry Hopkins to talk with Marshall about the appointment, hoping thereby to draw out Marshall's views on the subject. Unlike Churchill, who had left Brooke "bleeding and battered" over the Supreme Command decision,[85] Roosevelt was being careful with Marshall, hoping that he would make the decision himself. The command was his for the asking. The problem, of course, was that Marshall would not ask for the command, or deem it automatically his. Ever the good soldier, Marshall believed the decision was in the hands of his commander in chief. He had served with honor. He would not ask for anything. He would instead, he told Hopkins, "go along whole-heartedly with whatever decision the President made."[86] For Marshall, this was a matter of principle—the most fundamental principle of the American Republic. The commander in chief was the highest-ranking political and military official in the country. He gave the orders.

Disappointed that Marshall would not relieve him of his decision, the president invited the chief of staff to have lunch with him the next day in his Cairo villa. Marshall must have been aware that even discussing who should be commander meant that Roosevelt wanted to keep him in Washington. He had waited through the first Cairo meeting and the meeting in Tehran for Roosevelt to make the announcement. It had not happened. Marshall wanted the command, but he was determined that he would "not embarrass the President one way or the other—that he must be able to deal in this matter with a perfectly free hand in whatever he felt was in the best interests [of the country]."[87]

There followed what must have been one of the most uncomfortable meetings in the history of American civil-military relations. We have Marshall's account.

> As I recall, [President Roosevelt] asked me after a great deal of beating about the bush just what I wanted to do. Evidently it was left up to me. Well, having in mind all this business that had occurred in Washington . . . I just repeated again in as convincing language as I could that I wanted him to feel free to act in whatever way he felt was to the best interest of the country and to his satisfaction and not in any way to consider my feelings. I would cheerfully go whatever way he wanted me to go and I didn't express any desire one way or the other.[88]

Roosevelt thought about this for a moment and then turned to his chief of staff. "Well," he said, "I didn't feel I could sleep at ease if you were out of Washington." There was a silence then, and Roosevelt added: "Then it will be Eisenhower." Marshall left Roosevelt to sign the orders and to dictate messages to Stalin and Chiang Kai-shek. The announcement was made the same day: "The immediate appointment of General Eisenhower to command of 'Overlord' operation has been decided on."[89] The next day, December 7, 1943—two years to the day since the Japanese brought America into the war—and after yet another meeting with the British Chiefs of Staff, Marshall wrote to his lieutenant and included a copy of the order that he had written for Franklin Roosevelt. "Dear Eisenhower: I thought you might like to have this as a memento. It was written very hurriedly by me as the final meeting broke up yesterday, the President signing it immediately. G.C.M."[90]

SHINGLE

*"I merely wish to be certain that localitis is not
developing. . . ."*
*"So far as I am aware, no one here has tried to urge me to
present any particular view. . . ."*

O N NEW YEAR'S DAY 1944, American marines under the command
of Brigadier General Lemuel Shepherd struck southwest toward Borgen
Bay on the island of New Britain.[1] Shepherd's movement was a part of
Operation Cartwheel, a complex offensive that took place across thousands of
miles of ocean and across hundreds of tropical islands speckled in the southwest Pacific. Cartwheel was intended to isolate the strong Japanese garrison on
New Guinea, at Rabaul, and set the stage for the cracking of the Japanese defensive perimeter in the South Pacific.[2] That same day, U.S. carrier-based
fighter aircraft and land-based bombers attacked Rabaul as, farther south, troops
from the U.S., Australia, and New Zealand continued to slug it out with
Japanese forces entrenched in the steaming jungles of northern New Guinea.[3]
Within weeks the battle for the Bismarck Archipelago would be won, New
Guinea would be secured, and American and Allied forces would be poised for
a final push from the south toward the Philippines. While the Japanese outer
perimeter in the Pacific would thereby be successfully pierced, the victories had
already brought added worries. It had taken the Marines six months of hard
fighting to secure Guadalcanal and months more to launch attacks north and

then west toward the next Japanese defensive line — where the main battle fleet of the Japanese Empire remained.

Shepherd's offensive at Borgen Bay had been a long time coming. The fight for the Solomon Islands during the previous year had been costly, and Allied planning in the Pacific was hampered by Douglas MacArthur's continued sniping at Admiral Chester Nimitz and Chief of Naval Operations Ernest King, who were only too glad to snipe back. While Marshall reined in these disagreements, it was yet to be determined which line of advance — MacArthur's Army offensive in the southwest Pacific or Nimitz's Navy and Marine offensive in the central Pacific — would have priority. For Marshall, the MacArthur-Nimitz skirmish was particularly frustrating. While both men argued for increased resources by claiming that their operations provided the best prospects for victory against the Japanese, neither was celebrated for his altruism.[4] MacArthur stood in the front ranks of America's Army partisans, while the otherwise soft-spoken "hero of Midway" viewed the Pacific as the Navy's pond.[5] While Marshall had been able to rid himself of such rivalries in the Mediterranean by turning them over to Eisenhower, he found it impossible to shake free of the MacArthur-Nimitz competition, despite a number of high-level meetings he had held with Army and Navy senior commanders to sort through who would get what and when. Marshall was saved a soul-killing confrontation only by America's wartime industrial miracle, which produced eleven fleet and light fleet carriers and thousands of fighter aircraft in 1943, enough for Marshall to allow both commanders to carry through their plans. The production miracle enforced an uneasy Army-Navy truce, and by early 1944 the United States was fighting an Army war in the southwest Pacific and a Navy war in the central Pacific.[6]

The Pacific was not the only place where the Allies were on the offensive. Nearly ten thousand miles to the west of Borgen Bay, the New Year dawned cold along the Dnieper River, where the Red Army continued to launch dawn-to-dusk attacks across a nine-hundred-mile front from the Pripet Marshes in the north to the Crimea in the south. The immediate goal of the operation — called "Right Bank Ukraine" — was to methodically clear the Dnieper Valley of German Army Group A and German Army Group South by means of massed tank and infantry attacks by five separate "fronts."[7] Light snow and deep frost aided the initial offensive west of Kiev, though German resistance was tenacious. The battles along the Dnieper pitted over 2.6 million Russian troops and 2,400 tanks against 1.2 million German troops and 2,100 tanks. The success of these battles freed the Red Army's special mobile groups from the bitterly contested close-in battles for Kiev and the industrialized Donets Basin. The tank spearheads roamed across western Russia and the Ukraine, closing out what the Soviet high command had called the "second period of the war." Stalin believed that at the end of this second period the fully mobilized Red Army forces would be strong enough to contend with the Germans in men and matériel. Even so, as Stalin had made clear to Roosevelt and Churchill at Tehran, Hitler was playing for time and now, two years into the war, had the advantage of being able to shift troops along a constricted defensive front. The Germans could also, if necessary, call on reserve divisions from France, where panzer units were refitting and replacements were being trained. Stalin was insistent: Germany's final defeat would be assured only when Hitler was forced to drain troops from the Russian front and transfer them West—to meet an Allied force landing in France.

The Allies were on the move in the Pacific and in Russia. But the situation was quite different 2,400 miles south and west of the Dnieper, where Mark Clark and Harold Alexander, commanding eighteen Allied divisions, were still vainly struggling to breach Field Marshal Albert Kesselring's Gustav Line. New Year's Day found units of Clark's Fifth Army struggling to gain a foothold on the ridges below Monte Cassino, which loomed imposingly over the central Italian battlefield. The Monte Cassino position forced Clark to funnel his troops northward, as if into the neck of a bottle, with the German position at the Benedictine monastery its cork. If Clark could force the cork, his army would flow onto the plain beyond—spilling all the way to Rome. But such a movement was still months away. Clark and Alexander's straight-up- he-middle offensive was so effectively parried by Kesselring throughout the last weeks of 1943 that Eisenhower reluctantly approved yet another Salerno-like landing on Italy's western coast at Anzio.[8]

Called Operation Shingle, the landing at Anzio was scheduled for the end of January; its planners envisioned an over-the-beach assault by one British and four American divisions (the VI Corps) that would secure the area southwest of Rome, link up with Clark's troops, and sprint north, taking Italy's capital by storm.[9] If all went well, Kesselring's forces would disintegrate in the resulting retreat. The war in Italy would be over—won.[10] But Eisenhower had as many doubts about Shingle as he had had about Avalanche, his hesitation reflecting his views not only of Kesselring's abilities, but of the mounting chaos in the Allied command structure that attended his departure.

Indeed, Clark and Alexander's position in Italy was made more difficult by Eisenhower's move to London. The newly minted supreme Allied commander, Europe, had wanted to take Harold Alexander with him as his ground commander and invasion planner for Overlord, but Churchill wanted Alexander, whom he viewed as a brilliant strategist, to stay in Italy. Churchill maneuvered through December to keep Alexander where he was and to appoint Field Marshal Sir Henry Maitland Wilson as Eisenhower's replacement (and Alexander's superior) as the Allied Mediterranean commander. It was finally decided that with the SACEUR position firmly in the hands of an American, the big-eared Wilson (hence his nickname—"Jumbo") would command in the Mediterranean, while American major general Jacob Devers was appointed his deputy.[11] While the successful sandwiching of national commands between Americans and Englishmen thereby satisfied Roosevelt and Churchill's commitment to maintaining Anglo-American cooperation, it played havoc in Italy, where the competent and understated Devers held Clark in contempt, while Clark's disdain for Devers ("that dope") was nearly as public as his dislike of the British. The two fought so openly and with such bitterness that their staffs determined that they could not be in the same room for more than three minutes.[12] When Churchill insisted that Montgomery be Eisenhower's Overlord ground commander (a decision Eisenhower did not welcome), the prime minister appointed Lieutenant General Oliver Leese as his successor in command of the Eighth Army, then struggling up central Italy's German-infested ridges. Leese (who was as celebrated for his love of gardening as Brooke was for his love of birds) was notable for his solemnity; he was once described by a colleague as having the personality of "a suet pudding."[13] Eisenhower viewed all of this with trepidation, but he was reluctant to interfere with Churchill, whose heart was set on taking Rome.[14] After one last tour of the Italian battlefields, Eisenhower decided to leave well enough alone, and in any event, the new SACEUR now had new responsibilities. He spent the last two weeks of December ignoring Alexander and Clark's problems and turned his attention to making a list of commanders that he wanted to join him in London.

While Eisenhower was surprised by his appointment as supreme Allied commander in Europe, he moved quickly to reassure Marshall of his continued dependence on his guidance. "First, let me tell you how very deeply appreciative I am of your thoughtfulness in sending me the memorandum, in your handwriting, on which the agreement was made in Tehran that I was to command Overlord," Eisenhower wrote on December 17. "Of all possible assignments this was the one that I least expected, since I had assumed that the decision was firm that you were to take the job personally."[15] Eisenhower then reviewed the Mediterranean command arrangements—including his recommendation that Alexander be the planner and ground commander for Overlord—before hinting that he planned to travel to London to take command in Europe as soon as possible. But George Marshall had other plans. On December 28 he recommended that Eisenhower travel to Washington to meet with him and Roosevelt before taking up his London duties: "I suggest that you either come straight to the U.S. from Africa or if you go to England report here shortly thereafter to make the necessary contacts with the War Department, to see your family, and to get at least a brief rest," Marshall wrote.[16] When Eisenhower resisted this suggestion, Marshall came close to giving him an order. "You will be under terrific strain from now on," the chief of staff wrote. "I am interested that you are fully prepared to bear the strain and I am not interested in the usual rejoinder that you can take it. It is of vast importance that you be fresh mentally and you certainly will not be if you go straight from one great problem to another. Now come on home and see your wife and trust somebody else for 20 minutes in England."[17]

So on New Year's Day 1944, while Lemuel Shepherd's marines fought at Borgen Bay, the Red Army flung itself across the Dnieper, and Mark Clark and Harold Alexander continued their slog up the Italian peninsula,[18] Dwight Eisenhower boarded a C-54 bound for Washington for a "badly needed rest." But Marshall's advice to Eisenhower to spend time with his family was not a suggestion that the Army chief of staff applied to himself. After spending time with Katherine in Florida the previous March, Marshall had maintained a breakneck pace, visiting nearly every major American command, from North Africa to the southwest Pacific. He had just returned to Washington on December 22 after a thirty-five-thousand-mile journey that had taken him from Cairo to Tehran and back and thence to the Pacific, where he had conferred with MacArthur and America's senior naval commanders.[19] He celebrated his sixty-fourth birthday on the last day of 1943 with Henry Stimson. The secretary of war brought together a retinue of Marshall's friends and colleagues in the newly constructed Pentagon for a short celebration, which was followed by a less informal gathering at Stimson's home. Marshall was in a celebratory mood, buoyed by Stimson's laudatory comment that Marshall was the only American commander to lead U.S. troops "through an entire war."[20] Surprisingly, Marshall responded by shedding his normal reticence and grabbing Lieutenant General Brehon Burke Somervell, the head of U.S. Services of Supply, from a circle of admirers and leading a duet rendition of "We've Been Working on the Railroad."[21] George Marshall spent the next day, New Year's Day 1944, at home with Katherine. But he was not at ease: his Somervell duet had been a pointed reminder of his worries, which were now focused on U.S. railway workers, who had announced that they planned to go on strike. He had issued a withering condemnation of that decision during a press conference the previous week, and his words (that the strike would weaken the war effort and hamper U.S. operations against Germany) were in all the Sunday newspapers, along with a report that Marshall's private remarks were even more unusual than his decision to sing in public. For the first time in as long as anyone could remember, the Army chief of staff actually swore.[22]

MARSHALL AND Eisenhower were obsessed by the European invasion. While Marshall was certain the invasion would succeed and rarely took counsel of his fears, the new U.S. commander in Europe was worried that the planning for Overlord was not proceeding quickly enough to make a May invasion possible. Then too, Eisenhower's experiences in North Africa, Sicily, and, most particularly, at Salerno were convincing evidence that even the best plans and most detailed preparations could go awry. And they had, time and again: during the murderous commando assault at Oran in North Africa, during the friendly-fire incident that chewed up a regiment of the 82nd Airborne near Sicily, and then tragically at Salerno, where Kesselring's obstinate counterattacks had nearly pushed Allied soldiers back into the Bay of Naples. In each case, the ponderous weight of Allied men and matériel (what German field marshal Paul von Hindenburg had once described as America's "pitiless industry") had proven decisive, veiling several near defeats and miscalculations in a torrent of firepower.[23] The miscarried attack on Oran Harbor had been balanced by the missteps of its French defenders and the cavalry-to-the-rescue appearance of the Twelfth Air Force; the embarrassing lack of coordination among Allied troops in Sicily had been papered over by the ability of nearly one-quarter of a million Macs and Tommies to overwhelm sixty thousand Jerries; and the beachhead at Salerno had been saved by point-blank naval gunfire and a miraculously accurate airborne assault that was unlikely to be replicated. Marshall and Eisenhower both knew that firepower and leadership, pluck and self-sacrifice— and luck—had been vitally important to past Allied victories. But the just-in-the-nick-of-time appearance of bombers, the unpredicted missteps of an enemy, and point-blank artillery and naval gunfire were no guarantees of future success. Nor was simple brute courage. Good planning and "getting there the firstest with the mostest," in the words of Confederate cavalry commander Nathan Bedford Forrest, would make the difference. But any advantage in firepower during the first days of Overlord would be canceled by a large number of well-trained, highly mobile, well-led and experienced German panzer divisions, which for the first weeks after the invasion would outnumber the invaders. In Normandy, where the Allies now planned to land sometime on or after May 1, the Germans would be there first, they would have the most, and they would have Erwin Rommel—the new German commander in France.

Initial planning for the invasion of France had actually begun in February 1942, when Eisenhower, Gee Gerow, Generals Thomas Handy and Joseph McNarney, and Colonel Albert Wedemeyer at the War Plans Division began to exchange ideas on a cross-Channel operation.[24] All were concerned that the drain on U.S. and Allied resources, then being funneled to meet the crisis in the Pacific, could prove fatal to U.S. and British efforts in Europe. The longer an invasion was postponed, the more likely that Germany would gain in strength, particularly if its panzer divisions were victorious in Russia. There were three interrelated concerns: that Russia would be knocked out of the war; that Stalin would sign a separate peace that would keep German troops permanently in Poland and the Ukraine (as was then widely rumored); or, as seemed less likely, that the Red Army would weather the incessant battering it was taking from Hitler's panzers, recover lost ground, and gain control of most of Europe. Any of the three outcomes would be catastrophic. Convinced that a German defeat of Russia was then possible, Marshall instructed Eisenhower and his colleagues to write a plan for a diversionary invasion of Europe to take place in mid-1943—this was Sledgehammer. The invasion was necessary for political as well as military reasons: to liberate Western Europe, but also to keep the Red Army in the field.

Through the ensuing, often bitter debates on what kind of invasion should be launched and when, Marshall's planners detailed various estimates of probable enemy strengths, as well as likely Allied resources. Initially, U.S. planners estimated that victory in northwest Europe would come only with the deployment of forty-eight divisions and 5,800 aircraft.[25] The diversion of resources first to North Africa, then to Sicily, and finally to Italy sidetracked this initiative, frustrated Marshall, and threatened to institutionalize British thinking—to peel away German strength by attacks on its periphery. In the more than two years since, British insistence on invading Europe's soft underbelly, had provided endless teeth-gnashing moments for the chief of staff, but Marshall had come to understand the constant British hesitations. While the Americans were still capable of getting there "the firstest with the mostest," a methodical village-by-village war of attrition in France was a British nightmare. The British were scraping the bottom of the manpower barrel, and the effects of this were being felt on the field of battle. By mid-1943, Marshall later reflected, the quality of British divisions was deteriorating, an opinion he had come to after a close study of Montgomery's Eighth Army offensive against Rommel in North Africa. The situation worsened in Italy, where "the fighting spirit and aggressive quality of British divisions began again to decline, and for the reason of the sheer factor of exhaustion," he later reflected. "The British simply could not keep their battalions up to strength and it was very depressing to their men."[26] But Marshall knew that that explanation was not relevant. For a British soldier killed in Italy was not the same as a British soldier killed in France—the difference being that the Alp-less expanses of northern Europe beckoned to a man like Patton, whose armored spearheads could eviscerate the Reich. So why postpone the inevitable reckoning with Hitler's legions? That question was finally answered to Marshall's satisfaction when Churchill's physician sidled up to him during a particularly contentious debate with the British Chiefs: "You are fighting the Battle of the Somme," he said.[27]

Even so, and seen now through the lens of more than six decades of intervening history, it is clear that the price paid for North Africa, Sicily, and Italy had been worth it. Through all of the first two years of the war, the Russians were reeling, desperate for assistance, and keenly aware that if German troops garrisoning North Africa, Sicily, and Italy were suddenly transferred east, the weight of their arrival would tip the balance—and Russia would be out of the war. The Anglo-American alliance could not have sat idle and allowed this to happen. It *had* to fight. Eisenhower, Alexander, Anderson, Montgomery, Patton, Clark, and Bradley had tied down and then killed, wounded, or captured hundreds of thousands of German combat veterans who might have appeared outside of Moscow, just in the nick of time, tipping the balance in the east and ensuring a German victory. Stalin knew this, and presumably so did Hitler. So as Marshall confronted Churchill over the endless drain of resources to North Africa, Sicily, and Italy, he wondered why the German high command had defended Tripoli and Messina, and even Rome. Why not save your soldiers for the real battle in Western Europe or, better yet, ship them to the Moscow front, where they were desperately needed? It was Frederick the Great who had told his commanders that defending everything everywhere meant defending nothing anywhere. Hitler, who lionized Frederick, had failed to learn that lesson. Years later, Marshall was still puzzled by Germany's fatal decision to fight in North Africa and Italy, instead of shuttling its forces east, where panzer divisions were within sight of the Kremlin.[28] It is now clear that the German offensive in Russia weighed on Marshall even more than his concerns about preparing and waging the war in the Pacific or in North Africa. Russia's collapse, he believed, might even make the war unwinnable. "We had to go ahead brutally fast" in Europe, he said years later. "We could not indulge in a Seven Years War. A king can perhaps do that, but you cannot have such a protracted struggle in a democracy in the face of mounting casualties. I thought that the only place to achieve a positive and rapid military decision was on the lowlands of northwestern Europe. Speed was essential."[29] Even after the war, Marshall's reflections on global strategy were a reflection of Fox Conner's and as "pitiless" a judgment as Hindenburg's: democracies and free societies might be able to produce more tanks and aircraft than a dictatorship, but they could not discipline their people as effectively. Both Marshall and Eisenhower remained forever convinced that democracies could win only short wars, not protracted conflicts.

Marshall's laserlike focus on France as the key to shortening the war with Germany was insistently reinforced by Albert Wedemeyer, the foremost strategist on his staff and the military's leading intellectual. The ruggedly handsome, conservative, and articulate West Point graduate's brilliance resulted in his 1936 appointment to the Kriegsakademie, the prestigious German war college.[30] For two years, Wedemeyer studied German war thinking, rubbing shoulders with officers who would later lead German panzers into Poland, France, and Russia. In 1938, his German teachers took the unusual step of including him in a field test of their doctrines, despite the fact that he was an officer serving in the army of a potential future enemy. Wedemeyer was assigned to an antitank battalion, where he commanded a unit ordered to intercept and destroy a highly mobile tank unit. The experience was unique; no other American officer in World War II could speak with as much authority on German tactical operations. In 1938, Wedemeyer returned to Washington, where he presented a paper on his experiences to then–chief of staff Malin Craig. But his most ardent student was George Marshall. As the head of the Army Staff's War Plans Division in 1938, Marshall listened in fascination as Wedemeyer outlined German war thinking. What Patton and Eisenhower had done in taking apart and putting together a tank in a grimy garage at Fort Meade, Wedemeyer now did for Marshall in analyzing Germany's grand strategy: he dissected German thinking, taking it apart piece by piece, and then he put it back together again.

In July 1941, Roosevelt directed Marshall to provide a paper on "a strategic concept of how to defeat our potential enemies." Marshall passed the assignment to Wedemeyer. In the resulting paper, Wedemeyer said the U.S. needed to build highly maneuverable tank divisions, lots of tank divisions, capable of striking deep into enemy territory. Also, Wedemeyer argued, the U.S. should be prepared to put 8.8 million men into the field within two years of the opening of hostilities—by July 1943. Wedemeyer's supposition was prescient and brilliant: the United States trained and fielded almost precisely that many soldiers during its war with Japan and Germany. John Keegan, in his landmark study on the Normandy operation, summarized Wedemeyer's views: "And so, unlike the British army, which was building and training a host of small specialized units for raiding and diversion, the American army, in Wedemeyer's plan, was to contain only three sorts of formations: armored divisions, a few airborne divisions to operate with them on the blitzkrieg pattern, and a mass of infantry divisions to consolidate the gains won by the tanks. It was, in short, to be an army suitable for only one sort of operation: large-scale, tank-infantry battles on the continent of Europe."[31] In an introductory statement to his paper, Wedemeyer named America's most likely enemy and spelled out in the simplest terms all that he had learned through two decades of concentrated military thinking, and as a student in Berlin: "We must prepare to fight Germany by actually coming to grips with and defeating her ground forces and definitely break her will to combat. Air and sea forces will make important contributions, but effective and adequate ground forces must be available to close with and destroy the enemy inside his citadel."[32] The Eurasian landmass was the globe's "heartland," Germany's "citadel." It must be "pierced" by the surrounding industrialized maritime states. The only way to do this was to deploy massed tanks against the heartland's enemy on the plains of northern Europe.[33]

By the end of the North African campaign, Wedemeyer's ideas about an invasion of France so permeated American thinking that an indefinite postponement of the operation was out of the question. Despite continuing doubts (was Overlord really necessary? wouldn't Germany collapse anyway? couldn't it be bombed into submission?) and long, anxious looks at the potential casualty figures, the British agreed to begin writing a plan for the invasion of Europe. In March 1943, the Combined Chiefs of Staff appointed British general Frederick E. Morgan as the principal planning officer for the invasion. Morgan was given full powers, a staff to organize resources, and complete autonomy to ensure the maximum freedom in carrying out his mandate.[34] Christened COSSAC (after Morgan's title: chief of staff, supreme Allied commander—designate), Morgan appointed staff commanders responsible for determining naval, air, ground, intelligence, and logistics requirements. By July 1943, Morgan had designated the Second British Army, the First Canadian Army, and the U.S. First Army as the assault force, and named Normandy as the landing area. Normandy, Morgan believed, provided all that the Allies needed: firm and wide beaches for mounting armor, a predictable tidal schedule, nearby exit routes, good lateral roads to and from the region, and access to a port—Cherbourg. Morgan envisioned the creation of a three-division assault force that would land along a twenty-five-mile front, with two more divisions reinforcing the beachhead within twenty-four hours of the landings.[35]

On the same day that Eisenhower was landing in Washington, British field marshal Bernard Law Montgomery—cocksure, arrogant, ruthlessly ambitious, and an obsessive planner—arrived in London to review Morgan's plan. Montgomery's role was key. As in North Africa, Eisenhower would have three deputies charged with command of air, land, and sea assets. For Overlord, a fourth was added: a ground commander tasked with approving and implementing the final plan and overseeing the assault. The fear among the Americans in January 1944 was the same as it had been during Torch: that the British would attempt to "kick" Ike into the "stratosphere" and make Montgomery the designated hero of the operation. While that now seemed much less possible than it had in North Africa, just eight months before, Eisenhower was firm in his commitment to be as tough on Montgomery as he had been on Patton. Eisenhower had won the confidence of Winston Churchill, who seemed more likely to side with Eisenhower than with the hero of Alamein, who struck him as less a great commander than the ever-so-slow Harold Alexander. Marshall was confident that Eisenhower was now firmly in charge and that any decisions made by Montgomery would have to be approved by him. Montgomery had not been following COSSAC's planning, but immediately upon his arrival in London, Churchill insisted that he review Morgan's outline and report his first impressions. Montgomery spent hours leafing through Morgan's minutely detailed guide, focusing on his argument for a three-division, narrow-front assault. Montgomery was disdainful. Three divisions were not enough.[36] The Germans, with the Fifteenth Army in Pas-de-Calais and the Seventh Army in Caen, could match the Allied buildup soldier for soldier and unit for unit and, if they reacted quickly, could bring twenty-eight divisions to Normandy within the first forty-eight hours of the landings. The men in the assault waves, with minimal numbers of heavy weapons and tanks, would be slaughtered.

Montgomery determined that the argument for a three-division assault was built on rickety military logic: COSSAC planners argued for a narrow front because they assumed the Germans would be surprised by the landings and confused by the complex Allied deception. The deception plan consisted of creating a false army in England at the Channel's narrowest point, opposite the Pas-de-Calais, with a false headquarters and a false commandeer, George Patton.[37] Montgomery was dismissive. That the enemy would do what you hoped and that its commanders would believe what you wanted was perhaps the most specious

assumption in the history of warfare, and disproved in nearly every major contest from Cannae to Salerno. Montgomery did not discard Morgan's plan, for
its foundations were essentially sound, but he immediately pulled out a detailed map of Normandy and set about expanding its scope. "I'd like to assault
with twelve divisions," Eisenhower had told Beetle Smith back at his headquarters in North Africa.[38] Montgomery agreed with Eisenhower, but the divisions were simply not available. Still, a three-division assault, he believed, was
sure to fail, while a five-division assault might succeed. As Eisenhower and
Montgomery knew, the Allies had a painful history of bungling amphibious assaults, learning through bloody error the difficulties of coming ashore against
entrenched and fanatical defenders. George Marshall agreed with this viewpoint, for during his recent trip to the Pacific, the Army chief had closely questioned senior Marine commanders on their invasion of Tarawa, a rocky and
bleached island in the central Pacific that had been taken only after a loss of
3,300 American troops—an unacceptable casualty rate that shook the American
public's faith in the war. Unless Eisenhower and Montgomery learned the lessons of Tarawa, Marshall feared that Overlord could become a bloody cauldron,
a defeat from which the Allies might never recover.[39]

EISENHOWER HAD warned Mamie that he had changed, and now, in the first
moments after his arrival in Washington, during the early-morning hours of
January 2, she saw for herself the difference that time and high command
could make.[40] Her husband was more distant and seemed much older. He was
less patient, and her complaints about the difficulties of her daily life seemed
unimportant and niggling. He glared at her when she complained. He was
gruff, short-tempered, critical. He had filled out, and what was left of his once-
blond hair was now gray. But she and her neighbor and constant companion
Ruth Butcher were overjoyed to see their husbands. It had been eighteen
months since Ike and Mamie had been together, and despite some uncomfortable moments, they were pleased to finally see each other. Still, there was
a cool, unspoken distance between the two that was fueled by rumors: of his
dalliance with his driver, Kay Summersby (which, with little evidence, was
bruited about with winks and nods from other wives), and by quiet reports of
Mamie's "drinking problem." In truth, not only was Mamie's health fragile, but

she did not react well to being alone. Mamie missed her husband and was incapable of filling the role she had so proudly held through all of his years of thankless assignments and low pay. She felt unappreciated and isolated, alone.[41]

That the relationship of Eisenhower and his wife was strained, even uncomfortable, would not have come as a surprise to any senior military officer or, for that matter, to any married couple parted by war. The same cycle of separation and reunion was lived and relived tens of thousands of times in America during the war years. The best of marriages sometimes shattered under the stress. Even so, in comparison with many other marriages, Mamie and Ike's difficult reunion was unusual, even unique, for Mamie had a husband who *could* return. Her inability to grasp this fundamental fact angered Eisenhower and cast a pall over his visit. Millions of other American women had to wait interminably for husbands who could not take furloughs or who were under fire in Italy, the Pacific, or Burma or who lay wounded in hospitals or who were forever physically or mentally crippled. Many would never return at all. Eisenhower had tried to tell Mamie this in his letters, had attempted to steel her for the sacrifice she must make, had attempted to mollify her concerns about his health, his well-being, his personal sacrifices. There were others, many, many others, who did not have a personal staff, a personal driver, good meals, and friends. There were tens of thousands of others who had only a rifle, rations, and a cold and muddy pit and who depended for their lives on the courage of their friends and on the unpredictable wheel of fate. Through three decades of marriage and sacrifice, Mamie had shown remarkable resilience and loyalty. But now, in the midst of a world war, she had lost her stoicism.

On his first morning in Washington, Eisenhower, the stars on his shoulders hidden by a plain overcoat, said good-bye to Mamie and walked quickly down the back stairs of the Wardman Park Hotel to a waiting limousine that took him to the newly constructed Pentagon. Eisenhower's first meeting with Marshall in 1944 was more than friendly.[42] While Marshall was still Eisenhower's senior commander, their relationship had subtly changed. Eisenhower still deferred to Marshall, but during the briefings of the few senior staff officers that followed that morning's first personal meeting it was the younger man whose views held sway, whose opinions were solicited, whose plans and strategic views were reviewed, critiqued, accepted.[43] Slowly, inexorably, the relationship was beginning to be transformed. While Marshall would always remain the upperclassman and

Eisenhower his subordinate in both rank and seniority, Eisenhower was slowly becoming the senior partner in the relationship. Whether that fact was obvious to Marshall in January 1944 we will never know, for Marshall never said. But it was obvious that the Army chief of staff had been sorely disappointed by Roosevelt's decision to appoint Eisenhower to command in Europe, a feeling he shared with Secretary of War Stimson, who spent time with him on his birthday going through Roosevelt's decision-making process.[44] Marshall "showed his usual bigness about the whole thing," Stimson later commented.[45]

That evening, the Eisenhowers and the Butchers had a feast in Eisenhower's apartment, complete with steaks, oysters, and butter—which was tightly rationed.[46] The next morning, January 3, Eisenhower awoke to find that George Marshall had been named *Time*'s "Man of the Year."[47] The magazine praised the chief of staff for maintaining the principle of civilian control of the military: "He had armed the Republic," the accompanying article said. "In a general's uniform, he stood for the civilian substance of this democratic society. *Civis Americanus*, he had gained the world's undivided respect. In the name of the soldiers who had died, General George Catlett Marshall was entitled to accept his own nation's gratitude."[48] The *Time* cover seemed to belie Roosevelt's worry—that no one would remember a chief of staff, that he would become a World War II Halleck. Eisenhower returned to the Pentagon for several more meetings, and that evening the chief of staff hosted a dinner for him, sprinkling the guest list with senior officers and members of Congress. Major General J. Lawton "Lightning Joe" Collins talked of his command of the 25th Division, whose troops had wiped out Japanese resistance on Guadalcanal; Admiral Harold Stark spoke on the Battle of the Atlantic; and Lieutenant General George Kenney, responsible for the destruction of the Japanese Air Force at Rabaul, talked of the importance of air power in the reduction of enemy strongpoints.[49] Eisenhower then spoke briefly about Allied operations in North Africa and Italy but mentioned Overlord in only the most general terms. This was Ike's coming-out party, an inaugural briefing of politicians as well as senior commanders, and he spoke extemporaneously for twenty-five minutes. Marshall thought he did well, and after Eisenhower was finished he raised his glass in a toast to President Franklin Delano Roosevelt—and then raised his glass again, graciously, for a toast to General Dwight Eisenhower.[50]

Marshall and Eisenhower's meetings at the Pentagon over the next two days

were taken up with Ike's views on Overlord preparations and the Italian campaign. The two men agreed in nearly every particular, though that was hardly
a surprise: it was the reason Eisenhower had been sent to Europe, put in command in North Africa, and chosen for Overlord.[51] He exuded self-confidence,
but without understating the challenges that he faced in mounting the Normandy operation. On the morning of January 5 Eisenhower met with Roosevelt
at the White House, and he returned for a second visit on January 7. At Roosevelt's insistence, no notes were kept of these meetings, which were informal.
"Mr. Roosevelt was temporarily ill with influenza," Eisenhower later recounted,
"but seemed quite cheerful and kept me at his bedside for more than an hour
as we discussed a hundred details of past and future operations. As always he
amazed me with his intimate knowledge of world geography. The most obscure
places in faraway countries were always accurately placed on his mental map."[52]
After Eisenhower's last meeting with the president, again in the White House
private residence, the new supreme Allied commander asked about Roosevelt's
health. "I sincerely trust that you will quickly recover from your indisposition,"
Eisenhower said. Roosevelt responded: "Oh, I have not felt better in years. I'm
in bed only because the doctors are afraid I might have a relapse if I get up too
soon." Eisenhower was never to see him again.[53]

While Marshall and Eisenhower were in each other's company nearly constantly during Eisenhower's time in Washington, detailed discussions were impossible. But when they did have a quiet moment together, they reviewed what
both considered the war's most contentious issues. Eisenhower told Marshall
that he had grave doubts about the Allied landing at Anzio, despite Churchill's
Italy obsession. At the same time, he supported plans to carry out landings in
southern France, code-named Anvil, that would coincide with D-day. Marshall
agreed strongly on both points and noted his concern that in the immediate aftermath of Overlord the Allied right flank would be "in the air," unprotected
and vulnerable to a German counterattack.[54] Anvil, he said, must go forward.
Marshall was also worried that Eisenhower would be forced to concede resources to other combat theaters, resources that would be needed on
Normandy's beaches. The Anzio landing presented a major obstacle. A continued stalemate in Italy would rob Overlord of badly needed landing craft. The
landing-craft issue was particularly knotty, as continuing offensive operations in
the Pacific demanded the constant deployment of newly produced LSTs (landing ship, tank), LCIs (landing craft, infantry), LCAs (Landing craft, assault), and

LCTs (larger versions of LSTs), and the essential LCVPs (landing craft, vehicle, personnel)—which would ferry the first wave of U.S. soldiers to the beach—as well as prefabricated "Mulberry Harbors," behemoths built at Morgan's direction that would be towed into place as temporary harbors as Allied troops moved inland.[55] The landing-craft issue, Marshall knew, would be only superficially resolved by making sure that there were enough transports to bring three, or five, or twelve Allied divisions ashore. If the landings were not tightly scheduled, Allied troops would be more vulnerable to shore fire, but if they were too tightly scheduled, soldiers would be stuck offshore, steaming endlessly in circles. Unless the operation was planned in complete detail, down to the minute, men would not die on the beach—they would die trying to get there.

The terrible arithmetic of war placed almost insurmountable requirements on Allied planners. Each LCVP (or LCI, LCA, or LST) could carry a fully armed platoon of thirty-six men onto a beach, or twelve men and one jeep.[56] Thirty-six feet long and ten feet wide, the LCVP was initially constructed of wood and held together with taut ribbons of metal, though later models were made of stout metal and held together by ribbons of bolts. On the run into the beach the boats were open to small-arms and mortar fire, and the men they ferried were unable to shoot back. There were only two ways out of the boat: over the side (and into the water) or down the landing ramp (and into the teeth of withering defensive fire). *Ideally*, the landing-craft arithmetic worked in reverse: the number of men needed for a successful assault dictated the number of LCVPs needed to bring them ashore, which dictated the number of troop transports, which dictated the number of dock and warehouse facilities, which dictated the number of able-bodied men to sort, package, and load the ships— all of which subtracted from the number of men able to carry a rifle and kill the enemy.[57] This calculation did not count the numbers of larger landing craft that would be needed later to ferry the thousands of men and tanks that would come ashore after the landing sites were secured. In truth, however, the arithmetic never seemed to work in reverse, because there were never enough landing craft. War planners were particularly susceptible to ignoring this arithmetic. When faced with a shortage of landing craft, assault planners simply recalculated their assumption of enemy strength to make their plans match their lowered expectations.

Nor would any operation work ideally; there were simply too many intangibles. Overlord planners did not need simply to find the correct number of LCVPs to ferry the first wave to Normandy's beaches; they would have to calculate how many landing craft would be needed for the second and third waves. Finding the right number of landing craft was not a matter of addition or multiplication, but of division: the number of men in five divisions divided by the number of men per transport equaled the number of landing craft that would be needed for the invasion.[58] Except of course that those numbers didn't work at all, for after each exercise in long division, other calculations, chilling calculations, came into play. These were the inevitable subtractions—of boats destroyed, swamped, grounded, leaderless, or, through mechanical failing, unable to make the landing at all.[59] And for those craft that came bobbing through the surf from ten thousand yards offshore, there was a danger that early-morning demolition teams might be killed or drowned, and therefore unable to disarm the hundreds (or thousands—no one knew) of floating mines that would tear a platoon to pieces and destroy a landing craft needed for ferrying new waves of assault troops. Then too, the actual invasion had to take place in the best possible conditions, for if transport ships continued to steam endlessly in the Channel, waiting for the weather to clear, the men who landed would be groggy, seasick, and exhausted, and therefore easy targets for well-rested German gunners. D-day planners knew all of this and so calculated and recalculated their numbers again and again, only to determine what everyone already knew—which was that no one really knew just how many landing craft constituted the minimum needed for a successful invasion. And they did not know that minimum number because nothing on the scale of the Normandy landings had ever been done before.[60]

Such questions consumed Eisenhower, who was anxious to return to London to begin looking at the calculations that Montgomery was now studying. But Marshall had insisted that Ike take a break, so on the day following the Marshall dinner, Eisenhower and Mamie traveled to West Point to visit with John, who did not even know that his father was in the country.[61] Summoned from class, John was hurriedly bundled into a waiting sedan and taken to a nearby train, idling at a siding in Highland Falls. Ike was proud of his son, and he and Mamie spent several hours visiting with him, but even John could tell that his father was tense. "His no-nonsense life of the past eighteen months had sharpened his manner somewhat," he recalled. "Mother at one time chastened

him for his abruptness. He growled amicably, 'Hell, I'm going back to my theater where I can do what I want." That night Ike and Mamie hosted John and
five of his friends at a dinner. The visit with John was followed by time alone
with Mamie. The two stayed at a cottage reserved for them at the White
Sulphur Springs resort in West Virginia, during which Eisenhower reportedly
slipped at least twice, calling Mamie "Kay." Eisenhower later allowed that while
he was happy to see Mamie, "things did seem to be a bit upsetting," an observation that was pure Eisenhower: understated and uncomfortably true.[62] On
January 8, Eisenhower flew to Kansas to see his brothers Milton (now the president of Kansas State University) and Arthur and his mother, now eighty-two.
Once again, Eisenhower seemed withdrawn, his mind elsewhere. Before flying
to London, Eisenhower visited one more time with Marshall, then had a quiet
day with Mamie. When he left, she made only one comment: "Don't come
back till it's over, Ike—I can't stand losing you again."[63]

EISENHOWER ARRIVED at his new headquarters in London convinced that the
decisions on Overlord must be driven by facts, that his staff must be composed
of people whom he trusted, and that Allied commanders must be combat experienced. He insisted on knowing the bare statistics that would lead to victory, on stripping other commands of senior officers whom he trusted, on
ruthlessly culling out commanders who did not meet his standards. Everyone,
he told his staff, must exude confidence, must show that they believed they
would be victorious. The Allies would have only one chance at the invasion,
and it had to work. Managing the assault phase of Overlord demanded his immediate full attention. He now bent every effort to that task. Just days after his
arrival in London, Eisenhower wrote to Marshall reassuring him that he was
exercising control, and noted that a larger invasion force would be needed,
though this might mean reducing the strength of Anvil, the landings on the
southern French coast. Anvil was intended to support Overlord by diverting
German defensive assets and protecting Eisenhower's southern flank in
Normandy. Cutting back resources for Anvil was a negative, but it was the
only one noted by the new supreme Allied commander. Otherwise,
Eisenhower's first detailed missive to Marshall on the problems facing him in
London was positive, if realistic.

It is obvious that strong and positive action is needed here in several directions. The location of various headquarters, the exact pattern of command, the tactics of the assault, and the strength in units and equipment, are all questions that have not yet been definitely settled. The most important of all these questions is that of increasing the strength of the initial assault wave in Overlord. In order to assure themselves of what is deemed the necessary strength, most people here, including Montgomery, Smith and a number of others, have definitely recommended a serious reduction in Anvil. This seems to me to be justified only as a last resort. I clearly appreciate — in fact much more than do these people — that the coming venture is the decisive act of the War from the viewpoint of the British-American effort. I know that this attack *must* succeed.[64]

Eisenhower was convinced that looking beyond the first day of the invasion was a luxury. If American, British, and Canadian troops could not get ashore successfully, then the conquest of Normandy, the liberation of Paris, the defeat of Rommel's panzer divisions in northwestern France, and the ultimate defeat of Germany would not happen. Eisenhower quickly assembled his team, which included his indispensable chief of staff, Beetle Smith, and his U.S. ground commander, Omar Bradley. Senior British officers served as his primary subordinate commanders, as they had in North Africa: Admiral Bertram Ramsay and Air Marshal Trafford Leigh-Mallory were charged with overseeing Overlord's naval and air assets. Eisenhower's deputy commander was Air Chief Marshal Arthur Tedder, whom he had come to know well. The Allied high command, then, was composed of Eisenhower, Tedder, Montgomery, Ramsey, and Leigh-Mallory; but in practice the Overlord command team that would run the invasion on the ground (and assembled with liberal advice from both Marshall in Washington and Churchill in London) included the commanders of U.S. and British landing forces (U.S. First Army commander Omar Bradley and British Second Army commander General Miles Dempsey) and Canadian general Henry Crerar. U.S. naval forces in Europe were commanded by Admiral Harold Stark.[65] The air campaign, which targeted German and French rail assets in order to destroy German access to the landings zones, code-named "Pointblank," was put in the hands of Leigh-Mallory. Carl Spaatz was named chief of the U.S. Army Air Forces in Europe.[66]

On January 21, at London's Norfolk House, Eisenhower hosted the first senior briefing of Overlord commanders to review the troop buildup in England and to hear Field Marshal Montgomery's assessment of what it would take to make the landings a success.[67] The British commander was a brilliant briefer. With his pointer slapping against his graphs and maps, Montgomery was focused and blunt. His mien now, and so often after, was to assume that whatever he said was unassailable simply because he had said it. He was impatient with questions, as if to say that he had already *thought of that*. Historians, particularly American historians, critique Montgomery as cold, unsmiling, messianic, vain, and humorless. This is true of course, but in terms of Overlord it is also irrelevant. Montgomery was a gifted strategic thinker, and his plan for the invasion—for not just getting the troops to the beach but making certain they would stay there—has withstood history's test. The British commander might be rightly criticized for being incapable of fighting on the run (as would become painfully clear in Overlord's aftermath), but no one questioned his ability to plan and implement a set-piece battle. He was a master organizer, a compulsive and meticulous planner. Overlord was not Eisenhower's plan, it was Montgomery's—and it was nearly flawless.

The British field marshal argued persuasively for a five-division assault spread over fifty nautical miles.[68] The Americans would land to the west on two beaches (code-named "Utah" and "Omaha"), while the British and the Canadians would land on three beaches (code-named "Sword," "Juno," and "Gold") to the east. The landings would be flanked by airborne drops by three divisions, two inland from the American landings on the Allied right flank (by the 82nd and 101st Airborne divisions) and one inland from the Canadian and British landings on the Allied left flank (by the British 6th Airborne Division). The landings must take place under a full moon (in order to aid airborne troops) and in calm seas. It was essential that heavy weapons and armor come ashore as soon as possible to defend against German panzer counterattacks. "General Montgomery considered that, in view of the enemy's strength and rate of buildup, it was essential that we should obtain a quick success," the official notes of the briefing state, "and that an assault by three Divisions, as at present planned, was not sufficient to achieve this object. According to the original plan, we should be attacking on a relatively narrow front; [but] this would make it easier for the enemy to locate and hold us, and more difficult for us to emerge quickly and strike hard and deep."[69]

Montgomery then articulated the view of nearly all British senior officers, though his tone was matter-of-fact. The only way for a five-division attack to be supported, he argued, was to strip air and naval assets — and landing craft — from southern France. Anvil, he said, must be canceled. He then quickly went on to note that the capture of Cherbourg in the days following the assault was crucial; the Allies needed access to a deepwater port to exploit a breakout from Normandy and a pursuit of German forces through northern France. Montgomery detailed his view of Overlord's initial objective: "It should be the task of the US forces to capture Cherbourg and then to make a drive for the Loire Ports and Brest, while in the meantime the British-Canadian forces would deal with the enemy main body approaching from the East and South-East,"[70] he said. Boiled down, Montgomery's conception of Overlord was that the British and Canadians would grab the Germans and hold them while the Americans pummeled them. And with that, Montgomery ended his presentation. As always, his self-assurance seemed to brook no disagreement, and he took his seat only after peremptorily flashing a self-satisfied smile. Eisenhower was impressed. He agreed with Montgomery's five-division scheme but said that he did not believe that canceling Anvil would assure Overlord's success.[71] Alluding to his discussions with Marshall in Washington, Eisenhower noted that seven French divisions were then training in North Africa for the Anvil invasion. While he did not say so during the Montgomery briefing, the supreme Allied commander believed that French troops must come ashore on their homeland beaches on D-day or soon thereafter, and while he was loath to allow political decisions to affect military plans, he was determined that the U.S. and Great Britain remain sensitive to French national concerns.

The amiable, rail-thin Bertram Ramsay was the next to speak; he coolly noted that an expanded assault would mean an expansion of naval assets, including increasing the number of ports available in England to service the larger fleet. Port capacity was simply not then available, Ramsey added, so some ships would have to be docked as much as sixty hours sailing time from the beaches.[72] A widened front might mean more assault strength, but it also implied inherent weaknesses which could be countered only by an increase in warships and minesweepers. Despite these drawbacks, Ramsey reinforced Montgomery's views. The early capture of Cherbourg was essential, he said, as was the cancellation of Anvil. The landing forces would depend for support on the deployment of large prefabricated harbors (Mulberries), which would be towed to Normandy in the invasion's immediate aftermath. But the Mulberries were temporary, as they could never sustain the enormous weight of matériel that would need to be transferred to the fighting forces. Finally, a five-division assault would require more landing craft. Eisenhower leaned forward when Ramsey began to speak about landing craft, as the British admiral knew something about the subject. Ramsey was the unsung hero of Dunkirk, having patched together a fleet of landing craft to rescue the British Army. Since then, he had stayed awake nights thinking about the problem. Quick calculations showed that the Allies would be short by some 220 assault vehicles, including 120 LCTs, which would now (with the expansion of the lodgment area) come under fire from German heavy guns at Pointe du Hoc and Le Havre, Ramsey said. If Anvil was canceled or at least postponed, more landing craft would be available, he added.[73]

Air Chief Marshal Trafford Leigh-Mallory, a British private during World War I—and one of the pioneers of British aviation, followed Montgomery and Ramsey. He briefed Eisenhower's senior commanders on the Zuckerman Plan (code-named Operation Pointblank), named for British anatomist Solly Zuckerman, the British government's chief science adviser and a math whiz. The tweed-suited Zuckerman, a small man with large spectacles, was brought aboard by Leigh-Mallory to write an air plan for Overlord based on the successes (and failures) of similar campaigns in Sicily and Salerno and against the rail yards in Rome. After weeks of study, Zuckerman proposed creating a "railway desert" from Bonn through the Ruhr and then successively outward—toward the beaches—through Antwerp, Amiens, Paris, and Normandy. Rail yards, freight warehouses, transport assets, depots, boxcars, troop reinforcement points, sheds, major rail lines, airfields, runways, and switching stations would be targeted and destroyed. French rail capacity would be cut by two-thirds, which meant that the ability of the German Army to transport tanks, troops, ammunition, and supplies would be fatally undermined. On D-day, all available air assets would be assigned to destroy targets close to Normandy, isolating the beaches. If the air campaign succeeded, six panzer divisions in southern France, those refitting near Paris, and those few deployed along the Spanish border would be isolated and unable to move to Normandy.[74]

The Zuckerman Plan was immediately controversial, most especially among U.S. and British strategic air commanders, who believed that no more than thirty days of clear skies and twenty-four-hour bombing of German industry would cause the Reich to collapse. Diverting air resources to Normandy was a mistake: it meant ceasing the bombing of strategic targets. Eisenhower had heard this before and knew that he would have trouble selling the plan, particularly to Carl Spaatz, who had said in Cairo that he thought that continued around-the-clock strategic bombing of Germany would make Overlord unnecessary. Give me thirty days of clear weather and unlimited command, Spaatz had argued, and Germany would collapse.[75] Eisenhower was skeptical of Spaatz's claim, so he supported Leigh-Mallory. But he also knew that approval for Pointblank would come only when he, Eisenhower, had won control of all European air assets. Winning that battle would end the debate: Pointblank would be approved. Overlord would take precedence over any other European operation.

Eisenhower adjourned the January 21 meeting after Leigh-Mallory's presentation, but reconvened his senior commanders in the afternoon to determine the fate of Anvil. The resulting memorandum, sent to the Combined Chiefs of Staff by Eisenhower on January 23, included recommendations for a five-division assault at Normandy and the temporary postponement of the invasion of France along its southern coast.[76] Eisenhower also recommended an expansion of air and naval assets, and requested an additional 263 landing craft, twenty-four destroyers, five cruisers, and eight fighter squadrons. Eisenhower added that the forces should be in Britain at their jumping-off points twenty-eight days prior to the invasion. He then endorsed a postponement of the invasion for four additional weeks, until late May or early June. Eisenhower tackled the air controversy by bidding for control of all of Europe's air assets, which would carry out Pointblank. The Combined Chiefs of Staff and Marshall responded ten days later by approving an expanded assault, but they buried the air controversy in a torrent of meaningless directives: the support of Bomber Command for Overlord "should be maintained without detriment to the Combined Bomber offensive"—which seemed to imply that the Combined Chiefs believed that the Allies could both bomb Germany and support the Normandy assault.[77] The chiefs were no more specific on the issue of landing craft, saying that the need for the craft would have to be judged on "availability"—which was, after all, the question.

DESPITE HIS position as the leading senior Allied commander, Eisenhower remained highly sensitive to George Marshall's views, particularly when it came to Anvil. During Eisenhower's visit to Washington, the Army chief had made it clear that the invasion of southern France was essential. Anvil would get the French into the battle, would cover the invasion force's right flank, and would add badly needed combat divisions to the battle for France. No one must be left idle, Marshall had said, reflecting Abraham Lincoln's instruction to Ulysses S. Grant at the outset of the final campaign of the Civil War—this time, put in all of your forces. Anvil was the one way to do that, deploying idle divisions that could not get into the fight in Italy. Eisenhower also realized that Marshall was still suspicious of Alan Brooke's stated aim to kick Eisenhower into the stratosphere, a viewpoint that had not changed since Eisenhower had commanded in North Africa. Marshall believed Eisenhower might be susceptible to such a tactic, serving as the head of a London committee rather than as supreme Allied commander. If Eisenhower could not fight for Anvil in London, then Marshall was determined to do so in Washington, with the Combined Chiefs of Staff. By the end of January, Eisenhower realized he was caught in the middle, between British commanders, who believed Anvil was a diversion, and Marshall, who thought it a necessity. Ike tried to forge a compromise in a message to the Army chief that laid out the differences while signaling Marshall that things looked vastly different in London, where British resource pressures were more keenly felt than they were in Washington: "I feel that as long as you and I are in complete coordination as to the purpose then you in Washington and I here can do a great deal toward achieving the best overall results," Eisenhower wrote.[78] "I honestly believe that a five division assault is the minimum that gives us a really favorable chance of success. I have earnestly hoped that this could be achieved by the 31st of May without sacrificing a strong Anvil."[78]

Eisenhower's message was stark. Better a strong Overlord without Anvil than a weak Overlord with Anvil. Marshall rejected the trade-off—it was possible to do both—and he warned Eisenhower about his susceptibility to the British, hinting that promoting Anvil would not only provide increased forces against the Germans in France, but show the British who was in charge. Marshall couched his response to Eisenhower's plea for "complete coordination" by focusing on Eisenhower's "coordination" with Marshall, and not with the British. "Overlord of course is paramount and it must be launched on a reasonably secure basis of which you are the best judge. . . . Count up all the Divisions that will be in the Mediterranean, including two newly arrived U.S. Divisions, consider the requirements in Italy in view of the mountain masses north of Rome, and then consider what influence on your problem a sizeable number of Divisions heavily engaged or advancing rapidly in southern France will have on Overlord." So far so good, Eisenhower must have thought; Marshall agreed that the decision on Anvil was a matter of numbers. But the Army chief of staff then signaled his real concern. "I will use my influence here to agree with your desires. I merely wish to be certain that localitis is not developing and that the pressures on you have not warped your judgment."[79]

Eisenhower's response was immediate. He wanted to "disabuse" Marshall of any thought that he was unduly influenced by British pressures. He agreed that "we must strive in every way to promote a battle there that engages efficiently *all* of the combat forces we can make available," he wrote in early February, and added: "This is the point I have stressed in local conversations." Ike then reviewed what forces were available to the Allies and how they might be deployed, before rejecting Marshall's criticism: "In the various campaigns of this war I have occasionally had to modify slightly my own conceptions of campaign in order to achieve unity of purpose and effort," he wrote. "I think this is inescapable in Allied operations but I assure you that I have never yet failed to give you my own clear personal convictions about every project and plan in prospect. So far as I am aware, no one here has tried to urge me to present any particular view, nor do I believe that I am particularly affected by localitis."[80] But Eisenhower was bitten and, as he once had in North Africa, spent the night pacing, worried about his exchange with Marshall. The next morning, he sent Marshall yet another message. "Yesterday I sent you a long telegram in which I think for the first time since I became a Theater Commander I went a bit on the defensive in explaining my views to you," Eisenhower wrote. "The reason was that there seemed to be an implication in your telegram that I might, merely in the interests of local harmony, surrender my convictions as to operations. I hope I cleared up that point."[81] Marshall made no response, nor did he need to—his warning to Eisenhower had been heard.

The Marshall-Eisenhower colloquy of January 1944 was important for Allied war aims, as it reasserted Marshall's belief in American prerogatives. Marshall's view, if rarely articulated, was clear to all: the United States provided most of the resources for the war, so it would determine how it was fought; and Eisenhower would not be the supreme Allied coordinator of this effort, he would be the supreme Allied *commander*. Marshall had worked and fought with the British Chiefs of Staff for three years, and over those three years, he had learned a salient lesson. The British might retreat in the face of American political power, but they would never surrender. They had killed Sledgehammer and Roundup and had gotten their way in North Africa, Sicily, and Italy. They might now claim that they supported Overlord, but Marshall was cautioning Eisenhower not to be fooled. They played the international political game well, because they had in large part invented it. Churchill and Brooke would do anything to impose their vision of the war on the Americans, even if that meant hobbling or even killing Overlord. That Eisenhower was supreme Allied commander, that he was to head the largest military force in the world, meant nothing. Marshall girded himself for one final battle and signaled to his chief lieutenant that he expected and would demand his support. It is eminently clear from Marshall and Eisenhower's exchanges in the wake of Montgomery's Overlord briefing that while Eisenhower was the supreme Allied commander, George Marshall was still his commanding officer. And in the wake of that exchange, Eisenhower reasserted his control of the Overlord planning process and then quietly but firmly put Anvil, which the British were busy strangling, back on the table.

OVERLORD

"I am seriously contemplating the most drastic action. . . ."
"Consider only Overlord. . . ."

George Marshall's message to Dwight Eisenhower of early February 1944 warning him about "localitis"—his code word for capitulating to British desires—was not the only instance of the Army chief's intervention in Overlord's planning. While Marshall conceded that Montgomery's five-division plan provided the minimum number of troops for the invasion's success, he was taking no chances that British approval of Overlord would come at the cost of an invasion of southern France. On February 9, Marshall told the Combined Chiefs of Staff that Eisenhower's agreement to go forward with Anvil still "leaves in the air the question as to the sufficiency of landing craft."[1] Marshall's intention was to pressure the British to accept Eisenhower's Overlord plan (he purposely labeled it "Eisenhower's plan," not Montgomery's) at the same time that they committed the Allies to launch Anvil. Marshall's detailed memo included a veiled criticism of British planners, who had calculated that the current number of landing craft earmarked for Overlord could carry 20,160 soldiers onto Normandy's beaches. The British numbers were critical, for the number of landing craft they identified was not nearly enough to assure the Normandy landing's success. The British numbers implied that more landing craft would have to be found, which would make the cancellation of Anvil necessary. Marshall was not fooled and implied that British planners had purposely underestimated the number of soldiers who could be carried to the beaches in Overlord: "Combined planners in Washington figured a total personnel lift of 34,000," he said, and went on to note: "There was a further difference in bases of calculation regarding U.S. combat loaders. London planners calculated on a total of 960 men per vessel in order to permit unloading in two trips. U.S. calculations are based on 1400 and Navy advises that landing boats are sufficient for unloading in two trips."[2] Put simply, the British figures were wrong.

Marshall's message to the Combined Chiefs of Staff might seem best consigned to a footnote in Overlord's planning, but Marshall had correctly discovered a hidden political agenda in the landing craft figures put forward by the British. In scaling back the numbers of men and landing craft available for Overlord, the British hoped to pressure Marshall and Eisenhower to see the logic of canceling Anvil. But their second purpose was even more important. They wanted to make more landing craft available for Mediterranean operations, where, not incidentally, they were in command. In the Combined Chiefs' figures Marshall sniffed the nearly expunged odor of Arcadia, Casablanca, Quadrant, Trident, and Cairo, where the British prime minister and his chief lieutenant, Sir Alan Brooke, had continually opposed a landing in France in favor of lopping off the Germans in Italy. Marshall suspected that after three years of debate, the British—and Winston Churchill in particular— were still attempting to make more resources available to Wilson and Alexander. The memory of the Somme and the Marne was ever present in these British calculations. But Marshall was having none of it. When Churchill insisted that the landing craft issue be discussed in person, Marshall snapped back. Having warned Eisenhower that the Sledgehammer and Roundup game was still on, and having been reassured by his chief lieutenant that he would not cave in to "localitis," Marshall was determined to leave the issue of Anvil in his hands. Marshall's message to the British chiefs had its desired effect. By March 10 this last-gasp attempt to divert resources from Overlord was defeated and Anvil was reconfirmed. Churchill was disappointed, but Brooke, having already calculated that Marshall had won this round, was laconic. They would fight another day. Brooke went to Churchill to convince him to drop his Anvil objections.

We had a long COS [Chiefs of Staff meeting] which Eisenhower and Bedell Smith attended at 12 noon. They had prepared a paper showing the requirements for the cross Channel operation which coincided with our views. Marshall had also wired that he left it to Eisenhower to take final decision. Therefore all seems to be going well at present. We only await decision of experts on technical matters who are flying out. PM insisted on seeing us after our meeting with Ike. He was in bed looking ill and old. He still wanted to express tactical aspects of case and we had to fight him off them.[3]

Marshall was not finished. If the Army chief believed that Eisenhower's appointment as Overlord commander marginalized him, his instructions to the new Supreme Allied Command and the Combined Chiefs gave no hint of it. While he might have been satisfied with Montgomery's five-division front, he began a two-month barrage of messages to Ike and his planners, taking them to task on the plan's details. His discourse on landing craft on February 9 was followed by a lengthy memorandum on February 10 on the use of airborne troops. He made it clear to Eisenhower that he should plan a large airborne drop on the same day as the landings. "Up to the present time I have not felt that we have properly exploited air power as regards its combination with ground troops . . . ," Marshall wrote to Eisenhower. "It is my opinion that we now possess the means to give a proper application to this phase of air power in a combined operation."[4] Once again, as he had in the Anvil debate, Marshall intervened to impose his own vision of the war in Europe. He even cited his thinking about Overlord prior to Eisenhower's appointment. "I might say that it was my determination in the event I went to England to do this, even to the extent that should the British be in opposition I would carry it out exclusively with American troops," he said of his airborne plan. Marshall then laid out three airborne options for Eisenhower's review, adding that he supported the third — an airborne drop that would be made "south of Evreux" because it had "four excellent airfields."[5]

Eisenhower felt the pressure. Montgomery's conception of the airborne assault (on the flanks of the invasion force) accorded with his own, yet he was loath to defend it stridently in the wake of George Marshall's warning about "localitis." Then too, British air marshal Trafford Leigh-Mallory, whose opinions

Eisenhower valued, weighed in against Montgomery's airborne drops, saying that "losses will be seventy-five to eighty percent."[6] The percentages Leigh-Mallory cited underestimated the true impact of the air marshal's warning: Allied soldiers parachuted into Normandy to protect the landings would be slaughtered. In light of Leigh-Mallory's warning, Eisenhower must have wondered how the airborne troops would fare under Marshall's plan, in which they would be dropped south of a city well back of the landing zones, virtually opening a third front nearly one hundred miles from any supporting troops on Normandy's beaches. Eisenhower responded to Marshall's call for a separate airborne drop on February 19, more than one week after Marshall's proposal. Eisenhower called his reaction "tentative," signaling that he had not yet made up his mind whether to adopt Marshall's plan. In fact, he had no intention of doing so but was hesitant to be as blunt with the chief of staff as Marshall's proposal demanded. Privately, Eisenhower wanted nothing to do with parachuting three divisions into Evreux, where they would be undefended from Rommel's panzers. But he couldn't say that, particularly after Salerno, when Marshall had criticized him for a lack of boldness and creativity and most especially in the aftermath of the initial Anvil debate, when he had been accused of "localitis." Eisenhower included his response in a personal letter, the forty-second he sent the chief of staff during the war. It was a communication so thoroughly written and rewritten that it is nearly painful to read.

This is a long letter, in tentative answer to yours of 10 February on the subject of Airborne operations. . . .

My initial reaction to the specific proposal is that I agree thoroughly with the conception but disagree with the timing. Mass in vertical envelopments is sound. So the time for the mass vertical envelopment is after the beachhead has been gained and a striking force built up! . . .

An airborne landing carried out at too great a distance from other forces which will also be immobile for some time, will result in a much worse situation. The resistance to be expected by our landing forces at the beaches is far greater than anything we have yet encountered in the European War and I have felt that carefully planned airborne operations offer us an important means of increasing our chances in this regard. The American Division, which has first priority, dropping in the

Cherbourg Peninsula, gives us a reasonable expectation of preventing re-inforcement of that area and of seizing exits from the great flooded area that separates, in that region, our only practical landing beach from the interior of the Peninsula. Unless we throw a very strong force in the vicinity, the Division attempting to land there will be in a bad spot.

I instinctively dislike ever to uphold the conservative as opposed to the bold. You may be sure that I will earnestly study the idea [you pre-sented] because on one point of your letter I am in almost fanatical agreement—I believe we can lick the Hun only by being ahead of him in ideas as well as in material resources.[7]

Having thus raised saying no to an art form and for once following his in-stincts, Eisenhower must have wished that he had done so back in November, when common sense told him that Shingle, the landing of the Allies at Anzio, would not work. By mid-February, just four months later, it was clear not only that his judgment had been correct, but that the British claim that the Germans could be bled down by snipping at their periphery was having precisely the op-posite effect. Not only were thousands of American troops now penned in by the resourceful Albert Kesselring, but 263 landing craft that were supposed to come to Eisenhower in Shingle's wake might now have to be used to lift Allied troops off the Italian beaches. Anzio was a disaster.

WHEN DWIGHT EISENHOWER read the early reports of the Anzio landings on the morning of January 22, he breathed a sigh of relief. The invasion might have been copied from a textbook: the naval barrage prior to the assault had knocked out the German resistance, the landing craft coming into the beach rode to their destinations atop glass-flat water, British special forces teams quickly captured Anzio's port, and not a shot was fired as the landing craft disgorged their troops.[8] General John Lucas, a bespectacled, pipe-smoking combat veteran who commanded the combined British-American force, was ecstatic: "We achieved what is certainly one of the most complete surprises in history," he later wrote. "The Germans were caught off base and there was practically no oppo-sition to the landing."[9] By the end of the first day at Anzio, thirty-five thousand British and American troops were ashore, along with more than three thousand vehicles.[10] The Anzio plain, as inviting and as flat as any Iowa cornfield, lay before them. Beyond that, behind the Alban Hills, was Rome—the prize of Italy. As if to show just how vulnerable Rome was to Allied capture, just hours after the landings a small patrol, led by a jeep, drove up from the beachhead, heading east. It did not stop for nearly twenty miles, penetrating to the outskirts of the Italian capital. An officer of this small engineering reconnaissance unit reported his findings: "There was no sense of panic, apparently the people had not heard of the invasion," he said. "We stayed about an hour, met no enemy or civilians and returned to our unit, made out our report and went about our regular engineer duties."[11] The Germans were nowhere to be seen.

By the evening of the twenty-second, the unflappable Albert Kesselring stood on one of the rolling ridges of the Alban Hills, binoculars firmly in place, studying the Allied landings. As he gazed through his binoculars, he silently mouthed the words "Ja, ja, ja." In the distance he could see the British-American fleet, with barrage balloons floating above. He noted that there was little movement on the beach and no sign of tanks or troop transports moving east. It was just as he thought: the British and Americans were being cautious. Their strategy, to turn his German troopers out of their commanding positions to the south, could easily be countered. Kesselring ordered reserve units protecting Rome to move west, taking positions on the low rises over the beachhead, even though this left the Italian capital defenseless. Kesselring dismissed his senior commanders' concerns with a wave of his hand, then turned on his heel: if placed well enough, these troops would pin the Allied soldiers to Anzio's sands. Rome would not need defending. Certain that "time was our ally," Kesselring told his forces to hold firm, ordered three divisions refitting in northern Italy to come south, and then withdrew two divisions from their positions facing Clark and ordered them to Anzio.[12] While showing the appropriate élan to his soldiers, Kesselring was churning inside; he knew that the successful defense of Rome now depended on the early arrival of three German divisions refitting in northern Italy under the command of Colonel General Eberhard von Mackenson.[13] Mackenson, a dour, gruff, but thoroughly competent Prussian veteran of the eastern front, would not arrive for several days.[14] Still, Kesselring believed he would be successful; he had seen this before. American and British commanders were worried about their flanks.

Knowing your opponent is one of the keys to battlefield victory, and

Kesselring's response to Anzio was masterful. As Smiling Al stood gazing through his binoculars, John Lucas and Mark Clark were feasting on bacon and eggs on Anzio's beach.[15] Having outwitted the Germans, both felt it was only a matter of time before Kesselring packed up his forces in central Italy and moved north to protect Rome. Any commander in his position would do the same. It was plain to see: his line was untenable. And when he left, the Allied line to the south and Lucas's beachhead to the north would be united, providing a powerful fist that could punch its way into Italy's first city. Or so it seemed to Clark and Lucas. But then, Lucas was a careful soldier. With thirty-five thousand troops, he was concerned with protecting what he had gained. The "victory" at Anzio, the equivalent of threatening his opponent's queen (without, alas, having actually captured it), had been almost bloodless. Only sixteen soldiers had died since the beginning of the operation. Lucas also carefully calculated that a precipitate dash to Rome would be mad; it could undo all that he had so far gained and make the beachhead vulnerable to sudden attacks. Furthermore, he reasoned, for every mile forward, the balloon he had inflated would flatten out, since forward movement meant outward movement. The expansion of his perimeter would make it harder to defend. The line he formed to the east would grow tauter and weaker. Somewhere Kesselring was sure to break it. Clark agreed with Lucas in this, though for different reasons: "Don't stick your neck out, Johnny," Clark told Lucas. "I did at Salerno and got into trouble."[16] The two finished their bacon and eggs, and Lucas went off to see to his men and make sure that they did nothing to endanger the great victory they had already won.

On January 25, just three days after the landings, Mackenson and his divisions arrived in the foothills above the Anzio beachhead.[17] More German troops were arriving every hour: from the Balkans, even from the battlefields of Russia. Lucas watched the buildup with increasing worry, as his position was now becoming more tenuous. Worse yet from Lucas's viewpoint was that the three days after the Anzio landings seemed to show that Allied aircraft could do little to stop the flow of German forces to the beaches. This was bad news for Eisenhower and the Overlord planners, who placed great faith in U.S. and British bombers carrying out Pointblank to keep German units from flowing to the French beaches. While the situation was eased somewhat by the arrival of the 1st Armored Division and its commander, Ernest "Ernie" Harmon, Lucas's hold on Anzio continued to weaken. Still, Lucas began to plan his breakout, which he scheduled for the night of January 30. Lucas's plan was to attack on the German right while the British 1st Division attacked German units on the road to Rome. As a part of the operation against the German right a special combat team and the 1st Armored Division under Harmon would capture the small Italian crossroads town of Cisterna.[18] The attack on Cisterna was expected to roll forward with little resistance. In fact, Mackenson had heavily reinforced his units near Cisterna. As a result, a special Ranger unit ("Darby's Rangers," led by Colonel William Darby) assigned to pave the way for the assault was soon bogged down along the Isola Bella–Cisterna Road by elements of the Hermann Göring Division.[19] Pressed back into a series of ditches near the Mussolini Canal, the Rangers were soon fighting for their lives. "The Germans just ran tanks up to the edge of the ditch, lowered their guns and began slaughtering our troops. It was a dreadful way to die," a British journalist who witnessed the bloodletting reported.[20] Darby's unit was annihilated: out of 761 who made the foray, only 6 survived.

Harmon's 1st Armored Division was also running into trouble. Within minutes of his attack, Harmon's tanks were forced into a series of wide gullies, which had not shown up on Harmon's maps. Harmon's tank commanders were forced to backtrack and improvise by striking out through marshy bogs. When four tanks became stuck, Harmon ordered them salvaged. "I ordered an armored wrecker to pull them out," Harmon reported. "The wrecker was ambushed by the Germans. I sent four more tanks to rescue the wrecker. Then I sent more tanks after them. Apparently I could learn my first Anzio lesson only the hard way, [which]was not to send good money after bad. Because I was stubborn, I lost twenty-four tanks while trying to succor four."[21] The British, ordered to support Harmon and the Rangers, were also stymied when their troopers ran into the 3rd Panzergrenadier Division just east of Campaleone. The battle pitted British tanks against dug-in German machine-gun nests, antitank battalions, and reinforced infantry battalions. It was no contest. After losing dozens of tanks, the British pulled back into defensive positions.

It was no wonder that Eisenhower simmered with anger. Anzio was not Tarawa or Salerno—it was worse. Allied commanders failed to exploit their tactical opportunities, squandered U.S. and British air assets, underestimated the tenacity of their enemy, misused their armor, and overestimated the impact and power of their commando units. Allied commanders seemed more interested in bacon and eggs than in offensive action. One week after the failed attack on Cisterna, Harold Alexander and Mark Clark argued about Lucas's abilities, with Alexander blaming the American commander for failing to be more aggressive. Clark disagreed, pointedly telling Alexander that Lucas had actually done well. Alexander was stunned. Lucas should have taken Rome, he said. Clark responded that if Lucas had marched on Rome, all of his men would now be prisoners. The Clark-Alexander shouting match embittered senior commanders in both armies. In England, Churchill grew increasingly impatient. "You have not told me why the airborne troops were not used otherwise than as infantry," he said to Alexander. Alexander kicked the next two dogs down the line, arguing again with Clark and then, teeth gritted, upbraiding Lucas. "General Alexander is here," Lucas wrote in his diary on February 1. "He was kind enough but I am afraid is not pleased. My head will probably fall in the basket but I have done my best. There were just too many Germans here for me to lick."[22]

While Eisenhower was simmering over the Anzio debacle, he was calculating its impact on Overlord, believing the landings would now divert resources from the buildup in England and perhaps destroy Marshall's plan for an invasion of southern France. The failed landings also had political implications for Eisenhower's relationship with Churchill, whose disappointment was expressed by a number of verbal explosions so violent that they could be felt all the way to Italy. Having argued incessantly for Anzio (styling himself a battlefield commander and, at least in this instance, coming as close as he would ever become to actually being one), Churchill now dug in his heels: Anzio was the fault of Alexander (who was too soft) and Clark (who wasn't tough enough) and Lucas (who simply failed). "I had hoped we were hurling a wildcat on the shore," he railed, "but all we got was a stranded whale."[23] So it was that the Anzio operation exacerbated the tensions among Overlord planners in London, tensions that extended into the highest reaches of the Allied command. Churchill, once lionized by the Americans as the rock against which Hitler's legions were dashed and as cool and deft a political master as any American had ever met, now bellowed in frustration at Anzio, at the conduct of the war, at the summary dismissal of his plans, but most of all at his waning influence. He had good reason to bellow. By early 1944, the Americans were taking command of the war, providing the bulk of Allied resources and the majority of its fighters. Churchill's awareness of Britain's relegation to junior partner not only spread through the British high command, but cooled the prime minister's relationship with Roosevelt.[24] So as the Anzio situation worsened, Churchill decided that it was time for the Allies to commit to conquering Italy once and for all. It was obvious. The British and American stalemate in Italy meant that Wilson and Alexander needed more resources.

WHILE CHURCHILL saw in Anzio's failure a personal affront that could only be made good by shipping more guns, ammo, and landing craft to Italy, Eisenhower saw in Anzio's failure the evaporation of whatever chance there was of moving forward on an invasion of southern France. Believing that Churchill and Brooke would now strenuously argue for Anvil's cancellation, Eisenhower preempted them with a lengthy cable to the British chiefs on February 18, insisting that the landing craft he needed for Anvil be diverted immediately from the Mediterranean, in spite of the Anzio crisis. Eisenhower made certain to head his memorandum with his new designation—supreme Allied commander of SHAEF—Supreme Headquarters, Allied Expeditionary Force. "I am convinced that 'Anvil' will be of great assistance to 'Overlord,' " he wrote, "both by diverting German divisions from the build up against the lodgment and by opening a way into southern France for the French and U.S. divisions now in the Mediterranean to join in the decisive effort against Germany."[25] Eisenhower then upped the ante. Not only should the British approve Anvil, but they should sacrifice their own landing craft capacity to make it possible. "In the interest of balancing the national lift for both 'Overlord' and 'Anvil,' withdrawals from the Mediterranean should be British vessels," he wrote.[26] The February 18 memo had the desired explosive impact: the British chiefs called for a meeting on the morning of February 19 to discuss landing craft requirements and how best to retrieve the Anzio situation.

Eisenhower intended to be as tough on the British chiefs in person as he was in his letters, but he emerged from his meeting with them on the nineteenth chastened by their worries over the worsening Anzio situation. He immediately sat down to write to Marshall, labeling his cable "Eyes Only"— evidence of the delicacy of continuing British-American disagreements over

European strategy and of Eisenhower's sensitivity to Marshall's insistence that Anvil was an essential component of the Normandy invasion. After telling the Army chief that he had met with the British that morning, he carefully retreated from his support for the landings in southern France. "Developments of the past week in Italy have been leading me personally to the conclusion that Anvil will probably not be possible because of the tactical situation in that area," he wrote. "For this reason, I told the British Chiefs of Staff that I consider it of the utmost urgency that the Combined Chiefs of Staff quickly decide whether the prospects in the Mediterranean can really offer any reasonable chance of executing Anvil. Immediately upon any decision by the Combined Chiefs of Staff that Anvil cannot be executed on a full two division assault scale, then we should promptly be authorized to count on taking from the Mediterranean everything that we need."[27] If the resulting cable from Marshall, issued in the name of "The U.S. Joint Chiefs of Staff," is any indication, the Army chief could barely keep his temper. It seemed to him that Eisenhower had not only placed his conception of Anvil in jeopardy but overstepped his power as supreme Allied commander. The Joint Chiefs' response was barely civil: "You were delegated to represent United States Chiefs of Staff in conference with British COS on question of Overlord-Anvil. At present moment we have no clear cut statement of basis of your agreement or disagreement with them and the situation is therefore seriously complicated. Please seek an immediate conference and reach agreement or carefully stated disagreement."[28]

As these messages of mid-February make clear, the demands of Overlord, Anvil, and Anzio were severely straining the Marshall-Eisenhower relationship, as both men maneuvered to work through their disagreements with the British — and with each other. Marshall wanted Anvil to go forward no matter what, while Eisenhower was feeling the pressure of the Anzio debacle and the mounting calls for more resources and men to help Wilson, Alexander, Clark, and Lucas. Something would have to give, Eisenhower thought, and surveying the map of Europe from his headquarters in London, the supreme Allied commander believed that Anvil was the one operation that could be sacrificed. There were simply not enough landing craft to go around. Marshall dug in his heels, though this time he did not accuse Eisenhower of "localitis" or, as at Salerno, of not being "bold" or "creative." This time he dispensed with reason and, through sheer force of his will, imposed his vision of Overlord and Anvil on both the

British and his wobbly lieutenant. Marshall's reasoning was sound: the entire purpose of operations in the Mediterranean was not to make the Allies divert resources from Normandy, but to make the *Germans* divert forces from Normandy. Marshall would not allow the British to scrimp on Anvil so they could follow a course in Italy that was already proving costly—that would be to reward them for failing. In the end, he believed, the Allies would be rushing troops into Anzio's maw, just as Churchill had once reinforced Gallipoli. Nor would he allow the British Chiefs to drive a wedge between him and his chief lieutenant. "The shadow of Anvil is already cramping [British Field Marshal] Wilson," the British Chiefs of Staff had wired Marshall after the meeting with Eisenhower on the nineteenth. Anvil should be canceled, they said, and more resources made available for Italy, so that all efforts could be concentrated on "bleeding and burning German divisions."[29] Marshall must have cast a jaundiced eye on this outrageous claim: the only divisions "bleeding and burning" at Anzio were American and British. The Germans, sitting atop their bluffs, were shooting Allied soldiers as easily as if they were lining them up for execution.

On the morning of the twenty-first, Marshall went to Roosevelt, presented his argument for retaining Anvil, and gained the president's approval for sending a message to Eisenhower instructing him to tell the British chiefs that canceling Anvil was not an option. The British chiefs might be able to sway the supreme Allied commander, they might even be able to maneuver past the most important officer in the American military, but they would not cross Roosevelt. "Call attention that we are committed to a third power and I do not feel we have any right to abandon this commitment for Anvil without taking up the matter with the third power [the Soviet Union]," Roosevelt instructed.[30] Eisenhower made the argument to the British chiefs on the morning of the twenty-second.[31] They had no choice but to agree. The decision for Anvil was political, not military. Still, they maneuvered. According to a final agreement hammered out between Eisenhower and Churchill's military chief of staff, Hastings Ismay, Jumbo Wilson would have first call on any landing craft in the Mediterranean, but plans would be made to support Overlord with a ten-division assault landing that would take place in southern France. A review of the landings would be made on March 20, by which time it was hoped that the stalemate in Italy would have been broken. The British chiefs agreed that twenty LSTs and twenty-one LCIs would immediately be transferred to Anvil.[32] On the twenty-fifth, Roosevelt and the Joint Chiefs approved the agreement, and Eisenhower could breathe easier. But the strain had been enormous and had taxed the Marshall-Eisenhower partnership as had no other past crisis. The partnership they had forged had splintered, but it had not shattered. Eisenhower understood this and immediately set about repairing the damage, writing to Marshall reassuringly that in spite of the "incessant battling in Italy," he was confident that "the situation" would "automatically" resolve itself. It all depended on Anzio.

THE STRAIN in the Marshall-Eisenhower relationship in February 1944 was like a passing storm, bright and intense while it lasted, but eventually forgotten. The two had easily weathered previous storms—in North Africa, Sicily, and then Salerno. That such disagreements most often surfaced in the midst of crises is hardly surprising. Lifelong friendships among military commanders were often shattered by defeat or failure. The trusted Lloyd Fredendall was sent packing after Kasserine, Ike's good friend Wayne Clark was sidelined to his own "manure pile" during the Battle of Tunisia, Ernest Dawley prayed at Salerno but was then relieved, and Omar Bradley and George Patton learned to loathe each other during the bitter fighting for Sicily. Decades later, while crossing the White House lawn, President John F. Kennedy hailed Lieutenant General James Gavin while on the arm of General Maxwell Taylor. Gavin and Taylor fought together in France in World War II, as heads of the 82nd and 101st Airborne divisions. Taylor shook his head at Kennedy, nudged him slightly, and lowered his eyes. The two, who had fought side by side, could not stand each other.[33] Marshall and Eisenhower's relationship never broke under such strain, but the February 1944 debate over Anvil tested it to its limits. The relationship survived and was even strengthened because the two shared the same vision of putting American men and tanks ashore in France so that they could finally come to grips with the panzer divisions of Rommel and Guderian. Even the most basic disagreements could be forgotten or forgiven so long as this vision remained shared. The enemy was not the British or their warring visions of Overlord. The enemy was Germany.

The February 1944 debate also spurred Marshall and Eisenhower to turn away from the war, if only for a moment. Both men sought solace in their relationships with their families. Marshall penned several letters to his stepsons,

Clifton and Allen Brown. Clifton, who was never close to his stepfather, had volunteered for the Army and was now a captain in an antiaircraft battalion, while Allen was a tank commander in Italy. Allen had insisted on entering the military as a private and had made his own way into the officer corps. He had proven to be a competent and courageous soldier and the two exchanged long wartime letters. Marshall was proud of him and thought about him more and more during the height of the controversy over Anvil. Clifton was assigned to Italy and had told his stepfather that he would look for Allen, so now both of Marshall's stepsons were at the front. His wife, Katherine, worried about them in silence. Even in his letters to Clifton, Marshall's thoughts were on Allen: "Two letters from Allen came yesterday, written in early February, the last on the 8th."[34] He wrote to Allen at the beginning of March: "I find your mother following news of the Italian Campaign through the papers and on the radio. She doesn't talk about it much but it is constantly on her mind."[35] Soon thereafter Marshall wrote to Allen again, attempting to keep his worry hidden: "A report of deployments the other day created in my mind some doubt as to just where you were."[36]

Eisenhower also seemed to need relief from his trials. A letter from Mamie sparked him to write to his son John twice in two weeks, a veritable avalanche of words for him. He was worried about Mamie. "For about two or three weeks I went along in a complete state of bewilderment as to Mamie's whereabouts," he wrote, "but I know now she is in Fort Sam Houston, so at least I have a place to send my letters."[37] Just one week later he wrote again, commenting on his son's grades, which Mamie had sent to him. "By the way, Mamie just forwarded me your latest academic report. I was astonished at your standing in tactics. . . . I wrote Mamie a long letter telling her about a very wonderful present that was given me by a number of British Officers who served under me in the Mediterranean. I hope she forwards the letter to you but if she doesn't, let me know and I will tell you about it."[38] The letter to John only hinted at Eisenhower's feeling of isolation, of being (as he said) "continually jacked up" — criticized — over everything from Anzio to Anvil. The most recent tussle added to these criticisms as he wrestled with the British Chiefs of Staff over who would command the Normandy air campaign. The constant strain was exacerbated by a spate of reports on worsening relations between British and American soldiers, which spurred Ike to pen a particularly blunt missive to supply czar

J. C. H. Lee over the behavior of "a minority" of American troops. He was concerned, he said, that American soldiers not "damage the good name of the American Army in the United Kingdom." Eisenhower directed that all American servicemen be "especially careful" concerning "drinking in public places . . . excessive drinking . . . loud, profane or indecent language . . . slovenliness and . . . any discourtesy to civilians."[39] There was, in Eisenhower's tone, a clear sense that "Jesus Christ Himself" Lee was at least a part of the problem.

But the vast majority of Eisenhower's communications were to George Marshall. Between the beginning of the Anvil debate and the eve of Overlord, Eisenhower cabled Marshall nearly every day, and sometimes two or three times a day. The messages contained long and detailed accounts of Eisenhower's thinking and decisions, the state of Overlord planning, the status of the Allied fight in Italy, and his relations with the British. Marshall reciprocated, sending Eisenhower answering cables and directives, correcting only when he thought necessary, but monitoring Overlord's plans in detail. The Anvil debate resurfaced in March, with the British still trying to get it scaled back—to give Jumbo Wilson as many resources as in Italy as possible, and if not, then shuffling them back to London, where Montgomery could feed them into the Overlord mix. In fact, the British were keen to send more men and ammunition anywhere, so long as it did not end up helping Anvil. Eisenhower fought nearly every day for Marshall's vision, while admitting that the battle was exhausting. "The arguments, pro and con, on Anvil prospects versus efficiency in our own loading programs are getting a bit wearing," Eisenhower wrote to Marshall at the end of March. "We've been over the ground so often that more talk seems completely useless, while I must say that the past two months of argument have not, so far as I can see, changed the convictions of any single individual that has been involved."[40] Marshall was not surprised. The Army chief had been fighting the British since Arcadia—and not just in Europe. For every controversy in Europe, the Army chief faced many others, from Southeast Asia (where Joe Stilwell was at loggerheads with British commander Lord Louis Mountbatten) to the South Pacific, where Douglas MacArthur continued his sniping at the Navy. At least in the Pacific the Americans were fighting each other. Eisenhower knew about Marshall's troubles and he was intent on letting Marshall know that he knew: "When I think of all your problems, as compared to those the rest of us have to solve," he wrote, "I wonder how you do it."[41]

Finally, at the beginning of April, it seemed that, at long last, the Anvil debate was concluded. The British Chiefs of Staff agreed that the invasion of southern France could go forward on July 10, solidifying Eisenhower's right wing in Normandy. The landing would soon take a different name—"Dragoon"—and would take place later than Marshall had hoped, in August, but the chief of staff won his battle. It had been costly. To win British agreement, Marshall said that the U.S. would divert landing craft from the Pacific to the European theater. As a consequence, MacArthur and Nimitz would be forced to scale back offensive operations against the Japanese. This concession satisfied the British, who did not want to rob landing craft from Wilson's operations in Italy. Churchill was also pleased by the agreement, but just barely: "The destinies of two great empires seem to be tied up in some goddamn things called LSTs," he once bluntly told Eisenhower.[42] But even with Anvil approved, Churchill turned maudlin, even tearful. "When I think of the beaches of Normandy choked with the flowers of American and British youth and when in my mind's eye I see the tides running red with their blood I have my doubts—I have my doubts Ike, I have my doubts."[43] Marshall was not sympathetic, writing to Churchill that his insistence on maintaining a major effort in Italy meant hamstringing U.S. forces elsewhere. Marshall did not say everything he wanted to say to the prime minister, but he was blunt; he wanted Churchill's commitment and an end to the argument: "This sacrifice in the Pacific can be justified only with the assurance that we are to have an operation in the effectiveness of which we have complete faith."[44]

Churchill agreed, but the pugnacious British leader never gave up the fight. In the weeks leading up to Overlord, Churchill fought a rearguard action against Anvil, once again raising Marshall's ire. "We must throw our hearts into this battle [in Italy] for the sake of which so many American and British lives have already been sacrificed," Churchill said, "and make it like Overlord an all out conquer or die."[45] To Marshall it sounded as if Churchill were arguing that having expended thousands of lives in Italy to little perceivable benefit, he now wanted to expend more. It was not the beaches at Normandy that were "choked with flowers," the "tides running red with their blood." That was happening at Anzio—just as it had happened at Gallipoli. Marshall laid aside his anger, swallowed his impatience, and allowed Eisenhower to work his magic on the British prime minister. Eisenhower was more than equal to the task, visiting with

Churchill at least twice each week, sitting with him for hours talking about the war and staying up with him long into the night reflecting on British and American history and literature, shepherding him through his dark moods. The two smoked (Eisenhower puffing his ubiquitous cigarette, Churchill chomping at his cigar) and talked about the invasion. "It was very informal," Eisenhower later recalled. "There was no punctilio protocol."[46] Eisenhower also ushered Churchill on a regular schedule of visits to American and British units. Wherever the two went they were mobbed, Churchill in front, cigar firmly clamped in place, and Eisenhower behind, smiling broadly.

Churchill had the "touch," the ability to connect with the Americans, but surprisingly, so did Montgomery, who also made the rounds of American units. The Americans might be "oversexed" and "over here," but Montgomery made them feel welcome. When visiting the U.S. 2nd Armored Division, the British commander showed his human side, wading into the crowd of soldiers who stood off, making a circle for him. Some saluted. Some reached out to touch him. Here he was, the hero of Alamein. Montgomery swayed his back looking at them, in a typical Montgomery gesture, and his eyes sparkled. He rocked back and forth, his bushy eyebrows flaring, a smile just at the edge of his face, creasing it, his hands clasped behind his back. He then turned, looked almost quizzically into their faces, and then made everyone take off their helmets. He paused for a minute, nodding: "All right," he said, "put them back on. Now next time I see you, I shall know you."[47] Montgomery always made sure to praise American commanders, and his relationship with Eisenhower took on a surprising warmth. He was stunned by Eisenhower's immense capacity for work. "General Eisenhower is the captain of the team and I am proud to serve under him," he told one American unit. He confided the same sentiment to his diary. "Eisenhower is just the right man for the job. . . . He is a really 'big' man," he wrote, "and is in every way an Allied Commander—holding the balance between Allied contingents. I like him immensely; he has a generous and lovable character and I would trust him to the last gasp."[48]

Such sentiments trumped the disagreements over Anvil, overrode the harsh feelings and fears, and even the visions of the Channel choked with Allied blood. On a long rail journey to visit British and American troops, Eisenhower and Churchill sat silently side by side. Churchill fixed his vision on the passing gardens and homes of his British constituents. He was glum and moody, mired now in one of his regular bouts of deep doubt, caught by his own thoughts. He was also depressed. Eisenhower had told him that no matter what his arguments, Anvil would go forward. He had tried one last time: the invasion of southern France would take resources that were better expended in Italy, in Greece, in the Balkans, in his beloved "underbelly." He would *not* have it, he said. This was a replay of a tirade that he had once had in his office, with Eisenhower shocked by his vehemence. Churchill had exploded in a fit of pyrotechnic anger, wagging his finger at Eisenhower, demanding a reversal of the decision. Finally, caught up in his own emotion, he became tearful. Nonplussed, Eisenhower lit a cigarette, gazed at the floor and remained stony faced. "He [Churchill] painted a terrible picture if we didn't do it [cancel Anvil]. He said he would have to go to His Majesty 'and lay down the mantle of my high office.' "[49] But Eisenhower had made his decision. The only thing that would change, he said levelly, was that the name of the operation would change to Dragoon. Churchill, defeated, nodded his assent. Then, on that train ride Churchill, seated quietly beside Eisenhower, reviewed the Anvil debate, his regret still showing. But suddenly he flashed a sly smile at Eisenhower.

"There's only one thing worse than undertaking a war with allies," he said.

"What's that?" Eisenhower asked.

"Waging a war without allies."[50]

By the end of March 1944, Eisenhower and his senior commanders, Marshall and the Combined Chiefs of Staff, and Roosevelt and Churchill had all agreed on nearly every aspect of Overlord. Montgomery's conception of the assault— five divisions landing on five beaches supported by an additional three airborne divisions dropped inland to secure the Allied flanks—had been accepted. The assault would be supported by 6,500 ships forming seventy-five separate convoys that were now docked at dozens of ports along England's eastern and southern coasts. The guns of a flotilla of 1,213 naval combat ships would silence German shore batteries. The air over Normandy would be secured against the Luftwaffe by 11,590 Allied bombers and fighters. Over 156,000 American, British, and Canadian soldiers would be put ashore by 4,126 landing craft. The convoy carrying American soldiers would lower their craft into the sea eleven miles off of Normandy, while the British convoy would deposit its soldiers seven miles from the beaches.[51] Prior to the assault three airborne divisions would secure the approaches to the landing area: the U.S. 101st and 82nd Airborne Divisions would be dropped on the right flank of Utah Beach on the Cotentin Peninsula, west of the ancient Norman town of Sainte-Mère-Eglise, while the British 6th Airborne Division would be dropped east of the British beaches.[52] The airborne divisions would be landed in the dark, some of them in Normandy's most treacherous terrain, in forests, bogs, swamps, and farm fields, and on the outskirts of Normandy's sleepy rural villages. Some of the men would have to disentangle themselves from the thick shrubs that were planted in the Middle Ages—the *bocage*—ripping the cords of their chutes, releasing their safeties, and peering into the darkness.

Detailed plans and training were in force for each of the invasion beaches, from east to west: the British 6th Airborne would capture the bridges over the Orne River in advance of the landing of the British 3rd Division at Sword Beach at the same time that the Canadian 3rd Division would land at Juno Beach and the British 50th Division would come ashore at Gold Beach.[53] At the same moment, as near to clockwork as possible, American soldiers of the 1st and 29th divisions would assault Omaha Beach, while just farther west the 4th Infantry Division would be landed at Utah Beach. Already in place on the right, the 82nd and 101st Airborne divisions would secure the Normandy causeways on the high ground and secure the bridges leading to the crossroads town of Carentan. There was symmetry in Montgomery's plan that emphasized the use of combined (army, navy, air corps) arms and the overwhelming power of naval and air bombardments to shock the defenders and destroy their emplacements. If all went well, just after dark on the first day of the landings and for many days thereafter, larger ships would move in to disgorge the essential armored power that would secure the Allied foothold. Within days, the beaches would be studded with mobile ports, which would continue the flow of men and matériel into Normandy.

Opposing the Allied landings would be a formidable array of German forces, including all or parts of seven divisions and several infantry regiments. Hitler had assigned Erwin Rommel as the commander in France, and Montgomery's North African nemesis was determined to stop the Allied invasion at the water's edge. The coastline of France was studded with 155 mm and 75 mm guns, machine-gun nests, pillboxes, concrete fortifications, and reinforced seawalls.[54]

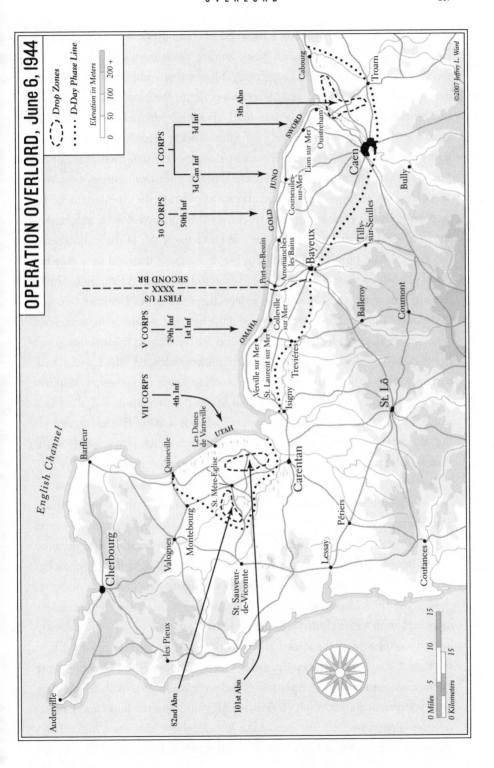

OPERATION OVERLORD, June 6, 1944

Drop Zones
D-Day Phase Line

Elevation in Meters
0   50   100   200 +

©2007 Jeffrey L. Ward

English Channel

Auderville
les Pieux
Barfleur
Cherbourg
Valognes
Quineville
Montebourg
St. Sauveur-de-Vicomte
Lessay
Périers
Coutances
St. Lô

Les Dunes de Varreville
UTAH
St. Mère-Eglise
Carentan

VII CORPS
4th Inf

82nd Abn
101st Abn

Vierville sur Mer
St. Laurent sur Mer
Isigny
Trevières
Colleville sur Mer
OMAHA

V CORPS
29th Inf
1st Inf

FIRST US
SECOND BR
XXXX

Port-en-Bessin
Arromanches les Bains
Bayeux
Ballerov
Coumont

GOLD
JUNO
SWORD

30 CORPS
50th Inf

1 CORPS
3d Can Inf   3d Inf

3th Abn

Courseulles-sur-Mer
Lion sur Mer
Ouistreham
Caen
Bully
Tilly-sur-Seulles
Cabourg
Troarn

It was Rommel's hope that sea mines and offshore obstacles would snarl incoming landing craft, making an Allied landing costly even before enemy soldiers made it to shore. But for Eisenhower, Montgomery, and the other Overlord commanders, the problem would not be getting to the beaches—it would be staying there. "Rommel is likely to hold his mobile divisions back from the coast until he is certain where our main effort is being made," Montgomery had told the assembled Overlord planners in January. "He will then concentrate them quickly and strike a hard blow. His static divisions will endeavor to hold on defensively to important ground and act as pivots to the counterattacks. By dusk on D minus 1 the enemy will be certain that the area is to be assaulted in strength. By the evening of D-day he will know the width of the frontage and the approximate number of our assaulting divisions."[55] It would be a race between the Allied ability to get men and matériel ashore and Rommel's ability to bring heavy armor to Normandy to stop them. This was Eisenhower's thin calculation: the landings would succeed *if* the men got ashore, *if* the beach and water obstacles were cleared, *if* the engineers arrived prior to the incoming tide, but only *if* German batteries on Omaha's bluffs were silenced, which would happen only *if* the Rangers landed on time, which depended on whether the transport ships could drop them on time and at the right location, and all of that would happen only *if* the weather cooperated. But none of this accounted for the ultimate if. The landings would succeed if the enemy was deceived, if Rommel did not know when and where the invasion was coming.

To deceive the Germans, Eisenhower and the Allied High Command approved and instituted Operation Fortitude, a detailed and sophisticated program whose purpose was to convince the Germans that the European invasion would not come at Normandy. Fortitude North included the creation of a fictional British Fourth Army, complete with fake radio traffic, to make the Germans believe that the Allies planned to invade Norway. Fortitude South was aimed at convincing the Germans that the Allies would invade across the Channel's narrowest point and included radio traffic from Montgomery's 21st Army Group (which would actually be aimed at Normandy) and a yet-to-be-deployed U.S. 1st Army Group under the command of George Patton.[56] The Germans were fed false documents on the plan, and Patton was outfitted with a complete headquarters, new (but empty) training camps, and dummy tanks and landing vehicles. Patton himself was one of the key deceivers, since the Allied High Command believed that Eisenhower's counterparts in Berlin would focus their energies on the legendary tank commander. Patton chafed at his new role, despite being promised that he would be given an important command after the Normandy landings had succeeded.

But Patton gave his word. He would make the deception work and he privately assured Eisenhower that his temper tantrums were a thing of the past. There would be no more slapping incidents, no more controversial speeches, no more offhand remarks. When Patton arrived in England, Eisenhower gritted his teeth at his old friend, for whom he still felt enormous warmth, and gave him "a severe bawling out for failing to follow Ike's instructions on counting to ten before issuing an order or by taking any abrupt action." This was the leftover from Sicily, and Patton knew it was coming. He was contrite and agreed that he would "be good," resorting to the worst sort of flattery. Patton told Eisenhower at a private dinner that it would be "foolish to contest the rightness of the Supreme Commander's views, particularly as he is now . . . 'the most powerful man in the world.' "[57] Eisenhower did not need such flattery, but he needed Patton's showmanship; it was an essential key to making the Fortitude deception work. While Eisenhower, Montgomery, Bradley, and other senior commanders planned and inspected troops, Patton set off on a tour to convince the British citizenry (and some fifty German agents sent to England to gather information) that he would soon be leading Allied forces onto the beaches of the Pas-de-Calais. In this Patton was masterful, as he proved in one speech to American soldiers.

> I am not supposed to be commanding this army—I am not even supposed to be in England. Let the first bastards to find out be the Germans. Some day I want them to rise on their hind legs and howl: "Jesus Christ. It's that goddamn Third Army and that son of a bitch Patton again." . . . There's one great thing you can say when it's all over and you're home once more. You can thank God that twenty years from now when you're sitting by the fireside with your grandson on your knee and he asks you what you did in the war, you won't have to shift him to the other knee and say, I shoveled shit in Louisiana.[58]

On the evening of April 25, Patton appeared before the Welcome Club of Knutsford, England, founded by a group of charitable women of the town to look after the homesick men of Patton's command. Patton was in his element, standing before sixty middle-aged women who beamed up at him as he slapped his shiny black gloves in his knotted hands. He said that he would make a few remarks but he made it clear that they would be off the record. What followed has entered American cultural lore, a speech made as legendary for Patton's easy and relaxed vision of American-British cooperation as for his flirtation with political controversy. "Until today," he began, "my only experience in welcoming has been to welcome Germans and Italians to the 'Infernal Regions.' In this I have been quite successful." As the ladies of Knutsford laughed, Patton warmed to his topic. Beaming broadly, he continued:

> I feel that such clubs as this are a very real value, because I believe with Mr. Bernard Shaw, I think it was he, that the British and Americans are two people separated by a common language, and since it is the evident destiny of the British and Americans, and, of course, the Russians to rule the world, the better we know each other, the better job we will do.
>
> A club like this is an ideal place for making such acquaintances and for promoting mutual understanding. Also, as soon as our soldiers meet and know the English ladies and write home and tell our women how truly lovely you are, the sooner the American ladies will get jealous and force this war to a quick termination, and I will get a chance to go and kill Japanese.[59]

The American press pounced, vying for front-page space by both criticizing Patton's statement that the British and Americans would rule the world and shrilly denouncing his apparent afterthought that they might be joined by the Russians. The British press thought the speech was innocuous, while a number of Patton's senior aides believed, in the wake of the Sicily incident, that he was simply being victimized. Others passed off Patton's remarks as fairly typical, if rather mild—"Oh, that's George for you." Omar Bradley got it right: "What would have passed as a local boner coming from anybody less than Patton had promptly exploded into a world crisis."[60] For George Marshall, the appearance of headlines and front-page articles on April 29 was simply the latest piece of evidence that George Patton, for all his genius, could not keep his mouth shut. Patton's remarks came at a particularly difficult time for Marshall, who had just sent Patton's name to the U.S. Senate for confirmation of his promotion to four-star rank.[61] An angry and disappointed Marshall, who had many more things to worry about than whether his recommendations for promotion would be approved by the Senate, cabled Eisenhower: "Newspapers today," he said, "carried reports of General Patton's statements reference Britain and American rule of the world. We were just about to get confirmation of the permanent makes [the promotion of Patton and others]. This I fear has killed them."[62] Eisenhower too was angry and disappointed and fed up with having to deal with Patton's numerous indiscretions, or the fear of such indiscretions, in the midst of the planning for the largest and most important U.S. military operation in history. He was blunt in his response to the chief of staff: "While his exact remarks on this occasion were incorrectly reported and somewhat misinterpreted in the press," Eisenhower wrote, "I have grown so weary of the trouble he constantly causes you and the War Department that I am seriously contemplating the most drastic action. I am deferring final action until I hear further from you."[63]

On April 30, Eisenhower summoned Patton for a meeting, cabling Marshall that "I will relieve him from command and send him home unless some new and unforeseen information should be developed in this case."[64] Marshall, now calmed, was inclined to allow Eisenhower to make up his own mind. "The decision is exclusively yours," he told his top European commander. "Send him home if you see fit, and in grade, or hold him there as surplus if you so desire, or . . . continue him in command if that promises best for Overlord. Do not consider War Department position in the matter. Consider only Overlord and your own heavy burden of responsibility for its success. Everything else is of minor importance."[65]

Eisenhower, with Marshall's cable in hand, met with Patton on May 1. It must have been a supremely uncomfortable moment for both men: Patton had once been Eisenhower's mentor and friend. But now Eisenhower outranked and outshone his friend and had his future in his hands. Eisenhower glowered at Patton. "George, you have gotten yourself into a very serious fix," he said.[66] Patton was effusive, embarrassed, contrite, and then pleading. "Before you go any farther," he said, "I want to say that your job is more important than mine, so if in trying to save me your are hurting yourself, throw me out."[67] Patton told his aides that his meeting with Eisenhower was cordial. The two old friends had a good, long talk. Eisenhower's account is quite different. While Patton stood at attention in front of his desk, Ike gave him the hiding of his life and then made it clear: if he remained, it would only be because of his battlefield skills. Patton believed he was finished.

> I feel like death, but I am not out yet. If they will let me fight, I will; but if not, I will resign so as to be able to talk; and then I will tell the truth, and possibly do the country more good. All the way home, 5 hours, I recited poetry to myself. . . . My final thought on the matter is that I am destined to achieve some great thing—I don't know, but this last incident was so trivial, but so terrible in its effect, that it is not the result of an accident, but the work of God. His Will be done.[68]

Two days later, Patton received a short note from Eisenhower: "I am once more taking the responsibility of retaining you in command in spite of damaging repercussions resulting from a personal indiscretion. I do this solely because of my faith in you as a battle leader and from no other motives."[69] In the end, Eisenhower determined, Marshall was right—he could think only of Overlord. And that meant he had to have Patton.

BY MAY 1944, Dwight Eisenhower could finally turn his full attention to Overlord without having to worry about Anzio, though the final breakout from the Italian beachhead had been accomplished only after bloody fighting. The Anzio debacle had also cost the hard-fighting John Lucas his job. Alexander relieved the American commander, telling Eisenhower that he had "lost confidence" in him.[70] Eisenhower was angered by the decision, believing that Lucas was being blamed for a bad plan, but he also believed that he must support Alexander. Still, Lucas's name shows up again and again in Eisenhower's messages to Marshall, as if Eisenhower could not bring himself to allow his relief. When Lucas arrived in London in mid-March, Eisenhower met with him and was briefed on Anzio. "Lucas has arrived," Eisenhower told Marshall in a cable on that day. "I must say he doesn't seem to me to be a 'defeated' man. I believe you'll get a lot of good out of him."[71] While Alexander recommended replacing Lucas with a British commander, Eisenhower advised that a shift in command nationalities could cause problems. On February 17, therefore, Alexander appointed Major General Lucien King Truscott as Lucas's replacement. Truscott was to become one of the most effective, fearsome, and creative senior commanders of the war. A Texan, Truscott joined the Army during World War I but saw no action. In the interwar years he became known as one of the nation's most talented polo players. His sophisticated exterior, his smiling visage in social settings, his ability to put people at ease belied a fierce inner life and an ambition that tick-tick-ticked every single day that he was an Army officer.[72] He served with Eisenhower at Fort Lewis in Washington and came to the attention of George Marshall—who admired his rasping voice, his command authority, and his considerable intellect. His name went into Marshall's book. By the time of Anzio, Truscott was renowned as the Army's leading expert on amphibious assaults and one of its most respected troop commanders.[73]

Truscott was unfazed under fire; in the midst of one battle, with shells raining down, he pinned a decoration on a fellow officer, remaining in full view of the enemy while nearby soldiers looked on in horror. "I can think of no finer way of presenting this decoration than under battle conditions," he said.[74] Truscott was also something of an eccentric (even when compared to Patton, with whom he served). He sported faded pink cavalry breeches (because they brought him luck), knee-high brown cavalry boots, and a white scarf. His soldiers were always well trained. Truscott believed in rigorous exercise and refused to have them "march into battle"—they ran at a clip that soon came to be known as the Truscott trot.[75] It is difficult to exaggerate the enormous impact he had on the soldiers at Anzio once he took command, but his senior aides could see, almost touch, the difference. He can perhaps best be summed up by a remark he made to his son: "Polo games aren't won by gentlemen," he is said to have told the young and wide-eyed boy. "They're won by men who can be first-class sonsofbitches when they have to be. It's as simple as that."[76]

The British-American command relationship in Italy was at an all-time low when Truscott stepped into Lucas's shoes: Lucas distrusted his British subordinates, cared little for Alexander (who returned the favor), and knew that Churchill was lobbying to replace him. The two armies at Anzio rarely talked, and meetings between senior American and British commanders were frigid. Truscott immediately set out to improve the command environment, making a great show of appearing among British units and listening carefully to British commanders. As a former aide to Lord Mountbatten, Truscott understood the

British, their fear of trench warfare, and their sensitivities to manpower issues. "Few comprehended the effect that Britain's ordeal and British manpower shortages had upon their tactical methods," he confirmed after the war. In his handling of troops, his fearlessness in combat, and his eccentricities, Truscott stood above his peers. He simply charged ahead, gaining a reputation even among the Germans as one of the few Americans who did not think of his flanks. While Truscott's abilities and confidence were immediately apparent at Anzio, it took the new commander time to dig out the beachhead created by Lucas and his British subordinates. Fortunately, the Germans—now pressing in on the Allied lodgment—seemed incapable of mounting a successful operation that would have determined the outcome of the battle. Through late February and into March, German divisions plunged ahead into the morass of the Carroceto-Factory salient, fighting a series of bloody battles whose names described the hellish ground on which they were fought: "the caves," "the boot," "the lobster claw."[77] When not plunging ahead on the left wing, Mackenson tried his luck at Truscott's center, only to meet with a curtain of Allied artillery fire and tons of bomber-dropped ordnance.

But while there is no question that the arrival of Truscott might have improved soldier morale and Allied cooperation, it did not immediately decide the battle. Instead, slowly but with increasing intensity, Truscott's counterpunching strategy began to wear down the Germans; he made the beachhead Kesselring's problem. The German commander understood Truscott's strategy, so he ordered Mackenson to dig in. In truth, Kesselring had little choice: German troops were exhausted by the endless fighting and demoralized by Allied firepower. Each day, Wehrmacht troops were subjected to endless strafing, to incessant bombardments, to a sheet of steel thrown into their positions by offshore warships.[78] The shelling was so effective that it took a superhuman effort to bring ammunition to the German divisions at Anzio, as Italy's railroad network—particularly in the burned areas south and west of Rome—had been destroyed. The constant shelling, the seemingly unremitting rain, the sense of chaos, the fields of mud and disintegrating foxholes all conspired to make Anzio one of the most brutal engagements of the war. The battles of February and March were particularly vicious, with Germans and Allies contending for ground in the belief that small but brutal skirmishes might tip the balance of the campaign. Some British units lost 100 percent of their officers and men in these hand-to-hand face-offs, so that by April nearly all British soldiers at Anzio had not been present when the invasion began.[79]

Inevitably, the Allied command determined that the key to unlocking Anzio lay farther south, along the Gustav Line, where repeated attempts by the Allied forces had failed to take Monte Cassino, the key to the German position. Finally, in late April, British lieutenant general John Harding, Harold Alexander's chief of staff, devised a plan that would ease the pressure on Truscott at the same time that it unhinged Kesselring's defenses.[80] Code-named "Diadem," Harding's plan called for mountaineers of the Free French Expeditionary Corps and the Polish 2nd Armored Division to pierce German defenses west of Monte Cassino, getting into and behind the German position.[81] At the same time, the newly reinforced Truscott would attempt a breakout from the Anzio beachhead. Somewhere, somehow, Harding believed, the German line would prove to be weak: there was simply too much ground for Kesselring to defend. The plan was put into operation on May 11, with the Free French Expeditionary Corps moving over the mountains just miles south of Anzio, while the Polish 2nd Armored Division drove straight forward toward Monte Cassino. After seven days of fierce fighting, the Poles took the town at the base of the monastery, then clambered up to storm its walls. On May 23, with Monte Cassino seized, and after months of fighting a static battle against dug-in and well-led German troops, the British XIII Corps breached the Gustav Line.[82] At Anzio, Truscott's solders battered their way out of their beachhead and headed for the Alban Hills. The 2nd Armored Division was in the lead, taking a swinging right hook first south and then north toward Rome. Unhinged, finally, Kesselring scuttled back, but not without exacting brutal losses on his attackers. On May 25, Truscott's and Clark's forces linked up. Route 7, the direct road into the Italian capital, was now open.[83]

On the last day of May 1944, six days before the Allied invasion at Normandy, George Marshall arrived at the Pentagon at his usual early hour, intending to tackle once again the mounting complexities of the war. As was his habit, he nodded and smiled at his staff before reading through the single-sheet overnight campaign and battle reports prepared for him. But this morning was different. On his desk was a sealed personal cable from Mark Clark. Clark told his commander that his stepson, twenty-seven-year-old Allen Brown had been killed in action, south of Rome, in the Alban Hills.[84] Marshall excused himself to his staff, then wordlessly drove to Quarters No. 1 at Fort Myer to tell Katherine of her son's death. Marshall consoled Katherine, but stayed out of the public eye. There were thousands of grieving parents; the Marshalls were not alone. Marshall dug out the details of Allen's death: he was killed by a German sniper on Route 7, apparently as he climbed out of his tank.[85] His body was buried at the Anzio beachhead, along with thousands of others. With less than one week to go before Eisenhower's troops came ashore at Sword, Juno, Gold, Omaha, and Utah beaches, Marshall ordered an aircraft to take him and his wife to New York so they could be with Allen's young widow. Two days later, Marshall returned to work.

MAY 29 was a beautiful spring day in southern England. It almost seemed like summer: warm and clear and calm. Eisenhower, Montgomery, Bradley, even the perpetually glum Leigh-Mallory could not believe their good fortune. If the weather would hold for just one week Allied troops would not only come ashore as scheduled, but be transported to France under a glowing full moon and across a glass-smooth sea. But as May turned to June the eastern Atlantic churned out a storm, throwing it east across England and then south toward Normandy. Eisenhower watched the balmy weather turn suddenly cold and windy. He was depressed, overworked, and short-tempered—and now he was helpless to do anything about the weather.[86] He continually corrected for his mood, forcing smiles, exuding confidence, reassuring his solders, his aides, his advisers. It was what he expected in others. To prepare for the invasion and to be nearer the new front, Ike moved from the nearly idyllic Telegraph Cottage to Southwick House in southern England, where he stayed in a command trailer. On June 2, Eisenhower directed Overlord's meteorologists to provide him and his senior officers with a twice-daily weather briefing. The first such briefing was not optimistic. Things might seem calm now, Eisenhower was told, but they would get much, much worse.[87]

Hearing this, Eisenhower directed the meteorologists to give him a five-day forecast. When told that to do so was to engage in sheer guesswork, he directed them to do the best they could. Captain J. M. Stagg was Eisenhower's weatherman; he remains perhaps one of the foremost meteorologists to go down in history—his name is immediately recognizable to any historian of D-day. In these last days before the invasion, Eisenhower regularly called on Stagg first. "Well, Stagg, what have you for us this time?" he would ask, and Stagg would respond, shaking his head: low clouds, rain and wind, "channel chop" and high tides.[88] The moon was out all right, but no one could see it. On June 3, Churchill arrived at Southwick, but he did not stay long. Eisenhower was detached, pensive, remote. It was clear to Churchill that he was not wanted, so he left. On the evening of June 3, Stagg confirmed his previous forecast. The bad weather would last until June 5, he said. It might last longer. Hearing this, Air Chief Leigh-Mallory advised Eisenhower to postpone the invasion. Admiral Bertram Ramsay, envisioning more than four thousand landing craft bobbing in the Channel, said he agreed. Only Montgomery stood alone: "I'm ready," he said.[89] Eisenhower made his decision: the invasion, scheduled for June 4, would be postponed.

Eisenhower paced outside of his trailer throughout the next day. Churchill arrived once more, this time with the commander of the Free French forces, Charles de Gaulle. The tall, spare, distant de Gaulle looked down the thin point of his nose at Eisenhower, bowed slightly, and tried to smile. Eisenhower responded with a firm handshake and a smile. No one liked de Gaulle. Roosevelt found him impossible to deal with and Churchill did not trust him. But Eisenhower was at his best. He spent twenty minutes with the prickly Frenchman, drawing him into the Allied circle. De Gaulle was flattered. He then offered Eisenhower some advice: "I will only tell you that if I were you, I should not delay."[90] Eisenhower's reply was not recorded. As he continued to brood, his subordinate commanders were not much help. Just the week before, with all of the Allied plans in place, Leigh-Mallory had railed at him, his eyes ablaze, pleading that Eisenhower cancel the airborne landings. They would not work, he said. The troopers would be slaughtered. Eisenhower listened and wondered why, now (just one week before the invasion), Leigh-Mallory had decided once again to express his worries. He took twenty-four hours to respond: the airborne landings would go forward. Now, on the night of June 4, he was faced with the inevitable result of his decision. If the airborne landings went forward in a gale, with gliders and parachutists punching blindly at the clouds, Leigh-Mallory's prediction might well come true.

On Sunday evening, June 4, Eisenhower convened yet another meeting of his senior commanders in the library of Southwick House. Stagg opened the briefing. This time, however, there was hope. The weather would remain mostly rainy and windy, Stagg said. But there was just a chance that the weather would clear enough for one twenty-four-hour period for the invasion to go forward. The clearing, Stagg said, would come on June 6. There was an air of expectation in the room, then smiles, then cheers. Eisenhower remained serious, then polled his commanders. Leigh-Mallory and Tedder remained pessimists, doubters, but Montgomery—egotistical, narrow-minded, faux aristocratic Bernard Law Montgomery—was emphatic: "No. I would say—go!" He banged the table. Eisenhower kept his own counsel, standing and pacing before his advisers, then saying aloud as if only to himself: "The question is, just how long can you hang this operation on the end of a limb and let it hang there?"[91] The meeting adjourned, but only for a short time. The following morning, before dawn, Eisenhower and his commanders met one last time. Once again, Stagg was optimistic. Exhausted and under enormous pressure, he allowed himself a modest smile. He confirmed his forecast. The weather would improve. June 6, he said, was likely to be clear. When Stagg finished, Eisenhower got up from his chair and paced the room. From time to time he turned to one of his commanders to ask a question. He then sat quietly on a nearby sofa for a full five minutes before once again looking at Stagg. He smiled only slightly: "Well, Stagg," he said, "if this forecast comes off, I promise you we'll have a celebration when the time comes." Other commanders gave their opinions before, once again, the room fell silent. "Okay," Eisenhower announced, "we'll go."[92]

That afternoon, Eisenhower slipped out of Southwick with Kay Summersby and drove to Newbury to visit American soldiers of the 101st Airborne. Standing in a circle around their commander, in full gear, their faces smeared with charcoal, they listened intently to Eisenhower. They smiled when he smiled, were grim when his face was set. He bantered with them, talked to them of the fight ahead, then wished them well. He left them in sober silence as their aircrews prepared for the flight to Normandy. They would depart one hour before midnight and, two hours later, would glide or float to their fates. By dawn, Eisenhower knew, many of them would be dead. In Washington, Marshall received a special cable from Eisenhower: "Halcyon plus 5 finally and definitely confirmed."[93] This was the code notifying the chief of staff that the invasion would take place on June 6. Marshall left his office at the normal hour for his trip home. It had been a difficult week for the chief of staff—

among the most difficult of his entire life—but now all that he had worked for through years of dedicated service was coming to fruition. Not one time, either then or in the long years following D-day, did Marshall speak of his emotions on that night. He remained, as ever, the modest, quiet, austere, and seemingly unemotional chief of staff. Dwight Eisenhower, the officer whose name Marshall had once written into his little black book, was now leading the most complex and largest invasion in human history. We might assume that Marshall did nothing this night that he had not done before. That was his way. He was a man of schedules and habits. He would eat dinner, talk with Katherine, read for a time, and go to bed. There was nothing that he could now do, nothing that he had not prepared. It was out of his hands. As he closed his eyes that night, the first American, British, and Canadian soldiers were wading ashore at Normandy.

COBRA

"The time has come for you to assume direct exercise of command. . . ."
"I am going to effect the reorganization of which you are already aware. . . ."

COMPANY A OF THE 116th Regimental Combat Team landed "on target" at "Dog Green" just below the Vierville draw on Omaha Beach at a little after 6:30 on the morning of June 6, 1944.[1] The Americans waded into a maelstrom. German machine-gun emplacements raked the sands, and artillery and mortar teams peppered the incoming LCAs with decimating fire. One of the six landing craft of Company A foundered one thousand yards from the beach. Soldiers in a nearby landing craft saw men "jumping overboard and being dragged down by their loads."[2] Six minutes later, the soldiers of the remaining five craft reached the beach and swung down their ramps. "Starting off the craft in three files, center file first and the flank files peeling right and left, the men were enveloped in accurate and intense fire from automatic weapons," an after-action report noted. "Order was quickly lost as the troops attempted to dive under water or dropped over the sides into surf over their heads. Mortar fire scored four direct hits on one LCA, which disintegrated. Casualties were suffered all the way to the sand, but when the survivors got there, some found they could not hold and came back into the water for cover, while others took refuge behind the nearest obstacles."[3]

The men of the 116th formed a tenuous firing line, but were easy targets for German emplacements on the bluffs. Within minutes, every officer of the company was dead or wounded. "The leaderless men gave up any attempt to move forward and confined their efforts to saving the wounded, many of whom drowned in the rising tide. Some troops were later able to make the sea wall by staying in the edge of the water and going up the beach with the tide."[4] A second wave of Americans came ashore twenty minutes later, but with the same results. Troops were scattered, pinned down, and leaderless, with engineers, still desperately attempting to clear beach obstacles, mixed with infantrymen. Artillery fire at the eastern end of the beach killed all the soldiers of two landing craft coming ashore at 7:40.[5] The German artillery, sited onto the beach from Pointe de la Percée, was to have been neutralized by tanks landing with the second or third wave, but the tanks were fighting for their lives against Germans dug in on the bluffs above the landing zones. Three hours after the landings, thousands of men were pinned beneath the bluffs. Many of them were wounded; many others were without weapons. Offshore, V Corps commander Gee Gerow, Eisenhower's friend and former boss, received his beach commander's grim dispatches. The beaches was jammed with leaderless infantrymen, and landing craft were circling offshore, unable to approach their deployment zones.[6] The beach commander could see piles of corpses on Omaha's sands.

At Utah Beach elements of the U.S. 4th Division landed west of their designated landing zones. The mistake was a blessing; the Americans came ashore nearly unopposed. The deputy commander of the 4th Division, Brigadier General Theodore Roosevelt Jr., had to make a snap decision—would he move his troops inland or reembark them for the actual landing areas farther north? "When it was realized that the landings had been made at the wrong place, [Roosevelt] personally made a reconnaissance of the area immediately to the rear of the beach to locate the causeways which were to be used for the advance inland. He then returned to the point of landing, contacted the commanders of the two battalions . . . and coordinated the attack on the enemy positions confronting them. These impromptu plans worked with complete success and little confusion."[7] By late on the morning of June 6, the 4th Division was pushing inland for its linkup with U.S. airborne troops, who had been deployed the night before by parachute and glider. On their right and inland from the 4th Division, the 82nd and 101st Airborne divisions were securing their drop zones. Both divisions had been scattered throughout the Cotentin Peninsula, but groups of paratroopers had organized themselves during the night into informal assault teams and attacked German artillery emplacements overlooking the American beaches.[8] By the early hours of the morning, the 101st Airborne Division had secured most of the crucial approaches to Utah Beach and occupied the line of the Douve River near Carentan.[9] The 82nd Airborne Division had a rougher time, dropping into the midst of the assembly area of the German 91st Division. None of the 82nd Airborne's D-day objectives were met (including the capture of the approaches to the Merderet River), except for one: by the evening of the sixth, the division had captured the town of Sainte-Mère-Eglise.[10]

As on Omaha, the troops on Juno Beach were simply attempting to stay alive. The Juno troops were assaulting beach sectors with code names that have gone down in Canadian history: "Nan White," "Nan Green," "Mike Red," and "Mike Green." Unlike any of the other landing groups, the first wave of six regiments of 3,500 Canadians had to fight their way through several French beach towns—Graye-sur-Mer, La Riviere-Saint-Sauveur, and Courseulles-sur-Mer—whose homes and stores provided invaluable firing positions for the defending Germans. The Canadians hit Juno twenty-five minutes after their American allies and "began the deadliest run of their lives."[11] Strung out below the Juno seawalls, the Canadians worked to clear German mines and pillboxes, then fought their way into the towns. The first assault waves suffered up to 50 percent casualties. "All morning long the battle raged along the precious strip of coast," one notable Canadian battle report reads. "The Regina Rifles and Royal Winnipeg Rifles fought their way through Courseulles and Graye-sur-Mer. The North Shore Regiment captured St. Aubin while the Queen's Own Rifles took the town of Bernières. Tanks and infantry struck inland all that day and pressed on through villages, fields and groves of trees defended by determined Germans."[12] Canadian commanders reported that while they had not reached their first-day objectives, by the night of June 6, Juno Beach was cleared of the enemy and twelve thousand Canadian troops were headed inland.[13]

The 3rd and 50th divisions of the British Army came ashore on Gold and Sword beaches and immediately took fire.[14] But within the first two hours of the British landings both beaches were secure, and by early afternoon they were jammed with British armor. The British moved away from the beaches quickly,

their primary objective being Caen, the inland crossroads city that controlled ·
the approaches to the Normandy beaches from the east. By the end of the day, the
British had landed thirty thousand troops and seven thousand vehicles
in Normandy.[15] The British were particularly intent on reaching the Orne
River bridge, where the British 6th Airborne Division was waiting to link up
with both British and Canadian troops. The British commander, Lieutenant
General John Crocker, was a hard driver. By the end of June 6, Crocker's troops
had successfully linked up with the Canadians from Juno and were fighting
against German troopers manning key artillery outposts. Crocker, known for his
negative views of America's fighting capabilities, had something to prove: he
had been pushed out of Dunkirk by the Germans in 1940 and wounded in a
training accident in North Africa. He had spent months in recovery. Crocker
was out to prove that his command could fight with the best and overcome enormous odds. And the odds were long, Crocker's men would be required to take
on the 21st German Panzer Division, which British intelligence said was in the
area. While neither the Orne River bridge nor Caen was captured on June 6,
by the end of the day Crocker's men were poised to storm German positions
on the outside of the French city.[16]

In spite of the enormous casualties suffered by the Americans in the first two
landing waves at Omaha, the beach was finally secured, but the combat was so
fierce and the contest so much in doubt that at one point American commanders considered withdrawing the beach's survivors. The eventual Omaha
victory was a classic example of tenacious small unit action. It was only through
the courage of American privates, corporals, and sergeants that the Germans
were finally routed from the defensive positions. Movement off Omaha took
place, finally, during the late morning when, here and there, units began to
move from the shelter of the beach wall up the bluffs. Offshore destroyers
steamed in close to the beach, targeting German machine-gun emplacements
near the beach's draws, with shells landing amid American units. "In the early
afternoon, destroyers continued their work of knocking out enemy gun emplacements along the beach front," a battle report notes. "The strongpoint
guarding the Vierville draw was silenced by 1300; somewhat later, the dangerous flanking positions near Pointe de la Percée were literally blown off the face
of the cliff. These actions greatly helped the situation on the beach, but by no
means ended all enemy opposition. Though the most dangerous enemy guns

were now neutralized and some emplacements were surrendered without a fight, there was still enough resistance to block three of the main exits."[17] By late afternoon most of the beach exits had been cleared, but fighting continued inland toward Saint-Laurent-sur-Mer and Colleville. By the evening of June 6, American units had penetrated no more than one mile inland, and resistance had toughened along the roads leading south.

By the end of D-day, American, British, and Canadian troops had successfully forced a shallow lodgment in Normandy. But the success of Overlord was still very much in doubt. While British and American troops were moving inland from Utah, Sword, and Gold beaches, and American and Canadian troops were scratching their way forward from Omaha and Juno beaches, a concerted German counterattack, especially if accompanied by the mailed fist of Hitler's panzer units, could force the Allies off the beaches. Despite the high casualty figures at Omaha and Juno, Dwight Eisenhower was pleased with the landings: by nightfall on June 6, 156,000 Allied troops were ashore in France. The news of the landings had now been beamed around the world, its import masked phlegmatically by Eisenhower's characteristic understatement: "Under the command of General Eisenhower, Allied naval forces, supported by strong air forces, began landing Allied armies this morning on the coast of France." In Rome, just liberated by Allied armies, Mark Clark's translator, Vernon A. Walters, told the general of the landings. Clark shook his head: "The sons-a-bitches," he said. "They didn't even let us have the newspaper headlines for the fall of Rome for one day." And so Wayne Clark, trailed by his ubiquitous retinue of reporters, was denied his most important headline. Everyone's mind was on Normandy. Even the reporters following him now ignored his Roman triumph.[18]

In the United States, news of the landings came to Mamie as she was attending the graduation of John from West Point. The proud mother and wife could hardly contain her joy. In Washington, George Marshall was at his office in the Pentagon. Waving off the congratulations from his staff, Marshall studied what little information there was coming in from the landing zones. Finally, at 8 a.m., midafternoon in Normandy, a cable from Eisenhower was placed on his desk: "All preliminary reports are satisfactory. Airborne formation apparently landed in good order. . . . Preliminary bombings by air went off as planned. Navy reports sweeping some mines, but so far as is known channels are clear and operations proceeding as planned. In early morning hours reaction from shore batteries was sufficiently light that some of the naval spotting planes have returned awaiting call."[19] Marshall was relieved. The slaughter of the American and British airborne brigades, so confidently predicted by Leigh-Mallory, had not taken place. But the Army chief of staff remained cautious: it was too soon to tell just how bloody the battle would be. The Germans had not yet awakened from their Normandy slumbers, but the chief of staff knew it was only a matter of time before they did.

Montgomery was unconcerned that his British troopers had failed to take Caen. But he was also cautious. With a picture of Rommel pinned to the bulletin board in his cabin aboard HMS *Faulknor*, Montgomery stared at a map of the Cotentin Peninsula and planned his next move. He sent a message to Eisenhower, emphasizing the importance of linking the U.S. beaches. With the Americans finally beginning to move through the draws above Omaha Beach, linking them with the 4th Division at Utah was essential, as Rommel was sure to exploit any weakness in the Allied line. Montgomery peered down at a map of the lodgment and studied the reports coming in from the beaches. What he saw on his map now—the Omaha lodgment outlined in a tentative red arc— was an exact reflection of the prediction he had made during his first briefing of Allied senior commanders back in January:

> Rommel is an energetic and determined commander: he has made a world of difference since he took over [the Normandy defenses]. He is best at the spoiling attack; his forte is disruption; he is too impulsive for the set-piece battle.
>
> He will do his level best to "Dunkirk" us—not to fight the armored battle on ground of his own choosing, but to avoid it altogether by preventing our tanks landing by using his own tanks well forward. On D-day he will try to:
> (a) Force us from the beaches.
> (b) Secure:
>   Caen
>   Bayeux
>   Carentan[20]

Montgomery leaned over the map, his eyes intently studying the names of the towns and villages of Normandy. His concentration was complete, as if studying the map would somehow unlock the key to the battle. Then standing upright, poised, Montgomery harrumphed and concluded that his plan had been good and his predictions of the coming battles sound. He nodded confidently to his staff, vindicated. He felt he was the man of the hour. Now it was time for the Allies to take the next step. The key to victory in Normandy was right there, in his battle plan, and lay in the crossroads town of Carentan.[21]

GEORGE MARSHALL was aglow—or so it seemed during a June 7 White House reception honoring Polish premier Stanislaw Mikolajczyk.[22] Resplendent in his full-dress uniform, his mouth curved with an unusual smile, Marshall greeted the president's guests with short nods, then listened closely and modestly to their praise of his work. Now, at last, the tide had turned. With an Allied toehold, no matter how tenuous, now a reality in France, Marshall was justly proud of the gains the Allies had made. On all fronts, from France to the Pacific, from Italy to Eastern Europe, the forces of the Axis were reeling in defeat. While he had not commanded the armies on the beaches at Normandy or stood in the trenches of New Guinea or appeared on a bridge of an aircraft carrier in the Marianas, the U.S. military was his creation, as was the arsenal that stood behind it. Even Joe Stalin in faraway Russia could attest to Marshall's brilliance: "The Soviet war economy had reached its zenith in 1944," German military historian Paul Carell notes. "By its appeal to Russian patriotism, the Bolshevik system had inspired a quite astonishing effort among the Soviet population. Military successes in the liberation of extensive areas and Hitler's disastrous occupation policy with its philosophy of 'inferior races' further emphasized this trend. And finally there was every kind of American aid, which by 1944 had reached its peak: many divisions of the Red Army moved on American trucks, fired American shells, lived on Canadian wheat, and wore uniforms of American cloth."[23] To cite just one statistic, from the summer of 1942 onward, the United States had supplied Stalin with 434,000 heavy trucks. The Germans, the engines of their trucks frozen by the Russian winter, the oil in their crankcases congealed by the frost, began to requisition horses.

While Marshall was pleased with the apparent success of Overlord, he refused to celebrate the Allied landings. Not only did he realize that there was much hard fighting yet to be done (and an eventual Allied victory was far from assured), but he was still deeply mourning the death of his stepson. Allen's wife came to Washington after her husband's death and was now living with Marshall and Katherine. Her presence provided some respite from their loss. While it would take some time for Katherine to recover from the shock of Allen's death, Marshall was determined to continue his work, which included an early visit to the Allied lines in Normandy. Marshall, Hap Arnold, and Ernest King departed for Normandy on the morning of June 8, just as Allied soldiers were facing off against German battalions that were holding Carentan. The delegation arrived in Wales on June 9 and took a train to London and thence to Eisenhower's forward headquarters southwest of the city.[24] The next morning, Marshall conferred with the British Chiefs of Staff, who presented a briefing of the war in Normandy. The next day, Marshall traveled to Chequers to confer with Winston Churchill. The two talked about Dragoon, the planned invasion of southern France. Now, with over 180,000 Allied soldiers ashore in Normandy, Churchill and Brooke were unwilling to argue about Dragoon, and American and British senior officers had some of their most cordial meetings of the war.[25] When Marshall argued that the Allies should halt their advance in Italy at the line of the Apennines, neither Churchill nor Brooke disagreed. Churchill was particularly jovial, engaging Marshall in an animated conversation about Overlord during a train ride to Portsmouth, where they were greeted by Eisenhower.[26] The delegation then boarded transports for the trip across the Channel to visit the beaches.

"We got Carentan today," Harry Butcher wrote in his diary on June 12, the day before Marshall arrived in Portsmouth. That was good news for the supreme Allied commander. While Eisenhower had been monitoring the Allied advance closely since the morning of the invasion, he, like Montgomery, was paying special attention to Carentan. German resistance was stiffening, and taking the town quickly was important. In many respects, the battle a Carentan would determine how quickly the Germans were reacting to the invasion and would be the first true large-unit combat test of the Allied armies as they penetrated the zones off the beaches. Eisenhower and his staff understood the battlefield's arithmetic: the Germans still outnumbered the Allies, with eighteen full-strength divisions near the landing zones and numerous others that Allied intelligence officers had yet to identify.[27] Not knowing was a problem, as it had been on D-day, when the landing parties at Omaha Beach had stumbled across the German 352nd Division, which was refitting nearby. After twenty-four hours of goading, Eisenhower was able to spark Montgomery to push units out of Omaha and Utah beaches onto the road to Carentan. If Carentan could be taken, then the Allied armies would be united. But it was the 101st Airborne that first ran into German resistance at Carentan, where the German 6th Parachute Regiment and leading elements of the 17th SS Panzergrenadier Division—two veteran, dedicated units—had dug in. Units of the 101st Airborne approached the town on the morning of June 9 and bumped into the Germans. The German resistance mounted over the next four days. As Marshall and Eisenhower were being ferried to the beaches on the morning of June 13, the 101st was battling the Germans on Carentan's outskirts. The battle was close-in and brutal. The small-arms fire was so intense that by the battle's end the tall poplars bordering the Carentan causeway had been stripped of their bark. The battle gave the Americans a taste of what was to come. After the war, Louis Simpson, who fought through Carentan's streets, penned one of the most memorable of the war's poems, using the town's name as his poem's title.

Trees in the old days used to stand
And shape a shady lane
Where lovers wandered hand in hand
Who came from Carentan . . .

There is a whistling in the leaves
And it is not the wind
The twigs are falling from the knives
That cut men to the ground . . .

Carentan O Carentan
Before we met with you
We never yet had lost a man
Or known what death could do.[28]

Just as the 101st was closing its envelopment of Carentan and fighting its way through and beyond the town, Marshall, King, and Arnold were walking on Omaha Beach, where Eisenhower and Omar Bradley were pointing out where German emplacements had poured murderous fire onto the first waves of Gerow's V Corps. Marshall was quiet, intense. Twenty-seven years earlier, nearly to the day, he had come ashore in France, one of the first Americans to arrive to reinforce British and French troops in World War I. Marshall, King, and Arnold walked up Omaha's tall bluffs and visited with a group of wounded men about to be evacuated to England. The Marshall delegation then traveled inland to some of the French towns taken in the first day's fighting and were then shepherded to Bradley's command post at Saint-Pierre-du-Mont, where they were briefed by American combat commanders Courtney Hodges, J. Lawton Collins, and Gerow.

Two days later, Marshall wrote of his impressions in a message to Franklin Roosevelt: "The Germans appear unable to muster a sizeable counterattack for some days to come," he wrote. "French Resistance good. Interruption of communications by air seems effective."[29] A crowd of officers and journalists joined the group of commanders. Famed American journalist Ernie Pyle ribbed Marshall that the closer to the front he got, the less he knew. Marshall smiled and then, as if to satisfy Pyle, announced that the Allies had that day invaded Guam.[30] There was bloody fighting going on just miles to the south, but Marshall and Eisenhower were optimistic, and impressed by the sheer weight of men and matériel pouring ashore in Normandy. The crowd at Bradley's headquarters made it impossible for Marshall and Eisenhower to have a private discussion, but the chief of staff had already seen Eisenhower's plan for breaking the German grip on France. The two were thinking ahead, and when Eisenhower returned to England that night, he shared his views with his staff, as well as the more personal moments he had had with Marshall. "Ike said last night that in conversation with General Marshall he had said that when the war is over he expected the younger men to take over the Army," Harry Butcher wrote in his diary. "Marshall said that Ike was a young man and, 'Why do you think we have been pushing you? You will have ten years of hard work in the Army after the war.' All Ike could say then was that he hoped to have a six months' rest."[31]

After Marshall returned to England with Eisenhower, he flew on to Italy to meet with Clark and Alexander and to visit the grave of his stepson. Eisenhower was also taken in by personal responsibilities, greeting his son John, a newly minted U.S. Army second lieutenant and recent West Point graduate. John looked healthy in his new uniform. He told his father that he wanted to get into combat, to do his part. The two sat up talking late into the night of June 14 and then visited Bradley's headquarters in France. John returned to the U.S. on the twentieth, where he was assigned to the Infantry School at Fort Benning.[32] In Italy, Marshall met with Jumbo Wilson, Mark Clark, Harold Alexander, and Jacob Devers. The chief of staff toured the Anzio beaches and then flew north, where he and Clark watched American units pursuing Kesselring's solders toward Pisa. He queried Clark on American deployments, pinned the Distinguished Service Medal on French marshal Alphonse Juin (the first such award given to a French commander), shared rations with groups of American soldiers, and visited the wounded. But finding his stepson's grave and discovering where he had fought during his last hours became nearly an obsession. Marshall toured the new Anzio cemetery, where the dead of Alexander and Clark's pursuit of Kesselring were still being interred. He then sat down to write to his stepson's widow, calmly laying out the last hours of her husband's life.

I flew down by Algiers and landed in Italy near Caserta late Saturday afternoon. The following morning I flew up to the Anzio beachhead and went out to the cemetery. I found they were just completing that day the last interments to be made in that plot of over 7,000, a new cemetery having been opened north of Rome. As soon as they have had an opportunity to place everything in the best order they will take and send me some photographs which of course I will send on to you. Allen's plot is on the main pathway through the cemetery, a short distance beyond the flagpole. . . .

After a brief reconnaissance over the beachhead site I embarked again and flew north, going by Velletri and the ground over which Allen had fought; I used the co-pilot's seat and we flew at about 300 feet so I had a very good view of the terrain. However, I did not know exactly where he had become engaged. General Clark met me in Rome and as it was too stormy for puddle-jumper planes which were all we could use in the forward zone . . . he and I motored north to his Headquarters, quite a long distance north of Rome. After an interview I had with the French and American Corps commanders and all the division commanders who were not then in the line, they brought in Lieutenant Druckenmiller of Nazareth, Pennsylvania, who commanded one of the platoons in Allen's company and was immediately behind him in the fight. Technician Clifford A. Doherty of Pittsfield, Maine, and Pvt. Wallace Bobo of Spartansburg, S.C.; also Technician William J. Spence of Red Bank, New Jersey. Captain Joseph Lieberstein, the battalion surgeon, was with these men. They gave me an account of what had occurred and spoke in very high terms of Allen. Lieutenant Druckenmiller had Allen's map, a much rumpled paper with the various lines and objectives noted in crayon, which he used to explain to me the details of the action.[33]

Marshall could not help providing his own military views of Allen's comrades, using his military judgment to comment on their morale: "These men looked in good shape and in high morale as they were engaged in a remarkably successful pursuit," he wrote. "The road north for forty or fifty miles was a litter of destroyed transportation, tanks, trucks, self-propelled artillery, etc., which the Air Corps had knocked out. Allen's division was moving toward the front at the time, to deliver an attack."[34]

Marshall loved being near the front, thrived on his meetings with soldiers, and enjoyed taking the measure of Wilson, Alexander, Clark, and Devers. His only uncomfortable moment in Italy came when Clark attempted to persuade him that the pursuit of Kesselring should continue northward. The Germans were on the run, their forces depleted, with Kesselring unable to find a strong defensive line, Clark said.[35] He should be pursued, fought, defeated. There was much that could be done to defeat the Germans in the Mediterranean. Perhaps, Clark noted tentatively, the Allies could take them on in the Balkans. Marshall listened politely and vetoed the idea. "Alexander wanted to go up in the Balkans where he would be in command. Clark said something about favoring it. . . . Like the others, he wanted something in his sphere," Marshall later remembered.[36] Marshall explained to Clark that he thought the war must be won in France, and for that to happen, Dragoon had to go forward. Resources for the invasion of southern France would come from Italy, he said; the decision had been made.[37] The Allies in Italy would pursue their offensive to the Apennines, and no farther.[38]

The Army chief of staff was in his element in Italy, marveling at the mountain of supplies that America brought to the field of battle, visiting with soldiers, observing the army he had created in pursuit of a beaten enemy. But his place was in Washington, and he returned there on June 22 after a long flight that took him to Casablanca, the Azores, Newfoundland, and then home to Fort Myer, where he told Katherine all that he had learned about her son's death. Marshall returned to his office at the Pentagon the next morning and wrote to Eisenhower that the supreme commander should pay attention to press reports about Overlord: "I find that no mention has been made in the press as to the name of any U.S. Overlord Commanders below Bradley except for some air men including [Army Air Corps lieutenant general Richard] Quesada. . . . Would it not be within the bounds of security, particularly since the division numerals in most cases have already been given time after time, to begin to mention by name some of the commanders."[39] Secretary of War Henry Stimson visited Marshall on the morning of the twenty-third. Stimson was relieved that the Army chief of staff was back in Washington: Marshall needed to continue to press the British on Dragoon, MacArthur was once again causing trouble in the Pacific, and planning for the postwar world would now take increasing amounts of his time. "He is as a matter of fact keeping his hand in on the control of the whole thing and his influence in driving ahead the war fast in the Pacific as well as in the Atlantic is a unique power nobody else could render," Stimson confided to his diary.[40]

In France, Dwight Eisenhower and his commanders were attempting to move a glacier. American, British, and Canadian soldiers were fighting hedgerow to hedgerow in brutal small-unit actions through Normandy and making little progress. At the end of June, Allied forces were hemmed in within an expanded but contained perimeter that included the landing beaches and Normandy's major western towns. [41] Nearly one million men were ashore, and tons of supplies continued to pour in over the D-day beaches. But all of that was of little use unless Eisenhower and his commanders could break through the hedgerows and set Patton's tanks loose on Rommel's formations. That had so far proved to be nearly impossible; Rommel was fighting a brilliant holding action, playing for time, until he could bring up his panzers and organize his infantry reinforcements. This was precisely the kind of combat that both Marshall and Eisenhower feared and that Winston Churchill, near tears, had warned Eisenhower about back in May.

What Marshall, Eisenhower, and Churchill wanted, desperately, was a war of movement led by Patton—now commanding the newly activated Third

Army—that would sweep through Normandy, Brittany, and Lorraine, and that would do to the Germans what they had done to the British back in 1940. Marshall was anxious, impatient, and irritated that Eisenhower seemed to have no plan of action—or, if he did, that the Army chief and the other senior commanders had not been informed of it. The Army chief followed the battle reports through all of June and July, as the Allies slowly fought their way, village by village, through Normandy. The casualty lists mounted. Marshall waited and waited until, finally, his patience ran out: "The Washington representatives of the British Chiefs of Staff have expressed lack of knowledge concerning your plans and your estimate of the situation," he cabled Eisenhower on July 31. ". . . It is true until your [Cable] 12493 arrived Saturday we had not received recently any information on your thoughts concerning the situation and your probable course of action. For instance, we received no information of Bradley's present offensive except an unexplained reference in a radio from Mr. Stimson referring to Cobra, whatever that was."[42]

THROUGH ALL of July, Montgomery pushed British divisions into Caen. But it was only in mid-July that he could claim to have taken even a very small part of the city. Rommel fought ferociously, moving men and matériel through Normandy's roads to weak points in his lines, then shifting entire divisions away from Montgomery to hit at Bradley's Americans. His movements were lateral: east to west and then back again, as he punched and counterpunched at the British and Americans. Montgomery pushed on, ignoring American whispers that he had once again exaggerated his fighting ability. It was rumored that Eisenhower was so disappointed in him, and his failure to take Caen, that he would be relieved.[43] Aware of these rumors, frustrated, and unable to show confidence in those divisions that had brought him success in North Africa, Montgomery planned Operation "Goodwood." The planned offensive would blast a hole in the German lines, allowing the British Second Army to take the rest of Caen and move onto the open and dry Vimont plain beyond.[44] Montgomery initially thought of Goodwood in modest terms, saying that he wanted to pin the Germans into Caen while Bradley's troops initiated a well-aimed right hook. But as his plans took shape he came to believe he might able to spill his tanks onto the Vimont plain and engage Rommel's panzers in

France's rolling countryside. In fact, however, Montgomery would not be facing Rommel during Goodwood, as the German commander was wounded on the evening of July 17 by an Allied fighter aircraft. He was replaced by Field Marshal Günther von Kluge, a hero of the German conquest of France and a veteran of the war on the eastern front. It was Kluge who would now bear the brunt of Goodwood. On the morning of July 18, 1,676 heavy bombers targeted German lines near Caen, what one commander called "the heaviest and most concentrated air attack in support of ground troops ever attempted."[45] The bombardment was so intense that bombardiers in the attack's second wave found their targets shrouded in smoke and fire. British tanks swarmed into the gaps, taking on the German defenses. For two days the British and Germans fought the largest tank battle in British military history,[46] but the offensive sputtered out after two days[47] with tanks from both sides hampered by a soaking rain that mired their treads in Normandy mud. Still, Montgomery cabled Eisenhower that he was satisfied with the results. He had captured the rest of Caen and forced Kluge to commit his reserves. And he had advanced seven miles.

Eisenhower was enraged. Seven miles? He told his senior commanders that if they followed Montgomery's example it would take them years to reach the Rhine. Even Arthur Tedder, a Montgomery partisan, wondered whether the British commander had taken leave of his senses. Perhaps, some British commanders quietly argued, Montgomery should be made a peer and sent into the House of Lords. Eisenhower was inclined to agree, but Montgomery was a national hero and Sir Alan Brooke's favorite commander. Still, that was not enough for Arthur Tedder, who told Eisenhower that as supreme commander he must take firm control of military operations. He had allowed Montgomery to take the lead during Overlord, and that was fine, but now it was time to take control of the battle, he said. That was a significant change for Tedder, who had agreed with Alan Brooke about Eisenhower in North Africa. Now key senior British officers had changed their minds, arguing that it was Montgomery who should be "kicked into the stratosphere," while Eisenhower should descend from his perch and start waging war. The bitter taste of Goodwood lasted for decades, providing fodder for military historians assessing Montgomery's character. At its worst, the argument came down to a question of whether Montgomery was even capable of fighting a modern war. Montgomery's testy replies to such whispers was that Eisenhower wasn't paying attention: Goodwood was never intended to end the war in France or to even win a major victory, he argued. Rather, it was a holding action undertaken to allow Bradley the chance to swing his flank forward. This was news to Eisenhower, who quietly pointed out to his closest commanders that in the midst of the Caen street battles, he had offered Monty an American armored division, but been turned down.[48] Of course Eisenhower could not prove this then, but the publication of Montgomery's communiqués after the war confirmed Eisenhower's claim. "I do not need an American armored division for use on my eastern flank; we really have all the armor we need," Montgomery told Eisenhower in the midst of his attack. "The great thing now is to get First and Third U.S. Armies up to a good strength, and to get them cracking on the southward thrust on the western flank, and then turn Patton westwards into the Brittany peninsula. To sum up. I think the battle is going well."[49] Even the British were stunned. "Absolute rubbish," one British commander exclaimed.[50] Eisenhower let the matter drop, but the misunderstanding festered. Arthur Tedder asked that Eisenhower show him his communiqués to Montgomery, a highly unusual request, and after studying them, pointed out that Ike needed to transform his suggestions into orders. Tedder—not Bradley or Patton—became Montgomery's fiercest critic.

While Eisenhower was embittered by Goodwood's outcome, he knew a good strategy when he saw it and so approved Bradley's plan to attempt on the Allied right wing what Montgomery had attempted on the left. This was Cobra. But Bradley's plan was different: he would avoid the "cratering" of key roads caused by massive aerial bombing, place his assault troops nearer the front lines, and move them forward right after the bombardment. Cobra was a good plan, but it was dangerous. The massive bombardment that Bradley planned had to be precise or it would kill many Americans. Bradley's goals were not simply to cut off the Cotentin Peninsula or take Caen or even enlarge the lodgment area. Rather, in the bombing's aftermath Bradley intended to set Patton loose on the plains of northwestern Europe, deep in the German rear, and then cut off German troops in Normandy.[51] If all went well, Patton might even be able to race German panzers all the way to the German border. "We must engage the enemy in battle unceasingly; we must 'write off' his troops, and generally we must kill Germans," Bradley told Eisenhower.[52]

Scheduled for July 24, Cobra was canceled at the last minute because of bad weather, though 1,600 bombers were already in the air. Tragically, some of the bombers "short-dropped" their loads, inadvertently killing scores of Americans. Undeterred, Bradley tried again on July 25, but again the bombers short-dropped and once again Americans were killed. Among the dead was the master trainer of U.S. ground troops, Lieutenant General Lesley McNair, who had come to Normandy to assess the effect of his training methods on America's frontline troops. McNair was killed while observing Bradley's bombing campaign from a forward post.[53] McNair's death was a talisman for Eisenhower, who had approved of both Montgomery and Bradley's use of strategic bombers in support of ground troops. The first day of Cobra confirmed his fears. "I gave them a green light on this show but this is the last one," he told one of Cobra's commanders.[54] Surprisingly, however, the July 25 bombardment shook the Germans far more than the Americans had hoped and accomplished much more than similar bombings had accomplished on Montgomery's front. This time, the gap blown in the German lines was exploited. The key to Bradley's success was the early positioning of two armored divisions near the front lines, ahead of the infantry. The armor would lead the way, just as Eisenhower and Patton had recommended years before, at Fort Meade. The commander of this Cobra spearhead was J. Lawton "Lightning Joe" Collins, commander of VII Corps and one of Marshall's black book generals. Six years Eisenhower's junior, Collins was celebrated for his leadership of the 25th ("Tropic Lightning") Infantry Division on Guadalcanal, where "Lightning Joe" had gotten his nickname. Marshall brought him to Europe to help Eisenhower understand amphibious operations. Ike studiously ignored Collins's views on landing craft, but he admired his handling of infantry and armor, and when a command slot opened in Overlord, Eisenhower made sure it went to Collins. Bradley was also a Collins partisan, primarily because, like Bradley, Collins was quick to anger and impatient and had a habit of breaking regimental commanders who did not meet his standards.[55] That was something that Bradley liked.

Collins's formations broke through the brittle German defenses along the Périers–Saint-Lô road on the morning of the twenty-sixth. Collins thought that fourteen German divisions were deployed against his forces, but only late on the twenty-sixth did he realize that the force facing him had been so weakened by the bombardment and the months-long fighting in the *bocage* that it was now nearly nonexistent.[56] With the ground still smoldering from Bradley's bombing, Günther von Kluge ordered Fritz Bayerlein, commander of the elite Panzer Lehr Armored Division, to hold his position. Not one man was to move from his position, he said. Bayerlein, who had been horrified by the bombing and doubted that anyone could have survived it, scoffed at the order. "Out in front, everyone is holding out. Everyone," Bayerlein screamed at his radio operator. "My grenadiers and my engineers and my tank crews—they're all holding their ground. Not a single man is leaving his post. They are lying silent in their fox-holes for they are dead. You may report to the Field-Marshal that the Panzer Lehr Division is annihilated."[57] With German formations that had survived streaming to the rear, Bradley instructed Patton to work with General Troy Middleton's VIII Corps as an unofficial adviser. Middleton was one of the U.S. Army's most creative and toughest fighters and didn't need Patton's help, but Bradley knew that he had to get the armored commander into the mix—and prepare him for the pursuit of the broken German formations that Bradley knew was only hours away.[58] But Bradley was not happy with having Patton on the battlefield. Patton's behavior in Sicily still rankled "the G.I. general": "I disliked the way he worked, upset technical plans, interfered in my orders," Bradley confirmed to Eisenhower as Cobra was getting under way. "His stubbornness on amphibious operations and his parade plans into Messina sickened me and soured me on Patton."[59] Still, there was no better fighter than Patton, and Bradley used him now because he knew how to push. On July 29, four of Collins's armored spearheads flowed south out of Saint-Lô headed for the Brittany coast. The carnage from Collins's attack on the retreating German units was, as an American officer described it, "the most Godless sight I have ever witnessed on any battlefield."[60]

George Patton's Third Army became operational on August 1, just in time to support Collins. During the early-morning hours of the first, Patton called his staff into his headquarters to give them their orders. The Third Army now had the opportunity to show the Germans (and the British, for that matter) just how good the Americans were at fighting a war, he said. With Collins exploiting the Cobra breakthrough, his Third Army would pour into Brittany. Patton thanked his staff for their loyalty through the long months when he was sidelined in England, then turned to the task ahead. An ounce of sweat was worth a gallon of blood, he said, and then he paused dramatically.

There's another thing I want you to remember. Forget this goddamn business of worrying about our flanks, but not to the extent we don't do anything else. Some Goddamned fool once said that flanks must be secured and since then sons of bitches all over the world have been going crazy guarding their flanks. We don't want any of that in the Third Army. Flanks are something for the enemy to worry about, not us. I don't want to get any message saying that 'We are holding our position.' We're not holding anything. Let the Hun do that. We are advancing constantly and we're not interested in holding on to anything except the enemy. We're going to hold on to him by the nose and we're going to kick him in the ass; we're going to kick the hell out of him all the time and we're going to go through him like crap through a goose.[61]

Two of Patton's armored divisions were now set loose on Brittany. The goal of Patton's armored spearheads was to secure Brittany's ports, allowing the Allied armies to bring more supplies into France's killing grounds. But seeing that much more could be done now, with his armor on the loose, Patton shifted ground. On August 3 he sent his armored spearheads plunging east, away from Brittany, in a long loop through the German rear. Bradley, tracing Patton's movements on the map of his headquarters trailer, worried. Like Montgomery, Bradley grew cautious. It was one thing to imagine a headlong armored race through France; it was another thing to approve it. Then too, Bradley calculated, by moving east Patton was leaving his flank open to attack. In England, Eisenhower, just returned from Bradley's headquarters, watched the arrows on his own map and immediately scrapped the Allied post-Overlord plans; now the Allied armies could conquer Brittany at the same time that they raced to the Seine.[62] "If the intercepts are right, we are to hell and gone in Brittany and slicing 'em up in Normandy," Eisenhower told Butcher.[63] But the supreme commander's joy at Patton's breakthrough was tempered by Marshall's letter and the Army chief's irritable tone—"Cobra, whatever that was." Eisenhower worked through the entire afternoon on August 2 and then on into the next day composing his reply, one of the most detailed he had ever written to the chief of staff. "I am sorry that I have not kept you more fully abreast of future plans as I did in North Africa," he wrote apologetically. "My excuse is that in my anxiety to push events the matter had merely slipped my mind. Hereafter I will have the staff draw up a suitable weekly appreciation for the Combined Chiefs of Staff."[64]

This was an odd construction for Eisenhower, and so it must have seemed to Marshall. Yet while Eisenhower had sent dozens of cables to the chief of staff in the wake of the Normandy landings, they had lacked the textured detail of his earlier messages, a sign perhaps that Ike simply did not know how to respond to Rommel's defense of Normandy and so was hesitant to describe his plans. Or perhaps it was a reflection of the subtle but certain shift in the Marshall-Eisenhower partnership, perceived first in the immediate wake of Roosevelt's decision that Ike would lead Overlord. Alone of all of Marshall's commanders, Eisenhower demanded less attention, less correction, less monitoring, less guidance—and gave Marshall the least trouble. Marshall expected America's combat commanders to show independence, but he had always intervened with them to smooth over problems and to impose on them his strategic vision of the war. He had done so with Eisenhower since the moment he had brought him to Washington. Now that was no longer necessary. Yet it was Marshall's vision that shaped the European battlefield and it was his commanders who fought the European war. Eisenhower, Bradley, Patton, Collins, Devers, Clark, and Truscott were in Europe because Marshall had put them there, had put their names in his book. It was only to be expected that now—with Patton finally poised to chase the legends of the German war machine across the rolling plains of France—George Marshall wanted to see it for himself. Wanted to be there. Or, barring that, wanted to know what it was like, wanted to feel it, wanted it described to him in terms he could understand and *see*. His irritable demand for more information was in part the cry of a warrior for the smell of a battle that he had always believed he would command. And now that battle was in Eisenhower hands. And Patton's.

We do not know whether the supreme Allied commander in Europe understood precisely that it was this *feel* that Marshall wanted, but we know that Eisenhower's cable of August 2 was among the most detailed and vivid of any he dictated for his mentor. It was the closest that Eisenhower ever came to a warrior's description of a battle, a narrative fit for the history books. "At this moment the enemy is bringing up such reinforcements as he can gather from within France to bolster up his lines and to establish a defensive position that will prevent us breaking into the open," Eisenhower wrote. "We are attacking

viciously in an effort to accomplish our purpose before the enemy can be successful in establishing new and strong lines."[65] "Should the Second Army succeed in getting firm hold of Vire while Bradley makes good his seizure of the
Avranches area and then both forces operate toward the rear of that portion of
the enemy now heavily engaged between these two attacks, we should not only
gain a real tactical victory but should destroy so many of his troops west of the
Vire that we will have created practically an open flank," the supreme commander wrote. A master of the battlefield map, who had exhibited his talent brilliantly for John J. Pershing, Marshall could visualize this "open flank," could
understand the thrill of moving along armored spearheads with nothing but
"air" to the south as far as France's southern coast. "An open flank"—Patton
would strike south and then east like a door on a hinge, spinning off lesser forces
to take the Brittany ports, while he raced suddenly toward the Swiss border and
then hook back north, coming in behind the Germans at Normandy. There
would be no one on his right, or if there was, Patton would be suddenly past
them, racing east and then north. The Germans would be shattered, retreating
before his tanks. Kluge would hardly have time to recover, and once he deployed his tanks to face him, Patton would not be there anymore. "Personally,"
Eisenhower concluded, "I am very hopeful as to immediate results, and believe
that within the next two or three days we will so manhandle the western flank
of the enemy's forces that we will secure for ourselves freedom of action through
destruction of a considerable portion of the forces facing us." So there it was:
the great battle of the West was now being waged in France between two armored forces, just as John J. Pershing, Fox Conner, George Marshall, and
Dwight Eisenhower had foreseen.

BY AUGUST 8, the Allied XV Corps in Normandy was pressing on to Argentan
in a short right hook while the British Second Army, having broken through the
German defenses, was moving quickly on the left toward Falaise. If Bradley's
Americans and Crerar's Canadians could meet behind Falaise, they would be
able to close off a pocket containing tens of thousands of German troops. But
the Canadian offensive stalled north of Falaise, held up by savage German
counterattacks. The Americans pushed the XV Corps to close the gap, but it
could not be done, in part because Omar Bradley feared a German counterattack east of the pocket.[66] He preferred, he said, "a solid shoulder at Argentan

to a broken neck at Falaise."[67] This was another opportunity missed. After the Cobra breakthrough, Patton pleaded with Bradley to allow him to turn his armored divisions even farther east, toward Paris. Bradley vetoed Patton's idea; he was worried about his flank. "We can't risk a loose hinge," he said.[68] Patton, believing that Bradley would complain about him to Eisenhower, kept silent, but he fumed at Bradley's conservatism. When Bradley should have been ordering a left hook into central France, he ordered Patton to assign most of his strength to make a right hook—into Brittany. When Bradley saw his chance and changed his mind, ordering Patton to send divisions to help close the Falaise Pocket, it was too late.[69] Disappointed, Patton watched helplessly as twenty thousand Germans escaped from Falaise.[70] Still, Eisenhower, Patton, and Bradley were consoled by the disintegration of the German defenses. The stalemate in Normandy was finally broken, and the German Army, stunned by the destruction around Saint-Lô and then in Brittany, began to disintegrate.

Over the next four weeks, German resistance in France collapsed, leaving the road to the German frontier open. The defeat was total. The vaunted armored and infantry divisions that had occupied France and fought through the *bocage* were shattered. The German Army lost ten divisions in two days near Caen alone, and now German soldiers were streaming toward the Reich, fighting rearguard actions in leaderless groups.[71] Eisenhower toured the Falaise battlefield just days after the German escape. "Forty-eight hours after the closing of the gap I was conducted through it on foot, to encounter scenes that could be described only by Dante. It was literally possible to walk for hundreds of yards at a time, stepping on nothing but dead and decaying flesh,"[72] Eisenhower recalled. The Germans used horses as their primary means of transport, and their corpses lay putrefying in the August sun. Allied spotter planes, tracking Patton's offensive, could smell the odors of their decaying bodies hundreds of feet in the air.[73] At the end of his tour of the battlefield, Eisenhower issued orders for Montgomery to move quickly into northeastern Europe to capture the German rocket sites then pummeling England, while Bradley was to continue clearing Brittany and then move east of Paris, taking up a position south of the Ardennes Forest. "The decision as to exactly what to do at this moment has taken a lot of anxious thought because of the fact that we do not have sufficient strength and supply possibilities to do everything that we should like to do simultaneously," Eisenhower wrote to Marshall.[74]

Allied commanders would have seconded Eisenhower's message to

Marshall: if only the Allies had more troops, more fuel, and more tanks, the war might be ended. At the end of August 1944, Eisenhower and his senior commanders could barely keep up with their own troops. Yet, strangely, in the midst of this overwhelming triumph—perhaps the most decisive Anglo-American victory of the entire war—and just as the armored formations of George Patton were racing across France, Winston Churchill and Field Marshal Alan Brooke made one last attempt to shift Marshall's and Eisenhower's attention to Italy. As Cobra was moving forward, Churchill reopened the debate over invading southern France by arguing that Alexander should be allowed to defeat the Germans in Italy. If reinforced, he said, Alexander could cross the Alps and deliver a decisive blow against the Reich "under the armpit."[75] Brooke agreed with his prime minister and was willing to reopen this old argument, but he doubted the Americans could be convinced. The British had "led the Americans by the nose from Casablanca to Florence," he wrote in his diary, "and it would not be easy to put this policy over the top of all that."[76] The British Chiefs of Staff became the official promoters of Churchill's plea, though couching their argument in more rational terms: if Eisenhower needed ports in France, they said, he could continue to use what he had in Normandy, and they would support him by sending along the rest of their landing craft. This was a strange offer indeed—to give Eisenhower landing craft when he didn't need them and arguing that he should be denied them when he did. Marshall could hardly believe that with victory in their grasp, the British would turn their attention to Italy. He gathered the U.S. Joint Chiefs of Staff and issued an unequivocal rejoinder: "British proposal to abandon 'Anvil' and commit everything to Italy is unacceptable." The end of the American paper bears Marshall's characteristically blunt imprimatur: "The British statements concerning Italy are not sound or in keeping with the early end of the war."[77] Marshall's words dripped with anger. The decision had already been made.

Eisenhower followed the debate while monitoring the combat in France, where Americans were fighting and dying at twice the rate of the British. While he had been inclined to postpone Anvil in the weeks leading up to Overlord, he now desperately needed the weight of men and armor that Anvil promised. Yet he remained positive. There was something not quite believable in the British position, he felt. He cabled Marshall that in spite of the British memo, he thought the British Chiefs of Staff would accept Anvil, though he predicted the British would make one last argument. Eisenhower proved prescient. Noting that Alexander still faced a formidable foe in Italy, the British chiefs cabled Marshall that they supported a continuation of a strong Italian campaign because of the benefits it could have for Eisenhower, attacking Anvil as an operation that, they said, would pay "small dividends." Their views were backed by Churchill's direct appeal to Roosevelt. Marshall drafted Roosevelt's reply: military operations that did not strike "at the heart of Germany" must be secondary to the Allies' primary military mission. Roosevelt's appeal was also personal. "At Tehran we agreed upon a plan," he wrote to Churchill. "That plan has done well up till now. Nothing has occurred to require a change. History would never forgive us if precious lives and time are lost as the result of indecision and debate." And then he concluded with a direct and emotional appeal: "My dear friend, I beg you to let us continue my plan."[78]

Turned down by the American president, Churchill appealed directly to Eisenhower, just as he had in North Africa. But the supreme commander was firm. The Allied armies in Normandy needed France's southern ports and Anvil, must go forward.[79] Eisenhower then cabled Marshall: "I have been informally advised that the Prime Minister will probably telegraph the President today agreeing to Anvil."[80] Suddenly, after months of fighting, Churchill surrendered. "Anvil," he agreed, could go forward. On August 10, Eisenhower signalled that the operation would go forward as planned and on August 15, three American and one French armored division, under the command of General Jacob Devers, came ashore in southern France between Cap Negre on the west and Saint-Raphaël on the right. The landings were virtually unopposed. Eisenhower was now reinforced by 94,000 troops and eleven thousand vehicles. Devers's troops moved quickly north, through the Rhône Valley, outstripping German defenses and herding disorganized German units into central France. The landings sparked the French Resistance to begin operations in Paris, and by August 20 German units were leaving the city.

GEORGE MARSHALL might well have felt satisfaction over the events of August 1944, but the seemingly endless and exasperating disagreements with Churchill, Brooke, and the British Chiefs of Staff were difficult to forget. The triumph of Allied arms in France had been due to his and Eisenhower's ability to overcome inter-Allied disagreements, to forge a unified command system, to organize and bring to bear the enormous resources that American industry provided, to work with and understand British war aims and worries—and to even acknowledge them with the adoption of British strategies where possible. But such cooperation had its limits, even for Fox Conner's most prized pupil. Marshall admired the British, understood the sacrifices they had made in fighting Germany alone, but he was also a patriot, and he would not stand by now as American soldiers bore the brunt of fighting while the British argued incessantly over a strategy that had already been decided. Nor would he allow the British to take the credit for the victories won by Eisenhower and his lieutenants. Marshall was particular angered by a London newspaper headline in mid-August trumpeting Montgomery's genius. Eisenhower, the accompanying story said, was a distant and uninvolved commander. The article was picked up in the U.S., where Montgomery's control was repeated by the anti-Roosevelt *Washington Times-Herald*: "It is generally recognized in congressional circles and common gossip in military circles that General Eisenhower is merely a figurehead and the actual command of the invasion is in the hands of the British General Staff and the British dominate the American War Department and Army."[81] The report was exacerbated by an accompanying story saying that Omar Bradley would be promoted to equal rank with Montgomery. The story implied that Bradley's promotion was planned to undermine the British commander's continued control over Allied ground forces.[82]

In France, Eisenhower worried that the *Times-Herald* report would cause a rupture in the Allied command structure. The British might respond to the Bradley report by promoting Montgomery another grade, making him the senior commander in the European Theater of Operations. That move, Eisenhower believed, would plunge the Allies into a war of promotions. Eisenhower fretted about the implications of the report: while it was true that Bradley would soon be named commander of all American ground forces and that, once the Normandy battle was won, Eisenhower would take direct command of all Allied units, the report of Bradley's promotion was premature. So Eisenhower issued a statement intended to calm British fears. He hoped his statement confirming that Montgomery would remain ground commander of Allied forces would not only undermine the growing criticism of the British commander but would put to rest the incessant British-American sniping over who was in control of what. Eisenhower's statement remained silent on the *Times-Herald* story, however, primarily because Eisenhower viewed it as an attempt by Roosevelt's opponents to undermine his political standing.

But in Washington, George Marshall had a different perspective and was less willing than Eisenhower to dampen the controversy. He viewed the *Times-Herald* story as evidence of Montgomery's attempts to take credit for American sacrifices—as another tactic to denigrate America's central role in the war. Coming so soon after the dustup over Anvil, Marshall was in no mood to give the British the benefit of the doubt. His patience was at an end. He had had enough. And he struck back. "The recent statement from your headquarters that Montgomery continues in command of all ground forces has produced a severe reaction in the *New York Times* and many other papers and I feel is to be deplored," Marshall cabled to Eisenhower on August 17. "Just what lay behind this confusion of announcements I do not know but the Secretary and I and apparently all America are strongly of the opinion that the time has come for you to assume direct exercise of command of the American contingent . . . The astonishing success of the campaign up to the present moment has evoked emphatic expression of confidence in you and in Bradley. The late announcement I have just referred to has cast a damper on the public enthusiasm."[83] Eisenhower responded that the command arrangements had been in place for months and that it was not true that he was not in control of Allied ground operations, but that as supreme Allied commander he was "directly responsible for approving major operational policies and principal features of all plans of every kind." Marshall understood this, but he also knew that if Brooke and Montgomery could not "kick Eisenhower into the stratosphere" in reality, they could at least try to do so in the newspapers.

Eisenhower mulled this over, attempting to balance the politics he was facing on the front lines and in the upper echelons of his own command structure with his need to satisfy his chief of staff. Finally, he cabled Marshall on August 25, the day that Paris was liberated by the Allied armies, that he would follow the chief of staff's command directive. But he would only do so at the right moment. "I am going to effect the reorganization of which you are already aware. This will cause some outcry and some uneasiness but I am sure that, all things considered, it is absolutely sound," he wrote to Marshall. "The principle argument that will be advanced against it is that we are trifling with a winning combination but the actual fact is that Bradley has operated with a considerable degree of independence for a long time. He and I are in constant touch and the change is really more obvious than real. Montgomery will necessarily have the right to effect tactical coordination between his own forces and the extreme left wing of Bradley's Army Group so that there will be no chance of any lack of cooperation in the day by day battling in that particular corridor." Eisenhower's message was confirmation of Marshall's wishes. Bradley and Montgomery would be equals whether Montgomery liked it or not.

Five days later, on August 30, Eisenhower held a press conference at the Ministry of Information in London announcing that he was assuming command of all Allied forces in Europe. Eisenhower "outlined the command setup in a perfectly honest, straightforward manner and, I think, has corrected the situation," Harry Butcher wrote in his diary. "He praised Monty and said that anyone who misinterpreted the transition of command as a demotion for General Montgomery simply did not look facts in the face. He said Montgomery is one of the great soldiers of this or any other war and he would now have the job of handling the battles on his side of the front . . . To the attentive correspondents, he made clear that when the initial beachhead was established, it was very restricted, and since there was only one tactical battle to be conducted, he had put General Montgomery in tactical control of the American land force." Eisenhower was at his best: defending Montgomery, calling him "a great and personal friend," rejecting criticism that he had moved too slowly in taking Caen. As for Allied cooperation, Eisenhower was vehement. There should not be "the slightest impression that any real fears need be entertained concerning the soundness of the Anglo-American military partnership in Europe," he said.[84] Had Marshall been in London he would have been pleased. The Germans were on the run and his great vision had been realized—Von Kluge's famed Tiger tanks were smoldering wrecks on the roads of Normandy, Brittany, and Lorraine. The British too, had been tamed, if only through the realization that, in any partnership, there must be a senior partner. The Americans now filled that role. Eisenhower was running the war.

13

BASTOGNE

". . . it would be convenient if my deputy were an experienced ground officer . . ."

"I will not remain as Chief of Staff . . ."

A PHOTOGRAPH OF George Marshall and Dwight Eisenhower was taken on the tarmac of La Bourget outside of Paris on October 6, 1944.[1] Marshall had just arrived in Europe and his aircraft can be seen in the background.[2] It is exactly five months to the day that Allied troops came ashore at Normandy. The army chief stands next to Eisenhower, his eyes on the Allied supreme commander while Ike, slightly shorter, has his hands on his hips and is looking into the distance. There is a broad and confident smile on his face. But it is Marshall's expression that draws the viewer's attention: he is looking at Eisenhower with a mix of pride and puzzlement. It is possible to read too much into this single photograph, yet the image of Eisenhower and Marshall in Paris provides stark evidence of the shift that had taken place in their partnership. While Marshall is still Eisenhower's commander and mentor, the upperclassman has now given way to the lower classman. The subtle and intangible transformation of Eisenhower from the deferential War Department colonel of December 1941 into a supreme commander in control of the largest military in American history in 1944 now seemed complete.

There is too, in this photograph, a growing sense that Marshall has aged, while Eisenhower retains his youth and vitality. There is good reason to suppose this is true. Marshall was sixty-four, one birthday away from the Army's mandatory retirement age. He was an old man by the era's standards and while it was expected that he would eventually pursue elected office (a possibility that, given his immense public popularity, was particularly worrisome to his political opponents on Capitol Hill), he had already hinted to Eisenhower that the supreme commander would someday become Army chief of staff. "Why do you think we have been pushing you? You will have ten years of hard work in the Army after the war," Marshall had said in June during his trip to Normandy.[3] Eisenhower was not simply the supreme Allied commander, he was Marshall's understudy as Army chief of staff. In the photograph, Marshall is looking at his successor.

MARSHALL AND Eisenhower were taken from the airport to Ike's headquarters at Versailles. During the subsequent briefing, Eisenhower reviewed Allied deployments and German strengths and summarized the battlefield situation, and the two discussed the strategy that needed to be followed in the weeks and months ahead. The Marshall-Eisenhower meetings continued the next day, though Marshall was exhausted from his nineteen hour trip.[4] Of primary concern to Eisenhower and Omar Bradley, who joined the discussion, was the War Department's officer replacement system. While the training of Army officers was good, Eisenhower and Bradley said, there was no substitute for combat experience; they requested that Marshall allow them to assign junior officers to noncombat units in their initial assignments in Europe.[5] They also requested that the chief of staff approve an accelerated program of battlefield commissions to restock the depleted American officers corps. This proposal reflected the reality of the European war. Great Britain had been facing a manpower crisis for many months, and now casualties from the close-in fighting in Normandy and the degrading of American combat units in the sprint across Lorraine imposed a remorseless arithmetic on Eisenhower. There were now three army groups operating in France: Bernard Law Montgomery's 21st Army Group, Omar Bradley's 12th Army Group, and Jacob Devers's 6th Army Group[6] —a total of more than thirty divisions (and dozens of independent brigades and regiments), comprising 1.5 million men, facing an increasingly strengthened German defensive line.[7] The American contingent comprised nearly two-thirds of the total number of soldiers on the western front, while British, Canadian, and French troops made up the balance. In all, the Allies deployed eighty-seven divisions and six thousand tanks. Still, to win an offensive war, the Allies needed roughly a three-to-one manpower advantage. With only 300,000 soldiers actually on the line in combat slots in northwestern Europe, Eisenhower did not have it.

Since August, Eisenhower had been calculating what it would take to defeat the Germans once the Allied armies reached the Rhine. While Montgomery believed it possible to end the war quickly, with a dash through the German defenses, Eisenhower dismissed such optimism. German manpower levels were actually increasing in western Germany, the result of Hitler's last-ditch conscription of old men and boys.[8] And the German formations— some seventy-four divisions and 1,600 tanks—were now under the command of the talented Gerd von Rundstedt.[9] The dour and nearly emaciated Prussian disciplinarian believed that Germany would lose the war, but he was a fighter and patriot and, while cool and aloof, a talented and creative military thinker.[10] Like Kesselring, Rundstedt might not be at his best as an attacker, but he had few peers as a defender. Eisenhower believed he would be a formidable foe.[11] Taking the measure of the German Army and Rundstedt, Eisenhower decided that he would attack on a broad front, moving his armies forward to the Rhine River, then using his armored formations to cut off and destroy pockets of German resistance once his armies penetrated Germany. The offensive would be deliberate, knocking ceaselessly against German entrenched positions, using Allied firepower to reduce enemy strongpoints. Eisenhower believed in this strategy. While conservative, it provided the best chance for victory at the same time that it held down casualties.

The supreme commander had no faith in a mad dash, the great slashing adventure that would miraculously unseat his adversary. His views were confirmed by the collapse of Montgomery's ill-fated airborne offensive across Holland in September. Operation Market Garden, as it was called, was conceived by Montgomery as a means of quickly securing the bridge over the Rhine River at Arnhem.[12] But Montgomery's offensive failed when the British 1st Airborne Division ran into the 9th and 10th SS Panzer Armored divisions at Arnhem. Later historians would claim that Monty's attempt to capture three bridges across three rivers both underestimated German strength and overestimated Allied capabilities. Monty went "a bridge too far," they said.[13] After bitter fighting, the British 1st Airborne had to be rescued from Arnhem by being ferried south across the Rhine.[14] Despite this, Montgomery still believed his northern front provided the Allies with the best prospect for victory, and he lobbied fiercely for increased troops and ammunition. Eisenhower, he argued, should put him in charge of an offensive against the Ruhr. When Eisenhower and his chief lieutenants adopted a policy of pressing the Germans along the entire Allied front, Montgomery was the only commander to oppose it.[15]

Eisenhower did not want to wage a broad-front war and knew that his strategy was controversial. But he thought he had little choice. While the Wehrmacht was deteriorating, Germany had put nine hundred thousand additional soldiers on the battlefield in the autumn of 1944 and enforced strict discipline on its combat units.[16] Then too, while a mad dash (or a "left hook" through Holland, as Montgomery would put it) might end the war quickly, such an adventuresome strategy could also result in a disaster, postponing the end of the war by months. A more conservative policy was painful, but it remained the best hope for an early and certain victory. Still, Eisenhower eyed his growing casualty lists with trepidation. The torrent of new troops and commanders that had poured into France in the aftermath of D-day had slowed to a trickle.[17] In June, George Marshall had established a ninety-division mobilization ceiling. The Army chief was adamant: Eisenhower would have to make do with what he had. The American people were tiring of the war. There were also political pressures on Marshall to begin diverting divisions from Europe to the Far East, where the Japanese were fighting a brutal island-to-island defense on their Pacific perimeter.[18] Nor could Eisenhower request that Marshall approve the transfer of American divisions in Italy to France, as such a transfer would only rekindle Winston Churchill's protest over America's European strategy. Besides, Harold Alexander and Mark Clark's forces were exhausted. In light of these facts, Eisenhower might have looked more closely at Montgomery's plan for a bold left hook. But Eisenhower knew the Allied armies lacked the trained mass of hardened, experienced, and aggressive officers that still characterized the Wehrmacht. While Eisenhower had great faith in his senior commanders, the headlong pursuit of the German Army across France had revealed some telling weaknesses, particularly among the Allied high command.

Montgomery had always been a cautious and conservative commander. He

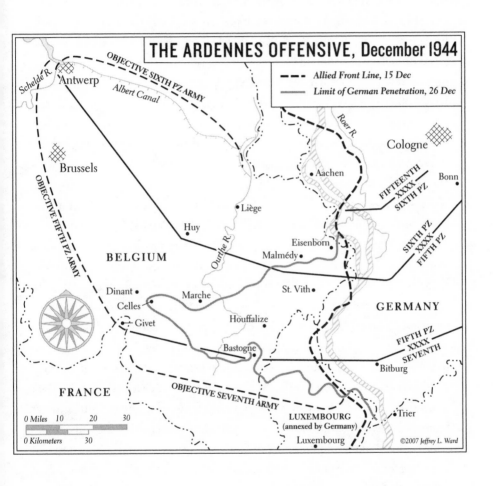

THE ARDENNES OFFENSIVE, December 1944

- - - Allied Front Line, 15 Dec
——— Limit of German Penetration, 26 Dec

would be even more so now after the one truly elegant (but flawed) airborne leap across the Rhine that he had designed, and that had so ignominiously collapsed at Arnhem. Bradley was a very good officer but not a great one, and at crucial moments in the attack across France he had held back. He lacked the kind of feel, of strategic intuition, for campaign strategy that made Kesselring and Rommel so brilliant. Then there was Patton. Patton was aggressive but mercurial. His reputation had fed his sense that destiny would grant him the victories his ego so desperately needed. Eisenhower knew better: Patton's forces had raced to Metz, where dug-in German defenders repulsed his every gambit, leaving his battlefield commanders bloodied and bitter. And Devers? Marshall liked Devers, though Devers's critics believed Marshall's patronage was the only reason that Devers was promoted. Bradley once described Devers as "overly garrulous (saying little of importance), egotistical, shallow, intolerant, not very smart, and much too inclined to rush off half cocked."[19] (That said, it is difficult now to determine whom exactly Bradley *did* like.) Finally, Eisenhower also realized that America's European army was facing a critical shortage of intelligent combat leaders—the majors, captains, and lieutenants of the front lines. Historian Max Hastings writes that the "educational standard of men shipped to combat arms ranked far below that of those posted to administrative branches,"[20] and he quotes a U.S. Army lieutenant colonel's observation that the replacements sent to his units were "not satisfactory. They never have been. It seems the infantry has been the last thing to be taken care of."[21] The opposite was true for the German Army, though Eisenhower might have been calmed by the knowledge that most of these midlevel officers, the cream of German youth, were already dead in the Soviet Union. Eisenhower could have used more soldiers of a higher caliber, would have done much better with another four or five divisions, but the American tradition of overwhelming force, of relying on technology and bombing to bludgeon an enemy into submission, did not allow for massed infantry attacks. Eisenhower would not send thousands of young men "over the top," as the British and French had in World War I. It was not then, and is not now, the American way of war.[22]

But perhaps Eisenhower's most pressing problem was logistical. George Patton's tanks had run out of gas on their way across France, and even with the opening of the harbor at Cherbourg, Allied resupply remained tenuous. To meet the increasing demands of his troops, Eisenhower approved the creation of a stopgap resupply network that included six thousand trucks running around the clock over a single highway. While the "Red Ball Express" consumed nearly as much fuel in a single day as an entire field army, it provided a respite from Ike's most pressing supply problems.[23] But the challenge for Eisenhower's commanders was not simply to overcome the Allies' cratered road system or its modest port capabilities. The problem was J.H.C. Lee, whose bungling of the supply services was well known to Marshall, Eisenhower, and the Army's senior commanders. Both Marshall and Eisenhower feared that Lee's strange habits would become public, sparking a storm of political investigations in Washington, so they worked around him. Even so, those habits were beginning to creep into public view. When "Jesus Christ Himself" scooped up the best available rooms in Paris after its liberation, the French joked that SHAEF actually stood for "Societé des Hoteliers Américains en France."[24] Worse yet, Lee had a habit of rewarding those he liked with the best supplies while punishing those he disliked by withholding supplies, a policy that should have led to his court-martial.

Though the solution of these problems was not immediately available to either Marshall or Eisenhower during their meetings at Versailles, the Army chief and supreme Allied commander recognized the looming crises they faced and began to take steps to solve them. Marshall and Eisenhower tackled the logistics problem first. The Army chief assigned three logistics experts to Ike's command, while Bedell Smith struggled behind the scenes to patch together a workable supply system.[25] The manpower issue was more difficult to resolve. Marshall was clear: there would be no additional call-up of troops in the U.S. Knowing this, Eisenhower decided the only way to address the issue effectively was to strip rear units of clerks who could carry a rifle. Of the 1.5 million Americans in France, only between 350,000 and 500,000 soldiers faced the Germans along the Siegfried Line, so Eisenhower cannibalized his army's long administrative tail, arming clerks and cooks with rifles and putting them on the firing line. To underscore his understanding of Eisenhower's manpower difficulties, Marshall brought Director of War Mobilization James Byrnes with him to Paris. While Marshall and Eisenhower conferred at Versailles, Byrnes went to Cherbourg to inspect the port and find ways to improve it. Byrnes's most important conclusion was that the European war was far from over and that more stringent workplace rules should be enforced in the U.S. to increase industrial production.[26]

The command problems facing Marshall and Eisenhower in the autumn of 1944, however, were of their own making. The two concluded that while Montgomery, Bradley, Devers, and Patton had personal foibles and military weaknesses, it was unlikely that their replacement by any of the handful of officers who formed the Allied second echelon would result in more aggressive leadership. Montgomery was imperious and egotistical, but his conservative outlook was matched perfectly to the drain on British manpower. Bradley was difficult and uncreative, but his disturbing lack of battlefield vision was balanced by his steady leadership. He would not sacrifice his men needlessly, and just now, that prudence was what Eisenhower needed. Devers might have been difficult, but he could fight. And while George Patton might have been obsessed by history's judgment, his attention to his own star provided Eisenhower with a commander who believed he could do the impossible. That quality, which might cost men lives, usually won wars. Of course, all of this ignores the strengths of the Allied armies: the U.S. fielded the best airborne units in the history of warfare, the toughest specialty regiments, and America's artillery and command of the air could blow holes in the lines of brave Germans who obeyed orders—and died in their trenches.[27] "Never send an infantryman to do a job that an artillery shell can do for him," Ninth Army commander William Simpson once said.[28] While uncompromising discipline and a Prussian mind-set might conquer nations, their ultimate result was defeat in one world war and certain defeat in a second. Finally, and most important, while the American people were loathe to produce a professional army along Prussian lines, the courage of individual American soldiers remained unquestioned—as the sacrifices at Salerno, Anzio, and Carentan showed.

AFTER GEORGE MARSHALL and Dwight Eisenhower concluded their private discussions on October 7, the Army chief flew over Verdun, then drove through Saint-Mihiel, his old battleground, before visiting George Patton at his headquarters in Metz.[29] Patton was ready for Marshall, providing a detailed briefing and a long discussion of German defenses. The next morning, Bradley escorted Marshall to Montgomery's headquarters in Belgium, where the British commander briefed the chief of staff on his deployments. Montgomery was filled with complaints: he complained about the supply problem, he complained about the soaking "German weather," and he complained about Eisenhower.

The supreme commander's strategy, Montgomery said, lacked direction and was "ragged and disjointed." As a result, the Allies had gotten themselves in a "real mess."[30] Marshall, who had disliked Montgomery from the moment he first met him in Algiers, kept his temper. But "I came pretty near to blowing off out of turn," he later told historian Forrest Pogue.[31] Marshall visited with Jacob Devers on October 9 and traveled south with him to see General Jean de Lattre de Tassigny, the commander of the First French Army, which guarded the French border just north of Switzerland. De Lattre made Montgomery's complaints sound modest, claiming that General Lucien Truscott's command success had come at the cost of French fuel—which, de Lattre claimed, Truscott had stolen. De Lattre later said that Marshall took his complaint seriously. But that's not how Marshall remembered it: "I just stopped the thing right where it was and walked out," he said. Marshall remembered the slight to Truscott years later, telling de Lattre that in his opinion, Truscott was a "fighter and not a talker."[32] De Lattre was insulted, which was Marshall's intent.

Marshall's whirlwind visit through the battlefields of the Allied armies, the most extensive of his wartime journeys, continued with another visit to Patton, an inspection of the 35th Division, and then, within the next three days, visits to two armored divisions and four infantry divisions. Everywhere he went, Marshall asked questions: about morale, battle plans, medical care, and ammunition supplies. On October 11, Marshall visited with three corps commanders: Troy Middleton, Gee Gerow, and J. Lawton Collins. He spent the evening of the eleventh at the command headquarters of the First Army, and on the twelfth he visited two more divisions and was briefed by commanders of XIX Corps. At each stop the Army chief made sure to visit frontline soldiers and award combat medals. He took notes of whom he saw and spoke with, and promised he would write to their families when he returned to Washington.[33] Marshall was looking forward to his return to America, but at the last minute he postponed his departure. While at Eisenhower's headquarters on the last afternoon of this visit, the Army chief was shown a long message that Bernard Montgomery had sent to Beetle Smith. In it, Montgomery complained to Smith about Eisenhower's decision to withhold American reinforcements from his front, claiming that his inability to capture Antwerp with its valuable port facilities was due not only to lack of troops, but to Eisenhower's failure to delegate authority.[34] The solution to these problems, Montgomery said, was for the Combined Chiefs to appoint an overall ground commander—presumably

Montgomery himself—which would free Ike to "coordinate" the Allied diplomatic, political, air, and sea efforts.

Enraged by Montgomery's bald power grab and suspecting that his ploy did
not have the support of his government, Marshall decided that any problems
at home could wait. He told Eisenhower that he would review his reply to
Montgomery. It was unusual for Marshall to intervene in Eisenhower's relationship with his subordinates, but Ike welcomed Marshall's suggestions. With
Marshall at his side, Eisenhower was free to take on Montgomery without his
normal studied courtesy.[35]

> I have read your letter to Smith on the subject of command. The ques-
> tions you raise are serious ones, and I will discuss them later in this let-
> ter. However, they do not constitute the real issue now at hand. That
> issue is Antwerp. . . . The Antwerp operation does not involve the ques-
> tion of command in any slightest degree. Everything that can be brought
> in to help, no matter of what nationality, belongs to you.
>
> In order that we may continue to operate in the same close and
> friendly association that, to me at least, has characterized our work in the
> past, I will again state, as clearly as possible, my conceptions of logical
> command arrangements for the future. If, having read these, you feel that
> you must still class them as "unsatisfactory," then indeed we have an issue
> that must be settled soon in the interests of future efficiency. I am quite
> well aware of the powers and limitations of an Allied Command, and if
> you, as the senior Commander in this Theater of one of the great Allies,
> feel that my conceptions and directives are such as to endanger the suc-
> cess of operations, it is our duty to refer the matter to higher authority
> for any action they may choose to take, however drastic.

In the same letter, obviously as a reflection of Marshall's views, Eisenhower
added his own conception of how Allied armies can successfully work together.

> But your letter brings up the question of nationalism as opposed to mil-
> itary considerations. It would be quite futile to deny that questions of na-
> tionalism often enter our problems. It is nations that make war, and when
> they find themselves associated as Allies, it is quite often necessary to
> make concessions that recognize the existence of inescapable national dif-

ferences. For example, due to difference in equipment, it is necessary that the 12th Army Group depend primarily upon a Line of Communications that is separate so far as possible from that of 21st Army Group. Wherever we can, we keep people of the same nations serving under their own commanders. It is the job of soldiers, as I see it, to meet their military problems sanely, sensibly, and logically, and, while not shutting our eyes to the fact that we are two different nations, produce solutions that can permit effective cooperation, mutual support and effective results. Good will and mutual confidence are, of course, mandatory.[36]

A more succinct statement of Marshall and Eisenhower's conception of coalition warfare and unity of command cannot be found in any document of the war. And while it is true that Eisenhower's staff had written a first draft of Ike's response to Montgomery, the final version of the Montgomery letter bears the unmistakable imprint of George Marshall. Marshall was not a gambler, and he played the one card that he knew was likely to silence Montgomery— particularly in the aftermath of Market Garden: if Monty did not like the command arrangements in Europe, then he could attempt to change them by arguing his case to Franklin Roosevelt and Winston Churchill. Marshall was certain that Montgomery would never dare go that far. Then too, while Eisenhower had withheld assigning American units to reinforce Montgomery at the height of September offensive, he had recently agreed to deploy Lieutenant General William Simpson's XIX Corps to reinforce the British push on Antwerp.[37] It was Eisenhower and the Americans who were sacrificing in the name of Allied unity; it was the Americans who were willing to have one of their commanders serve as a subordinate to a foreign field marshal; it was the Americans who were now to pour increased matériel and men into Monty's lines.

Montgomery received Eisenhower's response to his cable on October 13. The British commander read Eisenhower's message and made a quick calculation: Roosevelt would always stand behind Eisenhower, and Churchill was unlikely to support him. As for Alan Brooke, the chief of the Imperial General Staff, Montgomery had learned, was now among his most outspoken critics. The "Hero of Alamein" scrambled to redress the unfavorable impression he had made. "You will hear no more on the subject of command from me," he cabled to Eisenhower several days later, then pointedly added: "I have given you my views and you have given your answer. . . . I and all of us here will weigh in 100 percent to do what you want and we will pull it through without a doubt. I have given Antwerp top priority in all operations in 21 Army Group and all energies and efforts will be now devoted towards opening up that place."[38] For the first time during the war, Montgomery seemed humbled. While his divisions continued to reduce Antwerp, Monty stayed in his Brussels headquarters and sulked, certain that he would come under attack again. At the end of the month he returned to England for a rest.

George Marshall returned to Washington on October 14, Dwight Eisenhower's fifty-fourth birthday. The Army chief of staff was invigorated by his tour of the European theater, as well as by the outcome of Eisenhower's skirmish with Montgomery. While the Allied armies and their senior military leaders faced daunting problems, the command structure he had built since the first days of the war had been vindicated by the liberation of France. Eisenhower was firmly in control as the European commander; he was self-confident, aggressive, and respected by nearly everyone. More important, Marshall had made an extensive tour of European battlefields, and he liked what he had seen. While the Allies faced enormous logistical and manpower challenges, the Army chief of staff was pleased with his personal contact with America's soldiers. His first communication with Eisenhower after his return was warm, almost affectionate. "Dear Eisenhower," he wrote on October 16. ". . . The trip was immensely profitable to me and to those with me because I do believe that in a very short time we learned a great deal about conditions with you and therefore are much better prepared to meet your requirements from this end." Marshall then penned a more personal comment: "I am immensely indebted for your fine and generous hospitality and for all the arrangements made for me, and especially for the dinner the night of our arrival and the fine attention given Justice Byrnes. I always feel apologetic for burdening you in this way by taking up so much of your personal time."[39]

Eisenhower received Marshall's cable while retracing the chief of staff's tour. He visited nearly all the major Allied commands, assessing the offensive operations he had planned that would carry his forces through the cold winter ahead. Wherever he went, Eisenhower found his commanders battling the elements, the lack of supplies, and the Germans, now dug in and reinforced along the entire Siegfried Line. The problems Eisenhower identified were exacerbated by the fierce winter battles, the most costly of which was being fought in the Hurtgen Forest, where Courtney Hodges's First Army engaged in daily hand-to-hand combat against dug-in German infantry. The grim battle had gone on for weeks with little Allied penetration of German lines. Farther south, Jacob Devers was also running into trouble, fighting a series of crippling engagements that stalled just beyond the Belfort Gap on the west bank of the Rhine. Devers had taken Strasbourg, but it seemed now as if he might not be able to hold it. In the north, the Canadians made no progress in their bloody attempts to gain a foothold along the Scheldt. Even Patton was stuck, vainly throwing his infantry and armored columns at Metz. "How long, O Lord, how long?" Patton wrote in his diary. "We roll across France in less time than it takes Monty to say 'Regroup' and here we are stuck in the mud of Lorraine."[40] Everywhere along the front, the Allied armies grappled with the Germans in a series of close-in, brutal engagements, and all along the line the Germans held. "God, how wearying and wearing it all gets," Eisenhower wrote to Mamie. Later, the weather still casting a pall on his mood, Eisenhower detailed the suffering of American soldiers, squatting in their trenches beneath the cold rain. "It's all so terrible, so awful," he wrote to his wife, "that I constantly wonder how civilization can stand war at all."[41] Overcome by the bloody slogging of his troops, Eisenhower gave instructions that all shelter given to officers must be made available to the troops, an order that resulted from seeing a squad of soldiers huddled in the back of an uncovered truck. "I am getting exceedingly tired of the weather. Every day we have some report of weather that has broken records existing anywhere from twenty five to fifty years," Eisenhower wrote to Marshall.[42] There was no respite from the continuing cold, which actually worsened throughout December. Nothing was moving.

ON DECEMBER 16, 1944, preceded by a rolling artillery barrage, the Sixth SS Panzer Army and four SS panzer divisions struck west across the Ardennes Forest.[43] The *Schwerpunkt*, or main thrust, of the surprise offensive was directed by panzer commander Sepp Dietrich. Dietrich was supported on his left by Baron Hasso von Manteuffel's Fifth Panzer Army, and on Manteuffel's left by Lieutenant General Erich Brandenberger's Seventh Army.[44] The German force consisted of thirty-eight divisions and 250,000 troops, supported by numerous attached artillery brigades and a thousand fighter aircraft.[45] The targets of the German attack were the Meuse River crossings, the supply areas in the Allied rear, and the port of Antwerp. The Americans mustered only 83,000 troops to face the German onslaught. In the attack's first hours, the Germans punched gaping holes in the undermanned Allied front and surrounded a large number of infantry regiments who were now, through all of the sixteenth and on into the seventeenth, fighting for their survival.[46] By December 19, the German offensive posed a threat to the Meuse River crossings. The Allied losses were horrific; the 28th Division had been chewed to pieces, and the reinforcing 106th Infantry Division, untested in combat, was nearly destroyed.[47]

Omar Bradley told Eisenhower that he believed the Germans were simply launching a "spoiling" attack, aimed at disrupting Allied offensive plans in the north. But Eisenhower disagreed. German panzers had penetrated beyond Bastogne, and by the night of the eighteenth, pockets of Allied soldiers were surrounded in the Ardennes. With German panzers threatening to break through his last defenses, Eisenhower directed Bradley, Patton, Devers, and Air Marshal Arthur Tedder to attend a command meeting on the morning of December 19 in the conference room of the ornate Verdun casern—Bradley's forward headquarters.[48] Patton arrived with a flourish, standing in a jeep with Plexiglas doors that mounted .30 caliber machine guns. His jaw was clamped tightly on a cigar; the brass buttons on his overcoat sparkled in the chilly air.[49] In the cold conference room, Eisenhower eyed his commanders. "The present situation is to be regarded as one of opportunity for us and not disaster," he said. "There will only be cheerful faces at this conference table."[50] Patton smiled, then playfully joshed Eisenhower, suggesting that if that were the case perhaps the Allies should allow the Germans to go all the way to Paris. "Then we'll really cut 'em off and chew 'em up," he said. Eisenhower smiled and turned to his old friend. How soon could Patton break off his attacks against the Germans in the south and counterattack with six divisions against the German positions in the Ardennes? Patton was ready: his staff had already completed plans for a counterstroke. "I can attack on December 21, with three divisions, the 4th Armored, the 26th and the 80th," he said.[51] This was an astonishing proposal. "Don't be fatuous George," Eisenhower responded. "If you try to go that early, you won't have all three divisions ready and you'll go in piecemeal. You will start on the twenty-second and I want your initial blow to be a strong one! I'd even settle for the twenty-third if it takes that long to get three full divisions."[52] Patton agreed to the delay and left to issue orders to his commanders.[53] When Patton returned he and Eisenhower had a private chat. The two were suddenly back at Fort Meade, taking apart a tank and playing bridge. Eisenhower, recently promoted to five-star rank—general of the Army—shook his head. "Funny thing, George, every time I get another star I get attacked."[54] Patton smiled, ribbing his old friend and remembering North Africa. "And every time you get attacked Ike," he said, "I have to bail you out."[55]

George Marshall watched the battle reports from the Ardennes with increasing concern. Like Eisenhower, the Army chief was convinced that the German attack across the Ardennes was a major offensive—a drive to the Channel. But there was little he could do. In the office of the Operations Division, Colonel George "Abe" Lincoln—who would become an Army legend as the head of the West Point Social Science Department (his graduates, fighting in Vietnam, would be known as "the Lincoln Brigade")—studied Eisenhower's order of battle for northern France and began to pick out units that might reinforce Eisenhower.[56] Lincoln went to Marshall with a sheaf of papers, seeking guidance, but the Army chief of staff shook his head. No troops in England or bound for Europe would arrive in time to help the supreme commander. "We can't help Eisenhower in any way other than not bothering him," he told Lincoln. "No messages will go from here to the ETO [the European theater of operations] unless approved by me."[57] Marshall remained confident; he knew that Eisenhower's troops were cold and thinly placed in the Ardennes but he believed the Allies had enough units to fight off the Germans. Eisenhower might or might not have agreed, but after the Verdun conference he ordered the 11th Armored and 17th Airborne divisions in England to begin immediate deployment to France.[58] Then, to help manage the counteroffensive and give the British more firepower on the northern shoulder of the German breakthrough, Eisenhower transferred command of the First and Ninth armies from Bradley to Montgomery.

Given this new power, Montgomery strode into Courtney Hodges's First Army headquarters on December 18, as one observer noted, "like Christ come to cleanse the temple."[59] The offensive-minded Hodges, who was planning a way to first block the Germans and then send them reeling eastward, was told by Montgomery that the towns surrounded in the Ardennes would have to be evacuated. Montgomery then instructed "Lightning Joe" Collins to hold the line in front of the Meuse River. Like Hodges, Collins was not impressed by these orders, saying years later that he was certain that Montgomery wanted to order a full retreat, but he began to block the German path to the west.[60] It is clear that Montgomery's failure in Holland during Market Garden and his spat with Eisenhower over control of Allied ground forces made American commanders skeptical of his abilities, but Montgomery remained calm and determined and worked around the clock over the next three days to strip his own rear units to strengthen the Allied lines north of the German offensive. Meanwhile, on December 22—despite his pledge to Eisenhower that he would delay another day—George Patton's 4th Armored and 26th and 80th Infantry divisions made a ninety-degree left turn and attacked to the north. The counterthrust was thirty-five miles broad and caught the Germans unaware along the southern line of their salient.[61] While it was not apparent at the time, Patton's attack turned the battle's tide.

But even Montgomery's steady leadership and Patton's counteroffensive could not stem the offensive, and German panzer units continued to move west, cutting off Allied units in their rear. The greatest danger came at Bastogne, where VIII Corps commander Troy Middleton ordered his commanders to hold their positions despite being surrounded by German panzers.[62] Bradley quickly dispatched his reserves, the 101st and 82nd Airborne divisions, to help Middleton, who ordered what was left of his armor to impede the assault of the 2nd Panzer Division, diverting the German spearheads away from the town.[63] Four regiments of the 101st finally made it into Bastogne on the evening of the eighteenth, days before Patton's counteroffensive. They were immediately surrounded by a tide of German troops. The defenders of Saint-Vith, north of Bastogne, found themselves in the same predicament. A large salient, or bulge, now extended westward from the shoulders of the American lines, with American troops holding key towns inside the bulge opposing the German advance.[64] The salient was sixty miles long and fifty miles wide. By December 23, German armored spearheads were three miles from the Meuse River.[65] By Christmas Eve, the defenders of the small town of Bastogne—in the heart of the Ardennes—were entering their sixth day under siege. Behind the lines, at the farthest extent of the bulge, J. Lawton Collins's VII Corps waged a series of armored tank battles with the Fifth Panzer Army. Collins had been told by Montgomery that he must hold the Allied western lines "at all costs."[66] Collins said that he should be able to do so and passed on a vital piece of intelligence to Eisenhower headquarters: Manteuffel's Tigers, he said, were running out of fuel.

Finally, blessedly, the weather over Belgium began to clear. On the day before Christmas, as the 101st Airborne and elements of Middleton's VIII Corps spent another cold day at Bastogne, the Allies were able to put fighters into the air over Belgium. The "German weather" had broken. By Christmas Day, the Allied position had improved; Allied bombers began to pummel the German positions within the Ardennes salient.[67] On December 26, units of Patton's Third Army reached the Bastogne perimeter, and an exhausted Eisenhower urged Montgomery to support a proposal for a counterattack put forward by Omar Bradley. Surprisingly, Montgomery not only refused to agree to the plan, he criticized the 12th Army Group commander. Two days later, in a huff, Montgomery told Eisenhower that instead of a counterattack, all of Bradley's units should be assigned to his command for a thrust into the Ruhr basin. He then listed the failures suffered by the Allies since September—the lack of troops, poor morale, an indifferent supply chain, and the failure of Eisenhower and Bradley to foresee the Ardennes offensive. If Eisenhower had listened to him, he said, the Germans would not have attacked through the Ardennes. At his headquarters in Versailles, Eisenhower could barely bring himself to believe that, at this crucial moment, the British commander could criticize Bradley and concluded that Monty was making one last push to have himself named as Allied ground commander.[68] Or, barring that, Montgomery was conspiring to take control of Bradley's Army Group, thereby reinforcing his own depleted units.[69] Eisenhower did his best to ignore Montgomery's imperious demands as the fight in the Ardennes raged on, but the pressure from the field marshal proved relentless. Even so, after a cordial meeting with Montgomery on the twenty-eighth, Eisenhower returned to Versailles convinced that the British commander had finally agreed to a counteroffensive against the Germans. But upon his arrival at his headquarters, Eisenhower was handed a message in which Monty revived the "command coordination" issue that he had proposed back in October. After outlining his plan for reducing the Ardennes salient, Montgomery suggested he be given emergency military powers, which included control of Bradley's Army Group. He even suggested that Eisenhower adopt his language in the writing of a new command directive:

I would say that your directive will assign tasks and objective to the two Army Groups, allot boundaries, and so on. Thereafter preparations are made and battle is joined. *It is then that one commander must have powers to direct and control the operations; you cannot possibly do it yourself, and so you would have to nominate someone else.* . . . I would suggest that your directive should finish with this sentence: "*12 and 21 Army Groups will develop operations in accord with the above instructions. From now onwards full operational direction, control and co-ordination of these operations is vested in the C.-in-C. 21 Army Group, subject to such instructions as may be issued by the Supreme Commander from time to time.*"[70]

In the midst of this, Omar Bradley forwarded to SHAEF copies of British press stories implying that Eisenhower had been unnerved by the German offensive and that the Allies had been saved only by the timely arrival of Montgomery's northern forces. Patton was barely mentioned.[71] Enraged by Montgomery's demands, Eisenhower decided that it was time to put the British commander in his place. He would make an appeal directly to the Combined Chiefs of Staff: they could relieve Montgomery or they could relieve him.

Back in Belgium at Montgomery's headquarters, Montgomery's chief of staff, Major General Sir Francis "Freddie" de Guingand, watched this unfolding drama and decided that his boss was about to lose his job. On December 30 de Guingand flew from Brussels to Versailles in an attempt to dampen the controversy.[72] He was greeted by a glum and angry supreme commander, who was in no mood to let Montgomery escape punishment. "Does Monty realize the effects of the line taken by the British press?" Eisenhower asked de Guingand. "And I wonder if he recognizes the effects of his continued pressing for the establishment of a land commander? I am tired of the whole business and have come to the conclusion that it is now a matter for a decision of the Combined Chiefs of Staff."[73] Eisenhower handed de Guingand two documents; one was from George Marshall on the chief of staff's view of the Montgomery controversy; the second was a copy of the cable he intended to send to the combined chiefs. The Marshall cable had just arrived; it was the first Marshall had sent to Eisenhower since the beginning of the Ardennes campaign.

I am violating somewhat my own orders to the staff here in bringing up some question with you while you are in the turmoil of this German offensive. However, as you seem to be succeeding and my guess is that you will without much delay seize the offensive yourself, I feel free to make these comments.

They may or may not have brought to your attention articles in certain London papers proposing a British Deputy Commander for all your ground forces and implying that you have undertaken too much of a task yourself. My feeling is this: under no circumstances make any concessions of any kind whatsoever. You not only have our complete confidence but there would be a terrific resentment in this country following such action. I am not assuming that you had in mind such a concession. I just wish you to be certain of our attitude on this side. You are doing a grand job and go on and give them hell.

After reading the Marshall cable, de Guingand knew that Montgomery was in deep trouble. Winston Churchill might question Eisenhower, might be skeptical of American plans, might show frustration over the war in private, but he would not fight George Marshall, Dwight Eisenhower, and Franklin Roosevelt all at the same time. If asked to make a choice, de Guingand knew, Churchill would agree to the dismissal of the Hero of Alamein. De Guingand now turned his attention to Eisenhower's second cable, a blunt message to Marshall intended for the Combined Chiefs stating that the supreme commander could no longer work with the head of the 21st Army Group. Eisenhower suggested that Montgomery be replaced by Field Marshal Harold Alexander. "Freddie de Guingand earned a year's pay in the course of a few minutes," historian John S. D. Eisenhower notes. "Speaking in deadly earnest, he urged General Eisenhower to delay sending the wire to Marshall for twenty-four hours." Eisenhower, at the urging of Bedell Smith, reluctantly agreed and gave de Guingand twenty-four hours to bring Montgomery to his senses.[74]

De Guingand immediately flew back to Montgomery's headquarters. He literally took his life in his hands, flying through some of the worst winter weather ever recorded in European history. "I've just come from SHAEF and seen Ike," de Guingand told Montgomery in Brussels, "and it's in the cards that you might have to go." Montgomery was stunned. He seemed unaware that his demands

would cause such anger. When he was told that Alexander would be his re-
placement, he nearly collapsed. "What shall I do Freddie?" he asked. De
Guingand immediately produced a letter he had drafted to Eisenhower for
Montgomery to sign. It was as close to an apology as Montgomery would ever
issue. Montgomery read the letter and instructed de Guingand to send it to
Eisenhower. "Very distressed that my letter may have upset you," de Guingand
had written on Monty's behalf, "and I would ask you to tear it up."[75] But de
Guingand was not yet finished. Later that night, he spoke quietly with a group
of influential British war reporters and told them that their articles on the
Ardennes offensive had caused a crisis in the Allied high command that might
cost Montgomery his job. The reporters agreed to forward de Guingand's message to their editors.[76] Back in Versailles, Eisenhower was mollified by
Montgomery's apology but remained convinced that the British commander
had caused incalculable damage. Omar Bradley, in particular, was embittered
by British press reports and believed that in transferring the First Army and then
the Ninth Army to Montgomery, Eisenhower had shown a lack of confidence
in his abilities.[77]

The crisis in command that plagued the Allies in December 1944 could not
easily be so resolved or forgotten. But Dwight Eisenhower did his best to put it
in the past. He spent New Year's Eve drawing up plans for an Allied counterstroke against the Germans that would include a reduction of their remaining
forces in the Ardennes at the same time that Montgomery's Army group moved
into position to attack the Ruhr. Bradley's 12th Army Group would have only
a limited role in the offensive. At his own headquarters that night, Bradley was
nearly morose. As midnight struck, *Time* magazine correspondent Bill Walton
declared a toast: "Never has the world been plagued by a year less worth remembering," he announced, raising his glass. Bradley gave a wry smile.
Especially the last fifteen days, he thought.[78]

THE ALLIES had chased the Germans out of France and blunted their offensive in the Ardennes. The war was not won, but its end was in sight. Yet then,
in January 1945, the Marshall-Eisenhower partnership faced its greatest test.
Historians now judge the crisis that infected the high command in January
1945 as a predictable result of the German attack. Defeat breeds mistrust. So

while we rightly extol the "Patton to the rescue" narrative of the Battle of the Bulge and replay the triumphant defense of Bastogne by the brave men of the 101st Airborne, the truth is that German offensive shook Allied confidence. In the space of forty-eight hours, the Wehrmacht crushed Eisenhower's center. While the Allies turned the tide of the battle a mere six days after Sepp Dietrich's tanks destroyed their defenses, the German armored thrust so unsettled American and British policymakers that Eisenhower's plan for Hitler's final defeat was greeted with skepticism. Montgomery's poisonous maneuverings exacerbated this crisis. While defeated at Bastogne, the Germans fought on through the New Year, their retreat exacting a heavy toll in British and American lives. It hardly mattered to Eisenhower that on this New Years he was named *Time's* "Man of the Year." Nor did it occur to him that the previous "Man of the Year," George Marshall, was watching his handling of Allied forces more closely than at any previous time during the war. What Marshall observed did not give him confidence, for suddenly Eisenhower appeared off balance, his once deft hand seemingly numbed by the forces arrayed against him. At Versailles, Eisenhower was calmly working to recover from the Ardennes offensive and shape a strong response, but everywhere he looked it seemed as if the Germans were pressing in—as if energized by their near victory in Belgium.

Eisenhower looked first to his right wing, where Devers's forces, holding Alsace, were overextended. Seven German divisions were pressing the undermanned Devers, who informed Eisenhower that he would have to abandon his positions in Strasbourg. Carefully calculating Devers's losses, Eisenhower decided the Allies must abandon the city. Once known, the decision enraged Charles de Gaulle, the head of the Free French government, who stormed into Eisenhower's headquarters at the Trianon Palace at Versailles on January 2. Winston Churchill, in Europe to mediate the Montgomery-Eisenhower dispute, was with Eisenhower and attempted to mollify the French leader, but de Gaulle was adamant. If Strasbourg was abandoned, he said, he would withdraw French troops from SHAEF and form an independent French command. Unfazed, Eisenhower tried to reason with de Gaulle, but the French leader's criticism was withering. At one point, he patiently but bitingly gave Eisenhower a tutorial on the realities of French politics: "Retreat in Alsace," he said, "would yield French territory to the enemy. In the realm of strategy this would be only a maneuver, but to France, it would be a national disaster, for Alsace is sacred ground."[79] Slowly, prodded by Churchill, Eisenhower began to shift his ground. By the end of January 2, Churchill was able to shape an agreement: Devers would hold Strasbourg, but not "at all costs" as de Gaulle had demanded. Eisenhower agreed and Churchill was relieved: "You have done the wise and proper thing," he told Eisenhower.[80]

But Eisenhower's troubles were only beginning. While his threat to Montgomery had sent the field marshal scurrying for cover, the British Chiefs of Staff were skeptical that Eisenhower's plan to launch a post-Ardennes counteroffensive would work. Alan Brooke fed these doubts. In the next room at the Trianon Palace at Versailles during Eisenhower's argument with de Gaulle, Brooke decided that Eisenhower needed not only a tutorial on French politics, but a short lecture on his views of military strategy. When Eisenhower finished with de Gaulle, he appeared suddenly before Brooke, who had spread dozens of maps and papers on the floor of a large conference room. Brooke critiqued Eisenhower's plan, ticking off its weaknesses point by point, his finger wagging at the maps spread out beneath his feet. Eisenhower gazed patiently.[81] There was something else afoot here, he believed, and he thought he knew what it was. While Brooke and Churchill might not support Montgomery, they would do their best to appoint a British ground commander, perhaps Alexander, in his stead. Defeating Montgomery was not the same as defeating the British, whose manpower numbers were so crucial that Eisenhower's plan for an attack on all fronts seemed, particularly to Churchill, like a replay of the Somme. Alexander could solve that problem. Churchill confirmed this during a private discussion with Eisenhower in the wake of Brooke's lecture, saying that Alexander would not actually be the ground commander in Europe, but Eisenhower's "deputy supreme commander"—the position held by Air Marshal Arthur Tedder. Eisenhower thought this was reasonable, as he would still retain his command prerogatives.[82] In any event, the final word would come not from Churchill, but from Roosevelt. Any decision on new command arrangements would not be made until the conclusion of an Allied conference scheduled for the end of the month at Malta. Buoyed by Eisenhower's seeming acceptance of Alexander as a deputy commander, Churchill wrote a reassuring note to Roosevelt: "His Majesty's government have complete comfidence in General Eisenhower and feel acutely any attacks made on him," he said. "He and Montgomery are very closely knit, and also Bradley and Patton."[83]

But just as Eisenhower seemed relieved of the incessant military maneuverings of the British, the Marshall-Eisenhower relationship began to fray. Beginning the first week of January, Marshall bombarded Eisenhower with cables asking for details on his discussions with de Gaulle, warning him about the continued problems with General J. C. H. Lee, and, finally, forwarding Franklin Roosevelt's support for the Allied command during his State of the Union address. Marshall pointedly included Roosevelt's lukewarm praise for the American effort as an apparent warning that the administration was feeling the public malaise brought on by the shock of the German attack.[84] Roosevelt commended the American effort against the Germans but felt it necessary to offer a statement of confidence in Eisenhower's leadership—primarily because his leadership was under fire. "General Eisenhower has faced this period of trial with admirable calm and resolution and with steadily increasing success. He has my complete confidence," Roosevelt said.[85] Marshall did not let the moment pass. "I suppose you have seen so much of the text of the President's report on the State of the Union to Congress yesterday as refers to you and your battle," Marshall wrote. "Lest you may not have seen this I am having it sent to you by teletype. Might it not be a good thing to get the sense of the President's message down to your U.S. Armies, at least to the leaders?"[86] Eisenhower could hardly miss Marshall's meaning: Roosevelt would not have issued a public reassurance if one were not needed.

Marshall's cables never threatened the supreme commander's position, never betrayed any lack of confidence in Eisenhower's leadership. But their tone was worried, disapproving, strident. When word leaked out, once again in the British papers, that a new deputy commander might be appointed in Europe, Eisenhower explained his reasoning in a defensive letter to the chief of staff. This January 10 message began with a long explanation of Eisenhower's planned offensive against Germany, then explained his decisions to withdraw and then to retain Devers's forces in Strasbourg. Eisenhower then defended his agreement to appoint "a separate commander for ground operations" and his understanding with Churchill that Alexander would fill that role. Eisenhower sensed Marshall's disapproval, however, and so backed away from the idea of actually appointing a "ground commander." Knowing that his views might spark Marshall's strong censure, Eisenhower finessed what he had told the British prime minister, saying that it was simply his intention to appoint a "deputy supreme commander" who had infantry experience. The last paragraph of Eisenhower's letter to Marshall contained his most important argument.

> Because of the great size of the land forces now engaged on this front, it would be more convenient for me if my deputy supreme commander were an experienced ground officer rather than air. In spite of my personal and official admiration for Tedder he is not repeat not in position to help me by visits and conferences with troop commanders. If I could have a man of fine personality, respected by all and willing to serve as my deputy and not repeat not under independent charter from my superiors, it would be most helpful. As a corollary to such a scheme I would want Spaatz named air commander in chief. I am afraid it would be impossible to find such a deputy as I describe. The only one I could think of myself would be Alexander, and manifestly he is not repeat not available.[87]

If this last paragraph was intended to reassure Marshall it failed. The chief of staff's response was painfully precise and condemnatory, saying that Eisenhower's "last paragraph" indicated "a weakening on your part under the heavy pressure of the press and British officialdom to get some high British military official into your general management of the ground forces." Appointing a deputy commander, he said, would mean that "the British had won a major point in getting control of ground operations in which their divisions of necessity will play such a minor part and, for the same reason, we are bound to suffer very heavy casualties; and second, the man being who he is and our experience being what it has been, you would have great difficulty in offsetting the direct influence of the PM [prime minister]."[88] No more serious criticism could be leveled at a commander: his decision would cost lives, American lives. To punctuate this insistent tone, Marshall agreed to meet with Eisenhower at Marseille prior to the chief of staff's attendance at the Malta Conference.

As Eisenhower prepared for his crucial meeting with Marshall, the position of the Allies in France improved. By mid-January the Ardennes Pocket had been reduced, and Hodges's First Army was poised for the leap into Germany.[89] Montgomery, still subdued, had duly returned the First Army to Bradley's control and moved his forces closer to the Ruhr. In the east, the Russians were beginning their final march into East Prussia, herding hundreds of thousands of Germans before them. Jacob Devers, meanwhile, had successfully held on to Strasbourg and was beginning the arduous task of clearing German defenses along the Rhine south of the Siegfried Line. The Germans just to the east, he noted, were beginning to move some of their divisions out of the line, for transport to the eastern front to face the Russians. There was still seven inches of snow on the ground in Belgium, and American and British soldiers, strung out facing the German defenses, continued to fight the nasty war of attrition that had marked the campaign ever since December 16. But by mid-January, Eisenhower believed that he could give Marshall some good news—the Allies were beginning to move again.

THE STRAIN between Marshall and Eisenhower was clearly visible when the two met on January 26 at Marseille's Château Valmonte, as dark and cold an Old World edifice as Bradley's headquarters at Verdun. The testy exchange of cables between the two of the last weeks had taken its toll. After an exchange of pleasantries, the two commanders remained grim-faced. Eisenhower opened the conference with a list of his needs and an outline of his army's offensive plans. Marshall listened politely and nodded his approval.[90] Marshall began to speak then, his tones crisp and curt. He upbraided Eisenhower for agreeing to appoint a deputy commander for ground operations. As Eisenhower's notes on Marshall's presentation make clear, this exchange—after so many years of agreement—marked the most difficult moment of their command partnership. Looking directly at his subordinate, Marshall gave him specific instructions. His sentences were short. He left no room for misinterpretation. The Army chief of staff had fought the British for years on precisely this point—command in Europe. He was not going to give an inch now with victory so close at hand. As Eisenhower later wrote: "General Marshall will not agree to any proposal to set up a Ground Commander-in-Chief for this theater. If this is done he says he will not remain as Chief of Staff. He recognized the necessity of giving Montgomery an American Army." Uninterrrupted, Marshall continued in the same tone: "He [Marshall] agrees that crossing [the Rhine] in force should be preceded by well-conducted campaigns to eliminate the German forces west of the Rhine."[91] With this out of the way, the Army chief reviewed Eisenhower's plan. Marshall said that he disagreed with the British critique of his subordinate's strategy, as the supreme commander indicated that the offensives would be "so conducted as to employ in the front lines the fewest possible number of divisions so as to have well-rested and re-fitted the greatest number of divisions when the time comes for an all-out attack." Marshall added that Eisenhower would get reinforcements from Italy to conduct his operations. Marshall was finished, and Eisenhower concluded the meeting by requesting a promotion for Bradley. He pointed out that Bradley was a three-star general, while Montgomery held the equivalent of four-star rank. Marshall said that he needed more time to resolve the question, for giving the rank to Bradley meant giving it to other officers, including Patton. That was simply not possible.[92]

The Marshall-Eisenhower meeting at Château Valmonte was the last the two had during the war. While the meeting was filled with personal tension, Marshall left Marseille convinced not only that Eisenhower's plan to end the war was sound, but that his partner now fully understood why the Army chief was so adamant about defeating the British initiative to weaken Eisenhower's command over Allied troops. While appointing a deputy ground commander might reflect sound military realities, it violated America's growing sense of responsibility to build a postwar world. Marshall was so deeply committed to his view that he was willing to end his own career in its name.

The question of command in Europe in 1945 was *not* military, it was political. America's commitment to World War II was complete. Three-quarters of all the soldiers fighting in Europe in 1945 were American. The United States produced nearly half the world's armaments and two-thirds of its ships.[93] Bradley alone commanded more men in his Army group than the British and French put together. The stark realities of these sacrifices were clear to Marshall. The Americans were now the dominant force in the world and no matter how much Churchill or Brooke or Montgomery might protest, that needed to be recognized. Those who made the greatest sacrifices would retain the most power. As Franklin Roosevelt's most trusted military adviser, George Marshall had developed a keen sense of American political realities. The American people would not tolerate a British commander of American troops. Then too, Marshall had concluded, the only way to keep Europe from plunging itself into another European war was to keep America engaged in Europe. To make America the keeper of the European peace. To take control, finally, of Europe's destiny.

George Marshall arrived in Malta armed with Eisenhower's agreement that there would be no British deputy ground commander. Sensing Marshall's resolve, Alan Brooke slowly softened British demands, couching them in cooperative terms. Things had changed since Arcadia and now, with the Americans bearing the brunt of the European fighting, the chief of the Imperial General Staff had only one goal: to give British commanders the right to take the lion's share of the final victory. The final offensive should come in the north—on Montgomery's front—Brooke insisted to Marshall. Brooke was surprised by Marshall's answer. The Army chief of staff agreed, pointing out that this was a part of Eisenhower's plan. Beetle Smith, assigned to Malta as Eisenhower's personal representative, also agreed with Brooke's point. Eisenhower depended on Montgomery. Smiling slightly, the chief of the Imperial General Staff implied that that might not be good enough, and he shook his head, as if in disapproval of his colleagues. He wanted Eisenhower's commitment in writing, he said. The implied insult was clear—Alan Brooke would not trust the word of George Marshall. So, at Marshall's direction Smith contacted Eisenhower, who cabled Smith that Montgomery would lead the Ruhr offensive. "You may assure the Combined Chiefs of Staff that I will seize the Rhine crossings in the North immediately throughout its length," he replied.[94]

This should finally have satisfied Brooke, but it did not. On the sidelines of the conference, Brooke goaded Smith, telling him he did not think that Eisenhower was "strong enough" to do his job. Smith, who was not accustomed to Brooke's tone of voice, clenched his fists. The frustrations of four years finally boiled over: "Goddamn it," he said, "let's have it out right now." What exactly did Brooke mean? Brooke responded evenly that it was his opinion that Eisenhower was too easily influenced by his subordinates. Smith retorted that the supreme commander had always attempted to maintain cordial relations with all Allied officers and added that if the British chiefs had so many doubts about Eisenhower's abilities, they should appeal to the combined chiefs. Brooke retreated, waving Smith off and candidly admitted that no one but Eisenhower would ever be acceptable to George Marshall. Still, unbelievably, the matter did not end there. One week later Brooke raised questions about Eisenhower at Yalta, recommending that Arthur Tedder be transferred to the Mediterranean and that Alexander be reassigned as Eisenhower's deputy. Churchill and Roosevelt decided to postpone the issue. But this was only a diplomatic nicety. In Germany, Montgomery heard about the proposed change and told Eisenhower that he would not agree to it. It seems that in the end Montgomery concluded that Eisenhower should be in command; or perhaps, as seems more likely, he had determined that if he was not to be the deputy ground commander, then no one would. The war of the generals, waged now for four long years, was finally over. George Marshall had won.

ON MARCH 7, 1945, Signal Corps officers of Courtney Hodges's First Army scrambled across the Ludendorff Railroad Bridge at Remagen, Germany. American troops poured over the bridge. South of Remagen, George Patton's Third Army launched Operation "Lumberjack," a strike across south-central Germany. One week later, Bernard Law Montgomery began Operation Plunder—the huge pincer movement designed to trap hundreds of thousands of German soldiers in the Ruhr.[95] A jubilant Eisenhower cabled Marshall, and the Army chief of staff, buoyed by Ike's news, bantered with his subordinate— he had to juggle complaints from Congress about using young men in combat at the same time he had to juggle demands from MacArthur for more troops, he said. After Marshall's comment on the "illogical pressure" of these competing demands, Eisenhower told him that he understood Marshall's problems. "Sometimes when I get tired of trying to arrange the blankets smoothly over the several prima donnas in the same bed I think no one person in the world can have so many illogical problems. I read about your struggles concerning the eighteen year old men in combat . . . and went right back to work with a grin."[96]

George Patton, brass buttons shimmering, his gruff voice nearly a scream of triumph, crossed the Rhine on March 22 and began his race into Germany. Montgomery and Bradley began their offensive to the east of the Ruhr, their armored columns meeting finally behind the great industrial basin. While the Allies faced tough resistance in parts of western Germany, the Wehrmacht's ability to rally its forces for sustained resistance was at an end. The Germans were beaten. The overriding question remained whether Eisenhower would order Allied forces to move quickly to the east to Berlin. The decision was never made. Instead, on March 28, Eisenhower transferred command of the U.S. Ninth Army from Montgomery to Bradley.[97] For Montgomery, the decision seemed a last indignity. But for American commanders, the decision was meant to show the imperious "Hero of Alamein" who was in charge. Eisenhower was his own ground commander. The decision stunned the British government, for it meant that Montgomery's Army Group would not have the strength to fight its way to the German capital. Alan Brooke was particularly enraged, describing Eisenhower's move as "unintelligible," "unauthorized," and "a clear breach of promise" that Montgomery would lead the charge across northern Germany.[98]

Churchill, almost visibly exhausted now by the war, was less irritated than his chief of staff. He seemed deflated and admonished the British chiefs to face reality. Brooke and his colleagues might present their case to Marshall and the U.S. Chiefs of Staff, but the prime minister doubted it would have any impact. "I hope . . . we shall realise that we have only a quarter of the forces invading Germany, and that the situation has thus changed remarkably from the days of June 1944," he said.[99] In private, however, Churchill argued with Eisenhower that his orders condemned Montgomery to a "static role." It meant that Berlin would fall to the Red Army. Eisenhower maintained a diplomatic silence, supported by Marshall, who rallied the Joint Chiefs of Staff to his side: "General Eisenhower's course of action . . . appears to be in accord with agreed major strategy and with his directive, particularly in light of the present development of the battle in Germany . . . The United States Chiefs of Staff consider that to disperse the strong forces which probably would be required to reach and reduce the northern ports before the primary object of destroying the German armies is accomplished, would seriously limit the momentum of a decisive thrust straight through the center."[100] While speculation persists to this day that this was Marshall and Eisenhower fighting their final battle against Alan Brooke and Bernard Law Montgomery, in fact, Eisenhower's directive slowing Montgomery's advance was made in keeping with the philosophy that George Marshall and Dwight Eisenhower had learned from Fox Conner: wars should be fought alongside others and concluded quickly. American lives were precious, and no democracy, no matter how pressed, could afford to try the patience of its people. And no democracy could afford to expend lives casually for political purposes. Nor did Marshall or Eisenhower want to answer to any American for putting soldiers into a situation akin to what was then happening to the Russians in Berlin, where Germans fought house to house and building to building until the Germans in the last office on the topmost floor of the Reichstag were killed. Berlin would cost the Red Army 352,000 casualties.[101]

In early April, Omar Bradley's Army Group began its convergence on Essen and Hagen with its goal the Elbe River. Within days, Bradley's armored divisions were making their way along Germany's central autobahn, while massive lines of refugees numbering in the thousands headed to the west. Pockets of German resistance continued to be met but were easily overcome. The Third Reich was collapsing. On April 13, Eisenhower was told that Franklin Roosevelt had died at his home in Warm Springs, Georgia, the previous day. In Washington, George Marshall went immediately to the White House to speak with the first lady, then traveled to Warm Springs to accompany Roosevelt's body to Washington. The man whom Marshall had never allowed to call him George had depended on his chief of staff to organize and train young Americans for war. In return, Roosevelt had showed unsparing loyalty to his favorite soldier. Marshall quickly gathered an honor guard to accompany the president's remains from Warm Springs to Washington and then on to Hyde Park.[102] In Germany, Dwight Eisenhower cabled his sympathy to the first lady, then turned back to work: victory in Europe was near. On April 15, 317,000 German troops surrendered in the Ruhr—the largest mass surrender of the entire war.[103] The day of Roosevelt's death, Eisenhower cabled Marshall, telling him that he should come to Germany "to see the Army you have created."[104]

Marshall and Eisenhower had reason to celebrate their success. But the victory they had earned was tempered. Eisenhower wrote to Marshall of the death camps he had visited. What he had seen was beyond description, but he described it anyway, knowing that at some future date some might question the fact of the horrors. Eisenhower visited one camp and then another. He saw bodies piled to the ceiling: "I made the visit deliberately," he later said, "in order to be in position to give first-hand evidence of these things if ever, in the future, there develops a tendency to charge these allegations merely to 'propaganda.' "[105] Eisenhower's walk through the German death camps may be the single most important reason why, on the evening of May 6, 1945, he refused to meet with Generaloberst Alfred Jodl when the German commander arrived at Eisenhower's headquarters in Reims to sign the instrument of his country's unconditional surrender. The surrender ceremony took place early on the morning of May 7, when Jodl marched into the SHAEF conference room and bent over to append his signature to the surrender document. Bedell Smith then escorted Jodl into Eisenhower's office. The supreme commander asked Jodl if he understood the terms of surrender and would implement them. The German general stood erect. Months later, he would appear in the dock at Nuremberg, accused of crimes against humanity. Jodl stared at Eisenhower. "Ja," he said."[106]

"IKE"

"You have made history . . ."
"Our army and people have never been so deeply indebted
to any other soldier. . . ."

GEORGE MARSHALL LEARNED OF the surrender of Germany in a
cable written by Eisenhower to the Combined Chiefs of Staff:[1] "The
mission of this Allied force was fulfilled at 0241, local time, May 7th, 1945."[2]
Within hours, Marshall penned a confidential message to his subordinate. "You
have completed your mission with the greatest victory in the history of warfare.
You have commanded, with outstanding success, the most powerful military
force that has even been assembled. You have met and successfully disposed of
every conceivable difficulty incident to varied national interests and international political problems of unprecedented complications. . . . You have made
history, great history for the good of all mankind and you have stood for all we
hope for and admire in an officer of the United States Army. These are my tributes and my personal thanks."[3] In Reims, Eisenhower accepted the congratulations of his staff, then went to bed. "We had no local victory celebrations of
any kind," he said. The next day, after having read Marshall's tribute, he issued
a simple response ("I truly thank you for your message"), then reached into his
desk and retrieved a draft letter to the Army chief of staff that he had been writing over the previous days. After rereading it, he decided to send it without edits.

Since the day I first went to England, indeed since I first reported to you in the War Department, the strongest weapon that I have always had in my hand was a confident feeling that you trusted my judgment, believed in the objectivity of my approach to any problem and were ready to sustain to the full limit of your resources and your tremendous moral support, anything that we found necessary to undertake to accomplish the defeat of the enemy. This has had a tremendous effect on my staffs and principal subordinate commanders. Their conviction that you had basic faith in this headquarters and would invariably resist interference from any outside sources, has done far more to strengthen my personal position throughout the war than is realized even by those people who were affected by this circumstance. . . . Our army and people have never been so deeply indebted to any other soldier.[4]

These expressions of gratitude from Marshall to Eisenhower, and the supreme Allied commander's response, were characteristic of their relationship. The two were not friends in the way that Marshall was friends with Harold "Betty" Stark, or that Eisenhower was with Mark "Wayne" Clark. It is as difficult to imagine George Marshall being comfortable as a bridge-playing member of Club Eisenhower, as it is to imagine Dwight Eisenhower spending the afternoon with the Army chief of staff enjoying his solitary passions of riding or weeding a garden. There is a note of anticlimax in their tributes, as if the two realized their mutual expressions were both expected and necessary. Marshall needed Eisenhower's smooth diplomacy, his appreciation for the value of fighting with a coalition, and his ability to implement a military strategy that was global as much as Eisenhower needed Marshall's enormous capacity for ordering and organizing. Marshall understood that he could not equal the Eisenhower smile, while Ike understood he owed his position to Marshall's support. The Army chief was a man who recoiled from any demonstration of praise. An officer did his duty because that was his job. This was a part of the Marshall catechism. So the discomfort is there, just under the surface, of the chief of staff's message. "These are my tributes and my personal thanks," Marshall wrote. There would be no more.

Harry Truman named May 8 V-E Day, but the surrender of German forces went into effect at 12:01 A.M. London time on May 9. One million people crowded Whitehall to cheer Winston Churchill, and two million people in New York spontaneously took to the streets, celebrating in Times Square. The fighting did not end suddenly in Europe, as it had in 1918, but sputtered out. In the killing grounds of East Prussia there were Russian reprisals against the German population, and in the German capital the rape of Berlin was in full swing. Ethnic and national reprisals continued for weeks after May 8. Nor did the antagonists' armies automatically lay down their weapons. It took time for word of the surrender to reach through all of Germany and Eastern Europe. At the time of the surrender, a large American force was maneuvering carefully through southern Germany in an operation aimed at attacking the rumored Nazi national redoubt in Thuringia.[5] There was no such redoubt, and the attack was eventually canceled, but Allied commanders noted that parts of the population remained sullen. Half a year after May 8, a piano wire strung across a German roadway in Nuremberg decapitated several Allied soldiers. The final shots of the war in Europe were likely fired on May 13, when Soviet troops overcame the last German resistance in Czechoslovakia.[6] In Reims, Eisenhower issued "Victory Order of the Day," which praised Allied soldiers for their courage. Yet even in victory, Eisenhower could not forget the painful and divisive conflicts that had characterized relations between the U.S. and its allies: "Let us have no part in the profitless quarrels in which other men will inevitably engage as to what country, what service, won the Europe war," he wrote. "Every man, every woman, of every nation here represented has served according to his or her ability, and the efforts of each have contributed to the outcome."[7]

On Okinawa, 6,186 miles from Eisenhower's headquarters at Reims, marines of the 1st Division continued to blast their way into the caves on Nan Hill, where Japanese soldiers were mounting their last defense, ignoring calls for their surrender. Rain had fallen on Okinawa for several days, hampering American offensive operations, and conditions for the marines were miserable.[8] The combat was worse. By the end of the ruthless Japanese defense of the island, 12,500 Americans had been killed, along with 100,000 Japanese soldiers and 150,000 of Okinawa's civilians. On the day that George Marshall received Eisenhower's cable announcing the German surrender, the joint chiefs were planning Operation Downfall—the invasion of the Japanese home islands.[9] Marshall outlined the plan at the White House on June 1.[10] At the end of the meeting, Harry Truman asked Assistant Secretary of War John J. McCloy for his opinion. "Why not use the bomb?" McCloy asked.[11] According to Forrest

Pogue, Marshall agreed, saying later that the grim fighting on Okinawa convinced him it was necessary "to shock them [the Japanese] into action."[12] While
Marshall would work quickly over the next two months to release soldiers serving in Europe into civilian life, some units in Germany would be transferred
to the Pacific, including Courtney Hodges's battered First Army. Marshall
believed that casualties for the invasion would be heavy; one War Department
official predicted the United States would suffer upwards of four hundred thousand dead,[13] though others credibly predicted no more than sixty-thousand-
plus American combat deaths, at the most. It is not clear precisely what figures
Marshall was shown, though it now seems certain that Marshall believed the
casualty figures for the invasion would be appreciable. U.S. forces were ready-
ing for the leap into southern Japan when on August 6 the atom bomb was
dropped on Hiroshima. Three days later a second bomb targeted Nagasaki.
On September 2, Japanese officials surrendered aboard the USS *Missouri* in
Tokyo Harbor.[14] World War II was officially over.

While casualties for the war are difficult to come by, the most recent evidence shows that 72 million men and women served in the conflict.[15] At the
end of hostilities, more than 16 million had been killed, their bodies interred
in cemeteries and shallow graves, or scattered from Murmansk to Morocco,
from the Arctic to the Pacific. Nearly one in four men and women who served
in uniform died. The Soviet Union suffered the most casualties, with 7.5 million dead soldiers, sailors, and airmen. This was more than half of the total number mustered for service by Joseph Stalin. The United States, in comparison,
suffered 407,318 combat deaths—4,000 more than the British—with the deaths
almost evenly divided between the European theater of operations and the
Pacific. Civilian casualties are much more difficult to calculate. Twelve million
Russians, 6 million Jews (victims of Hitler's death camps and his extermination
squads), 5 million Poles, 2 million Chinese (the figure is probably low), 780,000
Germans, and 672,000 Japanese (the result of American incendiary bombings)
had died.[16] Final figures cannot be calculated within any precision, but a conservative estimate places the numbers of civilian deaths at 27 million. The total
dead for the war from all causes easily surpassed 40 million.[17] Large tracts of
land, hundreds of cities, and thousands of villages were destroyed. Entire regions
were depopulated. Jewish civilization in Europe had all but ceased to exist.
Tokyo, Nanking, Shanghai, Hiroshima, Kyoto, Nagasaki, Yokohama, Seoul,
Manila, and dozens of other cities in Asia were destroyed. Immediate prospects

for Europe were extremely dire: forty-nine population centers in Germany were in ruins, nearly all of its industrial capacity was destroyed, half the continent's population was near starvation, one-quarter of all the children in western Russia were orphaned, and millions of displaced persons were beginning the search for their homes.

THE MARSHALL-EISENHOWER command partnership ended with the war. Sixty years after V-E Day, its dynamics remain elusive. Marshall was the perfect "organizer of victory," in Winston Churchill's elegant phrase, while Eisenhower was the first, and perhaps ultimate, political general. The two were perfectly matched to their jobs. The United States might not have survived World War II with Douglas MacArthur as chief of staff, and the Allied armies would clearly not have performed so successfully under the leadership of Mark Clark. Proposing historical might-have-beens is always a risky business, but it is nearly impossible to suppose that the politically insensitive Douglas MacArthur would have remained staunchly loyal to Franklin Roosevelt, any more than it seems likely that the volatile Anglophobe Mark Clark would have remained patient with Bernard Law Montgomery. Much was lost during the war. George Marshall lost his stepson as well as his close friend and confidant, Field Marshal Sir John Greer Dill—the liaison between the British chiefs and the American Joint Chiefs of Staff—who died of a heart attack in Washington in 1944.[18] At times during the conflict, Marshall showed almost open affection for Dill. Learning that it was Dill's wish to be buried in Arlington National Cemetery, Marshall overcame regulations prohibiting the burial of a foreign national and won approval for the placement of an equestrian statue on his grave—the only one of its kind at Arlington.[19] Eisenhower suffered no comparable loss, but his prewar friendships with George Patton and Mark Clark did not survive his service in Europe. Eisenhower was no longer their friend, he was their superior officer. Paradoxically, Eisenhower's relationship with Bradley grew closer, and despite Bradley's open critique of Eisenhower in his two postwar books, the two remained friends.[20] At the end of the war, George Marshall's closest personal friend was Secretary of War Henry Stimson, thirteen years his senior, while Eisenhower's closest confidant was Walter Bedell Smith. The two, Stimson and Smith, have almost nothing in common, except for their self-abnegation in the face of what both believed was true greatness; Stimson's admiration for Marshall was unequaled, while Smith's loyalty to Eisenhower was complete.

There was never any question that George Marshall's marriage would survive the war. Marshall never allowed his work to intrude on his closely guarded private life. That was not true for Dwight Eisenhower. Rumors that Eisenhower was having an affair with his driver Kay Summersby followed him through the war—to the point where both Franklin Roosevelt and Winston Churchill gossiped about it.[21] It is said that after the war Eisenhower asked Marshall if he could divorce Mamie and marry Kay and that the Army chief, at Truman's insistence, turned him down.[22] It was not possible to be divorced and president, Truman reportedly said.[23] But claiming something is so does not make it so. It is hard to imagine Marshall participating in such an exchange. Truman, aging and carrying a grudge at the time is said to have told the story, enjoying such barbershop tattling. Rumors about the relationship continue to circulate, but they remain as unproven now as they did in North Africa six decades ago. Still, Eisenhower's relationship with Mamie was certainly strained during the conflict. When their son John was assigned as an officer of the 71st Division and ordered to Europe in January 1945, Mamie complained to Ike that he was doing nothing to keep his son out of harm's way.[24] Eisenhower blew up. "I constantly receive letters from bereaved mothers, sisters, and wives, and from others [who] are begging me to send their men home, or at least outside the battle zone, to a place of comparative safety," he responded to her. "So far as John is concerned, we can do nothing but pray. If I interfered even slightly or indirectly he would be so resentful for the remainder of his life that neither I (nor you, if he thought you had anything to do with it) could be comfortable with him. . . . I'd rather you didn't mention any of this mess again."[25]

Eisenhower was often angry with Mamie, but by the end of the conflict in Europe he was lonely for her. On June 4, 1945, Eisenhower wrote to Marshall asking permission for Mamie to join him in Europe. "I will admit that the last six weeks have been the hardest of the war," he told Marshall. "My trouble is that I just plain miss my family." Eisenhower then went on to talk about his wife. "The strain of the last three years has also been very considerable so far as my wife is concerned, and because of the fact that she has had trouble with her general nervous system for many years I would feel far more comfortable about her if she could be with me." Still, Eisenhower said he did not want to cause trouble and added that he would not have made the request at all, except that "I really would like to make it a bit easier on myself from the personal view-point."[26] Marshall had no objections to Eisenhower's request, but he took the matter to Harry Truman for his approval. Truman said no. Marshall was apparently chagrined by this and was forced to reply to Eisenhower that his request had been turned down. Eisenhower immediately responded with an apology, saying that he was sorry to bother the Army chief of staff with a private matter.[27] He knew Mamie would be disappointed: "You cannot be any more tired than I of this long separation," he told her, "particularly at my age."[28] What is remarkable about this exchange, as Eisenhower biographer Stephen Ambrose has pointed out, is that Eisenhower actually asked for Marshall's approval. The two were now equal in rank (Marshall, MacArthur, Arnold, and Eisenhower being the only five-star officers in the Army), and MacArthur had his wife with him at his headquarters in the Pacific throughout the war. "Eisenhower did not have to ask Marshall's permission in order to live with his wife," Ambrose rightly notes; "all he had to do was tell her to come over."[29] But he did not do that. Instead, Eisenhower remained deferential, the disciplined underclassman. While Eisenhower would protest at a description of his actions as somehow submissive, even after the end of the war General of the Army Dwight David Eisenhower still considered himself Marshall's subordinate. It seems unlikely that, in June 1945, Marshall would have so much as criticized Eisenhower for simply having his wife join him in Europe, but Eisenhower would act without the blessing of his Army chief. Then too, in June 1945, Dwight Eisenhower seemed unaware of how popular he had become since leading the Normandy invasion of June 1944. The supreme Allied commander and general of the Army was now one of the most popular men in America. But while Eisenhower seemed oblivious of his fame, George Marshall was not. "Yesterday I formalized the first phase of your moves in Washington . . . ," Marshall wrote to him on June 13. "I will meet you at the airport and ride with you to the Pentagon. . . . The column of cars containing your party will enter the inner court of the Pentagon where the workers in the War Department can see you and greet you either from the ground or the adjacent windows." Marshall then detailed Eisenhower's schedule for the rest of his planned visit, including an address to a joint session of Congress and a trip to New York, where Marshall and Eisenhower would be in a victory parade.[30] Eisenhower replied that he had "no general suggestion to make" to Marshall's plans, except that during his trip to the United States he hoped to attend a baseball game.[31]

Eisenhower arrived in Washington on June 16 and was greeted at the airport by Mamie, the Army chief of staff, and a bevy of senior commanders.[32] He
hugged Mamie and shook hands with Marshall: "Oh God," he said to him, "it's
swell to be back."[33] Unlike his previous visits, which had been cloaked in secrecy, Ike's arrival was covered by all the major newspapers, and his time in the
U.S. was a source of constant news. Thousands of Americans lined the route
from Washington's National Airport to the Pentagon. Marshall and Eisenhower
rode together, in the backseat of an open limousine. Eisenhower smiled and
waved. "Stand up so they can see you," Marshall said to him. Eisenhower, un-
steady, put his hand on the front seat and waved with the other.[34] Marshall, next
to him, worried about Eisenhower as cars of photographers weaved in and out
of the parade route. If there was an accident, Eisenhower would be pitched forward into the front seat. "Drive slowly," Marshall instructed the driver, a nervous Army corporal. "Avoid fast starts and stops. Be careful when you shift gears."
Eisenhower was overwhelmed by the welcome and in awe of the Pentagon
crowd that came to hear him in the building's courtyard. Eisenhower gave an
extemporaneous speech, praising the War Department's teamwork in the defeat of Germany. Apart from a private meeting with the Army chief to discuss
the return of troops from Europe, Marshall and Eisenhower had little to talk
about. The war against Germany was ended, its most contentious military issues now in the past, and while Marshall took time during Eisenhower's visit
to ensure that he was properly welcomed, the Army chief's mind was on the war
in the Pacific. For now, Eisenhower was the man of the hour—a fact made possible by Franklin Roosevelt's Cairo decision of late 1943 that he be the Overlord
commander. Marshall certainly knew then that Roosevelt's decision would not
only bring Eisenhower into the public eye, but might well put him in the
White House. He was being not being kicked "into the stratosphere," but into
the Oval Office.

This was no more apparent than after his time with Marshall at the
Pentagon, when Eisenhower was mobbed by crowds while driving to Capitol
Hill for his address to the joint session of Congress. The motorcade proceeded
at a snail's pace: "General Ike was standing, waving like a prize fighter," Harry
Butcher wrote.[35] He was greeted tumultuously on Capitol Hill and met with the
congressional leadership. After his appearance, he and Mamie attended a
luncheon in his honor. Then, in the late afternoon, Eisenhower went to the
White House, where Harry Truman presented him with his second oak-leaf

cluster for his Distinguished Service Medal.[36] In the early evening, Eisenhower visited John Pershing in his room at Walter Reed Army Hospital, and that night, Truman played host to Eisenhower and Marshall at a White House stag dinner which was "as simple and homey as a community supper in Missouri."[37] The next morning Eisenhower and Marshall traveled to New York City, where a crowd of millions greeted him, and he was the guest of honor at a private dinner at the Waldorf-Astoria Hotel. It was in New York that George Marshall's characteristic detachment finally broke down. While surveying the cheering crowds that greeted his most important field commander, the Army chief of staff suddenly draped his arm around Eisenhower's shoulder and proclaimed his own feeling of triumph. "Look at that, Ike," he fairly shouted. Eisenhower was taken aback. He looked at Marshall and then quickly turned away. It was the first time Marshall had ever referred to him as "Ike," the first time he had not addressed him as "General Eisenhower" or just "Eisenhower." Marshall remembered himself, then, and was chagrined—even embarrassed. As Eisenhower later related, Marshall quickly gathered himself and then, as if to make up for the slip, called Ike "Eisenhower" five times in the next sentence.[38] But Eisenhower was overwhelmed.

After his New York welcome, Eisenhower visited Franklin Roosevelt's grave at Hyde Park, appeared at West Point, and several days later visited his family in Abilene. He worried that his visit would upset his mother, who was aging and in frail health, but she seemed to be energized by his visit, and after falling sick the week of his arrival, she quickly recovered. It was only during the last week of his time in America that Eisenhower and Mamie could be alone. Marshall had arranged a quiet retreat for them in White Sulphur Springs and gave strict orders that they were not to be disturbed. Aside from this final week, however, Eisenhower's trip provided little time for contemplation. "In those few days the reaction from the war months and from a rapid series of celebrations was so great that I really didn't get to settle down and relax," he wrote to an old Abilene friend.[39] Nor was Eisenhower impressed with political Washington. "My hatred of Washington is even greater than it used to be," he wrote to Mamie after his visit. "Which is saying a lot."[40]

In fact, Eisenhower's name was now being circulated in Democratic Party circles as a prospective presidential candidate. Ike dismissed such talk. When he received a letter from Neill Baily, an old acquaintance, announcing that he was organizing an Eisenhower for President Club in San Antonio, Eisenhower's response was polite but firm. "I must tell you, with all the emphasis I can command," he wrote, "that nothing could be so distasteful to me as to engage in political activity of any kind. I trust that no friend of mine will ever attempt to put me in the position where I would even be called upon to deny political ambitions."[41] In spite of this protest, the former supreme commander (now officially the military governor of the U.S. Occupation Zone) began to emerge from his role as a military figure. He might dislike politics, but from the moment that Alfred Jodl signed the instrument of surrender on May 7, Eisenhower was making political decisions in Germany—on denazification, on fraternization between U.S. soldiers and Germans, on German rebuilding programs, and on the handling of German war criminals. In all of this he maintained an active correspondence with Marshall, though he slowly abandoned his wartime practice of always seeking Marshall's counsel.[42] And while Eisenhower liked Truman when he first met him, by the end of his tenure as a military governor in Germany, his respect for the president was beginning to erode. This was true despite Truman's obvious high regard for Eisenhower. The two got along well during Eisenhower's triumphant return to Washington, and quietly Truman became a part of the Eisenhower political bandwagon. He began surreptitiously to promote him as a future presidential nominee: "There is nothing you may want that I won't try to help you get," Truman once said to him. "That definitely and specifically includes the presidency in 1948. I'd be glad to serve as your Vice President."[43]

But the tentative emergence of Eisenhower as an independent political voice did not become apparent until the three-power Potsdam Conference, held on the grounds of a former German film studio, near Berlin in late July and early August 1945.[44] Eisenhower attended the conference at Truman's direction, but was quickly disenchanted by the fact that his views were not solicited by the president or his chief aides.[45] He was perceived as simply a military man who spent his time shifting troops from one point to another, a person who might be a great commander, but one with no political depth. Eisenhower resented this prejudice. The views of military officers, he felt, were especially valuable when it came to the development and deployment of weapons. In particular, Eisenhower resented that he had not been asked his opinion on the decision to use the atom bomb on Japanese cities. Eisenhower learned of the bomb from Stimson at his headquarters in Frankfurt, where Stimson had come to confer with him on German occupation policy. News of the bomb stunned Eisenhower. He later said that news of its development left him with a "feeling of depression."[46] Eisenhower was even more shocked when he learned from Stimson that Truman had decided to use the bomb on Japan and that Truman's advisers agreed with the decision. Eisenhower did not. He argued passionately against the policy. The Japanese were beaten, he told Stimson, and using the bomb would set a dangerous precedent. It would accomplish nothing. Stimson was surprised that Eisenhower felt so deeply about the issue and was taken aback by Eisenhower's almost angry refutation of Truman's views. This was not the general officer he had come to know over the years.[47] Despite his best efforts, Eisenhower seemed unable to forge a personal connection with Truman's top advisers.[48] After the confrontation in Frankfurt, Stimson remained aloof, while the U.S. ambassador to the Soviet Union, Averell Harriman, seemed focused on other problems. James Byrnes, the former head of War Mobilization whom Eisenhower had met in France just prior to the Ardennes offensive, also seemed removed from Eisenhower, paying little attention to his views. In spite of this, Eisenhower attempted to influence the American delegation's program: he urged Truman to relieve the military from administrative responsibility for running the U.S. Occupation Zone, argued against bringing Russia into the war against Japan, and said that—despite his support for Truman's tough denazification policy—the Germans should be allowed to maintain and rehabilitate their major industries. All of these recommendations were turned down by the president.[49] Eisenhower also argued that the Allies, including the Soviet Union, should set aside their occupation zones and create a political structure that would allow them to run Germany together. He feared that different zones would inevitably lead to friction between the U.S. and the Soviets and perhaps even to the division of Germany. Averell Harriman, for one, would have considered Eisenhower's views naïve at best, apostasy at worst. Harriman and other foreign policy advisers in the Truman administration had come to believe that a confrontation with the Soviets was inevitable. Eisenhower was dismayed by this view and when asked by a reporter about the possibility of a "Russo-American war," he gave a surprisingly harsh response. He saw no chance of it, he said, and his voice rose in anger, his finger stabbing at the air. "The peace lies, when you get down to it, with all peoples of the world," he said, "and not just . . . with some political leader. If all the peoples are friendly, we are going to have peace. I have found the individual Russian one of the friendliest persons in the world."[50]

Eisenhower's views on the Russians and the need to get along with them was so strongly held that when George Patton criticized denazification—saying that the Americans needed the Germans in order to mount an attack on the Russians—Eisenhower called him to his headquarters. Eisenhower had had his fill of his old friend, but he was not yet ready to dismiss him. The war might be over, but Ike was still Patton's commander and he was still capable of upbraiding a subordinate who stepped out of line. "I demand that you get off your bloody ass and carry out the denazification program as you are told instead of mollycoddling the Nazis," he reportedly screamed at him.[51] Eisenhower's aides could hear their commander in the hallway. Patton assured Eisenhower that he would more carefully watch what he said, pleaded for his patience, and said that he would make it clear that he was in favor of denazification. But when Patton visited a German detention center a few days later, he agreed with a German civilian that most of the internees should be freed. "It's sheer madness to intern these people," he said to a group of reporters. In Frankfurt, Ike read the comments and shook his head in disgust but decided to ignore the comment. That was a mistake. The more that Eisenhower shut his ears to Patton's verbal indiscretions, the more extreme they became. Eventually Eisenhower was forced to take action. When complaints reached his Frankfurt desk that the displaced-persons camps under Patton's control were being run poorly, Eisenhower went to see for himself. He was greeted by his recalcitrant subordinate, who shrugged his shoulders at the criticism. Aw hell, Ike, Patton said, it's not my fault. Some of the inmates, he said, were just "pissing and crapping all over the place." He laughed a bit. Hell. The situation was so bad that he was even "thinking of building" his own concentration camps "for some of these goddamn Jews." That was enough. Eisenhower wheeled on him: "Shut up, George." Patton was ordered to hold a press conference to explain his views and respond to reports that he was anti-Semitic. "I despise and abhor Nazis and Hitlerism as much as anyone," he said, but then cataloged his troubles as a commander. He rambled on and on, in true Patton fashion. "The way I see it," he said, "this Nazi thing is very much like a Democratic and Republican election fight."[52] That was the final straw. An enraged Eisenhower called Patton to Frankfurt and fired him. He was to be reassigned to head the Fifteenth Army, a paper force. Their parting, after twenty-five years of friendship, was unpleasant. Eisenhower said that Patton should join his new command immediately. In fact, Patton could be on the next train to Munich. Eisenhower glanced at his watch. "It's leaving in half an hour," he said.[53] It was the last time they saw each other.

ON NOVEMBER 18, 1945, George Marshall left his post as Army chief of staff.[54] Two days later, Harry Truman told the press that he had accepted Marshall's resignation and that he would be replaced as Army chief by Eisenhower. For Eisenhower this was much like an apostolic succession, particularly as he was succeeding one of his service's most storied officers and a man who had in turn received his scepter from an unbroken line that traced its genealogy to George Washington. While Eisenhower had commanded millions, received the surrender of an enemy army, presided over the largest combat force in American history, becoming Army chief of staff and successor to one of the greatest military officers in the nation's history was the culmination of all he had worked for. Marshall was less enthusiastic. "I'm playing an awful trick on you, getting out so fast," Marshall admitted to Eisenhower. "You're going to have an awful job. Everybody is going to want to get out right away, and you'll want to get them out, but you don't want to denude yourself. It's going to be very hard."[55] In fact, being Army chief of staff was more difficult than Eisenhower had imagined. For the first time in three years, his every decision had to be mediated through the Joint Chiefs of Staff—who were now his equal partners. He had once commanded millions; now he was presiding over their demobilization. He spent his first months wrangling with Congress over the Army's size, pleading for patience in shipping men home from the Pacific—it would take time, he said.[56] Just as Congress was pressing for accelerated demobilization, Eisenhower worried that the U.S. was stripping its military assets, just as it had after World War I. So when President Truman proposed that the U.S. military meet its needs through the passage of legislation calling for universal military training, Eisenhower enthusiastically supported it, though privately he supported the creation of a well-paid and highly trained all-volunteer force. But in the euphoria of the postwar era, when millions of American men were intent on coming home to start their families, any talk of military strength gained little support.

Finally, Eisenhower, turned his attention to institutionalizing what he and
Marshall had worked for during the war—the unified command of the armed
services. In this, at least, he and Truman saw eye to eye.

"We must never fight another war the way we fought the last two," Truman
had told his chief aide, Clark Clifford, after the surrender of Japan. "I have the
feeling that if the Army and the Navy fought our enemies as hard as they fought
each other, the war would have ended much earlier."[57] Truman added that in
his opinion the United States and its allies were "damn lucky" to have won
at all.[58] Eisenhower supported Truman's initiative to make the services ac-
countable to each other, but the civil war in China, the continued hammer-
ing over demobilization, and the interdepartmental debates over America's
nuclear policy derailed Eisenhower's efforts at unification and undermined
Truman's attempt to reform the military command structure. And Truman and
Eisenhower remained wary of each other, with Truman jealous of Eisenhower's
public standing. The Army chief was also noticeably cool toward the president
and irritated that Truman never seemed to seek his counsel. As he had in
Potsdam, Eisenhower took a different line from the administration's on nuclear-
weapons policy. When Truman proposed an international program control-
ling nuclear energy, Eisenhower offered his own critique. His views had
changed since Potsdam, however, and now he was decidedly more conservative. He opposed using the bomb, but he also opposed turning its technology
over to the international community: "If we enter too hurriedly into an international agreement," he said, "we may find ourselves in the position of having
no restraining means in the world capable of effective action if a great power
violates the agreement."[59] But Truman and his aides never asked Eisenhower
for his opinion.[60] George Marshall was undoubtedly aware of Eisenhower's
frustrations, though the nearly daily communications they had exchanged during the war now fell to a trickle. There was in fact little that Marshall could do
to help him. On the day of his retirement, Marshall was appointed by Truman
as the head of a U.S. mission to China with the rank of ambassador. Suddenly
he was out of retirement and back in uniform.[61] He was still a five-star general
of the Army. His mandate from Truman was to help end China's civil war,
which pitted American ally Chiang Kai-shek against Mao Tse-tung's Communists. These instructions would be difficult enough to fulfill, but when he
arrived in China he learned that he would also have to clean up the mess left

by Ambassador Patrick Hurley. Hurley had failed to forge an understanding between the warring parties, in large part because of his hatred of the Communists
and his habit of blaming the Truman State Department for his troubles. His job
would be made much easier, Hurley said, if it weren't for State Department
China experts, diplomats who were "endeavoring to support communism generally as well as specifically in China."[62] Such a claim was sweet music for congressional Republicans, whose anti-Communist leaders were beginning to
emerge as the Truman administration's most vocal critics. These Truman critics also noted, darkly, that when Marshall left Washington to take up his assignment he was seen off at the airport by State Department China expert Jay
Carter Vincent, the man Hurley had identified as his chief antagonist and the
premier Communist apologist. Vincent turned to his ten-year-old son when
Marshall was about to board his plane: "Son," he said, "there's goes the bravest
man in the world. He's going to try to unify China."[63]

The situation facing Marshall and the United States in the Far East was complex. U.S. troops in China were attempting to disarm the recalcitrant Japanese
(who worried that their weapons might be turned over to the Chinese
Communists), while Soviet divisions stood poised in the north, preparing to intervene in any argument between Chiang and Mao. At first, Marshall attempted
to convince the parties to agree to a simple cease-fire. That task, which he
feared might take months, was, much to his surprise, accomplished within
weeks of his arrival. But establishing a coalition government proved nearly impossible. Still, after eleven days of intense negotiations Marshall gained the
agreement of the Communists to integrate their guerrilla forces into the
Nationalist Army and to consider entering a broad-based government. The
Communists did not agree to Marshall's program until he promised that the
U.S. would help train Communist soldiers by sending a U.S. military mission
to China. The compact was signed, finally, on February 25, 1946, and for a time
the prospect of renewed civil war receded.[64] But the truce that Marshall engineered proved impossible to implement. The fault lay with the Nationalist
Chinese, a hopelessly corrupt cabal of Chiang supporters who viewed the truce
as a means of improving their deteriorating military position. Frustrated by his
inability to convince Chiang that building a coalition government was his only
chance of survival, Marshall accused the Nationalist leader of being "fatally
provocative and at times inexcusably stupid." Chiang responded by playing to

Truman's opponents. The U.S., he said, was not interested in peace in China, only in appeasing the Communists. Inevitably, the truce broke down and Communist and Nationalist forces began their campaign to gain control of the country. The fighting, coming in the wake of a bitter Japanese occupation, plunged the nation back into chaos.

Over the next eleven months, through a series of failed cease-fires and endless negotiations, Marshall struggled to bring peace to China. His only interlude came in May, when Dwight Eisenhower arrived in Nanking on an inspection tour assessing the readiness of U.S. units in the Far East.[65] Eisenhower's real mission, however, was to deliver a personal message from the president to Marshall. The two met at Marshall's Nanking home and passed the time reviewing Ike's problems as chief of staff and Marshall's inability to bring peace to China. Finally, Eisenhower told Marshall about Truman's concerns. Secretary of State James Byrnes was suffering from a stomach ailment, Eisenhower said, and Truman wanted Marshall to return to the U.S. to take his place. Marshall was weary but he nodded his agreement. "Eisenhower," he said, "I would do almost anything to get out of this place. I'd even enlist in the Army."[66] Marshall added that Eisenhower should tell Truman that he could not leave China before September, as it would take that long to get a new truce in place. Byrnes would just have to remain as secretary of state until then. Eisenhower stayed in China for several days before returning to the U.S. by way of Tokyo.

While in Japan, Eisenhower visited with his old commander Douglas MacArthur. It was not a visit that he relished—the last time he had seen MacArthur he was a major and "horse holder," and the two had not gotten along. Eisenhower and MacArthur met over dinner at the U.S. embassy in Tokyo, and their talk was formal and stunted. But after dinner, the tension seemed to ease and the two talked well into the morning, reviewing Eisenhower's career and catching up on mutual friends. When MacArthur said that he'd heard that the Navy was being honored with extra bugle calls because of its Pacific victories—even more bugle calls than for an Army chief of staff—Eisenhower passed off the comment. He wasn't really interested in military honors, he said. MacArthur laughed: "That's all right, Ike," he said. "Just so long as those Navy sons of bitches don't get ahead of us, I don't care either." Eisenhower changed the subject, but his curiosity finally got the best of him and he asked

MacArthur about his political plans. "General," he said, "you will surely be a candidate for the 1948 Republican party nomination." MacArthur responded that he was too old to run for president but added that he thought that one of them would surely be president—and that it would likely be Eisenhower. Eisenhower said that he didn't think so: "My country has given me everything I could possibly hope for," he said. "So I have no intention of running for the presidency." MacArthur guffawed at this and leaned over, patting Eisenhower on the knee: "That's right, Ike," he said. "You go on like that and you'll get it for sure." Eisenhower later said that MacArthur's comment so angered him that for several months he could not put it out of his mind.[67]

After Eisenhower's departure from Nanking, Marshall worked tirelessly for the remainder of his time to save the Nationalists' position in China. Their strength continued to deteriorate, however, and Marshall was convinced they would lose any military confrontation with the Communists. But, like Joseph Stilwell before him, Marshall thought the real problem with the Nationalists was not the lack of training in their army, but the intransigence of its leaders and their obsession with American domestic politics. Chiang, banking on his anti-Communist support among anti-Truman Republicans in Congress, stead-fastly refused to implement any of Marshall's initiatives, because he believed that in the end the U.S. would intervene on his behalf. Marshall knew that would never happen and cajoled Chiang to institute broad reforms in his move-ment. Nothing seemed to work. By late November 1946, Marshall was begin-ning to realize that his mission was failing and that the Nationalists were destined to lose their grip on their country. He also realized that his time in China was coming to an end. He had not been able to convince Chiang to shape a political agreement with the Communists. In a last desperate attempt to find a solution to China's problems, Harry Truman told Chiang that he would cut aid to the Nationalists unless he agreed to follow Marshall's advice. Chiang responded that he was prepared to turn over all of Manchuria to the Communists if need be—but he would not be blackmailed into accepting ei-ther a truce or a coalition government.[68] Marshall was disappointed but con-cluded that Chiang would remain incapable of instituting the reforms necessary to ensure his survival. Marshall blamed himself. "I tried to please everyone," he said. "The result was that by the time I left, nobody trusted me."[69]

Within hours of his departure from China, on January 10, 1947, word leaked that Marshall would be appointed secretary of state. As rumors of his appointment swirled through Washington, Republicans expressed concern about Truman's decision to replace Byrnes. They let it be known that despite his status as a military hero, Secretary of State George Marshall would not get the same consideration as Army Chief of Staff George Marshall. Republican senator Arthur Vandenberg, chairman of the Senate Foreign Relations Committee, was particularly concerned with Marshall's growing stature and believed that Marshall was being appointed by Truman in order to set up his run for the presidency as Truman's successor.[70] After nearly fifteen years of Democratic control of the White House that was the last thing that Vandenberg and his fellow Republicans wanted, so they began to maneuver to make Marshall's tenure difficult. Marshall understood the political implications of Vandenberg's worries and concluded that if he wanted to run a successful foreign policy, he would have to give the Republicans a reason to support him.[71] So when Marshall arrived on a cold and windy morning in Washington to take up his duties, he issued a statement intended to ease Vandenberg's mind: "I think this is as good a time as any to terminate speculation about me in a political way," he told a crowd of reporters who met his train. "I am assuming that the office of the Secretary of State, at least under present conditions, is nonpolitical and I am going to govern myself accordingly. I will never become involved in political matters and therefore I cannot be considered a candidate for any political office."[72]

GEORGE MARSHALL'S agreement to serve as secretary of state marked a distinctive and important break between his life as a military officer and his career as a political official. When he arrived in Washington on January 27, he owned exactly one dress suit.[73] Marshall's appointment as secretary of state also coincided with Dwight Eisenhower's transition to civilian life, for while he had four months remaining in his tenure as Army chief of staff, he had already begun the planning necessary to turn over many of his responsibilities to the next chief, Omar Bradley. He was beginning to consider what he would do once he retired. He hoped he might take on the presidency of a small college. Eisenhower continued to be disenchanted with his job at the Pentagon, which consumed hours of his time each day in briefings and meetings. He spent more hours reviewing programs and policies and initialing the stacks of paper that seemed to appear unbidden on his desk.

Marshall's appointment would have larger implications for the nation, however. The generation of Americans who were called to war in December 1941 and sacrificed themselves so readily in the conflict with the Axis would soon be called by Marshall and Eisenhower to participate in a new, less certain conflict. In November 1947, Marshall and Eisenhower were convinced the United States was facing a growing threat from the Soviet Union and its global allies. Eventually, both men committed themselves to shaping national policies that would respond to it.

The Soviet threat was the result of the military victory the Soviet Union had won. The defeat of Germany and Japan had so weakened Great Britain and France that, within two years of the war's end, the United States and the Soviet Union had emerged as the world's competing powers. The postwar diplomatic settlement did little to dampen this conflict, address the evils of colonialism, or meet the demands of emerging national movements. In the wake of the global conflagration with Germany and Japan, wars continued to break out in Africa and Asia, as the leaders of indigenous movements in colonial holdings were emboldened by the weakness of their overseers. Britain and France struggled to maintain their empires, but their economic and military weakness stretched their national abilities and their determination to maintain troops in their overseas holdings undermined their claims to be champions of self-determination. The short-term solution, undertaken in part to ease the emerging competition between the Soviet Union and the United States, was to implement a series of partition agreements to resolve these conflicts and adjudicate between competing religious and ethnic currents. Bearing the imprimatur of the new United Nations, these partitions were intended to provide a permanent settlement to competing claims, but for the next five decades a series of "partition wars" broke out in South Asia, Korea, Vietnam, and Palestine.

But the most serious division—the most crucial partition—was implemented in Europe, where the political processes agreed to for Eastern European nations by the Soviet Union at Yalta were subverted by national Communist movements answering to Moscow. Over a period of four years from the end of the war, Communist parties answerable to the Soviet Union emerged in Poland, Romania, Czechoslovakia, Hungary, Albania, Bulgaria, and (eventually) East

Germany. Estonia, Latvia, and Lithuania were absorbed as republics of the Soviet Union. The division of Europe was exacerbated by the continuing disagreement among the former allies over the administration of Berlin, which was divided between a Soviet eastern sector and a French, American, and British western sector. The informal division was quickly becoming a permanent division of the city. Nor was it certain that Soviet commitments made prior to the end of the conflict would be honored: Russian troops remained in northern Iran, and Soviet military advisers were providing assistance to the Chinese Communist Party. In Greece, a civil war had broken out between the Communist-dominated Democratic Army and the British-supported Hellenistic Army. So it was that by the time George Marshall became secretary of state, the United States and Russia were moving toward a confrontation on a continent still recovering from war.

Just two weeks after assuming his new position, Marshall was briefed on a February 9 speech by Joseph Stalin, in which the Soviet leader announced a new five-year program aimed at massive military rearmament. The plan was made necessary, Stalin said, because the prospect for continued world peace was "impossible" given the "present capitalist development of the world economy." In Washington, Supreme Court Justice William O. Douglas termed the speech "the Declaration of World War III."[74] Marshall also read Stalin's speech, and while he was not as willing as Douglas to declare that cooperation with the Soviet Union was impossible, much less that the world was on the verge of a new world war, he feared that diplomatic missteps and careless words might make it so. He was also heavily influenced by a telegram written by George Kennan, the career diplomat and Soviet expert whose career had taken him into Russia, where he served as the chief political aide to American ambassador William Bullitt. During his time in Moscow, Kennan witnessed Stalin's purges, and he emerged from his searing experiences as the State Department's foremost Soviet expert. At the outbreak of the war in Europe, Kennan was interned in Germany, but he returned to Moscow after World War II. At the end of his term there, in April 1946, Kennan wrote a cable on his impressions to Secretary of State James Byrnes. Marshall read this "long cable" within days of his arrival at the State Department and was impressed and disturbed by its conclusions: "Stalin and his associates," Kennan wrote, "are now elated with their recent military and political successes and think they see favorable prospects for extend-

ing their political influence over all of Europe through the devices of infiltra-
tion and subversion."[75] Kennan's sober words had a significant impact on
Marshall's thinking. The new secretary of state intuitively believed Kennan
and was inclined to fall back on his own experiences with Stalin during his
meeting with him in Tehran. Stalin was a man accustomed to the uses of violence, Marshall had said then. Stalin had helped his movement by robbing
banks. He was a thug.

One week after Stalin's speech, Marshall and Eisenhower traveled to New
York, where the two were to receive honorary degrees from Columbia
University, after which Marshall was to give a speech at a special convocation
marking Princeton's bicentennial. Katherine Marshall met her husband in
New York, and after the Columbia ceremony they continued by train to
Princeton. On that same afternoon, Undersecretary of State Dean Acheson received an aide-memoire from the British government saying that because of
Britain's increasingly dire economic situation, it would be forced to abandon
support for democratic forces in Greece. Acheson began to write a policy paper
for Marshall, recommending that the United States take Britain's place on the
side of the anti-Communist Greek forces. Acheson knew that doing so might
well bring the United States into an open confrontation with Stalin, but not
doing so would be to lose yet another European nation to Soviet influence.
While Marshall had not yet heard of Britain's decision to abandon Greece, his
remarks at Princeton reflected his belief that victory over Germany and Japan
made the United States responsible for keeping the peace. "You should fully
understand the special position that the United States occupies in the world ge-
ographically, financially, militarily, and scientifically, and the implications involved," Marshall said to Princeton's students. "The development of a sense of
responsibility for world order and security, the development of a sense of the
overwhelming importance of the country's acts, and failures to act in relation
to world order and security—these, in my opinion, are the great 'musts' for
your generation."[76]

While it was not yet clear to either Marshall or Eisenhower just how the
United States should meet its new responsibilities, or what structures it should
build to replace the rickety edifice left by the collapse of Europe's greatest nations, over a period of the next two years both men struggled to build the two
most important economic and military structures of the next five decades. The

Marshall Plan and the North Atlantic Treaty Organization did not emerge full-blown from the thinking of either George Marshall or Dwight Eisenhower, but their seeds were planted in the minds of both men at the end of 1947. In truth, the inception of both ideas can be found in the teachings of their mentor, Fox Conner. Neither Marshall nor Eisenhower believed that the United States alone could meet the challenge posed by the Soviet Union and its emerging allies in Eastern Europe and China. Nor could the United States so quickly mobilize the military strength necessary to confront the Soviet Union on the battlefields of Europe. The American people were exhausted by war, and as Conner had told Marshall and Eisenhower—and as Marshall was to say again and again in the years ahead—a democracy could not command its soldiers to fight, but must gain their trust through persuasion, through the consent of the governed. Never fight unless you have to, never fight alone, and never fight for long, Conner had said. Marshall and Eisenhower had followed this catechism in World War II, and now they would have to follow it again. It became their touchstone, the unstated but foundational belief of the Marshall Plan and the North Atlantic Treaty Organization.

"THE GENERAL"

". . . I sometimes find it difficult to adjust myself. . . ."
*"I pray especially for you in the choice of those to be near
you. . . ."*

EORGE MARSHALL WANTED TO avoid a rupture in relations with the
Soviet Union, but his trip to Moscow as secretary of state in April 1947
convinced him that that might not be possible. The Russians were intransigent
on all postwar settlement questions: on the reunification of Germany, on repa-
rations payments, on the status of Austria, on providing economic aid for
European recovery.[1] "We recognized that the Russians had a formidable setup,"
Marshall remembered. "We thought they could be negotiated with. Harriman
came back and said they could not be. I decided finally at Moscow, after the
war, that they could not be. I always thought we had to make a try to negotiate
with them, and I think the American people thought that."[2] When willing, the
Russians proved able negotiators, tough and dedicated. So they had seemed
throughout the war, when they relied on American aid. But now they dragged
out the talks, postponed meetings, and niggled over the use of language in
joint communiqués. Marshall did not believe they were serious about working
with the United States to solve the problems of Europe.

If Marshall was frustrated by the Russians, he was impressed by British and
French support for the U.S. as well as by their fear of the Soviet Union. The

British and French had sent their foreign ministers to Moscow, and the two, Ernest Bevin and Georges Bidault, worked with Marshall to convince the Russians that the Americans were not a threat but were only interested in European stability. But Britain and France were intent not only on establishing new political structures that could stave off another European war, they were also in dire need of American economic help. After listening closely to Bevin and Bidault, Marshall decided that Europe's economic woes posed a greater threat to Europe's political stability than the Soviet Union. So following his return to Washington from Moscow, Marshall gave a radio address on his trip, in which he focused a large portion of his attention on Europe's economic problems. While the Russians, he said, seemed more interested in "pernicious abstractions" than in negotiating real agreements, other European countries were crying out for solutions "which have to do with boundaries, with power to prevent military aggression, with people who have bitter memories, with the production and control of things which are essential to the lives of millions of people."[3] What was needed to prevent future wars, Marshall said, was not just military strength but also economic well-being, which included the immediate provision of fuel, food, and the other necessities of life for the people of those nations that had suffered most during the war.

Dean Acheson, Marshall's undersecretary of state, was thinking along the same lines. Prior to Marshall's departure for Russia, Acheson conducted a study focused on European economic needs, directing Assistant Secretary of State John Hildring to begin researching the possible requests for aid the U.S. would be receiving from around the world. He wanted to recommend policies to Marshall and Truman to meet these requests and he wanted to begin preparing the political ground to get the economic packages approved by Congress. At the Pentagon, meanwhile, Dwight Eisenhower turned his attention to possible European appeals for military assistance. Soon after Marshall began his tenure as secretary of state, Eisenhower wrote to General Lucius Clay, the military governor of Germany, expressing his concern about the deteriorating situation in Europe, adding that he intended to have a series of long discussions with Marshall about the global situation. But he was most concerned with Europe's slide into economic chaos. With Europe's economies sinking, the U.S. could be facing a crisis that might eventually lead to war. By the time that Marshall returned to Washington from Moscow, these combined efforts were coalescing in a government-wide initiative to structure a program that would lead to Europe's economic resuscitation.

A formidable array of government officials was involved in shaping the economic assistance effort: Marshall, Acheson, Kennan, and Hildring advised Marshall on drafting an aid package, while Eisenhower built support for increased administration attention to Europe's military problems. On May 15, George Kennan—the head of the State Department's Policy Planning Staff whose "long cable" had so impressed Marshall—reported that "the most important and urgent element in foreign policy planning is the question of restoration of hope and confidence in Western Europe and the early rehabilitation of the economies of the region."[4] Kennan recommended that the U.S. provide an immediate and large infusion of aid to Europe, adding that he believed the "formal initiative must come from Europe, the program must be evolved in Europe; and the Europeans must bear the basic responsibility for it."[5] Kennan's report was sobering, but eyewitness testimony from Will Clayton, the State Department's undersecretary for economic affairs, was even more serious. Clayton, a man of quiet influence, was a former cotton merchant and free trader who had been at Truman's side at Potsdam. A man of little formal education, Clayton was an American Bevin—when he spoke, everyone listened. Clayton toured Europe and was shocked by what he saw. When he returned he told Marshall that large-scale hunger and misery were undermining the U.S. position on the Continent and that only a massive relief and financial commitment could reverse the situation. "Europe is steadily deteriorating," he said. "The political position reflects the economic. Millions of people in the cities are slowly starving."[6]

In the wake of Clayton's report, Acheson recommended that Marshall begin preparing Congress to accept a program aimed at providing economic aid to Europe, though such an initiative was likely to be met with widespread skepticism.[7] Convincing Congress to once again turn the attention of the American people to Europe would be difficult at best. Acheson said that the only way to ensure congressional agreement was for Marshall to focus his efforts on gaining the support of Republican senator Arthur Vandenberg. But Marshall had to move fast to stave off a European economic collapse. Marshall visited Capitol Hill on the afternoon of May 28, 1947, to begin preparing Congress to accept his initiative; he visited members of the Senator Foreign Relations Committee and huddled with the skeptical Vandenberg. After hearing Marshall's report, Vandenberg said that he would not stand in the way of a modest initiative to save Europe but he warned Marshall that he would face a lot of criticism for the decision. That was enough for the secretary of state, who immediately accepted an invitation from Harvard University to speak at its upcoming commencement ceremonies.[8] On May 30, he directed his staff to begin drafting his remarks. Keep them short, he said—this was not to be a foreign policy speech, but an address focused solely on European economic recovery. Marshall also insisted that his remarks at Harvard not be released until the day of his speech, so as not to allow opposition to his program to build. Over the next five days, Charles Bohlen, of Marshall's staff, wrote and rewrote Marshall's address. Marshall edited the final text and added a number of key paragraphs. On June 5, Marshall flew to Boston with Omar Bradley (then head of the Veterans Administration), who also was to address the alumni. Marshall arrived in Cambridge and was placed at the head of the line of Harvard's commencement guests, which included the physicist J. Robert Oppenheimer, the poet T. S. Eliot, and newspaper publisher Hodding Carter. After the ceremony, Marshall and the other guests filed into the Fogg Museum for the traditional commencement luncheon. Marshall—now sixty-six and at the apogee of his public popularity—was the fourth speaker.[9]

Reflecting on his Harvard address years later, George Marshall expressed surprise at the attention it received. While the immediate response seemed tepid, and most observers thought Marshall's delivery was flat and without rhetorical flourishes ("typical of the man" was how Harry Truman put it), his address was front-page news in the next day's New York Times. "I need not tell you gentlemen that the world situation is very serious," he began. "That must be apparent to all intelligent people." Marshall then detailed "the breakdown of the business structure of Europe" and alluded to the difficulties the United States was having in its talks with the Soviet Union. Europe's problems were America's, he said. "Aside from the demoralizing effect on the world at large and the possibilities of disturbances arising as a result of the desperation of the people concerned, the consequences to the economy of the United States should be apparent to all." He then added: "It is logical that the United States should do whatever it is able to do to assist in the return of normal economic health in the world, without which there can be no political stability and no assured peace." This was the essence of the Marshall Plan—the view that peace would not be the result of American exceptionalism, but of its willingness to "face up to the vast responsibility which history has clearly placed upon our country . . ."[10] In England, Foreign Secretary Ernest Bevin read Marshall's remarks and telephoned French foreign minister Georges Bidault, seeking his agreement to convene a meeting on Marshall's proposal. Both men were overjoyed: the Americans had acted, and much more quickly than they had expected.

Over the next five months the Marshall Plan—officially the European Recovery Program—moved through Congress.[11] The initiative was a source of widespread public debate and comment. While Marshall's address at Harvard had caught the public's attention, the program's crucial importance as a major underpinning of American foreign policy became more apparent as Europe's economic position deteriorated, and as the American media sent reporters into the heart of Europe's bombed-out cities for eyewitness reports. Public polls showed early support for the program. In September, with congressional debate on the Marshall Plan going forward, European leaders met to determine their most pressing economic needs, with Bevin calling for a four-year, $17 billion program.[12] Soviet opposition to the Marshall Plan was not unexpected, though the United States made it clear that its financial help would not be restricted to Western European nations.[13] The Soviet leadership criticized the Marshall Plan, describing it as a veiled effort to make Europe "the forty-ninth state of America." The Soviet leaders, fearing a major American propaganda victory, determined that they would author a plan of their own, and on October 5, Communist delegates from Eastern Europe were called to Poland to establish an economic program for the Eastern bloc.[14] While Marshall was disappointed by the Soviet response, he was not surprised. Congressional opposition to the program, however, was worrying. By November, even with public sentiment growing for passage of the initiative, Marshall's European Recovery Program was mired in controversy. Isolationist Republican senator Robert A. Taft, a presidential contender, accused the State Department of conducting a propaganda campaign led by a cabal of internationalists on behalf of Marshall's program. Marshall responded by hardening his language. He characterized the European Recovery Program as a weapon in the "worldwide struggle between freedom and tyranny."[15]

Marshall appeared on Capitol Hill to defend his program throughout the early part of 1948. Often his appearances gave the political opponents of his plan a chance to question his views. He was pressed repeatedly to explain the shift in his opinion of the Russians, from extolling their sacrifices during World War II to condemning them as an enemy of freedom in 1948. He faced the criticism with little difficulty. The Russians were essential to winning World War II, he said. We could not ignore their help. He then pointed out that in the wake of the war, there was "a tremendous effort by the Communists to overthrow the governments of Italy and France, and it was done in a very barefaced manner. It was remarkable. There was little effort to disguise the central, dominating fact of what that was all about."[16] While Marshall's program sailed through the Senate Foreign Relations Committee (aided, at least in part, by the announcement that the secretary of state had once again been named *Time* magazine's "Man of the Year"), the initiative faced increasing difficulties in the House of Representatives. The turning point finally came with news of the collapse of the Czech government in Prague and the apparent murder of the Czech foreign minister, Jan Masaryk. Masaryk, it was rumored, was thrown from his office window by Communist agents. Marshall called the events in Czechoslovakia "a reign of terror."[17] On March 14, 1948, the U.S. Senate passed the Marshall Plan. On March 31 the House of Representatives followed suit. Marshall was relieved. "I worked on that as if I was running for the Senate or the presidency," Marshall told biographer Forrest Pogue. "It was just a struggle from start to finish and that's what I am proud of, that we actually did that and put it over."[18]

On February 7, 1948, Dwight Eisenhower attended the swearing-in of Omar Bradley as the new Army chief of staff.[19] Eisenhower and Mamie moved out of Fort Myer Headquarters No. 1 three months later and took a vacation in North Carolina, where Ike worked on his golf game and Mamie relaxed. In North Carolina, Eisenhower began to cultivate the friendship of a group of wealthy businessmen who, like him, held decidedly conservative views on domestic issues but were foreign policy internationalists. Eisenhower called his new friends "the gang." This substitute for Club Eisenhower consisted of well-heeled, prominent business executives, including Bill Robinson, the editor of the *New*

York Herald Tribune; New York investment banker Clifford Roberts; Coca-Cola chairman Robert Wood; W. Alton "Pete" Jones, the president of Cities Service Company; and Ellis Slater, the president of Frankfurt Distilleries. Eisenhower was now moving in unusual company, for each of these men was influential, Republican, and had contacts in every part of American industry, manufacturing, and finance. These were not the people he had grown up with in Abilene. Known unofficially as the *"Herald Tribune* wing" of the Republican Party, the gang was renowned as much for its dislike of Franklin Roosevelt's New Deal domestic programs as it was for its disdain for Robert Taft Republicans—as well as for the increasingly powerful anti-Communist wing of the conservative movement. Robinson, Roberts, Wood, Jones, and Slater liked Eisenhower and, unlike Harry Truman and his closest aides, solicited his views and listened carefully to his opinions.[20] Ike was entranced by these Republicans and enjoyed talking to them about Republican Party politics.

Ike and Mamie moved to New York in June 1948 when Eisenhower became the president of Columbia University. While Eisenhower continued to follow international events, he was intent on earning a large salary and thought the presidency of a prestigious institution like Columbia would suit his schedule and predispositions. He could not have been more wrong: he spent his days administering an institution as puzzling and as fraught with divisions as the Army. He was required to spend hours each day working through detailed policy papers. Most of his days focused on the minutiae of actually running a university, and much less on fine-tuning a large educational institution. What Eisenhower wanted to do was visit with students, talk with them in their classrooms, and be a part of the intellectual ferment of an urban university.[21] Instead, his days were taken up with meeting prominent visitors, mediating faculty disputes, and raising money. The work was "strange," "voluminous," and "bewildering."[22] By the end of each day he was exhausted. Just as he felt uncomfortable at Columbia, he also decided that he did not like New York. "I am a country boy born and bred, and cities never fail to irritate me," he told a friend. "I like the green grass better than paved streets and the sight of a well-fed cow more than that of a street car."[23]

While Eisenhower retained the respect of Columbia's board of trustees, there was a sense in the university leadership that Ike did not fit. Professors claimed that Eisenhower was inaccessible and they resented the fact that their university was now headed by a graduate of West Point. Many of Columbia's professors thought he was naïve, and looked down on his attempts to mix financiers, industrialists, and military officers with faculty during the global seminars he convened to discuss "real world issues."[24] Yet Eisenhower's tenure at Columbia was notable: he struggled to balance the university budget, and his name attracted scores of new funders. Under his leadership the university grew and became richer. Faculty and staff who were once quick to accuse him of anti-intellectualism and were often embarrassed by his guileless patriotism discovered that he was a staunch defender of faculty independence. Throughout his time at Columbia he successfully staved off claims that communism should not be taught in the classroom. Eisenhower responded that there would be "no intellectual iron curtain" at Columbia, and as biographer Stephen Ambrose noted, he "refused to interfere with the rights of students to form radical clubs and promote left-wing politics."[25] In spite of these notable successes, Eisenhower longed for a return to military life and the challenge of running an army. So when Harry Truman asked Eisenhower to return to Washington to lend his expertise to the newly created Department of Defense, he jumped at the chance. While he would not officially leave his position at Columbia, he scaled back his day-to-day activities as its president. He took the train to Washington once or twice each week to consult with the administration on U.S. military policy.

When Eisenhower first returned to Washington as Truman's military consultant he was appalled at what he found. While he had been out of the Pentagon for only a short time, the defense establishment seemed to have completely changed. The interservice rivalries and competition for appropriations between the Army, Navy, and newly created Air Force rivaled anything that he had experienced with the British in Europe. A "Revolt of the Admirals" over funding for Navy programs had broken out, Secretary of Defense James Forrestal was having difficulty managing senior military commanders, the Joint Chiefs of Staff were paralyzed by dissent and competing budget claims, the Army and Air Force were locked in a tight battle over recruiting, and the Navy wanted to build a new supercarrier. After several months observing this and reporting to Truman, Eisenhower was convinced that the interservice competition was beginning to hurt America's defense posture.[26] While he could not say so publicly, for fear of embarrassing Truman, Eisenhower was tempted to take

off his uniform and speak the blunt truth. "The whole performance is humili-
ating," he wrote in his diary. "I've seriously considered resigning my commission, so that I could say what I pleased, publicly."[27] Worse, the Truman
administration seemed strangely detached from these fights and, as in the past,
seemed unconcerned with Eisenhower's recommendations. Eisenhower was
forced to attempt to mediate interservice disputes on his own, without Truman's
guidance. Most frustrating of all, while Eisenhower was back in uniform and
was the highest-ranking officer in the Army, he had little actual influence. "The
situation grows intolerable," Eisenhower wrote to Hap Arnold. "I am so weary
of this interservice struggle for position, prestige and power that this morning I
practically 'blew my top.' I would hate to have my doctor take my blood pressure at the moment."[28]

While Eisenhower and Marshall corresponded rarely during this period,
they did see each other often and spoke regularly on the growing threat of the
Soviet bloc. Although the two had taken different paths since the end of the war,
both men maintained and extolled the principles that had won it. The Marshall
Plan was strongly supported by Eisenhower, while Marshall supported
Eisenhower's attempts to shape a unified military command structure.[29] Their
complimentary views were highlighted by the increasing Soviet threat and the
growing anti-Communist clamor in Congress. And while Eisenhower had stood
on the sidelines at Columbia during Marshall's most intensive jump into international diplomacy, both men were intrigued by the prospect of building an
emerging coalition of like-minded nations to meet the Soviet threat—just as
they had led the international coalition against the Axis. Eisenhower and
Marshall were advocates of international action and had determined that the
United States could not meet the emerging Communist threat alone, though
neither man can be credited with the sole authorship of the economic and defense structures that were being built to counter it. The American economic
and security establishment followed the lead of the Europeans in establishing
of both the Marshall Plan (the result of a plea by Great Britain's and France's
foreign ministers in Moscow in 1947) and North Atlantic Treaty Organization,
which was the brainchild of British foreign minister Ernest Bevin. But once the
Soviet threat began to be felt, both Eisenhower and Marshall shaped their response to it in accordance with their long-held views: Marshall was the most
public proponent of the European Recovery Program, while Eisenhower not

only became the Truman administration's chief exponent for NATO, but was given responsibility for organizing it.[30]

THE NORTH Atlantic Treaty Organization found its inception in a discussion that George Marshall had with British foreign secretary Ernest Bevin in London in November 1947, in the aftermath of yet another disappointing round of meetings with the Russians.[31] In this instance, the forum was a meeting of the Conference of the Council of Foreign Ministers, in which the Russians had proven as intransigent and uncooperative as they had back in April in Moscow. At the end of the conference, Marshall went to visit Bevin at the Foreign Office and found him deep in study. Bevin was a hard-nosed labor leader of little education who had begun his political career organizing transport workers. Yet, Marshall discovered, the square-faced Bevin was one of Great Britain's visionary thinkers and, during the war, had become Churchill's domestic field marshal, charged with overseeing of industrial production and supplying England's troops.[32] An idealist and dreamer (he believed in a world parliament, in which all nations would have votes), he was also a strong anti-Communist and constantly worried about Russia's designs on Western Europe. He was one of those celebrated European socialists who despised Stalin and was despised by him in turn. Morose now in the wake of yet another failed meeting with the Russians, Bevin asked Marshall a number of blunt questions: What are we going to do? What comes next? Can the Russians be stopped?[33] Before Marshall could answer, Bevin proposed the creation of an alliance of Western democracies to oppose the Soviets. The alliance would include the United States, Great Britain, France, and Italy. "It would be a sort of spiritual federation of the West," he said.[34] Marshall was intrigued by Bevin's idea and taken by his language. Over the next several months, Marshall discussed Bevin's ideas with the American policymaking establishment. When a group of European nations signed a mutual security pact in Brussels in March 1948, Truman not only endorsed it, he engaged the U.S. in secret talks with Canada and Great Britain to expand it.

Bevin supported the Truman initiative, but he wanted the administration to go further. A statement of American support was not enough, he said, just as it had not been enough in 1940 when England stood alone against the Axis. This time, Bevin said, Europe wanted America on its side from the beginning of a war—not only if it was attacked.[35] What Bevin was aiming for was a coalition of like-minded states that could act together toward a common goal and, if attacked, could fight together. Marshall knew exactly what Bevin wanted and agreed with him. But having only recently won congressional approval for the European Recovery Program, Marshall feared that an open discussion of engaging the U.S. in a military pact with Europe might spark strong reaction by Republican isolationists and by Stalin. Marshall wanted to move slowly, without provoking the Russians or solidifying Republican opposition. Maneuvering carefully through both the Senate and the House, Marshall eventually induced Congress to support a resolution calling for military help to Europe—the U.S., the Vandenberg Resolution implied, would be willing to consider a formal military association with the Brussels Pact countries and Canada.[36] By the end of the spring of 1948, support for this broad Atlantic Alliance was beginning to gain adherents, even among skeptical isolationists. In part, Marshall's effort was aided by the Russians, who reacted to the breakdown in four-party talks on the future of Germany by separating their zone of occupation from the British, French, and American zones. When the United States and its allies responded by establishing a currency in western Germany, the Soviets struck back. On June 24, they blocked all highway and rail access to West Berlin.

The Soviet blockade of West Berlin sparked a sense of deep crisis in Washington, particularly when the American commander in the German city, General Lucius Clay, recommended that the U.S. break the siege by sending armored spearheads along German highways into the Soviet Occupation Zone. The U.S. would be throwing down the gauntlet and the action could spark a war—but, Clay argued, it seemed likely there would be a war in any event, and such an American move might give the Russians pause. Harry Truman vetoed Clay's idea and agreed instead with Air Force General Curtis LeMay, who said that Berlin could be supplied by air. The Berlin airlift began within twenty-four hours of the Soviet blockade. Over a period of a few short weeks, the United States had built an air bridge into Berlin's Tempelhof Airport. The immediate crisis receded when it became apparent that the Soviets would not confront the Americans in the skies over Germany, but the near military confrontation accelerated American, British, and French discussions about forming a mutual defense pact. By the end of the summer of 1948, Marshall had convinced the

Pentagon, including Army Chief of Staff Omar Bradley, that U.S. military representatives should be sent to Europe to consult with their counterparts among Brussels Pact nations. Marshall was now fully committed, even conducting quiet talks with recalcitrant European foreign ministers in an effort to convince them that their nations should join the pact.[37] In September 1948, the U.S. agreed to send a group of military officers to a Western European Chiefs of Staff meeting; and at the end of October, Brussels Pact nations began negotiations with the U.S. and Canada on the details of a North Atlantic mutual defense treaty.[38] The meetings were held at the Pentagon, while diplomatic contacts were maintained by Marshall's State Department.[39]

George Marshall provided invaluable guidance to U.S. military officers during these early meetings, even though it was obvious to State Department officials that he was not in good health. Marshall always seemed fatigued. He had aged since the end of the war. The once handsome and tall man was beginning to walk with a stoop, his face was jowled, and his eyes were lidded with exhaustion. His closest friends were convinced that the ceaseless drumbeat of international issues, beginning with his inability to negotiate an end to the Chinese civil war—now winding its way to its bloody conclusion—had so exhausted him that his permanent retirement from public life was inevitable. So it seemed also to Marshall, who was quietly suffering from severe abdominal and back pains. At his yearly checkup at Walter Reed Army Hospital in June, Marshall was told that his right kidney was enlarged and that it must be removed. With the negotiations for the establishment of a Western military pact under way, the Berlin crisis still unresolved, and an important UN General Assembly meeting scheduled for November, Marshall asked his doctors to put off the surgery until December.[40] The doctors reluctantly agreed and Marshall seemed unconcerned. But his new frailty concerned him so much that he decided that it was now time to end his tenure at the State Department. He decided that he would resign his post after his surgery, but certainly no later than the end of Truman's first presidential term.

On December 7, 1948, Marshall had his right kidney removed. While doctors had expected his quick and full recovery, in fact it took months for Marshall to regain his strength. He kept his promise to Katherine—after Harry Truman's inauguration he resigned his post as secretary of state, turning over the reins to Dean Acheson. He retired to his home in Leesburg, Virginia, and returned to Washington only for short visits — including one on April 4, 1949, when he witnessed the signing of a pact establishing the North Atlantic Treaty Organization.[41]

"I AM not, now or in the future, going willingly into politics," Dwight Eisenhower wrote in his diary in 1949.[42] He had written this same passage many times and he believed it. Yet at the same time that he denied his desire to run for political office, Eisenhower willingly accepted numerous and obviously politically charged speaking invitations. He met openly with Republican Party officials, those people who could make his nomination as Harry Truman's successor a reality. And he began to take advice from political experts, who gauged his ability to reach out to the public. They did not like what they saw. Eisenhower's public speeches were often flat, when not flat they were controversial, and when not controversial they were tendentious. Ike tended to glibness, a habit he had picked up in World War II: "If all Americans want is security," he told a Texas audience, "they can go to prison."[43] Republican Party leaders winced. Ike needed to tone down the rhetoric, they said. Did Ike really want Americans to spend time in prison? He shook his head: that is not what he meant. Yes, but that's what he had said. He needed to talk about patriotism. Eisenhower listened. He met with the former executive director of the Republican National Committee, toured the country from Colorado to Illinois to Florida, met with defeated presidential nominee Thomas Dewey, talked with the chairman of the board of the Chase Manhattan Bank.[44] "I do not believe that anything can ever convince me that I have a duty to seek political office," he said.[45] This was his mantra, but he toured the country anyway. He toned down his rhetoric, he took the middle way, he talked about patriotism. He received standing ovations. People crowded around him to shake his hand. He shook his head in disbelief that what he said could be so important, telling a friend that his speeches were "a disjointed collection of empty platitudes and aphorisms."[46] In July 1950, Eisenhower was invited to the Bohemian Grove, the northern California retreat for American elites. A special train was provided for his transport by the chairman of the board of the Sante Fe Railway. These were the men who in no small part decided who would be president. Ike was a hit.[47]

While Eisenhower took time to position himself as a political figure, he remained deeply dissatisfied with his role at Columbia. He felt out of place in New York, almost as much as he did speaking "empty platitudes and aphorisms" before audiences in Texas. So when the North Korean Army invade South Korea on June 25, 1950, Eisenhower went directly to the Pentagon to talk with his old lieutenant, Omar Bradley.[48] Bradley, as irascible and irritable as ever, was struggling to balance military needs with political realities. It was a fight with which Eisenhower was familiar: isolationist Republicans wanted to cut the defense budget, while Truman wanted a military that would win a war against the Russians. Bradley was in the middle. Worse yet, as Bradley admitted to his old commander, the country was unprepared for the Korean conflict. Eisenhower did his best to help "Brad," urging Truman to begin a crash program of rearmament, cajoling Bradley to lobby Congress for more funds for the army, and talking with Dean Acheson about the need for an international response to Korean aggression.[49] While Eisenhower was not surprised that his recommendations seemed to have little impact on Truman, he was shocked that congressional Democrats were now blaming him for the Korean invasion. The military let down its guard in Korea when Eisenhower was chief of staff, they said. It was his fault. At first angered by these claims, Eisenhower soon realized that his public remarks of the last months, in which he had criticized the social programs of Franklin Roosevelt's New Deal, had had an impact—he was now being viewed by Truman and the Democrats as a likely Republican presidential candidate in 1952.[50] Even so, after a week in Washington, Eisenhower returned, if reluctantly, to New York. The Korean War, he decided, was in someone else's hands.

In fact, as Harry Truman would soon show, that was not exactly the case. Three months after the invasion, Truman called George Marshall and asked him to come to the White House. Marshall, then enjoying a fishing trip in Michigan with Katherine, agreed to meet with the president on September 6. When Marshall arrived Truman told him that he wanted him to be secretary of defense. He needed someone strong at the Pentagon, he said, to ride herd on the military and to keep an eye on the U.S. commander in Korea, Douglas MacArthur. Marshall, seemingly unfazed, told Truman that he would accept the appointment. "Mr. President," he said, "you have only to tell me what you want and I'll do it." But Marshall pointedly warned Truman that his appointment would likely be met with animosity by isolationist and anti-communist

Republicans. His nomination would certainly spark a tough and partisan fight in the Congress. In spite of his enormous stature and his unquestioned service, Marshall was now the target of Republican political operatives who blamed him for the downfall of Chiang's government in China. The defeat of the Nationalist Chinese and their removal to Taiwan the previous January was considered a major defeat for American interests in the Far East—and a chorus of critics blamed Truman and Marshall for the loss.[51] "I want to help, not hurt you," Marshall said.

The depth of political partisanship and fear of the Communist menace became painfully obvious to Marshall and to the American people during his confirmation hearings. A man once viewed as an American icon and who was credited with managing the most complex and bloody war in history was now the object of vicious political and even personal attacks. Wisconsin senator Joseph McCarthy led the opposition to Marshall's appointment, citing his record as Truman's ambassador to the Nationalist government as evidence that he was soft on communism. He had supported a cease-fire in China, McCarthy pointed out, and a partnership between Chiang and Mao. He was a compromiser with evil, a naïve believer in the soft words of evil men. But this was only the beginning. The debate grew more acrimonious, more bitterly partisan. McCarthy touted Douglas MacArthur as a solution to America's problems. Unlike Marshall, McCarthy said, MacArthur knew how to fight and win. He was uncompromising. And he was every bit as much a national legend as the former Army chief of staff. "Marshall should not be confirmed," McCarthy told reporters, "unless and until he convinces the Senate that he has learned the facts of life about communism, and that he will listen to MacArthur's advice rather than Acheson's advice on the Far East."[52] Indiana Republican William F. Jenner went further, issuing a shrill condemnation of Marshall on the floor of the Senate. Jenner's comments seemed so off balance and so filled with vitriol that he brought a stunned silence to his listeners.

> General Marshall is not only willing, he is eager to play the role of a front man for traitors. The truth is this is no new role for him, for General George C. Marshall is a living lie. . . . It is tragic that George Marshall is not enough of a patriot to tell the American people the truth of what has happened, and the terrifying story of what lies in store for us, instead

of joining hands once more with this criminal crowd of traitors and
Communist appeasers who, under the continuing influence and direction of Mr. Truman and Mr. Acheson, are still selling American down
the river.[53]

Jenner's speech was breathless, obsessed, hateful. The Senate was stunned by
his frothing denunciation. Massachusetts Republican senator Leverett Saltonstall took the floor, shaking with anger. "If there is any man whose public life
has been above censure," he said, "it is George C. Marshall. I wish I had
the vocabulary to answer the statement that the life of George Marshall is
a lie because if ever there was a life spent in the interest of our country, a
life that is not a lie, it is the life of George C. Marshall."[54] The dispute filled
the nation's front pages. But Marshall remained above the fray and seemingly
unconcerned—"Jenner? Jenner?" he asked. "I do not believe I know that
man."[55] But when Marshall was confirmed as Harry Truman's secretary of defense, the scars of the confirmation debate were observable in the thin firmness
of his face. He could barely disguise his contempt for his enemies.

Reviewing the confirmation fight from his home on Morningside Drive in
New York, Dwight Eisenhower could hardly believe what he read. The nation
seemed consumed by fear and hatred. Once again, he felt caught in the middle: his name was now being quietly circulated among the elite kingmakers of
the Republican Party, yet here were two Republican senators who had accused
his former commander of treason. Eisenhower seemed suddenly adrift. While
he had cultivated the gang, made himself available as a Republican speaking
before Republican crowds, disagreed strongly with many of Harry Truman's
policies, and felt ignored and snubbed by the Truman policymaking team, he
was much closer to Truman's circle of advisers than he was to Republicans of
McCarthy's or Jenner's ilk. He was close friends with John J. McCloy, for instance, whom McCarthy excoriated for his "unbelievable, inconceivable, un-
explainable record of deliberate, secret betrayal."[56] That's not how Eisenhower
saw it. McCloy had served as Henry Stimson's assistant secretary of war and had,
with Eisenhower, opposed the use of nuclear bombs on Japan. Ike was also uncomfortable with all this talk of "Godless Communism" and "a struggle that pitted Christianity against atheism." Nothing was that simple, Eisenhower
believed—this was about politics and power. This was a disagreement among

persons. It had nothing to do with God.[57] Of course these beliefs did not go down well with some Republicans, even those Republicans of Eisenhower's new gang. In many respects, Ike often appeared too soft to them and not public enough in his condemnation of the Truman administration. But not even the most conservative Republicans could argue with Ike's probusiness and internationalist viewpoint. The U.S. needed to be involved in the world, Eisenhower argued, because it needed to "obtain certain raw materials to sustain [our] economy and to preserve profitable foreign markets for our surpluses."[58] This could be done only by cultivating allies, particularly allies in Europe.[59] The members of his gang agreed. As for McCarthy and Jenner, Eisenhower would not compromise: they were "disciples of hate."[60]

Even so, in the summer of 1950, Dwight Eisenhower was walking a thin line, caught between his loyalty to George Marshall and his political ambition. It seemed as if he would always choose Marshall, forwarding him names of likely staffers for his new Pentagon position and supporting his appointment of experts hated by McCarthyite Republicans.[61] Republican moderate leaders watched this with growing worry and quietly counseled him to remain silent in the face of McCarthy's attacks. They pointed out that a public statement now might come back later to haunt him. He needed to be careful. Eisenhower agreed, but he had trouble thinking of just what line he could take that would satisfy everyone, and he despised those politicians who tried. He was caught in the middle of a vicious political fight inside of the Republican Party, between the waning influence of moderates (like Leverett Saltonstall), the bedrock midwestern strength of isolationists (like the influential Robert Taft), and the rising power of the conservative anti-Communist ideologues (like McCarthy and Jenner). Eisenhower did not like the balancing act of satisfying the most powerful voices of the Republican Party, but he liked being shunted aside by Truman Democrats even less. Once before, when he had been deliberately shunted aside, fate had intervened to change the course of his life—in December 1941, when George Marshall looked down a list of potential new staff members at the War Plans Division and picked Colonel Charles W. Bundy to help Gee Gerow plan World War II. Marshall called an aide to order Bundy to Washington, but was told that the young colonel had been killed the night before in a plane crash in Colorado. Marshall shook his head and looked further down the list.[62] Call Eisenhower, he said. Fate had saved his career. And

so it would now too. Just as Eisenhower was beginning to step out along a
very wobbly political tightrope, Harry Truman called him to Washington.
Eisenhower reported to the White House to see Truman on October 28 and
was quickly ushered into the Oval Office. The president was all business. Would
Ike become the first supreme commander in Europe for the new North Atlantic
Treaty Organization? he asked. Eisenhower immediately accepted. It was just
the assignment he was looking for.[63]

THE IRONY of Eisenhower's appointment was lost neither on Ike—now the
new NATO supreme Allied commander, Europe—nor on the new secretary
of defense. Eisenhower was called back to service for the first time since leaving his post as Army chief of staff, while Marshall had been called back to service three times. Five years after the end of the conflict in Europe and ten years
after Eisenhower's appearance in Marshall's doorway at the Old Munitions
Building on the National Mall, each man had come nearly full circle.
Technically, Eisenhower was once again acting under the instructions of his
mentor, although in this instance the Marshall-Eisenhower partnership was
wholly different. Eisenhower was now not simply one of many European experts; he was America's *premier* European expert. He knew more European military officers, political leaders and diplomats than any other American. As such,
he would no longer need to rely on Marshall's guidance or instructions—or be
required to filter his decisions through a solely military spectrum. Rather, and
oddly, Eisenhower was now required to reforge the alliance that he and the now-
secretary of defense had built from early 1942. Marshall, on the other hand, was
now relieved of his European worries; his work would be to rebuild American
military strength, guide American military policy in Korea, and mobilize a generation of Americans to fight in a new, if less certain, conflict.[64] Marshall and
Eisenhower were no longer partners in command; they were partners in making a new American foreign policy. And both men were precisely where they
were best suited to do that: NATO was in Eisenhower's hands, and the Defense
Department was in Marshall's.

Eisenhower welcomed Marshall's views on his new assignment, and the
two conferred prior to Ike's departure for the new NATO headquarters in Paris.
By now theirs was a well-worn procedure. Marshall, Eisenhower and Joint

Chiefs of Staff Chairman Omar Bradley informally reviewed American deployments and discussed how best Eisenhower might begin structuring his new command. Eisenhower's assignment was unprecedented in American military history. His job was to meld America's military structure in Europe into a larger, and more permanent, coalition structure—not in order to fight a war (as had happened in 1914 and 1941), but in order to prevent one. Eisenhower's job was to be a soldier and a diplomat. But his job was also more political than military; he would cajole and convince as much as order. On reflection, Eisenhower believed his first task was to assess the willingness of America's new military allies to contribute to the NATO force, so he spent January 1951 making a twelve-nation tour of NATO capitals, meeting with military commanders and introducing himself to Europe's new generation of postwar political leaders.[65] He then returned to the United States and briefed Truman on his tour. Then, almost immediately after that briefing, Ike and Mamie boarded the *Queen Mary* to take up residence in France. Their first residence was the Trianon Palace Hotel in Versailles, where Ike had met with Marshall during the most critical days of World War II and where the two had drafted the letter to Bernard Law Montgomery that ensured Eisenhower's continued power as supreme Allied commander.

Visiting the new NATO headquarters during his first days in France, Eisenhower decided that his military staff should be cut (from six hundred to two hundred officers) and that his first priority would be to put in place a series of policies to guide NATO through its first years. These policies had less to do with military strategies than with each nation's requirements under the NATO agreement. That Eisenhower's first job was political and not military suited him; the last thing that a NATO commander needed to do, he believed, was actually command NATO units. That would be left to NATO's cadre of national commanders. Ironically, Eisenhower's senior deputy at NATO was none other than Bernard Law Montgomery—now first Viscount Montgomery of Alamein, former chief of the Imperial General Staff, and former supreme commander of the Western Union's Commanders-in-Chief Committee (the precursor to NATO).[66] Eisenhower might have recoiled had he learned that Montgomery would once again be serving under him, but the craggy-faced commander had somehow changed. While he was still a priggish, self-referencing figure (his mother died shortly before he arrived in Paris but he did not attend the funeral—he said he was "too busy"), he proved to be an able and loyal lieutenant and an expert politician. The two agreed on nearly every point. Montgomery believed strongly in NATO and became one of Eisenhower's most important supporters.[67] Besides, as he told Eisenhower, it was in both their interests that their countries be defended from the line of the Elbe River rather than from the cliffs of Dover.

As chance would have it, the master planner of Normandy had already done much of Eisenhower's work for him. As head of the Commanders-in-Chief Committee, Montgomery had toured Europe examining its military needs.

We made plans to defend the West against aggression. But none of the plans could be carried out because the nations were unwilling to produce the necessary forces—properly trained, with a sound command structure and a reliable communication system. It was the more difficult as there was no true unity, and no nation was willing to make any sacrifice of sovereignty for the common good. The emphasis was on economic recovery. It was not understood that economic strength without military strength is useless; both are necessary, with a proper balance between the two. Military strength is necessary in order to have power behind the politics; power is essential when dealing with the Communist bloc. I quickly saw how difficult it was to obtain economic fusion and to build up military strength until the political association between the group of nations concerned had first been clearly defined and agreed.[68]

Montgomery had it precisely right. Eisenhower's job was to convince NATO's member military institutions to cede their command sovereignty to a single coalition structure—where all commanders would obey a single unified commander (of whatever nationality), would fight with the same weapons (American made), would speak the same language (English), and all with a common goal: to deter aggression and, if that deterrence failed, to fight as a single military unit.

Eisenhower returned to Washington from Paris at the end of January to brief Harry Truman's policymakers on what he had learned during his short tenure as NATO commander. A full panoply of administration officials greeted Eisenhower, including Truman, Acheson, and Marshall. For nearly three hours during a meeting at the White House, Eisenhower reviewed his trip through Europe, capital by capital, detailing the military strengths of each nation and the political willingness of their governments to increase defense spending to respond to Soviet rearmament. After the briefing, Eisenhower stayed in Washington for private discussions with Truman, Acheson, and Marshall, then returned to Europe to join Montgomery in building NATO's structure.[69] Eisenhower, Marshall, and Montgomery were certainly aware that in part they already had a model for this structure—that SHAEF (the Supreme Headquarters, Allied Expeditionary Force), which had existed during World War II, could easily be recast as SHAPE—Supreme Headquarters, Allied Powers Europe. Here finally, Eisenhower and Marshall knew, was the institutionalization, in the heart of Europe, of everything that they had worked for: a military coalition of like-minded nations that took Fox Conner's maxim one step further—never fight unless you have to, never fight alone, never fight for long, and create international coalitions that will deter wars so you don't have to fight them at all.

For the next seventeen months, Eisenhower and Montgomery created the structure of NATO, but for the last five of those months it was clear to Montgomery that Eisenhower's mind was elsewhere. Not only did Ike turn over many of his responsibilities to Monty, who seemed less impatient with French fears of German rearmament and eventual inclusion in NATO than Eisenhower (it was easier for a British officer to calm those fears, after all, than an American officer); he also began to put policies in place for his eventual successor. But Eisenhower was also trying to make up his mind about whether he should run for president. At first, Montgomery was against it. "I had told him he must not go," Montgomery remembered, "we needed him at SHAPE, and Europe needed him too." Eisenhower incessantly communicated his and Monty's difficulties in gaining European agreement to an arms buildup (and their difficulties with the French) to Truman and Marshall. But neither the president nor the secretary of defense could do much to help. The Korean War took much of Truman's and Marshall's attention. In late 1950, North Korean forces were finally forced back across the 38th Parallel by MacArthur's brilliant amphibious operation at Inchon, behind North Korean lines. But Truman was losing faith in MacArthur, who seemed bent on flouting his directives and using his status to energize Truman's congressional opponents. On April 5, 1951,

House Republican leader Joseph Martin released a letter he had received from MacArthur that implied that Harry Truman was interested not in a victory in Korea, but in a stalemate. If Truman were truly interested in victory, MacArthur wrote to Martin, then he would unleash "800,000 trained men" from Chiang Kai-shek's Nationalist forces on Taiwan against the Chinese. "If we are not in Korea to win," MacArthur wrote in his letter, "then this Truman administration should be indicted for the murder of thousands of American boys."[70]

The MacArthur letter was a bombshell that made headlines around the world. America's new NATO allies in Europe worried openly that MacArthur's call for using Chiang against the Chinese mainland meant that they would soon be engaged in another world war, with the Red Army pouring across the Elbe River. That was the last thing that Truman—or Marshall and Eisenhower—wanted. Europe was not ready for war and would likely be overrun. On April 6, Truman called together his foreign policy brain trust—Averell Harriman, Dean Acheson, Omar Bradley, and George Marshall—and solicited their views on MacArthur. Marshall's first concern was with Eisenhower and the newly formed Atlantic Alliance. MacArthur was out of line, Marshall said, but if he was fired it would be difficult to get Congress to appropriate more funds for NATO. Omar Bradley was undecided and said that he wanted time to confer with the other members of the Joint Chiefs of Staff. Acheson and Harriman were also cautious, but it was clear to them that MacArthur must be relieved. On Sunday, Truman told Bradley and the chiefs to "search their consciences" on the proper course to follow. The fight over MacArthur was now waged by Marshall and Bradley inside the Pentagon. For Marshall, the MacArthur controversy was reminiscent of one that he and Eisenhower had faced with Patton at the height of World War II: the Joint Chiefs were hesitant to relieve the Korea commander—while he was indiscreet, even insubordinate, he knew how to fight.[71] But slowly the tide turned, and after reviewing MacArthur's wartime record, the joint chiefs concluded that he had been insubordinate. On Sunday, April 8, the Joint Chiefs of Staff voted unanimously for MacArthur's dismissal "because the military must be controlled by civilian authority in this country." Marshall concurred.[72]

The next day Douglas MacArthur was ordered by Harry Truman to "turn over your commands, effective at once, to Lieutenant General Matthew B. Ridgway."[73]

In Paris, Eisenhower decided that he would remain silent on MacArthur's firing. Once again, he found himself caught uncomfortably in the middle. While he had no sympathy for MacArthur's position, and told his close military friends that he was not surprised by his old commander's indiscretions, he was now being pressured by moderate Republicans to separate himself from the administration.[74] That seemed particularly difficult for Ike just now. Eisenhower had attempted to take himself out of America's pugilistic political environment by going to Paris, but in doing so he had actually sparked widespread comments in conservative circles that by accepting the NATO job he was actually helping Truman. In New York, members of the Eisenhower gang engaged Bill Robinson to help refute these charges, but Eisenhower's new friends admitted that that might be difficult. Robinson contacted Eisenhower and told him to remain silent. Anything he said now, either way, could hurt him. Eisenhower agreed, but in the interim, he remained the loyal soldier. He refused to comment on the MacArthur crisis and focused on NATO and worked through all of late 1951 and into 1952 to build its military capacity. He traveled to London to give a speech on common defense and corresponded regularly with Secretary of State Dean Acheson on NATO's growth.[75] But his position was tenuous, and he felt he might come under fire at any moment. In fact, his own principles were now bumping up against his ambition. Eisenhower wanted to be a political leader who was an internationalist and supported strengthening NATO at the same time that he praised the virtues of a balanced federal budget—which meant turning down the Navy's call for a super carrier, as well as the Army's insistence on more and larger tanks.[76] He understood the contradictions in his position: he wanted a stronger NATO, but he wanted a smaller U.S. military. Yet, in all of this, Eisenhower was carefully positioning himself as the most moderate of moderate Republicans—a now extinct political animal that believed in a small military, free markets, balanced budgets, and common deterrence.[77]

In April 1952, Montgomery showed up in Eisenhower's office in Paris with a quizzical look on his face. "Ike," he said, "I've changed my mind. You must go back and run for President. European co-operation is in the doldrums and the only man who can get things moving is the President of the United States. You can do more good to us in the White House than you can here."[78] Shortly after hearing this, Eisenhower received a message from Bill Robinson in New York, saying that Douglas MacArthur was thinking about entering his name as a presidential candidate. Eisenhower moved quickly; he wrote a final NATO report to Truman and asked the president to accept his resignation as NATO commander. Truman agreed, and Ike and Mamie packed their belongings and planned their move back to the States. But they would not be returning to New York. Instead, Ike would announce his candidacy from his hometown of Abilene, and his campaign would be run from an office in Denver. On one of his final days as NATO commander, Eisenhower received a letter from an old friend, saying that he was pleased to hear that Ike was running for the White House. "Personally, I thank God that you have decided to do so, for I feel that the future security of the world depends on your now assuming this great office and of being in a position to guard the steps of your great country during the critical years to come."[79] The letter was signed by Field Marshal Alan Brooke.

DWIGHT EISENHOWER'S entry into political life began officially on June 4, 1952, a rainy day in Abilene, Kansas. He was a candidate for president of the United States, he said. The next day he held a press conference. It was a masterful Eisenhower performance. But once again, and now more than ever, Dwight Eisenhower felt he was walking a thin political line, satisfying everyone while keeping his own moderate and decidedly internationalist views hidden. Eisenhower was a very good politician, and while he imperceptibly winced at the backslapping informality of a run for the White House, he was a very good campaigner. His "hi, how are ya" methods and his "attaboy" Abilene personality went down well in the country, and everyone seemed to "like Ike." He played on his military service, but he had a right to. When hosting a group of Washington politicians at a picnic, he was asked if he could take the pressure of a national campaign. Anger flashed in his eyes, but only for a moment; then he relaxed and smiled: "That's a funny kind of question to put to a man who has spent forty years of his life fighting," he said.[80] At the Republican National Convention in August, Ike missed a first-ballot nomination by nine votes. Near midnight, the head of the Minnesota delegation announced that his state wanted to switch its votes to Eisenhower. This was done quickly, though over the protests of Taft partisans, and suddenly Dwight Eisenhower was the Republican Party's nominee for president.[81]

Marshall, now finally retired from public life, wrote to congratulate

Eisenhower. His former lieutenant quickly responded, saying that Marshall would probably never have believed that his old subordinate would someday run for the nation's highest office. He felt called to duty, he said. "But the whole atmosphere is so different from that to which soldiers of long service become accustomed that I sometimes find it difficult to adjust myself. Since you are well aware of this through your own experience, I will not belabor the point."[82] It is not known what George Marshall felt about Eisenhower's run for president—he never voted and he kept his political feelings to himself. This was his discipline; a military officer was not to have any political views, he thought, but to serve the nation, obey orders, and answer to the chief executive. Marshall watched from a distance and kept his feelings private. Eisenhower was a former comrade, a fellow Army commander, a great war planner, and a talented soldier-diplomat. He had been Marshall's partner during the most important period in both of their lives. But Eisenhower's opponent was Adlai Stevenson, who was also Marshall's friend. So Marshall wrote to both of them, wishing them luck.[83]

There was only one discordant note. In the midst of his campaign for the presidency, Dwight Eisenhower was asked whether he would endorse the bid of Senator Joseph McCarthy for another term as Wisconsin's senator. Eisenhower maintained his silence on the subject, but in private he hated McCarthy, resented his mindless criticisms of his old chief, and refused to forgive him. When the time came, he vowed, he would denounce him. Eisenhower had even written a speech defending Marshall, to be delivered in Milwaukee, when McCarthy was seated on the platform behind him. But the Republican gang, as well as leaders of the Republican Party and Wisconsin's governor, flew to Peoria, Illinois (where Eisenhower was campaigning), to urge Eisenhower to appear with McCarthy and say nothing. His criticism of McCarthy would do nothing to help Marshall now, they said, and it could hurt his majority in the state. Eisenhower reluctantly deleted the offending paragraphs, and one week later, in Milwaukee, he stood on the same stage as the senator. He remained silent. The next morning, the nation's papers commented on Eisenhower's apparent endorsement of McCarthy's views. That is what his silence meant, they said. Serving out his last months in the White House, Harry Truman was enraged. He denounced Eisenhower then and throughout the campaign. Eisenhower was surprised by Truman's vitriol; he had made his views on Marshall clear in public.[84] "There is nothing of disloyalty in General Marshall's soul," he told one audience. While never mentioning McCarthy's name, he told another audience that he had "no patience with anyone who can find in his [Marshall's] record of service for this country anything to criticize."[85] There was that and the fact that Katherine Marshall, in her nineties, defended Eisenhower: "Don't attack President Eisenhower about the McCarthy thing," she said; "he did everything in the world to make it up to George and me."[86] Even so, there it is: Eisenhower's silence remains a stain on the Eisenhower legacy.

When Dwight Eisenhower was elected President of the United States on November 4, 1952, Marshall sat down to write a letter to him. "I pray for you in the tremendous years you are facing," he wrote. "I pray especially for you in the choice of those to be near you. That choice, more than anything else, will determine the problems of the year and the record of history. Make them measure up to your standards." Eisenhower understood the implications of the Marshall message and saw that it contained a veiled compliment—perhaps the greatest compliment that the former Army chief of staff could ever give a subordinate: that a commander's success and ultimate victory depend on those he chose to help him. Marshall had chosen Eisenhower. Eisenhower invited Marshall to his inauguration and gave him a prominent place in the row of dignitaries seated behind him. Over the next years, Eisenhower would call on Marshall often. He asked for his guidance and was particularly pleased that one year after he became president, Marshall was named the recipient of the Nobel Peace Prize. It was a singular honor, a recognition of his greatest legacy—the Marshall Plan. Marshall's remarks upon receiving the award in Oslo were among the most eloquent he ever penned: "There has been considerable comment over the awarding of a Nobel Peace Prize to a soldier. I am afraid this does not seem quite so remarkable to me as it quite evidently appears to others. The cost of war is constantly spread before me, written neatly in many ledgers whose columns are gravestones."[87]

Marshall's trip to Oslo tired him and when he returned to the United States in February 1954, he was confined to his bed. His journeys to Walter Reed increased over the next several years and his health deteriorated. Eisenhower came to visit him at the hospital, making certain that he was always treated by his personal doctor. Marshall stayed in the hospital's Presidential Suite. When

Eisenhower visited, he sat near Marshall's bed and the two talked. But Eisenhower was president and Marshall was ill and there was not much time to reminisce. Marshall maintained his propriety. Dwight Eisenhower was no longer "General Eisenhower" or just "Eisenhower." He was now "Mr. President." Franklin Roosevelt once made the mistake of calling General Marshall "George," but Eisenhower never made that mistake. Even now, as president, his former commander—his eternal upperclassman—was "General Marshall." In August 1958, Marshall checked into the hospital to have a cyst removed from an eye. As always, Eisenhower sent flowers to brighten his room. Marshall penned his thanks: "I am comfortably situated in your fine suite and, again, you have my deepest thanks for this gracious gesture on your part."[88] In early 1959, Marshal suffered a stroke. His health now slid perilously downhill, and while he was able to attend some public events, he eventually returned to Walter Reed. He suffered from brain spasms and had a second stroke. Dwight Eisenhower brought Winston Churchill to visit him. Marshall was unconscious and Churchill, gaunt and stooped, stood in the doorway crying. George Marshall died in the early evening of October 16, 1959.

EPILOGUE:
"A MONSTROUS THING"

I N MAY 1957, two aging men stood silently, peering into the distance, on the modest eminence of Little Round Top. In the distance was the town of Gettysburg.[1] One of the men pointed out where the lines of the enemy armies had formed during three hot days in July 1863. Robert E. Lee's Confederate line was in the distance on a small rise called Seminary Ridge. The Union line was below, on Cemetery Ridge. The Union line curled north and then, in a fishhook, back to the east. Below them, in the Devil's Den and Peach Orchard, the New York brigades of Daniel Sickles formed, sticking out like a thumb. It was there, on July 2, that General James Longstreet attacked, rolling his regiments of the Deep South like a wave against the Union defenders. As one of the men pointed out these features, the other shook his head. "Why didn't he go around here?" he asked, and he took his cane and gestured to the south, where Longstreet might have launched his flanking movement and won the American Civil War. Later, standing on Seminary Ridge—where Lee had launched George Pickett's divisions on their famous assault across open ground—the first man turned to the other. "A monstrous thing to launch this charge," he said. "A monstrous thing. A monstrous thing." The other man turned to face him. "If you had, I would have sacked you," he said.[2]

One of these men, three years younger than his companion, was President Dwight David Eisenhower, now in his second term in office. His companion that day at Gettysburg was Field Marshal Bernard Law Montgomery. Their meeting and subsequent tour of the battlefield was a treat for the British general, who loved to walk the battlefields of northern France where he had begun his legendary career. Eisenhower also liked battlefields, but had bought the farm at Gettysburg only at Mamie's insistence. The two would have dinner there at the end of the day. Historians now comment on and debate Lee's failure at Gettysburg and Longstreet's plea that he "go around there"—and win the battle. Lee denied him. Other historians say the story of the battle is more complex. Lee did not win the battle, because the man who might have won it, Thomas Jonathan "Stonewall" Jackson, "was not there."[3] He had died two months before, after losing an arm at the Battle of Chancellorsville.

The two men who stood on Little Round Top that day won their fame on other battlefields in a later time. But the man who had made it possible for them to do so, George Marshall, was not on those battlefields with them. He was not in Europe, or at Bastogne, or even in Eisenhower's headquarters. He was back in Washington, behind a desk, thousands of miles from any World War II battlefield, studying maps and reviewing battlefield reports and even, on occasion, looking through the pages of a little black book in which he had written the names of officers he admired. It is perhaps a comment on the truth of recent wars that their greatest commanders followed in Marshall's footsteps—in an age of mechanized war, the victors are the best organizers. Then too, even retired generals enjoy the benefits of the armchair. Eisenhower agreed with Montgomery's judgment, pointing to the ground across which Pickett charged: "Why he would have gone across that field, I don't know," he said. But in the winter of 1944, Dwight Eisenhower sent thousands of young American men across similar fields, in a broad-front offensive against dug-in troops who served in the best-trained and best-disciplined army in human history. And Montgomery? Bernard Law Montgomery sent paratroopers up a single narrow highway into the teeth of Germany's toughest panzer units, hoping to surprise an army that had rarely been surprised before.

We rightly extol these warriors—and Bradley and Collins, Clark and Patton—and the soldiers who fought in World War II. It is worthwhile to recall their battles. But their history is not simply the history of battles won and lost. It is right also that in celebrating their victory we allow history to speak accurately of what they did. Sometimes the truth we find can be uncomfortable. The United States and Great Britain fought together in World War II, but not always well. The battles between Brooke and Marshall and Montgomery and

Eisenhower can teach us much about the difficulty of not only how to fight wars, but whether to fight them. "Men, this stuff we hear about America wanting to stay out of this war, not wanting to fight, is a crock of bullshit," George Patton told the soldiers of the Third Army just before D-day. "Americans love to fight—traditionally. All real Americans love the sting and clash of battle."[4]

No, actually, we don't. Americans have traditionally hated war. Americans have never loved a good fight, and thousands of otherwise patriotic American men have traditionally tried to stay *out* of war. That's a fact, proved by American desertion rates at the height of the Bastogne battle, where thousands of young men in the European theater of operations found themselves "separated from their units" and wandering in the rear. That is a conceit—these men were not just separated from their units. They were deserters. The desertion rate in the American Army in Europe in World War II reached such alarming proportions that Dwight Eisenhower read the provost marshal's report about it with growing concern—and shot a soldier for desertion as an example to others. That was not the only problem Eisenhower had. Rape became so common that at one point Eisenhower thought the only solution was to line up the perpetrators and mow them down. But he needed his soldiers, who were hanging on to their lines in Bastogne by a thread. "We're going to go through the Germans like shit through a goose," Patton said.

Historian Max Hastings, in *Armageddon*—his needed corrective to the triumphalist history of "the greatest generation"—termed the deserters from the American Army "a teeming horde" that engaged in "a huge traffic in stolen military rations, fuel, equipment and even vehicles."[5] This is not to detract from the sacrifices made by America's citizen-soldiers, but simply to point out the facts—and provide a needed coda for what George Marshall and Dwight Eisenhower understood about America. "Americans play to win all the time," Patton said. "I wouldn't give a hoot in hell for a man who lost and laughed. That's why American have never lost nor will ever lose a war; for the very idea of losing is hateful to an American." Of course that was not true then and it is not true now, and just because Patton said it was so did not make it so. Americans have lost wars and Fox Conner knew it. His goal was to teach George Marshall and Dwight Eisenhower how to win. Conner's simple axioms were based on what he knew about the American people and what he believed about democracies. He knew that Americans didn't like war and that, in truth, they weren't very good at it. The solution to this was for America never to agree to fight unless there was no other choice, to fight only with others, and then to do so quickly, before people got tired of spilling their children's blood. George Marshall and Dwight Eisenhower also believed that Americans thought war a monstrous thing—but they thought that it was a good thing.

Dwight Eisenhower and Bernard Law Montgomery climbed down from Little Round Top, continued their tour of the battlefield, and then talked during a quiet dinner. Montgomery enjoyed his visit, consulted with Eisenhower on NATO, and went back to England. Eisenhower finished his term as president. Before he retired he left us with the most poignant and pointed lesson he had learned from a lifetime in uniform. "In the councils of government, we must guard against the acquisition of unwarranted influence, whether sought or unsought, by the military-industrial complex," he said. "The potential for the disastrous rise of misplaced power exists and will persist." Eisenhower did not want to retire. But he reluctantly retreated from public life, turning over his mantle of office to a younger man. He had suffered a heart attack in 1955, and he suffered a second one ten years later. In 1968 he suffered a third heart attack. He was now confined to Walter Reed Army Hospital, where George Marshall had died. On March 28, 1969, his heart gave out.[6]

·   ·   ·

· HAROLD ALEXANDER—that is, Harold Rupert Leofric George Alexander, first Earl Alexander of Tunis—served as an immensely popular governor general of Canada after the end of the war, then returned to England to serve as minister of defense. He died in June 1969. He lived a life of great usefulness.

· Eisenhower's friend OMAR BRADLEY survived him by twelve years, dying in 1981. Bradley remained irascible to the last, though he reached Marshall's and Eisenhower's five-star rank.

· SIR ALAN BROOKE—that is, Alan Francis Brooke, first Viscount Alanbrooke—retired and served as the chancellor of Queens University, Belfast, until his death in 1963. The publication of his wartime diaries in 2002 caused a sensation in England.

· **CAPTAIN HARRY C. BUTCHER** published his diary of his time with Eisenhower under the title *My Three Years with Eisenhower* in 1946. The book embarrassed Eisenhower and the two exchanged angry letters. The book made him his fortune, but Eisenhower felt betrayed. Butcher retired from the Navy and from broadcasting and died in 1985.

· **WINSTON CHURCHILL** survived George Marshall by six years, dying in 1965.

· **MARK CLARK** never received the public accolades he so desired. After World War II he commanded the U.S. Sixth Army, served as commander of UN troops in Korea, and served as superintendent at the Citadel Military Academy, where he is buried. He died in 1984 at the age of eighty-eight.

· **JOSEPH L. "LIGHTNING JOE" COLLINS** served as chief of staff of the U.S. Army. He was a supporter of NATO and its most effective advocate. He retired in 1956 and died in 1987.

· **FOX CONNER** retired as a major general, never having commanded troops in combat. He retired in 1938, having been denied promotion to Army chief of staff. That appointment went to Douglas MacArthur. He watched with great interest the development of the Allied command in World War II and would occasionally write to Marshall about his admiration for the coalition he had established. He died in 1951.

· **JACOB DEVERS** was never given the credit he was due as a tough fighter and capable commander. Ambitious, with a biting delivery, he was trusted by Marshall, but Eisenhower never warmed to him. He received the command he coveted, as head of the Sixth Army Group, at the end of the war. He was an expert artilleryman. He died in 1979.

· **MAMIE EISENHOWER** continued to live in Gettysburg. Her husband continually worried about her health. She died at the age of eighty-two in 1979.

· **MILTON STOVER EISENHOWER** served as president of Kansas State University, Pennsylvania State University, and Johns Hopkins University. He is remembered as a great educator and champion of racial integration. He died in May 1985.

· **LEONARD "GEE" GEROW** was appointed commanding general, U.S. Second Army, after the war and retired in 1950. A charter member of "Club Eisenhower," he died in Petersburg, Virginia, where he was born, in 1972.

· **COURTNEY HODGES** was forced out of West Point because of bad grades, so enlisted in the Army as a private. He retired from the Army in 1949, but without the credit he deserved as a brilliant infantry commander. He died in San Antonio, Texas, in 1966.

· **FIELD MARSHAL ALBERT KESSELRING** was taken prisoner on May 6, 1945. He was put on trial by the Allies for ordering the shooting of partisans during the war, was found guilty, and was condemned to death. His guilt was based on flimsy evidence. He was released from prison in 1952 and died in Germany in 1960.

· After his dismissal by Harry Truman, **DOUGLAS MACARTHUR** made a triumphant return to the United States. His farewell address to the U.S. Military Academy at West Point is now the stuff of legend. "Old soldiers never die, they just fade away," he said. MacArthur died in 1964, hailed as a great American soldier and strategic genius.

· **KATHERINE MARSHALL** dropped out of public view and remained at her Leesburg home. She died nearly twenty years after her husband, in 1978.

· **LIEUTENANT GENERAL TROY MIDDLETON's** capable command of the U.S. VIII Corps during the Battle of the Bulge sealed his place as one of the great combat commanders in U.S. history. After the war he became commandant of cadets at Louisiana State University before being named as its president. He died in 1976.

· **BERNARD LAW MONTGOMERY** retired after serving under four NATO commanders, but his later life was filled with controversy. He praised Chinese

Communism and spoke out against the legalization of homosexuality, calling it "a charter for buggery." He noted: "This sort of thing may be tolerated by the French, but we're British—thank God." His monument should be the Normandy invasion, his masterpiece. He died, a tragic figure, in March 1976.

· **GEORGE PATTON** left the Third Army and prepared to take up his duties as commander of the Fifteenth Army. On December 9, 1945, he was badly injured in a car accident outside of Mannheim, Germany. Paralyzed from the neck down, he died of an embolism on December 21. He is buried in the Luxembourg American Cemetery and Memorial in Hamm, Luxembourg, beside the graves of those soldiers who died under his command. Twenty thousand soldiers volunteered to be his pallbearers. Marshall and Eisenhower were right— he was the greatest armored commander in the history of American warfare.

· **JOHN J. PERSHING** spent his last years battling illness. He was visited often during World War II by his student, George Marshall. He survived the war and died in 1948.

· **WALTER BEDELL "BEETLE" SMITH** served Eisenhower as the head of the CIA and as ambassador to the Soviet Union. He was promoted to four-star rank. He died, suddenly, of a heart attack in 1961.

· **KAY SUMMERSBY,** with Eisenhower's help, became an American citizen. She published *Eisenhower Was My Boss* in 1948. There was no mention of an affair in her writing. She published an autobiography in 1976 under the title *Past Forgetting: My Love Affair with Dwight D. Eisenhower.* She said that their attempts to make love failed. She said she published the book because she was short of money.

· **LUCIEN K. TRUSCOTT** succeeded George Patton as commander of the Third Army. He was promoted to the rank of general by an act of Congress in gratitude for his wartime service. After retirement he became an author. He died in 1965, remembered by his colleagues as perhaps the greatest combat commander of World War II.

NOTES

Prologue

1. *The Last Meeting of Lee and Jackson* was painted by Everett B. D. Fabrino Julio in 1864. Julio was born on the island of St. Helena and studied in Paris. He is remembered now for his brooding post–Civil War Louisiana landscapes. Julio had a short career. He suffered from tuberculosis and died in Kingston, Georgia, at the age of thirty-six.
2. Forrest C. Pogue, *George C. Marshall, Education of a General* (New York: Viking, 1963), pp. 43–45.
3. Ibid., p. 45.
4. Ibid., p. 46.
5. Shelby Foote, *The Civil War, a Narrative* (New York: Random House, 1963), vol. 2, p. 285.

Chapter 1: The WPD

1. General George Marshall conducted a series of five extensive interviews from August 1956 to April 1957 with historian Forrest Pogue. They provide the best firsthand account we have of Marshall's views. The Pogue interviews were followed by a series of command interviews conducted with senior officers deployed to the U.S. Defense Department and were not a part of Pogue's account of Marshall's life. Those interviews are available at the George C. Marshall Research Library and Foundation and are so cited in the notes. *The Papers of George Catlett Marshall* (Baltimore: The Johns Hopkins University Press) contains nearly all of his wartime correspondence and his messages to Eisenhower, as well as his most important military papers.

   The balance of Marshall's correspondence that is not published or available at the Virginia Military Institute can be accessed primarily in the General John J. Pershing Papers at the Library of Congress (for the prewar years). Correspondence and memoranda not yet published are cited in the notes and are available at the George C. Marshall Research Library, as are the complete records of Marshall's military service as well as all family papers. The George C. Marshall Research Library and Foundation also contains the papers of General Lucien K. Truscott, Lieutenant General Thomas T. Handy, Brigadier General Frank McCarthy, and Brigadier General Paul M. Robinett.
2. Dwight Eisenhower kept a diary of his prewar years, which is available at the Dwight D. Eisenhower Presidential Library in Abilene, Kansas. His World War II papers are compiled in an extensive published series, *The Papers of Dwight David Eisenhower* (Baltimore: Johns Hopkins University Press, 1970). The invaluable prewar and postwar personal correspondence of Eisenhower is at the presidential library. The extensive collection of letters sent by Eisenhower to Marshall during World War II—108 letters in all—is also at the Dwight D. Eisenhower Presidential Library. In the postwar period, Eisenhower, like Marshall, conducted a series of interviews with senior Army officers, providing an unprecedented firsthand account of his own views

of his career. Those interviews are available at the Dwight D. Eisenhower Presidential Library and are so cited in the notes.

3. Dwight D. Eisenhower, *Crusade in Europe* (New York: Doubleday, 1948), p. 17.

4. Ibid., p. 17. See also Carlo D'Este, *Eisenhower: A Soldier's Life* (New York: Henry Holt, 2002), p. 283.

5. "Walter Krueger," in *The Harper Encyclopedia of American Military Biography*, eds. Trevor N. Dupuy et al. (New York: HarperCollins, 1992), pp. 415–416.

    When recounting major battles of World War II, the author has relied on several general but authoritative studies that have formed the basis of scholarship on the war. *U.S. Army In World War II* is an eighty-volume work completed in the wake of the conflict by the Washington, D.C.–based Center of Military History. The work is complemented by the multivolume *History of the Army Air Forces in World War II*, published in Washington, D.C., in 1992 by the Center for Air Force History. For U.S. Navy operations in World War II, I have used Samuel Eliot Morison's fifteen-volume *History of United States Naval Operations in World War II*. (Boston: Little, Brown and Co., 1949).

6. Donald E. Houston, *Hell on Wheels: The 2d Armored Division* (San Rafael, Calif.: Presidio Press, 1977), pp. 122; also see "General Walter Krueger," Box 40, Krueger Papers, Dwight D. Eisenhower Presidential Library, Abilene, Kansas.

7. The George S. Patton Papers are housed at the United States Military Academy, West Point, New York (Special Collections, USMA, West Point). See also the Papers of George S. Patton, The Library of Congress, Manuscript Division, Washington, D.C.

8. Houston, *Hell on Wheels*, p. 123.

9. Eisenhower and Krueger remained close throughout the war, though Krueger was quite older, of Marshall's generation, and secretly resented the credit his chief of staff received for conceiving the "blue" forces plan. See also D'Este, *Eisenhower: A Soldier's Life*, pp. 280–281.

10. The Papers of J. Lawton Collins and General Joseph McNarney can be found at the United States Military Academy, West Point, New York. The Papers of General Carl Spaatz are at The Library of Congress, Manuscript Division, Washington, D.C.

11. Merle Miller, *Ike the Soldier, as They Knew Him* (New York: Putnam, 1987), p. 247.

12. Ibid.

13. Carlo D'Este made the interesting observation that Marshall's relationship with Eisenhower reminded Marshall of his own with General John J. Pershing—as the two were so unlike each other. See D'Este, *Eisenhower: A Soldier's Life*, p. 198.

14. Eisenhower recounted his meeting with Marshall several times to a number of biographers and journalists, particularly after the publication of his account of World War II, *Crusade in Europe*, in 1948. Eisenhower was sensitive about the fact that Pershing's two volumes of memoirs received the Pulitzer Prize, while *Crusade in Europe* did not. Eisenhower clearly felt that Pershing had come nowhere close to writing as good a book as he did. Eisenhower was rankled by this—particularly since he was right.

15. Forrest C. Pogue, *George C. Marshall: Ordeal and Hope* (New York: Viking, 1963), p. 237.

16. Ed Cray, *General of the Army: George C. Marshall, Soldier and Statesman* (New York: Rowman & Littlefield, 1990), pp. 54–56.

17. D'Este, *Eisenhower: A Soldier's Life*, pp. 268–269.

18. *The Harper Encyclopedia of Military Biography* "Gerow, Leonard Townsend," pp. 278–279.

19. Miller, *Ike the Soldier, as They Knew Him*, p. 212.

20. Pogue, *George C. Marshall: Ordeal and Hope*, p. 339.

21. "Assistance to the Far East" (OPD Exec 8, Book A), *The Papers of Dwight D. Eisenhower: The War Years*, vol. 1 (Baltimore: Johns Hopkins University Press, 1970), pp. 5–6, (hereinafter DDE).

22. Ibid.

23. Pogue, *George C. Marshall: Ordeal and Hope*, p. 239. See also Dwight D. Eisenhower, *Crusade in Europe* (New York: Doubleday, 1948), pp. 21–22.

24. "Chronology, 1941–1945," in *The U.S. Army in World War II*, Center of Military History, United States Army (Washington, D.C.: U.S. Government Printing Office, 1994), p. 5.

25. I. C. B. Deer, ed., *The Oxford Companion to World War II* (New York: Oxford University Press, 1995), pp. 929–935.
26. Ibid., p. 937.
27. Eric Larrabee, *Commander in Chief: Franklin Delano Roosevelt, His Lieutenants, and Their War* (New York: Harper & Row, 1987), p. 101.
28. Ibid., p. 100.
29. The Papers of Secretary of War Henry L. Stimson can be found at the Sterling Library, Yale University, New Haven, Connecticut.
30. Forrest C. Pogue, *George C. Marshall: Organizer of Victory 1943–1945* (New York: Viking, 1963), p. 61.
31. Forrest C. Pogue, *Education of a General* (New York: Viking, 1963), pp. 10–11.
32. Ibid., p. 43.
33. Ibid., p. 10.
34. The quote is from Larry I. Bland, ed., *George C. Marshall: Interviews and Reminiscences for Forrest C. Pogue*, (rev. ed.) (Lexington, VA, George C. Marshall Research Foundation: 1991), p. 221. The interviews by Pogue of General Marshall were taped, with prearranged questions. (In some cases the questions were put to Marshall prior to the recording sessions, and it appears that in some cases he is simply talking into a recorder without anyone present but with the questions typed out on a paper in front of him.) The interviews were conducted in 1957, after his retirement from public life.
35. Pogue, *George C. Marshall: Ordeal and Hope*, p. 157.
36. Ibid., p. 193.
37. Ibid., p. 210.
38. The differences and similarities between Marshall and Eisenhower were considered so important that they are mentioned explicitly in the official history of the Army in World War II; see Forrest C. Pogue, "The Supreme Command," in *U.S. Army in World War II: European Theatre of Operations*, U.S. Army Center of Military History, (Washington, D.C.: Government Printing Office, 1996), pp. 33–35.
39. Pogue, *George C. Marshall: Ordeal and Hope*, p. 338.
40. Thomas Parrish, *Roosevelt and Marshall: Partners in Politics and War* (New York: William Morrow, 1989), p. 242.
41. Daniel D. Holt and James W. Leyerzapt, *Eisenhower: The Prewar Diaries and Selected Papers, 1905–1941* (Baltimore: Johns Hopkins University Press, 1998), p. 52.
   The Eisenhower diaries are a compilation of five separate diaries kept by Eisenhower during various periods prior to World War II. At the end of the war, Eisenhower ordered all of his prewar diaries destroyed, in the interest of privacy, but they were saved by his family and aides. The diaries, particularly those for Eisenhower's time in the Philippines, were found by the widow of one of his aides and turned over to the Eisenhower Library after the death of Eisenhower. The diaries were cataloged by the staff at the Eisenhower Presidential Library, and the citations in them were checked against the records of prewar Eisenhower manuscripts. The diaries provide valuable insights into the views of Eisenhower and Marshall on a number of officers, many of whom would serve in senior commands later in the war. Eisenhower notes Marshall's views on Douglas MacArthur (p. 356 of the cited work), whom the later Army chief of staff viewed with "ill-concealed distaste."
42. Pogue, *George C. Marshall: Ordeal and Hope*, pp. 40, 92.
43. "To Lieutenant General Jacob L. Devers," April 22, 1944, Radio No. WAR-26520, in *The Papers of George Catlett Marshall* (Baltimore: Johns Hopkins University Press, 1996), vol. 4, p. 430.
   The Papers of George Catlett Marshall were compiled by an editorial staff of the George C. Marshall Research Library at the Virginia Military Institute. The papers have their foundation in a subgroup of papers compiled by the Miiltary History Department of the Office of the Secretary of Defense, Department of Defense, Washington, D.C. The papers in the collection were the result of letters, notes, memoranda, and staff studies dictated by Marshall to his secretary, Mona Nason. Radio messages from Marshall that are the result of staff reports are also in-

cluded in the compilation. Copies of the holdings of other repositories of Marshall papers during his service as secretary of state can be found in the National Archives. The Office of the Chief of Staff of the U.S. Army also contains papers of George C. Marshall which are not duplicated in these volumes, but are focused on internal staff matters and do not contain messages or memoranda to Dwight Eisenhower.

44. Trevor N. DePuy, ed., *Harper Encyclopedia of Military Biography* (New York: HarperCollins, 1992), p. 217.
45. At the beginning of World War II, President Roosevelt created a committee of staff commanders to coordinate strategy for the armed services. The group became known as the U.S. Joint Chiefs of Staff. The members of the new JCS were the counterparts of the British Chiefs of the Army, Navy, and Royal Air Force. The first members of the JCS were Admiral William D. Leahy, President Roosevelt's special military adviser, with the title of chief of staff to the commander in chief of the Army and Navy, who presided over the JCS; General George C. Marshall, chief of staff of the Army; Admiral Ernest J. King, chief of naval operations and commander in chief of the U.S. Fleet; and General Henry H. Arnold, deputy Army chief of staff for air and chief of the Army Air Corps.
46. Cray, *General of the Army: George C. Marshall, Soldier and Statesman*, pp. 54–56.
47. Ibid., p. 56.
48. *Education of a General*, Pogue, p. 198.
49. Ibid., pp 108–109.
50. Ibid., p. 109.
51. Ibid., p. 282.
52. *The Papers of George Catlett Marshall*, vol. 1, p. 714.
53. Miller, *Ike the Soldier*, p. 334.
54. Ibid., p. 337.
55. Ibid.
56. *DDE*, Vol. 1, p. 12 (December 17, 1941).
57. Stephen E. Ambrose, *The Supreme Commander* (New York: Doubleday, 1970), p. 6.
58. "Addresses Delivered at the Dedication Ceremonies of the George C. Marshall Research Library" (Eisenhower Remarks),Virginia Military Institute, in "Remembrances of General of the Army George C. Marshall," pp. 14–15.

CHAPTER 2: ARCADIA

1. Winston Churchill, *The Grand Alliance* (vol. 3, *The Second World War*) (Boston: Houghton Mifflin, 1950), pp. 544–548. See also John S. D. Eisenhower, *Allies: Pearl Harbor to D-Day* (New York: Doubleday, 1982), pp. 21–27.
2. "Churchill to Roosevelt" (Doc. 87), December 9, 1941, in *Roosevelt and Churchill, Their Secret Wartime Correspondence*, eds. Francis L. Loewenheim, Harold D. Langley, and Manfred Jonas (New York: Saturday Review Press Dutton, 1975), pp. 168–169.
3. John Eisenhower, *Allies*, p. 22.
4. Ibid., pp. 21–27.
5. Ibid., *Allies*, pp. 14–15.
6. Shelby Foote, *The Civil War: A Narrative* (New York: Random House, 1974), vol. 3, p. 17.
7. After the war, Churchill pointedly, and at some length, repudiated the notion that he opposed an all-out assault on the European continent. See Churchill, *The Grand Alliance*, pp. 581–582.
8. Ibid., p. 23.
9. Ibid., p. 24.
10. Maurice Matloff and Edwin M. Snell, *Strategic Planning for Coalition Warfare* (Washington, D.C.: Office of the Chief of Military History, Department of the Army), p. 100.
11. Dwight Eisenhower, *Crusade in Europe*, p. 22.
12. John Eisenhower, *Allies*, pp. 23–24.
13. Ibid., p. 18.
14. Admiral Ernest J. King had not yet been confirmed as the new chief of naval operations, but as

Stark's heir apparent and commander in chief, United States Fleet, King held a primary role. Roosevelt had faith in King, and much less in Stark. King was in a delicate position—he attended some Arcadia meetings, but not all. King and Stark both were members of the Joint Chiefs of Staff, according to Forrest C. Pogue (see his *The Supreme Command, U.S. Army in World War II*, Center of Military History, Government Printing Office, Washington, D.C., 1996), until March 1942 when King took over as CNO. See also John Eisenhower *Allies*, p. 17.

15. Pogue, *George C. Marshall: Ordeal and Hope*, pp. 263–265.
16. Ibid., p. 264.
17. John Eisenhower, *Allies*, p. 66. Brooke viewed Marshall as "filled with his own importance," while Marshall described Brooke as "icy and condescending." The relationship improved as the war went on, but it was never comfortable, and neither had charitable words for the other at the war's conclusion.
18. Lord Halifax, the British ambassador to the U.S., seemed to symbolize this British view: "They [the Americans] strike me as very crude and semi-educated," he said. And he was the ambassador and liked Americans.
19. *The Supreme Command*, p. 271. See also Deer, *The Oxford Companion to World War II*, p. 131. Brooke had replaced Dill as commander of the Imperial General Staff in 1941. After he successfully extracted British forces from Dunkirk, it was clear that Dill, who oversaw the operation, was near exhaustion from the pressures of the British defeat in France.

    Churchill and Brooke got along amazingly well, considering their different personalities, though they did not reach the level of understanding and empathy enjoyed by Marshall and Roosevelt. At one point in the war, Churchill exploded over one of Brooke's many disagreements with his views: "He hates me," he railed. "I don't hate him," Brooke responded when he learned of the incident. "I love him, but when the day comes that I tell him he is right when I believe him to be wrong, it will be time for him to get rid of me." At the height of the war, Britishers could sight Brooke in St. James Park, binoculars to eyes, bird-watching; he was an avid ornithologist.
20. David Eisenhower, *Eisenhower at War* (New York: Random House, 1986), pp. 75–77.
21. Ibid., p. 75.
22. Ibid.
23. "Notes Made by General Eisenhower after Conference with General Marshall at 7:45 p.m., December 23, 1941," *DDE*, vol. 1, p. 19.
24. The Papers of General Douglas MacArthur are contained at the MacArthur Memorial Bureau of Archives, Norfolk, Virginia. MacArthur and the papers of his top aides, excepting Eisenhower, can be found in Norfolk.
25. MacArthur maintained after the war that the Europe First strategy made his defense of the Philippines impossible—and he held Marshall and Eisenhower responsible for the decision. The claim is ludicrous: even if Eisenhower and Marshall had been able to find the transport to get troops and planes to the Philippines (a highly dubious proposition), and even if they had gotten them without major casualties (an even more dubious proposition), there were simply not enough of them to make a difference.
26. "To Douglas MacArthur," *DDE*, vol. 1, p. 21 (December 23, 1941).
27. "To Lesley James McNair, Delos Carleton Emmons, Walter Krueger, Ben Lear," *DDE*, vol. 1, p. 22 (December 23, 1941).
28. "Memorandum for Chief of Staff," December ———, 1941, in *DDE*, vol. 1, pp. 23–24. The editors note that "Eisenhower apparently prepared this memorandum just before the second meeting of the British and American Chiefs of Staff on Christmas Day, when Marshall first raised the question of unified command." That is to say, Eisenhower prepared the memorandum after the first meeting of the Chiefs of Staff, on December 24, and the second meeting on December 25. There is only time when Eisenhower could have prepared the memo—and that was on Christmas Eve 1941. Further, Eisenhower must have been directed to write the memo and the notes for the meeting of the twenty-fourth, as the records show he attended only the Arcadia Conference sessions of December 29, 30, and 31 and January 9 and 10.
29. Ibid.

30. Miller, *Ike the Soldier*, p. 52.
31. Ibid., pp. 53–54. See also Stephen E. Ambrose, *Eisenhower: Soldier, General of the Army, President-Elect, 1890–1952* (New York: Simon & Schuster, 1983), pp. 21–22 . Eisenhower was most expansive on the life of his father in Dwight D. Eisenhower, *At Ease: Stories I Tell to Friends* (New York: Doubleday, 1967).
32. Geoffrey Perret, *Eisenhower* (Avon, Mass.: Adams Media, 1999), p. 9. Geoffrey Perret notes: "In respectable families, the more flawed the father, the more it becomes important to obscure the truth."
33. Miller, *Ike the Soldier*, p. 63.
34. Ibid., p. 50.
35. Ibid., pp. 48–49.
36. Perret, *Eisenhower*, p. 31.
37. Dwight Eisenhower, *At Ease*, p. 12.
38. The General Omar N. Bradley Papers are housed at the United States Military Academy, West Point, New York. Miscellaneous correspondence and reports of General Omar N. Bradley can be found at the U.S. Army Military History Institute, Carlisle Barracks, Pennsylvania. The U.S. Military History Institute also houses the papers of Major General John P. Lucas, Major General Terry de la Mesa, Lieutenant General Robert L. Eichelberger, and Major General Orlando W. Ward, and contains Forrest Pogue's valuable monograph *World War II: The Supreme Command*, published now as a part of the U.S. Army in World War II series.
39. The *New York Times*, November 18, 1912.
40. Perret, *Eisenhower*, p. 49.
41. Miller, *Ike the Soldier*, p. 138.
42. Ambrose, *Eisenhower: Soldier, General*, pp. 49–51.
43. Dwight Eisenhower, *At Ease*, p. 152.
44. D'Este, *Eisenhower: A Soldier's Life*, p. 151.
45. Ibid., pp. 152–153.
46. Heinz Guderian, *Achtung—Panzer! Die Entwicklung der Panzerwaffe, ihre Kampftaktik und ihre operativen Maglichkeiten* (Stuttgart, 1937); trans.: *Achtung Panzer! The Development of Armored Forces, their Tactics and Operational Potential* (London: Arms and Armor Press, 1995), p. 57.
47. Dwight Eisenhower, *At Ease*, p. 173.
48. Carlo D'Este, *Patton: A Genius for War* (New York: HarperCollins, 1995), p. 294.
49. Ambrose, *Eisenhower: Soldier, General*, vol. 1, p. 73.
50. Dwight D. Eisenhower, "A Tank Discussion," in *Infantry Journal* 17 (November 20, 1920). Patton's article, "Tanks in Future Wars," appeared in *Infantry Journal* 17 (May 20, 1920).
51. D'Este, *Eisenhower: A Soldiers' Life*, p. 113.
52. Miller, *Ike the Soldier*, p. 192.
53. Eisenhower needed no convincing that a future war would come—but his ideas at this time were not nearly as well developed as Conner's. Looking back, he remembered that he and Patton had discussed the likelihood of a war in Europe while they were at Camp Meade. "George had become convinced . . . as I had—that the Treaty of Versailles had practically guaranteed the outbreak of another great war within something like a quarter century" (quoted in D'Este, *Eisenhower: A Soldier's Life*, p. 153).
54. Miller, *Ike the Soldier*, p. 224.
55. William Manchester, *American Caesar* (Boston: Little, Brown, 1978), p. 34.
56. D. Clayton James, *The Years of MacArthur* (Boston: Houghton Mifflin, 1970), vol. 1, pp. 386–389.
57. D'Este, *Eisenhower: A Soldier's Life*, p. 222.
58. Ibid., p. 224.
59. Miller, *Ike the Soldier*, p. 265.
60. Ibid., p. 221.
61. Ibid., pp. 268–269.
62. Ibid., p. 273.
63. Ibid., pp. 278–279.

64. Ibid., p. 278.
65. Ibid., p. 284.
66. Parrish, *Roosevelt and Marshall*, pp. 219–220.
67. Ibid., p. 221.
68. Ibid.
69. Pogue, *George C. Marshall: Ordeal and Hope*, p. 274.
70. Churchill, *The Grand Alliance*, pp. 574–585.
71. Arthur Bryant, *The Turn of the Tide* (New York: Collins, 1957), p. 82.
72. Parrish, *Roosevelt and Marshall*, p. 221.
73. Ibid. Oddly, a number of biographers of both Marshall and Eisenhower overlook this meeting, conflating it with Marshall's presentation during the Christmas lunch. The key source for the meeting is the unpublished diary of Colonel Paul M. Robinett of Marshall's staff. Robinett's unpublished diary is authoritative and detailed. Entitled "A Part of the Story," it can be found at the George C. Marshall Manuscript Collection at the Virginia Military Institute. (Hereinafter "Robinett Diary.")
74. Parrish, *Roosevelt and Marshall*, p. 221.
75. Ibid., p. 222. See also "Robinett Diary."
76. Parrish, *Roosevelt and Marshall*, p. 222.
77. Ed Cray, *General of the Army* (New York: Rowman and Littlefield, 1990), p. 272.
78. Ibid.
79. Ibid., pp. 272–273. The key to unifying the American command structure was Marshall's meeting with Admiral Harold Stark, who worried that the Navy would be marginalized in any unified command structure.
80. S. Woodburn Kirby, *Singapore: The Chain of Disaster* (London: Cassell, 1957), pp. 264–266.
81. Cray, *General of the Army*, p. 273.
82. Pogue, *George C. Marshall: Ordeal and Hope*, p. 280.
83. Ibid., p. 281. See also Cray, *General of the Army*, p. 274.
84. "War Department Diary," Dwight David Eisenhower, January 4, 1942, Box 22, Misc. File, Pre-Presidential Papers, Eisenhower Library, Abilene, Kansas.
85. Ibid.
86. Miller, *Ike the Soldier*, p. 344.
87. "Churchill and Marshall," August 24, 1967 (reminiscences), Box 8, Post-Presidential Papers, A-WR Series, Eisenhower Library, Abilene, Kansas.

CHAPTER 3: BOLERO

1. "Chronology, 1941–1945," in *The U.S. Army in World War II*, p. 12.
2. Ibid., p. 13.
3. Ibid., p. 14.
4. D'Este, *Eisenhower: A Soldier's Life*, p. 291.
5. "War Department Diary," Dwight David Eisenhower, February 16, 1942 [sic], Box 22, Misc. Files, Pre-Presidential Papers, the Eisenhower Library, Abilene, Kansas.
6. "War Department Diary," Dwight David Eisenhower, January 6, 1953 [sic], Box 22, Misc. Files, Pre-Presidential Papers, the Eisenhower Library, Abilene, Kansas. (The entry is misdated and should read January 6, 1942.)
7. Miller, *Ike the Soldier*, p. 346.
8. Ibid.
9. Ibid.
10. Ibid., p. 343.
11. Geoffrey Perret, *There's a War to Be Won: The United States Army In World War II* (New York: Random House, 1991), p. 54.
12. Ibid.
13. Miller, *Ike the Soldier*, p. 346.

14. *DDE*, vol. 1, p. 127.
15. Ibid., p. 129. Eisenhower is here referring to John Pope of the Civil War—a noted egoist who dillydallied at the Battle of Second Bull Run and so was beaten by Robert E. Lee—and the self-referencing self-made hero of the Revolutionary War, General Horatio Gates.
16. Manchester, *American Caesar*, p. 256.
17. Ibid.
18. "Special Studies, Chronology, 1941–1945," *U.S. Army in World War II*, p. 29.
19. Miller, *Ike the Soldier*, pp. 347–348.
20. Ibid., p. 348.
21. Larrabee, *Commander in Chief*, p. 209.
22. Ibid., p. 208.
23. Thomas M. Coffey, *Hap: The Story of the U.S. Air Force and the Man Who Built It* (New York: Viking, 1982), p. 199.
24. Larrabee, *Commander in Chief*, p. 214.
25. Pogue, *George C. Marshall: Ordeal and Hope*, p. 290.
26. Geoffrey Perret, *Eisenhower* (Adams Media, MA.: 1999), p. 151.
27. D'Este, *Eisenhower: A Soldier's Life*, p. 293.
28. Stephen E. Ambrose, *Eisenhower* (Simon & Schuster, New York: 1983), p. 162.
29. Ibid., p. 298.
30. Miller, *Ike the Soldier*, p. 49.
31. Ibid., p. 357.
32. Milton Eisenhower went on to become president of three universities—Kansas State University, the Pennsylvania State University, and Johns Hopkins University. His work relocating Japanese Americans during World War II is thought to be the reason behind his insistence on establishing the Milton S. Eisenhower Foundation, founded to "identify, fund, evaluate" and "build the capacities of and replicate multiple solution ventures for the inner city, the truly disadvantaged, children, youth and families." Milton Eisenhower viewed his role in the detention of Japanese Americans during World War II as a blot on his career. In part as a result of this experience, he worked diligently, and often under great pressure, to desegregate each of the institutions of higher learning at which he was president.
33. Cray, *General of the Army*, p. 240.
34. Pogue, *George C. Marshall: Ordeal and Hope*, p. 302.
35. Ibid., pp. 303–304.
36. Ibid., p. 304.
37. Ibid., 303.
38. Miller, *Ike the Soldier*, p. 342.
39. D'Este, *Eisenhower: A Soldier's Life*, p. 287.
40. Ibid., p. 302.
41. Miller, *Ike the Soldier*, pp. 351–353.
42. Pogue, *George C. Marshall: Ordeal and Hope*, p. 292.
43. Ibid., p. 293.
44. *DDE*, vol. 1, p. 205.
45. Ibid.
46. Ibid., p. 149.
47. Ibid., p. 174
48. Ibid.
49. Ibid., p. 197.
50. Pogue, *George C. Marshall: Ordeal and Hope*, p. 323.
51. Ibid., p. 304.
52. Ibid., pp. 306–307.
53. *DDE*, vol. 1, p. 205.
54. Pogue, *George C. Marshall: Ordeal and Hope*, p. 315.
55. "Special Studies, Chronology," in *U.S. Army In World War II, 1941–1945*, ed. Mary H. Williams (Washington, D.C.: U.S. Government Printing Office, 1994), p. 30.

56. Miller, *Ike the Soldier*, p. 353.
57. Pogue, *George C. Marshall, Ordeal and Hope*, p. 318. See also Winston S. Churchill, *The Hinge of Fate*, (Boston: Houghton Mifflin, 1950), pp. 280–288.
58. Churchill, *The Hinge of Fate*, p. 283.
59. Pogue, *George C. Marshall: Ordeal and Hope*, p. 319.
60. Hastings Ismay, *The Memoirs of General Lord Ismay* (New York: Viking, 1960), pp. 249–250.
61. Bernard Fergusson, *The Watery Maze, The Story of Combined Operations* (New York: Holt, Rienhart & Winston, 1981), p. 148.
62. Pogue, *George C. Marshall, Ordeal and Hope*, p. 324.
63. Bryant, *The Turn of the Tide*, pp. 288–289.
64. Miller, *Ike the Soldier*, pp. 354–355.
65. *DDE*, vol. 1, p. 267.
66. "Special Studies, Chronology," *U.S. Army In World War II*, p. 34.
67. *DDE*, vol. 1, p. 278.
68. John Keegan, ed., *The Oxford Companion to World War II* (Oxford, U.K.: Oxford University Press, 1995), p. 210.
69. Ibid.
70. Manchester, *American Caesar*, p. 289.
71. Ibid. pp. 289–290.

CHAPTER 4: SLEDGEHAMMER

1. Meirion and Susie Harries, *Soldiers of the Sun: The Rise and Fall of the Imperial Japanese Army* (New York: Random House, 1994), p. 309.
2. Gerhard L. Weinberg, *A World at Arms: A Global History of World War II* (Cambridge, U.K.: Cambridge University Press, 1994), p. 318.
3. Martin Gilbert, *The Second World War: A Complete History* (New York: Henry Holt, 1989), p. 322.
4. Weinberg, *A World at Arms*, p. 296.
5. *DDE*, vol. 1, pp. 260–261.
6. Ibid., pp. 263–264.
7. Miller, *Ike the Soldier*, p. 355.
8. "Memorandum for General Somervell and General Eisenhower," May 16, 1942, *The Papers of George Catlett Marshall*, vol. 3, pp. 203–204.
9. Ibid.
10. Miller, *Ike the Soldier*, p. 356.
11. Ibid.
12. The Papers of Lieutenant General Mark Clark can be found at the Citadel Archive, Charleston, South Carolina. See also Martin Blumenson, *Mark Clark* (New York: Random House, 1985), pp. 9–16; "To Admiral Harold R. Stark," *The Papers of George Catlett Marshall*, vol. 3, pp. 206–207.
13. Miller, *Ike the Soldier*, p. 360.
14. D'Este, *Eisenhower: A Soldier's Life*, p. 251.
15. Ibid., p. 275.
16. Kay Summersby, *Eisenhower Was My Boss* (New York: Prentice Hall, 1948), pp. 1–3.
17. Miller, *Ike the Soldier*, pp. 358–359.
18. Ibid., p. 359.
19. Depuy, *The Harper Encyclopedia of Military Biography*, pp. 520–521.
20. Nigel Hamilton, *Monty: The Making of a General* (New York: McGraw Hill, 1981), pp. 319–320.
21. "Mark Clark, an Oral History," The Papers of Lt. General Mark W. Clark, U.S. Army Military History Institute, Carlisle Barracks, Pennsylvania.
22. Miller, *Ike the Soldier*, p. 360.
23. Ibid.
24. Ambrose, *Supreme Commander, p. 45*.

25. Ibid., pp. 44–45.
26. Reflections on the Arcadia Conference," *The Papers of Dwight David Eisenhower*, Dwight David Eisenhower Library, Box 8, Post–Presidential Papers, A–WR Series.
27. Miller, *Ike the Soldier*, p. 362.
28. Ibid., p. 363.
29. Robert McHenry, ed., *Webster's American Military Biographies* (New York: Dover, 1978), pp. 408–409.
30. Samuel Eliot Morison, *History of United States Naval Operations in World War II*, vol. 1, *The Battle of the Atlantic* (Boston: Atlantic Monthly Press, 1955), p. 41.
31. "To Admiral Harold R. Stark," *The Papers of George Catlett Marshall*, vol. 3, pp. 240–241.
32. Ibid., p. 240. See also "Stark to Marshall," June 1, 1942, G. C. Marshall Papers, Office of Military History, Department of Defense.
33. Keegan, *The Oxford Companion to World War II*, pp. 585–586.
34. "Memorandum for the Commander in Chief, United States Fleet, Subject, Publicity on Pacific Operations," *The Papers of George Catlett Marshall*, vol. 3, p. 227.
35. Pogue, *George C. Marshall: Ordeal and Hope*, p. 327.
36. D'Este, *Eisenhower: A Soldier's Life*, p. 306.
37. "Command arrangements for Bolero," *DDE*, vol. 1, p. 327.
38. "Memorandum to the Chief of Staff," June 6, 1942, ibid., p. 332.
39. Miller, *Ike the Soldier*, p. 364. See also Dwight Eisenhower, *Crusade In Europe*, p. 50.
40. *DDE*, vol. 1, p. 333.
41. D'Este, *Eisenhower: A Soldier's Life*, p. 307.
42. Blumenson, *Mark Clark*, p. 58.
43. D'Este, *Eisenhower, A Soldier's Life*, p. 307.
44. *DDE*, vol. 1, p. 337.
45. Miller, *Ike the Soldier*, p. 357.
46. Parrish, *Roosevelt and Marshall*, p. 281.
47. Ibid., p. 282.
48. Pogue, *George C. Marshall: Ordeal and Hope*, p. 328.
49. *The Papers of George Catlett Marshall*, vol. 3, p. 243. See also *The Papers of Henry L. Stimson*, June 19, 1942 (Diary, 39:101), Yale University Library.
50. David Stone, *War Summits* (Washington, D.C.: Potomac Books, 2005), p. 53.
51. Miller, *Ike the Soldier*, p. 366.
52. Pogue, *George C. Marshall: Ordeal and Hope*, p. 328.
53. Forrest Pogue, "An Interview with George C. Marshall," October 5, 1956. See also Pogue, *George C. Marshall: Ordeal and Hope*, p. 330.
54. Pogue, *George C. Marshall: Ordeal and Hope*, p. 330.
55. Miller, *Ike the Soldier*, p. 367.
56. Ibid., p. 332. There is apparently much disagreement among historians about when Churchill received news of Tobruk. Rick Atkinson (*An Army at Dawn: The War in North Africa, 1942–1943* [New York: Henry Holt, 2002]) writes that Churchill received the news in the Oval Office from Marshall, while Churchill says that he received it from Ismay in his White House room. The dates for the Oval Office meeting are also different in the sources, though Churchill is authoritative, and used here.
57. Ibid., p. 332.
58. Atkinson, *An Army at Dawn, The War in North Africa, 1942–1943*, p. 16.
59. Winston Churchill, *The Hinge of Fate*, p. 333.
60. Ibid., p. 345.
61. D'Este, *Eisenhower: A Soldier's Life*, p. 309.
62. Dwight Eisenhower, *Crusade in Europe*, p. 51.
63. Pogue, *George C. Marshall: Ordeal and Hope*, pp. 334–335.
64. Ibid., p. 339.
65. Ibid., p. 338.
66. *DDE*, vol. 1, pp. 343–344.

CHAPTER 5: ETOUSA

1. Miller, *Ike the Soldier*, p. 372.
2. The letters are a part of *The Papers of Dwight David Eisenhower*, The War Years, vols. 1–5, Alfred D. Chandler, Jr. ed. (Baltimore: Johns Hopkins University Press, 1970). A portion of these (85 of 108) are printed in a separate volume, Joseph P. Hobbs, ed., *Dear General: Eisenhower's Wartime Letters to Marshall* (Baltimore: Johns Hopkins University Press, 1971).

    The 108 personal letters from Eisenhower to Marshall constitute only a small portion of the total correspondence of the two senior commanders during World War II. The primary means of communication was through coded radiograms or coded cables. From time to time, Eisenhower would send personal messages to Marshall couriered via returning officers to Washington from the front. Additionally, the senior commanders had intensive private meetings, during which there were no secretaries or note takers present. With some exceptions, neither Eisenhower nor Marshall characterized these private meetings in postmeeting notes or in their personal papers.
3. Hobbs, *Dear General*, p. 26 (Letter 1, dated June 26, 1942).
4. Pogue, *George C. Marshall: Ordeal and Hope*, p. 371.
5. Ibid., p. 373.
6. Ibid., p. 379.
7. Ibid., p. 380.
8. Ibid.
9. As Forrest Pogue in *George C. Marshall: Ordeal and Hope* summarizes the agreement: "The final directive divided the coming offensive into three parts: Task One, the attack on the Santa Cruz Islands, Tulagi, and adjacent positions to be under the control of Admiral Nimitz; Task Two, the capture of the remainder of the Solomon Islands and the seizure of Lae, Slamaua, and northeast New Guinea; and Task Three, the attack on Rabaul and adjacent position, were to be under General MacArthur. Amphibious forces in all three phases would be placed under naval task force commanders. The Joint Chiefs of Staff would decide on the composition of forces to be used, the timing of tasks, and the passage of command from Nimitz to MacArthur" (p. 381.)
10. Marshall's solution was brilliant. Halsey and MacArthur immediately became lasting friends, something that would never have happened had Nimitz been in Halsey's place. MacArthur loved Halsey (which is more than many others have said) and within minutes of meeting him said: "If you come with me, I'll make you a greater man than Nelson ever dreamed of being." That seemed to suit Halsey, who had such dreams. Likewise, Halsey's praise of MacArthur flows against almost everything we know of MacArthur's view of the Navy: "I have seldom seen a man who makes a quicker, stronger, more favorable impression." See Manchester, *American Caesar*, p. 333.
11. Arthur H. Vandenberg, *The Private Papers of Senator Vandenberg* (New York: Greenwood Press, 1974), p. 76.
12. Pogue, *George C. Marshall: Ordeal and Hope*, p. 374.
13. Forrest Pogue, "Interview with George C. Marshall," October 29, 1956.
14. Larrabee, *Commander in Chief*, p. 354. Nimitz's humor was so dry that it remains a part of Navy lore. His wife was surprised at his downcast look when Roosevelt promoted him to commander in chief, U.S. Fleet. "You always wanted to command the Pacific Fleet," she said in confusion. "Darling," he answered, "the fleet's at the bottom of the sea."
15. Pogue, *George C. Marshall: Ordeal and Hope*, p. 401.
16. *The Papers of George Catlett Marshall*, vol. 3, p. 251n. Brooke was not as impressed with the American training exercise he had witnessed at Fort Jackson during his trip to the U.S. in June. He noted afterward: "The American system of individual and elementary training seems excellent, but I am not so certain that their higher training is good enough, or that they have yet realized the standard of training required."
17. Pogue, *George C. Marshall: Ordeal and Hope*, p. 310.
18. Bryant, *Turn of the Tide*, p. 74. The Papers of Lord Alanbrooke (the title and general spelling of his name changed after he was named a lord at the end of World War II) are contained in the manuscript collection of the Imperial War Museum, London.

19. *The Papers of George Catlett Marshall*, vol. 3, pp. 246–248.

20. Hobbs, *Dear General*, pp. 28–29 (June 30, 1942).

21. *The Papers of George Catlett Marshall*, vol. 3, pp. 258–260.

22. *DDE*, vol. 1, pp. 378–379.

23. *The Papers of George Catlett Marshall*, vol. 3, p. 271.

24. "Memorandum for Admiral King," Colonel John R. Deane Memorandum, National Archives and Records Administration, #165 (Operations and Plans Division, General Staff), Executive Group File 8, Book 6.

25. "Memorandum for the President," George Marshall, Ernest King, and Henry H. Arnold Memorandum, National Archives and Records Administration, #165 (Operations and Plans Division, General Staff), Executive Group File 5, Item 1.

26. *Stimson Diary*, July 12, 1942.

27. Harry C. Butcher, *My Three Years with Eisenhower* (New York: Simon & Schuster, 1946), pp. 18–19. Butcher was asked to keep a running account of daily activities at Eisenhower's head-quarters as a part of his job. Butcher normally dictated these to a secretary at the end of each day, had them typed, then reread and edited them, adding his own comments at the end of each day or series of days. At the end of the war he compiled and edited the diary and put it into correct chronological order by checking against the official records. It is not known what Eisenhower wanted to do with the diary, but it is thought he wanted to refer to it as a check on his memory during the war years. Butcher does not cite any instance where Eisenhower did so.

28. *The Papers of George Catlett Marshall*, vol. 3, p. 274.

29. D'Este, *Eisenhower: A Soldier's Life*, p. 317.

30. Ibid.

31. Dominick Graham and Shelford Bidwell, *Coalitions, Politicians and Generals* (London: Brassey's, 1993), p. 238.

32. Harry Butcher met Eisenhower in 1926, and joined CBS in 1929. The Harry Butcher Papers are a part of the Papers of President Dwight D. Eisenhower, the Dwight D. Eisenhower Presidential Library, Abilene, Kansas. The Harry C. Butcher Papers in Abilene include the diary, clippings of Eisenhower from the period, early correspondence between Butcher and Eisenhower, and pho-tographs collected by Butcher. Parts of the Butcher book appeared in the *Saturday Evening Post* after the war.

33. Butcher, *My Three Years with Eisenhower*, p. 112.

34. McHenry, *Webster's American Military Biographies*, pp. 404–405. Spaatz added an extra *a* to his name in 1937, at the request of his wife, who wanted it spelled as it was pronounced ("spots"), and received his nickname because, like another West Point cadet, F. J. Toohey, he had red hair.

35. Hobbs, *Dear General*, p. 29.

36. Ibid.

37. Eisenhower did not request that Summersby be his driver, but recognized her about one month following his move to London. She was serving as Carl Spaatz's driver at the time, and Eisenhower appropriated her to work for him.

38. Miller, *Ike the Soldier*, p. 373.

39. Ibid., p. 374.

40. Ibid., p. 373.

41. Butcher, *My Three Years with Eisenhower*, p. 8.

42. Summersby, *Eisenhower Was My Boss*, p. 27.

43. While Marshall had arrived in England on the previous evening, Eisenhower sent him a hand-written note saying that owing to the lateness of the hour, he would brief him the following morn-ing.

44. *DDE*, vol. 1, pp. 400–401.

45. "The Diary of Field Marshal Lord Alanbrooke," July 15 and July 17, 1942, Liddell Hart Center for Military Archives, Kings College, London. Field Marshal Alan Brooke was invested with the title "Field Marshal the Viscount Alanbrooke" following the end of World War II.

46. "Conclusions as to the Practicability of Sledgehammer," *DDE*, vol. 1, p. 389.

47. "To George Catlett Marshall and Ernest Joseph King," ibid., pp. 393–396.
48. Churchill, *The Hinge of Fate*, p. 401. Churchill's six-volume treatment of the Second World War is primarily a compilation of government papers, memos, and correspondence, interspersed with Churchill's commentary. In parts it is unreadable. He received the Nobel Prize in Literature for the work.
49. D'Este, *Eisenhower: A Soldier's Life*, p. 335.
50. Miller, *Ike the Soldier*, p. 387.
51. "To Harry Cecil Butcher," *DDE*, vol. 1, p. 405.
52. Churchill, *The Hinge of Fate*, p. 404.
53. Forrest Pogue, "Interview with George C. Marshall," September 28, 1956.
54. D'Este, *Eisenhower: A Soldier's Life*, p. 332.
55. Ibid., p. 336.
56. Miller, *Ike the Soldier*, p. 388.
57. "To Lieutenant General Dwight D. Eisenhower," *The Papers of George Catlett Marshall*, vol. 3, p. 283.
58. Ibid., pp. 284–285.
59. D'Este, *Eisenhower: A Soldier's Life*, p. 336.
60. Ibid., p. 439
61. Major General Richard W. Stephens. "Northwest Africa: Seizing the Initiative in the West," *U.S. Army in World War II, Mediterranean Theater of Operations* (Washington, D.C.: Government Printing Office, 1956), p. 25.
62. John Slessor, *The Central Blue* (London: Cassel, 1956), p. 131.
63. Miller, *Ike the Soldier*, p. 388. Eisenhower was told by one senior British commander that it now seemed likely that the invasion of France would not come until 1944—after the German defeat in North Africa. "In other words," Eisenhower answered, "Roundup may be described in aviator's language as 'ticking without a load.'" This was the language aviators used to describe an idling propeller.
64. "To Fox Conner," *DDE*, vol. 1, p. 485.
65. Hobbs, *Dear General*, pp. 30–31.
66. Ibid., p. 31.
67. Stephens, "Northwest Africa," p. 15.
68. Ibid.
69. Ibid.
70. David Eisenhower, *Eisenhower at War*, p. 383.
71. John Eisenhower, *Allies*, p. 122.
72. Ibid., p. 82.
73. Dwight Eisenhower, *Crusade in Europe*, p. 76.
74. Rommel viewed Auchinleck as one of the greatest commanders he ever faced. Churchill criticized him ruthlessly, but Auchinleck is more sinned against than sinner: his subordinate officers were inferior, his army was poorly supplied, and any attack on Rommel at the time that Churchill proposed would have been disastrous. Auchinleck's career was marred by pitfalls and minor tragedies: he refused later commands when it would have meant replacing his friends (a self-abnegation that was not rewarded with praise), and his wife left him for another officer in the wake of the war. Churchill praised Montgomery for prompt action after he appointed him Auchinleck's successor, but in fact Montgomery's offensive took place well after one that had been planned by his predecessor—and was backed by Churchill's call for a resupply of the new commander that Auchinleck never enjoyed. See Dupuy, *Harper Encyclopedia of Military Biography*, pp. 53–54.
75. John Eisenhower, *Allies*, p. 122.
76. *Hobbs, Dear General*, p. 41.
77. Stephens, "Northwest Africa," pp. 34–35.
78. *The Papers of George Catlett Marshall*, vol. 3, p. 326.
79. Butchers, *My Three Years With Eisenhower*, pp. 83–87.

80. Ibid., pp. 39–42.
81. Ibid., pp. 46–48.
82. Ibid., pp. 50–53.
83. Ibid., p. 84.
84. Ladislas Farago, *Patton: Order and Triumph* (New York: Ivan Obolensky Publishing, 1963), p. 83.
85. "Patton Diary," United States Military History Institute, Carlisle, Pennsylvania, entry for "August 11, 1942."
86. Hobbs, *Dear General*, p. 31.
87. *The Papers of George Catlett Marshall*, vol. 3, p. 367.
88. Ibid., p. 368.
89. D'Este, *Eisenhower: A Soldier's Life*, p. 328.
90. Ibid., p. 329.
91. Churchill, *The Hinge of Fate*, p. 472.
92. Hobbs, *Dear General*, p. 50.
93. Ibid.
94. *The Papers of George Catlett Marshall*, vol. 3, pp. 428–429.
95. Ibid., p. 428.
96. Atkinson, *An Army at Dawn*, p. 94.
97. *DDE*, vol. 1, p. 655n.
98. Ibid., pp. 58–59.
99. *DDE*, vol. 2, p. 668.

Chapter 6: Torch

1. Pogue, *George C. Marshall: Ordeal and Hope*, p. 398.
2. Ibid.
3. Ibid., p. 399.
4. D'Este, *Eisenhower: A Soldier's Life*, p. 313.
5. "Mamie Doud Eisenhower to D. D. Eisenhower," August 28, 1942, Box 1 (John S. D. Eisenhower), Eisenhower Library, Abilene, Kansas.
6. "DDE to MDE," November 8, 1942, Box 1 (John S. D. Eisenhower), Eisenhower Library, Abilene, KS.
7. Butcher, *My Three Years with Eisenhower*, p. 248.
8. Ibid., p. 247.
9. Ibid., p. 248.
10. Ibid., p. 173.
11. Ibid., p. 174.
12. "November 8, 1942," *DDE*, vol. 2, p. 672. This was the second in a series of hundreds of detailed reports that Eisenhower would write to the combined chiefs, a habit he had undertaken at the beginning of the Torch operation. Eisenhower's focus in the early cables, and throughout, would be on diplomatic matters, with less emphasis on military operations.
13. *DDE*, vol. 2, p. 673. Eisenhower used Marshall's new code name in the transmission, instructing Smith "Transmit following personal to *wow.*"
14. The Academy of Political Science is a part of the American Political Science Association. Marshall's appearance at the dinner was a part of the organization's annual meeting. The organization included some of the most senior political science scholars in the nation, including a large number of government policymakers. The APSA circulated his remarks as a part of its quarterly journal. (Political Science Quarterly, "Remarks of General George C. Marshll . . . ," Spring 1943).
15. Stephens, "Northwest Africa," pp. 198–199.
16. Atkinson, *An Army at Dawn*, pp. 75–78.
17. Ibid., p. 76.

18. Ibid.
19. *DDE*, vol. 2, p. 594.
20. D'Este, *Patton: A Genius for War*, pp. 440–441. See also Pogue, *George C. Marshall: Ordeal and Hope*, p. 417.
21. Stephens, "Northwest Africa," pp. 262–263.
22. Ibid., p. 263. In all of the negotiations in North Africa, the primary difficulty became the inability of the Vichy government to determine its policy course. The differing orders issued from the Vichy government caught the French in North Africa by surprise, leading them to believe that the leaders of their government might be under threat from the Germans—as they certainly were. In the midst of the negotiations, the Allies (and Eisenhower) had to deal with two sets of French leaders, further complicating the negotiations.
23. Atkinson, *An Army at Dawn*, pp. 121–122.
24. *DDE*, vol. 2, p. 705.
25. Stephens, "Northwest Africa," p. 265.
26. Hobbs, *Dear General*, pp. 88–89 ("November 9, 1942").
27. *DDE*, vol. 2, p. 709.
28. Pogue, *George C. Marshall: Ordeal and Hope*, pp. 419–420.
29. Ibid., p. 420.
30. Ibid., p. 421.
31. *The Papers of George Catlett Marshall*, vol. 3, pp. 444–445.
32. Ibid., p. 447.
33. Stephen E. Ambrose and Richard H. Immerman, *Milton S. Eisenhower: Educational Statesman*, (Baltimore: Johns Hopkins University Press, 1983), p. 70.
34. Pogue, *George C. Marshall: Ordeal and Hope*, p. 421. See also Robert E. Sherwood, *Roosevelt and Hopkins: An Intimate History* (New York: Enigma Books, 1949). p. 653.
35. John Eisenhower, *Allies*, p. 207.
36. Eisenhower's villa was hardly palatial: the water had been cut as a result of the fight for Algiers, and the weather was cold. A second villa was put aside for Mark Clark. The Allied Forces Headquarters remained at the Hotel St. George, in Algiers, its rooms becoming a warren of offices and bedrooms that housed the Allied high command.
37. Milton Eisenhower, *The President Is Calling* (Garden City, Doubleday, 1974), p. 141.
38. Stephens, "North Africa," p. 357.
39. D'Este, *Eisenhower: A Soldier's Life*, p. 359.
40. Stephens, "Northwest Africa" pp. 280–283.
41. Ibid., pp. 283–284.
42. Ibid., p. 261.
43. Ibid., p. 326.
44. Ibid., pp. 330–331.
45. Hobbs, *Dear General*, p. 91.
46. *DDE*, vol. 2, p. 811.
47. *The Papers of George Catlett Marshall*, vol. 3, p. 488.
48. D'Este, *Patton: A Genius for War*, p. 464.
49. Butcher, *My Three Years with Eisenhower*, p. 229.
50. Ibid., p. 229.
51. D'Este, *Eisenhower: A Soldier's Life*, p. 377.
52. *DDE*, vol. 2, p. 846.
53. Butcher, *My Three Years with Eisenhower*, p. 230.
54. John Eisenhower, *Allies*, pp. 215–217.
55. Ibid., p, 227.
56. Pogue, *George C. Marshall: Organizer of Victory*, pp. 20–21.
57. Pogue, *George C. Marshall: Ordeal and Hope*, p. 425.
58. Pogue, *George C. Marshall: Organizer of Victory*, pp. 23–30.
59. Ibid., pp. 30–31.

60. Atkinson, *An Army at Dawn*, p. 281.
61. Field Marshal Lord Alanbrooke, *War Diaries, 1939–1945*, Alex Dancheve and Daniel Todman eds. (Berkeley: University of California Press, 2001), pp. 350–352.
62. *Eisenhower: A Soldier's Life*, p. 383.
63. John Eisenhower, *Allies*, p. 231.
64. Ibid., p. 248–249.
65. Ibid., pp. 251–252.
66. Stephens, "Northwest Africa," pp. 147–170.
67. Ibid. pp. 251–252, 349–355.
68. D'Este, *Eisenhower: A Soldier's Life*, p. 378.
69. Dwight Eisenhower, *Crusade in Europe*, p. 139.
70. Ibid.
71. D'Este, *Eisenhower: A Soldier's Life*, p. 386.
72. Butcher, *My Three Years with Eisenhower*, p. 248.
73. D'Este, *Eisenhower: A Soldier's Story*, p. 365.
74. Ibid., p. 251.
75. Ibid.
76. Field Marshal Earl Alexander of Tunis, *The Alexander Memoirs* (New York: McGraw-Hill, 1962), pp. 41–57.
77. Ambrose, *Supreme Commander*, p. 222.
78. Dwight Eisenhower, *Crusade in Europe*, p. 139.
79. Pogue, *George C. Marshall: Organizer of Victory*, p. 189.
80. Ambrose, *Supreme Commander*, p. 140.
81. D'Este, *Eisenhower: A Soldier's Life*, pp. 386–387.
82. *Ibid.*, p. 386.
83. Office of the Chief, Military History, U.S. Army, "Interviews with Marshall," Part 1, July 25, 1949.
84. Lord Alanbrooke, "Notes On My Life," Alanbrooke Papers, Imperial War Museum, London.
85. Ambrose, *Supreme Commander*, pp. 162–163.
86. Harold Macmillan, *The Blast of War, 1939–1945* (New York: Harper & Row, 1968), pp. 220–221.
87. D'Este, *Eisenhower: A Soldier's Life*, p. 386.
88. Ibid.
89. *DDE*, vol. 2, p. 946.

CHAPTER 7: KASSERINE

1. Stephens, "Northwest Africa," p. 407. Rommel had proposed the attack, arguing that the Axis had a small window of opportunity in combining his forces with Arnim prior to the linkup between Eisenhower and Montgomery's army.
2. Ibid., pp. 409–410.
3. Ibid., p. 411.
4. Atkinson, *An Army at Dawn*, p. 346.
5. Keegan, *The Oxford Companion to World War II*, pp. 505–506.
6. D'Este, *Eisenhower: A Soldier's Life*, p. 391.
7. Russell F. Weigley, *Eisenhower's Lieutenants* (Bloomington: Indiana University Press, 1981), p. 81.
8. D'Este, *Eisenhower: A Soldier's Life*, p. 393. See also *A Soldier's Story*, p. 27.
9. D'Este, *Eisenhower: A Soldier's Life*, p. 397.
10. Atkinson: *An Army at Dawn*, pp. 274–275.
11. Butcher, *My Three Years with Eisenhower*, p. 260.
12. Atkinson, *An Army at Dawn*, pp. 276–278.
13. Ibid., p. 279.
14. Ibid.
15. Stephens, "Northwest Africa," pp. 413–415. See also Atkinson, *An Army at Dawn*, p. 352. Given Ward's rage at Fredendall, we might suppose that he understood the enemy's intentions and was

working to build a stout defense. Not so: "The enemy was much stronger than the Americans realized," the official history notes.

16. Stephens, "Northwest Africa," p. 417.
17. Ibid., p. 423. Also see Atkinson, *An Army at Dawn*, p. 353.
18. Stephens, "Northwest Africa," p. 424.
19. Ibid., p. 425.
20. Ibid., p. 426.
21. Ibid., pp. 430–432.
22. Ibid., p. 432.
23. Field Marshal Earl Alexander of Tunis, *The Alexander Memoirs*, p. 131–132.
24. Pogue, *George C. Marshall: Ordeal and Hope*, p. 407. Marshall and Allen had served together in World War I. Many of Marshall's colleagues wondered why the chief of staff would have such confidence in a West Point washout, and a man whom Marshall had saved from imminent court-martial, or so the story goes.
25. Stephens, "Northwest Africa," pp. 456–457.
26. Ibid., p. 441.
27. Ibid., p. 443.
28. Ibid., pp. 465–466.
29. Ibid., pp. 469–470.
30. Ibid.
31. Pogue, *George C. Marshall: Organizer of Victory*, p. 182.
32. *The Papers of George Catlett Marshall*, vol. 3, pp. 553–554.
33. Pogue, *George C. Marshall: Organizer of Victory*, p. 184.
34. D'Este, *Eisenhower: A Soldier's Life*, p. 386.
35. Ibid., p. 395.
36. Michael J. McKeough and Richard Lockridge, *Sgt. Mickey and General Ike* (New York: Putnam, 1946), p. 73.
37. D'Este, *Eisenhower: A Soldier's Life*, p. 396.
38. Major General Ernest Harmon, *Combat Commander* (Englewood Cliffs, N.J.: Prentice-Hall, 1970), pp. 111–121.
39. D'Este, *Eisenhower: A Soldier's Life*, p. 396.
40. Atkinson, *An Army at Dawn*, p. 345.
41. Omar N. Bradley, *A Soldier's Story* (New York: Random House, 1999), p. 42.
42. Atkinson, *An Army at Dawn*, p. 274.
43. Dwight Eisenhower, *Crusade in Europe*, p. 147.
44. Ibid., p. 150.
45. Hobbs, *Dear General*, p. 104.
46. *The Papers of George Catlett Marshall*, vol. 3, p. 574.
47. *DDE*, vol. 2, p. 1010.
48. Butcher, *My Three Years with Eisenhower*, pp. 273–274.
49. Ibid., p. 274.
50. *The Papers of George Catlett Marshall*, vol. 3, p. 580.
51. *DDE*, vol. 2, p. 1007.
52. Historian Rick Atkinson called Eisenhower's comment "unctuous poppycock"—but Fredendall did perform well, as long as guns weren't firing.
53. Hobbs, *Dear General*, p. 105.
54. The most obvious example in U.S. military history may well be the dismissal of General Fitz–John Porter by General John Pope after the Battle of Second Manassas. Porter was convicted by a court-martial and dismissed from the service. The claims were manifestly unjust and politically motivated. It took nearly twenty years for Porter to clear his name; vindication finally came by verdict of a specially appointed commission, in 1886. There are few senior military officers of the U.S. military who are not familiar with the Porter case, which has had a profound and continuing impact on senior-level command relations.
55. Atkinson, *An Army at Dawn*, p. 400.

56. Ibid., p. 365.
57. *DDE*, vol. 2, pp. 965–966.
58. Stephens, "Northwest Africa," pp. 477–478.
59. Ambrose, *Supreme Commander*, p. 164.
60. Ibid., p. 188.
61. Atkinson, *An Army at Dawn*, p. 218.
62. Stephens, "Northwest Africa," p. 489.
63. Mary H. William, "Chronology," *U.S. Army in World War II* (Washington, D.C.: Center of Military History, 1994), p. 90. The Red Army gave the Germans no respite, beginning its drive on Rostov immediately after Paulus's surrender.
64. Keegan, *The Oxford Companion to World War II*, pp. 823–825.
65. John Erickson, *The Road to Berlin: Stalin's War with Germany* (New Haven, Conn.: Yale University Press, 1983), p. 23.
66. Stephens, "Northwest Africa," pp. 350, 509–511.
67. Weinberg, *A World at Arms*, p. 295.
68. Ibid., p. 452.
69. Stephens, "Northwest Africa," pp. 468–470.
70. Gilbert, *The Second World War*, p. 377.
71. *DDE*, vol. 2, p. 984.
72. D'Este, *Patton: A Genius for War*, p. 462.
73. Bradley, *A Soldier's Story*, p. 44–45.
74. D'Este, *Patton: A Genius for War*, p. 463.
75. Bradley, *A Soldier's Story*, p. 52.
76. Stephens, "Northwest Africa," pp. 521–523.
77. Ibid., p. 531.
78. Atkinson, *An Army at Dawn*, p. 443.
79. Ibid., p. 452.
80. "The Papers of George S. Patton, Jr.," Diary Collection, Manuscript Division, Library of Congress, March 28, 1943.
81. D'Este, *Patton: A Genius for War*, p. 480.
82. Ibid.
83. Arthur Tedder, *With Prejudice* (London: Cassel, 1966), p. 411. The cable to Marshall was apparently discarded by Eisenhower, as it is not contained in any of the official histories or in his papers.
84. D'Este, *A Soldier's Life*, p. 398.
85. Ibid.
86. "The Papers of George S. Patton, Jr.," Diary Collection, Manuscript Division, Library of Congress, April 9, 1943.
87. Ibid., April 11 and 12, 1943.
88. Bradley, *A Soldier's Story*, p. 208.
89. Atkinson, *An Army at Dawn*, p. 520.
90. Bradley, *A Soldier's Story*, p. 212.
91. *DDE*, vol. 2, p. 1071.
92. *The Papers of George Catlett Marshall*, vol. 3, pp. 643–644.
93. Ibid., p. 643.
94. Bradley, *A Soldier's Story*, p. 59.
95. D'Este, *Eisenhower: A Soldier's Life*, p. 402.
96. Ibid., p. 402. Bradley took umbrage at this, thinking Eisenhower was being patronizing. The tension between the two dated from this meeting and lasted through the war.
97. Stephens, "Northwest Africa," p. 609.
98. Atkinson, *An Army at Dawn*, p. 520.
99. Stephens, "Northwest Africa," p. 660–661.
100. *The Papers of George Catlett Marshall*, vol. 3, p. 681.

CHAPTER 8: HUSKY

1. Pogue, *George C. Marshall: Organizer of Victory*, p. 170.
2. Katherine Tupper Marshall, *Together: Annals of an Army Wife* (New York: Tupper & Love, 1946), pp. 140–142.
3. Marshall eventually folded up his chair and went inside. He ignored the original order, he said, because he thought he was close enough to his cottage to meet the regulations. The regulations had been in place for security purposes since December 7, 1941, along some American coastlines.
4. Marshall, *Together, Annals of an Army Wife*, p. 180.
5. *The Papers of George Catlett Marshall*, vol. 3, p. 583.
6. Conner's views, transmitted to Marshall during World War I and to Eisenhower during their service together in the Panama Canal Zone, were institutionalized in Army doctrine in the period 1920–1924, when Conner recast the Army's structure under the direction of General of the Army John J. Pershing. The restructuring, to make the U.S. Army more alliance friendly, has been the subject of a number of Army War College monographs that also touch on the Conner–Eisenhower relationship. See "Relations Between War Department and the Forces in the Field," November 4, 1920, WPD Course 6, 1920–21; "Replacements," February 4, 1921, Operations Course No. 22, 1920–21; "Supply Division WDGS," December 1, 1925, G–4 Course 5, 1925–26, Army War College Files, Carlisle, Pennsylvania.
7. David Eisenhower, *Eisenhower at War*, pp. 62–64.
8. Pogue, *George C. Marshall: Ordeal and Hope*, p. 338.
9. Marshall was careful about such proprieties. He addressed letters to retired officers by using their rank ("Dear Major General Martin," he wrote to a man who had retired in 1927); to less senior but foreign officers he wrote as he did to Eisenhower (he addressed Sir John Dill as "Dear Dill"); and to men of Eisenhower's generation who had yet to prove themselves he wrote using their full title, i.e., "To Major General Alexander M. Patch."
10. "Patton Diary," April 11 and 12, 1943.
11. Omar N. Bradley and Clay Blair, *A General's Life: An Autobiography* (New York: Simon & Schuster, 1993), p. 151. Historians have disagreed about whether Bradley would have allowed these opinions to be published had he lived—his book was finished by Clay Blair, an impeccable historian who showed transcripts of Bradley's interviews to subdue the critics. Those who knew Bradley best never doubted his views on Eisenhower.
12. *DDE*, vol. 2, p. 1016.
13. Ibid., p. 1132.
14. Ibid., p. 1129.
15. John Eisenhower, *Allies*, pp. 291–299. See also Stone, *War Summits*, pp. 78–79.
16. Pogue, *George C. Marshall: Organizer of Victory*, pp. 143–144.
17. Churchill, *The Hinge of Fate*, pp. 706–709. Churchill, pointedly, listed a direct assault on Europe through France as well down the list of Allied priorities: after invading Italy, taking the weight off Russia, the strategic bombing of Germany, and responding to Japanese aggression. The president was even more pointed, asking what should take place in Europe after Husky.
18. Ibid., p. 707.
19. Ibid., p. 708.
20. "Minutes of the Joint Chiefs of Staff 81st Meeting," May 14, 1943, in *Foreign Relations of the United States* (Washington, D.C.: Government Printing Office, 1961). See also Pogue, *George C. Marshall: Organizer of Victory*, p. 198.
21. Bryant, *The Turn of the Tide*, p. 508.
22. John Eisenhower, *Allies*, p. 295.
23. Ibid., p. 296.
24. Churchill, *The Hinge of Fate*, p. 709.
25. "Minutes of the Meetings of the Combined Chiefs of Staff," May 17, 1943, in *Foreign Relations of the United States*, Section 4.

26. Pogue, *George C. Marshall: Organizer of Victory*, pp. 203–205. See also David Eisenhower, *Eisenhower at War*, p. 20.
27. *The Papers of George Catlett Marshall*, vol. 3, p. 706. See also Bryant, *Turn of the Tide*, pp. 508–509, and Ismay, *Memoirs*, pp. 293–300.
28. Cray, *General of the Army*, pp. 397–398.
29. "Minutes of the Meetings of the Combined Chiefs of Staff," May 19, 1943, in *Foreign Relations of the United States*. See also John Eisenhower, *Allies*, p. 298.
30. John Eisenhower, *Allies*, p. 299.
31. Ibid.
32. "Stimson Diary," May 25, 1943. See also Pogue, *George C. Marshall: Organizer of Victory*, p. 213.
33. D'Este, *Eisenhower: A Soldier's Life*, p. 427.
34. Ibid., p. 428.
35. Pogue, *George C. Marshall: Organizer of Victory*, p. 217.
36. *Ibid*, p. 220.
37. Butcher, *My Three Years with Eisenhower*, p. 316.
38. Ibid.
39. Ibid., p. 317.
40. D'Este, *Eisenhower: A Soldier's Life*, p. 428.
41. Ibid.
42. Butcher, *My Three Years with Eisenhower*, pp. 320–321.
43. Ibid., p. 316.
44. Ibid., p. 323.
45. Bernard Law Montgomery, *Montgomery of Alamein: The Memoirs of Field Marshal Montgomery* (New York: World Publishing, 1958), p. 165.
46. Norman Gelb, *Ike and Monty, Generals at War* (New York: William Morrow, 1994), pp. 48–49.
47. Ibid., p. 219.
48. Ibid., p. 221.
49. Bryant, *Turn of the Tide*, p. 525. See also Pogue, *George C. Marshall: Organizer of Victory*, p. 218.
50. Lord Moran, *Churchill: Taken from the Diaries of Lord Moran* (Boston: Houghton Mifflin, 1966), p. 109.
51. Butcher, *My Three Years with Eisenhower*, p. 323.
52. Thomas Johnson, "America's Number 1 Soldier," *Readers Digest*, February 17, 1944.
53. Albert N. Garland and Howard McGaw Smyth, *Sicily and the Surrender of Italy* (Washington, D.C.: Center of Military History, Government Printing Office, 2002), pp. 64–65.
54. Ibid., pp. 123–124.
55. Ibid., pp. 115–132.
56. "Patton Diary," May 22, 1943.
57. D'Este, *Patton: A Genius for War*, p. 495.
58. Bradley, *A Soldier's Story*, p. 433. See also Butcher, *My Three Years with Eisenhower*, p. 360.
59. Butcher, *My Three Years with Eisenhower*, p. 360.
60. Bradley, *A Soldier's Story*, pp. 106–109.
61. Garland and Smyth, *Sicily and the Surrender of Italy*, pp. 206–208.
62. Bradley and Blair, *A General's Life*, pp. 188–189.
63. Ibid.
64. Garland and Smyth, *Sicily and the Surrender of Italy*, pp. 251–253.
65. Ibid., pp. 256–257.
66. *Ibid.*, pp. 305–306.
67. Ibid., p. 411. The official account of the battle by the U.S. Army notes that both Montgomery and Patton had innumerable opportunities to interdict the German ferrying operations but unaccountably failed to do so. Allied air power remained unfocused on the German escape. The Americans and British were certain that the Germans could only conduct their evacuation of Sicily during darkness, a major mistake (and one damning to Allied leadership): of holding the enemy's capabilities in contempt.
68. Ibid., pp. 382–384.

69. Ibid., pp. 411–412.
70. *DDE*, vol. 2, p. 1287.
71. Ibid.
72. *The Papers of George Catlett Marshall*, vol. 4, pp. 78–79.
73. Ibid., p. 84.
74. *DDE*, vol. 2, pp. 1258–1259.
75. D'Este, *Patton: A Genius for War*, p. 532.
76. "Conferences at Washington and Quebec," in *Foreign Relations of the United States*, pp. 467–472.
77. D'Este, *Eisenhower: A Soldier's Life*, p. 439.
78. Ibid.
79. "Patton Diaries," August 3, 1943, p. 243.
80. D'Este, *Eisenhower: A Soldier's Life*, p. 439. See also Butcher, *My Three Years with Eisenhower*, p. 393.
81. *DDE*, vol. 2, pp. 1340–1341.
82. D'Este, *Patton: A Genius for War*, pp. 537–539.
83. Dwight Eisenhower, *Crusade in Europe*, p. 201.
84. Butcher, *My Three Years with Eisenhower*, p. 403.
85. Ibid., p. 405.
86. *DDE*, vol. 2, p. 1353.
87. Ibid.
88. D'Este, *Eisenhower: A Soldier's Life*, p. 441.

CHAPTER 9: AVALANCHE

1. Stone, *War Summits*, pp. 85–91.
2. *The Papers of George Catlett Marshall*, vol. 4, p. 85.
3. Ibid., p. 84.
4. Ibid.
5. Ibid., p. 86.
6. "Stimson Diaries," 1944, pp. 84–85.
7. Bryant, *Turn of the Tide*, pp. 577–580.
8. *War Diaries*, pp. 437–39.
9. "Conferences at Washington and Quebec, 1943," in *Foreign Relations of the United States*, pp. 1024–1025.
10. Field Marshal Lord Alanbrooke, *War Diaries, 1939–1945*, Alex Damcheu and Daniel Todman, ed. (Berkeley, CA: University of California Press, 2001), p. 447.
11. *The Papers of George Catlett Marshall*, vol. 4, p. 91.
12. Winston S. Churchill, *Closing the Ring* (vol. 5 of *The Second World War*) (Boston: Houghton Mifflin, 1951), p. 116. Churchill expressed his desire that the Allies take a lunge into the Balkans ("... they are aflame," he said) in letters to South African prime minister Jan Smuts, who returned the thought by noting that preparations for the cross–Channel invasion should be "slowed down." Churchill realized when he heard this that he might have gone too far, and would incur the ire of Roosevelt—who might think that he had broken his pledge from Quebec. "There can be no question whatever of breaking arrangements we have made with the United States for 'Overlord,'" he wrote to Smuts on September 11.
13. Ibid., p. 104.
14. *DDE*, vol. 2, p. 1390.
15. Garland and Smyth, *Sicily and the Surrender of Italy*, pp. 482–483.
16. Martin Blumenson, *Salerno to Cassino, the US Army in World War II* (Washington, D.C.: Center for Military History, U.S. Government Printing Office, 1969), pp. 80–82.
17. Carlo D'Este, *Fatal Decision: Anzio and the Battle for Rome* (New York: HarperCollins, 1992), p. 41.
18. Blumenson, *Salerno to Cassino*, p. 99.
19. D'Este, *Fatal Decision*, p. 40.

20. Blumenson, *Salerno to Cassino*, p. 98.
21. Ibid., p. 103.
22. Mark Clark, *Calculated Risk* (New York: George G. Harrap, 1951), p. 91.
23. Blumenson, *Salerno to Cassino*, p. 116.
24. Ibid.
25. Ibid., p. 117.
26. Ibid., p. 150.
27. Ibid., pp. 118–119.
28. Ibid., p. 119.
29. Ibid., pp. 123–124.
30. Ibid., p. 126.
31. Ibid., p. 127.
32. Ibid., p. 130.
33. Ibid., p. 133.
34. *DDE*, vol. 3, p. 1411, 1416–1428.
35. Ibid., p. 1411.
36. Ibid., p. 1413.
37. Butcher, *My Three Years with Eisenhower*, p. 418.
38. Ibid., pp. 418–419.
39. Blumenson, *Salerno to Cassino*, p. 149.
40. Ibid. Blumenson's judgment is damning: "Sensitive of his prerogatives and understandably anxious to make good in this, his first command of combat operations in World War II, General Clark placed between himself and his American subordinates a distance that was perhaps more than the normal reserve consciously adopted for command purposes. He rarely, if ever, requested advice from his subordinate commanders or talked things over with them."
41. D'Este, *Eisenhower: A Soldier's Life*, p. 455.
42. Ibid.
43. Ibid.
44. *The Papers of George Catlett Marshall*, vol. 4, p. 136.
45. Butcher, *My Three Years with Eisenhower*, p. 424.
46. Ibid.
47. Ibid.
48. *DDE*, vol. 3, p. 1454.
49. Ibid. See also Churchill, *Closing the Ring*, p. 135.
50. *DDE*, vol. 3, p. 1454.
51. Blumenson, *Salerno to Cassino*, p. 166.
52. Miller, *Ike the Soldier*, p. 557.
53. Garland and Smyth, *Sicily and the Surrender of Italy*, p. 550.
54. Miller, *Ike the Soldier*, p. 558.
55. "Eisenhower Urged for President," *New York Post*, October 4, 1943.
56. Miller, *Ike the Soldier*, p. 558.
57. *The Papers of George Catlett Marshall*, vol. 4, p. 143.
58. Ibid., p. 154.
59. Ibid., p. 163.
60. Ibid., pp. 179–180.
61. Vincent J. Esposito, ed., *The West Point Atlas of American Wars* (U.S. Military Academy at West Point; Frederick A. Praeger, 1959), vol. 2, p. 171.
62. Miller, *Ike the Soldier*, p. 561.
63. Churchill, *Closing the Ring*, p. 288.
64. Miller, *Ike the Soldier*, pp. 560–561.
65. Pogue, *George C. Marshall: Organizer of Victory*, p. 272.
66. "John J. Pershing to Franklin D. Roosevelt," September 20, 1943, in Marshall Library Files, George C. Marshall Research Library, Virginia Military Institute, Lexington, Virginia.

67. "Roosevelt to Pershing," September 20, 1943, in Marshall Library Files, George C. Marshall Research Library, Virginia Military Institute, Lexington, Virginia.

68. Miller, *Ike the Soldier*, p. 561.

69. Dwight Eisenhower, *Crusade in Europe*, p. 195.

70. Ibid.

71. Ibid., p. 196.

72. The name of the chief of staff during the Civil War was Henry Halleck. Halleck's tenure is among the most forgettable in the history of the American high command. We must assume that Roosevelt was not comparing the two, but attempting to both reward Marshall for his service and assure his place in history.

73. Dwight Eisenhower, *Crusade in Europe*, p. 197. The quotation is extended in Sherwood, *Roosevelt and Hopkins*, to include President Roosevelt's statement that Marshall was "entitled to have his place in history" (p. 770). The Eisenhower quote is authoritative because the author of *Roosevelt and Hopkins, An Intimate History*, derives the quote from Hopkins' *Intimate History* papers, added to by Roosevelt's colleague after the event.

74. Pogue, *George C. Marshall: Organizer of Victory*, pp. 305–306.

75. Ibid., p. 304.

76. Ibid., p. 306.

77. Stone, *War Summits*, p. 116.

78. Pogue, *George C. Marshall: Organizer of Victory*, p. 310.

79. Ibid., p. 311.

80. Ibid.

81. Ibid., p. 313. The reminiscence is from a postwar interview of Marshall by Forrest C. Pogue.

82. Marshall's comment on Stalin is interesting: "I always thought they made a mistake of treating Stalin [as if he were] a product of the Foreign Service," he said after the war. "He was a rough SOB who made his way by murder and everything else and should be talked to that way." ("Dr. Sidney T. Matthews, Major Roy Lemson, Major David Hamilton Interview with George C. Marshall, July 25, 1949, in George C. Marshall Library, Microfilm Reel 332.")

83. Pogue, *George C. Marshall: Organizer of Victory*, p. 313.

84. Ibid., p. 318.

85. Ibid., p. 320.

86. Sherwood, *Roosevelt and Hopkins*, p. 803. The quote is contained in a letter written by Marshall to the author, Robert Sherwood.

87. Pogue, *George C. Marshall: Organizer of Victory*, p. 321.

88. "An Interview with George C. Marshall," Forrest C. Pogue, October 5, 1956 (Marshall Files, George C. Marshall Research Library, Virginia Military Institute, Lexington, Virginia).

89. Ibid., p. 322.

90. "Marshall to Eisenhower," December 7, 1943, Marshall Files, George C. Marshall Research Library, Virginia Military Institute, Lexington, Virginia.

CHAPTER 10: SHINGLE

1. Weinberg, *A World At War*, p. 643.

2. *Chronology, 1941–1945, U.S. Army in World War II*, pp. 156–163.

3. John Keegan, ed., *The Times Atlas of the Second World War*, (New York: Harper & Row, 1989, pp. 140–141. The attack at New Britain was a part of Douglas MacArthur's plan to prosecute the war from his position as commander in the southwest Pacific area. His offensive was complemented by a separate offensive in the central Pacific that cleared the Gilbert Islands.

4. MacArthur's concern that Nimitz would gain unwarranted attention was a near obsession. In late 1943, MacArthur was already planning a public relations blitz that would make it clear that Nimitz's victories were gained only with the help of MacArthur's forces. See Manchester, *American Caesar*, pp. 340–341.

5. Larrabee, *Commander In Chief*, pp. 282–283.

6. Keegan, *The Times Atlas of the Second World War*, p. 140.

7. Erickson, *The Road to Berlin*, pp. 162–165.

8. "Dr. Sidney T. Matthews, Major Roy Lemson, Major David Hamilton Interview with George C. Marshall," July 25, 1949, in George C. Marshall Library, Microfilm Reel 332. Marshall said Eisenhower was reluctant "because the place was too far away to have adequate air cover."

9. D'Este, *Fatal Decision*, pp. 70–75.

10. With a bow to Shelby Foote, whose use of the wine bottle analogy and repetition of "over" and "won" are lifted here from *The Civil War: A Narrative* as a most appropriate metaphor for describing the position in which Clark found himself.

11. The command arrangements in the Mediterranean mirrored those for Western Europe, where Eisenhower would have an English senior commander as his deputy. The accommodations had been agreed to between Roosevelt and Churchill in Cairo.

12. Peter Verney, *Anzio 1944: An Unexpected Fury* (London: David Charles, 1980), p. 64.

13. D'Este, *Eisenhower: A Soldier's Life*, p. 469.

14. Ibid., pp. 468–469.

15. Hobbs, *Dear General*, p. 131.

16. *The Papers of George Catlett Marshall*, vol. 4, p. 210.

17. Ibid., p. 215.

18. "Dr. Sidney T. Matthews, Major Roy Lemson, Major David Hamilton Interview with George C. Marshall," July 25, 1949, in George C. Marshall Library, Microfilm Reel 332. Surprisingly, in this interview Marshall said that it was never his intention that the Allies take all of Italy, but that they simply fight there to keep the Germans tied down until the cross–Channel operation could be launched.

19. Pogue, *George C. Marshall: Organizer of Victory*, pp. 348–349.

20. Ibid., p. 349.

21. Ibid.

22. Ibid., p. 350.

23. John Keegan, *Six Armies in Normandy: From D–Day to the Liberation of Paris* (New York: Penguin Books, 1982), p. 36.

24. Ibid., pp. 33–34.

25. Gordon A. Harrison *Cross–Channel Attack, U.S. Army in World War II* (Washington, D.C.: Center of Military History, Government Printing Office, 1950), pp. 11–13.

26. "Colonel L. M. Guyer and Col. C. H Donnelly Interview with George C. Marshall," February 11, 1949, in George C. Marshall Library, Modern Military Reference Collection, #5035. The Guyer–Donnelly interview was conducted with Marshall during a checkup Marshall was having at Walter Reed Army Hospital. The answers he gave in this interview are among the most interesting in all of his private comments (and he opened up considerably more than in the past), or even during his extensive interviews with Forrest C. Pogue, about his views on the British, on Sledgehammer, and on Roundup. See also "Dr. Sidney T. Matthews, Major Roy Lemson, Major David Hamilton Interview with George C. Marshall," July 25, 1949, in George C. Marshall Library, Microfilm Reel 332.

27. Ibid.

28. Ibid.

29. Ibid. Marshall was not alone in this view. Henry Stimson told the Army chief of staff that his worries about the Russians were so persistent that he prayed every night that they would survive until the U.S. and Great Britain could launch the cross–Channel operation.

30. Keegan, *Six Armies in Normandy*, p. 34.

31. Ibid., pp. 33–34.

32. Ibid., pp. 32–33.

33. This formula, from a midlevel major with no combat experience, vaulted Wedemeyer into the Army's senior ranks. In 1939 he was a major; in 1943 he was a major general.

34. Harrison, *Cross-Channel Attack*, pp. 41–43.

35. Ibid., pp. 52–53.

36. Nigel Hamilton, *Master of the Battlefield: Monty's War Years* (New York: Mcgraw–Hill, 1964), pp. 511–512.
37. Harrison, *Cross–Channel Attack*, p. 351.
38. Ibid., pp. 11–12. See also Miller, *Ike the Soldier*, p. 577.
39. *The Papers of George Catlett Marshall*, vol. 3, pp. 383–385.
40. Miller, *Ike the Soldier*, p. 577.
41. Ibid., p. 578.
42. Dwight Eisenhower, *Crusade in Europe*, pp. 216–217.
43. Because of the secrecy of Eisenhower's visit, his meeting with Marshall and the handful of senior commanders took place in the office of the secretary of war. Eisenhower was spirited into the Pentagon through a private entrance. One of Marshall's concerns was that the Germans would discover Eisenhower was in Washington; the Germans believed he was in London and were on guard because of rumors that his being there meant that the invasion of France would come within days.
44. Pogue, *George C. Marshall: Organizer of Victory*, p. 349.
45. "Stimson Diary," December 23, 1943.
46. Butcher, *My Three Years with Eisenhower*, p. 466.
47. Pogue, *George C. Marshall: Organizer of Victory*, p. 348.
48. "He Armed the Republic," *Time*, January 3, 1944.
49. Pogue, *George C. Marshall: Organizer of Victory*, p. 350.
50. Butcher, *My Three Years with Eisenhower*, p. 467.
51. Ibid.
52. Dwight Eisenhower, *Crusade in Europe*, p. 218.
53. Ibid.
54. "Colonel L. M. Guyer and Col. C. H. Donnelly Interview with George C. Marshall," February 11, 1949, in George C. Marshall Library, Modern Military Reference Collection, #5035.
55. Harrison, *Cross-Channel Attack*, pp. 100–105.
56. Ibid., pp. 63–65.
57. Ibid., pp. 170–171.
58. See, *DDE*, vol. 3, pp. 1688–1692. Among the longest messages from Eisenhower to the Joint Chiefs of Staff during the months of January, February, and March 1944 reviewed the landing craft issue, the debates surrounding the various numbers needed, the production rate of landing craft, and Eisenhower's detailed listing of what was available. At one point Eisenhower was so concerned with the issue that he recommended the invasion be postponed to allow for one more month of landing craft production.
59. Harrison, *Cross-Channel Attack*, pp. 169–173. The official history notes: "The serviceability rate of landing craft—or, in other words, the percentage of craft on hand which at any given date would be operationally available—was always a planning figure to conjure with. So narrow were the planning margins that a difference of 5 percent in the estimates of serviceability might mean the difference between adequate and inadequate lift for the assault."
60. The difficulties in determining an exact maximum number of landing craft that would be needed for Overlord became a bitterly contested issue, with splits between optimists (who thought the Allies needed a required minimum number) and pessimists (who believed the Allies needed as many as the offshore transports could hold). This empirical conflict was resolved as all such questions were—by a political decision: Overlord planners split the difference.
61. Miller, *Ike the Soldier*, p. 579.
62. Ibid., p. 580.
63. Ibid., p. 581.
64. Hobbs, *Dear General*, pp. 147–148.
65. Harrison, *Cross-Channel Attack*, pp. 159–163.
66. Ibid., p. 111.
67. Hamilton, *Master of the Battlefield*, pp. 511–514. Montgomery biographer Nigel Hamilton claims that Montgomery "demolished" Morgan's original Overlord plan, but that Eisenhower

took credit for it and ordered Harry Butcher to change his diary entry to suggest that the new Overlord plan was his idea. This is an old saw, meant to deny that Montgomery was innocent of charges that he intended to take Caen on the first day of the invasion. Of course the charges were made against Montgomery by senior American commanders, but not by Eisenhower. Then too, as attested to by Eisenhower and Smith, their view that a five-division assault should be made had been arrived at in late December 1943, and communicated to Montgomery.

68. Ibid., p. 513. Hamilton argues that Montgomery attempted to dissuade Eisenhower from going forward with Anvil, the invasion of southern France, but that he could not be dissuaded. True. Hamilton then notes that Montgomery was essentially right in arguing against it, as Shingle—Anzio—was a failure, thus proving the rightness of his position, and after all, Eisenhower was the "true progenitor" of Anzio. This is clever, but incorrect—Eisenhower went forward with Shingle, but it was not his plan and he did not support it. In fact, as Hamilton fails to note, Shingle was Churchill's idea, not Eisenhower's.

69. Ibid.

70. Ibid., pp. 513–514.

71. Harrison, *Cross-Channel Attack*, pp. 164–165.

72. David Eisenhower, *Eisenhower at War*, p. 122.

73. Ibid.

74. Ibid.

75. Ibid., p. 123.

76. *DDE*, vol. 3, pp. 1671–1672.

77. David Eisenhower, *Eisenhower at War*, p. 124.

78. *DDE*, vol. 3, p. 1707.

79. *The Papers of George Catlett Marshall*, vol. 4, pp. 272–274.

80. *DDE*, vol. 3, p. 1714.

81. Ibid., p. 1761.

CHAPTER 11: OVERLORD

1. *The Papers of George Catlett Marshall*, vol. 4, pp. 273–274.

2. Ibid., p. 274.

3. Alanbrooke, *War Diaries*, p. 520.

4. *The Papers of George Catlett Marshall*, vol. 4, pp. 282–283.

5. Ibid.

6. Butcher, *My Three Years with Eisenhower*, p. 475.

7. Hobbs, *Dear General*, pp. 153–155.

8. D'Este, *Fatal Decision*, pp. 119–122.

9. "The Papers and Diary of Major General John P. Lucas," United States Army Military History Institute, Carlisle Barracks, Carlisle, Pennsylvania, "January 22, 1944."

10. Keegan, *The Oxford Companion to World War II*, pp. 33–35.

11. D'Este, *Fatal Decision*, p. 124.

12. Ibid., p. 129.

13. Ibid., p. 130.

14. Albert Kesselring, *The Memoirs of Field-Marshal Kesselring* (1953; repr., London: Greenhill Books, 1967), pp. 90–91.

15. D'Este, *Fatal Decision*, p. 134.

16. "Lucas Diary," January 22, 1944. Clark would later deny to colleagues that he had ever said such a thing, though he admitted (albeit after the fact) that he did not support the landings. It is hard to find a military commander in the postwar period who did.

17. D'Este, *Fatal Decision*, pp. 146–147.

18. Keegan, *The Oxford Companion to World War II*, p. 34.

19. D'Este, *Fatal Decision*, pp. 160–163.

20. Verney, *Anzio 1944*, pp. 64–65.

21. Harmon, *Combat Commander*, pp. 163–164.
22. "Lucas Diary," February 1, 1944.
23. Churchill, *Closing the Ring*, p. 437.
24. Jon Meacham, *Franklin and Winston: An Intimate Portrait of an Epic Friendship* (New York: Random House, 2004), pp. 290–291.
25. *DDE*, vol. 3, pp. 1732–1733.
26. Ibid., p. 1733.
27. Ibid., p. 1735.
28. *The Papers of George Catlett Marshall*, vol. 4, p. 313.
29. *DDE.*, vol. 3, p. 1736.
30. Ibid., pp. 1745–1746.
31. Ibid.
32. Ibid., p. 1746.
33. Mark Perry, *Four Stars* (Boston: Houghton Mifflin, 1989), p. 121.
34. *The Papers of George Catlett Marshall*, vol. 4, p. 328.
35. Ibid., p. 329.
36. Ibid., 4, p. 342.
37. *DDE*, 3, p. 1742.
38. Ibid., pp. 1756–1757.
39. Ibid., pp. 1740–1742.
40. Ibid., p. 1779
41. Ibid.
42. James C. Humes, *Eisenhower and Churchill: The Partnership That Saved The World* (New York: Forum Books, 2001), p. 180.
43. Ibid., p. 181. Eisenhower was disturbed that on the eve of D-Day, he realized that Churchill disagreed with the landings and believed they would fail. Churchill was, until the very end, tied to a Mediterranean strategy. "It was quite a shocking discovery," Eisenhower said after the war.
41. *The Papers of George Catlett Marshall*, vol. 4, p. 404.
45. Quoted in ibid., p. 405.
46. Dwight Eisenhower, *Crusade in Europe*, p. 242.
47. Max Hastings, *D-Day and the Battle for Normandy* (New York: Random House, 1985), p. 92.
48. "The Diary of Bernard Law Montgomery," in the Imperial War Museum, Montgomery Papers, June 2, 1944.
49. Humes, *Eisenhower and Churchill*, p. 188. Churchill is reported to have said that Anvil's new name, Dragoon, was appropriate, as he had been "dragooned" into it. The story is apocryphal.
50. Ibid., pp. 189–190.
51. *The Oxford Companion to World War II*, pp. 662–667. See also Harrison, *Cross-Channel Attack*, pp. 269–273, 450–456.
52. Harrison, *Cross-Channel Attack*, pp. 75, 184, 289–293.
53. David Eisenhower, *Eisenhower at War*, pp. 123–124.
54. Keegan, *The Oxford Companion to World War II*, pp. 665–666.
55. Hamilton, *Master of the Battlefield*, pp. 512–513.
56. David Eisenhower, *Eisenhower at War*, p. 108, 351–352.
57. D'Este, *Patton, A Genius for War*, p. 567.
58. Ibid., pp. 585–586.
59. Ibid., pp. 587–588.
60. Ibid., p. 581.
61. Pogue, *George C. Marshall: Organizer of Victory*, p. 384.
62. *The Papers of George Catlett Marshall*, vol. 4, p. 437.
63. *DDE*, vol. 3, p. 1837.
64. Ibid.
65. *The Papers of George Catlett Marshall*, vol. 4, p. 445.
66. D'Este, *Patton: A Genius for War*, p. 588.

67. Ibid.

68. "Patton Diary," May 1, 1944.

69. D'Este, *Patton: A Genius for War*, p. 590.

70. D'Este, *Fatal Decision*, p, 269.

71. *DDE*, vol. 3, p. 1779. Lucas was considered for a senior command for the Normandy invasion but was returned to the United States, where he took command of the Fourth Army.

72. D'Este, *Fatal Decision*, p. 271.

73. Dupuy, *The Harper Encyclopedia of Military Biography*, pp. 754–755.

74. D'Este, *Fatal Decision*, p. 272.

75. Ibid., pp. 272–274.

76. Ibid., p. 272.

77. Ibid., p. 282.

78. Ibid., pp. 299–301.

79. Ibid., pp. 323–325.

80. Keegan, *The Oxford Companion to World War II*, p. 35.

81. Blumenson, *Salerno to Cassino*, pp. 404–406.

82. Ibid., p. 403.

83. D'Este, *Fatal Decision*, pp. 394–395.

84. Pogue, *George C. Marshall: Organizer of Victory*, p. 347.

85. *The Papers of George Catlett Marshall*, vol. 4, p. 468. Clifton Brown, in Italy at the time, was present at his brother's burial.

86. D'Este, *Eisenhower: A Soldier's Life*, p. 516.

87. Ibid.

88. Dwight Eisenhower, *Crusade in Europe*, p. 249.

89. D'Este, *Eisenhower: A Soldier's Life*, p. 520.

90. Ibid., p. 522.

91. Ibid., p. 525.

92. Ibid.

93. "Eisenhower to Marshall," S–52951 (Cable), "June 4, 1944," in SHAEF Files, Records of the Supreme Headquarters, Allied Expeditionary Force, National Archives, Washington, D.C.

CHAPTER 12: COBRA

1. Harrison, *Cross-Channel Attack*, pp. 305–306.

2. Ibid., p. 315.

3. Ibid., p. 317.

4. Ibid., p. 315.

5. Ibid., pp. 315–316.

6. Ibid., p. 320.

7. Ibid., p. 305.

8. Ibid., p. 285.

9. Ibid., p. 286.

10. Ibid., p. 289.

11. Stephen E. Ambrose, *D-Day, June 6, 1944: The Climactic Battle of World War II* (New York: Simon & Schuster, 1994), p. 342.

12. Keegan, *Six Armies in Normandy*, pp. 140–141.

13. Reginald H. Roy, *1944: The Canadians in Normandy* (Gage Distribution, Canadian War Museum Historical Publications, Ottawa, 1984,) p. 102.

14. Ambrose, *D-Day, June 6, 1944*, p. 515.

15. D'Este, *Decision in Normandy*, p. 114.

16. Ibid., pp. 120–122.

17. Harrison, *Cross-Channel Attack*, p. 325.

18. Eric Sevareid, *Not So Wild a Dream* (Columbia: University of Missouri Press, 1995), p. 92.

Clark held a press conference in Rome on the day the city fell and, with the French commander beside him, attributed the fall of the city to his own army—without mentioning the casualties of any other Allied army. Reporter Eric Sevareid remembered thinking that Clark's remarks were some of the most insensitive he had ever heard from an American commander. After the press conference, Clark ostentatiously spread a map on a hotel balustrade and began to instruct his commanders on their next moves. One of Sevareid's colleagues turned to Sevareid and said: "On this historic occasion, I feel like vomiting."

19. *DDE*, vol. 3, p. 1915. He added, perhaps unnecessarily, "I will keep you informed."
20. Hamilton: *Master of the Battlefield*, pp. 581–582.
21. Ibid., p. 561.
22. Pogue, *George C. Marshall: Organizer of Victory*, p. 390.
23. Paul Carell, *Scorched Earth*, (Atglen, PA: Schiffer Military History, 1994), p. 382. "Carell" is Paul Karl Schmidt, a historian whose works on the German Army on the eastern front provide some of the best historical writing of our era. He became a member of the Nazi Student Association at a young age and then an SS officer. He served as the German foreign ministry's press spokesman and was interned on suspicion of war crimes in 1945 for thirty months. He appeared as a witness for the prosecution during the Nuremberg war crimes trials. He denied that the German Army committed atrocities on the eastern front despite overwhelming evidence to the contrary. He was investigated for crimes against humanity by the Office of the State Prosecutor in Germany but was not indicted. His *Hitler Moves East* is among the best works of military history ever written. He never served in combat.
24. Pogue, *George C. Marshall: Organizer of Victory*, p. 391.
25. Ibid., p. 392.
26. Ibid., p. 394.
27. Butcher, *My Three Years with Eisenhower*, p. 571.
28. "Carentan O Carentan," in *The Norton Book of Modern War*, ed. Paul Fussell (New York: W.W. Norton, 1991), pp. 517–519. The poem here is quoted only in part.
29. "Marshall to Roosevelt" (Cable), "14 June 1944," in George C. Marshall Research Library, French Folder.
30. Butcher, *My Three Years with Eisenhower*, p. 579.
31. Ibid., p. 580.
32. Ibid., pp. 582–584.
33. *The Papers of George Catlett Marshall*, vol. 4, pp. 487–488.
34. Pogue, *George C. Marshall: Organizer of Victory*, p. 405.
35. Ibid., p. 404.
36. "George C. Marshall interview with Forrest C. Pogue," November 13, 1956.
37. Pogue, *George C. Marshall: Organizer of Victory*, p. 404.
38. Clark, *Calculated Risk*, pp. 380–381.
39. *The Papers of George Catlett Marshall*, vol. 4, p. 489.
40. "Stimson Diary," June 22, 1944.
41. Weigley, *Eisenhower's Lieutenants*, pp. 97–98.
42. *The Papers of George Catlett Marshall*, vol. 4, p. 535.
43. Ambrose, *Supreme Commander*, p. 439.
44. After the war, Montgomery insisted that it was always his intention to pin the Germans into Caen, not actually take the city. He added that his attacks at Goodwood drew troops away from Bradley's front—implying that the Americans had not taken advantage of his largesse.
45. Martin Blumenson, *Breakout and Pursuit* (Washington, D.C.: Government Printing Office, 1961), p. 193.
46. Francis de Guingand, *Operation Victory* (New York: Scribner, 1947), pp. 401–403.
47. Ibid., pp. 408–410.
48. In spite of Montgomery's cable spurning Eisenhower's offer of an armored division, there is evidence that Eisenhower might well have misinterpreted Goodwood's intentions. Then too, both Montgomery and Bradley were facing Rommel. Montgomery might well have failed in follow-

ing up the bombardments of July 18, but no one can argue with Rommel's deployments. He seemed prescient, and, having fought Montgomery, he knew how he would deploy his forces. That was not true for Bradley. Then too, as Martin Blumenson pointed out ("Some Reflections on the Immediate Post Assault Strategy," in *D-Day: The Normandy Invasion in Retrospect*, [Lawrence: University of Kansas Press, 1971]): Rommel had gathered most of his forces at precisely the place where Montgomery attacked, not because Montgomery was there, but because Rommel hoped to launch a counteroffensive around Caen to push the Allies back onto the beaches.

49. "M45, 2215 hours, 8.7.44" (Cable), "Montgomery Papers, Imperial War Museum. See also Hamilton, *Master of the Battlefield*, p. 721.

50. Gelb, *Ike and Monty*, p. 327.

51. Not all historians agree with this view. Carlo D'Este writes that Bradley never viewed Cobra as leading to a breakout. But D'Este also admits that Bradley and General Joseph Collins agreed that if Cobra worked the Allied armies would be in Avranches in a week. See D'Este *Decision in Normandy*, (New York: Dutton, 1983), p. 351.

52. "21st Army Group Directive M–510, 10 July 1944, in Eisenhower Papers, Dwight D. Eisenhower Library, Abilene, Kansas.

33. D'Este, *Decision in Normandy*, p. 410.

54. Ibid., p. 403.

55. D'Este, *Eisenhower: A Soldier's Life*, p. 482.

56. Max Hastings, *Overlord, D-Day and the Battle for Normandy* (New York: Simon & Schuster, 1984), p. 256.

57. Ibid.

58. John C. McManus, *The Americans at Normandy* (New York: Forge Books, 2004), pp. 339–341.

59. "Bradley to Eisenhower," 28 July 1944, in Eisenhower Papers, Dwight D. Eisenhower Library, Abilene, Kansas.

60. Weigley, *Eisenhower's Lieutenants*, p. 160.

61. The provenance of this quote seems suspect. It is quoted in D'Este, *Patton: A Genius for War*, and footnoted to Ladislas Farago, *Patton, Ordeal and Triumph* (Yardley, Pa.: Westholme Publishing) p. 463. The quote in Farago is unsourced, but it appears that this speech by Patton was to his staff at Third Army headquarters in France. The speech appeared in the movie *Patton* as an address to the Third Army—which has become is most popular attribution. That Patton said something like this is not in question.

62. Blumenson, *Breakout and Pursuit*, pp. 348–351.

63. Butcher, *My Three Years with Eisenhower*, p. 630.

64. *DDE*, vol. 4, p. 2048.

65. Ibid., p. 2049.

66. D'Este, *Decision in Normandy*, pp. 417–419.

67. Bradley, *A Soldier's Story*, p. 377.

68. Hastings, *Overlord, D-Day, and the Battle for Normandy*, p. 280.

69. Historian Max Hastings provides a needed corrective to the Patton legend: "At the beginning of August 1944, the posturing general was the man for the hour, performing feats of movement that probably no other Allied commander could have matched. But it would be absurd to suppose that he had discovered a key to the downfall of the German armies which escaped his peers. It was they who had made possible the glory that he now reaped with such relish" (*Overlord, D-Day, and the Battle for Normandy*, p. 281).

70. Fifty thousand Germans were taken prisoner and another ten thousand were killed.

71. Hastings, *Overlord, D-Day and the Battle for Normandy*, pp. 277–278.

72. Dwight Eisenhower, *Crusade in Europe*, p. 432.

73. D'Este, *Decision in Normandy*, p. 432.

74. *DDE*, vol. 4, p. 2092.

75. Pogue, *George C. Marshall: Organizer of Victory*, p. 409.

76. Ibid., pp. 409–410.

77. Ibid., p. 410.

78. *Triumph and Tragedy*, Winston S. Churchill, vol. 6, *The Second World War* (Boston: Houghton Mifflin Company, 1953), pp. 721–723.
79. Pogue, *George C. Marshall: Organizer of Victory*, p. 412.
80. Ibid., p. 413.
81. Butcher, *My Three Years with Eisenhower*, pp. 648–649.
82. Pogue, *George C. Marshall: Organizer of Victory*, p. 424.
83. *The Papers of George Catlett Marshall*, vol. 4, p. 551.
84. Butcher, *My Three Years with Eisenhower*, p. 654.

CHAPTER 13: BASTOGNE

1. "Photographic, Newspaper, and Radio Coverage of the Visit to the European Theater of Operations by General George C. Marshall, Chief of Staff, United States Army, October, 1944," George C. Marshall Research Library [Pentagon Offices, Scrapbook].
2. Marshall's flight from Newfoundland to La Bourget was the first nonstop flight of an aircraft from North America to Paris since Charles A. Lindbergh had made the flight in 1927. Marshall was aware of the historic significance of his journey.
3. *The Papers of George Catlett Marshall*, vol. 4, pp. 532–533.
4. Pogue, *George C. Marshall: Organizer of Victory*, p. 622.
5. Ibid.
6. Ibid., p. 623.
7. Shelby L. Stanton, *World War II Order of Battle: An Encyclopedic Reference to U.S. Army Ground Forces from Battalion through Division, 1939–1946* (Mechanisburg, Pa.: Stackpole Military Classics, 2006), pp. 45–72.
8. Max Hastings, *Armageddon: The Battle for Germany, 1944–1945* (New York: Macmillan, 2005), pp. 152–153.
9. Rundstedt hated Hitler and looked down on the Nazi Party, his primary allegiance being to the German Army. Still, Rundstedt was offended that a clique of German officers had plotted to kill Hitler by placing a bomb at his headquarters in East Prussia in July 1944. He served on an Army "Court of Honor" investigating the plot and dismissed hundreds of officers, turning them over to a special criminal court. Many were executed. Erwin Rommel, implicated in the plot, was given the option of committing suicide, and did so, on October 14, 1944. Rommel likely participated in the July Plot not because he opposed Hitler, but because he opposed Hitler's military strategy. There is no evidence that he disagreed with Hitler's racial policies.
10. Hastings, *Armageddon*, p. 198.
11. David Eisenhower, *Eisenhower at War*, p. 482.
12. Ibid., pp. 471–481.
13. The comment was made by a British commander after the battle and picked up as the title for Cornelius Ryan's popular account of the battle.
14. Hastings, *Armageddon*, pp. 39–41.
15. David Eisenhower, *Eisenhower at War*, p. 499.
16. Ibid., p. 521.
17. Ibid., p. 483.
18. Ibid., p. 484.
19. Bradley and Blair, *A General's Life*, p. 410.
20. Hastings, *Armageddon*, p. 214.
21. Ibid., p. 212.
22. Max Hastings's study of the American Army in France is a primer on how America fights and why—and the drawbacks of the American philosophy. The use of overwhelming firepower to subdue an enemy is neither new nor particularly controversial, and was inculcated in George Marshall's thinking about how the United States would fight World War II. To his and Fox Conner's view that the wars fought by democracies must be short must be added this proviso: that they must be as bloodless as possible.
23. *Eisenhower: A Soldier's Life*, p. 591.

24. Larrabee, *Commander in Chief*, p. 473.
25. Pogue, *George C. Marshall: Organizer of Victory*, pp. 497–498.
26. Ibid., p. 474.
27. Max Hastings adds to this judgment his own, undoubtedly correct, view that the U.S. Navy was the nation's strongest military branch, and the world's most effective fighting force.
28. Dwight Eisenhower, *Crusade in Europe*, p. 352.
29. Pogue, *George C. Marshall: Organizer of Victory*, pp. 474–475.
30. Bernard Law Montgomery, *Montgomery of Alamein*, p. 254.
31. "George C. Marshall Interview with Forrest C. Pogue," November 15, 1956, in Marshall Library Files, "Interviews of Forrest C. Pogue," George C. Marshall Research Library, Virginia Military Institute, Lexington, VA.
32. Ibid.
33. *The Papers of George Catlett Marshall*, vol. 4, pp. 624–626.
34. David Eisenhower, *Eisenhower at War*, p. 487.
35. The original draft was written by Smith and an aide, who then checked it with Eisenhower. The first draft was then rewritten and checked with Eisenhower again before being given to Marshall. Marshall apparently added some edits and reviewed the text with Eisenhower before it was sent on to Montgomery's headquarters.
36. *DDE*, vol. 4, pp. 2221–2225.
37. David Eisenhower, *Eisenhower at War*, p. 488.
38. *DDE*, vol. 4, p. 2225n.
39. *The Papers of George Catlett Marshall*, vol. 4, p. 626.
40. D'Este, *Patton: A Genius for War*, p. 667.
41. Ambrose, *Eisenhower: Soldier, General of the Army, President-Elect*, pp. 358–359.
42. *DDE*, vol. 4, p. 2296.
43. Trevor N. Dupuy, *Hitler's Last Gamble: The Battle of the Bulge*, December 1944–January 1945 (New York: Harper Collins, 1990), pp. 46–47.
44. Keegan, *The Oxford Companion to World War II*, pp. 39–40.
45. Keegan, *The Oxford Companion to American Military History* (New York: Oxford University Press, 1999), p. 93.
46. Weigley, *Eisenhower's Lieutenants*, p. 466.
47. *The Oxford Companion to American Military History*, p. 94.
48. Weigley, *Eisenhower's Lieutenants*, p. 497.
49. Ibid., p. 499.
50. Dwight Eisenhower, *Crusade in Europe*, p. 350.
51. Weigley, *Eisenhower's Lieutenants*, p. 500.
52. John S. D. Eisenhower *The Bitter Woods: The Battle of the Bulge* (New York: Putnam's Sons, 1969), p. 257.
53. Weigley, *Eisenhower's Lieutenants*, pp. 500–501.
54. Eisenhower had received his fourth star on the eve of the Battle of Kasserine Pass.
55. John Eisenhower, *The Bitter Woods*, p. 257.
56. Ibid., pp. 32–33.
57. Ibid., p. 33.
58. Weigley, *Eisenhower's Lieutenants*, p. 504.
59. David Eisenhower, *Eisenhower at War*, p. 576.
60. Ibid., p. 577.
61. Ibid., p. 579.
62. Weigley, *Eisenhower's Lieutenants*, p. 480.
63. Ibid., p. 483.
64. David Eisenhower, *Eisenhower at War*, p. 586.
65. Ibid., pp. 586–587.
66. Ibid., p. 587.
67. Ibid., p. 500.
68. Ibid., p. 596.

69. Ibid., p. 597
70. John Eisenhower, *The Bitter Woods*, pp. 381–382.
71. Ibid., p. 382.
72. *DDE*, vol. 4, p. 2387n.
73. John Eisenhower, *The Bitter Woods*, p. 383.
74. Ibid.
75. Ibid., pp. 384–385.
76. Francis de Guingand, *Generals At War* (London: Hodder & Stoughton, 1964), pp. 107–111. De Guingand was not only a master diplomat but also an accomplished writer. His postwar account of the Eisenhower–Montgomery crisis is authoritative. As was their habit, and quite predictably, Eisenhower and Montgomery tended to downplay the controversy in their postwar reminiscences.
77. David Eisenhower, *Eisenhower at War*, pp. 600–601.
78. Bradley, *A Soldier's Story*, p. 483.
79. David Eisenhower, *Eisenhower at War*, p. 603.
80. Dwight Eisenhower, *Crusade in Europe*, p. 363.
81. David Eisenhower, *Eisenhower at War*, p. 605.
82. Ibid., pp. 605–606.
83. Pogue, *George C. Marshall: Organizer of Victory*, p. 513.
84. *The Papers of George Catlett Marshall*, vol. 5, pp. 11–27.
85. Ibid., p. 18.
86. Ibid.
87. *DDE*, vol. 4, pp. 2415–2420.
88. *The Papers of George Catlett Marshall*, vol. 5, p. 27.
89. Butcher, *My Three Years With Eisenhower*, p. 742.
90. David Eisenhower, *Eisenhower at War*, pp. 638–639. There is some disagreement on who began the meeting. David Eisenhower says that the supreme commander reviewed his offensive operations and presented a list of his needs. Forrest C. Pogue says that Marshall opened the conference by talking of Allied command arrangements. David Eisenhower's account is the most recent authoritative account available.
91. Pogue, *George C. Marshall: Organizer of Victory*, pp. 511–513.
92. Ibid., p. 512.
93. Ambrose, *Supreme Commander*, p. 583.
94. Ibid., p. 586.
95. Ibid., p. 620.
96. *DDE*, vol. 4, p. 2521.
97. David Eisenhower, *Eisenhower at War*, p. 741.
98. Allanbrooke, *War Diaries*, p. 679.
99. Pogue, *George C. Marshall: Organizer of Victory*, pp. 555–556.
100. *The Papers of George Catlett Marshall*, vol. 5, p. 106.
101. Hastings, *Armageddon*, p. 548.
102. Pogue, *George C. Marshall: Organizer of Victory*, pp. 557–558.
103. Ambrose, *Supreme Commander*, p. 650.
104. *DDE*, vol. 4, p. 2616.
105. Ambrose, *Supreme Commander*, p. 659.
106. Dwight Eisenhower, *Crusade in Europe*, p. 426.

CHAPTER 14: "IKE"

1. A full account of the surrender ceremony and an explanation of why Eisenhower would not attend can be found in Walter Bedell Smith, *Eisenhower's Six Great Decisions* (New York: Longmans, Green, 1956), pp. 203–206.
2. *DDE*, vol. 4, p. 2696.
3. *The Papers of George Catlett Marshall*, p. 168.

4. Ibid., p. 169n.
5. Ibid., p. 397.
6. Williams, "Chronology," p. 537.
7. Dwight Eisenhower, *Crusade in Europe*, p. 428.
8. Williams, *Chronology*, p. 535.
9. Operation Downfall had two parts: Operation Coronet, the invasion of Honshu Island, near Tokyo; and Operation Olympic, the invasion of Kyushu Island, the southernmost of the Japanese home islands. Plans for the invasion were begun in 1943, and the Combined Chiefs of Staff determined after much wrangling that the final assault must take place less than one year after the surrender of Germany. Great Britain wanted to put the assault off until 1947, but Marshall strongly disagreed, believing that such a postponement would be bad for American morale.
10. Forrest C. Pogue, *George C. Marshall, Statesman, 1945–1959*, (New York: Viking, 1987), pp. 18–19.
11. Ibid., p. 18. According to historian and biographer Kai Bird, Pogue garbled the story of McCloy's response. There is, to be sure, some controversy about precisely what McCloy said during this meeting. It now seems certain that McCloy was not necessarily advocating use of the atomic bomb, but simply arguing that the scheduled invasion of Japan would not be necessary. McCloy's most critically important argument was that the U.S. needed to clarify the terms of Japan's surrender, allowing the Japanese to keep their emperor.
12. "George C. Marshall Interview with Forrest C. Pogue," February 11, 1957, Marshall Library Files, "Interviews of Forrest C. Pogue," George C. Marshall Research Library, Virginia, Military Institute, Lexington, VA.
13. Thomas B. Allen and Norman Polmar, *Code-Name Downfall* (New York: Simon & Schuster, 1995), p. 62. Historian Barton Bernstein (*The Atomic Bomb, the Critical Issues* [Little, Brown and Co., Boston, 1976] and *Hiroshima and Nagasaki reconsidered: The atomic bombings of Japan and the origins of the cold war*, 1941–1945 [University programs modular studies, General Learning Press, 1975] argues that Marshall was never shown any estimate of American deaths above 67,000.
14. Williams, *Chronology*, pp. 550–551.
15. Michael Clodfelter, *Warfare and Armed Conflict: A Statistical Reference* (Jefferson, N.C.: McFarland and Company, 1992), pp. 955–970.
16. Ibid., p. 956.
17. Ibid., pp. 953–955. We do not know the numbers of civilians killed in China in World War II, but most recent information indicates an undercount. Then too, Japan had been conducting its war in China from the early 1930s. When these figures are accumulated, it is possible that the total numbers of killed from World War II will exceed, by our best estimate, 50 million people.
18. Pogue, *George C. Marshall: Organizer of Victory*, p. 482.
19. Dill remains the sole foreign soldier interred at Arlington. Dill's widow wrote to Marshall: "He really loved you George, and your mutual affection meant a great deal to him—he trusted you implicitly."
20. Stephen E. Ambrose, *Eisenhower, the President*, (New York: Simon & Schuster, 1984), p. 15.
21. Ambrose, *Eisenhower: Soldier, General of the Army, President-Elect*, pp. 245–246.
22. Merle Miller, *Plain Speaking: An Oral Biography of Harry S. Truman* (New York: Berkley, 1973), pp. 339–340. Miller says that Truman and Marshall had received a letter from Eisenhower in 1945 asking permission to divorce Mamie and marry Kay Summersby and that the two met and decided against it, after which they destroyed the letter.
23. Ambrose, *Eisenhower: Soldier, General of the Army, President-Elect*, p. 415.
24. D'Este, *Eisenhower: A Soldier's Life*, p. 632.
25. "DDE to MDE," November 12, 1944, Box 1, (John S. D. Eisenhower), Eisenhower Library, Abilene, KS.
26. "DDE to George C. Marshall," June 4, 1945, DDE, vol. 6, p. 92, in *The Papers of Dwight David Eisenhower* (VI)—hereafter DDE, 6—Louis Galambos, ed., Johns Hopkins University Press, Baltimore, 1970.
27. Ambrose, *Eisenhower: Soldier, General of the Army, President-Elect*, p. 415.

28. John S. D. Eisenhower, ed., *Letters to Mamie* (New York: Doubleday, 1978), p. 259.
29. Ambrose, *Eisenhower: Soldier, General of the Army, President-Elect*, p. 415.
30. *The Papers of George Catlett Marshall*, vol. 5, pp. 227–228.
31. *DDE*, vol. 6, pp. 162–163.
32. Perret, *Eisenhower*, p. 351.
33. Miller, *Ike the Soldier*, p. 781. The statement appeared as the headline the next morning in the Washington newspaper, along with: "Mrs. Ike Gets a Quick Kiss and Steps Happily to the Side Lines."
34. Butcher, *My Three Years with Eisenhower*, p. 869.
35. Ibid., p. 870.
36. Ibid., p. 871.
37. Ibid.
38. Ambrose, *Supreme Commander*, p. 21. See also Dwight Eisenhower, *At Ease*, pp. 248–250. The story was originally related to historian Stephen Ambrose by Eisenhower himself in an interview. But the story has been variously reported since. One military legend has it that Marshall actually "slipped" during an Army–Navy football game, after Army scored a touchdown. "Oh, Ike," Marshall reportedly exclaimed, "we're going to win." The story is not reported by Pogue or referred to in any other context except in Eric Larrabee's *Commander in Chief*.
39. Ambrose, *Eisenhower: Soldier, General of the Army, President-Elect*, p. 416.
40. *DDE*, vol. 6, pp. 244–246.
41. Ibid., p. 251.
42. Eisenhower was particularly intent to show that the Allies would not treat Nazi war criminals simply as prisoners of war, but would deny them any rights due officers of a belligerent power. Eisenhower meant to show that senior German officers had operated outside of military convention and so would not be treated as military prisoners. This did not extend to harsh treatment, but took the form of an Eisenhower statement repudiating a photograph of American officers shaking hands with Hermann Göring. See *The Papers of George Catlett Marshall*, vol. 5, pp. 186–189.
43. "An Interview with Douglas Black," Columbia University Oral History Project, quoted in Perret, *Eisenhower*, p. 352. Black was the publisher of *Crusade in Europe* and he said that the story was related to him by Eisenhower. The comment was made, apparently, in Antwerp, when Eisenhower appeared to escort Truman to the Potsdam Conference.
46. Walter Isaacson and Evan Thomas, *The Wise Men: Six Friends and the World They Made* (New York: Simon & Schuster, 1986), pp. 299–308.
45. Ambrose, *Eisenhower: Soldier, General of the Army, President-Elect*, pp. 425–427.
46. Dwight D. Eisenhower, *Mandate for Change* (New York: Doubleday, 1963), pp. 312–313.
47. Ibid., p. 314.
48. Ambrose, *Eisenhower: Soldier, General of the Army, President-Elect*, p. 425.
49. Ibid.
50. Ibid., p. 427.
51. Ladislas Farago, *The Last Days of Patton*, (New York: McGraw-Hill, 1981), p. 358.
52. Ibid., pp. 196–197.
53. Perret, *Eisenhower*, p. 359.
54. *The Papers of George Catlett Marshall*, vol. 4, p. 363.
55. Perret, *Eisenhower*, p. 361.
56. Ibid., p. 362.
57. David Fromkin, *In the Time of the Americans* (New York: Knopf, 1995), p. 507.
58. Clark Clifford with Richard Holbrooke, *Counsel to the President*, (New York: Random House, 1991), p. 146.
59. Ambrose, *Eisenhower: Soldier, General of the Army, President-Elect*, p. 445.
60. Ibid., p. 446.
61. Katherine Marshall was enraged. "There is hell to pay," Marshall told Truman after hearing her out. But Marshall believed he might be able to help in China, one of his first assignments as a

soldier, so he did his best to mollify her. During Marshall's stopover in Tokyo on his way into the country, Douglas MacArthur noted that the former Army chief of staff looked exhausted.

62. Ambrose, *Eisenhower: Soldier, General of the Army, President-Elect*, p. 555.
63. Ibid., p. 562.
64. Pogue, *George C. Marshall: Statesman*, pp. 95–96.
65. Ibid., p. 113.
66. Dwight Eisenhower, *Mandate for Change*, p. 81.
67. Joseph Alsop and Adam Platt, *I've Seen the Best of It* (New York: W.W. Norton, 1992), p. 338.
68. Pogue, *George C. Marshall: Statesman*, pp. 131–132.
69. Cray, *General of the Army*, p. 585.
70. Pogue, *George C. Marshall: Statesman*, p. 144.
71. Cray, *General of the Army*, pp. 586–587.
72. Pogue, *George C. Marshall: Statesman*, p. 145.
73. Cray, *General of the Army*, p. 588.
74. Ibid., p. 592.
75. Ibid., p. 593.
76. Pogue, *George C. Marshall: Statesman*, 162.

CHAPTER 15: "THE GENERAL"

1. Pogue, *George C. Marshall: Statesman*, pp. 191–192.
2. "Forrest C. Pogue Interview with George C. Marshall," November 14, 1956, Marshall Library Files, "Interviews of Forrest C. Pogue," George C. Marshall Research Library, Virginia Military Institute, Lexington, VA.
3. Pogue, *George C. Marshall: Statesman*, p. 198.
4. Ibid., pp. 203–204. Surprisingly, Kennan's research did not show that Communist activities were undermining confidence in the U.S. in Western Europe; rather confidence was being undermined by the disruptive impact of the war on European economic well-being.
5. Ibid., p. 205.
6. Isaacson and Thomas, *The Wise Men*, pp. 410–411.
7. Robert L. Beisner, *Dean Acheson: A Life in the Cold War* (New York: Oxford University Press, 2006), pp. 73–74.
8. Marshall's address was not a "commencement address" in the normal sense of the term, but took place after the graduating students had accepted their diplomas.
9. Isaacson and Thomas, *The Wise Men*, p. 391.
10. *The Papers of George Catlett Marshall*, vol. 6, pp. 190–191.
11. William J. Hogan, *The Marshall Plan* (Cambridge, U.K.: Cambridge University Press, 1989), pp. 54–61.
12. Cray, *General of the Army*, p. 619.
13. Allen Dulles, *The Marshall Plan* (New York: Berg Publishers, 1993), pp. 92–95.
14. Ibid., p. 619.
15. "A World Wide Struggle," in *Los Angeles Times*, March 20, 1948.
16. U.S. Department of State, *United States Foreign Policy for a Post-War Recover Program*, part 1, (Washington, D.C.: Government Printing Office, 1948), p. 2019.
17. Cray, *General of the Army*, p. 625.
18. Ibid., p. 626.
19. Ambrose, *Eisenhower: Soldier, General of the Army, President-Elect*, p. 473.
20. Ibid., p. 477.
21. Ibid., pp. 477–478.
22. Ibid., p. 479.
23. "DDE to Drew Middleton," in *The Papers of Dwight David Eisenhower*, vol. 10, The Johns Hopkins University Press, Baltimore, pp. 138–139. Middleton was a well-known and accomplished reporter who covered the Pentagon. He befriended Eisenhower after the war and became a noted expert on military issues.

24. Ambrose, *Eisenhower: Soldier, General of the Army, President-Elect*, pp. 483–484.
25. Ibid., p. 484.
26. "DDE to Hap Arnold," *DDE*, vol. 10, p. 152.
27. "DDE Diary," vol. 10, p. 171–172.
28. "DDE to Hap Arnold," *DDE*, vol. 10, p. 177.
29. Pogue, *George C. Marshall: Statesman*, p. 263.
30. Herbert S. Parmet, *Eisenhower and the American Crusades*, (New York: Macmillan, 1972), p. 35.
31. Pogue, *George C. Marshall: Statesman*, p. 283.
32. Alan Bullock, *The Life and Times of Ernest Bevin* (Portsmouth, N.H.: Heinemann Publishing, 1960), pp. 92–98.
33. Pogue, *George C. Marshall: Statesman*, p. 285.
34. "British Memo of Conversation between Marshall and Bevin," in *Foreign Relations of the United States*, 1947, vol. 2, (Washington, D.C.: Government Printing Office), pp. 815–822.
35. Pogue, *George C. Marshall: Statesman*, p. 322.
36. Ibid., p. 328. See also Townsend Hoopes, *The Devil and John Foster Dulles* (Boston: Little, Brown, 1973), p. 76.
37. Pogue, *George C. Marshall: Statesman*, p. 332. Marshall's most difficult meeting on the topic was with Swedish foreign minister Osten Unden, who said that the U.S. could easily join the pact because it was a great power, while Sweden was not. Marshall asked Unden where the West would be if Roosevelt and Churchill had said that in 1941.
38. Ibid., p. 333.
39. Beisner, *Dean Acheson*, p. 129.
40. Pogue, *George C. Marshall: Statesman*, p. 413.
41. Cray, *General of the Army*, p. 670.
42. "DDE Diary," June 12, 1949, in vol. 12, *The Papers of Dwight David Eisenhower*, (Baltimore: Johns Hopkins University Press, 1996), p. 251.
43. Ambrose, *Eisenhower: Soldier, General of the Army, President-Elect*, p. 492.
44. "DDE Diary," July 7, 1949, vol. 12, p. 257.
45. Ambrose, *Eisenhower: Soldier, General of the Army, President-Elect*, p. 491.
46. "DDE to Swede Hazlett," August 20, 1950, *The Papers of Dwight David Eisenhower*, vol. 12, p. 192.
47. Ambrose, *Eisenhower: Soldier, General of the Army, President-Elect*, p. 492.
48. Ibid., p. 494.
49. Ibid.
50. Ibid., pp. 494–495.
51. Cray, *General of the Army*, p. 685.
52. "McCarthy Opens Hearings on Marshall," *New York Times*, September 14, 1950.
53. *Congressional Record*, September 15, 1950, pp. 14913–14914.
54. Pogue, *George C. Marshall: Statesman*, p. 428.
55. Isaacson and Thomas, *The Wise Men*, p. 570.
56. Ibid., p. 561. See also Ambrose, *Eisenhower: Soldier, General of the Army, President-Elect*, p. 512.
57. "DDE to Schaefer," December 27, 1951, *DDE*, vol.12, p. 222.
58. Ambrose, *Eisenhower: Soldier, General of the Army, President-Elect*, p. 512.
59. "DDE Diary," June 14, 1951, in *DDE*, vol. 10, p. 262–264.
60. Cray, *General of the Army*, pp. 687–688.
61. D'Este, *Eisenhower: A Soldier's Life*, p. 283.
62. Perret, *Eisenhower*, p. 389.
63. Cray, *General of the Army*, p. 689.
64. Perret, *Eisenhower*, p. 392.
65. Montgomery's official title was Field Marshal Bernard Law Montgomery, first Viscount Montgomery of Alamein, KG, GCB, DSO, PC; that is, Order of the Garter, Order of the Bath, Distinguished Service Order, and Member of the Privy Council of the United Kingdom.
66. Perret, *Eisenhower*, p. 393.
67. Montgomery, *Montgomery of Alamein*, p. 456.

68. "Meeting with General Eisenhower and the President," January 31, 1951, in Truman Presidential Museum and Library, NATO Files.
69. Manchester, *American Caesar*, p. 638.
70. Ibid., pp. 640–641.
71. Pogue, *George C. Marshall: Statesman*, p. 482.
72. Manchester, *American Caesar*, p. 642.
73. Ambrose, *Eisenhower: Soldier, General of the Army, President-Elect*, p. 508.
74. Ibid., p. 506.
75. "DDE to Mark Clark," DDE, vol. 12, p. 262, October 8, 1951. For an officer who had once rubbed shoulders with America's greatest armored commander, and even taken apart and put together a tank on the training fields of Camp Meade, this was an odd position for Eisenhower to take. But he was utterly serious, believing that new antitank weapons made the iron behemoth as useful as a hot-air balloon: the tank, he wrote to General Mark Clark, was "about as valuable as a piece of warm butter."
76. *DDE*, vol. 8, pp. 1150–1151.
77. Montgomery, *Montgomery of Alamein*, p. 462.
78. "Brooke to DDE," May 17, 1952, vol. 8, p. 1170.
79. Ambrose, *Eisenhower: Soldier, General of the Army, President-Elect*, p. 532.
80. Ibid., p. 541.
81. "Eisenhower to Marshall," Personal File, George C. Marshall Research Library, Lexington, Virginia.
82. Pogue, *George C. Marshall: Statesman*, pp. 498–499.
83. "Dwight Eisenhower Interview with Stephen Ambrose," in Ambrose, *Eisenhower: Soldier, General of the Army, President-Elect*, p. 548.
84. Thomas C. Reeves, *The Life and Times of Joe McCarthy* (New York: Stein & Day, 1983), pp. 436–437.
85. Pogue, *George C. Marshall: Statesman*, p. 497.
86. George C. Marshall, "Nobel Laureate Address," Oslo, Norway, 1953, in *The Papers of George Catlett Marshall*, vol. 6, pp. 232–235.
87. "Marshall to Eisenhower," August 14, 1958, Marshall Personal File, Marshall Research Library, Lexington, Virginia.

Epilogue

1. Glenn Tucker, *Lee and Longstreet at Gettysburg* (Gettysburg, Pa.: Morningside House, 1982), pp. 52–55, 62, 97.
2. "Ike and Monty at Gettysburg," *New York Times*, May 13, 1957.
3. Tucker, *Lee and Longstreet at Gettysburg*, pp. 21–22.
4. D'Este, *Patton: A Genius for War*, pp. 601–605. The speech is made famous in the movie *Patton*, where George C. Scott is shown giving the speech to the Third Army. In fact, Patton worked on the speech, honing it and practicing it among various groups of soldiers. Its final version was given on June 5, one day before the invasion of Normandy.
5. Hastings, *Armageddon*, pp. 212–213.
6. Ambrose, *Eisenhower, the President*, p. 675.

BIBLIOGRAPHY

PAPERS AND MANUSCRIPT COLLECTIONS

The Papers of Lord Alanbrooke, chief of the Imperial General Staff, are in the collection of the Imperial War Museum, London.

The General Omar N. Bradley Papers are housed at the United States Military Academy, West Point, New York. Miscellaneous correspondence and reports of General Omar N. Bradley can be found at the U.S. Army Military History Institute, Carlisle Barracks, Pennsylvania. The U.S. Military History Institute also houses the papers of Major General John P. Lucas, Major General Terry de la Mesa, Lieutenant General Robert L. Eichelberger, and Major General Orlando W. Ward.

The Papers of Lieutenant General Mark Clark can be found at the Citadel Archive, Charleston, South Carolina.

The Papers of J. Lawton Collins and General Joseph McNarney can be found at the United States Military Academy, West Point, New York.

The Papers of Brigadier General Fox Conner are housed at the U.S. Army War College. Correspondence between Conner and George C. Marshall can be found at the George C. Marshall Research Library and Foundation. Correspondence between Conner and Eisenhower can be found in the Papers of Dwight D. Eisenhower at the Dwight D. Eisenhower Presidential Library.

The Papers of Dwight David Eisenhower are housed at the Dwight D. Eisenhower Presidential Library in Abilene, Kansas. Eisenhower's extensive collection of World War II papers, memos, and diaries can be found at the library. The comprehensive series *The Papers of Dwight David Eisenhower* (Johns Hopkins University Press) contains his wartime and postwar correspondence. The extensive collection of letters sent by Eisenhower to Marshall during World War II is at the Dwight D. Eisenhower Presidential Library. In the postwar period, Eisenhower—like Marshall—conducted a series of interviews with senior Army officers, providing an unprecedented firsthand account of his own views of his career. Those interviews are available at the Dwight D. Eisenhower Presidential Library.

The papers of General Douglas MacArthur are contained at the MacArthur Memorial Bureau of Archives, Norfolk, Virginia. MacArthur and the papers of his top aides, excepting Eisenhower, can be found in Norfolk.

The Papers of General of the Army George C. Marshall can be found at the George C. Marshall Research Library and Foundation at the Virginia Military Institute, Lexington, Virginia. The Papers of George Catlett Marshall (Johns Hopkins University Press) contains nearly all of his wartime correspondence and his messages to Eisenhower, as well as his most important military papers. A series of extensive interviews with Marshall was conducted by historian Forrest C. Pogue and is available at the library. In the aftermath of the war and during his retirement, the U.S. Army War College conducted a series of interviews with General Marshall. These interviews can be found in the files of the U.S. Army War College in Carlisle, Pennsylvania.

The balance of Marshall's correspondence that is not published or available at the George C. Marshall

Research Library and Foundation can be accessed in the General John J. Pershing Papers at the Library of Congress. Correspondence and memoranda not yet published are cited in the notes and are available at the George C. Marshall Research Library, as are the complete records of Marshall's military service and all family papers. The George C. Marshall Research Library and Foundation also contains the papers of General Lucien K. Truscott, Lieutenant General Thomas T. Handy, Brigadier General Frank McCarthy, and Brigadier General Paul M. Robinett. A select but valuable set of Marshall papers can be found in "G. C. Marshall Papers," Office of Military History, Department of Defense.

The Papers of Bernard Law Montgomery can be found in the collection of the Imperial War Museum, London.

The George S. Patton Papers are housed at the United States Military Academy, West Point, New York (Special Collections, USMA, West Point). There is also a collection of the Papers of General George. S. Patton in the Manuscript Division of the Library of Congress, Washington, D.C.

The Papers of General Carl Spaatz are at the U.S. Library of Congress, Manuscript Division, Washington, D.C.

The Papers and Records of the Supreme Headquarters, Allied Expeditionary Force, can be found in the collections of the National Archives, Washington, D.C.

The author has used the generally accepted authoritative histories of the U.S. Army as compiled, edited, and written for the Washington, D.C.–based Center of Military History. *U.S. Army in World War II* is an eighty-volume work that focuses on the role of the U.S. Army in the war. Its companion work is the multivolume *History of the Army Air Forces in World War II*, published in Washington, D.C., in 1992 by the Center for Air Force History. For U.S. Navy operations in World War II, I have used Samuel Eliot Morison's fifteen-volume *History of United States Naval Operations in World War II*.

The U.S. Army Military History Institute, Carlisle Barracks, Pennsylvania—a part of the Army War College—contains invaluable files of extensive interviews of top commanders of World War II.

PUBLISHED WORKS

Abramson, Rudy, *Spanning the Century: The Life of W. Averell Harriman, 1891–1986* (New York, 1992).

Acheson, Dean, *Present at the Creation: My Years in the State Department* (New York, 1969).

Allen, Thomas B., and Norman Polmar, *Code-Name Downfall* (New York, 1995).

Alsop, Joseph, and Adam Platt, *I've Seen the Best of It* (New York, 1992).

Ambrose, Stephen E., *Duty, Honor, Country: A History of West Point* (Baltimore, 1966).

_____, *The Supreme Commander: The War Years of General Dwight D. Eisenhower* (New York, 1970).

_____, *Eisenhower* 2 vols., New York, 1983–84. Vol. 1, *Soldier, General of the Army, President Elect, 1890–1952* (1983); vol. 2, *The President* (1984).

Atkinson, Rick, *An Army at Dawn: The War in North Africa, 1942–1943* (New York, 2002).

Beisner, Robert L., *Dean Acheson: A Life in the Cold War* (New York, 2006).

Bissell, Richard M., Jr., *Reflections of a Cold Warrior: From Yalta to the Bay of Pigs* (New Haven, Conn., 1996).

Blumenson, Martin, *Mark Clark* (New York, 1985).

_____, *Salerno to Cassino, The U.S. Army in World War II* (Washington, D.C., 1969).

Bohlen, Charles E., *Witness to History, 1929–1969* (New York, 1973).

Borklund, C. W., *The Department of Defense* (New York, 1968).

Botti, Timothy J., *Ace in the Hole: Why the United States Did Not Use Nuclear Weapons in the Cold War, 1945 to 1965* (Westport, Conn., 1996).

Bradley, General Omar and Clay Blair, *A General's Life: An Autobiography* (New York, 1964).

Brands, H. W., Jr., *Cold Warriors: Eisenhower's Generation and American Foreign Policy* (New York, 1988).

Bryant, Sir Arthur, *The Turn of the Tide: A History of the War Years Based on the Diaries of Field-Marshal Lord Alanbrooke, Chief of the Imperial General Staff* (Garden City, N.Y., 1957).

_____, *Triumph in the West: A History of the War Years Based on the Diaries of Field-Marshal Lord Alanbrooke, Chief of the Imperial General Staff.* (Garden City, N.Y., 1959).

Bullock, Alan, *The Life and Times of Ernest Bevin* (Portsmouth, N.H., 1955).

Butcher, Harry C., *My Three Years with Eisenhower: The Personal Diary of Captain Harry C. Butcher, USNR* (New York, 1946).

Center of Military History, "Chronology, 1941–1945," *The U.S. Army in World War II* (Washington, D.C., 1994).

Churchill, Winston S., *A History of the English Speaking Peoples,* 4 vols. (London, 1956–58); Vol. III, *The Age of Revolution* (London, 1957).

_____, *Second World War: Memoirs of the Second World War* (Boston, 1959).

Clifford, Clark, with Richard Holbrooke, *Counsel to the President* (New York).

Clodfelter, Michael, *Warfare and Armed Conflict, A Statistical Reference,* Vol. 2 (Jefferson, N.C., 1992).

Coffey, Thomas M., *Hap: The Story of the U.S. Air Force and the Man Who Built It* (New York, 1982).

Cole, Alice C.; Alfred Goldberg; Samuel A. Tucker; and Rudolph A. Winnacker., eds., *The Department of Defense: Documents on Establishment and Organization, 1944–1978* (Washington, D.C., 1979).

Considine, Robert Bernard, *MacArthur the Magnificent* (Philadelphia, 1942).

Cray, Ed, *General of the Army: George C. Marshall, Soldier and Statesman* (New York, 1990).

Davis, James W., *The President as Party Leader* (New York, 1992).

Dedman, Martin J., *The Origins and Development of the European Union 1945–95* (London and New York, 1996).

Deer, I. C. B., ed., *The Oxford Companion to World War II* (New York, 1995).

D'Este, Carlo, *Fatal Decision: Anzio and the Battle for Rome* (New York, 1988).

_____, *Fatal Decision: Anzio and the Battle for Rome* (New York, 1992).

_____, *Patton, A Genius for War* (New York, 1995).

_____, *Eisenhower, A Soldier's Life* (New York, 2002).

De Gaulle, Charles, *The War Memoirs of Charles de Gaulle,* 3 vols. (New York, 1955–60). Vol. I.

Depuy, Trevor N., *Hitler's Last Gamble, The Battle of the Bulge* (December 1944–January 1945, New York, 1976).

_____, *The Harper Encyclopedia of American Military Biography* (New York, 1992).

Donovan, Robert J., *Eisenhower: The Inside Story* (New York, 1956).

_____, *Conflict and Crisis: The Presidency of Harry S. Truman, 1945–1948* (New York, 1977).

Dulles, Allen, *The Marshall Plan* (New York, 1993).

Eisenhower, David, *Eisenhower: At War, 1943–45* (New York, 1986).

Eisenhower, Dwight D., *Crusade in Europe* (Garden City, N.Y., 1948).

_____, *The White House Years: Mandate for Change, 1953–1956* (Garden City, N.Y., 1963).

_____, *The White House Years: Waging Peace, 1956–1961* (Garden City, N.Y., 1965).

_____, *At Ease: Stories I Tell to Friends* (Garden City, N.Y., 1967).

_____, *The Papers of Dwight David Eisenhower,* Baltimore, 1970–2001. Vols. I–V, *The War Years,* edited by Alfred D. Chandler, Jr. (1970); vol. VI, *Occupation, 1945,* edited by Alfred D. Chandler, Jr., and Louis Galambos (1978); vols. VII–IX, *The Chief of Staff,* edited by Louis Galambos (1978); vols. X–XI, *Columbia University,* edited by Louis Galambos (1983); vols. XII–XIII, *NATO and the Campaign of 1952,* edited by Louis Galambos (1989); vols. XIV–XVII, *The Presidency: The Middle Way,* edited by Louis Galambos and Daun van Ee (1996).

Eisenhower, John S. D., *The Bitter Woods: The Battle of the Bulge* (New York, 1969).

_____, *Strictly Personal* (Garden City, N.Y., 1974). *Allies: Pearl Harbor to D-Day* (New York, 1982).

Eisenhower, Milton S., *The Wine Is Bitter* (New York, 1963).

_____, *The President Is Calling* (New York, 1974).

Eisenhower, Susan, *Mrs. Ike: Memories and Reflections on the Life of Mamie Eisenhower* (New York, 1996).

Erickson, John, *The Road to Berlin: Stalin's War with Germany* (New Haven, Conn., 1983).

Esposito, Vincent J., *The West Point Atlas of American Wars* (New York, 1959).

Ewald, William Bragg, Jr., *Eisenhower the President: Crucial Days, 1951–1960* (Englewood Cliffs, N.J., 1981).

Farago, Ladislas, *The Last Days of Patton* (New York, 1981).

Fergusson, Bernard, *The Watery Maze: The Story of Combined Operations* (New York, 1981).

Foote, Shelby, *The Civil War, a Narrative*, Vol. 3 (New York, 1974).

Fromkin, David, *In the Time of the Americans* (New York, 1995).

Funk, Arthur L., *Charles de Gaulle: The Crucial Years* (Norman, Okla., 1959).

Garland, Albert N., and Howard McGaw Smyth, *Sicily and the Surrender of Italy* (Washington, D.C., 1974).

Gavin, James M., *War and Peace in the Space Age* (New York, 1958).

Gelb, Norman, *Ike and Monty, Generals at War* (New York, 1994).

Gilbert, Martin, *The Second World War, a Complete History* (New York, 1989).

Greene, John Robert, *The Crusade: The Presidential Election of 1952* (Lanham, Md., 1985).

Greenstein, Fred I., *The Hidden–Hand Presidency: Eisenhower as Leader* (New York, 1982).

Groves, Leslie M., *Now It Can Be Told: The Story of the Manhattan Project* (New York, 1983).

Guderian, Heinz, *Achtung—Panzer! Die Entwicklung der Panzerwaffe, ihre Kampftaktik und ihre operativen Maglichkeiten* (London, 1957).

Hagerty, James C., *The Diary of James C. Hagerty: Eisenhower in Mid-Course, 1954–1955*, edited by Robert H. Ferrell (Bloomington, Ind., 1983).

Halberstam, David, *The Fifties* (New York, 1993).

Hamby, Alonzo L., *Man of the People: A Life of Harry S. Truman* (New York, 1995).

Hamilton, Nigel, *Monty: The Making of a General* (New York, 1981).

Harmon, Ernest N., *Combat Commander: Autobiography of a Soldier* (Garden City, N.J., 1970).

Harrison, Gordon A., *Cross-Channel Attack, U.S. Army in World War II* (Washington, D.C., 1950).

Hastings, Max, *D–Day and the Battle for Normandy* (New York, 1985).

Hittle, J. D., *The Military Staff: Its History and Development* (Harrisburg, Penn., 1961).

Hogan, William J., *The Marshall Plan* (Cambridge, U. K., 1989).

Holt, Daniel D., and Leyerzapf, James W., *Eisenhower: The Prewar Diaries and Selected Papers, 1905–1941* (Baltimore, 1998).

Hoopes, Townsend, *The Devil and John Foster Dulles* (Boston, 1973).

Horne, Alistair, *Harold Macmillan*, 2 vols. (New York, 1988–89).

Houston, Donald E., *Hell on Wheels: The 2d Armored Division* (San Rafael, Calif., 1977).

Hughes, Emmet John, *America the Vincible* (Garden City, New York, 1959).

_____, *The Ordeal of Power: A Political Memoir of the Eisenhower Years* (New York, 1963).

Humes, James C., *Eisenhower and Churchill, The Partnership That Saved the World* (New York, 2001).

Immerman, Richard H., *John Foster Dulles: Piety, Pragmatism, and Power in U.S. Foreign Policy* (Wilmington, Del., 1999).

Irving, David, *The War Between the Generals* (New York, 1981).

Isaacson, Walter, and Evan Thomas, *The Wise Men: Six Friends and the World They Made* (New York, 1986).

Ismay, Hastings Lionel, *The Memoirs of General Lord Ismay* (New York, 1960).

James, D. Clayton, *The Years of MacArthur*, 3 vols. (Boston, 1970–85).

Jones, Vincent C., *Manhattan: The Army and the Atomic Bomb. Special Studies. U.S. Army in World War II* (Washington, D.C., 1985).

Keegan, John, *Six Armies in Normandy: From D-Day to the Liberation of Paris* (New York, 1986).

Keegan, John, ed., *The Times Atlas of the Second World War* (New York, 1989).

_____, *The Oxford Companion to World War II* (Oxford, 1995).

Kesselring, Field Marshal Albert, *The Memoirs of Field–Marshal Kesselring* (London, 1967, reprint of 1953 edition).

Kirby, S. Woodburn, *Singapore: The Chain of Disaster* (London, 1957).

Kluger, Richard, *The Paper: The Life and Death of the New York Herald Tribune* (New York, 1986).

Kornitzer, Bela, *The Great American Heritage: The Story of the Five Eisenhower Brothers* (New York, 1955).

LaFantasie, Glenn, "Monty and Ike Take Gettysburg," *MHQ: The Quarterly Journal of Military History*, vol. 8 (autumn 1995).

Larrabee, Eric, *Commander in Chief: Franklin Delano Roosevelt, His Lieutenants and Their War* (New York, 1987).

Larson, Arthur, *Eisenhower: The President Nobody Knew* (New York, 1968).

Loewenheim, Francis L., Harold D. Langley, and Manfred Jones, eds., *Roosevelt and Churchill, Their Secret Wartime Correspondence* (New York, 1975).

McCallum, John, *Six Roads from Abilene: Some Personal Recollections of Edgar Eisenhower* (Seattle, 1960).

McCullough, David, *Truman* (New York, 1992).

McHenry, Robert, *Webster's American Military Biographies* (New York, 1978).

Macmillan, Harold, *Riding the Storm, 1956–1959* (London, 1971).

Manchester, William, *American Caesar* (Boston, 1978).

Matloff, Maurice, and Edwin M. Snell, *Strategic Planning for Coalition Warfare* (Washington, D.C., 1973).

Meacham, Jon, *Franklin and Winston: An Intimate Portrait of an Epic Friendship* (New York, 2001).

Miller, Lawrence, *Truman: The Rise to Power* (New York, 1986).

Miller, Merle, *Plain Speaking: An Oral Biography of Harry S. Truman* (New York, 1973).

_____, Merle, *Ike the Soldier, As They Knew Him* (New York, 1987).

Mollenhoff, Clark R., *The Pentagon: Politics, Profits and Plunder* (New York, 1967).

Montgomery, Bernard Law, *Montgomery of Alamein: The Memoirs of Field-Marshal Montgomery the Viscount of Alamein, K.G.* (Cleveland and New York, 1958).

Moran, Lord Charles, *Churchill: Taken from the Diaries of Lord Moran* (Boston, 1966).

Morrison, Samuel Eliot, *History of United States Naval Operations in World War II* (Boston, 1955).

Murphy, Robert D., *Diplomat Among Warriors* (Garden City, N.Y., 1964).

Nevins, Arthur S., *Gettysburg's Five-Star Farmer* (New York, 1977).

Parmet, Herbert S., *Eisenhower and the American Crusades* (New York, 1972).

Parrish, Thomas, *Roosevelt and Marshall, Partners in Politics and War* (New York, 1989).

Patterson, James T., *Mr. Republican: A Biography of Robert A. Taft* (Boston, 1972).

Perret, Geoffrey, *There's a War to Be Won: The United States Army in World War II* (New York, 1991).

_____, *Eisenhower* (New York, 1999).

Perry, Mark, *Four Stars* (Boston, 1989).

Pogue, Forrest C., *George C. Marshall*, 4 vols. (New York, 1963–87).

Pogue, Forrest C., *The U.S. Army in World War II, European Theatre of Operations* (Washington, D.C., 1996).

Public Papers of the Presidents of the United States: Dwight D. Eisenhower, January 1 to December 31, 1955 (Washington, D.C., 1959).

Public Papers of the Presidents of the United States: Dwight D. Eisenhower, January 1 to December 31, 1956 (Washington, D.C., 1958).

Public Papers of the Presidents of the United States: Dwight D. Eisenhower, January 1 to December 31, 1957 (Washington, D.C., 1958).

Public Papers of the Presidents of the United States: Dwight D. Eisenhower, January 1 to December 31, 1958 (Washington, D.C., 1959).

Public Papers of the Presidents of the United States: Dwight D. Eisenhower, January 1 to December 31, 1959 (Washington, D.C., 1960).

Reeves, Thomas C., *The Life and Times of Joe McCarthy* (New York, 1983).

Richardson, James L., *Germany and the Atlantic Alliance: The Interaction of Strategy and Politics* (Cambridge, Mass., 1966).

Ruddy, T. Michael, *The Cautious Diplomat: Charles E. Bohlen and the Soviet Union, 1929–1969* (Kent, Ohio, 1986).

Slater, Ellis D., *The Ike I Knew* (Baltimore, 1980).

Smith, Richard Norton, *Thomas E. Dewey and His Times* (New York, 1982).

Smith, Walter Bedell, *Eisenhower's Six Great Decisions* (New York, 1956).

Stone, David, *War Summits* (Washington, D.C., 2005).
Taylor, Maxwell D., *Swords and Plowshares* (New York, 1972).
Terraine, John, ed., *The Life and Times of Lord Mountbatten* (London, 1969).
Truman, Margaret, *Harry S. Truman* (New York, 1974).
Tuchman, Barbara, *Joseph Stilwell and the American Experience in China* (New York, 1972).
Vandenberg, Arthur H., *The Private Papers of Senator Vandenberg* (New York, 1974).
Verney, Peter, *Anzio 1944: An Unexpected Fury* (London, 1980).
Weigley, Russell F., *The American Way of War: A History of United States Military Strategy and Policy* (Bloomington, Ind., and London, 1977).
Weinberg, Gerhard L., *A World at Arms, A Global History of World War II* (Cambridge, 1994).
Wilhelm, Peter, *The Nobel Prize* (Stockholm and London, 1983).

INDEX

ACKNOWLEDGMENTS

My gratitude to my editor, Scott Moyers, for his faith in this project, especially during its darkest days, and to Laura Stickney for her hard work to make this book possible. My love and appreciation to my wife, Nina, and to my children, Cal and Madeleine, for their continued patience during the sometimes long and moody periods of composition. My thanks to Gail Ross, who has been there from the beginning. My appreciation to my colleague Alastair Crooke, who allowed me to take time from our work to finish this book.

I have dedicated this book to Bobby Muller, in appreciation for his nearly thirty years of unswerving confidence, courage, loyalty and friendship. A book dedication can hardly compensate such trust.